D0371964

AMERICA'S FUTURE
WORK FORCE

America's Future Work Force

A HEALTH AND EDUCATION POLICY ISSUES HANDBOOK

Carl W. Stenberg III and
William G. Colman

GREENWOOD PRESS
Westport, Connecticut • London

Library of Congress Cataloging-in-Publication Data

Stenberg, Carl W.
   America's future work force : a health and education policy issues
handbook / Carl W. Stenberg III and William G. Colman.
      p.   cm.
   Includes bibliographical references and index.
   ISBN 0–313–27980–2 (alk. paper)
   1. Manpower policy—United States.   2. Medical policy—United
States.   3. Education and state—United States.   I. Colman, William
G.   II. Title.
HD5724.S677   1994
331.11′0973—dc20   93–25070

British Library Cataloguing in Publication Data is available.

Copyright © 1994 by Carl W. Stenberg III and William G. Colman

All rights reserved. No portion of this book may be
reproduced, by any process or technique, without the
express written consent of the publisher.

Library of Congress Catalog Card Number: 93–25070
ISBN: 0–313–27980–2

First published in 1994

Greenwood Press, 88 Post Road West, Westport, CT 06881
An imprint of Greenwood Publishing Group, Inc.

Printed in the United States of America

The paper used in this book complies with the
Permanent Paper Standard issued by the National
Information Standards Organization (Z39.48–1984).

10 9 8 7 6 5 4 3 2 1

To Erik and Kerry, CWS

To the late Joseph L. Fisher, Chairman of the Board, National
Academy of Public Administration, 1988–91, WGC

Contents

Illustrations

FIGURES

TABLES

APPENDIXES

Preface

As America approaches a new century, there are growing concerns about the capacity and commitment of its work force. As our world becomes more of a global community, the emphasis of competition has shifted from military to economic affairs. Many observers have concluded that unless significant remedial actions are taken, the United States' leadership position in the global economy and in world affairs generally will be adversely affected.

The future of America's youth, present and forthcoming, also is at stake. *Employability* is a prerequisite for both economic and social survival of the individual. The alternatives are dependency, discouragement, and alienation. Health and educational barriers to employability must be confronted and surmounted.

The focal points of many of these concerns are the changing workplace and the failures of the public health and education systems adequately to prepare the work force of the future to compete at home and abroad. Since the 1980s scores of commissions and task forces have issued reports and have made recommendations. Scholars and researchers have published volumes of statistical data and analyses. Politicians at all levels have made competitiveness, jobs, schools, and health care visible and sometimes heated campaign issues.

The results of this outpouring of information, ideas, and insights have produced much debate but insufficient action. To a certain degree, the public policy agenda has been overloaded with proposals and counterproposals. It has often been difficult to identify successful innovations and experiments and to disseminate information about them on a continuing and effective basis.

The purposes of this book are to "take stock" of the situation by collecting in one place vital statistics, recent analyses, and replicable case studies that relate to the conditions of and challenges confronting the workplace and work force of the future. Further, major policy options for improving our nation's health care and education systems are presented, and their pros and cons are analyzed.

No prescriptions or recommendations are offered; this is the task of others. Our intention is to help citizens, public-policy makers, and the business community better understand the nature of these problems and the ways they might be addressed.

Acknowledgments

A number of individuals and organizations played "behind the scenes" roles that proved critical to our research and writing efforts. We would like to acknowledge a few who have been particularly helpful.

This book could not have been prepared without the able assistance of the librarians at the Montgomery County (Maryland) Library System; Alderman, Clemons, and the Curry School of Education Libraries of the University of Virginia; the States Information Center at the Council of State Governments; and the Office of State Services in the Washington, D.C., headquarters of the major associations of state government officials.

The substance and style of the text benefited from the research, editorial, and production assistance furnished by several individuals. Special thanks are due to Joan Casey of the staff of the U.S. Advisory Commission on Intergovernmental Relations; Catherine Stover; and Lonce Bailey, a former graduate student at the University of Virginia, who provided research assistance for the education chapters and supervised production of the initial draft of the entire manuscript.

We are indebted to staff members of the University's Center for Public Service for their invaluable assistance, especially Frances Granger and Rhonda Katzman, who skillfully and cheerfully handled word processing and table preparation and coordinated production of draft chapters and the final manuscript; and Jayne Finkelstein and Jennifer Kleine, who designed the figures.

The authors also are grateful for the critical and constructive comments provided by two anonymous reviewers. Mildred Vasan of the Greenwood Publishing Group offered encouragement at each stage of the process.

Finally, we would like to express our gratitude to our wives—Marge Colman and Kirstin Thompson—for their support throughout the project.

AMERICA'S FUTURE
WORK FORCE

Chapter 1

The U.S. Labor Force: Present and Projected Economic, Social, and Fiscal Contexts

Beginning in the 1970s and accelerating thereafter, basic changes in the U.S. economy were occurring, causing widespread dislocations and growing public uncertainty and unease. In the early stages, these concerns focused upon industrial competitiveness in a globalizing economy, shifts within and among the agricultural, manufacturing, and service sectors, and, relative to competition from abroad, declines in productivity and product quality. By the mid–1980s and subsequently, concerns shifted to changes in labor force composition and higher skill requirements, inadequate education and training of future workers, and growing strains in the nation's social fabric.

The latter included weakening family structures, increased drug addiction, and acquired immunodeficiency syndrome (AIDS) infection, coupled with impaired access by lower-income persons and families to adequate health care. Also, violent crime and incarceration rates were increasing alarmingly. These health, crime, and other social problems were having a devastating impact upon school attendance and achievement in many districts, especially in large central cities, resulting in a severe hemorrhaging in the number and quality of potential future labor force participants.

By the early 1990s a consensus was beginning to form across a broad spectrum of public opinion and from leaders in both private and public sectors as to the nature, severity, and scope of these interdependent economic and social phenomena.

- From the national government, former labor secretary Elizabeth Dole: "At a time when the United States faces the stiffest international competition in our history, the basic skills of our work force are eroding at an alarming pace. . . . Many of our workers are unready—unready for the new jobs, unready for the new realities."[1]

- From the Committee for Economic Development (CED): "These trends, if left unattended, could precipitate a succession of painful economic and social crises because the U.S. workforce would lack the size and skills needed to sustain economic growth.''[2]

- From the chairman of IBM and of the Business Roundtable Education Task Force: ''Each school day, some 4,000 young Americans drop out [of school]—4,000 potential doctors, engineers, scientists and teachers lost to our future. That's about 700,000 a year. And, each year, our high schools graduate an equivalent number unprepared for the world of work.''[3]

- From the U.S. Census Bureau: ''In 1989 the poverty rate for all children under 18 years was 19.6 percent.''[4]

- From the Ford Foundation: ''In America today: One out of every four teenagers will drop out of high school. . . . Four out of every ten girls will become pregnant before they leave their teens. . . . One out of every four teenagers will become a problem drinker. . . . A teenager commits suicide almost every ninety minutes. . . . [In New York City] one out of every three young people grows up in a single-parent family.''[5]

- Even more frightening, from the bipartisan National Commission on Children (''Rockefeller Commission''): ''Homicide is now the second leading cause of death for all 15 to 24 year-olds in the United States . . . since 1978 homicide has been the leading cause of death for black males age 15 to 24,'' and from the U.S. Public Health Service: ''Homicide, using guns, was the leading cause of teen-age death in 1990.''[6]

- In the same vein, from then National Association for the Advancement of Colored People (NAACP) executive director Benjamin Hooks: ''As a minister I have counseled with young men and young women who really don't give a rap about living to be 30 years of age.''[7]

- From a social services coalition: ''Every day, thousands of youth workers, child care personnel, health workers, mental health counselors, members of the business community, volunteers, and policy makers face the responsibility of fostering success for our nation's children and families. . . . A growing proportion of America's children needs easy access to a broad array of high quality services and supports that seek to prevent, as well as to treat, their problems. . . . Instead, many . . . families are lost in a catch as catch can non-system of public and private services. Too often, this fragmented system offers too little, too late.''[8]

In contrast to broad agreement regarding the scope and severity of these problems, there are wide confusion and divergence as to the nature and direction of specific remedial public and private actions that should be taken. To identify the alternatives and assess the advantages and shortcomings of each are the basic purposes of this book.

As background for this review of public policy options, a substantive examination of each segment of the universe of problems must be undertaken. In this chapter, a five-part overview will be presented of the economic, social, fiscal, and other environments determining or influencing future labor force composition, including (1) economic growth and productivity trends; (2) demographic projections encompassing the aging of the indigenous population, changes in birth and mortality trends, and immigration estimates; (3) current labor force size and skill requirements and the likely future configuration of the civilian labor force; (4) some major implications of these projections; and (5) the fiscal and intergovernmental contexts within which public policy actions are taken.

Of critical importance to this examination is recognition of key population segments whose strengthening is essential to a vigorous labor force and a stable society and represents a pointed challenge to both public and private leadership over the next two decades. They include (1) economically, physically, or behaviorally vulnerable households having one or more children and usually only one parent; (2) at-risk students; (3) school dropouts; (4) high school graduates lacking entry-level skills; and (5) drug/alcohol addicted youth at all education-training levels. At present, this collection of vulnerable, disadvantaged groups receive an *unequal* start, *unequal* support in home, neighborhood, and school, and a consequent *unequal* chance for either work or subsequent education and training.

ECONOMIC TRENDS AND PROJECTIONS

During the final quarter of the twentieth century, technological advance had transferred the national economies of the major industrial countries into interdependent parts of a world economy. In this transformation, the U.S. economy lost ground, with its trade balance shifting from positive to negative, but with its economic growth rate keeping in general step with the world economy, leading in some periods and lagging in others. Not only were trade and commerce becoming "globalized" during this period, but so was the world's labor force. William Johnston commented: "For more than a century, companies have moved manufacturing operations to take advantage of cheap labor. Now human capital, once considered to be the most stationary factor in production, increasingly flows across national borders as easily as cars, computer chips and corporate bonds. . . . employers will increasingly reach across borders to find the skills they need."[9]

The 1975–90 period was also marked by substantial shifts among sectors in terms of employment—notably, away from manufacturing and agriculture over to the service industries, with productivity improving in manufacturing and lagging seriously in services. In 1991, manufacturing continued to account for about the same proportion of gross national product (GNP) as in former decades, but with a greatly reduced labor force. However, concerns continued to be expressed about the quality of American goods and services, compared with those developed by foreign competitors.

Economic Growth 1970–2000

A deteriorating U.S. position in foreign trade in the 1975–85 period brought forth alarmed reactions from corporate management and labor organizations, believing that national net losses in business and jobs were occurring. However, it was pointed out that for jobs lost through imports, others were being gained through exports. Charles Stone and Isabel Sawhill, in a study for the National Commission for Employment Policy in 1986, estimated that between 1972 and 1979 nearly a million more jobs were created by exports than were lost to imports. By contrast, between 1979 and 1984 trade contributed to declining employment across a broad range of industries that employed about a quarter of the U.S. labor force. Nearly 2 million jobs were estimated to have been lost to imports, most of them in manufacturing and most of the rest in agriculture. This represented only 2 percent of the 1984 labor force of 100 million but up to sizable proportions in particular industries, such as steel, autos, and apparel.[10]

By the late 1980s the declining U.S. trade position was viewed by many as the nation's number one problem. Subsequent years saw some improvement, and there emerged some consensus on certain steps that should be taken:

- Management-labor and public-private cooperation to permit quicker and more flexible responses to overseas developments.
- Cessation of reliance on foreign savings to reduce the U.S. budget deficit (partially manifested in 1990 with a combination of tax increases and ostensibly strengthened internal congressional expenditure discipline).
- Strong measures to improve productivity in the workplace, including corporate reorganization to flatten hierarchies, reduce the numbers and roles of middle managers, and remove "culture blinders"; introduction of cost- and labor-saving techniques, such as "just-in-time" parts deliveries to assembly lines and the use of robotics; and resurgence of interest in comprehensive quality management practices.

Following several years of sustained economic growth and the onset of a recession in 1990–91, the Congressional Budget Office (CBO) postulated some likely trends into the late nineties:[11]

- An average 2.6 percent growth per year in real GNP during the 1994–97 period, a moderate recovery rate, slowed by postrecession adjustments in commercial real estate, financial services, state-local governments, and other sectors.[12]
- A moderate inflation rate of 3.6 percent, real long-term interest rates remaining below prerecession levels, and some improvement in the national savings rate (0.6% above the 1986–89 period).
- A moderate picture on productivity, comprising about a 2.1 percent annual increase (better than the eighties), and the downsizing of the work forces in both manufacturing and private services sectors during the early nineties.

In 1987 a landmark study was completed for the U.S. Department of Labor projecting economic and labor market conditions from the base year of 1984 to 2000; its report contained economic estimates that subsequent CBO reports echoed in some respects. The 1987 estimates included the following:

- The national rate of economic growth would fall well below what it would be if the nation's population and work force were increasing at the rates of the 1960s and 1970s.

- Economic growth would depend more directly on increased demand for income-sensitive products such as restaurant meals, luxury goods, travel, tourism, and health care.
- Labor markets would be tighter, due to the slower growth of the work force and the smaller reservoir of well-qualified workers.[13]

While meeting with strong agreement in many quarters, some of these projections met with skepticism in others. Especially controversial were those relating to the escalation of skill requirements and the relative diminution of demand for unskilled labor.[14] Major reservations to the *Workforce 2000* projections included the following:

- The implication that the new workers would be largely racial minorities (derived from the inclusion in the projections of white women in the "minority" classification);
- The fact of need in the nineties for large numbers of low-wage, low-skill jobs in fast-food, retail trade and in protective, personal, and cleaning/maintenance services, concurrently with widespread downsizing within the services sector of middle management positions and in positions of all levels in the finance-insurance-real estate segment; and
- Undue emphasis upon the shortcomings of workers and schools rather than on the demand side of the labor market and the obligation of employers to meet international competition by creating more higher-skilled, higher-wage jobs. Those supporting the thrust of the original report continued to point to the existing rate of new job creation in the high-skill areas (e.g., nurses, medical technicians) at double the historic rate (pre–1970) and in the least-skilled categories at one-half the historic rate.[15]

Industrial Productivity

Beginning in the late 1970s and running through most of the 1980s, general agreement emerged that one of the major problems confronting the U.S. economy for the remainder of the century was lagging industrial productivity. *Business Week* magazine called productivity the nation's "No. 1 Underachiever"[16] and identified the United States as having the second-worst productivity record of the leading industrialized and industrializing countries for the 1981–85 period. This poor performance was attributed to various factors, including (1) the aging manufacturing capital plant, which was caused largely by a low national savings rate and a consequent high cost of capital; (2) the timidity of corporate management in light of economic uncertainty and danger of lawsuits arising from almost any kind of risk taking, especially product introduction in the manufacturing sector, and including the discharge of employees for cause;[17] (3) the unwillingness of top management to divert profits from dividends to increased research and development amid fears of corporate buyouts and takeovers; and (4) the costs of complying with environmental and other regulatory burdens.

Regarding litigation dangers, a 1991 *Wall Street Journal* editorial on "American Competitiveness" commented that the U.S. legal system tended to undermine, rather than protect, economic prosperity and that "our litigiousness stokes the trend [toward] risk phobia . . . [in that] every injury is supposed to have someone to blame, preferably for punitive damages. . . . It's only in the U.S. that safe products, notably drugs, are yanked from markets simply because the profit margin doesn't cover the cost of defending frivolous lawsuits."[18]

Manufacturing and Services. By the mid–1980s part of the productivity gloom began to lift, particularly in the manufacturing sector. Plants were automated, employment reduced, and output increased, with resulting decreases in unit costs. Two reports issued in February 1991 indicated that (1) manufacturing was more than holding its own as a percent of national GNP,[19] exceeding the previous peak reached in 1966, and (2) both manufacturing and service productivity were increasing at the end of the decade, with rates in 68 industries in the former sector recording higher annual rates of change in the post–1979 period than in 1973–79. In 6 of the 18 industries in the trade sector, productivity increased in 1989; 11 of these 18 had recorded increases in 1988.[20]

Arnold Packer contended that the manufacturing comparisons were faulty because the portion of GNP in earlier years had been downsized through changing the measurement base from 1972 dollars to 1982 dollars, thus retroactively reducing the manufacturing proportion of "real" GNP in 1950 from 25 to 20 percent.[21] Also, in 1992, economic recession in Japan and Germany was tending to reduce the volume of global trade, and despite productivity improvements in some of the export industries, the contribution of U.S. exports to economic growth was commensurately limited.[22]

A comparative study by the McKinsey Global Institute of labor productivity (output per worker) over the 1987–88 period in Germany, France, Japan, the United Kingdom, and the United States, in five service sectors—airlines, telecommunications, retail banking, general merchandise retailing, and restaurants—showed the United States leading in four and a narrow second to France in restaurants. These results were attributed principally to the lower intensity of governmental regulation in these sectors in the United States.[23]

In 1991, several segments of the service sector began to act vigorously in instituting automation and other labor-shrinking changes that had been undergone by manufacturers in the eighties. Stephen Roach, an economist with Morgan Stanley, pointed out that shrinkage was overdue in the service sector, where productivity had been stagnating; services had been employing about three times the work force of the manufacturing sector, and deregulation had combined with increased foreign competition finally to compel increased attention to cost cutting.[24] In summarizing the overall competitive situation, a *Business Week* editorial emphasized that "to compete internationally, U.S. companies need long-range planning, a commitment to quality, *generous R&D* [Research and Development] and a premium on risk-taking."[25]

Research and Development. Despite the improvements in manufacturing, both in proportion of GNP and in productivity, the United States was still lagging in a number of areas of new product initiation and in the translation of scientific research discoveries into product development and manufacturing processes. The

United States had long been a mecca for foreign students desiring to do graduate study in the physical and biological sciences. Foreign graduate students in science and engineering attending U.S. graduate degree-granting institutions in those fields, as a percent of such students, increased in the 1983–90 period (from 20.2 to 25.5).[26] Also, it had been apparent for several years that mathematics and science education in the elementary and secondary grades were not providing American youth with the basic numeracy and literacy skills needed in an increasingly technical and scientific world. This was amply demonstrated by poor scores on assessment and aptitude tests. This general problem and its numerous ramifications for educational policy are examined in chapters 5 and 6. In addition:

- The number of science/engineering doctoral degrees awarded in the United States increased annually from 1981 onward, and foreign students received 59.1 percent of engineering doctorates awarded in 1991 and 40.3 percent of those in the physical sciences, compared with 51.5 and 23.1 percent in 1981.[27]

- The number of scientists and engineers engaged in research and development (R&D) per each 10,000 labor force members showed the United States in 1987 with 75.9, followed by Japan (68.8), West Germany (53.7), Sweden (50.2), France (44.9), and the U.K. (35.9).[28]

- Women and racial/ethnic minorities continued to lag badly in science and engineering in the 1980s; however, by 1991, this representation improved, especially for women. Annual averages of household data by the Bureau of Labor Statistics showed that in a total labor force comprised of 45.6 percent women, 10.1 percent black, and 7.5 percent Hispanic, the engineering profession comprised 8.2 percent women, 3.6 percent black, and 2.4 percent Hispanic. The respective percentages in the natural sciences (chemistry, geology, and biological/life sciences) were 26.1, 3.3, and 3.6. Women were most heavily represented among biological and life sciences (37.9), compared with their 45.6 percent of the work force. Among mathematical and computer scientists, they represented 36.8 percent.[29] In a January 1992 update, the National Science Foundation (NSF) summarized:
  > The underrepresentation of women and minorities is most pronounced in . . . engineering . . . and physical sciences. In the [life, social, and behavioral sciences] women and minorities now constitute a significant proportion of the membership. . . . Americans of Asian origin [comprising 3% of the population and 2% of the total work force] account for 5 percent of all scientists and engineers employed in the United States.[30]

- The percent of GNP devoted to R&D in 1989 was 2.82 for the United States, compared with 2.98 for Japan, 2.88 for Germany, 2.34 for France, and 2.50 for the U.K.[31] However, for *nondefense* R&D, the 1989 percentages, as estimated by the NSF, were more discouraging: Japan (3.0), Germany (2.8), and the United States (1.9).[32] A mid–1992 report of the National Science Board (the governing body of NSF) declared:
  > The real rate of growth in United States industrial spending has declined since the late 1970s and early 1980s. In addition the nation's position has deteriorated relative to that of its major international competitors where investment in nondefense research and development has been growing at a faster pace than U.S. nondefense R&D since the mid–1980s.[33]

The status of nondefense R&D became especially critical with the end of the cold war. The congressional Office of Technology Assessment (OTA) pointed out in a 1992 report that a significant part of defense-related R&D had as much importance for commercial as for military application and that defense purchases had

launched whole new high-technology industries (e.g., semiconductors and computers) and have contributed both new technology and financial stability to others. . . . If national defense shrinks as . . . support for the advanced technologies and industries declines, and if no other institutions are created to take on these responsibilities, then the Nation will be the poorer.[34]

Perhaps recession-induced, industrial R&D spending (not including governmental contracts) began to level off; the NSF reported the following amounts, in billions of 1982 dollars: 1986, 52.7; 1987, 52.3; 1988, 54.1; 1989, 55.6; 1990, 56.5; and 1991 (est.), 55.4.[35]

Income Distribution

Debate arose in the early 1980s and continued thereafter regarding the effect of shifts in the nonagricultural sector of the economy upon the distribution of income and consequent standards of living among the U.S. population. Coincident with the 1983–88 economic recovery period, considerable controversy arose as to the effect the shift from manufacturing to services was having on the American middle class. A study conducted for the Joint Economic Committee of the Congress presented data on the proportion of low-, middle-, and high-income employees in new jobs created during two comparative recovery periods—1973–79 and 1979–84. The data showed that the proportion of net employment growth in low-income employment was 20 percent in the earlier period and 48 percent in 1979–84. Others offered contrary evidence from generally comparable, but different, periods.[36]

The congressional enactment of the Tax Reform Act of 1986 added to the debate. It eliminated or reduced the income tax burden on low-income taxpayers (while Social Security taxes continued to rise) and reduced tax rates on high incomes but simultaneously eliminated a number of tax shelters previously enjoyed by wealthy taxpayers. The act reduced the number of brackets and, in the view of most tax experts, improved the fairness of the federal tax code. As the economy slowed in 1990–92, sentiment for restoration of some of the tax shelters began to manifest itself.

In the early 1990s, an Urban Institute study on the economic future of American families predicted that college-educated 30-year-olds, by the time they became 50 in the twenty-first century, would make little more in real dollars per year than their fathers took home in *their* peak earning years. Increasing concern was also evidenced about the narrowing opportunities for anything approaching comfortable pay for relatively unskilled jobs.[37] One Brookings Institution study showed that for the period 1979–88 (1) real earnings declined more for young workers than for workers generally; (2) the fall in real earnings was limited to men, while the pay of women actually rose; (3) average earnings among blacks changed at roughly the same rate as for all workers; and (4) the earnings of the less educated declined the most, marking a break in a long-run trend toward reduced relative compensation for skill differentials.[38]

A more clear-cut aspect of personal economic change during the later portion of the 1978–90 period lay in asset ownership. Quadrennial Census Bureau surveys of household wealth in 1984 and 1988 showed median household net worth in constant 1988 dollars to be $35,752, basically unchanged over the four-year interval. In 1988, the lowest income quintile owned 7 percent of total net worth, and the top quintile owned 44 percent.[39]

Two reports issued in 1992, rather than looking at quintile incomes, examined the changing economic status of *individuals over time*. The first, by Sawhill and Condon, used data from a University of Michigan Panel Study of Income Dynamics, which had followed a representative group of households beginning in 1968. An examination was made of individuals age 25–54 in 1977–86. The conclusions included:

(1) When one follows individuals rather than statistical groups defined by income, one finds that [during the two decades] the rich got a little richer [5–6% increase] and the poor got much richer [72–77%]. . . . (2) Lifetime incomes may still be getting more unequal . . . if we rank all the . . . income-producing opportunities . . . we find a growing gap between the top and bottom.[40]

The other report, by the Office of Tax Analysis of the U.S. Treasury, tracked the tax returns of 14,000 households between 1979 and 1988. It found that nearly 9 of every 10 people who started out at the bottom climbed by at least one quintile, or 20 percent, and more broadly, "in the . . . lowest three quintiles, one-third or fewer of the taxpayers in [a] quintile at the beginning of the sample are in the same quintile at the end. . . . In the first (lowest) quintile a greater percentage . . . move to the . . . highest quintile over the 10-year sample period than remain in the first quintile." However, others questioned the representativeness of the sample, since a sizable number of people did not have sufficient income to file tax returns.[41] This issue of income fairness or unfairness seemed to be one of perception. Lynn Martin, labor secretary in the Bush administration, contended that the middle class was not disappearing, noting that "in fact, between 1983 and 1990, family income adjusted for inflation rose in every income group. Before the [1990–91] recession, income was at an all-time high for 80 percent of American families."[42]

DEMOGRAPHIC TRENDS AND PROJECTIONS, 1960–2020

In contrast to the economy, where most projections are really best estimates, based on extrapolations of existing situations, the projection of population numbers and categories is somewhat more precise; current age group counts establish outer perimeters for indigenous population totals. Nevertheless, numerous other variants exist, fertility rates in particular. Others include (1) health epidemics; (2) new diseases, such as AIDS, requiring considerable time to develop successful treatment; (3) quantum jumps in medical technology that reduce mortality and extend life span; (4) contraceptive developments such as RU 486 (the French abortion pill); and (5) cultural shifts in private decisions about family size, including ages at which childbearing occurs. Add the immigration factor, and estimates of total future population extending for more than a decade become subject to fairly wide variation.

Related to the foregoing uncertainties as to both economic and demographic projections may be the relative reliability of national statistics overall. *The Economist* conducted a survey of governmental statistical agencies in ten large OECD countries as to the *perceived* reliability of published figures, including frequency and extent of revisions and timeliness. Canada was an easy first, with several Western European countries next, followed by the United States, Japan, the U.K., and Italy in that order.[43]

Population Projections

The U.S. Bureau of the Census for many years has formulated population projections in three ranges—low, middle, and high assumptions. Principal factors underlying each of the three for census projections for 1986 to 2080 ranged as follows, with the 1986 base year and for low, middle, and high, respectively: (1) Lifetime births per 1,000 women at 1,825 in 1986—1,500, 1,800, and 2,200; (2) life expectancy at birth at 75.0 years—77.9, 81.2, and 88.0; and (3) yearly net immigration (inflow less out-migration) at 662,000—300,000, 500,000, and 800,000.[44]

Highlights of the 1988–2080 projections issued in January 1989, as modified in 1992, showed the following projections.[45] (A breakdown of the projections by age group appears in Appendix 1.A.)

- Total population, in millions, starting from 244.1 in 1987 (and 251.7 in 1990) was: 1995: 264.3; 2000: 276.4; 2005: 288.5; 2010: 301.1; 2015: 314.1; 2020: 327.0; 2030: 350.6; 2040: 372.4; 2050: 394.1; 2060: 417.2; 2070: 443.2; and 2080: 470.5 (a near doubling of population over a 90-year period).

- The median age, as initially projected, starting at 32.1 in 1987 and rising, ranged, in low, middle, and high at: 1995: 35.0, 34.7, 34.4; 2000: 36.8, 36.4; 35.8; 2010: 39.9, 38.9, 37.5; 2020: 41.9, 40.2, 38.0; 2080: 47.5, 43.9, 39.9 (a gradually aging population).

Other, more qualitative highlights were:[46]

• After 1995, the rate of population growth would likely be the lowest in the nation's history. (Future birth and immigration rates surrounded with many uncertainties.)

• The elderly (65 and over) segment of the population would grow more slowly in the 1990s than previously, then spurt upward until 2030, with the percent of elderly going from 12.6 in 1990 to 13.1 in 2010 and to 19 in 2030.

• The portion of population under 35 would decline from 55 percent in 1990 to the low 40s in 2020.

• The post–1990 white population would grow more slowly than heretofore and in 40 years begin to decline substantially; however, the black population would grow by 50 percent by 2030.

• The Hispanic population, in millions, would reach 26.5 in 1995, 31.2 in 2000; 41.9 in 2010, and 67.7 in 2030.[47]

• Both total births and white births would drop sharply in the 1990s.

• Despite a stable growth rate, by 2030, 12 percent of the total population would be post–1986 immigrants, numbering (including descendants) about 32 million.

• The elementary school population (age 5–13) would hover between 30 and 32 million, while high school numbers (age 14–17) would decline somewhat in the early 1990s, back to 14–15 million by the mid–1990s, and stabilize at that level until 2010. College population (ages 18–24) would fluctuate between 25 and 27 million until 2020. In 2015 the middle range projected percentages of white-black-other races within these younger age groups would be, for ages 5–13: 76.3, 17.3, and 6.4; for ages 14–17: 76.1, 17.5, and 6.4; and for ages 18–24: 77.5, 16.3, and 6.2.[48]

Table 1.1 shows the projected population for each major age group.

Table 1.2 shows estimated and projected population for 1960–2020, by race and sex. Under these projections, the white population would grow by about 60 million from 1990 to 2020, with its share of the total population increasing slightly, and the black population would grow by about 10 million, with a corresponding increase of two percentage points in its share of the total. The "other races" category (Asians, Pacific Islanders, Native Americans, et al.) was projected to increase most sharply (starting from a low base) by 2.5 percentage points. Using rates, rather than percentage points, an annual white growth rate of 0.75 percent was indicated. This rate decreased to 0.23 percent by 2020, compared with a black annual growth rate of 1.41 in 1990, slowing to 0.81 in 2020—still nearly four times the white rate. By 2080, the racial shares of the U.S. population were projected to be 73.3 percent white, 16.0 black, 10.7 other races, with the Hispanic percentage estimated at 19.3 by 2030.[49]

Immigration

Net immigration (number entering the country intending to remain minus the number of U.S. residents moving out of the country) is a significant factor in

Table 1.1

Estimated and Projected Population by Age Group, 1960–2020—Numbers and Percent of Total Population (numbers in millions)

Year	Total Pop.	Under 18 No.	Under 18 Pct.	18-24 No.	18-24 Pct.	25-34 No.	25-34 Pct.	35-44 No.	35-44 Pct.	45-64 No.	45-64 Pct.	65+ No.	65+ Pct.
Actual/Est.													
1960	180.7	64.5	35.8	16.1	8.9	22.9	12.7	24.2	13.4	36.2	20.0	.16.7	9.2
1970	205.1	69.8	34.0	24.7	12.1	25.3	12.3	23.2	11.3	42.0	20.5	22.7	9.8
1980	227.8	63.7	28.0	30.4	13.3	37.6	16.5	25.9	11.4	44.5	19.5	25.7	11.3
1985	239.3	63.0	26.3	28.7	12.0	42.2	17.7	31.8	13.3	44.9	18.8	28.5	11.9
1990A	248.7	63.6	25.6	26.7	10.8	43.4	17.7*	37.4	15.2*	46.4	18.6	31.2	12.6
Projected													
1995	264.3	68.8	26.0	24.7	9.3	41.7	15.8	42.6	16.1	52.8	20.0	33.8	12.8
2000	276.4	71.0	25.7	25.9	9.4	38.4	13.9	44.5	16.1	61.7	22.3	35.0	12.7
2005	288.5	72.8	25.2	27.8	9.6	37.6	13.0	42.0	14.6	71.9	24.9	36.4	12.6
2010	301.1	74.6	24.8	29.2	9.7	39.5	13.1	38.8	12.9	79.6	26.4	39.6	13.2
2015	314.1	78.6	25.0	29.6	9.4	42.4	13.4	38.0	12.1	81.6	26.0	45.4	14.5
2020	327.0	81.3	24.9	29.7	9.1	43.7	13.4	39.8	12.2	80.2	24.5	52.3	16.0

Sources: Bureau of the Census: Data on pre-1990 period from *Projections of the Population of the U.S., by Age, Sex, and Race: 1980 to 2080.* Series P-25 No. 1018, Table F. (January 1989), 7, 84, 85. 1990 data from press release CB 91-217, Table 1. (June 11, 1991) 5. Projections for 1995 period from Series P-25, No. 1018, Supplement, Series 18, Table 6. (March 1992), unnumbered pages of advance data.

Notes: A = Actual decennial count.
          * indicates combined total for age group 25-44 was 80.8 million, and 32.5 percent.

U.S. population growth. As of 1990, net immigration stood at around a half million persons annually. According to Census Bureau estimates, the population projections set forth earlier would be drastically lower, absent immigration. If there had been no immigration post–1986, the U.S. population would grow to 259 million in 2000, peak at 270 million around 2030, *and then proceed to decline to 220 million* (30 million less than the 1990 actual count) by 2080. The nation's relatively low fertility rate accounts for this. The "fertility replacement ratio" is about 2.1 or 2,100 for each 1,000 women (compared with the 1990 rate of 1,850).[50] Several Western European countries have already projected zero or minus population growth rates (Sweden, Austria, Belgium, Denmark, Hungary, and perhaps Germany, depending upon immigrant or refugee rates from the East and elsewhere.)[51]

Congressional legislation in 1990 contained an increased emphasis on future U.S. labor market considerations in the conduct of national immigration policy. The Immigration Act of 1990[52] established an annual limit of 675,000 immi-

Table 1.2

Estimated and Projected Population by Race and Hispanic Origin, 1960–2080— Numbers and Percent of Total Population (numbers in millions)

Year	All Races No.	Pct.	White No.	Pct.	Black No.	Pct.	Other Races No.	Pct.	Hispanic Orig. No.	Pct.*
1960	179.3	100	158.8	88.6	18.9	10.5	1.6	0.9	—	—
1970	203.3	100	178.1	87.6	22.6	11.1	2.6	1.3	—	—
1980	226.5	100	194.7	85.9	26.7	11.8	5.1	2.3	15.8	—
1985e	239.3	100	202.8	84.9	28.9	12.1	7.1	3.0	18.0	7.5
1990a	248.7	100	199.7	80.3	30.0	12.1	19.0	7.7**	22.4	9.0
Projected:										
1995	264.3	100	220.0	83.2	33.7	12.8	10.7	4.0	26.5	10.0
2000	276.4	100	227.6	82.3	36.2	13.1	12.6	4.6	31.2	11.3
2005	288.5	100	235.2	81.5	38.7	13.4	14.6	5.1	—	—
2010	301.1	100	243.0	80.7	41.4	13.7	16.8	5.6	41.9	13.9
2015	314.1	100	251.1	79.9	44.1	14.0	19.0	6.0	—	—
2020	327.0	100	259.3	79.2	46.8	14.2	21.2	6.5	54.3	16.6
2030	350.6	100	272.8	77.8	51.9	14.8	25.9	7.4	67.7	19.3
2040	372.4	100	284.9	76.5	56.8	15.3	30.6	8.2	81.9	22.0
2060	417.2	100	311.0	74.5	66.1	15.8	40.2	9.6	110.6	26.5
2080	470.5	100	344.9	73.3	75.5	16.0	50.2	10.7	140.7	30.0

Source: Bureau of the Census: For 1960–1985 period, *Projections of the Population of the U.S., by Age, Sex, and Race: 1988 to 2080.* Series P-25, # 1018, Table I. (January 1989) 9–10. For 1990: Press Release CB91-100, Table 2. March 11, 1991, 4. For 1995–2080 projections: Series P-25, 1018, Supplement, Series 18, Table 6. (March 1992) unnumbered pages of advance data. For Hispanic population: *Projections of Hispanic Population 1983–2080,* Table B, high series. (November 1989), 2.

Notes: a = Actual.
e = Estimated.
* Much of Hispanic population also counted as white; first estimated for 1983 and counted thereafter.
** Three reasons, among others, account for large increase in the "other races" category from the 1980 and 1985(e) numbers and the 1990 count: (1) Large increase in persons identifying themselves as American Indians (persons presumably identified earlier as white); (2) large Asian increase including those emigrating from Hong Kong; and (3) an increased fertility rate in the late eighties.

gration visas effective in 1995, with 700,000 authorized for fiscal years 1992–94. Within the seven immigration categories (relatives of U.S. citizens, family members of resident aliens, and so on) is an "employment-based" category comprising (1) priority workers with extraordinary skills; (2) professionals with advanced degrees in the sciences, arts, or business; (3) skilled workers; (4) certain special immigrants (ministers, religious workers, et al.); and (5) individuals who have a specified amount of money (usually $1 million) to invest in an enterprise that will create at least ten jobs for U.S. workers. Given the increased emphasis upon occupational skills in the new law, it should be noted that the 1988 immigration of natural scientists, engineers, and mathematical scientists/computer specialists totaled about 10,400, comprising 60 percent from Asia-Middle East, 23 percent from Europe, 11 percent from North and Central America, and the remainder from the rest of the world. In another break from preceding decades, the 1980s saw greatly increased immigration to the United States from the Third World. From both developed and developing countries in Asia came 2.6 million, or 44 percent of all legal immigrants during the decade.[53]

The census projections presented earlier assumed an average annual net immigration of 500,000, with 32.2 million post–1986 surviving immigrants and their descendants by 2030 and 72.0 million by 2080. Like the total population estimates, the revised immigration figures would tend toward higher ground (e.g., an average 800,000 net, with 49.5 million post–1986 survivors-descendants in 2030 and 112.6 million by 2080).[54] (Thus, as Franklin Roosevelt once addressed members of the Daughters of the American Revolution, an organization concerned about influxes of people from abroad, as "dear fellow immigrants," the United States appears destined over the foreseeable future to remain a "nation of immigrants.") Certainly, net immigration is one of the key components, not only in the country's population growth but in future labor force composition. It also affects the accessibility, affordability, and adequacy of the nation's health care and education systems. By 1993 this was becoming an increasingly controversial issue in federal-state relationships.

Geographic Distribution of Population Growth

The 1990 census contained an error range of 5.7 to 10.3 percent, according to estimates by the General Accounting Office (GAO) in a 1991 report. This range included from 4.4 to 10.2 million erroneous inclusions and from 9.7 to 15.5 erroneous omissions, resulting in a net undercount of 5.3 million persons. Under the GAO estimates, the minimal percentage of gross error of 5.7 percent compared with a minimal 3.4 percent for the 1980 census. The GAO concluded that the widely reported net undercount obscured the "true magnitude of the error in the census because, while millions of persons were missed . . . millions of other persons were improperly counted." The agency noted that it previously had pointed out to the Congress "the challenges that confronted the Bureau of the Census in taking the 1990 census . . . escalating census costs, a declining level of public cooperation, and a shrinking workforce available for temporary census employment—may well become even more difficult to address in the future" and that the amount of error reinforced "the importance of census reform."[55]

The 1990 census showed a continuation of the post–World War II trend of (1) movement away from the East and Middle West to the South and Far West; (2) concentration in metropolitan areas; and (3) within such areas, movement from central cities to suburbs and exurbs. With a total national population growth of 64.4 percent during the 1950–90 period, Nevada showed the largest percentage increase—650.8 (due to starting from a very low base). The greatest proportional losers and laggards (below 20 percent) in the 40-year period were District of Columbia (− 24.3%), West Virginia (− 10.6%), North Dakota (3.1), Iowa (5.9), South Dakota (6.6), Pennsylvania (13.2), and Mississippi (18.1). Large gainers in addition to Nevada were Arizona (389.0), Florida (366.9), California (181.1), Utah (150.1), New Mexico (122.4), and Texas (120.3), which also seemed certain to pass New York as the second most populous state by 1995.[56] The July 1992 estimates of resident population showed 1991 to 1992 percent increases of 3.5 (NV), 2.9 (AK), 2.7 (CO), 2.7 (ID), 2.5 (WA), and losses, including smallest increases of − 1.1 (DC), − 0.2 (CT), 0.1 (ME), 0.4 (NY), and 0.4 (PA).[57]

Metropolitan Areas. For the first time 1990 saw more than half (50.2%) of the nation's population living in metropolitan areas of 1 million or over.[58] However, five such areas lost population during the 1980–90 decade (Detroit, Cleveland, Pittsburgh, New Orleans, and Buffalo). The five areas with the largest proportionate gains were Phoenix (40.6%), San Diego (34.2), Dallas-Fort Worth (32.6), Atlanta (32.5), and Tampa-St. Petersburg (28.20). The 10 most populous metropolitan areas were New York, Los Angeles, Chicago, San Francisco Bay Area, Philadelphia, Detroit, Boston, Washington, Dallas-Fort Worth, and Houston. The ten most populous central cities in 1990 were New York, Los Angeles, Chicago, Houston, Philadelphia, San Diego, Detroit, Dallas, Phoenix, and San Antonio.[59]

Central Cities. Most metropolitan areas were growing, but numerous cities of over 100,000 were declining, and even in the cities showing population gains, the *proportion* of the metropolitan area's population and employment remaining in the central city was still declining, as illustrated in Table 1.3. Neither the proportionate losses nor the modest gains shown in the table necessarily indicate real change because the areal composition of either the city (through annexation or detachment) or the metropolitan area (through the addition of one or more suburban counties as they meet definitional standards maintained by the federal Office of Management and Budget, acting with information and expert advice from the Census Bureau) may have changed. However, both city population and its proportionate share of area population and employment still make up one of the several indicators that assist in distinguishing among growing, stable, stagnant, and declining central city economies. Ease or difficulty in changing city boundaries varies from state to state. For example, annexation laws historically have been relatively liberal toward cities in the South and very restrictive in the Northeast. In Table 1.3, these differences are still reflected, as illustrated by San Antonio, Houston, Dallas, Philadelphia, and Baltimore.

Various studies, beginning in the late sixties, examined socioeconomic and fiscal disparities between the larger central cities and their surrounding suburbs. The disparities were marked in economic, racial, and fiscal terms throughout much of the seventies.[60] By the mid-eighties they had begun to lessen somewhat

Table 1.3
Central City Population as a Percentage of Metro Area Population, 1970, 1980, and 1990 for 15 Largest Cities in 1990 (numbers in thousands)

	City Population			Metro Area Population			City Percent		
	1970	1980	1990	1970	1980	1990	'70	'80	'90
New York	7,896	7,072	7,323	9,077	8,275	8,547	87	85	86
Los Angeles	2,812	2,969	3,485	7,082	7,477	8,863	40	40	39
Chicago	3,369	3,005	2,784	6,093	6,060	6,070	55	50	46
Houston	1,234	1,595	1,631	1,891	2,735	3,302	65	59	49
Philadelphia*	1,950	1,688	1,586	4,824	4,717	4,857	40	36	33
San Diego	697	876	1,111	1,358	1,862	2,498	51	47	44
Detroit	1,514	1,203	1,028	4,554	4,448	4,382	33	27	23
Dallas	844	905	1,007	1,556	1,957	2,553	54	46	39
Phoenix	584	790	983	967	1,509	2,122	60	52	46
San Antonio	654	786	936	888	1,072	1,302	74	76	72
San Jose	460	629	782	1,065	1,295	1,498	43	49	52
Indianapolis*	737	712	742	1,111	1,167	1,250	66	60	59
Baltimore*	906	786	736	2,089	2,199	2,382	43	.36	31
San Francisco*	716	679	724	1,482	1,489	1,604	48	46	45
Jacksonville*	504	571	673	504	722	907	100	79	74

Source: Bureau of the Census, news release CB91-24, January 25, 1991.

Notes: * These are consolidated city-county in form and do not lie within an overlying county;
Indianapolis and Jacksonville, FL were consolidated with their overlying counties of Marion
and Duval during the 1960-90 period. New York comprises five boroughs, the latter being
somewhat comparable to counties.

in racial and economic terms due to minority middle-income movement to the suburbs and "gentrification" to central city neighborhoods, with some of the in-migrants coming from the suburbs.

However, in the late eighties and early nineties, drugs, crime, and other behavioral- and poverty-related problems worsened in a growing number of central cities. These serious social problems exacerbated the earlier fiscal disparities. They helped widen gaps in personal income between cities and suburbs, as found in a survey by the National League of Cities in the early nineties; (e.g., it showed city income as a percent of suburban for Philadelphia and San Antonio at 49 and 98%, respectively, mirroring the population/employment contrasts appearing in Table 1.3).[61] The inner-city schools continued to deteriorate, and poor rural districts began to join in litigation and other political action directed toward an increased state government role in fiscal equalization (examined in chapters 5 and 6).

However, there continued to be exceptions to these general economic and fiscal trends, and a feature closely related to small businesses of particular types might be noted here. Hourly manufacturing wages, especially for the lower skills, in central cities are often lower than in neighboring suburbs, due to lower industrial rents and minimization of commuting costs of time and money for the workers.[62]

Later in this chapter, data on employment as related to skills, residence, and job location illustrate, much more strikingly than population count, the socio-economic contrasts in metropolitan areas, especially as they relate to the health, education, and job preparation of children and adolescents in the nation's inner cities.

Household and Family Structure. During the period 1970–90, the proportion of households accounted for by two-parent families declined dramatically from 40 percent in 1970 to 26 percent in 1990. The increase in number of family households maintained by women alone was a major change in family composition in the 1970s but continued at a slower pace in the 1980s. The proportion of families maintained by women was much more prevalent for blacks than for whites (44 and 13%, respectively). For Hispanics the proportion was 23.[63] More children were living at home with parents for longer periods after finishing school and before marriage, and more were returning to parental households for sporadic periods between employments—a lengthening path from adolescence to independent adult living. The proportion of young adults age 18–24 living with parent(s) grew from 43 percent in 1960 to 52.8 in 1990; the age 25–34 group grew from 9.1 to 11.5 in the same period.[64]

Working-Age Population

In projecting the size, composition, and utilization of the U.S. labor force at various points in the future, it is necessary to begin with the estimated population of working age from which that force is primarily drawn. *Working age* is defined differently by demographers, public agencies, and private employers. The broadest view is taken by the U.S. Bureau of Labor Statistics (BLS) of the Department of Labor. It uses the "non-institutional population" (NIP) 16 years of age and over, which excludes only those in hospitals or confined to prisons, mental health, and other non-educational eleemosynary institutions. The NIP includes members of the armed forces; active-duty military personnel are, of course, not included in the civilian labor force (CLF).

There is a minimum (16), but no maximum, age for inclusion in either the NIP or CLF. Sixteen is the minimum working age under most federal and state laws and regulations, though with some exclusions, such as family members working on a farm or family-owned business. The reason for no maximum is obvious; the average CLF size for 1991 comprised 3.5 million persons age 65 and over, or 11.6 percent of the total NIP in that age group—193,000 of that group were 75 and over, comprising 4.4 and 3.9 percent, respectively, for the white and black NIP of that age subgroup.[65] A more restricted definition of *working age* is more appropriate here—18 to 65—because this is the group from which the bulk of the present and future labor force over the next 30 years must come. Further into the future it may be necessary to reexamine the question; subsequent to 2020, the retirement eligibility age for Social Security, under present law, is scheduled to go from 65 to 66, then to 67. Eighteen is the usual age for high school completion and the consequent eligibility of adolescents for full-time, year-round work.

From Table 1.1, the 1990 working age defined as 18–64 was approximately 155.4 million or 61.7 percent of the total population, with 1992 revised census projections for this group as follows: for 1995, 161.7 million and 61.2 percent; 2000—170.4 and 61.7; 2005—179.3 and 62.2; 2010—187.0 and 62.1; 2015—191.1 and 60.9; and 2020—193.2 and 59.1.[66]

Figure 1.1 indicates the nature of shifts and future projections of the three principal age segments of the working-age population.

Thus, during the period 1990–2020, the "core working-age" population would comprise between 60 and 65 percent of the total population, but the CLF would be augmented by some full-time and much part-time work by adolescents aged 16 and 17 and by those persons at or above "retirement age" but still part- or full-time members of the work force. *Dependency ratio* is the term used to reflect the numerical relationship between the working-age group and the group comprising minors and retired persons. A census table presents such ratios (number of "dependents" per 100 persons aged 18 through 64: 1990—62.0; 1995—63.5; 2000—62.2; 2010—61.0; and 2020—69.2). Subsequent to 2020, the projected ratios rise steeply—75.9 in 2050 and 76.7 in 2080.[67]

The term *dependency* can be misinterpreted easily, however, and the exceptions at both ends are sizable, as pointed out previously. In 1991 there were 2.7 million youth ages 16 and 17 in the labor force.[68] Millions of others were in high school and college preparing to enter the labor force and whose dependency was transitional. On the other hand, as described later, at any one time, several million persons are in the 18–64 "working-age" group who are truly dependent. They may be unemployed or not in the labor force for various reasons, such as nonworking women; unable to work; in school; in prison; or unwilling to work.

LABOR FORCE COMPOSITION AND TRENDS

Numerous variables enter into any attempted analysis of recent and current trends in composition of the U.S. labor force. Some of these are quantifiable and easily accounted for, such as size of the working-age population and of its component age groupings. Others, although quantifiable, are attributable to more general and sometimes elusive factors, such as human life-styles, which tend to vary by age group, ethnic culture, socioeconomic environment, and the "technological environment," with its changing skill, literacy, and other job requirements.

The principal considerations affecting work force composition and competence

Figure 1.1
The Aging of the Working-Age Population, Age Groups of 18 and Older, in Percent

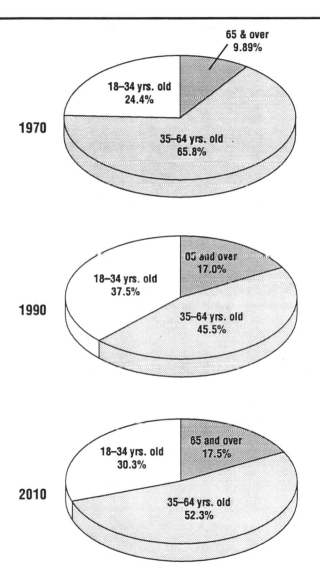

SOURCE: *Workforce 2000*, p. 81; U. S. Department of Commerce, Bureau of the Census, *Projections of the Population by Age, Sex, and Race 1988–2000*, Series P-25 No. 1018 (Washington, D.C.: U. S. Government Printing Office, January 1989), 9–10; and Bureau of the Census, Series P-25 No. 1018, Supplement Series 18, Table 6 (Washington, D.C.: U. S. Government Printing Office, March 1992), unnumbered pages.

are presented here, beginning with composition trends such as sex, race, and age and continuing with an examination of the non- and underutilized segments (unemployed, underemployed, and dropouts no longer seeking work). Also examined are work force skill requirements and projections, including formal education and employer-provided pre- and postentry training, with identification of major shortages and other labor force preparation problems over the next two decades.

Recent Trends and 1992 Civilian Labor Force Composition

The U.S. civilian labor force (CLF) comprises three major components: persons employed full-time; persons employed part-time; and unemployed workers seeking work. The Bureau of Labor Statistics (BLS) also reports regularly on the number of persons not in the labor force. In general this group includes those (1) not in a position to work, of which nonworking wives with young children are a major segment and full-time students are another; (2) disabled persons; and (3) persons too discouraged to seek work or uninterested or unwilling to work. Figure 1.2 shows the proportions of the major categories of the civilian noninstitutional population in 1990 and of the CLF itself, as between part- and full-time employed and unemployed members, including the proportions of males and females in each.

Between 1976 and 1988 the CLF grew from 97.8 million to 123.4 million, and it grew to 127.2 million at the beginning of 1992. The CLF composition by race and sex, and changes during the 1976–91 period are shown in Figure 1.3. Appendix 1.B gives a breakdown of the NIP as of mid-1992—the presumed bottom of the 1991–92 recession—along with employment by age group, sex, and race. During the 1976–91 period significant changes occurred in the degree of labor force participation by older workers, women, and blacks. Part of these changes are attributable to increases in the total population within the various age groups, as the impacts of the ''baby boom'' and ''bust'' cycles are manifested in succeeding periods. The increasing availability of, and eligibility for, private sector pension benefits and the rising real incomes of the upper-middle- and upper-income groups may have helped account for a decrease in the percent of older workers in the total population that remained in the labor force; however, this percentage began to increase somewhat in the late 1980s and early 1990s.

Labor force participation rates (number in labor force, at work or seeking work, as percents of noninstitutional population) for major age and racial/ethnic groups in 1990 were as follows.[69]

- Age 16 and over: By race and ethnic group—white (66.8); black (66.3); and Hispanic (67.0). By sex and race—white men (76.9), white women (57.4); black men (70.2); black women (57.8); Hispanic men (81.2); and Hispanic women (53.0).
- Ages 16–19: Both sexes, by race—white (57.5); black (39.0); and Hispanic (47.1). By

Figure 1.2
Major Components, U.S. Population and Labor Force, Age 16 and Over, 1990

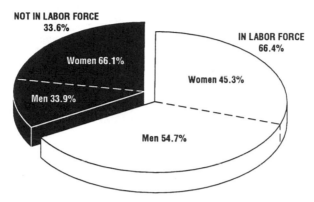

NOT IN LABOR FORCE
33.6%

Women 66.1%

Men 33.9%

IN LABOR FORCE
66.4%

Women 45.3%

Men 54.7%

CIVILIAN NON-INSTITUTIONAL POPULATION
188.0 million

Men: 89.65 million   Women: 98.4 million

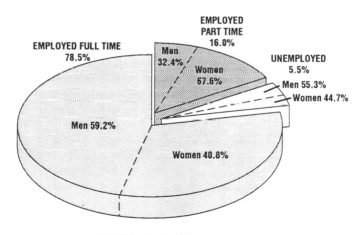

EMPLOYED FULL TIME
78.5%

EMPLOYED
PART TIME
16.0%

Men
32.4%

Women
67.6%

UNEMPLOYED
5.5%

Men 55.3%
Women 44.7%

Men 59.2%

Women 40.8%

CIVILIAN LABOR FORCE
124.8 million

Men: 68.30 million   Women: 56.50 million

SOURCE: U.S. Department of Labor, Bureau of Labor Statistics, *Employment and Earnings 1990 Annual Averages*, Tables 3 & 7. (Washington, D.C.: U. S. Government Printing Office, January 1991), pp. 164, 171. *Employment and Earnings* is published monthly, with each year's January issue containing annual averages for the preceding year.

Figure 1.3
U.S. Labor Force Composition, 1976–91, in Percents by Race/Ethnic Origin and Sex

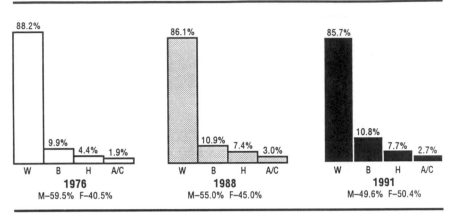

SOURCE: Fullerton, H., "New Labor Force Projections Spanning 1988 to 2000", Table 1. *Monthly Labor Review,* p. 4; 1991 data from *Employment and Earnings,* Jan., 1991, p. 183.

NOTES: W=White; B=Black; H=Hispanic Origin; A/C=Asian, other races. M=Male; F=Female.

race and sex—white men (59.5); white women (55.4); black men (41.1); black women (36.9); Hispanic men (55.4); and Hispanic women (38.6).

- Age 20 to 24: By race and sex—white men (86.0); white women (73.8); black men (76.8); black women (62.1); Hispanic men (89.5); and Hispanic women (59.5).

- For the age group 25–64 (which tends to neutralize differing proportions of age and sex categories that are in various simultaneous combinations of school and work and in the patterns of retirement-work), labor force participation rates in 1990 were: white men (90.1); white women (69.2); black men (83.0); black women (69.2); Hispanic men (89.4); and Hispanic women (59.4).

In the preceding two and one half decades, for males 20 or over, contrasting participation rates for whites and blacks were: 1955—white, 87.5, and black, 87.8; 1965—white, 83.9, and black, 83.7; 1975—white, 80.7, and black, 76.0; 1980—white, 79.8, and black, 75.1.[70] In addition to the shift in job-type availability away from assembly and fabrication, entry into military service by a higher proportion of blacks than whites helped offset this declining participation rate for blacks, insofar as the bases are civilian labor force as a proportion of the civilian noninstitutional population. Participation rates for women of all races in the age 25–64 group grew from 49.0 percent in 1970 to 52.0 in 1975, 64.7 in 1985, to 69.1 in 1990.[71] Major industry groupings of the CLF are shown in Figure 1.4. Substantial major increases and decreases in percentage points occurred over the period 1976–90: miscellaneous services (7); retail trade (1.9);

Figure 1.4
Employment by Industry, 1976 and 1990

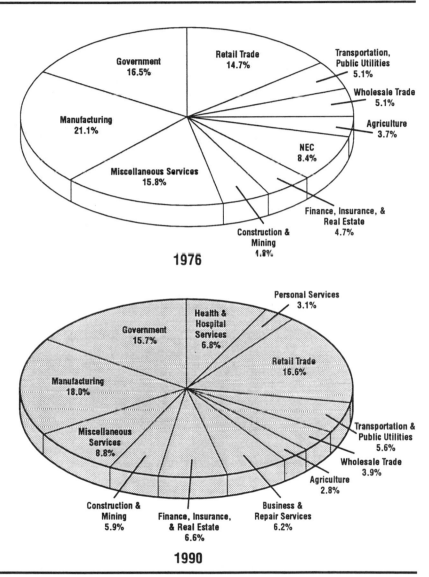

Government 16.5%
Retail Trade 14.7%
Transportation, Public Utilities 5.1%
Wholesale Trade 5.1%
Manufacturing 21.1%
Agriculture 3.7%
NEC 8.4%
Miscellaneous Services 15.8%
Finance, Insurance, & Real Estate 4.7%
Construction & Mining 1.8%

1976

Personal Services 3.1%
Health & Hospital Services 6.8%
Government 15.7%
Retail Trade 16.6%
Manufacturing 18.0%
Transportation & Public Utilities 5.6%
Miscellaneous Services 8.8%
Wholesale Trade 3.9%
Agriculture 2.8%
Construction & Mining 5.9%
Finance, Insurance, & Real Estate 6.6%
Business & Repair Services 6.2%

1990

SOURCE: 1976 data from Personick, V., "Industry Output and Employment," *Monthly Labor Review* (November 1989), 26. 1990 data from *Employment and Earnings 1990, Annual Averages*, Table 25 (January 1991), 193; and U. S. Department of Commerce, Bureau of the Census, *Public Employment: Government Employment 1990*, Tables 1, 3, and 5. (Washington, D.C.: U. S. Government Printing Office, September 1991), pp. 1, 3, 5.

Table 1.4
Employed Members of Civilian Labor Force by Major Occupational Group,
1972, 1982, and 1992 (numbers in thousands)

Occupational Group	1972		1982		1992	
	No.	Pct.	No.	Pct.	No.	Pct.
1	2	3	4	5	6	7
Total, all Occupations	82,153	100.0	99,526	100.0	117,598	100.0
Executive, administrative, managerial occupations	7,278	8.9	10,597	10.7	14,767	12.6
Professional & Specialty (Scientists, engineers, teachers, doctors, etc.)	8,830	10.7	12,555	12.6	16,386	13.9
Technicians & Related Support (e.g. health engineering, science)	1,928	2.3	3,013	3.0	4,253	3.6
Marketing & Sales	8,566	10.4	11,249	11.3	13,919	11.8
Administrative Support (e. g. clerical, and including supervisors and managers)	13,125	16.0	16,507	16.6	18,636	15.8
Service Occupations	10,831	13.2	13,494	13.6	16,096	13.7
Precision, Production, Craft and Repair	10,347	12.6	11,775	11.8	13,128	11.2
Operators, Fabricators, Laborers	17,384	21.2	16,550	16.6	16,957	14.4
Agriculture, Forestry, Fishing	3,843	4.7	3,751	3.8	3,456	2.9

Source: 1972 and 1982 data from Bureau of Labor Statistics (BLS), *Employment and Earnings* Table 1, January 1984, 13-14, with accompanying article by Klein, D., "Occupational Employment Statistics 1972-82." 1992 data from BLS, *Employment and Earnings*, Tables 20, 21. January 1993, 193-194.

manufacturing (-3.1); agriculture (-0.9); finance, insurance, real estate (1.9); and construction, mining (1.1).[72]

Occupational skill components of the labor force were in a state of proportionate flux to a slight, significant, or substantial degree in recent years, depending upon the skill or skill group involved. Data for 1972, 1982, and 1992 are summarized in Table 1.4. A more detailed breakdown within each occupational group as of 1992 is carried in Appendix 1.C.

Government is a major industrial grouping—a part of the services sector. In

October 1990, 18.4 million persons were employed full- or part-time by federal, state, or local governments; of these, approximately 3.1 million were in the federal government, 4.5 million in state government, and 10.8 million in local government. Nearly 8 million were in educational services (state and local), with 2.3 million in higher education; 5.6 million were employed in elementary and secondary education (K–12), mostly (4.9 million) by public school districts (numbering about 15,000).[73]

Unemployed and underutilized portions of the work force. The unemployed segment comprises those seeking either full-time or part-time work. The U.S. unemployment rate in the post–1955 period varied from a high of 9.5 percent in 1982–83 to a low of 3.7 in 1966–67. The lowest rate during the 1980s was 5.2 percent in 1989. In 1991, the rate averaged 6.6 percent, and in December 1991, of the 8.6 million unemployed, 7.1 million or 83.3 percent were seeking full-time work. The 1990–91 recession produced unemployment rates among civilian workers of an average rate of 6.7 for 1991 and 7.5 in May 1992.[74]

Unemployment rates reflect one segment of non- or underutilization of the labor force. Although a worker may be on a full-time schedule, he or she, for economic reasons—either within the firm or in the household—may not be able to keep to the schedule. Conversely, a number of workers on a part-time schedule really desire a full-time job, but none may be available. In December 1991, of 20.9 million part-time workers, 4.0 million, or about 19 percent, desired full-time work.[75]

Drop-outs from, and nonentrants into, the work force. In 1992, the NIP age 16 and over averaged about 191.5 million, of which 117.6 were employed in the CLF. The remainder of the NIP were either unemployed (about 9.4 million), or not in the labor force. The latter numbered over 64 million, of which about half were age 60 and over, with the other half comprising a relatively flexible pool of potential workers. The proportion of the NIP 16 and over not in the labor force headed steadily downward after 1960, during the 1956–91 period: 1956 (39.3); 1960 (40.0); 1970 (39.0); 1975 (38.3); 1980 (35.9); and 1992 (33.7).[76] This was due in considerable measure to a continuing increased percentage of women in the CLF; as this percentage flattens out, retirement ages may tend to increase. Table 1.5 summarizes the composition of this group by age and the reasons they did not want to be in the labor force. A further breakdown of the data by sex, race, and Hispanic origin, as well as reason, appears in Appendix 1.D. The portion of the group wanting but not seeking work is depicted in Figure 1.5.

The persons who "think they cannot get a job" and then drop out of the active labor force constitute a crucial category of "discouraged workers." This is especially the case for teenagers who have finished or dropped out of high school and those in the 20–24 age group.

For the discouraged group as a whole (1.03 million), the principal reasons, in percentages, for believing they could not get a job were job market/economic factors (67.6) and personal factors (32.4). Within the personal factor group, they

Table 1.5

Persons Not in the Labor Force, by Reason and Age Group, Annual Average, 1992 (numbers in thousands)

Reason	Total		16-19		20-24		25-59		60 & Over	
	No.	Pct.	No.	Pct.	No.	Pct.	No.	Pct.	No.	Pct.
1	2	3	4	5	6	7	8	9	10	11
Total not in LF	64,593	100.0	6,411	9.9	4,067	6.3	21,208	32.8	32,908	50.9
Don't want a job now	58,413	90.4	5,204	8.9	3,233	5.5	17,777	30.4	32,198	55.1
Reasons:										
Going to school	6,723	10.4	4,143	61.6	1,670	24.8	899	13.3	11	0.1
Ill, disabled	5,101	7.9	31	0.6	133	2.6	2,848	55.8	2,089	41.0
Keeping house	21,705	35.9	322	1.5	996	4.6	10,597	48.8	9,791	45.1
Retired	20,240	29.1	—	0.0	1	0.0	503	2.5	19,735	97.5
Other activity	4,644	7.0	709	15.3	434	9.3	2,930	63.1	571	12.3
Want a job now	6,181	8.9	1,207	19.5	833	13.5	3,430	55.5	710	11.5
Reason not looking										
School attendance	1,601	2.2	935	58.4	326	20.4	334	20.9	6	0.4
Ill health, disabled	1,078	1.5	17	1.6	58	5.4	820	76.1	182	16.9
Home responsibility	1,236	1.9	52	4.2	205	16.6	938	75.9	41	3.3
Think cannot get job	1,097	1.6	83	7.6	125	11.4	694	63.3	195	17.8
Job market factors	772	1.1	51	6.6	93	12.0	540	69.9	87	11.3
Personal factors	326	0.5	32	9.8	32	9.8	154	47.2	108	33.1
Other reasons*	1,169	1.7	119	10.2	118	10.1	645	55.2	286	24.5

Source: *Employment and Earnings*, January, 1993, Table 35, p. 214.

Note: * Included small number of men not looking for work because of "home responsibilities".

Figure 1.5
Males Age 16–59, Not in Labor Force, by Reason, 1990

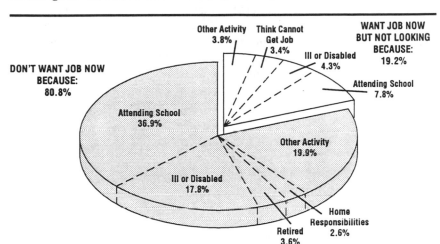

SOURCE: U. S. Department of Labor, Bureau of Labor Statistics, *Employment and Earnings 1990*, Table 35 (Washington, D.C.: U. S. Government Printing Office, January 1991), p. 204.

were too young or too old (36.7), they lacked education/training (43.7), or they had one or more other personal handicaps (19.6). The younger group (16–24) gave inadequate education/training as the principal reason, followed by age, and third, other personal handicap. The middle group (25–59) again felt education to be the principal handicap (59), followed by other personal handicap (26) and age (15). Not surprisingly, for the older group (60 and over), age was the overwhelming perceived handicap (83). Across all age groups, for blacks and those of Hispanic origin, education was perceived as the primary drawback, while for whites, the figures for relative factors were closer together: age (42), education (38), and other handicap (20). In the middle group, for all races, economic factors, such as the job market, were viewed as about three times as important in 1990 and 1991 as personal shortcomings.[77]

Blue-collar jobs and lower-skilled jobs in the white-collar category were much more at risk in the recession period, more so from a longer-range point of view. These workers faced the fact that despite an impending economic recovery, their lost jobs probably would never return; moonlighting continued at historically high levels; and most important, "the real culprit was technological change that made the skills of the educated more valuable, relative to those of the uneducated."[78]

Work Force Educational Requirement Trends and Projections

Among employers, labor economists, government officials, and the American public as a whole there is, and has been, for at least two decades a recognition of a continuing increase in training and skill levels necessary to perform adequately the majority of jobs in the labor market.[79] This recognition became sharper with the stiffening of foreign competition in the marketplace and the relative decline in numbers of lower-skilled and unskilled jobs, as well as growing complaints from private and public sector employers about the literacy and other abilities of job applicants and entrants. Noted earlier were differences of opinion among researchers, employers, and others as to the rapidity and scope of skill requirement escalation, both present and future. Data about the general thrust of these trends are presented here, followed by projections from several sources of educational requirements facing the future work force.

Educational attainment of the CLF, as measured by years of elementary-secondary education and college undergraduate and postgraduate study, improved during the 1970–90 period, as shown in Figure 1.6.

During the 1970–90 period, the percentage of men and women in the CLF age 25–64 with less than four years of high school dropped from 37.5 to 14.9 percent and from 33.5 to 11.2 percent, respectively; those with four or more years of college increased from 15.7 to 28.0 and from 11.2 to 24.6 percent, respectively.[80] The size and percent distribution of the CLF in the 25 to 64 age group by educational attainment, sex, and race are shown in Appendix 1.E.

Figure 1.7 shows in general terms the educational and employment status of the 31.6 million adolescent and young adults in the age 16–24 group in 1992. The proportion enrolled in high school or college stood at 40.6 percent of the population group, of whom a substantial number were working. Of this age group, who were not in school or college, many were working, but with sharply ascending proportions reaching higher educational attainment levels. A breakdown of these data by sex and by unemployment status as between full and part-time work being sought is shown in Table 1.6.

Appendix 1.F differentiates the educational and employment status of the 16–24 age group in the civilian labor force in terms of educational attainment, employment and unemployment status, sex, race, and Hispanic origin. These data present several discouraging aspects for the 16–24 age group as a whole for the current and impending employment problems of young persons with less than, or only, a high school education, particularly for certain minority racial and ethnic groups. The shortfalls of educational attainment in the light of projected job types and skill/knowledge requirements are examined later in this section.

Note should be taken at this point, however, of the progress in educational attainment made over the past two decades. While 36 percent of the labor force had less than a high school education in 1970, that figure declined by more than 50 percent by the end of the 1980s—to 14.7 in 1988, and for blacks a greater relative decline—from 55.5 percent to 22.6. The proportion with four or more years of college nearly doubled, with the black proportion going from 8.3 to 15.2 percent; as part of a growing middle class, many black workers increasingly moved into the more responsible, higher-paying occupations, with a larger pro-

Figure 1.6
Percent Distribution of Civilian Labor Force, Age 25–64, by Educational Attainment, Race, and Hispanic Origin, 1970 and 1990

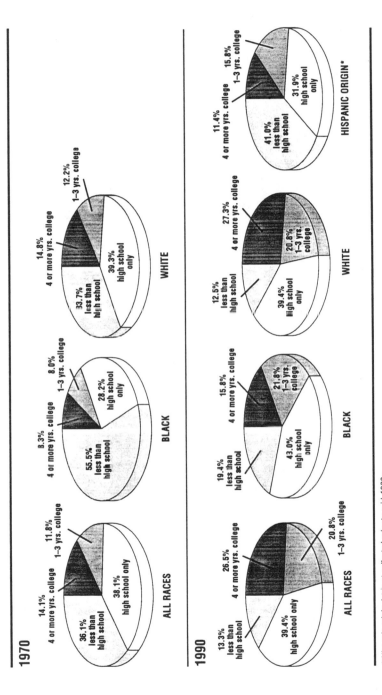

* Hispanic origin data not collected prior to mid-1980s.
SOURCE: U. S. Department of Labor, Bureau of Labor Statistics, *Handbook of Labor Statistics 1989* Table 65, 280–81, and Unpublished Tabulations from the Current Population Survey, 1990 Annual Averages (Washington, D.C.: U. S. Government Printing Office, 1991), Tables 1, 2, 9, 16, and 23.

Figure 1.7
Educational and Employment Status of Persons Age 16–24, 1992 (annual averages)

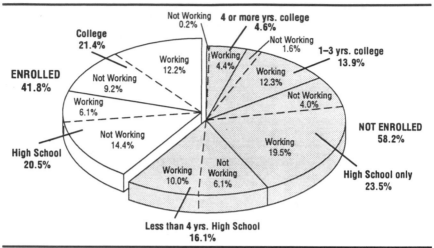

SOURCE: U. S. Department of Labor, Bureau of Labor Statistics, *Employment and Earnings 1992*, Table 6 (Washington, D.C.: U. S. Government Printing Office, January 1993), pp. 179–180.

portion among white-collar and skilled craft workers and a smaller proportion among domestic service and farm workers.[81] Conversely, for the 25–64 age group, a rather direct correlation is shown for all races between low educational attainment and both unemployment and dropping out or remaining out of the labor force. Data on these conditions are presented in Appendix 1.G.

PROJECTED 1990–2000 WORK FORCE OCCUPATIONAL COMPOSITION AND SKILL REQUIREMENTS

In the mid- and late-1980s, projections of U.S. work force numbers and occupational composition were issued by, or under the auspices of, the Department of Labor. The first of these was financed by the department, prepared by William Johnson and Arnold Packer and published by the Hudson Institute in June 1987 as *Workforce 2000: Work and Workers for the 21st Century*, carrying projections for the period 1984–2000. Subsequent projections were presented in issues of the *Monthly Labor Review*, 1989, 1991, and 1992, the latter two covering the period 1990–2005.[82] A Labor Department Commission on Workforce Quality and Labor Market Efficiency examined the implications of the projections, and another departmental group—Secretary's Commission on Achieving Necessary Skills (SCANS)—published an initial report in mid–1991 and a final report in April 1992.[83]

Table 1.6
Employment Status of Civilian Noninstitutional Population, Age 16–24 Not Enrolled in School, by Years of School Completed and Sex, 1992 (numbers in thousands)

Category	CNIP	In CLF	% In CLF	No. NICLF	% NICLF	Em- ployed	% of CNIP	Unem- ployed	Seeking Work F.T	Seeking Work P.T.	Unemp Rate
1	2	3	4	5	6	7	8	9	10	11	12
Total, all persons	17,987	14,285	79.4	3,720	19.8	12,250	71.2	2,035	1,728	312	14.2
Men	8,829	7,734	87.6	1,095	12.4	6,571	74.4	1,162	1,043	123	15.0
Less than high school	2,592	1,966	75.9	626	24.1	1,501	57.9	465	392	72	23.6
4 yrs. high school	3,623	3,319	91.6	304	8.4	2,830	78.1	489	458	31	14.7
1 - 3 yrs. college	1,975	1,832	92.8	143	7.2	1,667	84.4	165	149	16	9.0
4 or more yrs. college	637	613	96.2	24	3.8	565	88.7	47	44	3	7.7
Women	9,158	6,551	71.5	2,607	28.5	5,679	62.0	873	634	188	13.3
Less than high school	2,397	1,122	46.8	1,275	53.2	818	34.1	305	213	91	27.1
4 yrs. high school	3,642	2,711	74.5	931	25.6	2,360	64.8	351	294	58	13.0
1 - 3 yrs. college	2,313	1,959	84.7	354	15.3	1,785	77.2	175	139	36	8.9
4 or more yrs. college	810	763	94.3	47	5.8	721	89.0	42	39	4	5.5

Source: Bureau of Labor Statistics, *Employment and Earnings*, Table 6. January 1993, 179.

Notes: CNIP = Civilian non-institutional population; CLF = civilian labor force; NICLF = not in labor force; F.T. = Full time; P.T. = Part time.

Summary of Projections

Data on the occupational composition and educational attainment of the work force as of 1990 are presented in Appendix 1.H, along with the projected size and composition drawn from *Workforce 2000* and the referenced *Monthly Labor Review*. For the 1990–2005 period, drawing on the 1991 and 1992 referenced issues of the *Review*, the relative expansion and decline of industry groups and occupations can be summarized as follows, using the moderate or middle-range projections (where, as in census projections, high, middle and low alternative projections are issued):[84]

• Average annual growth rates of 1.3 percent for the labor force and 1.2 percent for employment were projected, compared with 1.9 and 2.3 in the 1975–90 period, with a 5.5 percent civilian unemployment rate in 2005, compared with 8.5 in 1975, 5.5 in 1990, and about 7.5 in the 1991–92 recession trough. The labor force in 2005 would number 150.7 million, and employment 147.2 million, a gain of 21.1 and 27.4 millions, from 129.6 and 119.8, respectively, in July 1992. (The 147.2 figure includes employment in agriculture and related fields as well as self-employed. The unemployment rates were calculated against a base of about 142 million, which includes the agricultural self-employed groups.) Employment had grown by about 35 million in the 1975–90 period. Thus employment growth would be at a slower rate than before, minus the powerful propelling factors of massive entry of women into the force and a sharp decrease in unemployment in the earlier period.

• The net 26 million job increase from 1990 would comprise 56 million new entrants and 30 million retirements and other departures.

• Practically all the increase would be in the service sector (only 0.3 million in the goods-producing sector, comprising an increase of 0.9 million in construction and a 0.6 million decline in manufacturing). With an average 20 percent increase in employment over the 15-year period, the fastest growing occupational groups, in percents, would be math and computer scientists (73); personal services (laundry, barbering, shoe repair, and so on) (44); health technologists/technicians (41); lawyers/judges (34); and protective services (32). The sharpest declines and slower growths would be in private household work (− 29); machine operators, assemblers, inspectors (− 9); financial records processing (− 4); farming, forestry, fishing (5); and handlers, equipment cleaners, helpers, and laborers (8).

• Labor force composition was projected to shift toward a slightly higher percent for women (from 45.3 to 47.4); blacks up from 10.7 to 13.0; Hispanics from 7.7 to 15.7; and Asians/other races from 3.1 to 6.0. White non-Hispanics comprised 78.6 percent of 1990's labor force but were projected to drop to 73.0 and would comprise 82 percent of the labor force leavers, but only 65 percent of new entrants.

• Perhaps the most significant findings regarding future labor force composition were the continuing above-average growth rate for jobs requiring relatively higher levels of education and training. The three major groups of (1) executive/managerial, (2) professional specialties, and (3) technicians/related support comprised about a fourth of total employment in 1990 but were projected to account for 41 percent of the employment increase during the 1990–2005 period.

- A continued direct correlation between the level of education and training and the level of compensation was projected, meaning that failure to complete high school usually results in a considerably lower wage or salary. On the other hand, the BLS projections concluded that the relative earnings increase for college graduates during the 1980s might well be the result of a worsening job market for male high school graduates, rather than a shortage of workers with college degrees. However, many employers recruit, or prefer to recruit, college graduates for most jobs in managerial and professional specialty groups and for many or most technician positions as well. It is expected that an increased supply may cause the proportion of college graduates who enter jobs requiring a degree to drop to 70 percent from the 80 percent prevailing during the 1984–90 period.

- When occupations were ranked by the Labor Department according to specific skill criteria—language, math, and reading—there was a direct correlation between skill requirements and rate of job growth.

- In addition to literacy and numeracy skills, holders of many of the newer-type jobs must be able to work both more autonomously, on the one hand, and as team members, on the other, in contrast to routine assembly work requiring a simple set of physical acts, a never-changing routine, or menial laborer chores.

- The continuing job shift among occupational categories and tightening of skill requirements in several of the growing groups listed above tend to have a strong negative impact upon blacks, Hispanics, and other disadvantaged groups, which are heavily represented in the lower-skill groups and more sparsely found in the higher-skill categories.

- When earnings are taken into account, it has been noted that in contrast to their respective 10.9 and 7.3 percent of the 1988 labor force, more than half the employed blacks and Hispanics in 1988 were found in three major occupational groups—service occupations; administrative support occupations, including clerical; and operators, fabricators, and laborers.

- The latter two of the preceding three groups are projected to have below-average growth in the period to 2000, with only the service occupations projected at a faster than average pace. Several of the service groups (e.g., household, building, and food) are in the lower-paying category). On the other hand, state and local government education (K–12 teachers and college faculty) was projected to increase by a million jobs, from 7.3 million in 1988 to 8.3 million.

The foregoing summary presented a broad range of challenges to all sectors of the U.S. economy, to all three levels of government, as well as to all young people. Already discussed were the challenges of higher productivity, especially in the services sector, and increased attention to overseas markets and a global, rather than a national, economy orientation. Apparent from the data on present and projected participation by women and minorities is the absolute imperative for integrating black and Hispanic workers fully into the economy and reconciling the conflicting personal and work needs of women and families.

Finally we come to the serious shortfalls in education and training. These shortfalls present private and public systems of elementary and secondary schools with "a new educational challenge," as aptly summarized by Robert Reich (subsequently secretary of labor in the Clinton administration):

The old system of education mirrored the old organization of production—most people spent eight to twelve years of their childhood [in] training for cog jobs, while a few were propelled toward top policy and planning positions. The new system must prepare for more people to take responsibility for their continuing education, and to collaborate with one another *so that their combined skills and insights add up to something more than the sum of their individual contributions.*[85]

The health and education aspects of future labor force preparation are the central foci of this book and are treated in succeeding chapters. However, our consideration of overall labor force needs will not be complete unless the challenge to employers to broaden and intensify postentry training and a continuous retraining process is examined carefully.

Increased Skill Requirements

As noted in *Workforce 2000*, education levels are only a generalized approximation for the skills necessary for employment.[86] For more specific criteria, six levels of skills were ascertained by the Labor Department, together with illustrative knowledge and tasks:

1. Language ability, including a vocabulary of 2,500 words, a reading rate of 95–125 words per minute, and capability of writing simple sentences.
2. Ability to write compound and more complex sentences and to use all tenses when speaking or writing, a vocabulary of 5,000–6,000 words, a reading rate of 190–215 words per minute, and a math skill of adding, subtracting, dividing, and figuring percents.
3. Ability to read and interpret safety rules and equipment instructions and to write simple reports.
4. Ability to read and understand journals and manuals and to compose business letters and reports.
5. Ability to read and understand scientific journals and financial reports and to write articles and speeches.
6. Public speaking and writing expertise and math abilities in advanced calculus and statistical probabilities.[87]

Compared with a mid–1980s average skill level of 2.6, embracing 70 percent of U.S. workers, a projected skill of 3.6 required in the year 2000 would include 58 percent of workers, with a full 40 percent needing a 5–6 level; *only 2 percent of the work force would be able to get by at levels 1 and 2.*[88] To attain these higher levels, enhanced preentry education and training alone will not suffice. Although a number of researchers and employers believed the projected difficulty levels and percents to be unduly high, the rapid changes in the workplace and work force over the past two decades support the general direction of these skill-level projections.

These skill levels can be acquired through a combination of preentry formal school education and postentry training. But for many young people in the United States, a bridge between school and work is absent or inadequate. A 1991 study by the General Accounting Office (GAO) found that

about half of U.S. youth do not go on to college and they receive little assistance in making the transition from school to work. Many flounder in the labor market, jobless or obtaining jobs with few opportunities for advancement. . . . High quality cooperative [school-work] programs show strong potential. . . . [whereby in the absence of apprenticeship programs] students attain work orientation, job skills, and often, permanent employment. They also are more likely to stay in school . . . employers gain access to a pre-screened pool of employees. . . . Efforts to expand cooperative education must overcome two major barriers: lack of awareness about programs and a negative perception of cooperation at the high school level [e.g., steered away by faculty and college counselors, parental fear that such a program might restrict options for college study].[89]

Various other problems of, and policy alternatives for, school-work transition are examined in chapters 5 and 6.

Postentry Training

Employer-provided formalized learning programs expanded considerably during the 1980s, driven both by technological advance and by the declining literacy and numeracy qualifications of many job applicants and entrants.[90] The private sector outlay for these programs had reached $30 billion in 1984,[91] and outlays for formal training alone by 1990 were estimated at $30 billion. In addition, the costs of informal training, which might include watching other workers at work or receiving other instruction outside formal settings, ranged everywhere from $90 billion to $100 billion.[92] Growing corporate recognition of the core necessity of employer investment in human capital development was illustrated by survey results of the decisions of most (80%) large businesses to maintain or expand training budgets in the face of recessionary influences in 1991–92, though 54 percent of them had laid off personnel during the same period. About a third reported an increase, a third a decrease, and the remainder, no change. Sixty-five percent contemplated increased training outlays in the postrecession period.[93]

Formal training might include outlays for middle management seminars as well as remedial education for entry-level workers. As the foregoing dollar ranges suggest, the cost estimates of employer-provided training are highly subjective, dependent on definitions and inadequate data. The tax treatment of training as between benefits and costs to employer and employee can vary as to training type and accounting methodology.

The scope and pace of work-based learning were broadening and quickening in the early 1990s. The time period for obsolescence of skills in many job categories shortened from 7–15 years to 3–5 years.[94] The skills toward which much pre- and postentry training has been directed comprise (1) preemployment and work maturity skills needed to find and hold a job; (2) basic education skills; and (3) job skills for the particular position involved. The first two should be, and often are, provided by the public or private K–12 school, supplemented by vocational education courses. With increasing frequency, however, it has been necessary for employing establishments to provide remedial cognitive, work maturity, and other social skills in addition to job-related technical training.

The Commission on Work Force Quality and Labor Market Efficiency, established by the U.S. secretary of labor in 1988, noted in its 1989 report that despite the magnitude of private sector annual spending in the $30 billion plus range, this outlay was spread across well over 100 million workers and came to only 1 to 2 percent of payroll. In addition, the expenditures tended to be concentrated in the higher-skill, higher-paid workers.[95]

Following the publication of *Workforce 2000* and in wake of the widespread public interest and favorable comment it received, agencies of the federal government, especially the Labor Department, began efforts to ascertain (1) what needed to be done to remedy the education and training shortfalls that had been identified and (2) how, and through what institutional changes and other arrangements, such steps should be undertaken.

It was apparent that attention needed to be directed to several areas of skill weakness: "basic" or "enabling" skills (literacy, numeracy, and so on); functional skills (the common abilities required to perform a range of jobs); technical skills peculiar to each suboccupation or skill; and integrative skills (use of information, social cooperation and interaction, such as negotiation and dealing with customers). Here we are concerned with the basic and functional skills, since our focus throughout is the preparation of youth for future labor force participation, covering the period from birth to stable employment or into postsecondary education.

Basic Skills. The "basic skills problem" was a growing complaint with many private employers through the 1980s. In the manufacturing sector this was placed into perspective with other factors by a survey done for the National Association of Manufacturers (NAM) by the personnel consulting firm of Towers Perrin, covering 360 companies. The average firm in the sample screened six applicants for each one hired. The most often cited reasons for rejection, in percentages were (1) will adapt poorly to work environment (about 60); (2) inadequate reading and writing skills (nearly 40); (3) no work experience (30); (4) deficient calculation skills (30); (5) poor verbal skills (25); and (6) failed medical or drug test (15).[96]

Training activity by employers to improve these skills may follow two major paths, among others: (1) provision of literacy and other basic cognitive training of probationary or other new employees for the purpose of filling in what the public or private high school failed to accomplish and (2) upgrading of regular employees whose basic skills no longer suffice to let them perform adequately within the establishment's work processes as the march of automation and other technology and the squeeze of the competitive marketplace requires lowered costs per unit and enhanced quality control of product.

A 1991 Rand Corporation report compared employer-provided entry-level training in the United States, Britain, and Australia, drawing on longitudinal studies of a total of over 14,000 young males in the 14–26 age group over a several year period in the three countries. Among the findings:

The data suggest that American youth get less formal training upon entry into the labor market, but more formal training [over time] in the labor market. . . . Between 30 and 40 percent of non-apprentices in Britain and Australia report some formal training. . . . [As they] acquire work experience a high (and rising) proportion of American youth report receiving training, while job training in Britain and Australia proceeds at a slower pace.[97]

Employer-provided basic skills training combined with job-related training under the same "program umbrella" has been illustrated in the Motorola Corporation. William Wiggenhorn, the vice president for training and education and the president of Motorola University, described early basic skills shortcomings thus:

We discovered to our utter astonishment that much of our work force was illiterate. They couldn't read. They couldn't do . . . percentages and fractions . . . our people were working by the color of the package, not by what it said. . . . We moved out in both directions: down, toward grade school basics as fundamental as the three R's; up, toward new concepts of work, quality, community, learning and leadership. . . . We came to spend $60 million annually—plus another $60 million in lost work time—and everyone thought it was money well invested.[98]

The report *The Bottom Line: Basic Skills in the Workplace*, published in 1988 jointly by the U.S. Departments of Labor and Education, addressed the challenges posed by *Workforce 2000*. It noted that an emphasis on school improvement alone would not

answer the needs of those young people who . . . drop out or those now of workforce age who will comprise 75 percent of the available pool for the next 15 years. So, even assuming the mastery of basic skills by all high school graduates, an increasing percentage of graduates [in the work force] will not address the basic skills problems of the current and near-term workforce.[99]

The report went on to note a wide range of literacy shortcomings in the then current work force, such as a third of secretaries not reading at job-required levels, half of managers/supervisors unable to write grammatically correct paragraphs, and numerous bookkeepers unable to use decimals and fractions. Finally, it placed the term *functional illiteracy* in a working context:

A clerk in the army, an executive in a bank, a nurse in a hospital, a city policeman, and a salesperson in a telecommunications company must all be able to read, write, reason, and calculate. Each must have command of the language and knowledge bases that are specific to their job tasks. In the absence of these skills, they would be functionally illiterate for the jobs they hold.[100]

Bottom Line proposed that firms conduct a "literacy audit," which would include determining basic skills needed through observation and collecting materials written in the course of the job, and from such determination, develop a basic skills improvement program. A variety of programs were cited that had been put into place (e.g., a Skill Enhancement Program operated jointly by Ford Motor and the United Auto Workers (UAW) in six areas—including adult basic education, high school completion, and enrichment education—to sharpen math, reading comprehension, and science needed for technical training, college courses, or other personal goals).[101]

Direct delivery of basic skills instruction/training by the employing establishment itself often is practicable for only the larger-size firms, especially if a literacy audit finds a large number of workers needing lengthy and intensive literacy upgrading. Much employer-financed training is delivered under contract with proprietary, nonprofit, or public providers.

Functional Skills. In April 1990, the Labor Department established a Secretary's Commission on Achieving Necessary Skills (SCANS), headed by former labor secretary William Brock, to define the essential skills needed to close the gap between educational achievement and workplace requirements. A statement of mission issued later in the year emphasized the teaching of functional skills.

The commission rendered an initial report in June 1991 and a final report in April 1992. The first report, *What Work Requires of Schools: A SCANS Report for America 2000*, opened with three conclusions: (1) all American high school students must develop a new set of competencies and foundation skills if they are to enjoy a productive, full, and satisfying life; (2) the qualities of high performance that characterize the most competitive companies must become the standard for the vast majority of U.S. companies—large and small, local and global; and (3) the nation's schools must be transformed into high-performance organizations in their own right. The commission's final report, *Learning a Living: A Blueprint for High Performance*, iterated the above conclusions.[102]

The reports identified five workplace competencies resting on three *foundations*, comprising (1) *basic skills*—reading, writing, arithmetic/math, speaking, and listening; (2) *thinking skills*—thinking creatively, making decisions, solving problems, seeing things in the mind's eye, knowing how to learn, and reasoning; and (3) *personal qualities*—individual responsibility, self-esteem, sociability, self-management, and integrity.[103]

The five competencies were (1) *resource use*—allocating time, money, materials, space, and staff; (2) *interpersonal skills*—working on teams, teaching others, serving customers, leading, negotiating, and working well with people from culturally diverse backgrounds; (3) *information*—acquiring and evaluating data, organizing and maintaining files, interpreting and communicating, and using computers to process information; (4) *systems*—understanding social, organizational, and technological systems, monitoring and correcting performance, and designing or improving systems; and (5) *technology*—selecting equipment and tools, applying technology to specific tasks, and maintaining and troubleshooting technologies.[104] Finally, the initial report specified three major implications for the U.S. educational system, especially K–12,[105] which are examined in a later chapter.

The commission's final report recast the foregoing broad principles as the context for its "action" recommendations: qualities of high performance characterizing our most competitive companies should become the standard for most employers; the nation's schools must be transformed into high-performance organizations; and all Americans should be entitled to multiple opportunities to learn the foundation skills and workplace competencies well enough to earn a decent living. More specifically, the commission recommended that:

- the nation's school systems should make the SCANS foundation skills and workplace competencies explicit objectives of instruction at all levels;
- assessment systems should provide students and workers with a résumé documenting attainment of the skills and competencies;
- all employers should incorporate these foundations, skills, and competencies into their human resource development efforts;
- the federal government should continue to bridge the gap between school and the high-performance workplace, by advancing the foregoing agenda; and
- every American employer should create its own strategic vision around the principles of the high-performance workplace.[106]

Subsequent to the final SCANS report, the Bush administration took the first formal step toward developing national testing standards for the workplace skills formulated by the commission and preceding studies and reports. The departments of labor and education began a series of joint public hearings on the subject in the spring of 1992. Following the hearings, the two departments launched 13 pilot projects designed to develop and validate industry-based skill standards. Provisions for the establishment of such standards were incorporated in one of the titles of education reform legislation proposed by the Clinton administration in 1993.[107]

The first SCANS report was met with a mixture of praise and criticism. In companion newspaper columns, Robert Samuelson termed it a "wrong-headed" opinion and full of jargon and failed to face up to the dilemma of "indifferent students and undemanding schools," while then Labor Secretary Lynn Martin argued that the worlds of school and work should be brought closer together and not rely on Samuelson's prescription for a "return to the good old days of the 19th-century school."[108] *The Economist* observed: "Pupils will keep more in their minds if their lessons are placed in context. Even the fact that the SCANS report has had a few raspberries need not depress the authors: abuse suggests that people may be taking the subject seriously."[109]

The earlier Commission on Work Force Quality and Labor Market Efficiency had noted an important economic obstacle to private employer outlay for human capital investment—*workers who leave a firm take their skills with them.* This obstacle is enlarged greatly with increases in employee mobility. The commission cited OECD mobility data showing the average stay on the job of a U.S. worker to be 7.2 years, *with Australia being the only other of the 14 OECD member countries having a lower average job tenure.*[110]

The Department of Labor's Advisory Commission on Work-Based Learning in a 1991 report expressed the view that the productivity gains from work-based learning were generally greater than those achieved from investments in capital and prework formal education. Among other suggestions for departmental action, the report proposed the development of (1) benchmark models for integrating training and technology through federal-state technology diffusion programs; (2) ways that large companies can leverage and assist small and midsize suppliers in implementing work-based learning programs; (3) benchmark programs that promote labor-management cooperation and involve workers in their design, installation, and administration; and (4) processes in large and small companies that maximize the potential of women and minorities.[111]

The latter two points—labor-management cooperation/worker involvement and increasing attention to training needs of women and minorities—lay at the heart of widespread criticisms voiced by scholars and other observers of employer-provided training in the early 1990s. Undue concentration on advanced skills and neglect of the lower skills, said the Economic Policy Institute; "too white and too male," said a *Business Week* editorial. It noted that while women comprised about 30 percent of all MBA candidates, in those programs paid for by corporations, only a token number of the participants were women (about 3% of the 180 executives in Stanford's advanced management program). It concluded: "There is only one real explanation and it is a damning one: many big corporations simply are not committed to helping women and minorities to the executive suite."[112]

Worker Retraining and Adjustment

The CED report *An America That Works* stated:

The old organization of work around a strict division of labor derived from the demands of machine-based production processes, with rank-and-file workers tightly controlled by supervisors. This model is rapidly giving way [to new approaches] based on different organizing principles. As the advance of automation . . . transform[s] the workplace, they are creating demands for workers who can operate more autonomously, making decisions and innovations on the job. In such a workplace, the ability to gain and apply new knowledge becomes crucial, and this creates a need for continuing education and training throughout the working life.[113]

These new situations mean an end, in most occupations and industry groups, to the previous pattern of a working life-career in a single occupation, often for a single firm. Whole new occupations will be appearing as others disappear. Consequently, workers are facing necessary changes in skill, employer, and often location, and these bring greatly increased need for worker adjustment and relocation. This is because, in numerous cases, it is not possible for the worker to retrain quickly, and the new job opportunity may be at another location and/ or another company. Although the nation may have gone through the most severe worker readjustment period with the shift of several million persons out of manufacturing and agriculture, and the subsequent 1990–93 downsizing of middle management and other white-collar work force, the lessons of those periods and measures used to ameliorate readjustment and relocation problems need to be kept in mind.

In addition to the long-standing federal-state program of unemployment insurance (UI), Congress enacted the Job Training Partnership Act (JTPA), Title III of which provided for adjustment assistance and further legislation to provide assistance to special groups of workers displaced by Clean Air Act amendments, reductions in defense expenditures, and increased imports (trade adjustment assistance). A CBO study of workers displaced during the 1980s found that "levels of displacement . . . and of the consequences for the [displaced workers] provide no evidence . . . that the displacement problem is about to get substantially worse." It also found, however, that "roughly half of the displaced workers who received UI benefits exhausted [them] without having found another job" and questioned whether a sufficient number of retraining opportunities were available under existing assistance programs.[114]

Changes in skill requirements, the formation of new occupations, and the decline of others will necessitate a higher degree of occupational movement and job location in the future. Not surprisingly, in the absence of structural or cyclical influences, the mobility of labor force members has tended to vary directly with education and inversely with age. In 1987–90, 7.6 percent of persons aged 55 to 64 moved during a 12-month period, compared with 37.9 and 33.4 percent in the 20–24 and 25–29 age brackets. Only 11.2 percent of persons with fewer than 8 years of schooling moved, while 17.9 percent of those with 4 years of college moved.[115] The 1990 decennial census showed 9.5 percent of the total population age 5 and over moved in the 1985–89 period. Of all ages in 1989, 8 percent of all homeowners and 36 percent of renters moved in the preceding year.[116]

Recommendations for relocation assistance in moving to new job opportunities were considered politically off-limits for most of the 1970s, as federal and state officials favored place-oriented, rather than people-oriented, approaches. The migration from manufacturing brought a reversal to that policy, as evidenced by the JTPA of 1982.

Tightened Corporate Management

As already noted, competition from abroad brought industrial productivity to the forefront of private and public sector concerns in the 1970s and 1980s. However, the competitive challenge to corporate management went much further. Product quality, customer satisfaction, and labor relations were likewise elevated to musts for boardroom consideration.

Quality Management. Despite widespread recognition by large firms that the lessons taught to the Japanese corporations in the 1950s by W. Edwards Deming had to be applied in America as well and despite considerable investment in disseminating the virtues of total quality management (TQM), it appeared in the early 1990s that many corporate managers were not yet attuned to its realities.

A survey conducted in 1990–91 by Ernst and Young and the American Quality Foundation, a New York research organization, of nearly 600 U.S., Canadian, German, and Japanese companies found that many TQM plans in the U.S. firms were too generalized and too far removed from day-to-day operations to be effective. The study covered four major industries—computers, autos, hospitals, and banking. In listing those criteria that the company considered most important in compensating senior managers, profitability, individual performance, and personal traits far outranked quality performance. The latter was chosen by only 10 percent of the firms in contrast to 40 plus for profitability in banking and computers and 30 plus in hospitals and autos. Computer companies involved only 12 percent of employees in idea and suggestion programs. The use of customer complaints about existing products in the identification and design of new products in the computer industry was found in 73, 60, and 26 percent of surveyed firms in Japan, Germany, and the United States, respectively. An Ernst and Young partner was quoted as finding that "a lot of companies read lots of books, formed teams, and tried to implement 9,000 new practices simultaneously. But you don't get results that way, it's just too much." Joshua Hammond, president of the American Quality Foundation, emphasized that "if quality is going to have a payoff it's got to be a routine part of the way you do business."[117]

The Malcolm Baldridge National Quality Award designed to stimulate productivity and management improvement was established in 1987. Ironically, 1990 winners in the manufacturing category—IBM and General Motors—were perceived by many to be in the catch-up rather than the trailblazing sections of the international competitive arena.[118]

The product liability aspects of the U.S. legal system (coupled at times with "consumerism" campaigns) appeared also to be operating against innovation and risk taking. Additionally, while the U.S. business community was endorsing quality management principles, many individual firms were saying that such strategic and preventive measures were beyond the affordability of the next quarter's profit-and-loss statements and balance sheet bottom lines.

Worker Involvement. Despite the certainty of an ethnically and culturally diverse work force in the years ahead, many private firms and governmental units and agencies have many changes to make in involving line supervisors and individual workers in work quality decisions, in broadening the participation base of employer-provided training, and in those management-worker relations affecting product quality and production processes.

Prior to the onset of global competition, evolving personnel supervisory practices both in industry and in government tended to encourage excessive overhead, especially in the middle management category. This was mainly due to the highly compartmentalized duties of individual groups of workers, necessitating the creation of coordinative positions. However, with the emergence of new and broader skill standards and the necessity for team approaches, both for economic efficiency and for product/service quality improvement, it became obvious that much unnecessary overhead existed. Consequently (in addition to broader values noted below), increased direct worker and supervisor involvement in the production process, overall productivity could be enhanced through the elimination of "many redundancies and non-value-added activities and personnel slots at the middle management level."[119]

In discussing "how Japan puts the 'human' in human capital," Alan Blinder emphasized that "the Japanese seem to have broken down the 'us vs. them' barriers that so often impair labor relations in American and European companies. They do so by creating the feeling that employees and managers share a common fate. . . . When an employee of Toyota thinks 'us vs. them,' 'them' is more likely to be Nissan or General Motors than Toyota management."[120] The "common fate" phenomenon, augmented by the partnership feeling engendered by the project team and other forms of worker involvement, seemed to be making considerable progress in many firms despite the adverse findings of the American Quality Foundation survey cited earlier.[121]

Likewise, local governments, especially in multiracial/ethnic urban areas, to meet the customer/taxpayer service satisfaction criterion in quality management, are adopting employment outreach programs. These governments must be able to see and understand the special needs of ethnic communities and neighborhoods through employees who understand how best to meet those needs and to deal with the residents on an equitable, but comfortable, basis. This is especially the case in regulatory functions such as code enforcement, police work, recreation, libraries, and firefighting. A diverse city or county work force not only can provide higher quality service to the customer but can go a long way to instill community harmony and stability.[122]

The "Industrial Policy" Issue

The general thrust of public policy at the national level traditionally was reluctance to engage in an "industrial policy," unlike Japan, with its Ministry for International Trade and Industry (MITI). The idea of government's trying to pick winners and losers in the marketplace has never been a persuasive one. Yet, throughout the 1980s and into the 1990s, state governments, and cities and counties to a growing extent, were effecting industrial policies of their own— not trying to pick and choose among competing firms and businesses but aggressively assisting *new* enterprises in getting started. This technical assistance role of state-local governments was being increasingly supported by the Congress, through programs of financial aid through the National Institute of Standards and Technology and the National Science Foundation.[123]

The end of the cold war and the phased reductions in defense expenditures seemed to precipitate an emerging consensus in 1991–92 that, rather than moving toward any picking of individual "winners and losers," national economic and fiscal policy should be directed toward (1) enhanced incentives for R&D in the high-tech industries, including continued and expanded governmental support for the dissemination of scientific and technical information, such as in communications infrastructure, and (2) continued federal support for those segments of defense R&D that already had demonstrated potential for industrial and commercial application. The earlier cited 1992 report of the National Science Board proposed (1) stimulating industrial R&D to match that of foreign competitors (e.g., tax credits); (2) reallocating R&D expenditures toward nondefense R&D, "process R&D" (technology transfer through extension centers and other means), engineering research, emerging and precompetitive technologies, and pioneering discoveries and inventions; (3) improving the speed and effectiveness of moving R&D results from lab to market; and (4) improving data quality and adequacy (e.g., a set of industrial science/technology indicators).[124]

A late 1991 report by the congressional OTA examined a range of policy options for the Congress to consider, including lower capital costs for long-term investment in technology development, improving the education and training of scientists and engineers, diffusion of technology to small and medium-size business (an industrial "extension service"), and possible sharing by government and industry in the development of risky, but potentially high-reward, technologies.[125]

SKILL SHORTAGE REMEDIATION ALTERNATIVES

Books, articles, reports, and other materials referenced so far, in addition to providing basic data, have presented various alternative proposals and possibilities for meeting the skills shortage that the nation's work force faces. The range of these proposals is described here, and their import summarized. Those applying to the education, other training, health, and environments of children and youth, in the age group of prenatal to 20, are examined comprehensively in succeeding chapters. Those proposals falling outside this group are discussed in somewhat more detail at this point, since they are not revisited subsequently, other than in passing reference.

Incentives to Older Workers to Remain in Labor Force and Empowerment of Others to Enter It

In the 1930s half of all men over 65 were in the labor force; at the beginning of the 1990s, the proportion had dropped to 15 percent. But numerous employers, both large and small, by that time were recognizing the benefits of retaining a larger percentage of this group as well as the costs, which include higher per capita health cost for that portion of health benefits provided to employees but not to retirees and lower mental and physical mobility, both in new skill training and in job location.

For those desiring to depart at retirement age, incentives for remaining include employer-provided flexible time and location arrangements, those that might be offered through federal and state tax systems, as well as those that involve both employers and governments, such as pension portability, which eases job mobility. It has often been suggested that the Social Security ceiling on earned income after retirement be eased or eliminated. While this change would cost the system money and would provide additional income to already financially comfortable persons, it could be made revenue-neutral by increasing the proportion of Social Security benefits of such higher-income persons subject to federal and state income taxation. Private pension plans could also be changed to raise retirement ages and consequent increased benefits for those working beyond regular retirement ages.[126]

In addition, steps were taken in the early 1990s to remove a number of physical and other barriers to disabled persons that had impeded their workplace and private lives. The increase of "telecommuting" and other options for employment at home eased the problems of the physically disabled. For the mentally retarded also, federal and state laws reducing discrimination in the workplace were put in place; and the utilization of illiterate workers had been enhanced through resort to talking and sign language computers.[127]

Increased Skill/Occupation-Based Immigration Quotas

A significant portion of future labor force needs *could* be met by resort to skill-based adjustment of immigration quotas and the consequent issuance of visas. As noted earlier, immigrants eventually make up an important share of the civilian labor force, regardless of the initial reason for their admittance. A further substantial increase of the labor market–connected portion to nearly half of all immigrants has been suggested. Also, the elevation of immigration to a more visible and powerful policy tool in the federal government would assure more careful and balanced consideration of labor market and other economic consequences of changes in immigration quotas.[128] However, by 1993, greatly increased economic-driven immigration into the United States and other Western democracies, often cloaked as seeking "political asylum," was turning public policy in a restrictive direction.

Increased Utilization of Part-time and Contract Workers

In 1991 19.2 percent of the employed members of the CLF were part-time workers. The growth of single-headed households and the preference of many married women for part-time work, as well as future labor force shortages, will dictate continued and growing use of measures to accommodate these preferences, including flextime and arrangements for the employee to work part- or full-time at home (''flexplace''). Also, the rapid rate of change in some occupations makes use of contract, rather than regular, employees more economical. However, a U.S. General Accounting Office (GAO) report has pointed out that part-time and temporary workers generally receive lower pay and fewer benefits than workers in comparable full-time jobs and often are not covered by retirement, health, or other benefit protection.[129]

Regarding the fringe benefit aspects, ''employee leasing'' arrangements provide an alternative for some types of firms. Unlike temporary workers, leased employees are de facto permanent employees of the firm at which they are working, but they are paid by, and draw benefits from, the lessor firm. In late 1991 an estimated 1 million persons were working for about 1,600 leasing or ''coemployment'' firms. By such an arrangement, the leased employees usually are provided higher benefits than the lessee firm could afford.[130]

Increased Investment in Labor-Saving Technologies

Most investment in technology, whether in the public or private sector, has in the past been directed principally to the manufacturing segment (computers, robots, integrated circuits). Little of the research funded by the national government is purposely aimed at improving productivity; rather, such improvements have been spin-offs from R&D support to defense and other operational missions of the government. Furthermore, few of the spin-offs are relevant to productivity improvement in the services sector of the economy.

In the areas of education and health care, however, governmental and privately supported research can be extremely useful in substituting technology for labor-intensive tasks (computer-assisted instruction in the schools and in health care, automated and computer-assisted billing, diagnosis, testing, treatment, and to a certain extent, care itself). Advances in information technology, allowing vastly more data to reach many more places, can do much to enhance productivity in all sectors and further stimulate economic growth.[131]

Public Sector Employment and Training Programs

Noted earlier were various data on income distribution in the United States, along with the relationship of education and training to salary and wage levels. In a 1992 article in the *American Economic Review*, two Michigan economists examined four alternative reasons for the large increase in the relative wages of highly educated workers in the 1980s: (1) decline in manufacturing employment associated with the trade deficit; (2) declines from overly high prior wages in manufacturing, associated with union power; (3) changes in technology, typified by the computer revolution; and (4) slowdown in growth rate of the college-educated population. The researchers concluded that the principal reason was "a combination of skill-biased technical change and changes in unmeasured labor quality." Applying hindsight to this conclusion could lead one to question the adequacy of public policy in the 1980s in largely neglecting the needs of further education and training of the non–college-bound youth, which would have shortened considerably the transition and adjustment to the drastic technological changes that were occurring.[132]

A number of federal-state training and placement programs were in operation in the early 1990s; two major elements of the federal-state effort consisted of the U.S. Employment Service dating to the early 1930s and the Job Opportunities and Basic Skills (JOBS) program, established as part of 1988 welfare reform legislation, the Family Support Act (PL 100–485). A GAO review of the JOBS program delivered to Congress in 1991 found that (1) state governments had made significant progress in establishing the program but were experiencing difficulties; (2) all states had had programs in place by the federally mandated deadline of October 1990, and 31 states were operating the program on a state-wide basis; (3) most states were moving in the new directions required by the program, especially targeting services to those facing employment barriers; and (4) major difficulties being experienced were shortages of such services as remedial education and transportation.[133]

Among the recommendations in its report *Investing in People*, the Commission on Work Force Quality and Labor Market Efficiency suggested three changes in the JTPA, the U.S. Employment Service (USES), and the federal-state unemployment compensation system. For the JTPA it proposed an increased targeting of resources to those in need of remedial education, improved coordination of JTPA programs with other human resource systems, and increased emphasis on basic skills remediation.

The commission found that ways should be developed to make the USES more effective and that the most promising way to improve it would be to install in it a system of accountability similar to that used in the JTPA program. Also, in the employment service and employment compensation area, it was proposed that state systems of unemployment insurance be modified to increase the extent of "experience rating" by changing the tax base, tax rates, and other features such as noncharged benefits.[134]

Balancing the Needs of Women, Families, and Work

Reconciling the needs of children, working mothers, and the labor force began receiving a great deal of public attention in the late 1980s and early 1990s and became a high public policy and corporate concern. In 1987 an estimated 7 of

10 mothers would have preferred part-time work, stay-at-home jobs, or flexible work hours, yet only half had such situations. As its early 1992 meeting, the National Governors' Association adopted a policy statement asserting that existing public and private policies were not well integrated and did not adequately reflect new realities in families and workplaces and called for new policies that were "family-friendly."[135]

Major work/family reconciliation aspects and developments included:

- *More time off for parents*. This includes flexible hours, use of sick leave to care for children, more part-time work, and pregnancy leaves for mothers and fathers. During the 1988–92 period a number of states enacted family leave legislation, especially following the repeated failure of congressional initiatives along those lines. (Finally, in early 1993, a Family and Medical Leave Act was passed and signed by President Clinton.) What had begun as maternity leave quickly became paternal leave, and then evolved into family leave. A Conference Board survey in the early 1990s found that major reasons that companies were initiating flextime policies were, in descending order of percents, employee requests (88); support of corporate image (70); part of "work-family" initiative (67); recruiting advantage (60); productivity increase (52); and prevention of unwanted turnover (51).[136] Another dimension of the labor market with an easing effect on "workfamily" stress was the evolution of income-generating home offices, including both telecommuting and the self-employed. The number of home offices was estimated at 20 million in a survey commissioned by the NYNEX corporation. The extent of telecommuting, estimated at 5.5 million according to another survey, had reached the point that employers were beginning to adopt rigorous new rules, including the prohibition of using the arrangement as a substitute for day care.[137]

- *More high-quality day care*. This was an early recognized need, as more mothers began to enter the labor force. Lack of adequate day care became a major deterrent to women who wished, through training and/or immediate employment, to work themselves off the welfare rolls. Day care as a remaining major deterrent is examined in chapter 2, along with trend data on providers and the extent of employer provision, subsidy, or other assistance.

- *Amalgam of work/family and women's issues*. As the August 1993 implementation date of the new federal family leave law neared, an increasing number of larger companies, and some smaller ones as well, were adopting comprehensive work/family policies. Traditional attitudes (working hour flexibility as an employee accommodation) were giving way to competition-conscious management (flexibility as a competitive issue and management tool) and to innovative management (risk-taking, results-oriented, respecting employees' needs while being sensitive to individual differences). For example, AT&T had found that the average cost of unpaid parental leave was 32 percent of salary, compared with 150 percent for a permanent replacement. Johnson and Johnson had found a 50 percent reduction among employees using flexible time/family leave arrangements compared to the rest of the company's work force. *Business Week* observed editorially that "learning to mesh personal and business work cycles can provide an unexpected dollop of productivity. Family-friendly companies are doing everyone a favor—especially themselves."[138]

- *Women in the workplace and contrasting private and public sector roles*. As a part of the civil rights and technological revolutions of the 1960–90 decades, the role of women changed drastically in America: in the household, workplace, politics, and the whole of society. However, there was another important dimension—the economic one. Economics professor Gary Becker pointed out the contrast between personal/emotional aspects, such as harassment, with women still often in defensive positions, and their rapid economic progress in occupations and earnings post–1970. In the early 1990s they were making up 40 percent of the students in law, medicine, business, and architecture and (as noted earlier in this chapter) a still small, but rapidly growing, share in physical sciences and engineering. This progress has muted (Becker claims for economic reasons; others might say, political) the earlier calls for nationwide legislation on "comparable worth." Finally, in light of most projections, labor force shortages to 2000 and beyond for well-qualified professional and technical workers could further reduce, possibly completely eliminate, or begin to reverse the professional-technical gender earnings gap that had declined to below 20 percent for persons working the same hours with the same experience.[139]

Unfortunately,

research on the effects of possible remedies [for work/family conflicts]: how much companies can save by offering family leave, job sharing, help with child and elder care, and other benefits is mostly flawed or incomplete. . . . The Labor Department [in 1992] is funding research at several employers to gauge whether work/family programs affect productivity, turnover, absenteeism and tardiness.[140]

Comparable public policy research might indicate the extent to which such policies and programs can effectively reduce poverty, welfare dependence, and other segments of public social and fiscal policy.

Reclaiming the At-Risk Youth Population

From a social, as well as economic, standpoint, this challenge is the most important of all to arise from the widespread restructuring of the U.S. labor force and the increased skill requirements accompanying it. Estimates of the size of this at-risk population ranges between 1 and 2 million teenagers. These vulnerable households and children are economically, physically, or behaviorally threatened. Most, but not all, of the nation's vulnerable children come from these households. They are at risk while in school; they may also be school dropouts or high school graduates lacking entry-level skills; or they may be drug- or alcohol-addicted youth of any educational or training level.

As already noted, increasing the effectiveness of school instruction and providing incentives, both material and psychological, to get these teenagers to finish high school and go into either stable employment or postsecondary college or other training is a prime requisite. Examining policy options, centering on education and health but involving certain aspects of other fields as well, is the main purpose of this book.

A new "American dream," with many critical "what ifs," was aptly described in the closing words of *Workforce 2000*:

If every child who reaches the age of seventeen . . . could read sophisticated materials, write clearly, speak articulately, and solve complex problems requiring algebra and statistics, the American economy could easily approach or exceed the 4 percent growth of the boom scenario. . . . Boosted by the productivity of a well qualified workforce, U.S.-based companies would reassert historic American leadership in old and new industries, and American workers would enjoy the rising standards of living they enjoyed in the 1950's and 1960's. . . . Promoting world growth, boosting . . . productivity . . . providing for the needs of working families with children, bringing minority workers into the workforce, and improving the educational preparation of workers . . . are issues that will not go away. . . . By addressing them now, the nation's decision-makers can help to assure that the economy and the workforce fulfill their potential to make the year 2000 the beginning of the next American century.[141]

These words were as relevant, and even more urgent, in the early 1990s as in 1987.

THE FISCAL AND INTERGOVERNMENTAL CONTEXT

To complete our overview of the factors affecting the changing work force and workplace and their public policy implications, it is essential to review the fiscal environment that will influence remedial actions in both the public and private sectors. If the "new American dream" envisioned in the above *Workforce 2000* report is to be realized, substantial investments, as well as basic structural changes, will be necessary. But where will the money come from?

At the outset, it is well to note the comparative public sector roles in the national economies of the industrialized countries. In 1989, as reported by the Organization for Economic Cooperation and Development (OECD), government tax revenue as a percent of gross domestic product (GDP) stood at an average of 38.4 among the 23 member countries, with OECD Europe at 39.7, and European Community countries, 39.9. Sweden was the highest (56.1), Turkey (29.0) the lowest, and the United States and Australia tied for the next lowest (30.1). Within the "G-7" nations, France (43.8) was highest, followed by Germany (38.1), Italy (37.8), United Kingdom (36.5), Canada (35.3), and Japan (30.6) with the United States last (30.1).[142]

While the American public sector is comparatively smaller than that of other industrialized countries, expectations about the desirability, feasibility, and impact of governmental intervention tend to run rather high, especially in the education and health care areas. Federal spending in 1991 accounted for 23.3 percent of GNP, while state and local governments accounted for 13.0 percent.[143] Major components of these public expenditures (combined federal, state, and local) in 1989–90 are illustrated in Figure 1.8. They totaled over $2 trillion, 219 billion.

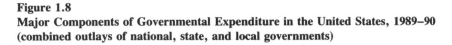

Figure 1.8
Major Components of Governmental Expenditure in the United States, 1989–90
(combined outlays of national, state, and local governments)

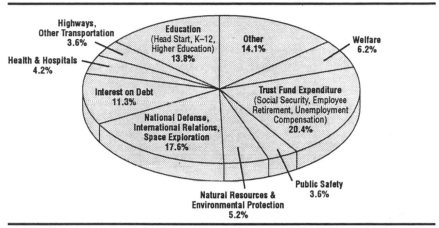

SOURCE: U. S. Department of Commerce, Bureau of the Census, *Government Finances 1989–1990*, GF 87-5, Table 2 (Washington, D.C.: U. S. Government Printing Office, December 1991), p. 3.

The two principal components were national defense-international relations-space exploration at $356 billion and insurance trust funds (Social Security, Medicare, employee retirement, unemployment compensation, other) at $454 billion. The next largest was education (K–12, higher, and other education) at $306 billion. Health/hospital expenditures—not including Medicare payments—were $92.5 billion.[144]

Overall governmental spending accelerated steadily after the Korean War, with the rate of state and local outlays generally outpacing both inflation and federal domestic expenditures until the 1990–91 recession. The growth of state and local spending was influenced by several factors, including population growth and migration, urbanization and suburbanization, and especially in the 1980s, budget surpluses. A major stimulus, however, was the rapid expansion of federal categorical grants-in-aid beginning in the early 1960s and continuing through much of the 1980s. Most of those federal programs contained matching requirements, calling for state and local financial contributions as well as compliance with a variety of administrative, process, and substantive policy conditions. The effects of these requirements on the scope of services and spending patterns of states and localities were significant.

As indicated in Table 1.7, federal aid reached its peak in 1980, with the total of $91.5 billion, representing 28 percent of state and local budgets and 22 percent of total domestic spending. During the Reagan and Bush presidencies, elimination and consolidation of some domestic programs and severe reductions in outlays for others diminished the portion of federal aid to 20 percent of state and local budgets and 20 percent of total domestic spending by 1990, even though the total amount of federal aid continued to grow to $135.4 billion by that year. These funds were dispersed through more than 500 separate programs, providing substantial assistance to a wide range of jurisdictions, programs, and individuals.

Changes in the magnitude, form, and fiscal impact of federal grants over the years were accompanied by shifts in the functional emphasis of these programs. As shown in Table 1.7,spending for education, training, employment, and social services grew from 10 percent of total federal grants in 1965 to 24 percent in 1975 but declined to 17 percent by 1985 and in the early 1990s was projected to fall to 15 percent by 1998. Over the same period, health grants rose from 6 to 18 to 23 percent of total federal aid, and they were projected to reach 51 percent by 1998. A large part of this projected increase is due to the rapid growth in federal outlays for Medicaid, providing for medical care to welfare recipients and to "medically indigent."

Turning to the subnational level, in 1990–91, state and local governments collected $748.1 billion of general revenue from "own sources" (exclusive of federal aid and of state aid to local governments) comprising $525.3 billion of tax revenue and $222.8 billion from user fees and miscellaneous general revenue. Their general expenditures (exclusive of utility, liquor store, and insurance trust expenditure) totaled $905.2 billion, which included pass-through federal aid for such programs as social services, transportation, health care, and education. Figure 1.9 shows the nature and proportions of state and local government general expenditures.

State aid to local governments was approximately comparable in dollar magnitude in 1990–91; in that year such aid approximated $182.7 billion, and about one-third of local general revenue was derived from the state governments, in contrast to 3.7 percent from federal aid. However, it must be noted that some of the state aid dollars going to local government were a "pass through" of federal aid, but this portion was quite modest, because 63 percent—nearly two-thirds—of state aid went to local public education, comprising mostly K–12 and community college segments, while the federal fiscal role in education was less than 10 percent of total public expenditure for that purpose. Local "own source revenue" in 1990–91 totaled $339.9 billion, with major portions consisting of property taxes (48%); user fees and charges (23%); other taxes (16%); and other revenues (13%).[145]

State, city, county, and school district governments are the public predominant financing and delivery agents through which public educational services are provided. State and local governments are also the principal deliverers of public health services, but the cost of a significant part of health care in the United States is borne either by the patient or by the federal government under its Medicare, Medicaid, and other health programs.

One final and crucial factor to be noted in this overview of the intergovernmental aid mix is the severe fiscal constraint that will be facing all three levels of government during the remainder of the decade. State and local governments faced large operating deficits for fiscal years 1991 through 1993, a trend that began in 1987, as shown in Figure 1.10. These shortfalls stemmed mainly from (1) growing citizen resistance to new or increased taxes, especially if the revenues to be derived from them were not earmarked for a particular, urgent, or popular purpose; (2) decreased revenue collections attributable to the 1990–91 economic recession; (3) increased construction needs to replace public physical infrastructure (roads, bridges, and other public works), practically all of which is supported by borrowing through bond issues; and (4) soaring costs of federally mandated expansions in Medicaid and environmental protection programs, which were not accompanied by compensatory federal aid. Likewise, high federal deficits were being forecast by the Congressional Budget Office through fiscal year 1997, due in large part to the costs of bailing out banking and savings and loan institutions, making interest payments on the growing federal debt, and increasing outlays for the federal share of Medicaid, estimated to grow from $53 billion in 1991 to $126 billion in 1997.[146]

SUMMARY

A broad array of trends and projections has been presented in this opening chapter. Because of their overriding importance in the consideration of detailed problems and public policy options in the ensuing chapters, the following deserve underscoring at this point.

- Technological advances, combined with global competition, will necessitate further downsizing dictated by productivity maintenance/improvement imperatives and a consequently less labor-intensive work force, illustrated by the maintenance of the manufacturing share of the GNP, but at the cost of scores of thousands of disappearing jobs over the past two decades continuing into 1993, with the strong likelihood of continuing over an extended period—hopefully at a reduced pace.

- The new facts of economic life, summarized above, would appear to dictate a smooth school-to-work transition and continuous education/training in the workplace in order to keep pace with an ever-changing world economy. Moreover, these changes will be necessary to help reduce the human costs of productivity improvements and to enhance the ability of individuals to contribute to the economy and society.

- Tighter labor markets are ahead due to slower work force growth and a relatively smaller pool of highly qualified workers.

- A somewhat slower growing and aging population portends reduced annual rates of economic growth over the long term.

- An income distribution pattern roughly following skill and educational levels, but with a continuing heavy political tilt toward the elderly population in income and asset accumulation.

- Growing importance of the immigration factor in work force composition, both in overall numbers and its use in meeting particular skill shortages.

- With scattered exceptions, continued relative decline in inner-city economic activity

Table 1.7
Trends in Federal Grants to State and Local Governments (outlays, dollar amounts in billions)

Grants	1960	1965	1970	1975	1980	1985	1990	1991	1992	1993	1994	1995	1996	1997
Percentage of distribution of grants by function:														
Natural resources and environment	2%	2%	2%	5%	6%	4%	3%	3%	2%	2%	2%	2%	1%	1%
Agriculture	3	5	3	1	1	2	1	1	1	1	1	1	*	*
Transportation	43	38	19	12	14	16	14	13	12	11	11	10	9	8
Comm. and regional devel.	2	6	7	6	7	5	4	3	3	2	2	2	1	1
Education, training, employ-ment & social services	7	10	27	24	24	17	17	17	16	15	14	13	13	12
Health	3	6	16	18	17	23	32	37	42	44	47	50	53	56
Income security	38	32	24	19	20	26	26	24	23	22	22	21	20	19
General government	2	2	2	14	9	6	2	1	1	1	2	1	1	1
Other functions	*	1	1	2	1	1	1	1	1	1	1	1	1	1
Total	100%	100%	100%	100%	100%	100%	100%	100%	100%	100%	100%	100%	100%	100%
Composition:														
Current dollars:														
Payments for individuals[1]	2.5	3.7	8.7	16.8	32.7	49.4	77.1	89.9	114.6	128.8	145.5	163.5	182.4	203.4
Physical capital[2]	3.3	5.0	7.0	10.9	22.5	24.8	25.7	26.5	28.1	29.4	28.6	29.1	29.1	30.5
Other grants	1.2	2.2	8.3	22.2	36.3	31.7	32.5	35.6	39.5	40.9	45.9	42.9	43.6	41.2
Total	7.0	10.9	24.1	49.8	91.5	105.9	135.4	152.0	182.2	199.1	220.1	235.5	255.1	275.2
Percentage of total grants:														
Payments for individuals[1]	35%	34%	36%	34%	36%	47%	57%	59%	63%	65%	66%	69%	71%	74%
Physical capital[2]	47	46	29	22	25	23	19	17	15	15	13	12	11	11
Other grants	17	20	34	45	40	30	24	23	22	21	21	18	17	15
Total	100%	100%	100%	100%	100%	100%	100%	100%	100%	100%	100%	100%	100%	100%
Constant (FY 1987) dollars:														
Payments for individuals[1]	9.0	12.5	24.7	35.1	46.3	53.0	67.4	75.0	93.0	101.3	110.9	120.7	130.5	141.0
Physical capital[2]	13.8	19.5	21.9	20.6	27.6	25.8	23.6	23.8	24.5	24.8	23.3	22.9	22.1	22.4
Other grants	6.4	9.8	26.7	49.6	53.7	34.2	28.7	30.1	32.4	32.4	35.2	31.7	31.1	28.3
Total	29.1	41.8	73.6	105.4	127.6	113.0	119.7	129.0	149.9	158.4	169.3	175.3	183.7	191.7

Total grants as a percent of:														
Federal outlays:														
Total	8%	9%	12%	15%	15%	11%	11%	11%	13%	13%	15%	15%	16%	16%
Domestic programs [2]	18	18	23	22	22	18	17	17	19	20	22	22	23	23
State and local expenditures	15	16	20	24	28	23	20	N/A	N/A	N/A	N/A	N/A	N/A	N/A
Gross domestic product	1	2	2	3	3	3	3	3	3	3	3	3	3	3
As a share of total state and local capital spending:														
Federal capital grants	25%	25%	27%	37%	31%	22%	N/A	N/A	N/A	N/A	N/A	N/A	N/A	N/A
State and local own-source financing	75	75	73	63	69	78	N/A	N/A	N/A	N/A	N/A	N/A	N/A	N/A
Total:	100%	100%	100%	100%	100%	100%	100%	100%	100%	100%	100%	100%	100%	100%

[1] Excludes capital grants that are included as payments for individuals.
[2] Excludes national defense, international affairs, net interest, and undistributed offsetting receipts.

Source: U.S. Office of Management and Budget, *Budget of the United States Government: Fiscal Year 1993*, part one-438.

Figure 1.9
Combined General Expenditure by State and Local Governments, 1989–90

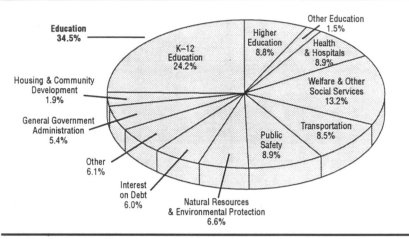

SOURCE: U. S. Department of Commerce, Bureau of the Census, *Government Finances 1989–1990* (Washington, D.C.: U. S. Government Printing Office, December 1991), Table 5, p. 6.

overall, but with historic patterns of boundary formation and adjustment playing a crucial role in economic growth or decline.

• Growing problems for many working couples in dealing with child care and balancing work and home responsibilities.

• Increasingly direct correlation between educational attainment and occupational advancement.

• Continued and intensified fiscal constraints upon public revenues and expenditure flexibility at all levels of government, arising from national economic conditions, the federal deficit, and taxpayer resistance to unearmarked taxation.

• The issue of a major shift in public and private resources toward reclamation and preventive measures to maximize survival of, and opportunity for, the increasingly at-risk child, youth, and young adult populations, especially in the poverty areas of America's central cities.

The following chapters treat principal potentialities and deterrents to employ-ability as applied to the fields of health care and education.

NOTES

1. U.S. Department of Labor press release 90–172, April 5, 1990, 1.

2. Committee for Economic Development (CED), Research and Policy Committee, *An America That Works: The Life-Cycle Approach to a Competitive Work Force* (New York: CED, 1990), 6.

Figure 1.10
State and Local Surpluses and Deficits as a Percent of GDP

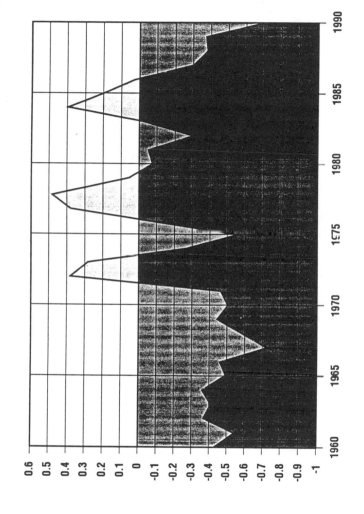

SOURCE: U.S. Office of Management and Budget, *Budget of the United States Government: Fiscal Year 1993*, Part One–441

3. Akers, J., "Let's Get to Work on Education," *Wall Street Journal*, March 20, 1991, editorial page.

4. U.S. Bureau of the Census, *Characteristics of the Population: Below the Poverty Level 1989*. Series P–60, no. 168, 1991, 7.

5. *The Ford Foundation Letter* 21, no. 3, Fall/Winter 1990, 1. See also "Children in Crises: The Struggle to Save America's Kids," *Fortune* Special Report, August 10, 1992, 34–96.

6. National Commission on Children, *Beyond Rhetoric: A New American Agenda for Children and Families* (Final Report) (Washington, DC: National Commission on Children, 1991), 122. See also U.S. Department of Health and Human Services (HHS), U.S. Public Health Service (USPHS), and National Center for Health Statistics (NCHS), "Firearm Mortality Among Children, Youth, and Young Adults 1–34 Years of Age, Trends and Current Status: United States, 1979–88," *Monthly Vital Statistics Report* Supplement, March 14, 1991, 3.

7. Interview in the *Washington Times*, August 30, 1991, A–1.

8. Education and Human Services Consortium, *What It Takes: Structuring Interagency Partnerships to Connect Children and Families with Comprehensive Services* (Washington, DC: Education and Human Services Consortium, 1991), 6.

9. Johnston, W., "Global Work Force 2000: The New World Labor Market," *Harvard Business Review*, March-April 1991, 115–27. See also Becker, G., "As Nations Splinter, Global Markets Are Merging," *Business Week*, April 22, 1991, 16; Belsie, L., "Global Unions: Labor Seeks International Reach," *Christian Science Monitor*, October 23, 1990, 7.

10. "Reduction of Trade and Budget Deficits: Key to Reviving Manufacturing," *Policy and Research Report* 17, no. 1 (Washington, DC: Urban Institute, April 1987), 9 (a summary based on Stone, C., and Sawhill, I., "Labor Market Implications of the Growing Internationalization of the U.S. Economy," an Urban Institute Changing Domestic Priorities paper prepared for the National Commission for Employment Policy).

11. Congressional Budget Office (CBO), *The Economic and Budget Outlook: Fiscal Years 1993–1997*, January 1992, 1–26. See also U.S. Department of Commerce, International Trade Administration (ITA), *U.S. Industrial Outlook '92: Business Forecasts for 350 Industries* (Washington, DC: ITA, January 1992), 6–18.

12. Ibid., xiii–xiv. See also Kuttner, R., "America Is Saving More Now, Not Less—If You Count It Right." (Is U.S. Department of Commerce using a faulty statistic in not counting as savings: capital gains, pension contributions, and house equity?) *Business Week*, Economic Viewpoint, April 13, 1992, 18.

13. Johnson, W., and Packer, A., *Workforce 2000: Work and Workers for the 21st Century* (Indianapolis: Hudson Institute, June 1987), 78–79.

14. The Urban Institute, "Will There Be a Skills Shortage in the Year 2000?" *Policy and Research Report*, Winter/Spring 1991, 22 (from Mincy, R., "Workforce 2000: Silver Bullet or Dud?" Research Paper [Washington, DC: Urban Institute, November 1990]). See also Reich, R., *The Work of Nations* (New York: Knopf, 1991).

15. Mishel, L., and Teixeira, R., *The Myth of the Coming Labor Shortage* (Washington, DC: Economic Policy Institute, July 1991).

16. "Productivity: Why It's the No. 1 Underachiever," *Business Week*, April 20, 1987, 54–55. On relation of education reform to productivity, see Chubb, J., and Hanushek, E., "Reforming Educational Reform" in Aaron, H. (ed.), *Setting National Priorities* (Washington, DC: Brookings Institution, 1990), 213–19.

17. "[Knowing] someone could be looking over their shoulders [managers] really have to be on the ball," a quote from Frank Beneski, a CIGNA vice president; however, consultants FCI, Inc., found in a poll of 60 major firms that management proclaimed in employee handbooks and job applications their right to fire at will, as reported in Labor Letter, *Wall Street Journal*, May 12, 1992, A–1.

18. "American Competitiveness" (editorial), *Wall Street Journal*, August 14, 1991, A–8.

19. DeLeeuw, F., Mohr, M., and Parker, R., "Gross Product by Industry, 1977–88: A Progress Report on Improving the Estimates," *Survey of Current Business*, January 1991, Tables 5–6, 33–34. See also Nasar, S., "Boom in Manufactured Exports Provides Hope for U.S. Economy," *New York Times*, April 21, 1991, A–1; Gleckman, H., "Itching to Get onto the Factory Floor: Manufacturing Jobs Attracting More MBAs as Wall Street Shrinks and Global Competition Grows," *Business Week*, October 14, 1991, 64–66.

20. U.S. Department of Labor (USDL), Bureau of Labor Statistics (BLS), "Productivity by Industry: 1989," News Release USDL 91–41; data in release derived from News Release USDL 89–570, November 28, 1989, BLS Bulletin 2349, February 1990, and Table 47 in the *Monthly Labor Review*, February 1990.

21. Packer, A., "Did America Ever Make Anything? How Official Statistics Keep Shrinking the Industrial Past," *Washington Post*, April 19, 1992, C–2.

22. Myers, H., "U.S. Exports May Set the Course of the Job Market," *Wall Street Journal*, Outlook column, May 18, 1992, A–1

23. *Service Sector Productivity* (Washington, DC: McKinsey Global Institute, October 1992), 1–4. See also Mandel, M., "There's a Silver Lining in the Service Sector," *Business Week*, March 4, 1991, 60–61.

24. From "Desktop America," *The Economist*, February 2, 1991, 66. See also Uchitelle, L., "A Growing Drag from Services," *New York Times*, Business Scene, September 24, 1991, D–2.

25. *Business Week* (editorial), "Consolidation: Cure or Disease," October 14, 1991, 166 (emphasis added). See also "The Business Week Plan to Spur Economic Growth: Promote Business Investment (Tax Incentives); Invest in People (Spend More on Training, Improved Access to Health Care); Fortify the Infrastructure; Remake Budget Policy (Expenditure Cuts, Targeted Tax Increases); Encourage Innovation; Don't Fight the Global Economy (Free Trade); and Ease Governmental Regulation," *Business Week Reinventing America* special issue, Fall 1992, 26, 224–25.

26. National Science Foundation (NSF), *Science and Engineering Indicators 1991*, 10th ed. (Washington, DC: NSF, December 1991), 260.

27. NSF, *International Science and Technology Update: 1991*, NSF 91–309 (Washington, DC: NSF, 1991), 47.

28. Organization for Economic Cooperation and Development (OECD), *OECD in Figures: Statistics on the Member Countries*, Paris, June-July 1992, 52–53. See also NSF, *Science and Engineering Indicators*, 341–42.

29. BLS, *Employment and Earnings*, Table 22, January 1992, 185.

30. NSF, *Women and Minorities in Science and Engineering: An Update*. NSF 92–303, January 1992, xi, xii.

31. OECD, *OECD in Figures*, 51–52.

32. NSF, *Science and Engineering Indicators*, 342.

33. National Science Board, *The Competitive Strengths of U.S. Industrial Science*

and Technology: Strategic Issues NSB 92–138 (Washington, DC: NSF, August 1992), ii.

34. Congress, Office of Technology Assessment (OTA), *After the Cold War: Living with Lower Defense Spending* (Summary) OTA-ITE–525 (Washington, DC: OTA, February 1992), 3–4.

35. NSF, *Science and Engineering Indicators*, 307.

36. Bluestone, B., and Harrison, B., *The Great American Job Machine: The Proliferation of Low Wage Employment in the U.S. Economy* (Prepared for the Joint Economic Committee of the Congress, December 1986). See also McMahon, P., and Tschetter, J., "The Declining Middle Class: A Further Analysis," *Monthly Labor Review*, August 1985, 9–22.

37. Levy, F., and Michel, R., *The Economic Future of American Families* (Washington, DC: Urban Institute), 1990. See also Silk, L., "Keeping a Chicken in Every Pot," *New York Times*, February 6, 1991, D2; Burtless, G. (ed.), *A Future of Lousy Jobs* (Washington, DC: Brookings Institution), 1990.

38. Blackburn, M., Bloom, D., and Freeman, R., "An Era of Falling Earnings and Rising Inequality?" *The Brookings Review*, Winter 1990/1991, 38–43.

39. U.S. Department of Commerce, Bureau of the Census, *Household Wealth and Asset Ownership 1988*, Series P–70, no. 22, December 1990, 1, 19.

40. Sawhill, I., and Condon, M., "Is U.S. Income Inequality Really Growing? Sorting Out the Fairness Question," *Policy Bites*, no. 13, Urban Institute, June 1992, 1–4.

41. U.S. Department of the Treasury, Office of Tax Analysis, "Household Income Mobility During the 1980s," June 1, 1992, 1. See also Nasar, S., "A Statistical Assessment Based on Tax Return Data: One Study's Rags to Riches Is Another's Rut of Poverty," *New York Times*, June 17, 1992, D–1; *Wall Street Journal* (editorial), "Income Dynamics," June 16, 1992, A–12.

42. Martin, L., "The Middle Class Is Not Disappearing," *Washington Post*, December 31, 1991, A–17.

43. "Official Numbers: The Good Statistics Guide," *The Economist*, September 7, 1991, 88.

44. Bureau of the Census, *Projections of the Population of the United States, by Age, Sex, and Race: 1988 to 2080*, Series P–25, no. 1018 (Washington, DC: Bureau of the Census, January 1989), 1.

45. (1) Bureau of the Census, *Projections*, Series P–25, no. 1018 and Supplement: March 1992, unpublished, Table 6, unnumbered pages. This shifted the 1989 projections toward the higher assumption category as they applied to fertility, Hispanic origin, and immigration. (2) Bureau of the Census, *Projections of the Hispanic Population 1983–2080*, Series 25, no. 995, Table B, November 1986, 2.

46. Ibid., (1), 6–9.

47. Ibid., (2), 2.

48. Ibid., (1), 9–10 and (2), 13–14.

49. Ibid., (1), Table K, 11–12.

50. World Bank, *World Development Report 1988* (Washington, DC: Oxford University Press, 1988), Table 27. See also Census Bureau, *Projections of the U.S. Population*, Table O, 13.

51. Immigration Act of 1990 (PL 101–649). See also Urban Institute, "Special

Section on Immigration Reform: Overview of Recent Urban Institute Immigration Policy Research," *Policy and Research Report*, Winter/Spring 1991, 11–19.

52. NSF, *Immigrant Scientists and Engineers 1988*, Report NSF 90–13, 1990, 7.

53. "The New Americans: Yes, They'll Fit In," *The Economist*, May 11, 1991, 17.

54. *Projections of the U.S. Population*, Table O, 13, as modified by No. 1018 Supplement.

55. U.S. General Accounting Office (GAO), *1990 Census: Reported Net Undercount Obscured Magnitude of Error*, GAO/GGD–91–113 (Washington, DC: GAO, August 1991), 1, 5. The prior report referred to was *Decennial Census: Preliminary 1990 Lessons Learned Indicate Need to Rethink Census Approach*, GAO/T/GGD–90–18, August 8, 1990.

56. U.S. Department of Commerce, Bureau of the Census, news release CB91–07, January 1991; Bureau of the Census, *Census and You*, 27, no. 2, February 1992, 5.

57. Bureau of the Census, news release CB92–276, Table 1, December 30, 1993, 3.

58. Ibid., CB91–66, February 21, 1991.

59. Ibid., CB91–24, January 25, 1991.

60. Manson, D., and Schnare, A., "Changes in the City/Suburban Income Gap, 1970–84," *Urban Institute Project 3376*, November 1985.

61. Ledebur, L., *City Fiscal Distress: Structural, Demographic, and Institutional Causes* (Washington, DC: National League of Cities, March 1991), 3 and unnumbered Appendix. See also Peirce, N., "Class Divisions Within States Growing Worse," *Messenger-Inquirer*, Owensboro, KY, June 16, 1991, 3E.

62. Marsh, B., "Some Small Businesses Are Heading Back to the Cities," *Wall Street Journal*, June 21, 1991, B–2.

63. Bureau of the Census, *Household and Family Characteristics March 1990 and 1989*, Population Characteristics, Series P–20, no. 447, December 1990, 1–7.

64. Bureau of the Census, *Marital Status and Living Arrangements 1990*, Series P–20, no. 450, Table J, May 1991, 10. See also Vobejda, B., "The Future Deferred: Longer Road from Adolescence to Adulthood Often Leads Back Through Parents' Home," *Washington Post*, September 15, 1991, A–1.

65. U.S. Department of Labor, Bureau of Labor Statistics (BLS), *Employment and Earnings*, January 1992, 164–66.

66. Census, *Projections*, P–25 no. 1018, Supplement Series 18, March 1992, Table 6.

67. Ibid.

68. BLS, *Employment and Earnings*, January 1992, 164.

69. BLS, unpublished tabulations from the Current Population Survey, 1990 Annual Averages, Table 1, 1991, 10–24.

70. BLS, *Handbook of Labor Statistics 1988*, Table 66 (Washington, DC: BLS, 1989), 282–83. For 1990 data and Hispanic participation rates post–1982: BLS unpublished tabulations cited in note 69.

71. Le Grande, L., "Adult Black Workers: The Progress of Some," Economics Division, Congressional Research Service, Library of Congress, December 1984, 22–23.

72. Personick, V., "Industry Output and Employment: A Slower Trend for the Nineties," *Monthly Labor Review*, Table 1, November 1989, 26. See also Shack-Marquez, J., "Issues in Labor Supply," *Federal Reserve Bulletin*, 77, no. 6, June 1991,

375–87; Myers, H., "Look for Jobless Rate to Remain High," *Wall Street Journal*, Outlook column, March 2, 1992, A–1.

73. Bureau of the Census, *Public Employment: Government Employment 1990*, GE 90–1, Tables 1, 3, and 5, September 1991, 1, 3, 5.

74. U.S. Department of Labor, BLS, *Employment and Earnings*, Tables A–1, A–9, January 1992, 14; "The Employment Situation: May 1992," *News* (BLS), USDL 92–337, June 5, 1992, 1.

75. U.S. Department of Labor, BLS, Table 3, 174, January 1993.

76. Ibid., Tables A–1, 35, 14, 204. See also, Murray, A., "Retirees Pose Burden for Economy," *Wall Street Journal*, Outlook column, September 16, 1991, A–1; Koretz, G., "Job Worries Obscure a Looming Labor Shortage . . . and Fewer Workers Could Mean Later Retirement," *Business Week*, Economic Trends, November 11, 1991, 26.

77. U.S. Department of Labor, BLS, *Employment and Earnings*, January 1992, Tables 35, 37, 204, 206.

78. Kohr, S., "Accepting the Harsh Truth of a Blue-Collar Recession: Old Way of Work, and Life, May Never Return," *New York Times*, December 25, 1991, A–1.

79. U.S. Departments of Labor and Education (joint report), *The Bottom Line: Basic Skills in the Workplace* (Washington, DC: U.S. Government Printing Office, 1988), ii–iii. See also U.S. Department of Labor, *Work-Based Learning: Training America's Workers*, November 1989, i–vi; U.S. National Science Foundation, Science Resources Section, *Human Talent for Competitiveness*, 1987; Committee for Economic Development, *An America That Works*, 1990, 1–2.

80. BLS, *Handbook of Labor Statistics*, 280–81 and unpublished tabulations, 1990 annual averages, Table 1, 1–2, 8–9, 15–16, 22–23.

81. La Grande, "Adult Black Workers," 1. See also Mann, T., *African-Americans in the 1990s: Growth, Change, and Diversity* (Washington, DC: Population Reference Bureau, July 1991).

82. *Workforce 2000*, 96–102; Silvestri, G., and Lukasiewicz, J., "Projections of Occupational Employment 1988–2000," *Monthly Labor Review*, November 1989, 60–65.

83. U.S. Department of Labor, Commission on Workforce Quality and Labor Market Efficiency, *Investing in People: A Strategy to Address America's Workforce Crisis*, September 1989; the Secretary's Commission on Achieving Necessary Skills (SCANS), *What Work Requires of Schools: A SCANS Report for America 2000*, June 1991 (interim report) and a final report: *Learning a Living: A Blueprint for High Performance*, April 1992.

84. *Monthly Labor Review*, November 1991; Kutscher, R., "Outlook 1990–2005—New BLS Projections: Findings and Implications," 3–12; Fullerton, H., Jr., "Outlook 1990–2005—Labor Force Projections: The Baby Boom Moves On," 31–44; Carey, M., and Franklin, J., "Outlook 1990–2005—Industry Output and Job Growth Continues Slow into Next Century," 45–63; Silvestri, G., and Lukasiewicz, J., "Outlook 1990–2005—Occupational Employment Projections," 64–94, *Monthly Labor Review*, July 1992; Hecker, D., "Reconciling Conflicting Data on Jobs for College Graduates," 3–17. See also *Review* February 1992: Braddock, D., "Scientific and Technical Employment 1990–2005," 28–40.

85. Reich, R., *Education and the Next Economy* (Washington, DC: National Education Association, 1988), 17 (emphasis added). See also Kolberg, W., and Smith, F., "A New Track for Blue-Collar Workers," *New York Times*, February 8, 1992, D–2.

86. *Workforce 2000*, 97–101.

87. Ibid., 98–99. See also Packer, A., "Job Training—Retooling the American Worker," *Washington Post*, July 10, 1988, C3.

88. *Workforce 2000*, 100.

89. GAO, *Transition from School to Work: Linking Education and Work Training*, GAO/HRD–91–105, August 1991, 2, 3, 30–31, 34. See also GAO, *Training Strategies: Preparing Noncollege Youth for Employment in the U.S. and Foreign Countries*, GAO/HRD–90–88, May 1990; Peirce, N., "Taking a Page from Europe's Book," *National Journal*, March 27, 1993, 772.

90. CED, *An America That Works*, 82.

91. Ibid.

92. Carnavale, A., "The Learning Enterprise," *Training and Development Journal*, (Arlington, VA: American Society for Training and Development [ASTD], January 1986), 1.

93. ASTD, *National HRD Executive Survey: The Effect of the Recession on Training and Development Survey Administered February 1991* (Arlington, VA: ASTD, June 1992), 1, 2.

94. U.S. Department of Labor, Employment and Training Administration, *Work Based Learning: Training America's Workers* (Washington, DC, November 1989).

95. U.S. Department of Labor, Commission on Workforce Quality and Labor Market Efficiency, *Investing in People* (Washington, DC, September 1989), 16.

96. As reported by Barker, R., "A Shortage of Basic Skills," *Business Week*, January 13, 1992, 39.

97. Tan, H., Chapman, B., Peterson, C., and Booth, A., *Youth Training in the United States, Britain and Australia*, R–4022–ED, supported by the U.S. Department of Education (Santa Monica, CA: Rand Corporation, 1991), 3, 38.

98. Wiggenhorn, W., "Motorola U: When Training Becomes Education," *Harvard Business Review*, July-August 1990, 71–83.

99. *The Bottom Line*, 12, 24. See also CED, *An America That Works* for description of the Aetna Institute for Corporate Education and Nissan's training program for a new work force at its Symrna, TN, plant, 78, 83.

100. Ibid., 13.

101. Ibid., 13–15.

102. (1) U.S. Department of Labor, the Secretary's Commission on Achieving Necessary Skills (SCANS), *What Work Requires of Schools: A SCANS Report for America 2000*, Interim report, June 1991, vi. (2) SCANS, *Learning a Living: A Blueprint for High Performance*, Final report, April 1992, xiv. See also Kane, M., et al., "Identifying and Describing the Skills Required by Work," prepared for SCANS, Employment and Training Administration, U.S. Department of Labor, September 1990, 10, 12.

103. Ibid., (1), vii; (2), xiv.

104. Ibid., (1), 12.

105. Ibid., (1), 19.

106. SCANS, *Learning a Living*, xv.

107. *Industry-Based Skill Standards Analysis of Public Hearings* (Department of Labor, Employment and Training Administration, 1993). Proposed legislation in S.1150 and H.R.1804, 102nd Cong., 1st sess.

108. Samuelson, R., "Gibberish on Job Skills"; Martin, L., "Teaching Tomorrow's Skills: We Need Both Basic and Work-Related Education," *Washington Post*, July 22, 1991, A–11.

109. *The Economist*, "Beyond the Basics," August 17, 1991, 83.

110. *Investing in People*, 16.

111. U.S. Department of Labor, National Advisory Commission on Work-Based Learning, Memorandum on Commission's Recommendations, October 11, 1991, 1, 2.

112. As reported in Conte, C., *Wall Street Journal*, Labor Letter, October 22, 1991, A–1; *Business Week* (editorial), October 28, 1991, 150; also in same issue, "Back to School—The B-Schools That Are Bent on Executive Education," 102–9. See also Gaiter, D., "Short-Term Despair, Long-Term Promise: As Traditional Black-Owned Businesses Lose Ground, Hope Rests on a New Generation of Entrepreneurs," and other articles in *Wall Street Journal* special section on black entrepreneurship, April 3, 1992, R–1–14.

113. *An America That Works*, 82. On the issue of extent to which government should require firms to provide a given level of postentry training, see Dentzer, S., "How to Train Workers for the 21st Century," *U.S. News and World Report*, September 21, 1992, 72–78.

114. CBO, *Displaced Workers: Trends in the 1980s and Implications for the Future*, February 1993, ix–xv, 35–36.

115. Bureau of the Census, Current Population Reports, *Geographic Mobility, March 1987–March 1990*, Series P–20, No. 456, Table F, December, 1991, 8–9.

116. Bureau of the Census, "The Nation's Economic, Social and Housing 'Portrait' Drawn from Census Long Form," press release CB92–87, May 29, 1992, 2; "We're on the Move," *Census and You*, 27, no. 2, February 1992, 2; data from *Housing Characteristics of Recent Movers 1989*.

117. As reported in Fuchsberg, F., "Quality Programs Show Shoddy Results," *Wall Street Journal* May 14, 1992, B–1. See also Walters, J., "The Cult of Total Quality," *Governing*, May 1992, 38–42.

118. "A Bolder Baldridge," *The Economist*, July 20, 1991, 83, 84.

119. As reported by Peterson, T., "Can Corporate America Get Out from Under Its Overhead?" *Business Week*, May 18, 1992, 102.

120. Blinder, A., "How Japan Puts the 'Human' in Human Capital," *Business Week*, November 11, 1991, 22.

121. Lublin, J., "Trying to Increase Worker Productivity More Employers Alter Management Style" (1 in 5 employers operating self-managed teams, up from 1 in 20 ten years ago), *Wall Street Journal*, February 3, 1992, B–1.

122. Ream, D., "Employment Outreach: A Quality Approach to Workforce Diversity," *PM* (Public Management), June 1992, 18–20.

123. Holusha, J., "An Industrial Policy, Piece by Piece," *New York Times*, July 30, 1991, D–1. See also Pilcher, D., "The Third Wave of Economic Development," *State Legislatures*, November 1991, 34–37.

124. National Science Board, *Competitive Strengths of U.S. Industrial Science and Technology*, 50–54. See also "Industrial Policy," *Business Week*, cover story, April 6, 1992, 70–76; Pennar, K., "Defense Cuts Don't Have to Wound the Economy," *Business Week*, February 24, 1992, 82. For comprehensive analyses of the industrial policy issue, see Krugman, P., *Age of Diminished Expectations* (Cambridge, MA: MIT Press, 1990) and Thurow, L., *Head to Head* (New York: Morrow, 1992).

125. Office of Technology Assessment (OTA), *Competing Economies: America, Europe and the Pacific Rim* (Washington, DC: OTA Report Brief, October 1991), 2, full report from U.S. Government Printing Office.

126. *An America That Works*, 140–55; *Workforce 2000*, on pension portability, 110–11.

127. Freudenheim, M., "New Law to Bring Wider Job Rights for Mentally Ill," *New York Times*, September 23, 1991; Bulkeley, W., "Computer Use by Illiterates Grows at Work," *Wall Street Journal*, June 9, 1992, B–1.

128. *An America That Works*, for detailed proposals, 130–39; *Investing in People*, 32. Both sources agree that labor market needs should be achieved without compromising humanitarian needs and that upgrading the skills of American citizens should always come first.

129. U.S. General Accounting Office, *Workers at Risk: Increased Numbers in Contingent Employment Lack Insurance, Other Benefits*, Report GAO/HRD–91–56, March 8, 1991.

130. For further description of leasing arrangements, see Willey, T., *The Business of Employee Leasing* (San Bernadino, CA: Aegis Group, 1988); *The NSLA Report* 2, no. 6 (Arlington, VA: National Staff Leasing Association October 1991).

131. "The Technology Pay Off," *Business Week*, Special Report, June 14, 1993, 57–79; *Workforce 2000*, 109–10.

132. Bond, J., and Johnson, G., "Changes in the Structure of Wages in the 1980's: An Evaluation of Alternative Explanations," *The American Economic Review* 82, no. 3, June 1992, 371–92; Passell, P., "The Wage Gap: Sins of Omission," Economic Scene, *New York Times*, May 27, 1992. See also Greenhouse, S., "The Coming Crisis of the American Work Force: Are Urban Youth Prepared for the Rigors of Work in the 21st Century?" *New York Times*, June 7, 1992, F–14.

133. GAO, *Welfare to Work: States Begin JOBS, But Fiscal and Other Problems May Impede Progress*, GAO/HRD–91–106, September 1991, 2–3.

134. Commission on Workforce Quality and Labor Market Efficiency, *Investing in People*, 22, 29–32. See also GAO, *Employment Service: Improved Leadership Needed for Better Performance*, GAO/HRD–91–88, August 1991, 3, 35–40.

135. National Governors' Association, Committee on Human Resources, February 1992, 1.

136. Sylvester, K., "Family Leave: Alive in the States," *Governing*, March 1991, 23–24; Trost, C., "To Cut Costs and Keep the Best People, More Concerns Offer Flexible Work Plans," *Wall Street Journal*, February 18, 1992, B–1. See also Conley, J., "Dade, the First County to Adopt a Family Leave Ordinance," *County News*, January 20, 1992, 7.

137. Bowers, B., Enterprise, *Wall Street Journal*, September 23, 1991, B–1; Shellenbarger, S., Work and Family, *Wall Street Journal*, "Employers Set Rules for Doing Home Work" (work at home), August 16, 1991, B–1.

138. As reported in "Work and Family" and "The Right Family Values in the Workplace," *Business Week*, June 18, 1993, 80–89, 248.

139. Becker, G., "Working Women's Staunchest Allies: Supply and Demand," Economic Viewpoint, *Business Week*, December 2, 1991, 18.

140. Shellenbarger, S., "Employers Try to See if Family Benefits Pay," Work and Family, *Wall Street Journal*, April 3, 1992, B–1.

141. *Workforce 2000*, 116–17.

142. OECD, *Revenue Statistics of OECD Member Countries, 1965–1990*, Table 3 (Paris: OECD, 1991), 73.

143. ACIR, *Significant Features of Fiscal Federalism 1992* 2, Tables 20, 24, September 1992, 52, 57.

144. Census Bureau, *Government Finances 1989–90*, Table 2, February 1992, 3.

145. Bureau of the Census, "State and Local Government Finances, by Level of Government and State 1990–91," *Government Finances 1991* (Preliminary), GF91–5.

146. Congressional Budget Office, *The Economic and Budget Outlook: Fiscal Years 1993–1997*, January 1992, 56.

Chapter 2 _____

General Deterrents to Future Labor Force Employability of American Youth

If the nation's institutions for health care and education are to deal successfully with the challenges identified in chapter 1, significant weaknesses in these services must be overcome. These problems impede optimal mental and physical development of the individual from the time of conception to initial stable employment or secure enrollment in post-secondary education/training.

There are five factors external to both the individual and the two sets of institutions. They can interpose substantial additional deterrents to physical and mental development. These are (1) economic status, especially poverty and parent unemployment or nonparticipation in the labor force; (2) neighborhood environments, particularly economically depressed and/or crime- or drug-ridden areas; (3) the plague of homelessness, wherein child and adult acquaintances are out of the economic and/or behavioral mainstream; (4) family structure that is disintegrating or fragmented, including parental death, separation, divorce, or desertion, and unmarried motherhood and consequent female headed family and/or household; and (5) parents and peers who are uncaring, abusive, or discouraged and who place a low value on, or disparage, educational achievement and good health practices.

HOUSEHOLDS AND CHILDREN IN POVERTY

For children, the incidence of poverty in a geographic or an employment context is often similar. The combination of economic disadvantage at home and growing up in a neighborhood where the cultural home-school-peer and surrounding environment discourages schooling, work, and societally legal or otherwise acceptable behavior can easily be disastrous. The noneconomic environmental factors are examined subsequently, but the following data include separate summations of poverty in general and its geographically concentrated incidence.

Extent of Poverty and Its Measurement

Table 2.1 shows the numbers and percentages of families and persons below the federal poverty "thresholds" in 1990 and 1991, which for 1990 varied from $6,652 for a person living alone to $26,848 for a family of nine or more members. It also shows for 1990 those below the threshold after taking account of taxes, on one hand, and noncash benefit transfers (including Medicaid, Medicare, food stamps, and housing subsidies), on the other.

Poverty Rate Measurement. Presented here are two sets of poverty rates: the official rate, based on pretax cash income, and a broader measure, including noncash benefits and related factors. Such a presentation is warranted because each is controversial, and experimentation with measurement improvements accelerated during the 1980s.

Before drawing any conclusions as to degrees of personal and national economic severity, three major methodological problems should be noted: (1) whether the consumer price index (CPI) is reliable when applied to urban areas of widely differing price levels for food, shelter, medical care, and other consumption items (the CPI already distinguishes between urban and rural areas); (2) whether a separate CPI should be established for the retired population, whose consumption pattern varies so greatly from the working group; and (3) whether the poverty-level threshold should take into account noncash government transfers as well as cash income, and whether such threshold level should be based on pretax or after-tax income.

Researchers in the poverty and income fields developed three principal methods of treating noncash transfers. Initially, the Census Bureau, in determining which of the many kinds of noncash transfers should be counted if the poverty measure were expanded from cash income only, decided that based on data availability and reliability, four categories should be counted—food stamps, free or discounted school lunches, housing assistance, and medical care made available through Medicaid, Medicare, and employer-provided or other types of private health insurance.[1]

The Census Bureau noted:

Traditionally, income and poverty data presented in . . . Bureau reports have been based on the amount of money income received during a calendar year before any taxes and excluding capital gains. This definition of income is narrow and does not provide a completely satisfactory measure of the distribution of income. The omission of data on taxes, capital gains, and the value of non-cash benefits has an effect on comparisons over time and between population sub-groups.[2]

The new, more inclusive methodology adopted by the bureau presents income and poverty data based on a 15-step approach:

Table 2.1
Numbers and Percents* of Persons, Families, and Children Below Poverty Level (BPL) by Race, Hispanic Origin, and Family Type, 1990, and Percents for 1991 (numbers in millions)

Category	All Races Total No.	BPL No.	Pcts. (1)	Pcts. (2)	1991 %	White Total No.	BPL No.	Pcts. (1)	Pcts. (2)	1991 %	Black Total No.	BPL No.	Pcts. (1)	Pcts. (2)	1991 %	Hispanic Total No.	BPL No.	Pcts. (1)	Pcts. (2)	1991 %
Persons																				
All Ages	248.64	33.59	13.5	11.0	14.2	208.61	22.33	10.7	9.0	11.3	30.81	9.84	31.9	24.3	32.7	21.41	6.01	28.1	22.7	28.7
Under 18	65.05	13.43	20.6	15.8	21.8	51.93	8.23	15.9	12.5	16.8	10.16	4.55	44.8	33.0	45.9	7.46	2.87	38.4	29.6	40.4
Under 18, Related, in Families	63.91	12.72	19.9	15.1	21.1	51.03	7.70	15.1	11.7	16.1	9.98	4.41	44.2	32.5	45.6	7.30	2.75	37.7	28.7	39.8
Families & Persons																				
All Families**	66.32	7.10	10.7	8.4	11.5	56.80	4.62	8.1	6.6	8.8	7.47	2.19	29.3	21.9	30.4	4.99	1.24	25.0	19.6	26.5
Families W/Related Children over 18	34.50	5.68	16.4	N/A	17.7	28.12	3.55	12.6	N/A	13.7	5.07	1.89	37.2	N/A	39.2	3.50	1.09	31.0	N/A	33.7
Married Couple Families	52.15	2.98	5.7	4.7	6.0	47.01	2.39	5.1	4.3	5.5	3.57	.45	12.6	8.8	11.0	3.45	.61	17.5	14.4	19.1
W/Rel. Chldrn over 18	25.41	1.99	7.8	6.1	8.3	22.29	1.57	7.1	5.6	7.7	2.10	.30	14.3	9.7	12.4	2.41	.50	20.8	17.0	23.5
Female Headed Families	11.27	3.77	33.4	25.3	35.6	7.51	2.01	26.8	20.3	28.4	3.43	1.65	48.1	36.1	51.2	1.19	.57	48.3	35.6	49.7
W/Rel. Chldrn over 18	7.71	3.43	44.5	33.0	47.1	4.79	1.81	37.9	28.1	39.6	2.70	1.51	56.1	41.8	60.5	.92	.54	58.2	42.4	60.1

Sources: For 1990 data: Bureau of the Census. *Poverty in the United States: 1990.* Current Population Reports, Consumer Income, Series P-60, No. 175, Tables 2, 3, 4. August 1991, 16-23; and *Measuring the Effect of Benefits and Taxes on Income and Poverty: 1990.* Series P-60 No. 176-RD, Tables 2, 3. August 1991, 40-55. For 1991 data: Census, *Poverty in the United States: 1991.* P-60, No. 181, Tables 2, 3, 4. August, 1991, 2-9.

Note: * 1991 percentages based on official definition only.
For 1990: (1) and (2) percentages are based respectively on (1) The official census definition of income — pretax cash income, excluding capital gains and (2) Census definition of income step #14 as presented in Report 176 RD — after-tax cash income, plus cash and selected non-cash government transfers; excludes step # 15: imputed return on equity in own home.
** Beginning in 1979, unrelated subfamilies were excluded from "all families."

1. The official definition of income (recognized by Congress and the federal executive branch in establishing program eligibility thresholds for assistance programs) as "money income excluding capital gains, before taxes," then proceeding as follows:

2. Definition (1) less government cash transfers, including nonmeans-tested ones such as Social Security benefits and means-tested ones such as Aid to Families with Dependent Children (AFDC).

3. Definition (2) plus capital gains.

4. Addition of health insurance supplements to wage/salary income.

5., 6., 7., 8. Successive subtraction of Social Security payroll taxes, federal income taxes, including the effect of counting or not counting the Earned Income Tax Credit, and state income taxes.

9. Addition of nonmeans-tested transfers (Social Security et al.).

10., 11., 12. Successive addition of values of Medicare, regular-priced school lunches, and means-tested cash transfers (AFDC et al.).

13. Addition of value of Medicaid.

14. Addition of values of other means-tested government noncash transfers, including food stamps, rent subsidies, and free or reduced-price school lunches.

15. Addition of net imputed return on equity on owned home.[3]

Through the above incremental process, users of the census data can draw the line wherever they desire to suit their particular purposes. Values of Medicare and Medicaid benefits are included to the extent of their fungible value, that is, the extent that they free up resources that could have been spent on medical care. Appendix 2.A shows the percentage of persons in poverty according to each of the 15 above steps, broken down by age group.

The following poverty rates for 1990 are adjusted to encompass tax burdens and transfers based on fungible value as described above, stopping after step 14; step 15, imputed return of equity on own home, although theoretically sound from an economic point of view, is not readily understood by noneconomists. The official and alternate rates would be, respectively: all persons—13.5 and 11.0; persons under 18—20.6 and 15.8; persons 65 and over—12.2 and 9.5; and persons age 45–64—8.6 and 7.6 The disparate effect of counting noncash transfers is attributable to the much larger absolute and relative amounts of such transfers going to the elderly through Medicare (eligibility largely limited to those 65 and over) and Medicaid (nearly half the expenditures for which are for long-term care in nursing homes). Typically, while median family incomes, in constant dollar terms, remained essentially static between 1989 and 1990, families with a householder 65 or over experienced a 3 percent increase, "*the only age group to experience a positive change in real income*," according to a Census Bureau report.[4]

Acquisition of Assets. Although poverty is generally measured in terms of income, however defined, the value of assets acquired minus debts—or net worth—is an important aspect of personal financial independence and security.

Table 2.2
Median Net Worth, by Type of Household and Age Group, 1988

Type of Household by Age of Householder	No. of Households (Thousands)	Median Monthly Income	Total	Median Net Worth Excl. Equity in Own Home
Married Couple Households	51,697	$2,566	$57,134	$16,293
Less than 35 years	13,357	2,430	12,041	4,705
35 to 54 years	21,437	3,173	60,611	16,922
55 to 64 years	8,186	2,589	120,158	42,737
65 years and over	8,736	1,733	124,419	45,890
Male Householders	14,383	1,661	13,053	5,454
Less than 35 years	5,592	1,790	4,959	3,395
35 to 54 years	4,587	1,999	17,055	6,099
55 to 64 years	1,586	1,430	34,722	10,682
65 years and over	2,346	1,023	48,883	15,914
Female Householders	25,437	1,109	13,571	3,633
Less than 35 years	6,430	1,187	1,378	978
35 to 54 years	7,236	1,616	10,945	2,936
55 to 64 years	3,336	1,209	40,796	7,004
65 years and over	8,471	780	47,233	10,693

Source: Census Bureau, *Household Wealth and Asset Ownership: 1988*, Series P-70, No. 22, Table K, December, 1990, 10.

Typically, asset acquisition and consequent net worth starts essentially from a modest nominal figure, zero, or a net liability, for the young person leaving high school or college and beginning work. As the person advances in his or her line of work, earns more, and buys a car, furniture, house, and other property, net worth increases. In the 1970–90 period, the ratio of debt to net worth in the household sector of the economy moved from about 25 percent in 1970 to 10 percent in 1980 and upward during the boom years to 35 percent where it began to stabilize as debts were refinanced at lower interest rates.[5] In the case of parents and children, greater financial security of the former lessens worry or stress that "rubs off on" the children, and vice versa. Table 2.2 shows net worth by various age groups and type of household. Female householders fare badly in comparison with male householders and married-couple households.

Poverty Rate Highlights and Comparisons. The highlights of the foregoing tabulations, plus other data included in Census Bureau reports, are:[6]

• Between 24 and 34 million persons were below the poverty level (BPL) in 1990, depending upon whether the alternate (definition 15) or official measure of income is used, comprising a BPL rate range of 9.8 to 13.5 percent nationally. In official rate terms, this was below the 1983 rate of 15.2 percent but above the 1974 rate of 11.2 percent.

• For persons below age 18, the poverty rate ranged from 14.9 to 20.6 percent (from approximately one in seven to one in five). The rate at definition step 9 (after-tax income plus nonmeans-tested government cash transfers) was 21.8 percent, slightly above the official rate. Successive definition steps produced rates of (10) Medicare, 20.3; (11) regular-priced school lunches, 21.5; (12) AFDC and other means-tested cash transfers, 20.2; (13) Medicaid, 18.7; (14) food stamps and other means-tested noncash transfer, 15.8; and (14) imputed return on home equity, 14.9.

- Under the official measure, of the 33.6 million persons below poverty level, one-half were either children under 18 (40%) or elderly (10.9%).

- Of the 5.7 million poverty families with children, three out of five were maintained by women with no husband present; by race/ethnic origin, under the official measure, the percents of poverty families with children headed by a female were white (51.0), black (80.2), and Hispanic (49.4).

- For female-headed households with children the overall official poverty rate was 47.2: for whites, it was 40.3; for blacks, 57.9; and for Hispanics, 60.4. Where such householder's age was in the 18–24 range, the percentages were much closer: all, 73.6; white, 69.9; black, 80.5; and Hispanic, 79.7.

- Contrastingly, for families comprising married couples with related children, the BPL rate was 8.9 nationally: for white, 7.9; black, 16.0; and Hispanic, 22.6.

- Of BPL family householders, 49.8 percent worked during 1990, with 24.1 percent working year-round, full-time.

- Poverty rates varied inversely with school years completed (21.8 for householders with less than 12 years and 2.2 for 12 or more years).

- The regional BPL rates were: South, 15.8; West, 13.0; Midwest, 12.4; and Northeast, 11.4.

- Farm and nonfarm household BPL rates were 11.2 and 13.6, respectively.

Employment Rates and Labor Force Nonparticipation

In 1990, 40 percent of individuals below poverty level who were age 15 and over worked, and 9 percent worked full-time, year-round. Forty-four percent of female-householder families with no husband present worked, with 8 percent working year-round. However, of all female-headed households with children, nearly three-fifths were below poverty level, and of those 44 percent worked, but only 6 percent worked full-time.[7]

Table 2.3 presents March 1990 census data on the interrelation of family poverty and employment.

With further reference to employment, a 1991 U.S. General Accounting Office (GAO) report concluded that many single mothers were suffering particular disadvantages in seeking and keeping work. Using data from the National Longitudinal Survey of Youth conducted at Ohio State University under Department of Labor support, the GAO found:

Many single mothers will remain near or below the poverty line even if they work at full-time jobs. Problems they are likely to face include low earnings; vulnerability to

Table 2.3

Poverty Status* of Families with Children Under 18 and Employment Status of Householder, by Race and Hispanic Origin, as of March 1990 (numbers in thousands)

Type of Family and Employment Status	Total				White				Black				Hispanic			
	No.	% of Total	BPL No.	%	Total No.	% of Total	BPL No.	%	Total No.	% of Total	BPL No.	%	Total No.	% of Total	BPL No.	%
All Families																
With Children	34,279	100.0	5,308	100.0	27,977	100.0	3,290	11.8	5,031	100.0	1,783	35.4	3,314	100.0	986	100.0
Employed	27,725	80.9	2,251	8.1	23,545	84.2	1,592	6.8	3,192	63.4	568	17.8	2,387	72.1	438	18.3
Unemployed	1,432	4.2	586	40.9	1,020	3.6	333	32.6	369	7.3	234	63.4	185	5.6	97	52.3
Not In Labor Force	4,545	13.3	2,452	53.9	2,953	10.6	1,355	45.9	1,367	27.2	972	71.1	700	21.1	449	64.2
In Armed Forces	577	1.7	19	3.3	459	1.6	10	2.1	103	2.0	9	9.0	40	1.2	2	5.0**
Married Couples																
With Children	25,476	100.0	1,872	7.3	22,271	100.0	1,457	6.5	2,179	100.0	291	13.3	2,309	100.0	453	19.6
Employed	22,180	87.1	1,121	5.1	19,653	88.2	908	4.6	1,672	76.7	151	9.0	1,897	82.2	291	15.3
Unemployed	839	3.3	201	23.9	697	3.1	154	22.1	111	5.1	36	32.3	104	4.5	40	38.4
Not In Labor Force	1,904	7.5	534	26.0	1,483	6.7	387	25.1	295	13.5	95	32.2	273	11.8	120	44.0
In Armed Forces	553	2.2	17	3.1	437	2.0	8	1.8	102	4.7	9	9.2	35	1.6	2	5.6**
Female Householder With Children, No Husband Present																
	7,445	100.0	3,190	42.8	4,627	100.0	1,671	36.1	2,624	100.0	1,415	53.9	848	100.0	491	57.9
Employed	4,479	60.2	993	22.2	3,015	65.2	578	19.2	1,371	52.2	388	28.3	373	44.0	124	33.2
Unemployed	512	6.9	357	69.7	260	5.6	158	60.6	241	9.2	191	79.2	67	7.9	49	73.1**
Not In Labor Force	2,453	32.9	1,840	75.0	1,351	29.3	934	69.2	1,011	38.5	836	82.7	408	48.1	318	78.0
In Armed Forces	Neg.	-	-	-	Neg.	-	-	-	Neg.	-	-	-	Neg.	-	-	-

Source: Census Bureau, Money Income and Poverty Status in the United States 1989. Current Population Reports, Consumer Income. Series P-60 No. 168, Table 23. September, 1990, 67-74.

Note: * Official definition.
** Not significant due to small number BPL.

layoffs and other work interruptions; lack of important fringe benefits such as paid sick leave and health insurance; and relatively high expenses for child care.[8] . . . Poor women in our sample tend to have less education, less work experience, and, as a result, lower earnings potential than women who are not poor . . . Nearly half of poor single mothers in our sample had not finished high school, compared with 17 percent of single mothers who were not poor.[9]

A crucial and growing problem, associated both with economic realities and with labor force wage patterns, on one hand, and behavioral traits, on the other, has been the increasing unattractiveness of leaving public assistance rolls for an entry-level job. This reluctance is based largely on the long-standing penalties in federal welfare legislation that essentially reduced the federal share of welfare benefits on a dollar-for-dollar basis as wage income begins and, in the case of unmarried female householders, if marriage to an employed individual occurs.[10] (To remedy this problem by easing or phasing in the welfare payment reductions or by most alternatives thereto would require considerable up-front additional public expenditure, as discussed in chapter 4.)

Access to, and Costs of, Child Care

An important barrier to employment opportunity for women with below school-age children is the substantial cost and arrangement difficulties for child care while the mother is at work. The two-worker married couple became the norm in many married couple households, partly through economic necessity or preference (a two-earner household being able to enjoy a higher standard of economic consumption and/or saving) and partly from the motivation of women toward career accomplishment and recognition. Consequently, the availability of adequate young child and day care became a must for working couples; but availability and access are only one part of the equation. Such care, especially if rendered outside the family, kindergarten, or other noncost or low-cost arrangement, like any other service, costs money.

Child-care arrangements fall into six general census categories: (1) care in child's home, with subcategories of care by father, grandparent, other relative, and nonrelative; (2) care in another home, with subcategories of care by grandparent, other relative, or nonrelative; (3) care in a group-care center; (4) care by the mother herself while working; (5) care of child in school; and (6) child taking care of self. Table 2.4 summarizes these arrangements by working mothers with young children over the period 1977–88.

A more recent study and report, *The Demand and Supply of Child Care in 1990,* produced the following findings:[11]

- The proportion of all mothers with children below 18 rose from 39 to 62 percent in the 1970–90 period.
- Nearly half of employed mothers and a third of nonemployed mothers were using care in a center as the principal arrangement, supplemental to care in own home.

Table 2.4
Principal Types of Child-Care Arrangements Used by Working Mothers, 18 to 44 Years Old, for Youngest Child Under Age 5, by Full- or Part-Time, June 1977 and Fall 1988 (numbers in thousands)*

Arrangement	June, 1977			Fall, 1988		
	Total	F. T.	P. T.	Total	F. T.	P. T.
No. of Children	3,987	2,645	1,342	9,483	5,969	3,514
Percent	100.0	100.0	100.0	100.0	100.0	100.0
Care: In own home	31.9	27.6	40.3	28.2	20.8	40.9
Father or relative	25.6	21.7	33.2	23.0	16.2	34.6
Non-relative	6.3	5.9	7.1	5.2	4.6	6.3
Care: Another home	40.4	46.1	29.4	36.8	41.6	28.6
Relative	18.0	20.3	13.6	13.2	14.4	11.2
Non-relative	22.4	25.8	15.8	23.6	27.2	17.4
Organized facility**	12.5	14.3	8.9	25.8	30.8	17.4
Care: Mother, while working	10.7	7.3	17.3	7.6	5.1	11.9
Other***	4.4	4.6	4.0	1.5	1.6	1.3

Source: 1977 data excerpted from Census Bureau, *Child Care Arrangements of Working Mothers: June 1982*, Current Population Reports, P-23, No. 129, Table A, p. 4, 1988 data from Census Bureau, *Who's Minding the Kids? Fall 1988*. Table 1. P-70 No. 30, August, 1992, p. 23.

Notes: *1977 data based on number of mothers.
** e. g. group centers.
*** "Other" includes child taking care of self and care by school. 1977 census survey also included nonresponses and "don't knows."

• Overall, enough child-care openings existed to meet demand, but numerous mismatches existed in meeting needs of low-income families and children with special needs.

• Competition and a tighter economy were keeping fees relatively low, but child-staff ratios increased to near unacceptable levels.

• Use of family day care and in-home care remained relatively static over an extended period (30–35 percent).

• The proportion of income spent on child care ranged from 23 percent for lower-income (below $15,000 yearly) families to 6 percent for higher incomes ($50,000).

In 1989–90 the Bureau of Labor Statistics conducted surveys of employer-provided benefits for child care and other family purposes. For full-time employees in medium and large-size firms in 1989, 23 percent had reimbursement accounts, often funded solely by employees, but with tax advantages (lower salaries being reported to the Internal Revenue Service), and sometimes with employer financial participation. Five percent (up from 2% in 1985) of employees were eligible for child-care benefits at on- or off-site facilities. In 1990, full-time employees in 9 percent of state and local governments and 1 percent in small firms (less than 100 employees) were provided subsidized child care. Assistance through reimbursement accounts, often employee-funded, was available to 31 percent of state-local government employees and somewhat less than 10 percent in small firms.[12] Despite the continued modest percentages for private firm employees, the employers were trying a variety of approaches to child-care subsidization, including multifirm consortia in which expenses, risks, and benefits involved in day-care center operation were shared; child-care home networks managed by the employer; and child-care vouchers usable at a care provider of the employee's choice.[13]

NEIGHBORHOOD AND OTHER AREA ENVIRONMENTS

Table 2.5 presents a breakdown of poverty levels inside and outside metropolitan areas. At the state level, based on the official poverty rate over the three-year period 1988, 1989, and 1990, the Census Bureau in 1991 published for the first time poverty levels for each state. A three-year average was used to minimize sampling error, which remained large in comparison with national and regional estimates. In broad groupings, with a national three-year average poverty rate of 13.1 percent, states with rates above 20 percent were, in alphabetical order, Louisiana, Mississippi, and New Mexico; those below 9 percent were Connecticut, Delaware, New Hampshire, New Jersey, Rhode Island, Utah, and Wisconsin. Rates for the Consolidated Metropolitan Statistical Areas (CMSAs) of Los Angeles and New York were close to the national average at 14.4 and 12.7, respectively, as were the two largest states, with California at 13.3 and New York at 13.4.[14]

The data in Table 2.5 show a somewhat higher poverty rate in nonmetropolitan than in metropolitan areas, although the poor are more concentrated in the latter, especially where the central city population is a relatively high proportion (half or more) of the metropolitan area. In those metropolitan areas where the central city population is in the 25–35 percent range, the high suburban portion would shift the balance of the poverty population in the other direction. However, the relative economic distress in the city might well exercise a much stronger influence on the poverty rate than concentration per se.

Often, "poverty areas" as defined by the Census Bureau and shown in Table 2.5 comprise all or parts of "underclass" areas as defined specifically in 1986 by Ricketts and Sawhill of the Urban Institute and generally (by other urban research organizations and scholars) as areas having a high proportion of persons with "nonmainstream behaviors"—high school dropouts, men not regularly attached to the labor force, criminal activities, nonworking welfare recipients, and households headed by single mothers with children. Institute researchers identified 880 census tracts as having an above average prevalence of all four conditions. Of the 880, 40 percent were not in extreme poverty areas, and 72

Table 2.5
Below Poverty Level (BPL) for Persons In and Outside Metropolitan, Central City, and Suburban Areas, by Race and Hispanic Origin, in 1990 (numbers in thousands)

Residence	Total Persons				White				Black				Hispanic Origin			
	All	No.	(1)*	(2)*	Total	No.	(1)	(2)	Total	No.	(1)	(2)	Total	No.	(1)	(2)
Total	248,644	33,585	13.5	9.8	208,611	22,326	10.7	7.9	30,806	9,837	31.9	22.3	21,405	6,006	28.1	21.4
Inside Metro Areas	193,052	24,510	12.7	9.3	159,443	15,711	9.9	7.4	25,561	7,696	30.1	21.1	19,883	5,519	27.8	20.9
In Central Cities	74,936	14,254	19.0	14.0	53,686	7,664	13.2	9.6	17,344	5,870	33.1	22.7	11,116	3,524	31.7	24.0
In Poverty Areas**	19,283	7,404	38.4	N/A	9,052	3,141	34.7	N/A	9,272	3,928	42.4	N/A	4,904	2,163	44.1	N/A
Out of Central Cities	118,116	10,255	8.7	6.3	105,757	8,047	7.6	5.6	8,218	1,826	22.2	16.9	8,767	1,995	22.8	14.6
In Poverty Areas	5,184	1,632	31.5	N/A	3,567	890	25.0	N/A	1,470	691	47.0	N/A	1,307	455	34.8	N/A
Outside Metro Areas	55,592	9,075	15.3	11.6	49,168	6,615	13.5	9.7	5,245	2,141	40.8	27.9	1,522	487	32.0	28.0
In Poverty Areas	13,212	3,511	26.6	N/A	9,644	1,915	19.9	N/A	3,167	1,454	45.9	N/A	524	214	40.9	N/A

Source: Bureau of the Census, *Poverty in the United States: 1990.* Current Population Reports, Series P-60, No. 175, Table 9. August 1991, 73-79. *Measuring the Effect of Benefits and Taxes on Income and Poverty: 1990.* Series P-60 No. 176-RD, Table 2. August 1991, 40-47.

Note: * (1) and (2) percentages are based respectively on: (1) The official Census definition of income and (2) Census definition No.15 of income as presented in Report 176RD. Estimated numbers of persons in poverty under definition step 15 would be a product of the no. (2) percentage applied to the total number of persons in the respective categories. Step 15 comprises imputed return on equity in own home.

** "Poverty Areas" are defined as census tracts in metropolitan counties and minor civil divisions in nonmetropolitan counties with a poverty rate of 20 percent or more in 1990 based on the 1980 census. In 1990, the overall poverty rate in such areas was 33.0 percent, up from 32.9 in 1989 and about 2 1/2 times the national average.

N/A = Data not available.

percent of the poverty areas were not underclass areas. Of the 2.6 million persons living in the underclass areas, only about 40 percent, or 500,000, had no regular attachment to the labor force, either directly through a job or indirectly through marriage.[15]

Because a great many of the "underclass areas" are in large cities, contain neighborhoods of high residential density, and have a population that is disproportionately black, there has been a tendency to equate concentrations of black populations with "underclass areas." Roland Mincy in an Urban Institute research paper emphasized that many white underclass neighborhoods exist in small- and medium-size cities. These areas represent about 19 percent of all underclass neighborhoods nationwide. Also, Mincy argued that contrary to the belief that racial and ethnic minorities living in underclass areas are worse off than their white counterparts, minorities and whites in such areas have statistically insignificant differences in mean poverty rates and mean values of other social problem indicators.[16] This viewpoint was largely affirmed by another study finding that poverty tended to be more permanent for the poor in rural than in urban areas, with more than half of the rural underclass being white and two-thirds located in the South. However, the proportion of unmarried mothers was considerably lower in rural than in urban areas.[17]

In *The Urban Underclass,* published in 1991, Christopher Jencks advanced a more general concept, considering four ranking arrangements, with each implying a different definition of the underclass and with its size depending upon which of the four carry the most weight: (1) "income level," wherein the underclass includes only those whose poverty is attributable to a violation of one or more widely held "moral norms" and excludes those who are in a poverty condition through no fault of their own; (2) "moral norms," including the propositions that nondisabled, working-age men should have a steady job, females should avoid childbearing until married, and all individuals should refrain from violent behavior and other crime; (3) "income sources," where irregular work, crime, welfare, and panhandling are primary; and (4) "cultural skills," where basic literacy and numeracy abilities are lacking.[18]

William Prosser, in a 1991 article, expressed the belief that scholars deeply involved in research on underclass issues tended to fall into two groups. "Structuralists," epitomized by William Julius Wilson, who had done much of the original research in the field, had defined the underclass as a "heterogeneous grouping of families and individuals outside the mainstream of the American occupational system," emphasizing the economic aspects. "Behavioralists [e.g., Nathan, Sawhill, Ricketts, and Mincy] had focused on individuals and categorized them on the basis of groups of behaviors."[19] Terminology aside, our focus here will be those geographic areas whose environments pose a severe deterrent to healthy birth, childhood, and adolescence and to acquisition of necessary cognitive and social skills. Those areas comprise a large proportion—often a majority—of persons with combined characteristics of chronic joblessness and antisocial and/or illegal behavior.

Second only to the economic fact of poverty itself and the insecurity of chronic unemployment, the prevalence of crime and violence in the above-described areas comprises the principal deterrent to the health and safety of growing children. Crime, violent behavior, and illegal drug traffic and use are interlocked and constitute a growing social problem in the United States and many other countries. A draft report by the Advisory Commission on Intergovernmental Relations (ACIR) summarized the situation in early 1992 as follows:

The 1980s drug trade was distinguished, first, by its level of violence, fostered in part by the fact that most drugs of current choice produce an aggressive rather than a passive physiological response and by the increased firepower of the weapons used. Second, as never before, organized crime has used juveniles. Juveniles are recruited as young as age 10 and are often using high-powered weapons by their mid-teens. These guns and individuals with the inclination to use them will be on the streets for years to come.[20]

In 1990 homicide was one of the leading causes of premature death in the United States and the leading cause for young blacks. Because it is the extreme manifestation of violent behavior, homicide itself gains more attention than the biological, psychiatric, and cultural elements that go into violence as a whole.[21]

Youth gangs comprised a second major manifestation of violent and other antisocial behavior in the late 1980s and early 1990s. In late 1991, a National Conference on Youth Gangs and Violent Juvenile Behavior was convened by the National Governors' Association, the U.S. Department of Justice, and the National Criminal Justice Association (a Washington-based interest group representing state governments on crime and public safety matters). Among the principal viewpoints emphasized in the conference were:[22] (1) it is difficult to ascertain the reasons youths join gangs; (2) apparently gangs often are the only "family" structure available to many of their members and often provide stability, protection, reinforcement, and financial support absent in many youth's lives; (3) the socioeconomic need of youths and their families, especially minorities and the underprivileged, must be met before law enforcement and delinquency prevention programs will be effective in curbing violent crime; and (4) "participants agreed that there is no one answer to the problem of youth violence."

By 1992, getting at the root causes of youth crime and violence was being recognized as top priority by public health officials and scholars in that field. One of the more ambitious efforts was initiated, and partial funding secured, by the Harvard School of Public Health for a 10-year longitudinal study examining how and why inner-city children change over time, drawing on a cross-section of academic disciplines, including sociology, psychiatry, education, public health, pediatrics, and human behavior.[23]

HOMELESSNESS

The 1980s witnessed the emergence and continued growth of a homeless population—men, women, and children, many of them poor, but some of the adults in full-time employment—beset with a combination of problems. The principal ones included mental health, alcohol and drug addiction, and housing unaffordability. For children under 18, the homeless condition carries a severe restriction upon adequate health care and educational opportunity.

Magnitudes of the Homeless Population

In the early and mid-1980s, estimates of the size of the homeless population varied greatly ranging from 250,000 to 3 million.[24] However, a physical count by the Urban Institute was made in the spring of 1987 of a sample of persons using homeless shelters or soup kitchens in American cities of 100,000 or more. This effort resulted in an estimate of 500,000 to 600,000 over a seven-day period, and subsequent assessments of population size began to draw closer together. The CBO projected a one-day homeless population of about 700,000 for 1991.[25] Based on the Urban Institute sample, a seven-day estimate would expand the 700,000 figure to something over 800,000.

In March 1990 the Census Bureau supplemented its 1990 census to include a nationwide, onetime Shelter and Street Night count of persons at locations where homeless persons tended to congregate or stay. This effort met with mixed results and much skepticism.

At the state level, the Council of State Governments (CSG) conducted a survey in late 1988 to gather qualitative perspectives on the homeless problem. The following groups of public officials in each of the 50 states were queried: governors' offices; legislative committee chairpersons; community affairs agencies; social service and human resource agencies; legislative service and research agencies; and state budget offices. Responses included the following assessments: (1) governors and all of the health/social service respondents said homelessness was a significant problem, and 95 percent of the respondents found it increasing and its severity not likely to be reduced in the immediate future; (2) many states did not have methods for counting the homeless, and most states that did have them could well be using unreliable methods; (3) only 8 of the governors' offices felt the federal government should have principal responsibility in dealing with the problem, 10 thought local governments should have it, but most believed federal programs for the homeless were inadequate; and (4) most states were relying on nonprofit service providers to shoulder much of the direct assistance responsibility.[26]

Composition of the Homeless Population

In contrast to variations in estimates of total size, the estimated proportion of the homeless categories has consistently encountered less disagreement. The Interagency Council on the Homeless was created by congressional enactment in 1987 as part of the McKinney Homeless Assistance Act (PL 100–77), with responsibility for coordinating and directing federal activities in this area. The council estimated in its 1990 annual report the following approximations of the homeless population composition:[27]

- 85 percent adults, 15 percent children (making 100,000 to 150,000 children under 1991 estimates);
- Adults were nearly three-quarters unattached single men, 8 percent unattached single women, and 6 percent in couples with no children.
- Adults in families with children made up 10 percent of the adult homeless, and 80 percent of the adults in homeless families were single women with children.
- In round figures, the homeless population comprised 45 percent non-Hispanic white, 40 percent black, 10 percent Hispanic, and 5 percent other races. Blacks were over-represented compared with their proportion among the poor population in the United States.
- In 1989 the average cash income of the homeless was about $125 monthly, with half of them receiving less than $60.
- The proportion of homeless that were employed was in the 20–25 percent range.
- One-third of the homeless suffered from severe or disabling mental illness, and this condition was most prevalent among single adults.

A considerable number of homeless mentally ill had been hospitalized in state institutions and had been "deinstitutionalized" because it was thought that the patient would be better served by community-based facilities. These facilities subsequently were found to be extremely difficult to fund due to state hospital union opposition and violent neighborhood opposition when community sites were proposed—the "not in my backyard" (*NIMBY*) syndrome.[28]

The U.S. Conference of Mayors (USCM) conducted periodic surveys in the 1980s of the homeless in major cities whose mayors were members of the USCM Task Force on Hunger and Homeless. The report became an annual document in 1990. Among all the national organizations representing state and local government, USCM tended to address the homeless problem in the most specific terms. That was understandable, because the problem had been concentrated in the large central cities, and the mayor had to lead local efforts to address, and hopefully improve, the situation. The size of the 30 cities surveyed in 1990 ranged from very large jurisdictions—such as New York, Los Angeles, Chicago, Philadelphia, San Antonio, and San Diego—to medium-large areas—such as Alexandria, Virginia; Charleston, South Carolina; Hartford; Providence; and Trenton, New Jersey; as well as San Juan, Puerto Rico. Findings, in addition to those cited above from other sources, as to composition and causes of homelessness in 1990 were:[29]

- 35–40 percent suffered from chronic alcohol problems, while 10–20 percent had chronic problems with drugs other than alcohol.
- Considerable overlap existed among the mentally ill and alcohol and other drug addicts.

One year later (1991) the USCM survey showed a 40 percent incidence of substance abuse and 7 percent tested human immunodeficiency virus (HIV) positive. Eighteen percent were employed full- or part-time and 23 percent were veterans of the armed services. The high incidence of substance abuse was a substantial barrier to move homeless people into temporary or other transitional housing that could serve as intermediate steps away from the streets or shelters and into permanent housing.[30]

Hardening of Public and Official Attitudes

The 1991–92 period saw a substantial shift in public opinion and local government policies from empathy toward the homeless to attitude of impatience, avoidance, and harassment, responding to antisocial behavior by homeless persons, aggressive panhandling, and other irritants. "Over the course of a decade, shock at the mounting numbers of 'street people' has given way to weariness, and now to intolerance. . . . In New York the city has just evicted [the homeless from a park] . . . Chicago's O'Hare airport has been closed to the homeless, Santa Barbara has banned sleeping on public streets and Atlanta's mayor has proposed . . . criminal penalties . . . for aggressive begging."[31]

With the change in attitudes on the part of many urban residents came the realization by public-policy makers that problems much more deep-seated than low-income housing availability had to be addressed. Fortunately, homeless mothers with children continued to be viewed with sympathy and were not being targeted by "public nuisance" crackdowns. Drug/alcohol abuse and its treatment and adequate care for the mentally ill began to receive more serious attention from state and local governments and the nonprofit and civic sectors.

Homeless Children

In October 1988 the U.S. General Accounting Office undertook a survey of the number, condition, and characteristics of children and youth age 16 and under who were homeless in one sense or another. On a given night in that period, about 68,000 such persons were estimated to be "literally homeless"— that is, they were in homeless shelters or sleeping in abandoned buildings, cars, parks, or other public places. In addition, nearly 186,000 were in the "precariously housed" category—spending the night in doubled-up or "shared housing" circumstances.[32]

A breakdown of the range of GAO estimates appears in Table 2.6, along with fiscal year 1991 data from surveys of state education agencies.[33] In a 1991 report, the Children's Defense Fund (CDF) reviewed various estimates of the number of homeless children, including those of the GAO, the Urban Institute, and the National Institute of Medicine, as well as annual estimates from the California state government, Western Center on Law and Poverty, and others. It concluded that 100,000 was a "fairly conservative estimate." (The National Institute of

Table 2.6
Estimated Number of U.S. Homeless Children and Youths, Age 16 and Under, in 1988, and of Homeless School-Age Children and Youths in Fiscal Year 1991

Facility/Location	1988 Best Estimate No.	%	Range* Low	High	FY 1991 Facility Type	No.	%
Urban:	46,313	68.0					
Shelters & hotels	25,552	37.5	18,265	32,779	Shelters (PbF)	63,683	17.5
Churches	4,094	6.0	2,340	6,570	Shelters (Pv F)	166,787	44.8
Public Places	9,016	13.2	4,512	24,072	Family/Friends	79,440	21.8
Other	7,651	11.2	5,168	10,446	Other	54,532	14.9
Suburban	14,427	21.2	7,213	21,641			
Rural	7,357	10.9	3,678	11,035			
Total	68,067	100.0	41,176	106,543			

Source: 1988 data from U.S. General Accounting Office (GAO), *Children and Youth* GAO/PEMD-89-14, 1989, 2. GAO's primary data sources were: GAO survey of shelter providers and agencies; application of homeless rates to a population base; and expert opinion. The 1988 figures cited here were classified by GAO as "literally homeless." Another category of "precariously housed," not shown, was estimated at 185,512 within a low-high range of 39,362 and 296,452.

FY 1991 data from surveys by state education agencies in all 50 states, District of Columbia, Puerto Rico, Virgin Islands, American Samoa, and the Northern Mariana Islands and covered grades K-12, school-age children both in and out of school. Included in the totals were preschool children in a few states. Reported in U. S. Department of Education, *Report to Congress: Final Reports Submitted by States Authorized by Education for Homeless Children and Youth Program Fiscal Year 1991*, September 1992, Enclosure A.

Notes: * High and low estimates represent a plausible range of values based on various assumptions.

Medicine study had produced a similar figure two years earlier.) The CDF report pointed out that 100,000 approximated the total number of children in a fairly large city, such as Atlanta, Boston, Miami, or Newark, and that at any given time, the number of the nation's homeless children would represent the total child population of one of those cities. The report went on to emphasize that "homeless children and their parents must have access to programs for which they are eligible" and that the "lack of a permanent address should not be a barrier to participation in any such program."[34]

As the CDF report and other studies have pointed out, adequate pre-natal and young child health care, including immunizations and other preventive and treatment measures for mothers and children, are more difficult to achieve for those many homeless dependent upon Medicaid, AFDC, or other governmental programs. This is due to lack of fixed address and legal residence and of the persistence required on the part of an applicant in order to complete necessary forms and comply with other procedures. Where emergency and other medical care is provided as part of shelter facilities and services, these deterrents to health care access are mitigated. A lack of legal residence in a school district can be a formidable barrier to adequate educational opportunity, and frequent changes in family or shelter locations exacerbate the problem.

FRAGMENTING FAMILY STRUCTURES

Following the end of World War II, the traditional American family structure— married couple with children—began to change in a number of respects, and most of these tended to accelerate in the 1960–90 period.[35]

- Divorce became ordinary instead of somewhat exceptional; the ratio in 1990 of divorced and not remarried persons per 1,000 married persons with spouse present was four times that of 1960.

- One-parent households with children increased dramatically; the proportion of children living with one- and two-parent families, respectively, moved from 9.1 and 87.7 in 1960 to 21.6 and 72.5 in 1990. Of all families with children in 1990, 28.1 percent were one-parent, compared with 12.9 percent in 1970.

- The proportion of children in single-parent situations living with a divorced, never remarried, or never-married parent, increased from 23 and 4 percent, respectively, in 1960, to 36 and 11 in 1975, and to 39 and 31 in 1990.

- Despite continued advances in contraceptive technology and the full, nationwide legalization of abortions in the 1970s, out-of-wedlock births and teenage pregnancies in the United States reached the highest points among the industrialized nations; the proportion of children under 18 living with a never-married parent grew from 4.2 in 1960 to 30.6 in 1990, with percentages of 19.2, 51.8, and 32.6 for whites, blacks, and Hispanic origin, respectively.

- Female-headed families with children were concentrated in the central cities of the larger metropolitan areas; the proportion of female householders of all family types in central cities and outside metropolitan areas in 1990 was 29.9 and 13.5.

Figure 2.1 illustrates the overall composition of households, and Figure 2.2 presents in graphic form the differential parental environments for children in one- and two-parent households.

The nearly half-century trend away from the former near-universal norm of two-parent families has been raising the odds against a substantially equal socioeconomic start for all young children, especially in areas of concentrated poverty. The national income aggregates shown in Figure 2.2 understate greatly the extent of single motherhood in large cities. As early as 1980, William Julius Wilson noted that of the 27,000 families living in public or subsidized projects of the Chicago Housing Authority, only 11 percent were married couple families.[36]

Female-headed families arise from three general conditions and circumstances. First, married mothers may become the household head as a result of divorce,

Figure 2.1
Composition of U.S. Households, 1990

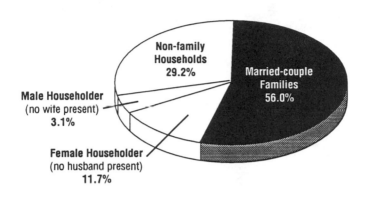

SOURCE: U. S. Department of Commerce, Bureau of the Census, *Household and Family Characteristics, March 1990 and 1989.* Series P-20, No. 447, Table B (Washington, D.C.: U. S. Government Printing Office, December 1990), p. 3.

desertion, or death of the husband and a decision to forego remarriage. Second, a single woman may become pregnant by intent or accident, opt for carrying the fetus to term (after being subject to much pro and con pressure as to having an abortion), further opt for keeping the child rather than putting it up for adoption, and finally choose to forego marriage to the father or other male, deciding instead to live with her own parents or other relatives or to establish her own household. A third condition, comparatively less frequent but becoming more common, has been the decision of single career women, approaching the mid-thirties, or earlier, and with comfortable or adequate income or other financial resources, to proceed to have one or more children, avoiding the perceived distractions and responsibilities of marriage.

Divorce and Remarriage

In 1990, 15.1 million divorced persons had not remarried, or 8 percent of the total adult population. The number was higher for women than for men—8.8 versus 6.3 million, because women were less likely to remarry after divorce. The ratio of divorced to married persons living with spouses was 142 per thousand, three times the ratio in 1970. The divorce ratio for blacks was higher than for whites (282 versus 133), and the ratio for Hispanics was not statistically significant from that for non-Hispanic whites.[37] A breakdown by decade appears in Table 2.7.

Figure 2.2
Children Under 18 Living with One or Two Parents, by Characteristics of the Parent(s), 1990

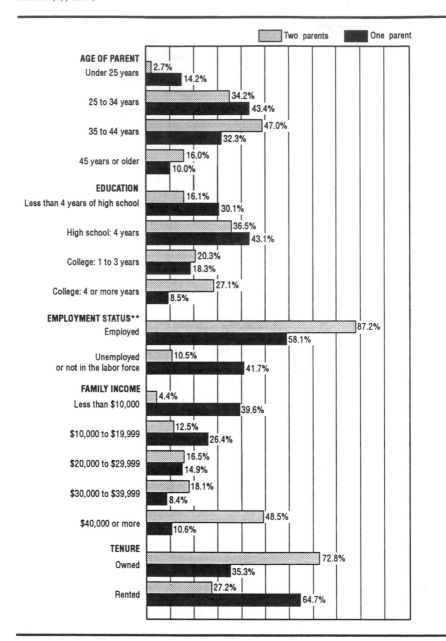

SOURCE: U. S. Department of Commerce, Bureau of the Census, *Marital Status and Living Arrangements: March 1990.* Table H. (Washington, D.C.: U. S. Government Printing Office, May 1991), p. 7.

NOTES: **Persons in the Armed Forces are not included.
Characteristics of the reference person are shown for children living with two parents. Tenure refers to tenure of the householder (who may not be the child's parent).

Table 2.7
Ratio* of Divorced Persons per 1,000 Married Persons with Spouse Present, by Decade, Sex, Race, and Hispanic Origin, 1960–90

Year and Sex	Total	White	Black	Hispanic
Both Sexes				
1990	142	133	282	129
1980	100	92	203	98
1970	47	44	83	61
1960	35	33	62	N/A
Male				
1990	118	112	208	103
1980	79	74	149	64
1970	35	32	62	40
1960	28	27	45	N/A
Female				
1990	166	153	358	155
1980	120	110	258	132
1970	60	56	104	81
1960	42	38	78	N/A

Source: Census Bureau, *Marital Status and Living Arrangements: March 1990* Series P-20, No. 450, Table C. May, 1991, 3.

Note: *The divorce ratio is cumulative and therefore affected by rates of marriage, divorce and remarriage in prior years. The annual divorce rate (number occurring in a given year) was 4.8 per thousand for 1989.
N/A = Data not available.

Living Arrangements of Children

In 1990, 72.5 percent of the nation's 64.1 million children were living with two parents, a drastic drop from 87.7 percent in 1960. The percentages by race and ethnic origin were: white (79.0), black (37.7), and Hispanic (66.8). Nearly one-quarter of all children were living with one parent and 2.2 percent with other relatives; of those living with one parent, about seven out of eight were with the mother. There were no significant differences of the mother-father ratio among whites, blacks, and Hispanics.[38]

Figure 2.3 illustrates the 1960–90 trend in the relationship between the two major causes of one-parent families—divorce and failure to marry before, or subsequent to, the birth of children.

Table 2.8 shows the marital status of the parent in one-parent families with children in 1960 and 1990. A more detailed breakdown, including numbers in preceding decades, is carried in Appendix 2.B.

The proportion of children under 18 living with a grandparent who was the householder stood at 4.9 percent in 1990, up from 3.8 percent in 1960. By race

Figure 2.3
Children of Single Parents, by Marital Status of Parent, 1960–90

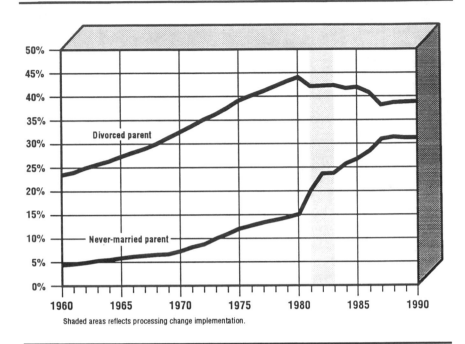

Shaded areas reflects processing change implementation.

SOURCE: U. S. Department of Commerce, Bureau of the Census, *Marital Status and Living Arrangements: March 1990.*
Series P-20, No. 450 (Washington, D.C.: U. S. Government Printing Office, May 1991), p. 6.

and Hispanic origin, the figures for 1990 were: white, (3.6); black, (12.1); and Hispanic (5.8).[39] Further details on the custodial and householder role of grandparents and other relatives in 1990 are presented in Table 2.9.

Respective educational attainment contrasts between two- and one-parent living arrangements in 1990 are shown in Figure 2.4.

Although the percent of grandparent involvement is relatively modest when the universe of comparison is all children, as in Table 2.9, it becomes quite important when the large number of children living with both parents is disregarded. Of children living with the mother only, 11.3 percent were grandchildren of the householder (10.2, white; 18.9, black; and 21, Hispanic). Of those living with neither parent, 54.1 percent were grandchildren of the householder (49.7, white; 62.8, black; and 39.3, Hispanic).

Single Motherhood and Teenage Pregnancy

Although the largest proportion of single-parent children lived with a divorced parent in 1990 (39%), this was slightly lower than in 1980 (42%). The next

Table 2.8
Children Under 18 Living with One Parent, by Marital Status of Parent, Race, and Hispanic Origin for 1960 and 1990 (in percents of children)

Parent Marital Status	All Races 1990	All Races 1960	White 1990	White 1960	Black 1990	Black 1960	Hispanic 1990	Hispanic 1980*
Total	100	100	100	100	100	100	100	100
Divorced	38.6	23.0	49.1	28.4	20.4	11.9	26.6	30.6
Married, S.A.	23.7	46.3	23.9	41.1	22.8	57.2	33.8	40.6
Separated	20.3	27.6	20.1	19.8	20.5	34.0	26.8	34.7
Other	3.4	18.7	3.8	21.3	2.3	13.5	7.0	5.9
Widowed	7.1	26.5	7.8	29.0	5.1	21.3	6.9	8.9
Never Married	30.6	4.2	19.2	1.6	51.8	9.6	32.6	19.8

Source: Census Bureau, *Marital Status and Living Arrangements: March 1990*, Table F, 6.

Notes: * Decennial Hispanic data not available pre-1980.
S.A. = Spouse absent.

highest and fastest growing percentage of children lived with a parent who had never married (see Figure 2.3). Between 1960 and 1990, the proportion living with a never-married parent rose from 4 to 31 percent as childbearing among never-married women increased as they postponed marriage, and as more teenage women bore out-of-wedlock children. For 24 percent of the "single-parent children," the reason for absence of the spouse was separation or desertion, and for 7 percent it was spousal death.[40]

The National Commission on Children (NCC) in its 1991 report stated:

Today, more than a million babies each year are born to unmarried women. Births to adolescents are especially likely to occur outside of marriage. Approximately 40 percent of White babies and 90 percent of Black babies of teenage mothers are born into single-parent families. Even when teenagers do marry, their marriages tend to be unstable, and for this reason the children of teenage mothers are even more likely than other children to spend a substantial portion of their formative years in a single-parent family.

A striking feature of the growth of mother-only families over the past generation has been the difference between Blacks and Whites. For Whites, the increase is primarily due to divorce and separation; for Blacks, it is primarily the result of childbearing outside of marriage. Yet taken together the result of these trends is that more than half of all White children and three-quarters of all Black children born in the 1970s and 1980s are likely to live for some portion of their formative years with only their mothers.[41]

Foregoing data in this chapter concerning poverty, unemployment, and homelessness demonstrate conclusively the various disadvantages besetting mothers

Table 2.9

Role of Grandparents and Presence of Parents in Living Arrangements for Children Under 18 Years, by Age, Race, and Hispanic Origin, March 1990 (numbers in thousands)

Living Arrangement	All Races Under 18 No.	%	Under 6 No.	%	White Under 18 No.	%	Under 6 No.	%	Black Under 18 No.	%	Under 6 No.	%	Hispanic Origin Under 18 No.	%	Under 6 No.	%
Total	64,137	100.0	22,625	100.0	51,930	100.0	18,114	100.0	10,018	100.0	3,510	100.0	7,174	100.0	2,689	100.0
In Households	64,097	99.9	22,612	99.9	51,372	98.9	18,101	99.9	10,003	99.9	3,510	100.0	7,162	99.8	2,680	99.7
GC of Householder	3,155	4.9	1,642	7.3	1,831	3.5	984	5.4	1,215	12.7	588	16.8	415	5.8	232	8.6
With Both Parents	46,503	72.5	16,562	73.2	41,571	80.4	13,781	73.7	4,789	66.8	1,202	34.2	4,789	66.8	1,781	66.2
GC of Householder	467	0.7	313	1.4	385	0.7	252	1.4	36	0.4	25	0.7	74	1.0	51	1.9
With Mother Only	13,874	21.6	4,906	21.7	8,321	16.0	2,767	15.3	5,132	51.2	1,969	56.1	1,943	27.1	747	27.8
GC of Householder	1,563	2.4	960	4.2	851	1.6	518	2.9	671	6.7	414	11.8	227	3.2	148	5.5
With Father Only	1,993	3.1	652	2.9	1,549	3.0	503	2.8	353	3.5	129	3.7	211	2.9	104	3.9
GC of Householder	191	0.3	74	0.3	143	0.3	60	0.3	45	0.4	13	0.4	28	0.4	14	0.5
With Neither Parent	1,727	2.7	492	2.2	910	1.8	260	1.4	737	7.4	210	6.0	219	3.1	48	1.8
GC of Householder	935	1.5	296	0.5	45	0.2	191	1.9	33	0.9	91	1.3	86	1.2	19	0.7
Other Relative of Householder	487	0.8	89	0.4	256	0.5	45	0.2	191	1.9	33	0.9	91	1.3	17	0.6
Non-relative of Householder	306	0.5	106	0.5	202	0.4	62	0.3	83	0.8	42	1.2	42	0.6	13	0.5
Foster Child	139	0.2	68	0.3	89	0.2	39	0.2	40	0.4	25	0.7	7	0.1	-	0.0
In Group Quarters	40	0.1	13	0.1	18	Neg.	13	0.1	15	Neg.	-	0.0	12	0.2	9	0.3

Source: Census Bureau, *Marital Status* Table 4, May, 1991, 37-40.
Note: GC = Grandchild.

Figure 2.4
**Education of Parent in One- and Two-Parent Families Living with Children
Under 18, 1990**

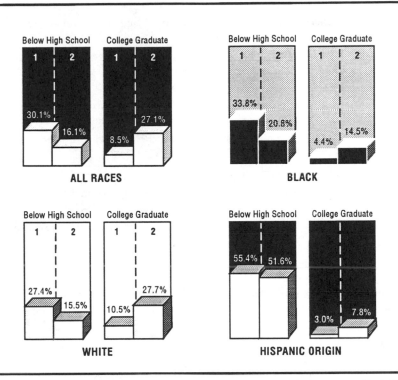

ALL RACES

BLACK

WHITE

HISPANIC ORIGIN

SOURCE: U. S. Department of Commerce, Bureau of the Census, *Marital Status and Living Arrangements: March 1990.*
Series P-20, No. 450 (Washington, D.C.: U. S. Government Printing Office), Table H.

and children in single-parent families and in households headed by the mother.
Yet, the conception and attempted rearing of children by unmarried women
without significant sources of financial support have continued to increase.

Increases averaging 4–7 percent were reported for child-bearing by unmarried
women in 1990, the sixth successive year of such increases, reaching a record
level of nearly 1.2 million in 1990. Such births occurred at a rate, for all age
groups, of 28 percent of live births. Rates by age group were under 15, 91.6;
15–19, 67.1; 20–24, 36.9; and 25–29, 18.0. The rate for age 15 was 86.9, the
highest for any given age. The 15–19 rates for whites was 56.4, blacks, 92.0,
and 90.0 for other races. However, the rate for white unmarried women of all
ages was 32.9 in 1990, compared to 18.1 in 1980; the comparable rates for
blacks, although at a much higher level, were 90.5 and 81.1, a smaller *relative*
increase over the decade than for whites.[42] The question then arises, Why do
the pregnancy, abortion, and birthrates for the teenage group continue to rise,

given the unfavorable odds facing young unmarried women without assured means of support and given continuing advances in contraceptive technology? Various motivating factors have been cited for these trends, including:

*   to show independence from, or rebellion against, parental control or other home conditions;
*   a combination of low grades in school, low educational expectations, early physical maturity, and disillusion about, or unwillingness to consider, the future prospects of marriage to any known or available male acquaintances;
*   desires for a child of her own, strong enough to avoid contraception, to choose birth over abortion, and to opt for retention of the child over adoption;
*   especially in deciding to have additional children, the availability of increased AFDC benefits;
*   for some, no access to contraceptive information;
*   unwillingness of the male to use contraceptives or to acquiesce in the female's use of them;
*   peer pressure toward sexual activity and scorn toward protective measures; and
*   increasing employment opportunities for women, providing a basis for anticipating an independent life-style.[43]

The National Commission on Children generalized as follows on other causes and motivations:

Some analysts suggest that declining opportunities for economically disadvantaged young men have made it nearly impossible for them to support families, making them less attractive marriage partners. Others highlight the growing social acceptance of premarital sex and early, unmarried childbearing, especially in low income communities. Still others point to the growing number of young people who perceive their opportunities for the future as so limited that bearing a child is one of the few achievements they can look forward to.[44]

In the mid-1980s the Rand Corporation analyzed data from the National Center for Educational Statistics and tracked 13,000 sophomore women for two years, comparing the group that became unmarried mothers and those that did not. Multivariate analyses were used, producing findings that low family socioeconomic status was significant for blacks, less so for Hispanics, and not a factor for whites. Parent-child communication was most important for whites, parental supervision for blacks, and religion for Hispanics.[45]

Inner-city environment has been stressed by a number of researchers. There "peer pressure, ignorance, passion, luck, intent, conquest, religion, love, and even profound hostility between young men and women" are factors. For the young woman: "A large part of her identity is provided by the baby, the symbolic passage to adulthood . . . for many street-oriented girls there is no quicker way to grow up. Becoming a mother can be a strong play for authority, maturity, and respect."[46]

A strong correlation has also been found in "very bad neighborhoods" between the percentage of high-status (managerial or professional) workers in the neighborhood and the probability of teenage childbearing, with a sharp drop in such probability for both blacks and whites when the high status percentage increased beyond the 10–15 percent range. This factor was found considerably less important for both races in less severely impacted areas. Despite the prevalence of economic and sociological assumptions that teenage motherhood causes school dropout and ensures long-term unemployment and poverty, some research supports the opposite proposition that the cycle begins with poverty, with a consequent attitude of hopelessness and "nothing further to lose."[47] In any event, the health and educational risks for both teenage mother and offspring described here are awesome and growing more so. They are analyzed in further detail in the two subsequent chapters.

Child Support

Closely associated with single motherhood and one-parent households is the lack in many instances of adequate financial support to the mother and child(ren). For many mothers, adolescent ones in particular, this financial support may come from a mix of private and public sources. The potential private sources comprise her parent(s) and other relatives, her own earnings, and her husband or the father of her child(ren). The first two of these—labor market participation and living arrangements—were examined earlier. Support from private sources and potential public sources are now examined.

Support from Absent Fathers. The concepts and laws governing paternal child support cover all marital status and income classes. Federal law provides an underpinning of support framework and process, directed mainly toward fathers and former husbands of AFDC recipients. State laws vary in severity and enforcement vigor. Figure 2.5 shows the award status of mothers from absent fathers. According to the Census Bureau's report showing the status of child support awards as of spring 1990, 55 percent of the absent fathers had visitation privileges, another 7 percent had joint custody with the mother, the other 38 percent had neither. Of the 2.7 million mothers who initially wanted support but were not awarded it, about one-half were below the poverty level. The reasons (in percents) for failing to get a support award, for all women and women below poverty level, respectively, were: (1) father unable to pay, 23 and 26; (2) father not locatable, 21 and 23; (3) mother finally decided not to pursue the award, 3 and 27; and (4) other reasons, including inability to establish paternity, 26 and 27.[48]

Table 2.10 shows the status of parental child support in the 1987–89 period, based on census data. Most of the contrasts in this table are similar to data in a different context presented earlier regarding the relationships among poverty, educational attainment, and single motherhood. The highest proportion of child

Figure 2.5
Award Status of Child Support Payments as of March 1990

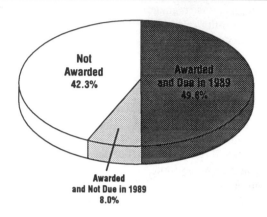

Not
Awarded
42.3%

Awarded
and Due in 1989
49.6%

Awarded
and Not Due in 1989
8.0%

SOURCE: U. S. Department of Commerce, Bureau of the Census, *Child Support and Alimony: 1989,* Current Population Reports, Consumer Income. P-60, No. 173 (Washington, D.C.: U. S. Government Printing Office, September 1991), p. 6.

support payments (CSPs) went to the better-educated, white, married, or divorced women, whereas less than a fifth of the never-married women were helped. A much lower proportion of women below the poverty level were awarded support, probably because the absent father lacked the income or assets from which to provide it. Once awarded support, however, delinquencies did not seem to vary much among the categories of mothers.

Federal and state child support policies and enforcement procedures have been an important public policy and fiscal issue throughout the 1980s to the present. Nationally, child support payments due in fiscal year 1990, as reported by 47 of the 54 states and jurisdictions, amounted to $23.8 billion for that year and prior years; the total collected was $5.5 billion. The amount of support owed in that year was $7.8 billion; of that amount, $4.2 billion was collected, or 53 percent. The amount due for prior years in the 47 jurisdictions was $15.8 billion, of which just $1.2 billion was collected, or 8 percent of the amount owed.

The federal Family Support Act of 1988 (PL 100–485, 102 Stat. 2343) strengthened earlier child support requirements that had focused rather exclusively on partial reimbursements to the federal and state governments for AFDC payments and foster care (FC) for AFDC children. The 1988 legislation emphasized that collection procedures should apply to non-AFDC families as well. In fiscal year 1990, total child support collections within the federally required collection system came to slightly over $6 billion, of which $1.7 billion was for AFDC reimbursement and $11 million for FC; $4.26 billion was for non-AFDC mothers. Percentages of AFDC payments recovered via child support from absent

Table 2.10
Child Support Payments (CSPs) Awarded and Received by All Women with Own Children Under 21 and Women with Incomes Below the Poverty Level in 1987 and 1989 (numbers in thousands)

Category	Number		% Awarded CSP's		No. Due CSP's		% Rec. CSP's		Mean Amount		% of Total Income	
	1987	1989	1987	1989	1987	1989	1987	1989	1987	1989	1987	1989
All women	9,415	9,955	59.0	57.7	4,829	4,953	76.1	75.2	$2,215	$2,995	19.0	18.5
Married*	2,386	2,531	82.0	79.0	1,656	1,685	72.9	72.1	2,540	2,931	20.2	20.3
Divorced	2,958	3,056	77.2	76.8	2,087	2,123	78.0	77.0	3,073	3,322	17.6	17.1
Separated	1,381	1,352	54.8	47.9	628	527	74.0	79.7	2,745	3,060	21.5	20.5
Never Married	2,625	2,950	19.7	23.9	430	583	83.3	73.2	1,632	1,888	22.7	19.9
Education												
Below 12th	2,349	2,372	42.9	36.9	855	741	69.7	66.7	1,872	1,754	28.9	21.4
H. S. Graduate	4,486	4,704	59.4	62.0	2,285	2,470	75.6	76.4	2,518	2,698	20.6	19.9
1-3 Yrs. College	1,739	1,988	71.0	65.0	1,105	1,139	77.5	76.6	2,570	2,338	16.5	18.1
4 + Yrs. College	842	891	77.0	74.5	584	603	85.1	77.9	4,310	4,850	16.3	15.7
Race												
White	6,437	6,905	58.8	67.5	3,910	4,048	76.6	76.5	2,950	3,132	19.7	18.8
Black	2,686	2,770	35.6	34.5	787	791	73.2	69.7	1,503	2,263	14.7	16.3
Hispanic	937	1,112	42.4	40.6	344	364	75.6	69.8	2,628	2,965	28.6	20.1
Below Poverty Level	3,191	3,206	44.3	43.3	1,241	1,190	71.9	68.3	1,673	1,889	36.6	37.4

Source: Census, Child Support and Alimony: 1987, Series P-23 No. 167. June, 1990, p. 5; Child Support and Alimony: 1989, Series P-60 No. 173. Sept. 1991, p. 5.

Note: * Remarried women, post-divorce.

parents ranged from a high of 35.7 percent (Idaho) to 4.4 percent (Arizona), with a national average of 10.3 percent.[49]

Important procedural weapons under the 1988 federal-state child support enforcement program included:[50]

- Location of noncustodial parent through inquiries to banks, insurance companies, and government agencies.

- Establishment of paternity through court orders for tests and other appropriate means.

- Credit agency reporting, which encourages states to provide such information if the amount of overdue support exceeds $1,000.

- Federal and state tax intercepts, under which tax refunds due the absent parent are intercepted and seized to satisfy overdue support payments.

- Garnishment proceedings to seize wages, bank accounts, pension, workers' compensation, and other income.

- Imposition of liens upon the assets of the person whose support payments are delinquent.

By the early 1990s most states were looking for additional approaches to make child support programs more effective, and the possible need for further legislation was being explored. One of these was the interstate collection system. The Family Support Act of 1988 established a 15-member Commission on Interstate Child Support, with 8 members appointed by Congress and 7 by the HHS secretary. The commission issued its report in August 1992, calling for a number of changes in federal and state child support laws and procedures. Its recommendations to the Congress and the state and territorial governments were based on the objectives of achieving (1) uniformity of state laws and procedures that are not only uniform in nature but consistent in application; (2) simplicity and ease of case processing; and (3) availability of dedicated funding to process interstate cases. The specific recommendations to achieve these objectives included:[51]

- Congressional action to use the Federal Parent Locate Service to create a federal-state network linking statewide automated child support systems with federal locate resources.

- Congressional authorization to modify the W-4 tax withholding form and its processing to require persons with a child support order or health care support obligation to so indicate on the form, including an authorization to begin withholding on the first paycheck, with employers required to forward a copy of the W-4 to the state employment service, with the resulting W-4 database accessible to the state child support enforcing agency.

- Federal action, in conjunction with employers and states, to develop a national income withholding notice; if income withholding were contested by the liable parent, any hearing would be held where the employer received notice, with the responsible state agency appearing in behalf of the person due the support.

- A federal requirement that states enact the Uniform Interstate Family Support Act, formulated earlier by the National Conference of Commissioners on Uniform State

Laws, after receiving input from the commission, which, in effect, was a revision, expansion, and tightening of the Uniform Reciprocal Enforcement of Support Act, which had been enacted by most of the states.

- A federal requirement that states establish presumptions of parentage based on a threshold resulting from genetic tests.

- A change in federal law to require the health insurance industry to cooperate with states in providing health benefits to the child(ren) included in the support award.

- Changes to strengthen and make more effective the federal aid formula used to determine the incentives states receive for collecting child support.

At least one commission member dissented from the report on the grounds that it did not go far enough and that more national action was required. Some members of the Congress from both parties were already advancing proposals along those lines, "federalizing" virtually all of the enforcement aspects of child support except the issuance of initial support orders, but even those would need to meet national guidelines specified in the legislation, based on federal income tax filings.

The quantitative financial benefits of the child support enforcement program are apparent. The personal qualitative benefits and ramifications for child, mother, father, and society in general, especially in the case of heretofore unknown fathers, are illustrated in Appendix 2.C, reproduced from a report by the GAO.[52] It shows major public and private effects associated with paternity establishment, including a force for change in male out-of-wedlock procreative behavior as a societal benefit.

Sources of Public Financial Support. Governmental aid in support of low-income mothers and their children comes in a variety of forms—cash payments, in-kind assistance such as food stamps, and health and other services. The principal programs in these categories, in addition to child support enforcement, have been:[53]

- *Cash Assistance*: (1) Aid to Families with Dependent Children for single- and some two-parent families, which is federal-state in financing, with local government financial participation in some states; (2) general assistance in a number of states, wholly state or state-local in financing, which can be used for a variety of purposes.

- *In-Kind Assistance*: (1) Free or low-cost medical care through the Medicaid program; (2) Food stamps, which are vouchers for food purchases by poor families and persons; (3) subsidized housing, either through public housing projects or rental subsidy certificates; (4) supplemental food program for women, infants, and children (WIC); (5) Job Training Partnership Act (JTPA) for work-related training and services; (6) social services block grant, under priorities determined by each state, including child care, family planning information and referral, adoption, foster care, and a variety of other authorized purposes; (7) maternal and child health block grant for authorized health services, with priorities determined by recipient states.

PARENTAL NEGLECT, ABUSE, AND ABANDONMENT OF CHILDREN

In its report chapter on *Protecting Vulnerable Children and Their Families,* the National Commission on Children stated:

Children need strong, stable families and enduring supportive relationships . . . in families experiencing severe stress, love often turns into neglect, affection withers into hostility and discipline becomes abuse. Poverty, single parenthood, mental illness, drug abuse, and social isolation can weaken families and impair some parents' ability to care for their children. When families are in turmoil, children are often the helpless victims of their parents' frustration and despair. In the absence of adequate support . . . these children are frequently removed from their families and placed in the custody of the state . . . to protect them from physical, emotional, or sexual abuse.[54]

Child Abuse and Neglect

Reports of child abuse and neglect, with or without substantiation, rose dramatically between 1976 (numbering 669,000) and 1986 (over 2 million), to a general estimate of over 2.7 million in 1990.[55] It should be noted that collection and maintenance of child abuse data have been extremely difficult to manage, due both to the delicacy of the subject matter and to the time required to assemble, recheck, and aggregate reports from each of the states. A new national data system was congressionally mandated in the Child Abuse Prevention, Adoption and Family Services Act of 1988 (PL 100–294). An initial quantitative report under the new system was issued in 1992, embracing state reports of abuse and maltreatment for the year 1990.[56] A breakdown by type of maltreatment over the 1976–90 period is shown in Table 2.11.

Following substantiation of a serious incident, repetition of such a pattern of abuse or neglect by a state or local child welfare or other public agency and following unheeded warnings, a local court typically assumes temporary jurisdiction over the situation, often delegating the supervision to a social, health, or other appropriate agency. The agency attempts, through counseling and other persuasive approaches to improve conditions, looking toward stabilization and lifting of state jurisdiction. Often during this period, the child is removed physically to a protective group home or other facility. If efforts to effect a return to a safe condition appear to be impossible or highly unlikely, the agency then looks toward placement in a foster home. In the latter case, the householder(s) receives a support stipend from public authorities. Marian Edelman cited estimates in 1990 that more than 50 percent of out-of-home placements (foster homes and custodial facilities) were for children who needed protection from adults in their own homes.[57]

Table 2.11
Child Maltreatment Cases Reported, 1976–90, by Type of Maltreatment and Characteristics of Child and Perpetrator (in percents, except for total number in thousands)

Item	1976	1980	1984	1986	1990[1]
Number children reported	669	1,154	1,727	2,086	2,734
Rate per 10,000 chldren	101	181	273	328	420
Type of maltreatment:					
Deprivation of necessities	70.7	60.7	54.6	54.9	45.0
Minor physical injury	18.9	19.8	17.7	13.9	25.6
Sexual maltreatment	3.2	6.8	13.3	15.7	15.5
Emotional maltreatment	21.6	13.5	11.2	8.3	6.4
Other maltreatment	11.2	14.7	16.5	21.6	6.6
Child Characteristics:					
Average age (years)	7.7	7.3	7.2	7.2	7.0[2]
Male	50.0	49.8	48.0	47.5	45.9
Female	50.0	50.2	52.0	52.5	52.3
Perpetrator Characteristics:					
Average age (years)	32.3	31.4	31.5	31.7	N/A[3]
Male	39.0	41.2	43.0	44.1	N/A
Female	61.0	58.8	57.0	55.9	N/A

Sources: For pre-1990 data: American Humane Association, Denver, *National Study on Child Neglect and Abuse Reporting* (annual) carried in *Statistical Abstract of the United States 1990*. Table 297, p. 176. For 1990 data: U.S. Department of Health and Human Services (HHS), National Center on Child Abuse and Neglect (NCCAN), *National Child Abuse and Neglect Data System Working Paper 1: 1990 Summary Data Component*. Tabular sections I, IV, and V. (Washington DC: HHS, April 1992), 8, 13-16, 18-21.

Notes: [1] Initial data report emanating from formation of a National Data System on Child Abuse and Neglect reports received by state authorities. 1990 data reported from 49 states (except KS), DC, and one territory. Most but not all states reported on each set of characteristics. 47 states reported that 833,000 cases substantiated after investigation. Number of states reporting on table categories were: Type of maltreatment (47), age (46), sex (47) and perpetrators' relation to victims (40).

[2] Median age; mean not available.

[3] Perpetrator age and sex not reported.

Foster Homes

The children in foster care may be located there under circumstances described above or may have been abandoned after birth or placed there for other reasons. The National Commission on Children pointed out that information on the population of children living apart from their families is limited by inadequate data collection. According to then-existing sources, it estimated that the number of children in foster care had been increasing over the years immediately preceding

1991—from an estimated 502,000 in 1977 to 275,000 in 1983 to 340,000 in 1989—and was heading for an estimated 550,000 in 1995—reversing declines in the late 1970s and early 1980s. The increase under way in the early 1990s was overwhelming the judicial and child welfare systems. Child welfare agencies were responsible for investigating and overseeing out-of-home placements, including a number of children who were placed in residential group care facilities outside the home state. They have also been providing counseling for the growing number of children who require protective services.[58]

The commission reported that increasingly the foster care population was comprising seriously troubled adolescents at one end of the age spectrum and medically fragile infants and young children at the other. Growing numbers of adolescents in foster care are youth who have dropped out of school, and unable to find jobs, and are pregnant or already have babies of their own.[59] As in the case of the homeless population discussed earlier, policies mandating the deinstitutionalization of the mentally ill and the decriminalization of status offenders (runaways, truants, or "ungovernables") increased the number of emotionally disturbed, developmentally disabled, and delinquent children in foster care.

The country has been experiencing a growing population of infants and very young children born to, or being raised by drug-abusing parents, with many of them having been exposed to drugs in utero and experiencing physical, psychological, and other disabilities. Others are at risk of developing AIDS. Many of these children are beginning their lives as "boarder babies." These infants have been abandoned by their mothers, and finding even temporary placements is becoming extremely difficult. Consequently, such infants were spending much more time in hospitals than medically necessary.[60]

Detention, Custodial, and Shelter Facilities

In 1989, 93,945 juveniles were in detention, custodial, and shelter facilities, according to a count by the Census Bureau for the U.S. Department of Justice (Office of Juvenile Justice and Delinquency Prevention). This census of 1,100 public and 2,167 private juvenile facilities found a majority of juveniles (56,123) being held in public facilities, with the rest in private ones. In the two years following the 1987 census, the population in custody had increased by 3 percent and the public facility population was up by 5 percent, while the private population decreased by 1 percent.[61] A further breakdown of the juvenile custodial population is shown in Table 2.12.

In the two years following the 1987 census, minorities passed whites in the custodial population (52%), while having only about 29 percent of the total 1990 population. Between 1987 and 1989, the proportion being held for delinquent offenses (against persons, such as murder, rape, and other violent crimes; against property; probation violation; drug/alcohol/public order, and other offenses) increased by 5 percent, while the number held for status offenses (that would not be criminal if they were adults, such as runaways) decreased by 2 percent. Of

Table 2.12
Juveniles Held in Public and Private Custody: Residents and Facilities, 1985 and 1989

Characteristic	1985 Public Custody No.	1985 Public Custody %	1985 Private Custody No.	1985 Private Custody %	1989 Public Custody No.	1989 Public Custody %	1989 Private Custody No.	1989 Private Custody %
No. Residents (1,000)	49.3	100.0	34.1	100.0	56.1	100.0	37.8	100.0
Male	42.5	86.3	23.8	70.0	49.4	88.1	26.6	70.4
Female	6.8	13.7	10.2	30.0	6.7	11.9	11.2	29.6
White	30.0	60.8	24.0	70.4	22.2	39.6	22.8	60.3
Black	18.3	37.0	9.2	27.0	23.8	42.4	10.9	28.8
Hispanic Origin	6.6	13.3	2.5	7.4	8.7	15.5	3.1	8.2
Other	1.1	2.2	0.9	2.6	1.4	2.5	1.1	2.9
Detained/Committed for:		100.0		100.0		100.0		100.0
Delinquent Offenses	46.1	93.4	11.7	34.2	53.0	94.5	13.1	34.7
Person	12.2	24.8	1.8	5.4	14.3	25.5	2.5	6.6
Property	22.0	44.6	5.9	17.3	22.8	40.6	7.0	18.5
Alcohol/drugs	2.7	5.4	.7	2.0	6.6	11.8	1.8	4.8
Public order	6.5	13.2	.7	1.9	2.8	5.0	.3	0.8
Probation violator	----	----	----	----	4.9	8.7	.3	0.8
Other offenses	2.7	5.4	2.6	7.5	1.6	2.9	1.2	3.2
Non-delinquent	3.1	6.6	22.3	65.8	3.0	5.3	24.7	65.3
Status* offenses	2.3	4.6	6.7	19.7	2.2	3.9	6.9	18.3
Abuse, neglect	.4	0.8	6.9	20.3	.4	0.7	8.5	22.5
Other**	.1	0.4	1.6	5.6	.1	0.1	2.4	6.3
Voluntarily admitted	.3	0.6	6.9	20.1	.3	0.5	7.0	18.5

Source: U.S. Department of Justice, Bureau of Justice Statistics, *Census of Public and Private Juvenile Detention, Correctional and Shelter Facilities, 1975-85,* Tables 31, 41; May 1989, 39, 50. *1989 Census of Public and Private Juvenile Detention, Correctional and Shelter Facilities,* February 1991.

Notes: * Offenses that would not be criminal for adults (e.g. runaways).
          ** All other unspecified reasons for detention or commitment, including emotional disturbance or mental retardation cases in private custody.

youths in private facilities, nearly two-thirds were held for nondelinquent reasons. Of those held for reasons of abuse and neglect, nearly all (96%) were housed in private facilities.[62]

SUMMARY OF GENERAL DETERRENTS

Significant barriers to the physical health and educational attainment of American children and youth exist outside the public and private institutions delivering those services. Some factors are external to the child and parent(s); others involve household and family structures and parent-child relationships. These common deterrents and the ways in which they may affect child and youth development can be summarized as follows.

- A child reared in poverty conditions undergoes many deprivations, including (1) lack of adequate health care and/or access to it; (2) necessity of working part- or full-time during adolescent years in order to meet personal and/or family needs; and (3) interpersonal stress within the household due to financial worries and setbacks.
- In 1990, the proportion of children under 18 living below the poverty level ranged from more than one in seven to one in five, depending on the poverty measure—whether based on cash income alone or on total income, including noncash benefits.
- The poverty proportion of families with children lay in a range of 1 in 10 to 1 in 14; however, for female-headed families, the range was from a third to a half. Of all families in poverty, a majority were headed by never-married women.
- Access to child and day care has become essential for a majority of young families and a critical must for a single mother with children below school age, unless she has independent means or is on welfare. Employer-provided day care became increasingly available during the eighties, but was concentrated in larger firms.
- Residence in a poverty area carries external deterrents to health and educational progress, especially when the neighborhood poverty condition is combined with a high incidence of school dropouts, unemployed or not-interested-in-working youths, drug dealing, and other illegal activity. Over 800 census tracts—many in large central cities—were identified as permeated with the poverty/nonmainstream behavior combination in the late 1980s.
- Homelessness has been an increasingly difficult problem, stemming from multiple sources—mental health institution overcrowding, drug or alcohol addiction, and housing affordability, among others—with a visibility growth that disturbed the public and perplexed public officials. At any one time, at least 100,000 children were homeless and 250,000 others were precariously housed in 1990, and adequate prenatal and young child health care and educational opportunities were becoming more serious among the general homeless population, which was approaching or exceeding 1 million persons.
- Unstable and disintegrating family structure emerged as perhaps the most pervasive and hard-to-attack general deterrent to child and youth development. One-parent households were increasing dramatically, divorce had become ever more common, and female-headed households were becoming the norm in many poverty and minority population concentrations. Characteristics of these mothers in comparison with two-parent families included low educational attainment (e.g., a fourth versus a tenth with 16 or more years of schooling), unemployed or not in the labor force (three to one), and low annual income.
- Lack of adequate child support from absent fathers was especially marked for never-married women, with only one-fifth receiving such support. The largest proportion of payments went to better-educated, white, married, or divorced women.
- The incidence of child abuse and neglect grew considerably. The rate of reported cases apparently quadrupled between 1976 and 1990, and the proportionate reporting of sexual abuse cases quintupled. Based on anecdotal and other news reporting, the magnitude of the problem was still increasing in 1992.

• The numbers of foster home children increased. There was a rapidly growing backlog of children removed from custody of parent(s) but not yet placed in a foster home.

The foregoing underscores the number and extent of economic, social, and others ills threatening the nation's youth in the first half of the 1990s. Taken together, they mean that from a fifth to a quarter of the below-18 population, including especially large proportions of black and Hispanic youth, are vulnerable in varying degrees to physical or personal failure or to work lives that produce far less than optimal results, both for the individual and for American society. From the standpoints of social conscience, national policy, and international competitiveness, this is a present and future weakness that might appear to many as both unaffordable and unforgivable.

To all of the above must be added the specific shortcomings in institutional structures and processes in the delivery of health and educational services that affect the quality of life and employability of youth. Those are examined in the ensuring chapters.

NOTES

1. Congressional Budget Office (CBO), *Reducing Poverty Among Children*, Appendix A, "Measuring Poverty," May 1985, 149–73. See also Garfinkel, I. (ed.), *Income-Tested Transfer Programs: The Case For and Against* (New York: Academic Press, 1982), 12–14; Bureau of the Census, *Alternative Methods for Valuing Selected In-Kind Transfer Benefits and Measuring Their Effect on Poverty*, Technical Paper 50, March 1982, 28–31, 38–44, 58–69, 127–34; Danziger, Sheldon, and Gottschalk, P., "The Measurement of Poverty: Implications for Antipoverty Policy," Discussion Paper No. 709–82 (Madison, WI: Institute for Research on Poverty [IRP], 1982); Ruggles, P., "Measuring Poverty," *Focus* (published by IRP) 14, no. 1, Spring 1992, 1–9; Congress, House Committee on Ways and Means, *Background Material and Data on Programs Within the Jurisdiction of the Committee on Ways and Means*, May 7, 1991, 1167–68.

2. U.S. Department of Commerce, Bureau of the Census, *Measuring the Effect of Benefits and Taxes on Income and Poverty: 1989*, Current Population Reports, Consumer Income, Series P–60, no. 169RD, September 1990, 1.

3. Bureau of the Census, *Measuring the Effect of Benefits and Taxes on Income and Poverty: 1990*, Current Population Reports, Consumer Income, Series P–60, no. 176RD, Tables 2, 3, August 1991, 1–17, 40–55.

4. Bureau of the Census, Release CB–91–288, September 26, 1991, 3 (emphasis added).

5. CBO, *The Economic and Budget Outlook: Fiscal Years 1993–1997*, January 1992, 14.

6. Bureau of the Census, *Poverty in the United States: 1990*, Current Population Reports—Consumer Income, P–60, no. 175, Tables 2–4, 10, 14, August 1991, 1–14, 16–23, 84–87.

7. Ibid., 8–9. See also Danziger, Sheldon, "Anti-Poverty Policy and Welfare Reform," paper prepared for Rockefeller Foundation Conference on Welfare Reform, Williamsburg, VA, February 16–18, 1988; Danziger, S., and Gottschalk, P., "Work, Poverty

and the Working Poor: A Multifaceted Problem," *Monthly Labor Review*, September 1986, 17–21.

8. Committee on Ways and Means, Subcommittee on Human Resources, *Background Material on Family Income and Benefit Changes*, December 1991, 28–29.

9. Center for Human Resources Research, *NLS Handbook, 1987* (Columbus: Ohio State University, 1987).

10. GAO, *Mother-Only Families: Low Earnings Will Keep Many Children in Poverty*, Report GAO/HRD–91–62, April 1991, 3.

11. As summarized in "The Child Care Market Today," *Urban Institute Policy and Research Report*, Winter/Spring 1992, 11–12. The full reports were Hofferth, S., Brayfield, A., Deich, S., and Holcomb, P., *The 1990 Child Care Survey* (Washington, DC: Urban Institute Press, 1991); National Association for the Education of Young Children (NAEYC), Doc. no. 136 (Washington, DC: U.S. Department of Education, 1990).

12. U.S. Department of Labor, Bureau of Labor Statistics (BLS), *Employee Benefits in Small Private Establishments 1990*, Bulletin 2388 (Washington, DC: BLS, September 1991), summarized in "BLS Reports Its First Survey of Employee Benefits in Small Private Establishments," USDL 91–260, June 10, 1991, 2; BLS, *Employee Benefits in Medium and Large Firms 1989*, Bulletin 2363 (Washington, DC: BLS, June 1990), summarized in "Employee Benefits Focus on Family Concerns in 1989," USDL 90–160, March 30, 1990, 1; BLS, *Employee Benefits in State and Local Government 1990*, Bulletin 2398 (Washington, DC: BLS, February 1992), as summarized in "Employee Benefits in State and Local Government," USDL 91–549, October 31, 1991, 2, 7.

13. Hyland, S., "Helping Employees with Family Care," *Monthly Labor Review*, September 1990, 22–26. See also Marsh, B., "Firms Offer Parents Help Caring for Kids," *Wall Street Journal*, September 6, 1991, B–1, reporting on a study of 29 small-company programs conducted by Child Care Action Campaign, a New York–based nonprofit child advocacy group.

14. Bureau of the Census, *Census and You* 26, no. 11, November 1991, 4. See also "Improverishment, State by State," *Governing*, December 1991, 58–59; Voith, R., "City and Surburban Growth: Substitutes or Complements?" *Federal Reserve Bank of Philadelphia* (Bulletin), September/October 1992, 21–33.

15. Ricketts, E., and Sawhill, I., "Defining and Measuring the Underclass," Research Paper (Washington, DC: Urban Institute, 1986), 8–9. Also, Richard Nathan noted that it "consists of such groups as long-term welfare recipients, street criminals, and delinquent youth—on the whole, people who are hard to love, and thus politically hard to assist," in "The Underclass Challenges the Social Sciences," *Wall Street Journal*, July 8, 1983, op-ed.

16. As summarized in "The White Underclass," *Urban Institute Policy and Research Report*, Winter/Spring 1991, 24. Full report: Mincy, R., "Underclass Variations by Race and Place: Have Large Cities Darkened Our Picture of the Underclass?" Research Paper (Washington, DC: The Urban Institute, 1991).

17. O'Hare, W., and Curry-White, B., *The Rural Underclass: Examination of Multiple-Problem Populations in Rural and Urban Settings* (Washington, DC: Population Reference Bureau, January 1992).

18. Jencks, C., "Is the Urban Underclass Growing," in Peterson, P., and Jencks, C. (eds.), *The Urban Underclass* (Washington, DC: Brookings Institution, 1991), 28–100. See also "Britain: How the Other Tenth Lives," *Economist*, September 12, 1992, 63–64.

19. Prosser, W., "The Underclass: Assessing What We Have Learned," *Focus* 13, no. 2, Summer 1991, 1–5, 9. See also Clark, R., "Neighborhood Effects on Dropping Out of School: No Epidemic Effect," summarized in Urban Institute Policy and Research Report, Fall 1992, 9–10.

20. Advisory Commission on Intergovernmental Relations (ACIR), *The Role of General Government Elected Officials in Criminal Justice,* Report A–125 (Washington, DC: ACIR, May 1993), 20. Data from U.S. Department of Justice (DOJ), *Uniform Crime Reports 1990* (Washington, DC: DOJ, August 1991), 20, 27, 178, 180–81. See also Peirce, N., "L.A. Six Months Later," (Baltimore) *Sun,* November 2, 1992.

21. Stark, E., "Rethinking Homicide, Violence, and the Politics of Gender," *International Journal of Health Services* 20, no. 1, 1990, 4.

22. National Criminal Justice Association (NCJA), National Governors' Association, *National Conference on Youth Gangs and Violent Crime* (Proceedings) (Washington, DC: NCJA, January 1992), 1. See also Jankowski, M., *Islands in the Street: Gangs in American Urban Society* (Berkeley: University of California Press, 1991), 382 pp.; reviewed by Wartell, J., in *Law Enforcement News* 18, no. 358, May 15, 1992, 15.

23. As reported in Geyelin, M., "Study to Focus on What Leads Youth to Crime," Law, *Wall Street Journal,* June 5, 1992, B–1.

24. Office of Policy Development and Research, U.S. Department of Housing and Urban Development (HUD), *A Report to the Secretary on the Homeless and Emergency Shelters,* May 1984, 8–19.

25. CBO Memorandum, "Preliminary Cost Estimate for the Homeless Outreach Act of 1990," May 7, 1990.

26. Council of State Governments (CSG), *Homelessness in the States* (Lexington, KY: CSG, 1980), 1, 5, 18, 20.

27. *The 1990 Annual Report of the Interagency Council on the Homeless* (ICH) (Washington, DC: U.S. Department of HUD, February 1991, 30. See also the council's 1991–92 report of similar title, which showed no major change in composition from 1990.

28. Reflected in 10 studies supported by the National Institute for Mental Health between 1983 and 1986; these included Hoch, C., and Slayton, R., *New Homeless and Old—Community and the Skid Row Hotel* (1989); Rossi, P., *Down and Out in America—The Origins of Homelessness* (1989) and *Homelessness in America—Selected Topics* (1989); Main, T., "What Do We Know About the Homeless," *Commentary,* May 1988; National Institute of Mental Health (NIMH), *Deinstitutionalization Policy and Homelessness,* a Report to the U.S. Congress (May 1990); Tessler, R., and Dennis, D., *A Synthesis of NIMH-Funded Research Concerning Persons Who Are Homeless and Mentally Ill III* (February 9, 1989), 35. See also Lamb, H., "The Deinstitutionalization of the Mentally Ill," *Assisting the Homeless: State and Local Responses in an Era of Limited Resources* (Washington, DC: U.S. Advisory Commission on Intergovernmental Relations [ACIR], Report M–161, November 1988), 21–30.

29. Waxman, L., *A Status Report on Hunger and Homelessness in America's Cities: 1990* (Washington, DC: U.S. Conference of Mayors (USCM), December 1990), 33.

30. Waxman, L., *A Status Report on Hunger and Homelessness in America's Cities: 1991* (Washington, DC: USCM, December 1991), summary, 2. See also USCM, *Mentally Ill and Homeless: A 22-City Survey,* November 1991; Berlin, G., and McAllister, W., "Homelessness: Why Nothing Has Worked and What Will" (temporary housing tied to drug treatment and other services), *Brookings Review,* Fall 1992, 12–15, GAO, *Home-*

lessness: Transitional Housing Shows Initial Success but Long-Term Effects Unknown, GAO/RCED–91–200, September 1991, 2–5.

31. "Rougher and Tougher," American Survey, *The Economist,* June 29, 1991, 21. Further examples: McCarron, K., "A Crackdown Focused on the Homeless," *Governing,* September 1991, 19; Wilkerson, I., "Shift in Feelings on the Homeless: Empathy Turns into Frustration," *New York Times,* September 2, 1991, A–1; "The Homeless Revisited" (editorial), *Wall Street Journal,* April 27, 1992, A–14 (pointing to a New York state proposal to redirect "governmental homeless budgets to small non-profit shelters that also provide drug treatment and care for the mentally ill").

32. General Accounting Office (GAO), *Children and Youths: About 68,000 Homeless and 186,000 in Shared Housing at Any Given Time,* Report GAO/PEMD–89–14, June 1989, 1–2; U.S. Department of Education, Report to Congress, *Final Reports Submitted by States Authorized by Education for Homeless Children and Youth Program Fiscal Year 1991,* September 1992, Enclosure A, Table 2. See also Stevens, L. N., "Counting the Homeless: Limitations of 1990 Census Results and Methodology" (Testimony before Subcommittee on Government Information and Regulation, Senate Committee on Governmental Affairs, Report GAO/T-GGD–91–29, May 9, 1991).

33. U.S. Department of Education, Report to Congress, *Final Reports Submitted by Status Authorized by Education for Homeless Children and Youth Program Fiscal Year 1991,* September 1992, Enclosure A, Table 2.

34. Children's Defense Fund (CDF), *Homeless Families: Failed Policies and Young Victims* (Washington, DC: CDF, January 1991), 2, 22–23. See also *Homelessness, Health and Human Needs* (Washington, DC: National Institute of Medicine, National Academy of Sciences, 1988); Goetcheus, J., "Healing the Homeless: They Need Medical Care, Shelter, Solace," *Washington Post,* Health Section, October 15, 1991, 6; McGeady, M., *God's Lost Children* (New York: Covenant House, 1991), 115 pp.

35. Bureau of the Census, *Marital Status with Living Arrangements: March 1990,* Current Population Reports, Population Characteristics Series P–20, no. 450, May 1991, 1–11; *Household and Family Characteristics: 1990 and 1989,* P–20, no. 447, December 1990, 18.

36. Wilson, W., "The Urban Underclass," in Peterson, P. (ed.), *The New Urban Reality* (Washington, DC: Brookings Institution, 1985), 138.

37. Bureau of the Census, *Marital Status,* 1–3.

38. Ibid.

39. Ibid, Table I, 9.

40. Ibid., Table H, 7.

41. *Beyond Rhetoric: A New American Agenda for Children and Families* (Final Report) (Washington, DC: National Commission on Children, 1991), 20–21. References cited by the commission for the figures given in the quoted paragraphs included 1988 natality data contained in *Vital Statistics* (National Center for Health Statistics of the U.S. Public Health Service) and Hayes, C. (ed.), *Risking the Future: Adolescent Sexuality, Pregnancy, and Childbearing* (Washington, DC: National Academy Press, 1987).

42. National Center for Health Statistics (NCHS), *Advance Report of Final Natality Statistics,* 41, no. 9, Supplement, February 25, 1993, 9, 33.

43. Garfinkel, I., and McLanahan, S., *Single Mothers and Their Children: A New American Dilemma* (Washington, DC: Urban Institute Press, 1986), 46–47, 55–85. See also Danziger, Sandra, "Teenaged Childbearing and Welfare Policy," *Focus* 10, no. 1, Spring 1987, 16–20; Wilson, W., *The Truly Disadvantaged: The Inner City, the Un-*

derclass, and Public Policy (Chicago: University of Chicago Press, 1987), 90–92; Christensen, *The Retreat from Marriage: Causes and Consequences* (Lanham, MD: University Press of America, 1990), ix–x.

44. *Beyond Rhetoric,* 252.

45. Abrahamse, A., Morrison, P., and Waite, L., *Beyond Stereotypes: Who Becomes a Single Teenage Mother?* R–3489–HHS/NICHD (Santa Monica, CA: Rand Corporation, 1988), 62.

46. Anderson, E., "Neighborhood Effects on Teenage Pregnancy," *Urban Underclass,* 362.

47. Crane, J., "Dropping Out and Teenage Childbearing," *Urban Underclass,* 301–19; discussion of high school completion rates in relation to age of mother at first birth in Children's Defense Fund (CDF), *A Vision for America's Children* (Washington, DC: CDF, 1990), 92. Contrastingly, Geronimus, A., and Korenman, S., contend that such correlation does not mean causality; study of sets of sisters in sample of families, both of whom were young mothers but not with consistent negative outcomes discussed in Blinder, A., "If You Think Teen Motherhood Causes Poverty, Think Again," Economic Viewpoint, *Business Week,* May 27, 1991, 20.

48. Bureau of the Census, *Child Support and Alimony: 1989,* CPR, Consumer Income, 60, no. 173, September 1991, 6–7.

49. U.S. Department of Health and Human Services (HHS), Office of Child Support Enforcement, *Fifteenth Annual Report to Congress for the Period Ending September 30, 1990,* November 1992, 7–11.

50. Ibid., 11.

51. U.S. Department of Health and Human Services (HHS), U.S. Commission on Interstate Child Support, *Supporting Our Children: A Blueprint for Reform,* chapter 3 (Washington, DC: HHS, August 1992), 49. See also "Child Support Assurance," *Urban Institute Policy and Research Report,* Summer 1991, 23; Juffras, J., Institute Research Paper, "Issues in Child Support Assurance"; Ponessa, J., "Delaware to Dads-To-Be: Sign Here," *Governing,* March 1992, 23; Meyer, D., and Garasky, S., "Custodial Fathers: Myths, Realities, and Child Support Policy," Technical Analysis Paper #42, *Focus,* Summer 1992, 12–15; "Child Support," *Insights* (Newsletter by Institute for Research on Poverty, University of Wisconsin, Madison), no. 8, March 1993, 1–2.

52. U.S. General Accounting Office (GAO), *Child Support Enforcement: A Framework for Evaluating Costs, Benefits, and Effects,* GAO/PEMD–91–6, March 1991, 32–35, 42–43. See also Richter, M., "Information Technology and the Missing Parent," *Governing,* March 1992, 57.

53. CBO, *Sources of Support for Adolescent Mothers,* September 1990, 35–39.

54. *Beyond Rhetoric,* 281. See also Schor, L., *Within Our Reach: Breaking the Cycle of Disadvantage.* (New York: Doubleday, 1988), 151.

55. *Statistical Abstract 1990,* Table 296, 176.

56. U.S. Department of HHS, National Center on Child Abuse and Neglect (NCCAN), *National Child Abuse and Neglect Data System Working Paper 1: 1990 Summary Data Component* (Washington, DC: NCCAN, April 1992) (Distributed by Clearinghouse on Child Abuse and Neglect Information, P.O. Box 1182, Washington, DC 20013). See also ibid., *Executive Summary: Study of National Incidence and Prevalence of Child Abuse and Neglect 1988*; Sedlok, A., "Technical Amendment" thereto, May 23, 1990, both distributed by Clearinghouse.

57. Edelman, M., "Building an Achieving America," in *SOS America! A Children's Defense Budget* (Washington, DC: Children's Defense Fund, 1990), 12–13. See also GAO, *Child Welfare: Monitoring Out-of-State Placements*, GAO/HRD–91–107BR, September 1991, 1–5.

58. *Beyond Rhetoric*, 284. Source cited for estimate was U.S. Congress, House of Representatives, Select Committee on Children, Youth and Families, *No Place to Call Home: Discarded Children in America* (Washington, DC: U.S. Government Printing Office, 1990), 19. See also *Beyond Rhetoric*, 285–87.

59. *Beyond Rhetoric*, 284. Source cited for estimate was HHS, National Institute of Mental Health, "Provisional Estimate of Census Data," Statistical Research Branch, Division of Applied and Services Research, unpublished data, 1988.

60. Ibid., 286–87.

61. U.S. Department of Justice (DJ), Office of Juvenile Justice and Delinquency Prevention (OJJDP), *Fact Sheet on Children in Custody 1989*, February 1991, 1; DJ, Bureau of Justice Statistics, *Children in Custody, 1975–85: Census of Public and Private Juvenile Detention, Correctional and Shelter Facilities*, Table 41, May 1989, 50. See also Department of Justice, Bureau of Justice Statistics, OJJDP, *Children in Custody in 1987: A Comparison of Public and Private Juvenile Custody Facilities*, March 1991; Allen-Hagen, B., "Public Juvenile Facilities: Children in Custody, 1989," *OJJDP Update on Statistics*, January 1991.

62. OJJDP, *Fact Sheet*, 1–2.

Chapter 3 _____

Deterrents to Adequate Health Care

For several years, health care in the United States has been a critical, contentious, and pervasive issue of public and private sector policy, confronting not only national, state, and local governments but corporate management, labor unions, and other segments of the national economy. In the 1990s, it is a serious and omnipresent personal issue facing most Americans and their families. Three major aspects of the health care system present serious problems: high and escalating costs, including those for insurance coverage; access—informational, financial, physical, and professional (e.g., willingness of hospitals and/or doctors to treat); and health practices and behaviors of individuals and families.

Another aspect—health care quality—has been largely positive, despite its unevenness among geographic areas and categories of persons served. The notable achievements of American medicine are indisputable. The United States continues to attract many persons from the rest of the world. Medical students and practitioners are drawn to our teaching hospitals and medical schools to learn advanced procedures, and public and private officials from abroad travel across the nation, learning about innovative medical and health care methods. Americans not only are grateful for computerized axial tomography (CAT) scans, magnetic resonance imaging (MRI), sonograms, and other marvels, but when surveyed in opinion polls, typically express satisfaction with the care they themselves receive. A 1990 Gallup Poll showed a 92 percent excellent or good rating for the respondents' family physician, but 56 percent of the same respondents characterized the U.S. health care system as fair or poor![1]

For the at-risk population with which this book is concerned, problems of access, cost, client behavior, and motivation became increasingly serious through the 1980s and early 1990s. The 1991 report of the National Commission on Children (NCC) stated:

Perhaps no set of issues moved members of the . . . Commission more than the wrenching consequences of poor health and limited access to medical care. In urban centers and rural counties, we saw young children with avoidable illnesses and injuries, pregnant women without access to prenatal care, families whose emotional and financial resources were exhausted from providing special care for children with chronic illnesses and disabilities, and burned-out health care providers.[2]

The commission noted that "minority children, low-income children, children who live in geographically isolated areas, and those whose parents are poorly educated often have difficulty getting the health care they need."[3]

In the ensuing sections, both general and specialized aspects of the health care system are examined and weakness highlighted, beginning with an overview of the delivery and financing institutions and processes as a whole. This overview is followed by a consideration of insurance, malpractice liability, technological duplication, and other cost issues; prenatal and postnatal care; immunization, nutrition, and other aspects of young child care; adolescent health, including the problems of unsafe sex and sex education; drug, alcohol, and tobacco addiction; AIDS; and violent behavior and associated mental health problems.

DELIVERY OF HEALTH SERVICES

People have never been happy to leave health care to the vagaries of buyers and sellers in competing private markets. . . . Egyptian pharaohs tried vainly to avert plagues. . . . In 2200 BC Hammurabi, King of Babylon, brought in laws that limited doctors' fees and punished them for treatments that injured their patients. In ancient China the mandarins gave preventive medicine a boost by paying doctors only if their patients were well. . . . By the 14th century most parts of the Holy Roman Empire had laws about medical training, the licensing of doctors and physicians' fees.[4]

Most health care services in the United States are delivered by private solo, group, or other providers—physicians, dentists, and other specialists in "private practice"; by hospitals, many of which are nonprofit organizations; and by nursing homes for the elderly and permanently disabled, many of which are operated by proprietary, for-profit organizations. All of these private providers function under state and local regulation, such as the licensure of professional personnel and facilities. Local regulation may cover such activities as sanitary inspection, but all regulation is pursuant to provisions of state law, and some of it comes under indirect federal controls where federal funds are involved. The roles of these providers have been undergoing substantial change over the past two decades—a period marked by such phenomena as rising costs, an accelerating shift away from general practitioner/fee-for-service medicine to group practice in numerous patterns, a growing role for various types of "third-party" payers, and an increased role for governmental financing. These dynamic changes have been driven by increasingly successful medical technology and by governmental and other third-party reimbursement policies and processes.

Health maintenance organizations (HMOs) and other forms of group practice that usually provide health care services on a prepaid basis comprise a growing proportion of private providers. In addition to hospitals, private fee-for-service practitioners, and HMOs, the "health industry" includes medical supply houses; pharmaceutical research, manufacturing, wholesale, and retail businesses; and many other types of facilities and services. Most of this additional network is in the for-profit category.

Governmentally delivered health services include principally veterans' hospitals and other health facilities operated by the U.S. Veterans Administration; medical facilities of the U.S. Department of Defense, serving all active-duty personnel of the armed forces and their dependents as well as a significant proportion of retired and reserve military personnel; state hospitals and health centers for the mentally ill; city and county hospitals; the U.S. Public Health Service and the National Institutes of Health, within the Department of Health and Human Services (HHS); and state and local public health clinics and other facilities staffed by physicians, nurses, and support personnel.

As noted in chapter 1, the health services sector has been, and is projected to be, a continually growing and attractive part of the U.S. labor force. Wage and salary professional employees in direct health services and delivery totaled 1.8 million in 1990, of which 1.4 million (77%) were in the private sector; 0.4 million (22%) were employed by government; and a remaining 282,000 were self-employed.[5] Employment in the whole health care industry is considerably larger (e.g., health research, pharmaceutical manufacture and distribution, and medical/dental device/instrument manufacturing). Total public employment of health personnel—both professional and other—in 1989 was 1.73 million; of these, 265,000 (15%) were in the federal government, and the remainder were in state or local government.[6]

Health Care Costs

For reasons to be detailed, the United States spends much more for health care than other industrialized countries. The Organization for Economic Co-operation and Development (OECD) estimated that in 1990, the United States was spending 12.4 percent of GDP on health care, compared with 9 in Canada, 8.1 in Germany, 6.5 in Japan, and 6.2 in the United Kingdom. Spending by the United States in 1992 was estimated at $838.5 billion, or 14 percent of GDP, by the U.S. Department of Commerce, and 1993 expenditures were expected to rise 12.1 percent to $939.9 billion in 1993. Furthermore, U.S. national health spending was projected "to rise by about 12–15 percent per annum during the next 5 years unless significant changes in the health care delivery system occur." The expenditures are offset to some degree by significant export balances in medical and dental instruments, devices, and supplies, in the $3 billion range in 1992. In 1980, 11 percent of the federal budget went to health care, rising to 14.3 in 1991. The Congressional Budget Office in 1993 projected a 23.6 percent portion of the federal budget by 1998 in the absence of significant changes in health policy. It also projected a real annual rise in health spending of 6 percent during the 1990s, reaching $1.3 trillion by the year 2000.[7]

When health care financial inputs in some of the principal industrialized countries are placed in juxtaposition with health care outcomes, however, a serious question arises as to the real effectiveness of the American health care system. For a somewhat different set of OECD member countries, male-female life expectancy and infant mortality (per 1,000 live births) rates in 1990 were: Holland (ages 73.8–80.1 and 6.9); France (72.7–80.9 and 7.2); Belgium (72.4–79.1 and 7.9); Australia (73.9–80.0 and 1.8); and United States (72.1–79.0 and 9.2). Some argue that the effects of diet, personal habits/way of life, crime, housing, education, and ways of dealing with poverty have much greater impact on health outcomes than does paid-for health care.[8] The rising tide of urban violence over the past two decades, which is examined later in the context of adolescent health, undoubtedly comprises another significant element in growing U.S. health care costs.

As shown in Table 3.1, the approximate proportions of health care costs borne by patients, insurers, and governments changed significantly in the three-decade period from 1965 to 1991. In 1991 the proportions stood at roughly one-fifth patient, one-third private insurance, and two-fifths government, with the largest shift being from consumer out-of-pocket to private insurers and governments. On the other hand, relative shares of health expenditures among hospitals, physicians, and nursing homes changed relatively little during the same period. However, total expenditures, after adjusting for inflation, rose in 1991 dollars, from $121 billion to $752 billion.[9] A detailed breakdown appears in Appendix 3.A.

Factors contributing to these rising costs included (1) an aging population; (2) intensive medical research, translated through expeditious conversion into availability of new and often costly medical treatments driven by technological innovation; (3) failure of the marketplace to limit the quantity and level of services used, resulting from low "out-of-pocket" or "consumer" share; and (4) the tort liability system with large malpractice awards, allegedly forcing many physicians into "defensive medicine," including multiple opinions and intensive testing.[10]

The scope and future implications of an aging population were discussed in chapter 1. Following is a summary of the other factors contributing to cost escalation.

Rapidly Expanding Medical Technology. While advances in medical technology often lengthen life spans and provide more effective care, they can stimulate unnecessary costs through (1) duplication of highly expensive equipment by competing hospitals, clinics, and other providers, in a sort of "medical arms race," in order to gain prestige and to retain patients and doctors and (2) overutilization of the new processes and equipment. This phenomenon has been attributed to prescribing physicians and third-party payers who offer a "blank check" to the providers and not to technology itself. A 1989 study by the American Medical Association (AMA) found that on a per capita basis, the

Table 3.1
Proportions of Health Care Costs Borne by Patients, Insurers, Governments, and Other Private Sources, 1965 and 1991

Service Type	All Payers		Private Health Insurance		Consumer Out-of-Pocket		Federal Government		State & Local Governments		Other Private Providers	
	1965	1991	1965	1991	1965	1991	1965	1991	1965	1991	1965	1991
1	2	3	4	5	6	7	8	9	10	11	12	13
Total	100.0	100.0	24.0	32.5	45.7	19.2	11.6	29.6	13.2	14.2	5.5	4.4
Hospitals	33.7	38.4	40.9	35.2	19.6	3.3	15.5	41.3	22.2	15.1	2.0	5.1
Physicians	19.7	18.9	32.4	47.0	60.5	18.1	1.5	27.5	5.6	7.3	0	*
Nursing Homes	4.1	8.0	*	1.0	64.2	43.1	13.4	32.6	16.4	21.4	6.0	1.8
Drugs/other non-durables	14.2	8.1	1.7	14.8	95.7	73.0	0.9	5.9	1.3	6.1	0	0
Other	28.3	26.7	12.7	33.2	38.6	19.2	19.1	20.7	13.1	18.3	16.3	8.6

Source: Congressional Budget Office (CBO), based on data from HHS, Health Care Financing Administration (HCFA), Office of the Actuary, 1992.

Note: * = Negligible

United States had four times as many MRI machines as Germany and eight times as many as Canada.[11]

Imbalances in Supply of Health Care Workers. George Lundberg, editor of the *Journal of the American Medical Association* (*JAMA*) listed "an increased number of health professionals, particularly too many specialists" as one of the causes of the "runaway trend" in health costs.[12] As a result of the peculiar nature of health care and the inability or hesitance of patients and insurers alike to question the need for a particular test or procedure, "health care providers can generate their own demand and increase their revenues and profits despite declines in the demand," according to former HHS secretary Dr. Otis Bowen.[13]

The CBO report on health care costs described the supply-demand imbalance thus: "The complexity of medical services . . . and uncertainty about the efficacy of treatment have led consumers to delegate much decision-making to providers"[14] The report also noted that the increased supply of physicians throughout the 1980s, although bringing better access to rural and other areas that were previously less well served, had not led to lower incomes for physicians. Like health care costs in general, earnings of physicians increased well above the inflation rate. In 1970 physicians earned on average $113,192 in 1987 dollars after expenses but before taxes; by 1988, average net earnings had risen to $132,300. The AMA reported that incomes increased another 9 percent in 1988 and 8 percent in 1989.[15]

To meet the problem of supply of general practitioners, the number of "physician extenders" (physician assistants [PAs], nurse practitioners [NPs], and midwives) expanded greatly, in thousands, from a very few, other than midwives, in 1970 to 11.4 PAs and 13.1 NPs in 1980 to 23.9 PAs and 25.0 NPs in 1990, according to data from the American Academy of Physicians Assistants and the American Nurses Association. The expansion of extenders was due in large part to the shrinkage in the proportion of family doctors in the total physician population, which dropped from 17 percent in 1970 to 12 in 1980 to 11 in 1990, according to the AMA.[16]

Excess Tests and Referrals and Defensive Medicine. These included what Lundberg referred to as "inappropriate use of diagnostic and therapeutic procedures."[17] Partially driven by the medical technology "arms race" were the increased referrals by physicians to diagnostic and test centers and clinics with the most advanced equipment, often partially or wholly owned by one or a group of physicians. A study of ownership of 2,200 clinics, laboratories, and imaging centers in Florida by that state's Health Care Cost Containment Board found that, although partially limited by federal rules on the Medicare and Medicaid portion of medical practice, nearly half of all physicians practicing in Florida had invested in joint clinics to which they could refer patients. The proportion of substantial doctor ownership of facilities ranged from 92 percent for diagnostic imaging to 12 and 5 percent, respectively, for hospitals and nursing homes.[18]

Malpractice Insurance and Product Liability. Another driving force of probably greater importance in terms of excess tests and procedures during the 1980s was the skyrocketing size of medical malpractice awards. This tendency was not targeted toward malpractice as such but toward the nation's tort liability system, in which juries often sensed the "deep pockets" of insurance companies, hospitals, pharmaceutical and medical equipment manufacturers, and other large corporations in reaching their decisions. The CBO concluded in a 1992 report that this tendency, rather than malpractice liability and defensive medicine, was a principal factor in rising costs, pointing out that malpractice premiums amounted to less than 1 percent of national health expenditures (nevertheless amounting to nearly $7.5 billion in 1992). To defend against potential liability suits and to pay rising malpractice insurance premiums, hospitals, doctors, and other health professionals resorted to exhaustive diagnostic procedures, with more and more tests at every stage of a patient's treatment. This circle of actions and reactions could only increase health care costs.

Conversely, physicians often resorted to procedures that their own professional judgment told them *might* be helpful to the patient. It was reported that a sizable proportion of surgical procedures was unnecessary or inappropriate in a substantial number of cases. A typical allegation—from a study of procedures for Medicare beneficiaries in eight states—was that 14 percent of coronary bypasses and 20 percent of pacemaker implants fell into the unnecessary/inappropriate category.[19] ("Appropriateness" is a contentious issue and is examined in the next chapter in connection with policy options.)

Insurance Tilt Toward Acute, in Contrast to Preventive, Care. The cost-benefit ratios for preventive care have been well established—sex education, precaution, and restraint/abstinence instead of unwanted pregnancy, abortion, or childbirth to female teenagers; prenatal care instead of low birth weight deliveries; and early childhood immunization. Failure to practice preventive measures and to obtain preventive health care incurs enormous subsequent financial costs as well as premature death, injury, or continuing disability. Most insurance and other health benefit plans have tended to meet full or most initial hospital costs, including emergency room care, but except for prepaid capitation plans, have not covered, or have otherwise neglected, the preventive side of health care. Throughout the late 1980s, the U.S. General Accounting Office (GAO) and the U.S. House Select Committee on Children, Youth, and Families conducted a number of reviews and studies, all of which seemed conclusive as to the cost advantages of preventive care in areas such as prenatal care, immunization, and nutrition education.[20] (These findings are examined subsequently.)

Consumer Overutilization of Health Care Resources. Practitioners and researchers in health care approached a general consensus by the early 1990s that the earlier shift in medical care costs from consumer out-of-pocket to third-party payers had produced unnecessary use and overuse of medical care by the insured population, with the low-income, noninsured, and unemployed suffering most of the consequences. A 1987 Rand Corporation report noted:

The dominant form of financing health care has been open-ended payment by "third parties"—private insurers and government programs that passively reimburse patients for medical bills, with only minimal questioning of the price or the appropriateness of the service to the patient's condition. With neither the physician nor the patient concerned about the cost of treatment, little restrains physicians from prescribing all services that *might* be effective, regardless of their cost and how small or unproven their effectiveness.[21]

(The reimbursement often appears "passive" to the patient but often is preceded by much haggling and paperwork among insurers and providers.)

Perverse Tax Incentives. This is another factor associated with the decline in the consumer out-of-pocket share of health care costs. For federal individual income tax purposes, consumer health care outlays are deductible to the salary- or wage-earning individual only to the extent that they surpass a threshold of 7.5 percent of adjusted gross income. Health insurance premiums are counted as medical expenses, but only rarely do they approach the 7.5 percent threshold. For many self-employed persons, the premiums are partially or largely deductible as a business expense. However, employer outlays for health benefits to the employee are fully deductible to the employer on his or her corporate income tax but are not counted as income to the employee for income tax purposes.

The CBO report on rising health care costs illustrated the effect of this tax policy on health costs as follows:

For an employee with a marginal income tax rate of 15 percent, a federal payroll tax rate of about 8 percent, and a state income tax rate of 5 percent, this tax exclusion [of employer contributions to the employee's health benefit plan] means that $1 spent by the employer generates $1 of health insurance at a cost to the employee equivalent to 72 cents of after-tax cash income. As a result, employees have considerable incentive to negotiate for generous health insurance benefits, with the employer paying for a substantial proportion of them. In fact, the average employer contribution was about 83 percent of total premium costs in 1987. This exclusion will save individuals and businesses about $56 billion to $58 billion to federal, state, and local taxes in 1991 [with an equal revenue loss to those governments].[22]

Alain Enthoven characterized the tax exclusion of health benefits from employee income thus: "From the point of view of cost to the federal budget, it is the second largest health care program after Medicare," and he went on to cite the foregoing CBO estimate.[23]

Stuart Butler of the Heritage Foundation pointed out that "because the current system gives a tax break only for company-provided insurance, not for out of pocket medical expenses . . . it encourages employees to press for insurance that covers even the most minor medical services and to resist employer attempts to introduce higher deductibles or co-payments."[24] Essentially, the commentaries of CBO, Enthoven, and Butler might be summed as a proposition that employer-provided, "gold-plated" insurance coverage has caused excessive health care spending and overutilization.

Between 1970 and 1980 the number of Americans with coverage for dental expenses jumped from 12 to 80 million.[25] This is an important segment of the health care system.

State Mandates upon Insurance Carriers. These mandates include (1) financial status requirements as to assets, reserves, and investments and financial reporting coupled with state insurance department audits, all as conditions of state licensure to sell insurance; (2) prescribed individual and group policy forms and, in some states, regulation of rates and premium charges; and (3) in practically all states, statutory mandates of particular benefits (e.g., osteopathy, optometry), with this mandated expanded coverage often going beyond what many people wanted or could afford and, at the time, precluding the offering of lower-cost, basic, or "bare bones" coverage. In the early 1990s, several states began to enable the issuance of such policies as a consumer option. In addition to state mandates, various federal and state antitrust and consumer protection laws and regulations apply to health care providers and the health insurance industry.[26]

High Overhead Costs and Excess Paperwork. Partially due to the complexity of the health care delivery system and the accompanying regulatory activity, administrative costs have become very high. The CBO reported that administrative costs of third-party payers comprised 4.9 percent of U.S. health care spending in 1987, compared with 2.5 percent in Canada and 2.6 percent in the United Kingdom. The report explained the disparity thus:

Higher administrative costs of insurance in the United States are, in part, accounted for by the costs of determining eligibility for coverage, risk assessment, marketing, and coordination of benefits. In addition the presence of multiple payers, negotiated prices and the need for eligibility determination imposes significant administrative costs on providers who must collect payments from multiple sources, each with different procedures and paperwork requirements. These costs are reflected in higher prices for health services and health insurance.[27]

The per capita cost of the administrative overhead portion of health insurance is much higher for small business—the segment of the economy having most of the uninsured employees.

The Health Care Insured and Noninsured

Close to seven-eighths of the American population were covered by some kind of health care benefit program in 1990, while the other one-eighth to 15 percent were not. Practically all of the nation's 65 and over population are covered by Medicare, a federal health insurance program tied to Social Security benefits. Those 65 or over in a no-low-income status are also eligible for Medicaid. The population universe with which we are concerned here is the below 65 category and, within that group, primarily those families with children under age 18. This universe comprises approximately 64 million children plus their parent(s), particularly the one-fifth to one-fourth of that group in poverty and those whose

Figure 3.1
Proportionate Sources of Health Insurance Coverage for the Under 65
Population, 1990

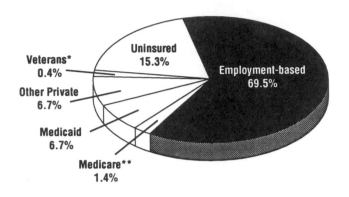

SOURCE: Congressional Budget Office, *Rising Health Care Costs: Causes, Implications, and Strategies.* Table B-2. (Washington, D.C.: U. S. Government Printing Office, April 1991), p. 69.

NOTES: *Care primarily from Veterans Administration facilities; active-duty personnel and dependents included in employer-based category.

** Persons below 65 covered by Social Security disability benefits.

parent(s) is part of the ''working poor'' category. Medicaid, a federal-state program for low-income (official poverty level and below) and for otherwise ''medically indigent'' persons, is not an insurance program as such, but being a ''safety net,'' it is included in initial tabulations here. Similarly, persons eligible for Veterans Administration health care and active-duty military personnel and their dependents are included in the ''insured category.'' Figure 3.1 shows the proportions of the below 65 population covered by health insurance and health benefit programs.

The Insured Population. Until the 1950s, insurers established premiums based on ''community rating.'' That is, when an entire community's claims experience was used to set rates, insurers could rely on the law of averages: claims of high-cost patients would usually be offset by those of low-cost patients. As costs rose, many medium and large employers became ''self-insuring,'' serving as their own insurance companies, saving the overhead costs, and contracting directly with hospitals, HMOs, or other groups of physicians to provide the health care required by the employer's particular plan. Consequently, smaller businesses increased as a proportion of the private insurance market.

Small firms thus narrowed the scope of the ''community rating'' and became subject instead to an ''experience rating.'' For a small firm of 25 or fewer employees, a single high-cost illness could change the experience rating of the firm and make the following insurance premium much higher and quite possibly

Figure 3.2
Employment Status of Uninsured Population Under 65, 1990

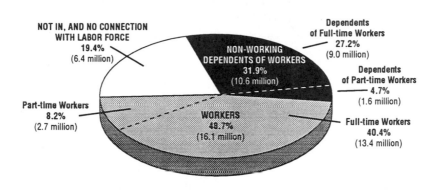

NOT IN, AND NO CONNECTION
WITH LABOR FORCE
19.4%
(6.4 million)

NON-WORKING
DEPENDENTS OF WORKERS
31.9%
(10.6 million)

Dependents
of Full-time Workers
27.2%
(9.0 million)

Dependents
of Part-time Workers
4.7%
(1.6 million)

Part-time Workers
8.2%
(2.7 million)

WORKERS
48.7%
(16.1 million)

Full-time Workers
40.4%
(13.4 million)

SOURCE: Congressional Budget Office, *Rising Health Care Costs: Causes, Implications, and Strategies.* Table B-3, (Washington, D.C.: U. S. Government Printing Office, April 1991), p. 70.

unaffordable. As a result, by the late 1980s, many small firms were staying away from health insurance coverage plans, and by 1987 nearly two-thirds of all uninsured workers were in firms with 25 or fewer employees.[28] The 1989 employer survey by the Health Insurance Association of America showed that employer-based insurance was available for only one-third of firms employing fewer than 10 people, with only 40 percent of the employees in such firms being eligible to utilize the coverage. Thirty-nine percent of firms employing fewer than 25 were making insurance available, but 100 percent of firms of 500 or more employees were providing coverage. Since most business firms are small, only 43 percent of all firms were offering insurance.[29] (Presumably, insurance cost was a constant factor in this trend, sometimes a primary cause, and in other cases an exacerbation.)

The financial noose also tightened on the larger firms, but in a different context. In the early 1990s, the Financial Accounting Standards Board (FASB) issued a ruling, effective in 1993, requiring firms to include on their balance sheets the estimated unfunded liability for future health care benefits of employees; the GAO estimated this liability at $227 billion at 1988 health care prices.[30]

Understandably, insurance coverage is significantly lower for part-time workers and for those having voluntary or involuntary work interruptions. The employment status of insured and uninsured persons in 1990 is shown in Figure 3.2. In many firms, part-time workers are provided with limited or no coverage; often new employees are temporarily ineligible for coverage for a probationary or other waiting period. About 10 percent of workers were refusing coverage in 1988, but about half of this group were covered by their spouse's firms.[31]

The Uninsured. Only 1 percent of the over 65 population was uninsured as of March 1990; 33.1 million persons or 15.3 percent of the below 65 population was uninsured, ranging from 25.1 percent for the 18–24 group to 12 percent for those 45 to 64.[32] The younger group was in the process of getting established in employment, many probably were serving probationary periods, and others were in college. As noted earlier, young adults in good health, especially if unmarried without family responsibilities, are least concerned about health insurance.

The U.S. General Accounting Office conducted a study to compare characteristics among the uninsured population, using results of the Census Bureau's March 1989 *Current Population Survey*. In addition to the use of national data, the GAO study included a follow-up of the census sample in 15 selected states. The results were reflective of the approximately two-thirds of the nation's uninsured population residing in those states.[33]

- Uninsured rates among all 50 states and the District of Columbia ranged from 8 percent (Michigan and Rhode Island) to 26 percent (New Mexico and Texas), with much higher rates in the Southwest and lower in the Upper Midwest and Northeast.

- Most of the insured were under employer-provided or employer-employee negotiated plans. States with higher incidence of these plans (Illinois, Michigan, New Jersey, Ohio, and Pennsylvania) tended to have a lower portion of their populations without health insurance.

- The proportions of uninsured in the service sector and service-related industries like agriculture, mining, utilities, and transportation were higher than in the manufacturing sector. The service and service-related group had a respective 15 and 21 percent uninsured rate, compared with 11 percent for manufacturing.

- Not surprisingly, families with lower incomes were more likely to be uninsured. Nationally, 34 percent of the families below the poverty level were uninsured, with the percent of noninsurance for this group ranging from 17 (New York) to 58 (Texas); most of the uninsured (61 percent) were in families with incomes less than twice the poverty level, with about 30 percent each in the under 1 and the 1 to 2 multiples of the poverty level.

- Of the uninsured population, 31 percent had incomes of $20,000 to $40,000, and 13 percent had incomes of over $40,000. The rest (54%) had incomes below $20,000.

- Unemployed people had the highest uninsured rate (50%) in the 19–64 age group; most of the employed but uninsured were part-time or seasonal workers, but over a third of the uninsured had full-time jobs.

- As with the incidence of poverty, the likelihood of being uninsured was greater among young adults, the unmarried, minorities, and those with less than a high school education. In 1988, 33 percent of Hispanics and 21 percent of blacks were uninsured, compared with 12 percent for whites. In absolute numbers, whites were in the majority of the uninsured population nationwide and in 12 of the 15 states studied, with the exceptions being California, Texas, and Georgia.

A breakdown of the insured and noninsured populations by insurance status, sex, race and ethnic origin, residence, and other selected characteristics appears in Appendix 3.B.

In contrast to the foregoing "snapshot" profiles of the uninsured at a particular time, Urban Institute researchers conducted a longitudinal study covering four characteristics—age, income, employment status, and prior insurance type— over a 28-month period, with the study continuing as of 1991. Partial returns as of late 1990 showed the following:[34]

- Half of all uninsured periods were under four months; 15 percent were more than two years.

- Young adults (18–24) were less likely to have long periods of being uncovered than older persons (25–54).

- Low-income persons had a longer noncoverage period than those with higher incomes.

- Workers losing their employer-provided health insurance when job switching were likely to have brief periods of noncoverage, often due to lack of eligibility during a probationary or other fixed period after initial employment.

- Persons unemployed or out of the labor force during the first month of noncoverage were more likely to have had long periods of noncoverage.

- Duration of noncoverage for both part- and full-time workers was nearly the same, but for both it was likely to end within a year.

Government Health Care Safety Nets

As noted earlier, the national government delivers direct health care services to active-duty military personnel and dependents via the Department of Defense and to service veterans through the Veterans Administration. Though not providing a safety net, the National Institutes of Health (NIH) expend several billions of dollars annually for health research, an indispensable part of the health care system.

Major Safety Net Programs for Families with Children. The national government programs most directly connected with families and households with children under 18 consist of financial aid to state and local governments for the provision or assurance of health care or, as in the case of food stamps, for assistance in the administrative costs of those governments. In addition to Medicaid, major programs for health care delivery or closely associated services serving the at-risk population of expectant mothers and of children under 18 and where, by 1990, federal appropriations were exceeding $100 million, are shown in Table 3.2.

Specialized health care programs for mothers and children in addition to Medicaid include the following.

Food Stamps. This program, administered by the U.S. Department of Agriculture, reached an average of 25.4 million persons in fiscal year 1992, at

Table 3.2
Major Selected Federal Financial Assistance Programs to State and Local
Governments for Health Care and Appropriations for Fiscal Years 1990, 1992,
and 1993 (amounts in billions of dollars)

Program	Admin. Agency	Type	Channeled to	FY 1990	Appropriations FY 1992	FY 1993
1	2	3	4	5	6	7
Food Stamps	USDA	A	S	14.16	22.30	27.06
School Lunch Program	USDA	A	S	4.11	4.25	4.60
Special Supplemental Food Prog. (WIC)	USDA	A	S,L	2.12	2.60	2.86
State Admin. Matching for Food Stamp Program	USDA	A	S	1.40	1.27	1.32
Alcohol, Drug Abuse, Mental Health Block Grant	HHS	A	S	1.13	1.36	1.32
Child and Adult Care Food Program	USDA	A	S	.88	1.10	1.30
School Breakfast Program	USDA	A	S	.59	.79	.90
Maternal & Child Health Block Grant	HHS	A	S	.47	.65	.66
Drug Free Schools & Communities; State Program	DEd	A	S	.46	.50	.49
Community Health Centers	HHS	B	S,L	.43	.53	.56
Child Welfare Services	HHS	A	S	.25	.27	.29
Summer Food Service for Children	USDA	A	S	.17	.19	.22
Family Planning Services	HHS	B	S,L	.13	.15	.18
Childhood Immunization	HHS	B	S,L	.13	.30	.34
Adoption Assistance	HHS	A	S	.13	.20	.24
Handicapped Infants and Toddlers	DEd	A	S	.12*	.18	.21

Source: For 1990 appropriations: GAO, *Federal Aid: Programs Available to State and Local Governments.* GAO/HRD
91-93 FS. May, 1991, 6-16. FY 1992 and 1993 data were obtained directly from administering agencies.

Key: DEd = Dept. of Education; USDA = Dept. of Agriculture; HHS = Health & Human Services. Type: A = Funds
allocated by formula; B = Project grants to individual jurisdictions. Channel: S = State; L = Local.
* $79.5 million after sequestration.

an average total monthly cost of $1.9 billion, or a total annual cost of $22.5
billion.[35]

Supplemental Food Program for Women, Infants, and Children (WIC). The
WIC program was established in 1972 as an amendment to the Child Nutrition
Act of 1966. WIC distributes funds to states and certain recognized Indian groups
to provide supplemental foods to low-income (below 185 percent of poverty
level), pregnant, postpartum, and nursing mothers, and infants and children up
to age five who are diagnosed as being at nutritional risk. The program provides
food benefits specifically prescribed according to nutritional needs of the individual. It also provides counseling and education in food habits. Annual partic-

ipation in 1990 was 4.5 million, out of an estimated eligible population of 8.7 million in fiscal year 1991.[36]

Prenatal Care Programs. These include the Maternal and Child Health (MCH) Services block grant, authorized in 1981 under Title V of the Social Security Act, and grants to community health care centers under Section 330 of the Public Health Service Act, providing primary health care services to residents of medically underserved areas and persons, including pregnant women and infants. The goals of these program categories include reduction in infant mortality, low birth weight, and premature births and elimination or reduction of diseases and disorders during pregnancy that can threaten mother and/or infant health.[37]

Home Visiting. This service delivery method is employed in many public and nonprofit social service and education programs, including health. This approach brings important services and social support to the homes of needy persons using home health aides, trained community workers, paraprofessionals, and nurses. Home visiting programs are also targeted to reducing the incidence of child abuse and neglect.[38]

Supplemental Security Income (SSI). A part of this broad federal public assistance program, which states may supplement, is directed to lower-income families with blind or disabled children. In December 1991, about 440,000 children were receiving SSI payments averaging $387 monthly per child.[39]

Childhood Immunization. This program was authorized under PL 100–177, an amendment to Section 317 of the Public Health Service Act, and helps states and localities establish and maintain immunization programs for the control of vaccine-preventable childhood diseases, such as measles, rubella, polio, diphtheria, tetanus, and mumps. Vaccination has been found the most cost-effective method of preventing human suffering and reducing economic costs of diseases such as those mentioned above. The Public Health Service in the mid-1980s set a goal of immunizing 90 percent of preschool children by 1990. The GAO, however, after reviewing the situation, reported in 1992 congressional testimony that the United States had one of the lowest rates in the Western Hemisphere, that the PHS had estimated the national rate to be significantly less than 59 percent, and that "only about one-third of all urban preschool children were fully immunized." At the time of the report, about half of the children were being vaccinated by private physicians and half by public providers.[40]

Medicaid. This federal program, dating from the mid-1960s, is a health care safety net for low-income and "medically indigent" Americans. It is really three programs in one: a program for low-income women and children; a program for the blind and disabled; and a program for the elderly in need of long-term care.[41] The last group must be in, or acquire, a low-income and -asset status in order to qualify for Medicaid financing of nursing home bills. Medicaid covered approximately 25.3 million persons in 1990, with total expenditures of $75.2 billion, of which outlays by state and local governments totaled $32.3 billion.[42] Estimated matching ratios for 1993 ranged from a maximum federal share of 79 percent for Mississippi, downward to the statutory federal minimum of 50 percent

Table 3.3
Medicaid Users, Payments, and Services Rendered to Children in Low-Income Families, by Number, Percent of Total Medicaid Population, and Type of Service, 1980, 1989, and 1991 (users in thousands; payments in millions of dollars)

Type of Service	1980				1989				1991			
	Users No.	% of Tot.	Paymts Amt.	% of Tot.	Users No.	% of Tot.	Paymts Amt.	% of Tot.	Users No.	% of Tot.	Paymts Amt.	% of Tot.
1	2	3	4	5	6	7	8	9	10	11	12	13
Total, All Services	9,333	43.2	$3,123	13.4	10,318	43.9	$6,892	12.6	12,855	46.0	$11,600	15.1
Inpatient Hospital	978	4.5	1,476	6.3	1,138	4.8	3,270	6.0	1,472	5.3	5,376	7.0
ICF*, Mentally Retarded	5	Neg.	22	0.1	1	Neg.	20	Neg.	1	Neg.	38	Neg
ICF*, Other	6	Neg.	16	0.1	0	0	1	Neg.	0	0	2	Neg
SNF**	3	Neg.	8	Neg.	0	0	5	Neg.	1	Neg.	18	Neg
Physician	6,085	28.2	528	2.3	6,908	29.4	950	1.7	8,911	31.9	1,518	2.0
Outpatient Hospital	4,238	19.6	381	1.6	4,662	19.8	793	1.5	6,157	22.0	1,333	1.3
Home Health Care	72	0.3	8	Neg.	59	0.3	38	0.1	103	0.4	93	0.1
Prescription Drugs	5,590	25.9	156	0.7	6,454	27.5	343	0.6	8,605	30.8	590	0.8

Source: Pine, P., Baugh, D., and Clauser, S., "Trends in Medicaid Payments and Users of Covered Services, 1975-1991," *Health Care Financing Review 1992*, Medicare and Medicaid Statistical Supplement. Chapter 1.
Key: * ICF = Intermediate Care Facility. ** SNF = Skilled Nursing Facility.

for 12 states (Connecticut, Delaware, Massachusetts, Maryland, New Hampshire, New Jersey, Virginia, New York, Illinois, California, Hawaii, and Alaska) and the District of Columbia.[43]

Medicaid is one of the three major bases of financial support of low-income mothers with children below 18; the other two are food stamps and Aid to Families with Dependent Children (AFDC), commonly referred to as "welfare." AFDC is one of four "public assistance" programs, the other three being aid to the partially or totally disabled, supplemental security income (SSI), limited, for adults, to the financially needy over 65, and "general assistance," which is financed and administered entirely by state governments in most states and partially or wholly by local governments in a few. A combination of AFDC and Medicaid comprises a financial safety net for many never-married mothers with children. Table 3.3 shows for the low-income group of children the number of Medicaid recipients, amount of expenditure, and type of health care service rendered in the 1980–91 period.

In 1988, congressional legislation expanded Medicaid to additional low-income children. The following year, over 70 percent of payments for these children were for inpatient hospital, physician, and outpatient hospital services. They did not use expensive long-term care facilities, as is the case for nursing homes for the elderly.[44]

Some of the general problems and/or weaknesses in the Medicaid program are summarized here. Those associated with particular health care needs, such as in prenatal care, are identified and discussed later in this chapter. Issues besetting the program in the early 1990s included:[45]

- Federal mandates that tied continued federal sharing in Medicaid costs to expanded coverage of designated population groups; for states this meant compulsory added spending in a period of recession-induced reductions in tax revenues and increased AFDC and general assistance spending.

- Mandate-driven new state initiatives to gain increased federal Medicaid funds through such means as provider taxes and donations and to shift the support of services to Medicaid formerly financed with other state and federal dollars. Use of provider taxes/ donations was most productive for state treasuries when hospitals were the intermediary. This tended to increase referrals of Medicaid patients to hospitals, the most expensive of the provider alternatives available.

- Increased demand for nursing home and other care for the elderly, blind, and disabled.

- Already noted universal increases in medical care costs.

- Increased personnel layoffs in the private sector, induced both by international competition and the 1990–91 recession, resulting in losses of health insurance coverage for the released workers, with subsequent increased reliance upon Medicaid. The absence of a universal insurance system made Medicaid the primary health care safety net for the non-elderly.

- Aside from health care cost factors, a structural complicating factor in the Medicaid program was the interstate and, for some states, intrastate diversity in eligibility standards and levels of payment, with poverty level thresholds ranging from 36 percent of poverty to 112 percent for Missouri and Vermont, respectively.

PERINATAL CARE

Upon learning of pregnancy, whether it was intended or accidental, a woman has had the choice of carrying the fetus to term or, during the first trimester for most cases, the option of obtaining an abortion. Preliminary data for 1988, issued in 1991, showed legal abortion ratios per each live birth at approximately 1 for each birth to women under 15, 0.7 for ages 15–19, dropping to 0.4 and .25 for ages 20–24 and 25–29, respectively, and climbing to 0.5 plus for ages above 40.[46]

Following a decision to carry a fetus to term, immediate contact with a physician, nurse, clinic, or other health care provider is essential to the future health of both the expectant mother and the fetus. Abstention from use of illicit drugs is required; also, cessation of tobacco and alcohol use and proper nutrition are essential if premature birth, low birth weight, and other hazards to the embryo and subsequent infant are to be avoided.

In the mid-1980s, the Institute of Medicine (IOM) traced the evolution of rates for infant mortality and low birth weight as follows:

Between 1965 and 1980, the infant mortality rate in the United States dropped by almost 50 percent, from 24.7 to 13.1 per 1,000 live births. This decrease has not been matched by a comparable decline in the rate of low birth weight. Between 1971 and 1982, low-weight births declined moderately from 76 to 68 per 1,000 live births. . . . No decline has been observed in the proportion of very low birth weight infants.[47]

The provisional nationwide mortality rate for the 12-month period ending in February 1992, with all but three states reporting (California, Connecticut, and New York), was 8.8, slightly lower than the 9 rate for the same 12-month period ending in early 1991. The four states with the lowest provisional rates for the year ending in February 1992 were New Hampshire (6), Vermont (6.1), Utah (6.3), and Maine (6.3), all well below 7. For the largest states in 1990–91 (California and New York data not being available in 1991–92), the rates were: California (7.6), New York (9.3), Texas (7.9), Pennsylvania (9.6), and Florida (9.7). States with the highest rates in 1990–91 (11 or more) were District of Columbia (21), Delaware (12.4), Mississippi (11), and Georgia (11).[48]

In its 1991 report, the National Commission on Children (NCC) underscored the importance of prenatal care as follows:

Each year, nearly 40,000 babies born in the United States die before their first birthdays. Black babies are twice as likely to die as white babies. This nation's infant mortality rate is higher than those of 21 other industrialized countries. . . . After rapid progress in re-ducing U.S. infant mortality in the 1960s and 1970s, the pace of decline has slowed considerably. In 1990, the U.S. infant mortality rate was 9.1 per 1000 live births. . . . Low weight at birth (5.5 pounds or less) is the leading factor contributing to the nation's dismal infant mortality record. Low-birth weight babies are 40 times more likely to die in the first month of life and 5 times more likely to die later in the first year. . . . They are much more likely to suffer from chronic conditions, including neuro-development disabilities. . . . Many require intensive, high technology hospital care immediately after birth . . . often two or three months. Since 1980, no progress has been made in reducing the [rate of premature or low birth-weight births]. For blacks, the rate has actually increased.[49]

The above noted intensive, high-tech care given to low-weight infants is an important factor in rising health care costs. Table 3.4 shows the incidence of low-weight births, infant mortality, and the extent of prenatal care. More than a quarter of all births failed to have been preceded by early prenatal care (ranging from one-fifth for whites to two-fifths for blacks and Hispanics). A state-by-state incidence breakdown of the data in Table 3.4 is shown in Appendix 3.C.

In hardly any or no, aspect of health care is the crucial contrast between early preventive care and subsequent acute care more evident than in perinatal (pre- and postnatal) care. The NCC report noted:

Table 3.4
Rates for Low Birth-Weight Babies, Infant Mortality, and Births to Single Mothers, in Selected States, 1989–92, and Initial Prenatal Care, by Race and Ethnic Origin, for 1970–90 Period

Year	Low Birth Weight (Under 2,500 gr.)	Infant Mortality (Death in 12 Mos.)	Live Births to Unmarried Mothers
U.S. 1970	7.9	20.0	10.7
U.S. 1980	6.8	12.6	18.4
U.S. 1985	6.8	10.6	22.0
U.S. 1989	7.0	9.0	27.0
U.S. 1990	7.0	9.2	28.0
U.S. 1991		8.9	
U.S. 1992		8.5	

State	1990 Percents	1991 Percents	1992* Percents	1990 Percents
Hawaii	7.1	7.4	6.5	24.8
Minnesota	5.1	7.5	7.3	20.9
North Dakota	5.5	8.1	9.0	18.4
Utah	5.7	6.1	6.0	13.5
Vermont	5.3	5.8	6.1	20.1
California	5.8	7.6	7.8	31.6
Florida	7.4	9.0	8.9	31.7
Illinois	7.6	10.7	10.3	31.7
New York	7.6	9.4	9.4	33.0
Texas	6.9	7.7	7.7	17.5
Delaware	7.6	11.8	12.7	29.1
Dist. of Columbia	15.1	21.0	20.0	64.9
Georgia	8.7	11.4	12.4	32.8
Mississippi	9.6	11.4	11.3	40.5

Initial Pre-Natal Care, by Per Cent of Live Births and Race/Ethnicity

Year	First Trimester				Third Trimester or None			
	All	White	Black	Hispanic	All	White	Black	Hispanic
1970	68.0	72.4	44.4	N/A	7.9	6.2	16.6	N/A
1980	76.3	79.3	62.7	60.2	5.1	4.3	8.8	12.0
1985	76.2	79.4	61.8	61.2	5.7	4.7	10.0	12.4
1989	75.5	78.9	60.0	59.5	6.4	5.2	11.9	13.0

Source: For 1990 data: NCHS, "Advance Report of Final Natality Statistics 1990," *Monthly Vital Statistics Report* (41:9 Supplement), Tables 14 and 18, February 25, 1993, 32 and 36. For historical 1970-1989 data: USPHS, "Prenatal Care and Maternal Education for Live Births," *Health, United States, 1991*, Table 8, April 1992, 130-131. For 1991 data: NCHS, "Advance Report of Final Mortality Statistics, 1991," *Monthly Vital Statistics Report* (42:2 Supplement), Table 24, August 31, 1993, 53. For 1992 provisional data: "Annual Summary of Births, Marriages, Divorces, and Deaths, United Sates, 1992" *Monthly Vital Statistics Report* (41:13 Supplement), Table 3, September 28, 1993, 12.

Note: * = Provisional data.

Women who do not receive routine care are approximately three times as likely to deliver low-birth weight infants as those who do. Advanced medical technology can now save the lives of many of these children, but the human and financial costs are very high. Low-birth weight babies are at a substantially greater risk of chronic illnesses and disabilities, including cerebral palsy, retardation, autism, and vision and learning disabilities. The cost of a very-low-birth weight [3.3 pounds] infant's stay in a neonatal intensive care unit can reach $150,000 or more. In contrast, the cost of providing prenatal care . . . can be as little as $400.[50]

Two separate but closely related factors are critical during the first trimester—action by the expectant mother to establish initial contact with the health care system and maintenance by her of healthy habits throughout her pregnancy. Several deterrents stand in the way of a successful outcome. Some of these are "system-based," such as financial and physical access to prenatal care, availability of appropriate professional attention when needed, and availability of information and its dissemination to high-risk women. Others are behavioral and are referred to as "client-based," such as the failure to show up for appointments, continued use of alcohol/drugs/tobacco, and failure to take seriously the importance of good nutritional and other health habits.

Informational Impediments

Information about health measures to be taken during pregnancy should be available to all women of childbearing age who are expecting to be, or likely to become, pregnant and is absolutely essential to those women in the high-risk category (e.g., low-income, below high school education, residing in poverty and/or drug-use concentrated areas). Numerous system- and client-based barriers stand in the way of assuring (1) the availability of necessary information, (2) delivery of this information to the high-risk targets, and (3) recipient action to carry out the measures called for.

Too often information availability and delivery are limited to notices in the media about its availability, with the suggestion that the expectant mother telephone or visit an agency, clinic, or other source to get the necessary examinations and accompanying instructions. Sometimes notices are placed in envelopes containing the welfare check or food stamps being sent to female-headed households or to all food stamp and AFDC recipients. However, the recipient may be illiterate in English, or in any language. Within the health care and public welfare delivery systems, even the envelope enclosures are a periodic expense item. Public service radio or television announcements of this type are far removed from prime time or even from all daylight and early evening hours. More effective outreach efforts by system personnel, such as the initiation of prenatal care information and/or attention to all, or high-risk, women found positive in pregnancy tests at public health clinics, are labor-intensive and quite expensive.[51]

For fiscally hard-pressed state and local governments, a conscious or subconscious avoidance of, or resistance to, a new group of potential public aid recipients is understandable, though not excusable, given the much larger long-term public costs that result from failure to obtain prenatal care. The high-risk women most difficult to reach are those in remote rural areas; those living in extreme poverty in central city ghettos; those suffering from alcohol and drug dependence; and those in, or on the borderline of, illegal activities (drug dealing, prostitution, shoplifting) and consequently fearful of contact with a governmental, community health, or social agency. The difficulty in "case-finding" new pregnancies among these very hard-to-reach groups through informational networking among public housing project managers, school officials, and others comprises a major impediment to prenatal care, with the consequent bearing of low-birth weight or other unhealthy infants.

Upon the receipt of information about prenatal care, the response of the recipient may be, and unfortunately often is hesitancy, unwillingness, or disdain. This is a significant behavioral barrier to adequate care, especially among the high-risk population. It may include not knowing if she is pregnant, as well as hiding the pregnancy from others.[52]

Other women may turn away from prenatal care because of a language barrier; a cultural belief that women should receive such care only from other women; conflicts over the life-style changes, such as in smoking, drinking, or drug use, required for a healthy pregnancy; or previous unfortunate experiences with the U.S. health care system.[53] Regarding prior experiences with the system, procedural complexities are given by women as reasons to stay away from the bureaucracy, system, or government itself. (This barrier is a mixture of a client- and system-based one.)

Access Impediments

These impediments include financial access and, especially for low-income women, the establishment of eligibility for food stamps, Medicaid, WIC, MCH, and other public assistance programs; physical access, including shortages of health facilities and personnel in some areas and transportation difficulties in reaching them; and personnel access to health professionals and/or facilities willing to treat low-income, especially Medicaid, patients.

Financial Access. For below-poverty and other low-income women, especially those who are unmarried, obtaining adequate care is dependent on (1) becoming a "charity patient" at a clinic or physician's office or (2) establishing eligibility for Medicaid or other public assistance programs that will underwrite all or part of the cost of care during the prenatal, delivery, and postnatal period. The principal means of financial access for low-income persons has been through the Medicaid program.

From its inception in 1965 until the end of the 1980s, eligibility for AFDC was sufficient to establish initial eligibility for Medicaid; consequently, applicants were directed first to the welfare office. However, as the share of Medicaid outlays for long-term care of the elderly grew, the application process became more cumbersome in order to allow a close examination of any recent transfers of assets by elderly applicants to their heirs, thereby to bring their net worth and income down to the Medicaid eligibility threshold. This resulted in forms, documents, and other procedures of seemingly unlimited length. Finally, in response to state government's and other concerns about infant mortality and the "welfare stigma" syndrome that deterred some women from applying for Medicaid, the umbilical cord linking Medicaid to welfare was loosened through a series of congressional enactments beginning in 1984 that broadened Medicaid eligibility for pregnant women and young children.

In brief, the successive legislative changes broadening eligibility for women, infants (below age one), and young children comprised the following.[54] A more detailed description appears in Appendix 3.D.

- 1984: Coverage of all children meeting other state AFDC requirements, regardless of family structure; coverage from beginning of pregnancy if qualifying for AFDC after birth; and automatic coverage of infants of Medicaid mothers for one year after birth.
- 1985: Coverage without exception of all pregnant women with family income or assets below state AFDC levels for 60 days after birth and required coverage of "special needs" children regardless of income/assets of adoptive/foster parents.
- 1986: Continuation of eligibility for young children if they were hospital patients when maximum age was reached.
- 1987–88: Coverage for all pregnant women and infants up to 100 percent of federal poverty line (official measure) and increased required period of Medicaid coverage if AFDC cash assistance was stopped because of increased household earnings.
- 1989: Mandated coverage of pregnant women, infants, and children under age 6 below 133 percent of federal poverty line.
- 1990: Child coverage up to age 18 if below 100 percent of poverty line; states required to receive and process applications at convenient outreach sites.

During the 1970–90 period, the state-local share of Medicaid outlays rose from $2.5 billion to $11.8 billion in 1980, to $32.3 billion in 1990. As a share of state "own-source" general revenues, Medicaid outlays grew from 4.3 to 6.9, to 8.3 percent in the corresponding years.[55]

Although the foregoing changes widened greatly the Medicaid coverage of low-income mothers and their children, state fiscal problems and other system-based factors continued to impede efforts to remove or mitigate various nonfiscal impediments to prenatal care. These are examined below.

Physical Access. The 1991 Advisory Council on Social Security (ACSS) dealt with a number of health issues, partly due to the connection between Medicare and Social Security. Its report issued in late 1991 identified several aspects of the access problem, including the fact that:

the geographic distribution of physicians in the United States remains very uneven. Although a quarter of the population resides in rural areas, only 12 percent of physicians practice there, and even a smaller share of specialists. . . . Another factor . . . is income. The average annual salary for a family practitioner is $96,000, while [a surgeon's] can exceed $200,000. . . . Many medical students graduate with large debts . . . and [this obligation] often causes them to choose subspecialty practice over primary care. . . . During the Council's . . . hearings, providers in rural areas described several reasons why it is more difficult to attract providers. . . . Medicaid reimbursement rates are generally lower for rural physicians. . . . Rural hospitals and community health centers cannot afford to pay physicians as well as hospitals in urban and suburban areas. . . . In remote areas, there is no one to rely on for back-up. . . . Inner-city communities . . . have difficulties attracting and retaining physicians due to high costs of living, scarcity of housing, inadequate transportation and concerns for safety.[56]

From the patients' point of view, physical access falls into three procedural categories: (1) access to agencies and offices for the purpose of acquiring information; (2) where eligibility for Medicaid or other financial aid is necessary before the first visit to a health care provider, access to transportation to the place where applications must be filed and interviews take place; and (3) initial and successive visits to health care professionals during and following the prenatal period and for the delivery, which may involve in going to two or more different health facilities located in disparate parts of the city, town, or county.

For physical access to these locations, the expectant mother usually must travel to them, although under special circumstances, after the initial contacts have been made, home visits by public health or social service personnel may occur. Consequently, transportation distance and cost are often major access impediments. Transportation distance is an important factor, both in rural and in urban areas, with distances being greater in the former, but costs per mile considerably higher in the latter. Furthermore, public transportation is often nonexistent in rural areas and in urban areas is often complex and frustrating, dependent upon number of transfers and other characteristics of the route between the woman's home and the facility being visited.

In some rural areas, however, distance can become a nearly insurmountable barrier, due to the declining rural population and the closure of hospitals, clinics, and physicians' offices. In a 1990 report, *Health Care in Rural America,* the congressional Office of Technology Assessment (OTA) noted that rural areas had lower mortality rates than their urban counterparts but a higher morbidity rate, particularly chronic disease and disability.[57] The General Accounting Office found in a series of reports and noted in testimony that rural hospitals were representing one-fourth of all acute care beds and about half of all acute care hospitals in the country. More rural than urban hospitals were small, government-owned, and in areas with weak economies and provide care for less complex medical conditions. The reports concluded that although most closures did not significantly reduce access to care, about a third of the rural closures in the immediately preceding years might have created or worsened access problems for low-income residents and patients needing emergency care.[58]

With the growing shortage of facilities and health care personnel in rural areas, transportation obviously becomes more difficult. In both urban and rural areas, transportation cost is legally one of the lesser problems for those on Medicaid. As the National Governors' Association (NGA) pointed out in a 1989 report:

Two sections of the *Code of Federal Regulations* (CFR) address the transportation issue. One requires that a Medicaid state plan must . . . "specify that there will be provision for assuring necessary transportation of recipients to and from providers of services, and describe the methods that will be used" (42 CFR 431.53). While this is an administrative requirement, a second section has always provided states with the flexibility to cover transportation as an optional medical service (42 CFR 440.170). However, *these regulations rarely have been enforced, and states have been unable to consistently meet the transportation needs of recipient populations.*[59]

Access to Health Care Professionals. The low-income expectant mother who has acquired Medicaid eligibility or otherwise met the financial access problem and has transportation available to visit an office, clinic, or other facility must still find a physician available and willing to provide her with prenatal care. Sometimes there may be subtle barriers of race, nationality, and culture; more often, difficult language barriers are encountered. A 1988 survey of provider participation by the NGA found maternal and child health and Medicaid administrators from 35 of the 50 states reporting participation problems in at least some localities.

The most severe problems of physician nonparticipation in Medicaid and other health programs for low-income mothers and children were occurring in rural areas, with greater difficulty encountered in the non-Medicaid program areas. This perhaps was due largely to the fact that alternatives to a family physician (e.g., hospitals, clinics, and community health centers) were available in urban areas where a large majority of prenatal Medicaid recipients were located.[60]

State agency perceptions of the major reasons for providers' being unwilling to participate included low fees, malpractice fears, complicated paperwork and other procedural difficulties, client problems, and delays in the reimbursement process. In the Medicaid program, fees and malpractice comprised nearly three-quarters of the state agency perceived reasons. Numerous providers were dropping out of obstetrical/gynecological (OB-GYN) care or declining to take new patients. Reasons often given by physicians for not participating or being reluctant to do so, included (1) fees do not cover malpractice premium costs; (2) poor patients are erratic; (3) poor patients sue more; (4) poor patients do not get prenatal care and thus are high risk at delivery; and (5) doctor cannot afford to give charity care.[61]

Behavioral Impediments

The NCC report emphasized:

A mother's responsibility begins before her child's birth, because her own health and healthful behavior during pregnancy are fundamental to the health of her unborn child.

Unless pregnant women recognize the importance of maintaining healthful lifestyles, getting proper nutrition, and avoiding harmful substances . . . they are likely to severely compromise their children's health from the very beginning of life. . . . [They] must obtain adequate prenatal care, beginning early and continuing throughout pregnancy.[62]

The relative negative impacts of the major behavioral or life-style deterrents had not been established in quantitative terms much prior to 1990. But there was a growing consensus that the major threats of fatal, irreparable, or long-term disability of the infant lay in infection of the mother with AIDS prior to, or during, pregnancy; the prolonged illicit and licit use of certain drugs, especially crack (smoked cocaine); heavy alcohol use; and smoking.

Birth of AIDS-Infected Infants. The NCC observed:

AIDS threatens a growing number of children each year, primarily through transmission from their mothers before or at birth. By 1990, approximately 2,000 cases of pediatric AIDS had been diagnosed, and many more are expected over the decade. At current rates, the number of children with this fatal but preventable disease will reach 13,000 by the year 2000. By 1991, 10,000 children under the age of 13 are expected to have the HIV virus, which can develop into AIDS.[63]

Table 3.5 shows the incidence of AIDS mortality among age and ethnic groups and the manner in which the virus had been transmitted to females.

At a conference on Women and AIDS sponsored by the Department of HHS in December 1990, Dr. Antonia Novello, then surgeon general of the U.S. Public Health Service, stated that the issue of women and HIV is "a major public health challenge. Women need education, testing, and counseling."[64] It was estimated that based on trends at that time, AIDS would be one of the five leading causes of death in women of childbearing age in 1991, as reported in *JAMA,* the AMA journal.[65] Many women are unaware they are at risk for HIV infection, and an infected woman often remains undiagnosed until the onset of AIDS or until a perinatally infected child becomes ill.

Therefore, it is apparent that major policy and procedural weaknesses in the child health care system respecting AIDS and the HIV virus center around the acquisition of early information regarding extent of the mother's exposure and the acquisition of information before pregnancy if possible and if not, as soon as pregnancy is ascertained. This involves the controversial issue of screening and testing, with or without consent of the patient.

Knowledge of virus presence or high-risk exposures (especially among IV drug users) early in the first trimester raises the question of abortion, another controversial issue. At the very least, early knowledge allows more time for the woman, her physician, and maternal and child health (MCH) personnel to counsel with one another and plan other next steps, including foster care and "boarder baby" homes.

Drug-Addicted Mothers and Infants. In contrast to the difficulty of quantifying, except in very broad terms, the presence in particular cases and the demographic

Table 3.5

Cases of Acquired Immunodeficiency Syndrome (AIDS), by Year of Report, Sex, and Transmission Category, 1984[1] and 1990[2]

Categories	All Years			1984			1990		
	Male	Female	Children	Male	Female	Children	Male	Female	Children
All Races:	131,390	13,666	2,469	4,110	276	50	29,050	3,599	566
White (Non-Hispanic)	79,414	3,852	565	2,602	78	10	16,865	969	127
Black (Non-Hispanic)	33,831	7,531	1,352	949	142	28	8,156	2,042	300
Hispanic Origin	16,797	2,147	531	537	56	12	3,696	560	135
Other Races	1,348	136	21	22	–	–	333	28	4

Numbers and Percents

Transmission Categories for Females:	All Years		1984		1990	
	No.	Percent	No.	Percent	No.	Percent
All Categories	13,667	100.0	276	100.0	3,599	100.0
I.V.[3] Drug Use	6,967	51.0	170	61.6	1,727	48.0
Hemophelia/Coagulation Disorder	34	0.2	2	0.7	9	0.3
Born in C/A[4]	532	3.9	17	6.2	96	2.7
Heterosexual Contact[5]	3,828	28.0	46	16.7	1,077	29.9
Contact with I.V. Drug User	2,672	19.6	33	19.6	737	20.5
Transfusion	1,300	9.5	21	7.6	279	7.8
Undetermined[6]	1,005	7.4	20	7.2	411	11.4

Source: *Health USA 1990*, Tables 44 and 46, 109, 111-112.
Notes: 1 Includes cases prior to 1984.
2 Data as of September 30, 1990, and reflect reporting delays.
3 Intravenous drug use.
4 Born in Caribbean or African countries.
5 Includes persons who have had heterosexual contact with a person with HIV infection or at risk of HIV infection.
6 Includes persons for whom information is still incomplete.

incidence of the HIV-infected persons (due to the incubation period after infection), quantifying the incidence of drug addiction among expectant mothers and the extent of risks to offspring is more precise. Two successive GAO reports in May and June 1991 dealt, respectively, with a special set-aside for drug treatment of pregnant women within the MCH federal block grant and with the eligibility of financing such treatment from Medicaid funds. The reports contained several estimates.

In the first report, GAO estimated the range of infants born prenatally exposed to crack cocaine at 100,000 to 375,000 annually.[66] The second report noted: that (1) the National Institute of Drug Abuse had estimated that in 1988, 5 million women of childbearing age used illicit drugs (e.g., crack cocaine, heroin, phencyclidine (PCP), marijuana, amphetamines, and barbiturates), and (2) a 1990 survey conducted by the National Association of State Alcohol and Drug Abuse Directors estimated that 280,000 pregnant women nationwide were in need of drug treatment, yet less than 11 percent of them were receiving it.[67]

Drug-exposed infants have significantly lower birth weights, are more likely to be premature, and have longer, more serious, and much more expensive hospital stays. In the postnatal period, the children are often unfed, unsupervised, and generally uncared-for, having emotional as well as developmental problems, and are more likely to be subject to physical abuse. Still another GAO report, *Drug-Exposed Infants: A Generation at Risk,* issued in 1990, found a large gap between the number of women who could benefit from drug treatment and the number of treatment slots.[68] For a number of years, beginning in the mid-1980s, waiting lists for persons *desiring* drug treatment had existed over indefinite periods of time in many of the nation's largest cities.

The same GAO study reviewed the number of drug-exposed infants ascertained through testing by several hospitals. The average incidence ranged from three to five times as high where rigorous tests were applied to the mother (16% compared with 3%). Rigorous testing included a review of prior medical history and testing for urine toxicology. The incidence at a large Detroit hospital using meconium, a very sensitive test for drug use, found nearly 3,000 out of over 7,000 births in 1989 to have been drug-exposed, or about 42 percent. In contrast, when self-reporting of drug use by the mother was the base for determining exposure, only about 600, or 8 percent, were identified. Another study anonymously tested for drug use among women entering private obstetric care and women at public prenatal care clinics and found that the overall incidence of drug use was similar between the two groups—16.3 percent at public clinics and 13.1 at private offices.[69]

The GAO study found further that in addition to insufficient drug treatment slots for pregnant women, some programs were refusing to provide such services because of legal liability, treatment medications, and lack of prenatal care that might well have adverse effects on the fetus. Some pregnant addicts told GAO interviewers that because they had other children, the lack of day-care services made it difficult for them to get away for treatment. Other barriers to seeking treatment included fear of criminal prosecution and fear of incarceration and consequently losing children to foster care with the risk of never getting them back. Hospital officials interviewed said that in addition to not seeking prenatal care, some drug-using women were delivering their infants at home in order to avoid being reported to child welfare authorities.[70]

On the other hand, in some large cities in 1991, including New York, in order to slow the sharp increase in numbers of children being sent to foster homes as a result of the cocaine "epidemic," judicial and child welfare authorities were beginning to encourage drug treatment for mothers while permitting them to retain custody. The mother, if found to be addicted as a result of a test on the infant, could take the child home, if agreeing to drug treatment, attendance at classes on child rearing, and other conditions, instead of transferring the infant to foster care.[71]

The earlier of the 1991 GAO reports was concerned primarily with a review of the extent to which state governments were utilizing a particular federal grant program. Under this program, states were required to set aside at least 10 percent of an already existing block grant for alcohol, drug abuse, and mental health services, for the purpose of initiating or continuing "new or expanded alcohol and drug abuse services for women." The block grant program was under federal cognizance of the Alcohol, Drug Abuse, and Mental Health Administration (ADAMHA); the "10 percent" program was known as the ADAMS Set-Aside (the S for services). In the course of the study, data were collected from seven states (California, Florida, Nevada, New York, South Carolina, Texas, and Washington). Estimates of drug-abusing pregnant women in those states as of June 1990 ranged from 65,000 in California to 7,000 in Washington, with New York at 24,000, and Florida at 10,175.[72]

Financial access impediments stood in the way of a sizable proportion of the pregnant women desiring drug treatment. This type of treatment was often not available under the Medicaid program, despite the intent of the Congress to broaden and intensify coverage for pregnant women and small children. The 1991 GAO report on Medicaid funding of drug treatment stated that in fiscal year 1991, neither Medicaid laws nor regulations specified substance abuse treatment as a service that could be reimbursed. However, states could be reimbursed if the treatment were provided under a service category that qualified for federal matching funds such as inpatient hospital services. (If a patient was receiving inpatient treatment that included alcohol detoxification, the detoxification would have been reimbursable.) The report stated: *"The amount of state and federal Medicaid funding for substance abuse treatments is not known because neither HCFA* [Health Care Financing Administration, a part of HHS and responsible for administering the Medicaid program] *nor the states we visited maintained data that identify services specifically provided for substance abuse."*[73]

Smoking and Alcohol Abuse. In the early 1980s, the National Institute of Medicine (IOM) of the National Academy of Sciences-National Research Council convened an interdisciplinary committee to study the causes and prevention of premature birth and intrauterine growth retardation (UGR), the two major contributions at that time to low birth weight. The resulting report commented as follows on the adverse effects of smoking and alcohol use during pregnancy: "Smoking is one of the most important and preventable determinants of low birth weight. [Studies] indicate that smoking during pregnancy is associated with a reduction in birth weight ranging from 150 to 250 grams. This relationship has persisted for at least 20 years, despite reported reductions in the average tar and nicotine yields of cigarettes on the market."[74] Later estimates appeared in 1992 in the *Monthly Vital Statistics Report* to the effect that babies born to low-income mothers who smoked during pregnancy were "74 percent more likely to be of low birth weight than were infants [whose mothers] did not smoke." Another study had indicated that "21–39 percent of all low weight births occur as a consequence of maternal smoking."

The study also showed that white mothers were slightly more likely to smoke than black mothers; more important, black mothers who were smokers smoked fewer cigarettes. Thirty-eight percent of white mothers smoked 16 or more cigarettes a day compared with 21 percent of black mothers. Finally, 8 percent of Hispanic mothers smoked during pregnancy compared with 22 percent of white, non Hispanic mothers.[75]

Improper/Inadequate Eating and Nutritional Habits. In contrast to the specificity of findings in several other aspects of perinatal care, particularly the precise harmful effects of drug use and smoking and the direct correlation between types of birth outcomes and socioeconomic status, the extent of improved outcomes that are directly attributable to good nutritional habits has been consistently more generalized.

The 1985 IOM report, cited previously, stated: "Four types of research have been used to examine the effect of nutrition during pregnancy on birth outcomes: animal studies, human war famine studies, nutritional intake/fetal outcome correlational studies, and experimental nutrition intervention studies. They all point to the common conclusion that good nutrition has a positive influence on birth weight, but the extent of the effect is unclear."[76] The majority report on health by the NCC took a less equivocal approach:

Pregnant women and children need adequate nutrition if children are to grow and develop normally. Nutritional deprivation during pregnancy and the early months of life can cause damage that can never be repaired. When infants and young children fail to receive adequate nutrition, their growth is often slowed, they are more susceptible to illness, and they are at greater risk of neuro-developmental problems that impair learning. Malnourishment that results in a condition known as "failure to thrive" often requires hospitalization and has serious lasting effects on growth and socio-emotional functioning.[77]

However, the minority report on health (health being the only chapter of the commission's report on which there was disagreement), in a section on "Adequate Nutrition," argued: "Low birth-weight births . . . are much more frequently due to other adult behavior such as drug abuse, smoking, and stress . . . [and cited a nutrition/pediatrics professor at Johns Hopkins University who had written]: 'Studies of whites, blacks and Puerto Ricans all suggest that [low birth weight] births . . . correlate strongly with behavior, not nutrition.' "[78]

A 1992 GAO report stated: "The WIC program served an estimated 75 percent of all income-eligible pregnant women who would have given birth in 1990. . . . GAO estimated that serving all income-eligible who gave birth in 1990 would have cost about $407 million, or about $111 million more than was spent on pregnant women, but could have returned more than $1.3 billion in avoided expenditures over the next 18 years."[79]

Despite some of the foregoing expressed uncertainties about the precise extent of nutritional influence, no exceptions were taken to the positive thrust of a healthy diet. Within that context, it must be emphasized that malnutrition and a poor diet can be both a behavioral as well as an access impediment to adequate perinatal care. On postnatal nutrition, the National Commission observed:

Breast feeding has clearly demonstrated health benefits . . . often overlooked. . . . Children who are breast-fed . . . are usually healthier than those who are fed formula [and it] helps promote attachment between mothers and children. . . . Although breast-feeding has become less popular in recent years among some groups of mothers including some . . . at highest risk of having . . . unhealthy babies, it has clear health and cost benefits.[80]

In 1989, the National Governors' Association reported that of the 24 states enhancing perinatal care, 17 added additional coverage of nutritional counseling and education to their refined Medicaid-financed prenatal series, making a total of 35 states providing this service in mid-1992. Some states specified intervention for women at special nutritional risk, such as those with gestational diabetes mellitus, gastrointestinal/renal disease, and metabolic problems.[81]

Research and Evaluation Shortcomings

Federal and state agencies have emphasized repeatedly the need for increased research as to causes of unfavorable outcomes in the perinatal period and improved design of evaluation models that could be used in assessing comparative costs and benefits resulting from alternative approaches. This is a general need in young child and adolescent health care as well. Relative to perinatal care, the GAO has emphasized the particular difficulties associated with drug treatment of addicted expectant mothers. Although drug abuse research at the National Institute on Drug Abuse (NIDA) grew substantially during the 1975–91 period, research of any kind remained only a small part (4%) of the $10.5 billion of federal drug control spending. Furthermore, among research on causality, prevention, and treatment, and latter two continued to receive primary attention, with causality research receiving only a small part (3–5%) share of NIDA expenditures. GAO found a high consensus among experts in the drug abuse field on the need for increased causality research. It was pointed out that understanding the causes of abuse could be a useful basis for prevention and treatment ideas. Without such understanding, interventions are often mere guesswork, with cumulative learning depending largely on after-the-fact evaluations.[82]

The NGA pointed out that while there was an overwhelming body of literature pointing to the effectiveness of prenatal care in reducing low birth weight and infant mortality, major concerns had been expressed about the adequacy of the research designs and methodologies in many of those studies. This was especially the case in the early 1990s because with the cost of several billions of dollars of additional Medicaid expenditure mandated upon the states by the federal government in the perinatal area, it was crucial that evaluations of the enhanced coverages and new approaches being initiated in the states be evaluated as expeditiously, methodologically, and soundly as possible. The four key elements of program impact evaluation emphasized by the report were (1) process of care; (2) health service access; (3) birth outcomes; and (4) costs.[83]

Summary

In the perinatal period, especially the prenatal stage, much irreversible harm can befall the developing fetus and newly born infant, and in the first year thereafter, through inadequate and/or irresponsible health care of, and by, the mother. The most serious shortcoming is failure of such a high proportion of at-risk women to make and maintain contact with the health care system during the first trimester of pregnancy. This arises from neglect and irresponsibility on the part of the system, the woman, or both.

Equally serious for the mother and devastating for the birth outcome are AIDS infection and drug abuse—especially crack cocaine—by the mother. This results in the birth of a critically ill and sometimes addicted or permanently mentally or physically disabled infant. In the case of drug abuse, the health care system is terribly at fault for those cases where the woman desperately desires, but is rejected for, treatment. Treatment for those desiring it, especially expectant mothers, is a critical health and social need.

Those infants born and remaining healthy during the first year start childhood with favorable odds. A high majority of white infants do so, but a typically large percentage of black and Hispanic infants do not. Many view that as both a social and economic tragedy—high public expenditures to care for the resulting disabled persons and a deprivation of the future American society and economy of a precious ingredient, human capital.

YOUNG CHILD CARE

This section spans the period from the end of infancy (1 year) through age 14. Quantitative data presented are drawn largely from vital statistics publications of the U.S. Public Health Service (USPHS), which are derived in turn from vital statistics agencies in each of the 50 states and the District of Columbia. Most of the data covering young persons are broken into four groupings: below 1 year, 1–4, 5–14, and 15–24. The final period to be covered in this book is adolescence through age 19.

In contrast to perinatal and infant care and mortality, where the general quantitative picture is mixed at best and alarming in several respects, the overall status of the physical health of young children was continuing to show gradual improvement at the beginning of the 1990s. The National Center for Social Policy, a nonprofit organization supported by the Annie E. Casey Foundation, in the second of an annual report series, *Kids Count,* showed in the 1991 report a profile by state of child health.

The report summarized the young child health situation in the 1986–88 period as follows: "In 48 states and the District of Columbia, young child death rates for children ages 1–14 improved between 1980 and 1988. The rate of improvement for white children was twice that for black children. If current progress continues, the United States will meet the U.S. Public Health Service national goal for the year 2000 for young deaths."[84] The 2000 goal had been set at 28 per 100,000; the 1988 rate stood at 33.2. For the 1–4 age group it had declined from 139.4 per 100,000 in 1950 to 84.5 in 1970, to 63.9 in 1980, to 50.9 in 1988. Corresponding rates for the 5–14 group were 60.1, 41.3, 30.6, and 25.8. The highest state death rate for the 1–14 group was Alaska at 45.6, while Rhode Island had the lowest at 21.0, followed by Hawaii at 22.4. The national rates for this group in 1990 and 1991 were 30.1 and 30.7, respectively.[85]

Although the mortality rate for the 1–14 group decreased significantly during the 1970s and 1980s, several determinants of future life expectancy and the incidence of morbidity over lifetime continued to erode. In a few respects, the future physical health of the 1–14 group itself showed signs of deterioration. These included a declining rate of immunization against childhood diseases and infections. Increasingly violent environments for the 15–24 age group in inner-city poverty areas and elsewhere also threaten death or disability to the 1–14 group. The continued growth in the teenage unmarried pregnancy rate, especially among blacks and Hispanics, cannot help but threaten the physical health of their offspring during the age 1–14 period. Table 3.6 shows leading causes of death to young children in the 1–4 and 5–14 groups over the 1970–91 period.

Appendix 3.E breaks down Table 3.6 data by race and sex. Major categories of deterrents to adequate young child health care (a few of which parallel those discussed earlier for the perinatal period) examined here are (1) informational, physical, financial, and professional provider access and willingness to treat; (2) access to, and follow-through with, early and periodic screening, diagnosis, and treatment (EPSDT); (3) lack of timely immunizations; (4) safety hazards and protection, including restraint seating in autos, household poisons, and lead poison in paint; (5) violence and other child abuse; (6) weaknesses in parenting skills; (7) foster care deficiencies; (8) chronic disease and physical disability;

Table 3.6

Death Rates for 10 Leading Causes of Death in Age Group 1–14 for 1979, 1988, 1990,* and 1991* (rate is number per 100,000 group population)

Cause	1979		1988		1990*	1991*
	1-4	5-14	1-4	5-14	1-14	1-14
1. Accidents and adverse effects	26.5	16.1	19.6	12.2	12.4	12.4
Motor vehicle	9.8	8.3	6.9	7.0	6.0	6.0
Other	16.7	7.7	12.7	5.2	6.4	6.5
2. Malignant neoplasms, including neoplasms of lymphatic and hematopoietic tissues	4.6	4.4	3.7	3.2	3.0	3.3
3. Homicide and legal intervention	2.5	1.1	2.6	1.3	1.8	1.9
4. Diseases of heart	2.1	0.8	2.4	0.9	1.1	1.1
5. Suicide	—	0.8	—	0.7	0.5	0.5
6. Pneumonia/Influenza	2.0	0.6	1.3	0.4	0.4	0.6
7. Conditions originating in perinatal period	0.6	0.0	0.9	0.1	0.4	0.3
8. Meningitis			0.9	0.2	**	**
9. Human immunodeficiency virus infection (HIV)***	—	—	0.8		0.7	0.7
10. Septicemia	0.5	0.1	0.6	0.1	0.2	0.3
11. Cerebrovascular diseases	0.3	0.3	0.4	0.2	0.3	0.3
All Causes	64.2	31.5	50.9	25.8	24.1	30.7

Sources: U.S. Department of Health and Human Services, Public Health Service, Centers for Disease Control, National Center for Health Statistics, "Advance Report of Final Mortality Statistics, 1988," Tables 5, 9. *Monthly Vital Statistics Report* (39:7), Supplement. November 28, 1990, 17-19; 24-25. For 1990 and 1991: Same agencies, "Annual Summary of Births, Marriages, Divorces, and Deaths: United States, 1990," *Monthly Vital Statistics Report* (39:13), Table 5 and same title in corresponding 1991 issue (40:13), Table 5, September 30, 1992, 17-18.

Notes: * Provisional data. ** Not in top 15. *** Including those under 1 year in 1990 and 1991.

(9) hunger and improper food; (10) child behavior and life-style; (11) fragmentation and complexity of the health care delivery system as it applies to child health care; and (12) lack of community responsibility and concern.

A common thread running through many of the foregoing deterrents is the need to focus on prevention and preventive care, in contrast to delayed treatment until the emergency room or other acute care need is reached. The lack of regular, preventive care is particularly marked for black and Hispanic children in low-income families. The National Commission on Children noted:

Metabolic disorders that can be detected through routine new-born screening and that are readily treatable can lead to mental retardation if they are overlooked. Immunizations protect individual children as well as whole communities from the devastating effects of preventable diseases. Physical examinations and routine tests can lead to the early correction of conditions that might otherwise severely impair intellectual and social development. Yet many children . . . do not get the regular preventive care all children need. Nor do they receive timely acute care when health problems occur. . . . A common earache left untreated, for example, can lead to significant hearing loss. A vision problem, correctable with glasses, can inhibit learning. Nearly 20 percent of children report no contact with a physician in the past year. Low-income black and Hispanic children are even less likely to have regular preventive and acute care than other groups, especially if their families have no health insurance.[86]

Informational, Physical, Financial, and Professional Access

Many of the aspects of access to the health care system by the pregnant woman in the perinatal period continue through the preschool period, including the need for continued parental attention and motivation. These are discussed below.

Informational Access. Professional contacts made during the earlier period continue to be relevant and useful. In many cases, initiative of an outreach nature from a health care provider, maternal and child health (MCH), or other agency may be necessary. Prior to 1990, the influence of congressional mandates for concentrated attention to pregnant women and infants caused the perinatal stage to preoccupy the outreach activities of state governments, with little time or resources left for programs aimed at young children. Officials in 13 states noted that outreach and marketing efforts had been focusing almost exclusively on persuading pregnant women to seek prenatal care assistance. Exacerbating this problem was the permission granted to providers to bill against a mother's Medicaid ID number any services rendered the infant just after birth and causing the parent(s), providers, and others not to become conscious of the fact that new Medicaid eligibility for the infant needed to be established.[87]

Physical Access. This problem has been somewhat less severe in scope than in prenatal care because of the range of young child care services available from general practitioners and from community and migrant health centers. Pediatric care, in contrast to OB-GYN care, had been more often available in the small health centers. Many community health centers grew out of neighborhood health centers initiated and supported as part of the economic opportunity initiatives under the War on Poverty program of the late 1960s and early 1970s. As of 1991 it was estimated that 550 grantees were operating nearly 2,000 clinics but serving only 6 million of the 32 million medically underserved persons.[88] The Children's Defense Fund stated in its 1991 report on the *State of America's Children* that these health centers were a "highly effective but seriously underfunded federal program" and were serving nearly 6 million low-income patients a year, with a third being under 14. The fund estimated that the existing and projected centers would be able to serve about 20 percent of all people living in medically underserved areas.[89]

Financial Access. As shown in Appendix 3.D, minimum Medicaid eligibility levels were mandated, becoming effective beginning in 1990, to cover children below the age of 6 in households with incomes less than 133 percent of the federal poverty figure, with coverage stepping up a year at a time until age 19. As of January 1990 a sizable number of states had gone beyond the mandates of 1985, 1986, and 1987 and had already begun to phase in requirements above and beyond those later mandated by Congress in 1989 for children below age 7. The 1990–91 recession, however, caused many states to tighten their budgets and complain ever more vigorously about unfunded federal mandates. Nevertheless, by mid-1992, 31 states and the District of Columbia had expanded coverage of pregnant women and infants above the mandated 133 percent of poverty; several states had extended these expansions beyond infants (e.g., Delaware—up to age 18; Maine—through 19 up to 125 percent of the poverty level (PL); Minnesota—below age 18, up to 185%; Wisconsin—age 2 to age 5, up to 155%).[90]

As in perinatal care, eligibility needed to be established or reestablished for infants of mothers covered during the perinatal period. Consequently, Medicaid has been the major source of financial coverage for young children in low-income households. More difficult is the case of working mothers earning too much to qualify for Medicaid but not enough to afford private health insurance or to take the preventive steps necessary for a healthy childhood. In these instances the individual must turn to state or local health or welfare agencies or to private charity for free or discounted health service. In any case, the mother in such circumstances often tends to be reluctant to visit a physician until or unless the child becomes noticeably ill.[91]

Access to Health Care Professionals. The ACSS report pointed out:

From 1975 through 1988, the number of active physicians engaged in primary care has increased dramatically. Despite this increase, some 360,000 people live in the 221 counties that have no physicians whatsoever, and substantially larger numbers live in counties containing only one or two physicians. Typically, the per capita income in these counties is low . . . in almost 90 percent of the counties having no physicians, per capita income is below the national average.[92]

In contrast to widespread reluctance and downright refusal of OB-GYN specialists to participate in Medicaid-funded perinatal services, particularly through fear of malpractice litigation, Medicaid and MCH administrators were having quite good relations with the pediatric segment of the health care system in the early 1990s.

Surveys and studies by the National Governors' Association (NGA) and the American Academy of Pediatrics found declining proportions of pediatricians willing to treat all Medicaid beneficiaries requesting care—dropping from 85 to 77 percent. But in NGA's 1990 Survey of State Children's Health Initiatives, malpractice liability was perceived as a significant participation drawback in only three states, compared with inadequate fees in 36 states; excess paperwork in 30; client problems in 21; and delayed payments in 14. In another encouraging contrast with perinatal care, the willingness of pediatricians to care for low-income populations seemed to be much greater than that of obstetricians.[93]

EPSDT: Early and Periodic Screening, Diagnosis, and Treatment

The Committee on Practice and Ambulatory Medicine of the American Academy of Pediatrics in a September 1987 report issued recommendations for a preventive pediatric health care schedule, the key parts of which were visits for physical examinations, monthly during infancy; at 15, 18, and 24 months; annually at ages 3 through 6; and biennially until adulthood. Immunizations were to occur at 2, 4, 6, 15, 18, and 24 months and at age 5.[94]

Within the Medicaid financing structure, a program was established by PL 90–248 in 1967 for early and periodic screening, diagnosis, and treatment (EPSDT), specifically designed to permit the delivery of comprehensive preventive pediatric care to Medicaid-eligible children. A congressional mandate for its expansion was enacted in 1989. Despite its obvious health, economic, and fiscal advantages, participation rates were low during the 1967–89 period, with only about one out of five eligible children receiving EPSDT services, representing only 1 percent of state Medicaid budgets.

Major barriers to access and use of EPDST services appear to have been (1) entanglement in the whole Medicaid eligibility process; (2) procedural difficulty in directing and quality-monitoring an integrated system through individual private providers in separate specialties under Medicaid reimbursement; (3) fiscal-political difficulties in going step-by-step in an expensive case management approach, using state public health personnel; (4) difficulty in linking treatment with screening and the diagnosis and resulting recommendations; and (5) reaching and convincing parent(s) of young children to adhere to a preventive care program, rather than waiting for crises.[95]

Immunization

In contrast to the progress in extending life expectancy and reducing death rates and in several other quantifiable segments of young child health care, rates of immunization against childhood diseases were in alarming decline in the 1980s. The NCC reported:

Even though most communicable diseases can be prevented with immunizations, thousands of American children are not immunized. In 1979 the Surgeon General set the goal of immunizing 90 percent of two-year olds against common childhood diseases by 1990. Yet in 1990 only about 70 percent were immunized against measles, mumps, and rubella. In many inner cities only about half of these young children were protected. Recent information concerning immunization rates for other communicable diseases, including polio and whopping cough, are unavailable because *the federal government suspended data collection in 1985*. Nevertheless, many experts fear that immunization rates for these diseases are also low. . . . Failure to immunize children has resulted in measles outbreaks in many U.S. cities. . . . In 1990 more than 26,000 cases of measles were reported, a huge increase over the average of 3,000 cases a year between 1981 and 1988. Most were among children in poor, inner-city families. . . . Cases of rubella and whooping cough have also increased, and many experts express concern that serious outbreaks of these and other preventable diseases may follow.[96]

The minority chapter on health care in the commission's report commented:

Some observers cite federal cutbacks as the primary reason for failure to vaccinate young children. But it is at least as likely that in taking responsibility for these decisions away from parents, public health officials have unintentionally diminished the need for parents to act responsibly. . . . Well-intended plans that reduce parents' primary responsibility for the immunization of their children may unintentionally . . . discourage individual initiative and healthful behaviors.[97]

In light of cessation of regular reporting of vaccination data and the substitution of sporadic sample surveys, Table 3.7 contains no post–1985 information but shows 1970–85 trends.

In October 1991, the World Health Organization (WHO) announced that 80 percent of the world's children had been vaccinated against the diseases listed in Table 3.7, except for mumps. WHO data showed, for measles among one-year-olds, rates of 87 and 98 percent for India and China, respectively. For continents, the measles vaccination rates were Asia, 86; Americas, 82; Europe, 80; and Africa, 58. In early 1991, a USPHS Centers for Disease Control (CDC) survey of nine large U.S. cities found immunization rates for two-year-olds, having received 4- and 3-doses, respectively, ranging from a low of 10–40 percent in Houston to 42–61 percent in New Orleans. More or less concurrently, 28,000 cases of measles were reported for 1990—more than 18 times the number

Table 3.7
Vaccinations of Children Age 1–4 for Selected Diseases, by Race and Residence for 1970, 1976, and 1985 (in percents of population in age group)

Vaccinations and Year	Total	Race White	Other	Inside CC	MSA's OCC	Outside MSA
Measles:						
1970	57.2	60.4	41.9	55.2	61.7	54.3
1976	65.9	68.3	54.8	62.5	67.2	67.3
1985	60.8	63.6	48.8	55.5	63.3	61.9
Rubella						
1970	37.2	38.3	31.8	38.3	39.2	34.3
1976	61.7	63.8	51.5	59.5	63.5	61.3
1985	58.9	61.6	47.7	53.9	61.0	60.3
DTP*						
1970	76.1	79.7	58.8	68.9	80.7	77.1
1976	71.4	75.3	53.2	64.1	75.7	72.9
1985	64.9	68.7	48.7	55.5	68.4	67.9
Polio						
1970	65.9	69.2	50.1	61.0	70.8	64.7
1976	61.6	66.2	39.9	53.8	65.3	63.9
1985	55.3	58.9	40.1	47.1	58.4	58.0
Mumps						
1970	----	----	----	----	----	----
1976	48.3	50.3	38.7	45.6	50.7	47.9
1985	58.9	61.9	47.0	52.4	61.0	61.4

MSA's = Metropolitan Statistical Areas
CC = Central City
OCC = Outside Central City
*DPT = Diphtheria-tetanus-pertussis. Three doses or more.

Sources: 1970-85 data from *Health USA 1990*. Table 42. 1990,107.

of 1983 and more than 50 times the goal of 500 cases annually that the U.S. surgeon general had set for 1990.[98]

In contrast to the shockingly disparate immunization rates between the United States and other continents, including Third World countries, by the time American children enter school, most have been immunized through a combination of Head Start, day-care centers, and other sources. WHO and national officials in poorer countries carry on aggressive campaigns to eradicate childhood diseases completely. In New York City only 40 percent of children had completed their vaccination series by age 1, compared with 89, 77, and 76 percent by age 21, respectively, in Algeria, El Salvador, and Uganda. The low level of immunization among poor preschoolers was causing measles epidemics in Chicago, Houston, and Los Angeles and in New York State and New Jersey in the early 1990s, according to state and local health authorities.[99]

Clearly, USPHS data services and state-local public health regulations and activities were highly deficient in the early 1990s concerning immunization of very young children against the dangerous childhood diseases. The Children's Defense Fund in its 1991 report stated, under the heading of "A Collapsing Public Health System:"

In the case of vaccines, maintaining the public health system means having an adequate supply of vaccines and enough health providers to deliver them. But since the early 1980s, the vaccine system has collapsed. The National Vaccine Advisory Committee, a congressionally mandated body of experts that advises the U.S. Department of Health and Human Services on vaccine policy, recently reported that the principal cause of the current national measles epidemic (and other epidemics of preventable childhood illnesses that may be looming on the horizon) is "failure to deliver vaccines to vulnerable preschool children on schedule."[100]

Accidents, Safety Precautions, and Violence

Accidents, excluding those from motor vehicles, comprised the leading cause of deaths in 1988 and apparently also in 1990, both for the 1–4 and 5–14 age groups. Motor vehicle accidents alone were the second leading cause for both age groups. Homicide and legal intervention ranked fourth after the two accident categories and malignant neoplasms. Suicide was one of the 10 leading causes in the 5–19 group.

The House Select Committee on Children, Youth, and Families in its 1990 report summarized the childhood injury situation as follows:

The cost of these deaths and injuries for children ages birth to 15 are estimated to exceed $14 billion annually in direct medical expenditures, long-term care and lost productivity due to premature death. . . . Injury has surpassed diseases as the leading cause of childhood mortality and disability. Minority and low-income children are at greatest risk of accidental injury and death [African-American death rates are twice the white rate].

A 1987 survey of state health agencies found that only 10 had comprehensive injury prevention programs. Most devoted less than one-half of 1 percent of the state's annual health department budget to injury prevention.[101]

For motor vehicle accidents, the respective 1990 death rates for the 1–4 and 5–14 age groups were: all races, 6.3 and 5.9. For 1988 the rates by race and sex were: white males, 6.9 and 8.7; black males, 9.2 and 9.5; white females, 6.2 and 5.2; and black females, 7.5 and 5.6.[102] The congressional OTA reported in 1988 that although all states at that time had laws requiring infant or child restraints, 38 had no restraint requirements applicable over age 5 and many others with no restraints over age 3 or 4.[103]

Household hazards that harm or kill thousands of children each year include exposure to lead, dilapidated (and thus dangerous) housing, passive smoking, and careless handling of medicines, household cleaning agents, and other chemicals. For low-income children living in substandard housing, these risks are multiplied many times over.[104] Of these, lead poisoning is especially widespread and is considered to be among the most preventable of childhood afflictions. It causes decreased intelligence, developmental disturbances, and behavioral disorders. Screening is essential to detect elevated blood levels, as these effects may occur in children who show no obvious signs of lead poisoning. It was estimated that from 3 to 4 million preschool children have blood levels above the level associated with the onset of early detectable adverse effects, and 400,000 infants are born with toxic blood lead levels every year. Investigations at the beginning of the 1990s found rates of 20 percent and higher in some urban areas. State regulation and requirements for lead screening were far from comprehensive.[105]

Concentrated attention to violence and the threat/fear of violence and to suicide is undertaken in the next major section, which deals with adolescent health. These tendencies appear well before age 15. The death rate for suicide in the 5–14 age group stood at zero in the 1950s and 1960s, appearing first at 0.2 (per 100,000 age group population) and holding at that level through 1987 but rising to 0.5 in 1988. White and black female rates were 0.4 and 0.5; and for white and black males, 1.1 and 0.6. For homicide during infancy, the rate of 4.4 in 1950 gradually rose to 5.9 in 1980 to 8.2 in 1988 (for the most part presumably committed by a parent, as the extreme form of child abuse).[106]

Chronic Disease and Physical Disability

Children with a wide range of disabling or potentially disabling conditions have routine health care needs like those of other children. In addition, they also usually require specialized diagnostic and therapeutic care, medical and surgical care, and home care. They may also need special educational, vocational, and family services. The physical and financial burdens of their care and sometimes its lack of availability at any cost jeopardize their health and constitute an overwhelming family burden.

Particularly troubling in the early 1990s have been the following problems: AIDS-infected and drug-addicted children those with chronic afflictions, with death rates for the two age groups from malignancies at 3.7 and 3.2 and from heart diseases at 2.4 and 0.9; prevalent infectious diseases, such as repeated ear infections (experienced by 28–29% of the 1–4 and 5–11 age groups as of 1988); repeated tonsillitis (by 5 and 14%); and pneumonia (by 5 and 7%).[107] For all children under 18, AIDS cases numbered: 1984—50; 1987—321; 1989—605. For deaths from AIDS: 1984—49; 1987—260; 1989—295. Total cases and deaths, respectively, for all ages, numbered: 1984—4,436, 3,276; 1987—21,114, 14,710; 1989—33,710, 22,616.[108] The helpless children born infected with the HIV virus constitute probably the most tragic aspect of this global catastrophe, although the contracting of the virus by adolescents, discussed in the next section, is equally, if not more, tragic in ultimate national consequences.

A 1990 study by the National Governors' Association of home care options for disabled children estimated the scope and intensity of disability among children thus:

Nationwide, children with severe chronic physical or mental illnesses number about 2 million. Of these, approximately 500,000 are impaired so severely that they are unable to participate in major life activities, which for young children generally includes attending school. Chronically ill children are intensive users of health care services and, on average, their annual health care costs are three times those of healthy children.[109]

Securing medical attention to chronically ill or physically handicapped children in the 1–4 age group faces the earlier discussed barriers in the health care system and parental behavioral lapses. Financial assistance to lower-income blind and disabled children (under the Supplemental Security Income provisions of the Social Security Act) has been subject to numerous delays and to under-enrollment due to lack of information and outreach about its existence and eligibility conditions.[110] Child-care centers are able to provide or arrange attention to apparently ill toddlers and others too young for nursery school, Head Start, or other preschool programs. Once into such a preschool setting, access to appropriate health care— at least to and through the testing and diagnostic phase—becomes easier. But for treatment, especially the kind that requires repeated visits or hospital admission, the financial and other access barriers reappear. The same general situation prevails through the elementary and middle school years but varies among school districts and local government jurisdictions, depending upon the scope and concentration with which public health services are delivered at, or under the aegis of, public and private school authorities.

Mental Health and Learning Disability

According to estimates of the USPHS, the congressional Office of Technology Assessment (OTA), and others, the incidence of mental health disorders sufficiently serious to warrant treatment, including autism and depression, among the nation's children in the early 1990s, was at least 10 percent of the child population, or about 6.5 million.[111] These mental health data include a substantial number of adolescents suffering severe emotional problems arising from environmental, economic, and social factors particularly pertinent to the teenage and young adult age group. The NCC emphasized:

Children with mental health problems require special care. Yet many of these children do not receive the full range of services they need to treat their problems and enable them to lead better and richer lives. Traditional psychotherapy is often unavailable to children in low-income families. Even if ... available, it is typically isolated from other health, education, and social services that these children ... need. Fragmentation often renders these services less useful and less effective than they might otherwise be.[112]

Learning Disability. Beginning in the 1960s, national and state governments and local school districts began to give increased attention and support to the provision of special education to pupils suffering from varying degrees of learning difficulty and to establish separate classes and schools for these children. These steps were dedicated to the objectives of either (1) preparing the child to reenter the regular classroom (''mainstreaming'') as soon as appropriate or (2) educating the child to his or her maximum potential in terms of being able to survive and function in society, with permanent institutionalization only as a last resort.

By 1991, a growing proportion of learning-disabled pupils in preschool, kindergarten, and first grade were ''crack's children,'' whose bodies and minds had developed in wombs contaminated with crack cocaine. A newspaper staff writer described the school environment in striking terms:

There is the little boy who is unable to sit still for more than a few minutes. He fidgets in his seat so feverishly that his desk is out of position with its row. ... Another child has such problems controlling his hands that he sometimes drops his face into his plate ... picking up spoon or fork is too taxing. ... The vast majority of these children ... share textbooks and lunchrooms with other students. [The unaffected students] will suffer as their teachers become preoccupied with the crack-affected youngsters' overwhelming problems.

The New York State comptroller was reported as estimating that in nine years there would be about 72,000 children in New York City who had been exposed to crack in the womb. Similar problems and magnitudes over the 1986–91 time period were reported for Los Angeles, Miami, Houston, Boston, and other cities.[113]

Barriers to Mental Health and Learning Disability Services. In addition to lack of adequate prenatal testing of expectant mothers, the shortage of drug treatment slots for them, and the failure to acquire EPSDT (early and periodic screening, diagnosis, and treatment), several other weaknesses pervaded the health care system and the state, local, and school system processes as they apply to mental health and learning disability. In the various contexts of the foregoing cited references, these problems can be summarized as follows:

- Isolation of mental health services from general health, child welfare, and other social services, with consequent unnecessary paperwork in Medicaid eligibility establishment.

- An inappropriate and expensive ''tilt'' toward institutionalization arising from the fact of easier financial and other access in qualifying for inpatient treatment, in contrast to individual counseling, outpatient treatment, and other noninstitutional alternatives.

- Necessity for a complex federal waiver procedure for the use of Medicaid funds for home care, especially the calculation of such costs and their relation to estimated total institutional costs and the Medicaid share thereof.

- A large underserved or nonserved population (estimated by OTA and the National Conference of State Legislatures [NCSL] at one-half to two-thirds of those needing service.
- A growing incidence of prenatal, drug-induced child learning disability for school systems to handle.

Nutrition and Hunger

Estimates of the number of children who experience hunger have ranged from 2 million to 5.5 million. These relate closely to the high rates of childhood poverty. Nutritional problems, most prominently iron deficiency anemia, are associated frequently with poverty.[114] According to a 1991 study by the Congressional Research Service (CRS) of the Library of Congress on issues and funding associated with the WIC supplemental food program, about 4.5 million persons and almost one-third of all infants in the country were being served by the program. Since program eligibility in terms of family incomes was standing at 185 percent of the federal poverty level, the coverage appeared to be nearly complete for infants. Unlike many other domestic social programs, WIC grew continuously during the 1980s. Service priority of the program had always been focused on pregnant women and infants with poor health conditions. Despite the nearly complete coverage of eligible infants, the CRS study estimated that only about half the eligible children ages one to five and their mothers were being served.[115]

The WIC program is entirely federally funded, with no state or local government matching required; separate federal grants are provided to the states for administrative costs in handling the program. Such grants are made from the initial appropriation, and the remainder of each state's allocation goes to cover food costs. The food grant is divided into two parts, the first being the amount necessary, after inflation, to maintain the previous year's caseload and the other part going toward meeting total needs. Total need comprises the state's arithmetic portion of the national total of (1) all women, infants, and children with family incomes below 185 percent of poverty; (2) infant mortality; and (3) low-weight births. Although the WIC program has had strong bipartisan support in the Congress, each year's funding in the late 1980s and early 1990s was falling short of total needs, due to annual pressures to reduce the federal deficit expressed at the reconciliation stage of the congressional budget process.

In fiscal year (FY) 1990 the program was operating out of 8,330 clinics and serving a monthly average of 4.5 million persons; 23 percent of those were women, 31 percent infants, and 46 percent children age one to five. More than two-thirds of those served were below the federal poverty level, although 46 of the 51 states and the District of Columbia had set 185 percent of the poverty level as the maximum income permitted for eligibility. The CRS study noted that no data had been available from the Agriculture Department on the health circumstances of WIC participants, rendering somewhat murky the estimates of proportions of eligibles being served.[116]

Not surprisingly, a less optimistic picture of proportions of eligibles being served by the WIC program than that postulated by the CRS study and by the U.S. Department of Agriculture and of the incidence of hunger among the U.S. population came from a 1989–90, prerecession study conducted by the Food Research and Action Center, a nonprofit antihunger advocacy group. The study comprised a sample of over 2,300 low-income households in seven localities and produced an overall estimate of 5.5 million hungry children under age 12. The projected proportion of eligibles being served by the program was 45 percent. Among the WIC participating families interviewed, almost one-third said they were hungry.[117]

Major weaknesses in the program, in addition to an uncertain year-to-year fiscal base, maintenance of adequate data, and administrative complexities involved, such as the required recertification of program eligibility of children every six months between the age of infancy and termination at the fifth birthday, appeared to lie in the nutrition education phase and ensuing client behaviors. In light of the increasing importance of motivation and other client characteristics, a key weakness on the nutrition front may be the lack of outreach programs (stopped for food stamps in 1981) to inform and convince eligible parent(s) of the availability of food stamp and WIC programs. In terms of nutrition content, the law establishing the WIC program required that foods being provided contain protein, iron, calcium, vitamin A, and vitamin C. In addition to food benefits, recipients also must receive nutrition education.[118] Seemingly, nutrition education falls on the deaf ears of many young children and their parent(s), especially those in low-income households. A *Wall Street Journal* story quoted comments from Dr. Harold Freeman, chief of surgery at a Harlem hospital and former president of the American Cancer Society, who had heard a cancer patient say she was eating "soul food most every day including pigs feet, pork rinds and fried chicken." Dr. Freeman observed: "This is a pervasive problem in poor America, especially poor black America. This is the way people eat." The Reverend Jesse Jackson commented, "Low-income Americans, with a certain desperation that there might not be any more food tomorrow, are eating themselves to death." Then HHS secretary Louis Sullivan, in the same story, said: "We have to develop better strategies to get the nutrition message across. This is a very serious problem and one that isn't really recognized as such."[119]

Child Behavior and Life-style

The NCC in its 1991 report stated:

Childhood is an important time to promote health and prevent disease. Because lifestyles formed in childhood and adolescence can last a lifetime, early positive influences can have long-term beneficial effects on health. And it is easier both to establish healthful habits and to prevent the formation of unhealthful habits early in life. The . . . Commission concurs with the Surgeon General and other[s] . . . that improving children's health is a widely shared responsibility. Parents must take responsibility for promoting healthful lifestyles at home. . . . Others in the community . . . must also help children form attitudes and develop behaviors and lifestyles that will protect their health during childhood . . . and they must help ensure that essential health services are available.[120]

Too often, alternation of adult life-styles in order to provide better role models for young children in the preadolescent stage of development, although necessary and helpful, still is insufficient to convince the child to avoid harmful habits, because neighborhood environments and peer pressures can be extremely strong. Discipline, household management, and skill in arousing and holding the love and companionability of the growing child are also necessary.

Parenting Skills. An increasingly critical segment of child welfare and health services in the early 1990s was the larger proportion of households with young children who were being classified as vulnerable or "at risk." The growing multiplicity of, and interrelationships among, economic, health, and social ills converging upon the developing child were becoming apparent, and the increasing incidence of teenage motherhood demonstrated conclusively that many adolescents and young adult women were becoming mothers with little understanding of the responsibilities involved. Beginning in the early 1980s, efforts were initiated to bring together the skills, disciplines, and agencies that could begin at the prenatal period and continue to assist the household for so long as the mother and/or growing child continued to be seriously at risk. Consequently, help during the prenatal period expanded beyond the medical and health aspects to embrace counseling the parent(s)-to-be on their imminent new responsibilities. This became known as "parenting," and the major delivery method for the multidisciplinary service became known as "home visiting."

More than 4,500 programs have been identified that employ home visiting to provide health, social, or educational services to families. These programs are universally available in many European countries as an integral part of the health care delivery system. They have a variety of goals; what unites them is the process of delivery. Using home health aides, trained community workers, paraprofessionals, and nurses, home visiting programs have begun to address a myriad of issues that keep families from obtaining adequate care. These programs also have been useful in reducing child abuse and neglect.[121]

A 1990 report by the GAO focused on home visiting as a means of delivering early intervention services to at-risk families with young children, such as parenting education, home-based preschool, and referrals to other agencies and services. The GAO study leading to the report included (1) review of the home visiting literature; (2) interviews with medical, educational, and social service agencies and various researchers in the field; and (3) review of eight programs in the United States, United Kingdom, and Denmark that used home visiting.

The GAO report concluded, "Home visiting is a promising strategy for delivering or improving access to early intervention services that can help at-risk families become healthier and more self-sufficient." But it went on to say that "the cost-effectiveness of home visiting, compared to other strategies . . . has not been well researched."[122]

Home visiting, by its nature, is labor-intensive and involves much lower caseloads than where clients must visit agency offices. The GAO review of evaluations of several programs showed that not all programs using home visiting had been successful. The causes for lack of success included (1) failure to use objectives to guide the program and its services; (2) poorly designed and structured services; (3) insufficient training and supervision of home visitors; and (4) inability to provide or access the range of services multiproblem families need because the program was not linked to other community services.[123]

Community and Media Responsibilities

The NCC emphasized in its report that to fulfill their responsibilities for promoting and protecting their children's health, parents need support from their communities and that just to grow up, "children need to live in environments where they are physically safe and can feel secure that they will not be harmed by adults or other children. Communities have a basic responsibility to create and maintain safe environments for all their residents."[124]

The commission also pointed out that

children are exposed to countless media messages that affect decisions about health. [Positive] messages come from news, documentary, and public affairs programs. Indirect but equally powerful messages are contained in advertising, the plots of television shows, and the lyrics of rock music. These . . . are not always benign. . . . The media, especially television, are major purveyors of popular culture. Most American children spend more time watching television than attending school. . . . Pervasive images of crime, violence and sexuality expose children to situations and problems [that often conflict with the common values of our society].[125]

ADOLESCENT HEALTH CARE

For most growing children, the adolescent years are highly determinative and predictive of future personal physical and mental health. Personal habits and life-styles are formed and, once formed, are difficult to change. They are stressful, painful, and very difficult years. They became more so for American children in the post–World War II period and by the early 1990s had become highly volatile.

The National Commission on Children (NCC) stated:

In adolescence, young people assume increasing responsibility for their own behavior. Yet during this period, parents have a major role to play in guiding their children toward wise choices. They also should monitor their teenagers' behavior to help them avoid risks that can have devastating short and long-term health consequences, including premature and unprotected sexual activity, smoking, alcohol and drug use, unsafe driving and delinquent behavior.[126]

Many at-risk adolescents are in that category because of not a single problem but a variety of interlocking ones: alcohol/drug abuse, poor school performance or dropout, promiscuous sexual activity, and others. The Carnegie Council on Adolescent Development (CCAD) found in 1989 that a sizeable number of American children of high school age were seriously at risk. Subsequent to several working papers and follow-up studies, the CCAD held a national conference in Washington, DC, called "Crossroads: Critical Choices for the Development of Healthy Adolescents." Some of the critical conditions examined were (1) many adolescents live in one-parent families, many of them poor or near poor (20, 50, and 30%, respectively, of white, black, and Hispanic adolescents); (2) by age 16, 17, and 29 percent of girls and boys had had sexual intercourse; (3) between 1960 and 1988, gonorrhea had increased 4 times among adolescents age 10–14; and (4) American adolescents were 15 times more likely than their English counterparts to die from homicide.[127] This would mean that up to one half of adolescent youth in the United States were in a health/education danger zone or on the verge of it as the mid-1990s neared.

The nature and magnitude of each of these health hazards and others are examined here, and the education ones subsequently. First, morbidity, and other quantitative data as to the overall health picture for adolescents are reviewed, followed by consideration of the major problem areas: (1) sexual activity and the hazards of sexually transmitted diseases (STDs), pregnancy, and AIDS; (2) teenage pregnancy and the agonizing choices of abortion, carrying to term, and adoption; (3) drug and alcohol abuse, smoking, and other unhealthy life-styles; (4) antisocial behavior, violence, and crime; and (5) the drug-alcohol-violence connection.

Overall Health and Mortality Rates

The overall mortality rate in 1991 for adolescents and young adults (15–24) was 107.1 per 100,000 resident population, and increase from 104.1 in 1990. The five leading death rates, by cause, were (1) accidents with a motor vehicle (33.9), (2) homicide and legal intervention (24.1), (3) suicide (13.8), (4) accidents other than motor vehicle (11.2), and (5) malignant neoplasms (5.8). A disturbing aspect was the comparative male-female death rates. These were, for the age group population as a whole, 160.8 and 52.2, respectively, or a ratio of slightly over 3 males to 1 female; for whites, the ratio was 3 to 1 (142.7 and 48.2), and for blacks, 3.6 to 1 (277.1 and 77.3). For all ages and races, the comparative 1991 rates were 909.1 and 801.6; whites, 924.3 and 837.6; and blacks 961.5 and 721.3.[128]

Most of the male-female disparity is found in the first four of the leading causes of death. The respective male-female rates for those causes in the 15–24 age group in 1988 were: motor vehicle accidents, 51.3 and 22.6; other accidents, 15.8 and 2.8; homicide, 18.8 and 4.4; suicide, 18.0 and 4.4; and malignant neoplasms, 5.2 and 3.6. By race for males, the 1988 rates for whites and blacks for motor vehicle accidents were 56.3 and 28.9; other accidents, 15.5 and 17.0; homicide, 8.1 and 77.4; suicide, 19.6 and 9.7; and malignant neoplasms, 5.3 and 5.0.[129]

In terms of mortality rates, if one sets aside the nondisease categories (accident, homicide, and suicide causes) and AIDS, the survival rates for adolescent youth can be viewed as good, with gradual further improvement. This is due in part to improved medical technology and the one-half or more of the adolescent population that appeared to be receptive to warnings and urging from parent(s), teachers, and the media/public opinion on the desirability of healthy food and habits, indicated by declines in cigarette smoking. But longer-term survival, life expectancy, and a healthy and productive adulthood are threatened from several sides.

Earlier and Increased Adolescent Sexual Activity

Increased sexual activity involves the adolescent in three risks—pregnancy of the female, contraction of one of the sexually transmitted diseases (STDs), and infection with the HIV virus, with consequent illness and death from AIDS.

National health objectives for the year 2000, promulgated by the USPHS, included efforts to reduce the proportion of adolescents who have engaged in sexual intercourse to no less than 15 percent by age 15 and less than 40 percent by age 17. The USPHS estimated in early 1992 that to reach these objectives, the percentage of students who report ever having had sexual intercourse will have to be reduced substantially, and the percentage of sexually active students who use contraception will have to increase by 16 percent.[130]

Incidence of Adolescent Sexual Activity. Some progress toward the above objectives was reported in the CDC's Youth Risk Behavior System, which periodically measures the prevalence of priority health-risk behaviors among youth through comparable national, state, and local surveys. In 1990, a three-stage sample design was used to obtain a representative sample of over 11,000 students in grades 9–12 from the 50 states, District of Columbia, and the territories. Students were asked if they had ever had sexual intercourse and if they had had intercourse during the three months preceding the survey. The results of the survey are summarized in Table 3.8 below.

Avoidance of Pregnancy and Teenage Motherhood. The socioeconomic impact of unmarried motherhood was discussed earlier. One of the health/education goals of the USPHS has been to reduce pregnancies among girls 17 and under to no more than 50 per 1,000. This proceeded from a base of 71.1 pregnancies per 1,000 girls in 1985.[131]

Table 3.8
Percentage of High School Students Reporting Having Had Sexual Intercourse,*
by Sex, Race/Ethnic Origin (EO), and School Grade, 1990**

Category	Ever Had Intercourse			Intercourse During Past Three Months		
	Total	Female	Male	Total	Female	Male
Race & EO						
White	51.6	47.0	56.4	38.0	37.1	39.0
Black	72.3	60.0	87.8	53.9	42.3	68.1
Hispanic	53.4	45.0	63.0	37.5	31.4	44.6
Grade						
9th	39.6	31.9	48.7	24.7	20.8	29.1
10th	47.6	42.9	52.5	34.3	32.4	36.4
11th	57.3	52.7	62.6	43.1	41.3	45.1
12th	71.9	66.6	76.3	55.0	52.7	56.9
Total	54.2	48.0	60.8	39.4	36.4	42.5

Notes: *Ever, and during the three months preceding the survey.
   **Unweighted sample size = 11,631 students.
   Due to self-reporting basis, confidence interval varied; range of plus or minus 2.1 percent for
   total female response on preceding 3 months to 6.9 per cent for 10th grade male response on "ever
   had."

Source: Centers for Disease Control (CDC) Youth Risk Behavior Survey 1990 as reported in CDC,
Morbidity and Mortality Weekly Report, 40 (51, 52), January 3, 1992, Table 1, 886.

The need for unmarried teenagers to avoid pregnancy has been recognized
widely in the United States, both by those who, on the basis of moral values or
religious belief, urge abstention as the only course and by others who urge either
abstinence or contraception. Charles Murray stated the socioeconomic basis for
pregnancy avoidance:

If you follow a set of modest requirements, you are almost surely going to avoid poverty.
... For women, one option is to get an education, acquire skills, and get a job. . . .
Another option is to marry a man who will be a good and conscientious provider. . . .
Whatever else she does: A poor woman who wishes to get out of poverty ought not to
have a baby out of wedlock. This is not a moral statement but an empirical one.[132]

Likewise, the Children's Defense Fund noted: "In the decades before 1970,
teen parents were likely to be married, and the father was likely to be employed
or to have reasonable prospects of earning a wage enough to support a family.
Today a teenage mother is likely to be unmarried, and both she and her child
are very likely to live in poverty."[133]

Teenage youth obviously are not abstaining from unmarried sexual activity, as the preceding data have indicated. Here, the extent to which contraception is utilized to avoid pregnancy is noted. The CDC survey ascertained the extent to which contraceptives were being used in 1990 on the occasion of the last previous intercourse. Overall, three-fourths of the students (77.7%) reported such use (+ or −2.5%), equally divided between male and female. Four-fifths of the white females reported similar use, in contrast to 71 percent for black and 63 percent for Hispanic females. Given the self-reporting nature of the survey on an intimate topic, one might expect some exaggeration in stated usage; in any case, the survey results fell considerably below the USPHS goal of 90 percent usage (up from 78% in 1985).[134]

A substantial proportion of teenage pregnancies are terminated by abortion. For females in the below age 15 group, the number of abortions per 100 live births fluctuated from a 1 to 1 ratio (101.5) in 1975, up to 1.5 to 1 (145.8) in 1984, and back to 1 to 1 in 1988 (101.7). For the 15–19 age group, the rate per 100 live births stood at 46.4 in 1975, 71.4 in 1984, and 69.9 in 1988.[135]

Sexually Transmitted Diseases (STDs) and AIDS. As of 1990, 86 percent of all STDs were occurring in the 15–19 age group.[136] The principal diseases in this group are gonorrhea, syphilis, and genital herpes. The first two are "notifiable" under public health laws (i.e., must be reported by physicians to vital statistics or public health authorities). Genital herpes, the most prevalent, is not. The incidence of gonorrhea and syphilis varied greatly over the 1950–85 period, with the former more than tripling and the latter decreasing by a third in overall numbers; 1990 rates per 100,000 of the total population were 276.6 for the former and 53.8 for the latter, with a comparable HIV infection rate of 16.7. The syphilis rate increased from 32.0 in 1981 to 53.8 in 1990. For the adolescent age groups, in 1990 the numbers and rates for gonorrhea and syphilis, respectively, were: for the 10–14 group—11,020 (64.6) and 303 (1.8); for the 15–19 group—183,865 (1,028.3) and 5,184 (28.7). For all age groups, the CDC reported for gonorrhea a national total of 690,169, with 94,416 for white non-Hispanic, 550,112 for blacks, 26,037 for Hispanics, and 5,487 for other races; in 14,117 other reported cases race was not stated.[137]

The Children's Defense Fund noted that for teenagers, the 1989 rate was 1,123 for every 100,000 adolescents 15 to 19. Experts had reported a rate for black males at 15 times that for whites, and for females the comparable ratio was 10 to 1.[138] In the CDC student survey, 4 percent reported having had an STD. According to the report, black students (8.4%) were significantly more likely than white (3.1%) or Hispanic (3.5%) students to report having had an STD. Among then currently sexually active students 49.4 percent of males and 40 percent of females reported that they or their partner used a condom during the last preceding intercourse.[139]

In reporting the preceding data, the CDC stated: "Two of the national health objectives are to increase the use of condoms to 60–75% among sexually active, unmarried persons aged 15–19 during last sexual intercourse. To reach these objectives sexually active students must increase their use of condoms by 50%.''[140]

The Children's Defense Fund noted that a high teenage rate of STD infection indicated widespread unprotected intercourse with more than one partner, a behavioral pattern bound to raise the chances of HIV infection and consequent AIDS. Final 1988 morbidity data had shown that one-third of young women ages 15 to 19 reported using no protection during their first intercourse.[141]

From the foregoing it can be concluded that:

- Increased sexual activity among teenagers has serious health implications.
- Without either abstention, precautions, or a highly unlikely long-term independent source of income, the results for unmarried teenagers are either increased abortion rates or lifelong socioeconomic consequences, to say nothing of the cost and care implications for the public health system and for federal, state, and local government treasuries and taxpayers.

In sum, serious gaps in private behavior and public policy in these areas were extant and widening in the early 1990s.

Drug and Alcohol Abuse

The very serious threat of these two addictive categories to healthy adolescent development was aptly summarized in a Rand Corporation study published in 1990:

Drug use among teenagers is a cause of major national concern. It not only threatens the health, safety, and development of the nation's young people, it also jeopardizes their future functioning as adults. The business of adolescence is development, that is, acquiring the coping skills that are critical for becoming healthy, productive adults. The changes that adolescents go through—cognitive, emotional, social and physical—are an integral part of the process. However, drug use can push this process off track, interfering with motivation and ability to learn, to finish school, to hold a job, or eventually to maintain a stable marriage. Moreover, the earlier young people start using drugs, the longer the period during which they are at risk of damage and the more likely that use will become abuse.[142]

The report went on to delineate among addictive drugs, between the "gateway" drugs—alcohol, cigarettes, and marijuana—and the hard drugs—cocaine/ crack, heroin, and others. Cigarette smoking is discussed later; although eventually life-threatening, nicotine is not a mind-altering drug.

Incidence and Scope. The NCC assessed the scope of the drug problem as having increased rapidly between the mid-1960s and mid-1970s and leveling off subsequently, presumably affected by intensified law enforcement and stricter penalties and the increasingly apparent health consequences of drug use. Surveys by the National Institute on Drug Abuse (NIDA) and other surveys placed the beginning of meaningful decline at different times for different drugs. But ascertaining the incidence of illicit drug use and even general trends in their use among adolescents is inherently difficult. First, the typical survey technique of interviewing a representative sample of the population raises in the minds of respondents the fear that in some way or other, an admissive statement about drug use may get back to law enforcement authorities. Also, swings in society's tolerance or disapproval can affect greatly the willingness of users to respond freely. Second, and conversely, there may be temptations for teenagers to exaggerate (as also on surveys of sexual activity) in emulation of "adult" behavior.

NIDA obtains data on drug use in three major ways, among others: (1) household surveys of a representative sample of the population; (2) surveys of high school students, both on a onetime and on a longitudinal basis (i.e., following a particular category, such as graduating seniors, over a period of time); and (3) surveillance reports, such as episodes of drug overdose or other drug-connected appearances at hospital emergency rooms. Data from these three approaches are presented below.

The U.S. General Accounting Office issued a report in early 1991 on the incidence of teenage drug use and its linkages, if any, with teenage pregnancy or school dropout. (On the linkage question, insufficient data were found to warrant a firm conclusion.) GAO found the annual interviewing of high school seniors (a sample of 17,000 a year) to be a somewhat firmer basis for estimating trends in use than the annual household surveys. It noted, however, that student interviewing missed absent students and school dropouts, which in some city districts go into the 30, 40, or higher percents. The report stated: " . . . Assuming that drug use among dropouts has not changed much in recent years, the trend estimates are probably unaffected, because dropout rates have not changed dramatically." The GAO report noted that by sampling only households, the NIDA household surveys did not reach institutionalized or homeless populations or those living in dormitories or other group quarters and that they had oversampled blacks, Hispanics, and young people.[143]

Based on a sample of hospital emergency rooms (ERs) in 21 metropolitan areas in the mid- to late 1980s, numbers of adolescents and young adults in cocaine-related ER episodes showed the first year-to-year decline in 1988–89. All race, ethnic origin, and sex categories showed 1988 to 1989 declines except white females in the 12–17 group; all categories in the 18–24 group declined. For all ages, only black females showed a small (0.8%) increase from 1988 to 1989.[144] However, the NIDA Drug Abuse Warning System (DAWN) reported an increase of 13 percent in ER cocaine-related visits in the July to September 1991 time period from the preceding quarter and reported for all drug-related visits, a 7.7 percent increase from the first quarter of 1991 to the first quarter of 1992.[145]

Table 3.9 indicates use of alcohol, marijuana, and cocaine by the adolescent/

Table 3.9
Use of Alcohol, Marijuana, and Cocaine in the Preceding Month, by Youths Ages 12–17 and 18–25, by Age and Sex, 1976, 1979, 1985, and 1990

Substance and Sex	Age	*Percent* 1976	1979	1985	1990
Alcohol *					
Both Sexes	12-17	32	37	31	25
	18-25	69	76	71	25
Male	12-17	36	39	34	25
	18-25	70	84	78	74
Female	12-17	29	36	28	24
	18-25	58	68	64	53
Marijuana					
Both Sexes	12-17	12	17	12	5
	18-25	25	35	22	13
Male	12-17	14	19	13	6
	18-25	31	45	27	17
Female	12-17	11	14	11	4
	18-25	19	26	17	9
Cocaine					
Both Sexes	12-17	**1.0	1.4	1.5	0.6
	18-25	2.0	9.3	7.6	2.2
Male	12-17	—	—	2.0	0.7
	18-25	—	—	9.0	2.8
Female	12-17	—	—	**1.0	**
	18-25	—	—	6.3	1.6

Notes: * In 1979, 1985 and 1990 private answer sheets were used for alcohol questions; in 1976, respondents answered aloud.
** Relative standard error greater than 30 per cent.
— Data not available.

Source: USPHS, *Health United States 1990*, Table 57. 126. Major source cited: National Institute on Drug Abuse; National Household Survey on Drug Abuse for years pre-1990. Same source as before for 1990, but unpublished data as of publication date of *Health United States 1990*.

young adult population over the 1976–90 period, showing cocaine incidence in the preceding month at 2.8 percent in 1990 for males.[146]

A NIDA survey of the high school graduating class of 1987 revealed, as did a similar 1982 survey, a significant regional difference in use. For cocaine, with similar differentials in the other categories, the "annual prevalence of current use" was Northeast, 13.3 percent; North Central, 7.5 percent; South, 7 percent; and West, 16.4 percent. Additionally the NIDA 1987 study covered a representative sample of private and public high school graduates of the classes of 1975 through 1986, essentially representing all high school graduates age 19–

29, including those attending college. Drug use for this group rose in the early 1970s, with peaking at different times: nonmedical use of tranquilizers and barbiturates occurred in the mid-1970s; marijuana in 1978; PCP, 1979; LSD, 1980; and amphetamines, 1982. Cocaine did not peak until 1986, with "reported use in prior year" dropping from 20 to 16 percent in 1987. For eight years prior to 1986, there had been relatively no change in the rate of cocaine experimentation. The 19–29 age group studied included no high school dropouts.[147]

The Rand Corporation's Drug Policy Research Center (DPRC) assessed the situation thus in early 1992:

It appears . . . the [1990s] cocaine epidemic may now be subsiding, leaving in its wake large numbers of people with long-term dependencies . . . the steepest reductions in drug use have occurred in suburban areas and among the educated middle class. . . . The data point to [a strong] connection between cocaine use and health problems and cocaine use and crime . . . we may see continued or even increasing drug-related health problems and violence in . . . inner cities.[148]

The Children's Defense Fund in early 1991 indicated that the racial/gender use of the major drugs and alcohol differed from some other behavioral problems for adolescents, with white use of drugs and alcohol at least as great as, and probably somewhat more likely than, use by black teenagers.[149] (However, the difficulties in many drug use surveys, including the heavier use among school dropouts—not counted in the high school surveys—must be kept in mind.)

Weaknesses in Health System Response to Adolescent Alcohol and Drug Use. Three major weaknesses are apparent: (1) inconclusive data and analyses as to incidence of use and the interconnection with other adolescent health/education/ behavioral problems; (2) inadequate research on the relative efficacy of treatment methods and the consequent adaptation of public health policies accordingly; and (3) shortage of drug treatment "slots" and inadequate public, nonprofit, and private financial resources for expansion and improvement of drug/alcohol treatment facilities and personnel. The first of these—inconclusive data on use— has already been described.

The principal approaches to drug abuse treatment as they developed over the 1970s and 1980s comprised both short- and long-term and inpatient and outpatient combinations. Detoxification, usually inpatient and intensive programs, have been directed toward physical addiction per se. Most comprehensive have been the residential treatment communities with stays of a year to 18 months for patients in a rigorous, structured environment to end their addiction.

Specifically directed to the heroin addiction were the methadone maintenance programs, where methadone dosages substituted for heroin and the user is weaned away gradually from the methadone. The methadone blocks the heroin craving and eliminates the withdrawal pains but can become somewhat, or seriously addictive itself; on the other hand, it permits the individual to continue a normal living and working pattern. Similarly, outpatient clinics and support groups like

Narcotics Anonymous, patterned somewhat on Alcoholics Anonymous, provide counseling and support to those who want to quit drugs. In the middle range of intensity are private inpatient or residential three to four-week programs, furnishing medical treatment and services to treat and hopefully reduce or eliminate the addiction.

A 1990 GAO report on drug abuse treatment summarized in strong and unambiguous terms the status of treatment efficacy research:

Research knowledge applicable to drug abuse treatment has not significantly advanced in the last decade. There are no recently completed national evaluations of treatment programs, and earlier evaluations may have limited applicability to today's population of drug abusers. Treatment effectiveness depends, in part, on matching patient needs to appropriate types of treatment. However, knowledge on patient-treatment matching is limited. Although cocaine abuse became a widespread problem during the 1980s, knowledge on how to treat it is in the early stages of development.[150]

The report continued:

Knowledge about drug abuse treatment is limited in significant ways. Knowledge concerning the effectiveness of drug abuse treatments is limited by the lack of recent large-scale evaluations of treatment programs and methodological shortcomings of existing evaluations. . . . Despite the recent cocaine and crack epidemic, NIDA's treatment research program has given priority to developing therapies for addiction to heroin and other opiates. NIDA has recently begun to place additional emphasis on developing therapies for cocaine abuse, but results from this research are not expected for several years.[151]

Low Policy Priority to Drug Treatment. In the early 1980s, the Reagan administration began to express alarm about the national drug problem; the Bush administration launched a "War on Drugs." Throughout this period and into the 1990s, it was argued repeatedly by many knowledgeable professionals and numerous public officials and political leaders that priorities were getting skewed. It was contended that most of the effort and money was being directed to the interdiction of international drug traffic into the United States and the vigorous investigation, apprehension, and incarceration of drug users (many first-time offenders) and dealers—the supply side of the equation—with only mediocre, minimal, or absent attention to the demand side—education and other preventive measures—and to the treatment of the millions of persons already addicted and of those in the process of becoming so. The Clinton administration announced in early 1993 an increased emphasis upon the "demand side" of the drug problem and on education and treatment. By mid-1993 the congressional appropriation actions, in the midst of a deficit reduction program, were showing very limited responses.

Consistent with poverty concentration, antisocial behavior, and school dropout patterns, the drug use problem was considerably more devastating in inner-city neighborhoods than in suburban areas but was becoming increasingly serious in the latter also. Drug education in the public schools began on an incremental, tentative basis in the late 1960s, but it was 1991 before the nation's first public school system (in Little Rock, Arkansas) assured a full range of early intervention and medical treatment (including up to three months' hospitalization) of student drug abusers.[152]

Before leaving office in 1988, HHS secretary Otis Bowen set forth some facts about, and reasons for, the dismal drug treatment situation. He pointed out that at that time, over 70 million Americans had used illicit drugs and about 6.5 million were severely dependent on cocaine, heroin, and other opiates. Yet treatment facilities were serving as few as 10 percent of the severely addicted, and some institutions and facilities had waiting lists as long as two years. He then listed some of the barriers standing in the way of meeting these needs and called for more research on treatment modalities.[153]

• Many people oppose the establishment of treatment facilities in, or anywhere near, the areas in which they reside, with local zoning regulations and legal procedural delays combining to create an absolute veto.

• The cost of treating a single addict might run into many thousands of dollars, with no assurance that he or she would remain drug-free.

• Treatment is not a panacea because drug use is a chronic, relapsing disease, underscoring the need for a goal of keeping people drug-free for as long as possible.

• Because there are no easy solutions, necessary fiscal and political support could not be obtained and maintained.

Four years and a full presidential term later, the total treatment slot situation had not improved appreciably, and in a growing number of state and local governments, public funding was being decreased under severe budgetary pressures. Fortunately, in some instances nonprofit organizations and business establishments were moving to fill part of the gap. Ironically, the recognized need for more research on treatment methods tended to delay even further the expansion of some treatment facilities until more certain medical outcomes were in sight.

Not only is alcohol and drug abuse a threat to adolescent health and long-term survival but adults of all ages are addicted. Many of those so addicted are potentially costly to society in terms of remedial care and, although productively employed, are an unstable asset both to the employer and to the American labor force in general and to its international competitive strength.

Smoking. Like the drugs just discussed, cigarettes and other nicotine use are highly addictive; additionally, linkage between smoking and lung cancer was established in the mid-1960s and continually strengthened in subsequent years. For the 18 plus age group, the proportion of cigarette smokers declined from 42.3 percent in 1965 to 28.7 percent in 1987; for all males, from 51.6 to 31.0 percent, and for females, from 34.0 to 26.7 percent.[154]

Cigarette use in 1990 among 9th through 12th grade students is shown in

Table 3.10
Cigarette Use Among High School Students, by Gender, Race/Ethnicity, and Grade, 1990 (in percents)

Category	Use*	Frequent Use**
Total	32.3	12.8
Gender		
Female	31.3	12.5
Male	33.2	13.0
Race/Ethnicity		
White	36.4	15.9
Female	36.0	16.6
Male	36.8	15.2
Black	16.1	2.3
Female	15.7	1.8
Male	16.8	3.0
Hispanic	30.8	7.4
Female	27.2	5.5
Male	34.7	9.6
Grade		
9th	29.5	9.9
10th	30.0	10.8
11th	32.8	12.6
12th	36.7	17.7

Notes: * Smoking cigarettes at any time during the 30 days preceding the survey.
  ** Smoking cigarettes on more than 25 of the 30 days preceding the survey. Confidence interval: 95%.

Source: CDC, "Tobacco Use Among High School Students—United States," *MMWR Morbidity and Mortality Weekly Report* (40:36), Table 1, September 13, 1991, 617-619.

combined data from two surveys by NIDA and state departments of education in 22 states and four cities. Current use (during preceding 30 days) in percents was: national, 32; high states—West Virginia, 37; Kentucky, 37; South Dakota, 34; low states—Utah, 20; Georgia, 25; Massachusetts, 29; for the four cities: Ft. Lauderdale, 24; Jersey City, 23; Dallas, 19; and Miami, 14.[155] Table 3.10 shows the incidence of smoking among high school students in 1990, based on a nationwide sample.

In 1988, cigarettes had been the second "drug of choice" among high school seniors, being used in the preceding month by 29 percent of respondents, compared with 64 percent for alcohol and 18 percent for marijuana, with cocaine at 3.4 percent.[156] While still a health hazard, cigarettes in the early 1990s seemed to be on a more solid declining path than the harder drugs.

Antisocial Behavior, Violence, and Criminal Activity

Adolescent youth in the nation's inner cities began to show substantial unrest and alienation in the 1970s; combined discouragement and disorder in the class-room and violence on the streets began to escalate. As adolescent antisocial behavior and violence spread in the 1980s to suburbs and rural areas, the visual media, seemingly endeavoring to keep step with "social reality," gave increasingly vivid portrayals of violent behavior. By the early 1990s, these portrayals were sometimes producing violent behavior at public showings, including some homicides at theaters. "Violence in the United States is a public health emergency," stated Antonia Novello, M.D., former U.S. surgeon general in June 1992 in the *Journal of the American Medical Association (JAMA)*.[157]

The annual report *Crime in the United States 1991* showed that of all murder offender arrests in 1991, 13 percent were under 18 and 77 percent were in the 15–34 age group. The 15 through 19 age group accounted for 16.7 percent of the total. Of that age group, 94.5 percent were male, 62.6 percent were black, 34.8 percent white, and the remainder of other races or race unknown. The report summarized the juvenile crime situation thus: "Nationwide there is a growing concern over an escalation in juvenile delinquency, a perception supported by the unprecedented level of juvenile violence confronting the Nation."[158]

Mortality Rates from Violence. In the above-cited *JAMA* article, Dr. Novello stated: "Suicide has become the third leading cause of death for 15- to 34-year-old Americans and the second-leading cause . . . for 15- to 34-year-old Native Americans. These rates are growing. Since 1950 the suicide rate among children and adolescents has nearly tripled . . . in 1989 the suicide rate among our country's young was the highest it has ever been."[159] Comparative rates for suicide and homicide for the 15–19 and 20–24 age groups in 1980 and 1989 are shown in Table 3.11. Following is a summary of rates for these two causes over the 1950–80 period for the 15–24 age group as a whole.

Rates for suicide for the 15–24 age group (combining the two age groups in the table) for the years 1950 and 1980 were, for all races and both sexes—4.5 and 12.3; white males—6.6 and 21.4; black males—4.9 and 12.3; white females—2.7 and 4.6; black females—1.8 and 2.3. Rates for homicide in the same order were, for all races and both sexes—6.3 and 15.6; white males—3.7 and 15.5; black males—58.9 and 84.3; white females—1.3 and 4.7; black females—16.5 and 18.4.[160] Thus, during the three-decade period, adolescent youth violence seemed to be directed both to themselves and to one another, but with the overall suicide rate declining modestly between 1960 and 1989 and the homicide rate continuing to grow.

The CDC Youth Risk Behavior Survey (YRBS) in 1990 interviewed over 11,000 high school students in the 50 states and District of Columbia: 8.3 percent had attempted suicide; 27.3 percent had thought seriously about it. Of those surveyed who had attempted suicide, females represented 10.3 percent and males

Table 3.11
Mortality Rates for Suicide and Homicide/Legal Intervention for Age Groups 15–19 and 20–24, by Race and Sex, 1980 and 1989 (deaths per 100,000 resident population)

		15-19				20-24		
	Suicide		Homicide		Suicide		Homicide	
Sex and Race	1980	1989	1980	1989	1980	1989	1980	1989
1	2	3	4	5	6	7	8	9
Total								
Both Sexes/All Races	8.5	11.3	10.6	13.7	16.1	15.3	20.6	20.0
Male, All Races	13.8	18.0	16.2	22.4	26.8	26.4	33.0	32.8
Female, All Races	3.0	4.3	4.9	4.6	5.5	4.2	8.3	7.2
White, Total	9.2	12.2	7.5	6.5	16.9	15.6	12.7	10.1
Male	15.0	19.4	10.9	9.6	27.8	26.8	19.9	15.7
Female	3.3	4.5	3.9	3.3	5.9	4.3	5.4	4.4
Black, Total	3.6	6.3	29.9	52.6	11.2	13.2	73.2	78.8
Male	5.6	10.3	48.8	92.7	20.0	23.7	124.9	138.9
Female	1.6	2.3	11.0	11.6	3.1	3.4	26.0	22.9
Other Races, Total	4.7	7.7	26.7	43.4	11.9	13.8	64.7	65.5
Male	7.5	12.1	43.3	75.7	20.9	24.1	109.4	113.4
Female	1.8	3.1	10.1	10.0	3.6	3.9	23.3	19.6

Source: *Vital Health Statistics of the U.S., 1989,* Vol. 2, Part A, 1993, 1288-92, 1320-23.

6.2 percent. Also considered at risk of suicide attempts were those suffering depression, alcohol and other drug use, social isolation, and child abuse. Similarly, results from the 1991 YRBS by CDC were combined with state and local YRBS's conducted by education departments in 23 states, both sets of data being self-reported. Female-male percentages of reporting students for thinking seriously about suicide were 37–21; making suicide plans, 25–13; and actually attempting, 11–4. From the state-local surveys in percents: those having been in a physical fight (42); having carried a weapon (26); and "usually carried a hand gun" (11).[161] Here, as in other aspects of adolescent health, there appeared to be direct correlations among family structure, school years completed, alcohol and drug use, and, last but not least, poverty.

Dr. C. Everett Koop, former surgeon general, and Dr. George Lundberg, editor of *JAMA,* in a joint editorial pointed out that:[162]

• One million U.S. inhabitants die prematurely each year [from] intentional suicide or gunshot wounds. . . .

• The leading cause of death in both white and black teenage boys in America is gunshot wounds. . . .

• The number of deaths [from] firearms is seven times greater in the United States than in the United Kingdom. . . .

• Armed assaults in California schools are on a sharp increase. . . .

• Of the fatalities in the 1992 Los Angeles . . . riots the vast majority [were from] gunshot wounds.

The relationship between drug use and violence also seemed to be especially strong in the early 1990s, as explored below.

The Drug-Alcohol-Violence-Delinquency Connection

The transition from high school student from a poor family in a poor and crime-ridden neighborhood to drug user, to school dropout, to drug dealer, to violence in protecting territory, and into the criminal justice system became tempting, easy, disastrous, and deadly for many adolescent youth in the eighties and early nineties.

Drug Dealing. A 1988 Rand Corporation study of the dynamics of the drug trade in the District of Columbia found that:

Despite high rates of imprisonment, injury and even death, street dealing in the late 1980s was an increasingly common activity for young, poorly educated District males. . . . Extravagant incomes of the kind frequently reported in the media were rare. But in general participants earned far more—typical net tax-free earnings of $24,000 a year for those who sold on a daily basis—than in the legitimate jobs most of them simultaneously held.[163]

Using 1989 data from the U.S. Department of Labor and from samples from the 11,430 District residents charged with drug selling, Rand researchers produced a comparative wage scale embracing occupational group members working full-time in the District. The median earnings were: food counter/fast food, $8,684; custodial-domestic services, $9,620; waiters-waitresses, $10,556; salesclerks, $12,220; machine operators, $16,276; clerical-administrative, $17,212; *drug dealers, $24,000*; engineers, $40,300; doctors, $41,184; and lawyers, $51,480. Other findings were: feeding a personal habit seemed to be a prime motive for involvement in dealing, with 70 percent being users; two-thirds of those arrested for drug dealing were legitimately employed; there were an estimated 22 percent chance of imprisonment, a 7 percent chance of serious injury, and a 1.4 percent chance of being killed—a fatality rate 100 times greater than that of the general work force.[164]

Other Juvenile Justice Problems. A 1987 survey of youth in long-term, state-operated juvenile institutions showed that at the time of current offense for which they were in custody, 3.19 percent of those under 18 were under the influence of alcohol and 39.1 percent were under the influence of drugs. In the same age group, 50.2 percent had lived with mother only while growing up.[165] In 1986, over 80 percent of state prison inmates had been previously sentenced to probation or incarceration as a juvenile or adult and 43 percent had been using illegal drugs on a daily basis in the month before the last offense. Use at the time of offense was 33 percent for murder, 32 for rape, and 42 for robbery.[166]

The congruence of strong adverse influences bearing upon adolescent youth is found in many public housing projects. Big city housing projects, described by columnist Neal Peirce as having "degenerated into America's most foul and fearsome killing fields," were typified by the Chicago Housing Authority: comprising "150,000 people officially, but with perhaps 50,000 additional squatters . . . More than nine of 10 families . . . headed by females, black and destitute (median annual income $5,000) . . . three-quarters of the adults jobless." Project cleanups under way were estimated to take three years beyond the completion of the first 25 in 1991.[167]

SUMMARY OF HEALTH DETERRENTS

Deterrents to employability of American youth and to an adequately skilled and physically capable U.S. labor force fall into three categories: (1) those that increase morbidity and mortality among adolescents and young adults and shorten life expectancy and/or the period during which they are able to carry on a productive work life; (2) those health habits and life-styles that prevent, or lengthen the odds against, being able to complete high school or other preparatory training schedule adequate to permit them to enter the labor force; and (3) those that threaten both health and the completion of cognitive, social, and other preparatory education and training.

Deterrents of the third category—because of their double-threat nature—present the most serious and urgent danger to the physical and economic survival of millions of young Americans. It and the other two categories embrace weaknesses of both substantive content, such as the low rate of childhood immunization, and financial, administrative, and other aspects of the health care delivery system. This third category calls most clearly and loudly for the attention of, and action by, public, community, and private leadership.

- The drug-violence combination continues to grow, in both number and severity. The mind-altering drugs
  —stimulate bravado, violence, and often murder;
  —virtually assure school dropout and either early death or intermittent incarceration; and
  —terrorize neighborhoods and destabilize societal order throughout large urban areas.
- Much of the drug-violence combination arises initially from the failure of parent(s), schools, and communities to take strong action to identify, educate, treat, and reclaim potential and active drug users for completion of their education.
- Unhealthy habits on the part of expectant mothers in the use of tobacco, alcohol, and hard drugs, thus weakening and permanently disabling the developing child and arising

—from the failure of community and health authorities to reach, counsel, and treat these women; and

—from the failure of parent(s) and schools to provide effective health and guidance to avoid teenage motherhood.

• Failure of communities and governments to mount effective home intervention of a multipurpose nature to assist families and children facing difficulties.

Prominent in the strictly health weaknesses are the following:

• The large and growing number of the uninsured population, thus depriving millions of Americans of adequate access to the health care system.
• A continuing neglect of preventive, in contrast to acute inpatient, health care.
• Lagging research efforts to ascertain the most effective drug treatment modalities.
• A breakdown in childhood disease immunization in the preschool years.
• An organizational and procedural fragmentation of the health care delivery system, with an absence of incentives for comprehensive preventive approaches and for overhauling the malpractice tort system.

In the second category of deterrents that lengthen the odds against optimum labor force participation are these overarching factors:

• A growing poverty population, underpinned by a public assistance system that has failed to provide an effective exit from welfare into work.
• A disintegration of family structure, in turn raising the odds against adequate health care, educational opportunity, and labor force participation of parent(s) and children.
• Parental neglect, abuse, and abandonment of children and an overloaded and chaotic system of foster care.
• Deteriorating neighborhood environments, with concentrated poverty, hopelessness, homelessness, alienation, and violence.

It is clear that the nation as a whole faces a formidable array of challenges to improve the economic, financial, and organizational bases of health care and its interconnections with other human services and the private and nonprofit sectors in such a way that incentives are created to drive human behavior into more careful and responsible postures in health care. This will require the collaborative efforts of all parts of the health industry and of national, state, and local governments.

NOTES

1. U.S. General Accounting Office (GAO), *U.S. Health Care Spending: Trends, Contributing Factors, and Proposals for Reform,* GAO/HRD 91–102 (Testimony of U.S. Comptroller General Charles Bowsher before the House Committee on Ways and Means, April 17, 1991). Opinion poll cited was conducted by the Employee Benefits Research

Institute and the Gallup Organization. See also Jajich-Toth, C., and Roper, B., "Americans' Views on Health Care: A Study in Contradictions," *Health Affairs*, Winter 1990, 149–57.

2. *Beyond Rhetoric*, 118.

3. Ibid., 147.

4. "A Survey of Health Care: Surgery Needed," *The Economist*, July 6, 1991, 3.

5. BLS, *Employment and Earnings 1990*, Household Data Annual Averages, Table 24, 192.

6. Bureau of the Census, *Public Employment: Government Employment 1989*, Table 1, October 1990, 1.

7. For proportion of GDP: OECD, *OECD in Figures*, June/July 1992, 44; 1992 estimates, five-year projections, and trade balance estimates from U.S. Department of Commerce, "Health and Medical Services," *U.S. Industrial Outlook 1993*, January 1993, 42-4; and for trade balance, Table 1, 44-4. Percent of federal budget from CBO, *Trends in Health Spending: An Update* (Washington, DC: CBO, June 1993), xiv, 2. See also Health Industry Manufacturers Association (HIMA), "Competitiveness of the U.S. Health Care Technology Industry: Contributions to the U.S. Economy and Trade," Report 91–2 (Washington, DC: HIMA, 1991).

8. For life expectancy/infant mortality: *OECD in Figures*, 46. Observations about diet, and so on from "A Survey of Health Care," *The Economist*, 5.

9. CBO, based on data from the Office of Actuary, Health Care Financing Administration (HCFA), 1992; for 1989 and related data, see CBO, *Rising Health Care Costs. Causes, Implications, and Strategies*, April 1991, ix, x, 22–27.

10. Ratner, J., "The High Cost of Health," *GAO Journal*, Summer/Fall 1991, 6; Health Industry Manufacturers Association (HIMA), *Straight Talk About Health Care Technology and the Rising Cost of Medical Care* (Washington, DC: HIMA, 1991), 1.

11. As reported by Pollack, A., "Medical Technology 'Arms Race' Adds Billions to the Nation's Bills," *New York Times*, April 29, 1991, A–1. See also Stout, H., "Soaring Health Costs Have a Silver Lining: A Host of New Jobs," *Wall Street Journal*, September 6, 1991, A–1.

12. In Ratner, J., "The High Cost of Health," 6.

13. Bowen, O., and Burke, T., "The Power Vacuum in U.S. Health Care," *Journal of Health Care Benefits*, November/December 1991, 9–15.

14. CBO, *Rising Health Care Costs*, 9.

15. Ibid., 20–21.

16. As reported in Khanna, P., "While Physician Extenders Proliferate, Doctors Worry About Competition, Care," Medicine, *Wall Street Journal*, August 5, 1992, B–1.

17. Ratner, J., "The High Cost of Health," 7.

18. Pear, R., "Study Says Fees Are Often Higher When Doctor Has Stake in Clinic," *New York Times*, August 8, 1991, A–1. See also Winslow, R., "Studies Confirm Patients Pay More for Care When Doctors Own Facilities," *Wall Street Journal*, October 21, 1992, B–6.

19. CBO, *Economic Implications of Rising Health Care Costs*, October 1992, 27. See also Ratner, J., 4, citing: Winslow, C., et al., "The Appropriateness of Performing Coronary Artery Bypass Surgery," *Journal of the American Medical Association* 260, no. 4, July 22–29, 1988, 505–9; Enthoven, A., "What Can Europeans Learn from Americans?" *Health Care Financing Review 1990 Annual Supplement*, 49–63.

20. U.S. General Accounting Office (GAO), *Early Intervention: Federal Initiatives Like WIC Can Produce Savings*, GAO/HRD–92–18, April 1992, 2; U.S. House of Representatives, Select Committee on Children, Youth and Families, *Opportunities for Success: Cost-Effective Programs for Children Update 1990* (Washington, DC: U.S. Government Printing Office, October 1990), 6–10.

21. Ginsburg, P., and Sunshine, J., *Cost Management in Employee Health Plans* (Santa Monica, CA: Rand Corporation, 1987), 7. See also *Rising Health Care Costs*, 26–27; Haislmaier, E., "Why America's Health Care System Is in Trouble," in Butler, S., and Haislmaier, E. (eds), *Critical Issues: A National Health System for America* (Washington, DC: Heritage Foundation, 1989), 1–31.

22. *Rising Health Care Costs*, 12.

23. Enthoven, A., "Reforming Tax Treatment of Health Insurance: A Step Toward Universal Health Insurance and Cost Containment," in proceedings of a symposium on *Tax Policy: New Perspectives* (in Arlington, VA, May 8–10, 1991), *National Tax Journal*, 44, no. 3, 145.

24. Butler, S., in "The High Cost of Health," 13. See also Friedman, M., "Gammon's Law Points to Health Care Solution" (quoting British physician Gammon, who expressed a theory that "in a bureaucratic system . . . increase in expenditure will be matched by fall in production"), *Wall Street Journal*, op-ed, November 12, 1991; Haislmaier, E., 9–10.

25. Health Insurance Association of America (HIAA), *Sourcebook of Health Insurance Data 1984–85*, as reported in Haislmaier, E., 9.

26. *Rising Health Care Costs*, 12–13. See also GAO, *Health Care: Antitrust Issues Relating to Physicians and Third-Party Payers*, GAO/HRD–91–120, July 1991.

27. *Rising Health Care Costs*, 30.

28. Employee Benefit Research Institute (EBRI), "A Profile of the Nonelderly Population Without Health Insurance," Issue Brief no. 66, May 1987, 5 (cited by Haislmaier, E., 15). See also GAO, *U.S. Health Care Spending*, 9.

29. As reported in *Rising Health Care Costs*, 72.

30. GAO, *U.S. Health Care Spending*, 9.

31. *Rising Health Care Costs*, 75.

32. Ibid., 67.

33. GAO, *Health Insurance: A Profile of the Uninsured in Selected States*, GAO/HRD 9–31 FS, February 1991, 2–5.

34. Urban Institute, "People Without Health Insurance: How Many and How Long?" *Policy and Research Report*, Fall 1990, 9.

35. U.S. Department of Agriculture, Food and Nutrition Service, "Program Information Report," June 30, 1993, 2.

36. House Select Committee, *Opportunities for Success*, 12–13. (Eligibility data cited in the report were derived from estimates of the CBO and GAO.)

37. Ibid., 25–26.

38. Ibid., 141–42.

39. Kennedy, L., "Children Receiving SSI Payments, December 1991," *Social Security Bulletin* 55, no. 2, Summer 1992, 48–51.

40. GAO, *Childhood Immunization: Opportunities to Improve Immunization Rates at Lower Costs*, GAO/T-HRD–92–36 (Testimony of Mark Nadel, associate director, National Public Health Issues, Human Resources Division, GAO), June 1, 1992, 1.

41. U.S. Advisory Commission on Intergovernmental Relations (ACIR), *Medicaid:*

Intergovernmental Trends and Options, Report A–119, Table 3–4 (Washington, DC: ACIR, June 1992), 17, 28. See also Altman, D., and Beatrice, D., "Perspectives on the Medicaid Program," *Health Care Financing Review/1990 Annual Supplement,* December 1990, 2.

42. PHS, Centers for Disease Control (CDC), National Center for Health Statistics (NCHS), "Advance Report of Final Natality Statistics," *Monthly Vital Statistics Report* 41 no. 9 (Supplement), February 25, 1993, 9.

43. ACIR, *Medicaid: Intergovernmental Trends,* 17. For additional data, see the Kaiser Commission on the Future of Medicaid, *Medicaid at the Crossroads* (Baltimore, MD: Henry J. Kaiser Family Foundation, November 1992), Appendixes 61–70.

44. U.S. Department of Health and Human Services, Social Security Administration, *Social Security Bulletin Annual Statistical Supplement 1990,* Table 7.E1, 281.

45. The Kaiser Commission on the Future of Medicaid, *The Medicaid Cost Explosion: Causes and Consequences* (Baltimore, MD: The Henry J. Kaiser Foundation, 1993), xi–xii, 11–35; The Urban Institute, "The Crisis in Medicaid Spending," *Policy and Research Report,* Winter/Spring 1993, 8–10.

46. U.S. Public Health Service, *Health United States 1990,* Table 10, March 1991, 62.

47. Institute of Medicine (IOM), Committee to Study the Prevention of Low Birthweight, *Preventing Low Birthweight: Summary* (Washington, DC: National Academy Press, 1985), 3.

48. PHS, Centers for Disease Control (CDC), National Center for Health Statistics (NCHS), "Births, Marriages, and Deaths for February 1992," *Monthly Vital Statistics Report* 41, no. 2, June 26, 1992, 3, 4, 12. See also "Overview of Findings," *Kids Count Data Book 1993* (Washington, DC: Center for the Study of Social Policy, Annie E. Casey Foundation, 1993), 9–11.

49. *Beyond Rhetoric,* 119.

50. Ibid., 122.

51. Hill, I., *Reaching Women Who Need Prenatal Care* (Washington, DC: National Governors' Association, 1988), 1–8; 39–51. See also GAO, *Prenatal Care: Medicaid Recipients and Uninsured Women Obtain Insufficient Care,* September 1987.

52. *Reaching Women,* 1–8, 39–51. Also cited were Hughes, D., Johnson, K., Rosenbaum, S., Butler, W., and Simons, J., *The Health of America's Children: Maternal and Child Health Data Book* (Washington, DC: Children's Defense Fund, 1988).

53. IOM, *Preventing Low Birthweight,* 24.

54. GAO, *Medicaid Expansions: Coverage Improves But State Fiscal Problems Jeopardize Continued Progress,* GAO/HRD–91–78, June 1991, 11–12.

55. ACIR, *Medicaid: Intergovernmental Trends,* Table 3–4, 28. See also NGA, "State Coverage of Pregnant Women and Children—July 1992," *MCH Update* (Washington, DC: NGA, 1992), 3.

56. U.S. Department of Health and Human Services, 1991 Advisory Council on Social Security (ACSS), *Commitment to Change: Foundations for Reform* (Washington, DC: ACSS, December 1991), 79–80.

57. Congressional Office of Technology Assessment (OTA), "OTA Says Rural Health Care Access Will Deteriorate Without Government Intervention," Press Advisory, September 12, 1990, 1 (based on OTA, *Health Care in Rural America* (GPO stock number 052–003–01205–7) (Washington, DC: Superintendent of Documents, 1990).

58. "Rural Hospitals: Closures and Issues of Access" (Testimony of Nadel, M.,

GAO associate director for National and Public Health Issues before a task force of House Select Committee on Aging), GAO/T-HRD–01–46, September 4, 1991, 1–2.

59. Hill, I., and Bennet, T., *Enhancing the Scope of Prenatal Services* (Washington, DC: National Governors' Association, 1989), 27 (emphasis added).

60. Lewis-Idema, D., *Increasing Provider Participation* (Washington, DC: National Governors' Association, 1988), 3–4.

61. Ibid., 7–8, 23–24.

62. *Beyond Rhetoric,* 127–28.

63. Ibid., 121.

64. Orsena, J., "Women and HIV: More than a Matter of Numbers," *County Health Report* 2, no. 1, February 4, 1991, 3, as a supplement to *County News,* of same date (biweekly by National Association of Counties).

65. Chu, S., Buehler, J., and Berkelman, R., "Impact of the HIV Virus Epidemic on Mortality in Women of Reproductive Age in the United States," *Journal of the American Medical Association* 264, no. 2, July 11, 1990, 225–29.

66. GAO, *ADMS Block Grant: Women's Set-Aside Does Not Assure Drug Treatment for Pregnant Women,* GAO/HRD–91–80, May 1991, 2–3. Sources for low and high estimates cited were *National Drug Control Strategy,* the White House, September 1989, and the president of the National Association for Perinatal Addiction Research and Education. Neither estimate was based on a nationally representative sample of births.

67. GAO, *Substance Abuse Treatment: Medicaid Allows Some Services But Generally Limits Coverage,* GAO/HRD–91–92, June 1991, 1–2.

68. GAO, *Drug-Exposed Infants: A Generation at Risk,* GAO/HRD–90–138, June 1990, 4–6.

69. Ibid., 6. The source for the anonymous testing and public-private comparisons referred to on p. 6 was Chasnoff, I., Landress, H., and Barrett, M., "The Prevalence of Illicit-Drug or Alcohol Use During Pregnancy and Discrepancies in Mandatory Reporting in Pinellas County, Florida," *New England Journal of Medicine,* April 26, 1990, 1202–6.

70. Ibid., 9–10.

71. Treaster, J., "Plan Lets Addicted Mothers Take Their Newborns Home," *New York Times,* September 19, 1991, A–1.

72. GAO, *ADMS Block Grant,* 6–7.

73. GAO, *Substance Abuse Treatment,* 4 (emphasis added).

74. Institute of Medicine (IOM), *Preventing Low Birthweights,* 11–12.

75. NCHS, *Monthly Vital Statistics Report* 40, no. 125, April 15, 1992, 2–16.

76. IOM, *Preventing Low Birthweight,* 11.

77. *Beyond Rhetoric,* 124.

78. Ibid., 163. The nutrition/pediatrics source cited was Graham, G., "Mothers, Not Nutrition Cause Infant Mortality," *Wall Street Journal,* April 2, 1991.

79. GAO, *Early Intervention,* 2–3.

80. *Beyond Rhetoric,* 128, 13–14; minority views, 155–63.

81. Hill, *Enhancing Prenatal Services,* ix, 21–23; NGA, *MCH Update,* July 1992, 14.

82. GAO, *Drug Abuse Research: Federal Funding and Future Needs,* GAO/T-PEMD–91–14, September 1991, 9–14.

83. Biltheimer, L., *Designing Program Evaluations* (Washington, DC: National Governors' Association, 1989), v-xiii, 9–20.

84. *Kids Count: State Profiles of Child Well-Being*, Appendix 1 (Washington, DC: Center for the Study of Social Policy, 1991), 4.

85. Ibid., 65–73; NCHS, *Monthly Vital Statistics Report* 40, no. 13, Table 8, September 30, 1992, 17.

86. *Beyond Rhetoric*, 125. Sources cited included U.S. Congress, Office of Technology Assessment, *Healthy Children: Investing in the Future*, 11–14; National Center for Health Statistics, *Estimates from the National Health Interview Survey*, 72; Bloom, B., *Health Insurance and Medical Care: Health of Our Nation's Children, United States, 1988* (Advance Data from Vital and Health Statistics, no. 188, Washington, DC: NCHS, 1990).

87. Hill, I., and Breyel, J., *Caring for Kids* (Washington, DC: National Governors' Association, 1991), 21.

88. *Beyond Rhetoric*, 149. See also GAO, *Community Health Centers: Hospitals Can Become Centers Under Certain Conditions*, GAO/HRD-91-77FS, March 1991, 1–3, 6–7.

89. Children's Defense Fund, *The State of America's Children 1991*, 1991, 68.

90. NGA, *MCH Update*, 2–3.

91. Katz, J., "A Health Care Safety Net," *Governing*, October 1990, 42, 45.

92. ACSS, *Commitment to Change*, 258.

93. Hill and Breyel, 32, 34.

94. Ibid., 9.

95. Ibid., 14, 39–44.

96. *Beyond Rhetoric*, 119–21 (emphasis added). Cited sources included Henderson, D., White House Office of Science and Technology, quoted in Okie, S., "Vaccination Record in U.S. Falls Sharply," *Washington Post*, March 24, 1991, A–1, A22–23; Department of Health and Human Services, Centers for Disease Control (CDC), "Measles Vaccination Levels Among Selected Groups of Pre-School Age Children," *Morbidity and Mortality Weekly Report* 40, January 18, 1991, 36.

97. *Beyond Rhetoric*, 161.

98. As reported by Brown, D., and Taylor, P., "Worldwide Vaccination Progresses," *Washington Post*, October 9, 1991, A–16. Official sources for the city data cited were CDC, "Retrospective Assessment of Vaccination Coverage Among School-Aged Children—Selected U.S. Cities, 1991," Table 1; *Morbidity and Mortality Weekly Report* 41, no. 6, February 14, 1992, 103–7.

99. Lee, F., "Immunization of Children Is Said to Lag," *New York Times*, October 16, 1991, B1, B5.

100. *State of America's Children 1991*, 59.

101. House Select Committee, *Opportunities for Success*, 119–20.

102. 1990 data from "Advance Report of Final Mortality Statistics," *Monthly Vital Statistics Report* 41, no. 7, January 7, 1993, 25; PHS, *Health USA 1990*, Table 33, 95–96.

103. OTA, "Healthy Children: Investing in the Future," *OTA Report Brief*, February 1988, 1.

104. *Beyond Rhetoric*, 128, which cited Children's Defense Fund, *SOS America*, 59.

105. House Select Committee, 125; "Lead Poisoning Screening: Despite the Risk Only Two States Mandate Childhood Screening," *State Health Notes*, November 4, 1991, 4–5. See also Bayhurst, P., et al., "Environmental Exposure to Lead and Children's

Intelligence at the Age of Seven Years—The Port Pirie Study,'' *New England Journal of Medicine* 327, no. 18, October 29, 1992, 1279–84.

106. *Health USA 1990*, Tables 34–35, 99–100.

107. "Incidence and Impact of Selected Infectious Diseases in Childhood," NCHS, *Vital and Health Statistics Series*, Series 10, no. 180, Table 1, October 1, 1991, 9.

108. *Health USA 1990*, Tables 44, 45, 1990, 109, 110.

109. Hall, L., *Medicaid Home Care Options for Disabled Children* (Washington, DC: National Governors' Association, 1990), vii.

110. As reported in Rich, S., ''Aid to Disabled Children Still in Dispute,'' *Washington Post*, October 28, 1991. See also Kennedy, L., ''Children Receiving SSS Payments,'' 48–51.

111. OTA, *Children's Mental Health: Problems and Services—A Background Paper*, 4; U.S. Public Health Service, *Healthy People 2000*, 211–13.

112. *Beyond Rhetoric*, 125–26.

113. Norris, M., ''And the Children Shall Need: Drug-Induced Disabilities Will Tax School Resources'' (second of three articles), *Washington Post*, July 1, 1991, A1, A8.

114. *Beyond Rhetoric*, 124. Sources cited for 2–5 million estimates were the 1990 House Agriculture Committee Hearings and a 1991 Food Research Action Center report.

115. Jones, J., ''The WIC Program: Funding and Issues,'' *CRS Issue Brief* (Congressional Research Service, Library of Congress, March 1991), 1. See also GAO, *Early Intervention*, 32–33.

116. Jones, J. ''The WIC Program,'' 3–5.

117. Pear, R., ''Hungry Children Put at 5.5 million,'' *New York Times*, March 27, 1991, A–18.

118. Jones, J., *CRS Issue Brief*, 2.

119. Friedman, A., ''Deadly Diet: Amid Ghetto Hunger, Many More Suffer Eating Wrong Foods—High-Fat, Salty, Sugary Fare Exerts a Powerful Draw for Poor and Uneducated,'' *Wall Street Journal*, December 18, 1990, A–1, A–6.

120. *Beyond Rhetoric*, 127.

121. House Select Committee, *Opportunities for Success*, 141.

122. GAO, *Home Visiting: A Promising Early Intervention Strategy for At-Risk Families*, GAO/HRD 90–83, July 1990, 1–5.

123. Ibid., 39.

124. *Beyond Rhetoric*, 130. See also Kyle, J., *Children, Families, and Cities: Programs That Work at the Local Level* (Washington, DC: National League of Cities, 1987), 7–34.

125. *Beyond Rhetoric*, 133, 75.

126. Ibid., 74–75. See also ''Results from the National Adolescent Student Health Survey'' (1987 assessment of risks to adolescent health and student perception of such risks—e.g., accidents, violence, suicide, tobacco, alcohol, drugs, AIDS, sexually transmitted diseases (STDs), nutrition, health products and extent of school instruction about such risks), *Morbidity and Mortality Weekly Report* 38, no. 9, March 10, 1989, 147–50.

127. ''Adolescent Health: A Generation at Risk,'' *Carnegie Quarterly* 37, no. 4, Fall 1992, 2–12. See also Urban Institute, ''Identifying Adolescents at Risk,'' *Policy and Research Report*, Winter/Spring 1993, 11–19.

128. NCHS, ''Annual Summary of Births, Marriages, Divorces and Deaths: United

Deterrents to Adequate Health Care 177

States, 1990," *Monthly Vital Statistics Report* 40, no. 13, Tables G, 4, 8, September 30, 1992, 6, 13, 17–18.

129. USPHS, *Vital Statistics of the United States 1988,* 2A, Mortality, Table 1–9, 18, 30.

130. USPHS, Centers for Disease Control (CDC), "Health Objectives for the Nation: Sexual Behavior Among High School Students United States, 1990," *Morbidity and Mortality Weekly Report* 40, nos. 51, and 52, January 3, 1992, 887.

131. USPHS, *Healthy People: National Health Promotion and Disease Prevention Objectives.* (Washington, DC: USPHS, September 1990), 573.

132. Murray, C., "No, Welfare Isn't the Problem," *Public Interest,* Summer 1986, 90.

133. CDF, *State of America's Children 1991,* 93–94.

134. "Sexual Behavior," 887.

135. *Health USA 1990,* Table 10, 62.

136. CDC, Division of STD/HIV Preventive annual report for 1990 (Atlanta: PHS, CDC, 1991).

137. USPHS, CDC, "Summary of Notifiable Diseases, United States, 1990," *Morbidity and Mortality Report* 39, no. 53, October 4, 1991, 10–11.

138. Ibid., 10; CDF, 94.

139. "Sexual Behavior," 886.

140. Ibid., 887.

141. CDF, *State of America's Children 1991,* 96.

142. Ellickson, P., and Bell, R., *Prospects for Preventing Drug Use Among Young Adolescents.* (Santa Monica, CA: Rand Corporation, 1990), 1.

143. GAO, *Teenage Drug Use: Uncertain Linkages with Either Pregnancy or School Dropout,* GAO/PEMD–91–3, January 1991, 11 (emphasis added).

144. *Health USA 1990,* Table 58, 127.

145. *HHS News,* May 12, 1991, 1, Ibid., October 23, 1992, 1.

146. NIDA, *National Survey on Drug Abuse: Main Findings, 1982,* 83–1263; *NIDA Capsules,* C–86–13, 1986, 1–4. See also "Current Tobacco, Alcohol, Marijuana and Cocaine Use Among High School Students, United States, 1990," *Morbidity and Mortality Weekly Report,* September 27, 1991, 659–63.

147. *Health USA 1990,* 127.

148. Rand Corporation, Drug Policy Research Center, *DPRC Issue Letter* 1, no. 1, Santa Monica, CA: Rand Corporation, April 1992, 1.

149. CDF, *State of America's Children 1991,* 96.

150. GAO, *Drug Abuse: Research on Treatment May Not Address Current Needs,* GAO/HRD–90–114, September 1990, 3.

151. Ibid., 3, 15–19.

152. "Little Rock Schools Insure Drug Treatment," *New York Times,* September 8, 1991, A–19.

153. Bowen, O., "The Quiet Side of the War on Drugs—We're Not Doing Enough to Treat the Users," *Washington Post,* October 14, 1988, A–25.

154. *Health United States 1990,* Table 55, 124.

155. "Health Objectives for the Nation: Current Tobacco, Alcohol, Marijuana, Cocaine Use Among High School Students—United States, 1990," *Morbidity and Mortality Weekly Report* 40, no. 38, September 27, 1991, 659–63.

156. Ellickson, 5.

157. Novello, A., "From the Surgeon General U.S. Public Health Service," *JAMA* 267, no. 22, June 10, 1992, 3007. See also Uva, J., "Urban Violence: A Health Care Issue," *JAMA* 263, no. 1, January 5, 1990, 135, 139.

158. U.S. Department of Justice, Federal Bureau of Investigation, *Crime in the United States 1991: Uniform Crime Reports*, Table 2.5, August 30, 1992, 16, 279.

159. "From the Surgeon General," 3007.

160. *Health USA 1990*, Tables 34, 35, 97–100.

161. For 1990: CDC, *Weekly Morbidity and Mortality Report*, September 20, 1991, 633–35. 1991: *WMMR*, October 16, 1992, 760–65, 771–72.

162. Koop, C. E., and Lundberg, G., "Violence in America: A Public Health Emergency: Time to Bite the Bullet Back," *JAMA*, June 10, 1992, 3075. See also Chartrand, S., "Gunshot Wounds Labeled Epidemic: American Medical Association Recommends Licensing of All Gun Owners in U.S.," *New York Times*, June 11, 1992, B–10.

163. "Work Legal Jobs Too: Washington Drug Dealers Take Modest Profits, Major Risks," *Rand Research Review* 14, no. 2, Fall 1990, 1.

164. Ibid., 1–2.

165. National Governors' Association, *Kids in Trouble*, 1991, citing source as U.S. Department of Justice, Bureau of Justice Statistics, *Survey of Youth in Custody 1987*, September 1987. See also Watts, D., and Wright, L., "The Relationship of Alcohol, Tobacco, Marijuana, and Other Illegal Drug Use to Delinquency Among Mexican-American, Black, and White Adolescent Males," *Adolescence* 25, no. 97, Spring 1990, 171–81.

166. U.S. Department of Justice press release, January 21, 1988, 1.

167. Peirce, N., "Getting Tough in Public Housing," *Philadelphia Inquirer* (and other newspapers), April 29, 1991, A11.

Chapter 4 ⸻

Public-Private Policy Options for Restructuring the U.S. Health Care System

In contrast to public K–12 education, health care for infants, young children, and adolescents, both in its delivery and financing, is both private and public. In brief, the nation's future course in revising its health care system to address the shortcomings identified earlier will be determined in Washington and state capitols, in local courthouses and city halls, and in corporate boardrooms across America. These determinations will be greatly influenced (1) by public opinion in general and powerful special interest groups and (2) by company management, stockholders, and customer/consumer considerations.

In both public and private sectors particularly difficult barriers to change exist: (1) highly compartmentalized public opinion as it relates to public policy issues and lawmakers and (2) the inexorable tilt in corporate decisionmaking toward the short term, with consequent serious impediments to long-term strategic planning and to the achievement of long term objectives. In the post–World War II period, corporate concern with human capital investment was limited, until international competition and productivity imperatives began to manifest themselves in the late 1980s. In the public sector, Daniel Yankelovich described the public policy dilemma created by "compartmentalized" public opinion this way:

In today's America, the chief cause of poor-quality public opinion is the failure to confront the inevitable costs and trade-offs involved in making choices. Among the many devices people have for avoiding reality, the most common is to keep related aspects of an issue mentally separated, failing to make the proper connections between them. By compartmentalizing their thinking, people can maintain contradictory and conflicting opinions without being . . . discomforted. When people think about preserving American jobs, they endorse protectionism. When they think about consumer values—lower prices, better quality, and more choice—they oppose protectionism. As long as their thinking is compartmentalized, they are unable to take a firm and unwavering stand on the issue.[1]

This compartmentalized approach was being evidenced during the early 1990s regarding health care. Large majorities said consistently and often that the health care system was grievously in need of overhaul from top to bottom but said at the same time that their own particular doctor was doing just fine, thank you. (Similarly, the performance of the national Congress was being roundly condemned in opinion polls, but the individual respondents were expressing full satisfaction with their particular representative or senator.) In health as in other public policy areas, there was strong opposition to new or increased taxes to pay for needed change.

Health care in 1991–93 was at the forefront of the national Congress and the state legislatures. Among the major state legislative issues being considered were public school issues, prenatal care, extension of health insurance coverage, childhood lead poisoning, Medicaid cost containment, and alternative prison sentencing, especially for young people. (Term limits, worker's compensation, privatization of public services, and sexual harassment rounded out the list.)[2]

In this chapter, the principal policy options for change in health care that are needed to deal with the major weaknesses already identified are presented and are accompanied by pro and con arguments associated with each approach and by additional references cited that support and oppose each viewpoint.

Identified earlier were many serious weaknesses both in the health conditions of the nation's children and families, especially those of lower income, and in the equity, economic efficiency, and overall effectiveness of the U.S. health care system. We now explore alternative ways in which health care may be made more fair, efficient, affordable, and accessible to parents and growing children and in which parents and their young and adolescent children may be encouraged and persuaded—or even required—to adopt or change life-styles in such ways as to avoid ill health.

At the outset, to place U.S. health care costs in perspective, a sizable segment of these costs is incurred by individuals and families well beyond the population group with which this book is concerned (age 0 to 20 and their parent(s) during that particular period of childbirth, growth, and development). The parents of children age 0 to 18 depend on three major sources of health care cost balancing: (1) employer-provided insurance, (2) Medicaid, and (3) their own out-of-pocket resources, assisted partially by individually purchased insurance.

At the beginning of the 1990s and reaching a crescendo in 1992–93, national concern with health care reform mounted, especially its cost and the plight of the several million uninsured children and families. It was becoming apparent that new governmental and private sector action was going to be necessary. The collection of such nationwide system reform proposals in various states of debate and legislative consideration ranged from minor to major incremental changes in the private-public insurance systems to extreme change from the private insurance system to a totally governmental one. The nature of the three types of major national change, plus several variations thereof, is presented in an overview fashion, along with the principal arguments for and against, followed by an analysis of the major segments of incremental reform that might be incorporated into one or more of the major system changes or undertaken separately prior to, or concurrently with, a more general overhaul of the system.

OVERVIEW OF MAJOR HEALTH INSURANCE
REFORM PLANS

At the beginning of 1992, a variety of nationwide reform plans was advanced, and some were converted into congressional bills. Most of them recognized three growing problems with the public-private insurance system, which had been in effect since the late 1960s. These were: (1) the growing numbers and percents of the uninsured, especially young children, approximating 15 percent of the nation's population, (2) the distorting effect of employer-provided insurance, whereby worker movement from one employer to another increasingly depended upon health insurance considerations and thus impeded optimum deployment of the labor force,[3] (3) runaway costs of the then-existing health insurance system, especially in consideration of international comparisons of both costs and health outcomes. Dr. Everett Koop, former U.S. surgeon general during most of the eight year Reagan administration, in a 1991 autobiography, emphasized the seriousness of lapses in U.S. health outcomes and the various weaknesses in the insurance and delivery systems. In early 1992 he stated a firm belief that *it would require a full decade* to effect the many changes needed in the system and that phase-in periods would be required, due to the size and complexity of the problems.[4]

In the broadest sense, the three principal approaches by which the U.S. health care system would be transformed under the reform proposals extant in 1992 and early 1993 were:

1. A *universal coverage, single-payer system*, run by a single entity—a governmental one under most proposals, tending toward a replica of the Canadian Health Insurance (NHI) system.

2. A *universal coverage, multipayer system*, using both private and government insurance and relying heavily upon employer-provided insurance or, at the employer's option, employer payment of a payroll tax into a governmental insurance fund ("play or pay"), such system incorporating the concept of "managed competition" and comprising the expansion of Medicaid to encompass all unemployed and not-in-labor-force persons. (This approach of universal access coupled with cost containment through a national cap—or at least a target—was advocated by President Clinton during the 1992 presidential campaign.)

3. *Universal coverage, requiring purchase by every individual or household of a basic health insurance policy*, with purchases by lower-income groups governmentally subsidized and free choice of provider(s) by the individual/household but completely erasing employer-provided insurance.

Several of the plans in the first and second category embraced various elements of cost containment (managed care, caps on malpractice awards, maximum fee schedules, curbing technological and facility duplication and/or overuse, and so on). Four variations within the three overall approaches just described should be noted.

The broadest of the published plans, the most "liberal" (in terms of coverage, benefit levels, and the role of government), and very much in the nature of the Canadian NHI system was described (not proposed) in a 1991 Congressional Budget Office (CBO) report. It outlined the features of a single-payer, universal health insurance system, using the Medicare payment rate structure as the principal element of cost containment. Private health insurance policies would be restricted to the coverage of services excluded from the nationwide plan. The uniform benefit package would cover basic medical services, resembling 1991-type comprehensive plans being offered by large corporate employers. The plan would be tax-financed, as would be the residual Medicaid program. Medicare rates would govern physician and hospital services. A consumer copayment rate would be required, but Medicaid would supplement the universal plan's coverage of low-income people and would cover their copayments.[5]

Actually, the broadest of any of the plans was formulated by the American Association of Retired Persons (AARP) and in early 1992 was circulating among the association's membership. Its main features were universal coverage—every individual would have a "Medicard." Long-term care, along with all other "basic health needs," including drugs, would be covered. Affordable limits would be place on out-of-pocket expenses, with no copayment whatever required for preventive, prenatal, and well-baby care. Medicare and Medicaid would be folded in. The federal government, using the states as intermediaries, would run a national risk pool. The plan would be financed by a combination of "sin taxes;" corporate income surtax; monthly premium averaging $50 per capita; an 8 percent employer payroll tax on those employers not covering the "basic health needs;" and remaining gaps filled by a 3 percent special income tax or a 5 percent value-added tax on all goods and services excepting food, housing, and medical care and with a refundable tax credit for low-income persons.[6] The Urban Institute and the Brookings Institution proposed the "play or pay" approach, combined with various new governmental control powers. Proposals introduced in the Congress in late 1991 by the House Ways and Means chairman and the Senate majority leader, respectively, were based on play or pay, with the House version conferring some cost containment powers upon the HHS secretary to enforce legislative standards.[7] Appendix 4.A presents in chart form the principal features of these proposals. To the foregoing, an additional factor that had been gaining increased attention was what former Colorado governor Richard Lamm and Lester Thurow of the Massachusetts Institute of Technology (MIT) termed ''an ethic of restraint and a concept of 'appropriate care'/'cost-effective medicine.' ''[8] (This concept was mirrored by a subsequently discussed "health rationing" plan in Oregon.)

A number of states enacted legislation in the 1980s to (1) establish an employer-based health insurance safety net for the otherwise uninsured and/or (2) create an insurance risk pool to cover basic needs of targeted populations. Hawaii enacted legislation to implement the first category in 1974 (just before Congress preempted, in the Employment and Income Security Act—ERISA—the power of states to *require* employers to offer health coverage). About two dozen states passed legislation in the second category. Major 1992 state enactments occurred in Florida, Vermont, and Minnesota. The first two endeavored to pressure insurers and employers into providing coverage for all workers, while Minnesota enacted a new cigarette tax and a tax on hospitals and other health providers, beginning in 1996. Tax credits were given Kentucky employers starting insurance plans for their workers. Oregon combined tax credits with pay or play. All states trying to implement pay-or-play plans were running the risk of federal estoppel under ERISA or disability legislation.[9] (A summary of the 1992 state initiatives appears in Appendix 4.B.)

Breaking Health Care Chains in Labor Force Deployment

A major advantage cited by supporters of categories 1 and 3 plans—either a fully government or free market system—was the removal of employees and their careers, as well as the U.S. labor force as a whole, from the tightening grip of health insurance captivity to a particular employer or the health insurance plan of which the employer was a member. Also cited was a substantial reduction in paperwork and other overhead costs inherent in a multitiered system.

On the other hand, serious disadvantages cited in these two approaches were, in the case of the government-dominated system, the substitution of layers of government bureaucracies for the insurance carriers and, for the free market approach, (1) the absence of any effective cost constraints—the free market having done little in the past to restrain the overuse (either through physician referral, patient choice, or unnecessary expansion) of costly equipment and technology by medical providers—and (2) the compulsion factor involved in requiring all citizens to purchase health insurance.

Preserving Competition While Providing for Universal Coverage

Major advantages cited for play-or-pay plans were (1) achieving universal coverage, while leaving in place the far-flung and flexible employer-provided health insurance systems; (2) providing numerous avenues for the initiation of cost containment strategies at the initiative of employer(s)—individually or collectively—insurers, governments, or combinations thereof; and (3) making it affordable for small businesses to participate in the health insurance system without facing the inequities of experience rating. (In broad terms this approach acquired the name "managed competition." The initial position of the Clinton administration was to couple managed competition with cost controls of some sort.)

Conversely, some argued that many large, as well as small, employers would opt for "paying" rather than "playing," thus producing a very large government-insured group—comprising "a weigh station on the road to a giant Medicaid program for all Americans."[10] Former surgeon general Koop expressed a preference for achieving universal coverage in a way similar to the free market approach, but with one major concern about play or pay that a number of small businesses might have to lay off a portion of their work force in order to produce savings sufficient to cover the payroll tax.[11]

The possibility of layoffs in small business to absorb a payroll tax of 7 to 8 percent (the level often projected as that required to achieve universal coverage) was echoed by other critics of play or pay. Michael Morrisey contended:

If society wants the individual to have coverage, the most efficient way to do this is to directly subsidize the individual's purchase of health insurance, not to subsidize particular types of firms. . . . The questions . . . are not about whether employers should pay their fair share . . . but should be: (1) Does this society wish to compel individuals to purchase health insurance? (2) If so, how much insurance and how much compulsion? (3) Should general tax revenues be used to subsidize the purchase of health insurance? (4) If so, how much of a subsidy, to whom should it be provided, and in what form?[12]

It was also argued that mandating employer contributions to health insurance, while having the political attraction of keeping additional health care costs out of the federal budget, was very costly in other ways. It places another burden on management/labor relations in small businesses, while distracting attention from crucial issues of productivity and competitiveness.[13]

On the other hand, Victor Fuchs noted that the problem was not that small businesses could not afford it (most employees of small professional firms such as law and accounting had health insurance) but that "many workers in small firms cannot afford health insurance." Like Koop, Fuchs predicted a long road ahead:

In the long run, though, national health insurance is not dead. The need to curb costs will push the country toward a national system, although the timing will depend largely on political factors producing a major change in the political climate. Short of that we should expect modest attempts from Washington to increase coverage and contain costs, accompanied by immodest amounts of sound and fury.[14]

Reconciliation Between Ends and Means

A conflict between the required carrying of health insurance by all citizens, as embodied in the "free" market approach of category 3 and the obvious need for cost containment, which was part of most category 1 and 2 proposals, was noted by Mark Pauly: "The paradox is this: What is [economically and administratively] efficient to do does not provide strong promise of cost containment and what seems to work for cost containment—government control of one sort or another—cannot be guaranteed to be efficient.''[15]

The U.S. GAO in its 1991 annual report to the Congress summed up the tasks ahead. It noted several common elements in the health care systems of France, Germany, Japan, and Canada and concluded that the following elements should be embraced by the United States: insuring each individual; instituting uniform payment rules; and setting targets or caps on total expenditures in major categories, such as hospitals, physicians, and the purchase of high-cost capital equipment. The specific features of any broad-based reform program—the role that government would play, the extent to which employers might be required to provide coverage, the assignment of responsibility for expanding coverage to the uninsured—would need to be decided through debate. But the need for health care reform was becoming clear as costs and inequities continued to grow.[16]

The Advisory Council on Social Security, a permanent institutional part of the social insurance system, in completing its 1991 deliberations, found itself also divided, with a minority in favor of proposing a single universal health care plan, but a majority favoring and recommending a course of important but segmental reforms. The council's report stated,

The Council also heard clearly that the obvious right choice for reform from one person or group is abhorrent and unacceptable to another. The real implications of change are unclear. . . . A majority of the Council concluded that at this time there is no one right choice. The national consensus so essential to the successful systemic reform the Council believes necessary has clearly not developed. This is, however, exactly the right time to prepare the country for reform. Now is the time to lay the foundation for change. . . . Change can be gradual, but it must be deliberate, focused and timely. We must tend to the immediate and urgent needs of our citizens and at the same time . . . move systematically forward to the system of our future.[17]

The council recommended a series of immediately needed reforms, referenced at various points in this chapter, and a summary listing of them presented in Appendix 4.C.

In 1993 the legislative and executive branches of the national and state governments, major segments of the medical profession, many larger private employers, and other substantial sectors of American society were in overall agreement that basic reforms were needed in the country's health insurance and delivery systems. But on the form and financing of such reforms, the major segments of government, business, and the general public were far apart as the Clinton administration began formulating its health care and financing reform package. In the meantime state governors and legislatures had not been idle, as shown in Appendix 4.B. Florida legislation (SB 2390, 1992) provided for area-based purchasing cooperatives (managed competition); a 1993 Maryland statute (HB 1359, 1993) expanded a long-standing state hospital rate control body to cover physicians and other medical services (cost containment).

We now move to the particular segments of either a broad ''macro'' reform measure or of a series of incremental or "micro" approaches to health care revision. The major policy options examined here include those addressed to:

1. Aspects of employer-provided and other health insurance plans and the tax treatment thereof that converge with provider/patient incentives to overuse medical resources; the "medical arms race"; physician referrals to entities in which he or she has an equity interest; and malpractice awards and consequent practice of defensive medicine, all of these tending to drive up health care costs in one way or another.

2. The somewhat lessening, but still persisting, strong tilt in the health care system toward acute, inpatient care, all too often initiated by emergency room treatment, to the detriment of preventive care—a tilt with serious health outcome and financial consequences.

3. Various impediments to physical access to health care facilities and personnel by low-income mothers and their children.

4. The need for incentives/sanctions directed against those client behaviors that highly risk or insure adverse health outcomes.

5. The need for countervailing influences against the forces that tend to encourage, abet, or cause violent and other antisocial behavior in families and by adolescents and that deter rehabilitation of young offenders.

6. The need for improvement in health care data and in research/monitoring/evaluation of the effectiveness of remedial programs.

ADDRESSING ECONOMIC, EQUITY, AND HEALTH WEAKNESSES IN THE INSURANCE SYSTEM

The following reviews and alternatives encompass three major population groups and, within each, concentrate on children, adolescents, and their families: (1) group-insured by public or private employer, falling primarily into two categories, employer self-insurance or the purchase by the employer of coverage, usually an insurance company but increasingly per capita payments to a HMO or some other "managed care" intermediary, (2) working poor and employees of small businesses who find insurance unaffordable on an individual or small group basis, (3) low-income individuals and families covered by Medicaid or other publicly subsidized sources. For all three of these groups, the underlying public-private policy objective would seem to be to reduce economic inefficiencies, improve equity, and increase emphasis upon, and incentives for, preventive care, in contrast to acute or other crisis care.

Two factors influenced strongly the evolution of the health insurance industry in the 1950–90 period: (1) a centering of health care insurance reimbursement in hospital and hospital-related coverage and (2) disassociation of the consumer from the *economic consequences* of his or her health care choices.

The Health Insurance Association of America (HIAA) in 1991 assessed the evolution of the system thus:

From its beginning, the emphasis of health care reimbursement has been on hospital coverage, since the hospital has been the center of medical technology and since it claims the largest share of medical expense dollars. . . . In 1969, per capita expenditures for health care were $268 in this country. By 1990, [they were] $2,567. . . . Three leading reasons for health care cost escalation [are]: (1) increases in coverage . . . raised levels of expectation and demand; (2) incentives for providers and consumers have encouraged high levels of utilization, discouraged cost consciousness, and created tolerance for inefficiency and provision of marginally useful care; and (3) new technologies have usually brought improvements in quality at substantial increases in the cost of treating an episode of illness.[18]

Abetting these forces was the complex and uncertain nature of many medical treatments, which tended to cause consumers to leave most or all decision making to the physician.

A more specific listing of the economic disincentives came from Mitchell Rabkin, a Boston hospital president and Harvard Medical School professor:

Cost reimbursement and fee-for-service [have not] . . . encouraged behavior that would restrain costs. [Nor] has the ability of employers to tax deductions on their insurance payments, [and] employees to take those benefits tax free. [Nor] the many economic opportunities . . . the current system provides for equipment manufacturers, pharmaceutical companies, and entrepreneurial physicians and other providers. These people and organizations are not necessarily motivated by greed, but they undoubtedly respond to the influence of economic incentives. . . . Laissez-faire cost reimbursement has made it easy for the physician to order a test or procedure because it *might* do some good, and after all, "the patient isn't paying for it."[19]

A much higher degree of consumer cost participation might offer an alternative offset to the foregoing disincentives. A capitation advance payment approach places with the physician or other provider both economic and medical incentives to make the treatment process as cost-effective as possible. But there is substantial disagreement on both points.

Increasing Employee Share of Health Insurance Cost

The director of the medical assistance division of the North Carolina state government observed that "most of us believe access to health care is a right; unfortunately many mistakenly believe it is free. Consumers expect medical services to be conveniently located, easily accessible and technologically advanced—all at little or no direct cost to them."[20] The disassociation of the insured consumer from the question of "where is the money coming from?" was reflected in a 1992 admonition from the American Association of Retired Persons (AARP) to its members: "Americans make clear in poll after poll that they want major health care change—but they don't want to pay for it. They don't seem to understand that they will have to pay higher taxes to get the very health reforms they seek."[21]

The National Commission on Children (NCC) in its 1991 report stated:

Another important approach to containing health care costs is consumer cost sharing. When consumers are required to share a portion of the costs of care, they are usually more sensitive to price and the usefulness of medical services they use. Therefore the Commission would hold families responsible for a portion of premium and service costs for both public and private health coverage.[22]

An eight-year research project (1974–82) by the Rand Corporation as to the effect of coinsurance requirements concluded that "free medical care [although resulting in more visits] does not appreciably improve the health of adults receiving it."[23] The free-care patients made approximately 33 percent more visits than the other groups.

To implement a recommendation for an increase in the consumer share would necessitate action either (1) by the employer or employer group providing the coverage to make the cost-sharing adjustment through a plan modification or (2) by state or national governments or both, as a regulatory action in the state's role as insurance regulator or as a condition enacted by the Congress, probably as an amendment to the federal tax code. In the latter case, the tax deductibility of health costs as a business expense would be established at a specified minimum level of employee cost-sharing or as a condition to the continued exclusion of employer-provided insurance from being counted as income to the employee. A state having an income tax could, of course, attach the same kind of conditions to its tax code.

The NCC suggested as a condition to its proposal quoted earlier that "to encourage the use of essential preventive health care (prenatal care, well-child care, and immunizations)," cost-sharing for these services be excluded from the cost-sharing requirement. It pointed out that parent-consumers would be more motivated to avail themselves and their children of preventive care that would reduce the need for more expensive treatment and hospitalization later if cost of the preventive care were not a barrier.[24] Such an exclusion might help redress the unwarranted system tilt toward acute, rather than preventive, care.

There has been widespread, but not unanimous, agreement that the drastic lowering and, in many cases, complete disappearance of any consumer cost consciousness associated with employer-provided health insurance have been a major factor in unnecessary health care cost escalation. Even where the employee bears a modest or significant share of a premium cost, no incentive is provided for consumers to search for reasonable fees when getting medical care. Only a moderate copayment associated *with each episode* provides such an incentive. Some progress would be made at no increase in cost to employees *as a group within a particular establishment*, if employer action were taken to substitute copayments for premiums or premiums were reduced and a commensurate amount imposed as a copayment. The employee argument against such a trade-off might be that it is either discrimination against lower-paid employees or, if pay levels were made a factor in premium rates, a means testing of what has become an employee right.

It is clear that despite the economic savings to the health insurance system as a whole through increasing the consumer share of costs, intense opposition from large segments of the public would be encountered. Not only would this include the general opposition to any increase in taxes or charges, but labor unions would strongly object to a "give-back" or the watering down of a hard-won gain at earlier bargaining tables. Inclusion of such a step as part of a larger package of health insurance might be feasible, depending upon other surrounding circumstances.

Eliminating or Modifying Federal and State Disincentives to Economically Efficient and Equitable Health Care Financing

These disincentives fall into two categories—tax disincentives and wasteful state health insurance regulations. A major reason most employees covered by employer-provided health insurance view the coverage as free is that the value of the employer's contribution—often in the 80–90 percent range and not infrequently, 100 percent—is not counted as income to the employee for federal income tax purposes. In the late 1940s in a mistaken attempt to widen health insurance coverage, the Internal Revenue Service ruled that health care benefits to employees would be tax-free. A cash bonus of $5,000 to an employee obviously is taxable income; a $5,000 health insurance policy is not. Consequently, employer-provided health insurance constitutes a nearly unbreakable bond between employer and employee, and it grows tighter with each increment of health cost increase.

Many argue that this bond interferes with optimum deployment of the nation's labor force. A survey commissioned by the U.S. Advisory Council on Social Security found that nearly 30 percent of all Americans reported that they or a family member stayed in an unsatisfactory job out of fear of losing health insurance if they moved to another employer. Furthermore, in a recession, when an unusually large number of firms file for bankruptcy or go out of business, employee health insurance, in contrast to retirement, has not enjoyed the vested liability status.

Alain Enthoven cited four additional inequities and inefficiencies in the tax exclusion of employer contributions as income to the employee:

First, it greatly attenuates the incentive for employment groups and individuals to accept economical managed-care arrangements. Considering all . . . taxes, a group or individual who chooses a health plan that costs an additional $100 will pay only $60 to $70 in net after-tax dollars. . . . Second, the cost to the federal budget is very large; like health care, it is growing faster than the GNP. Third, as a method of subsidizing health insurance, it is unfair. Most of the revenue loss goes to people with above average incomes [as shown in a CBO report]. [This revenue loss] does nothing for people without employer-provided health insurance, arguably the ones most in need of help. Fourth, as an incentive to people to purchase insurance, it is inefficient; most of the dollars go to people who would buy [such] insurance without the incentive.[25]

The exclusion of employer-provided health benefits began to receive wide attention at the beginning of the 1990s as a way to offset part or all of the cost of financing a refundable tax credit that could provide "bare bones" health insurance coverage to those not insured, particularly those not in the labor force, the unemployed, and the working poor. Stuart Butler, director of domestic/economic studies at the Heritage Foundation, framed the proposal thus:

Congress should end the tax exclusion for company based plans and use the revenue (about $50 billion) to finance a system of refundable tax credits for health care spending by individuals and families. . . . These changes would . . . shield most families—especially lower income [ones]—from the full cost of their medical care. . . . People would have the incentive to seek the best value for their money because they, not their employers would pocket the savings from wise purchases of insurance.[26]

In some respects such a trade-off, while equitable, would intensify objections from the employer-insured population, who would consider that Peter was being robbed to pay Paul.

Objections to a cancellation of the health benefit exclusion from the federal, and most state, income tax codes are obvious. Many of the same people addressed in the *AARP Bulletin* cited earlier probably would be in the forefront. To cancel the exclusion completely would, in all probability, increase the number of employed people choosing to go without health insurance. Most proponents of a tax change in this direction would begin the cancellation at a moderately high level of adjusted gross income (e.g., $60,000) or, alternately, not to exceed a proportion (e.g., 80%) of the average price of a "basic benefit package" limited to essential services.[27] Such a compromise would reduce considerably the revenue that would be retrieved through a complete cancellation of the exclusion but could be said to be more equitable in terms of progressive taxation.

Redirecting State Regulatory Activity

Prior to the early 1990s much of the state regulation of health insurance had been perverse in its effects, driving up the cost of health insurance.

- Pre-1990, state legislatures and regulatory agencies were responding to innumerable special interest pressures to add to an already long and growing list of diseases, afflictions, procedures, and professions that any insurance policy issued by a company or outlet in the state was required to cover, as a condition of permission to operate. Often services were required to be provided that many enrollees would not buy if they had any choice. As the list lengthened, policy premiums had to go up if the insurer was to remain solvent. As the results of this kind of regulation became apparent, states began to authorize the issuance of basic, "bare bones" policies at greatly reduced premiums.

- On another front, state regulatory activity initially had tended toward abolishing or modifying regulatory action by the medical and associated professions that had been taking the form of limiting professional entry or otherwise impeding competition within the profession (e.g., prohibition of advertising). In general, the state medical associations strongly opposed these state deregulatory actions, on the ground that medicine, with its life-death decisions, required close professional monitoring and supervision. States tended to respond by increasing pressure on the associations to be more vigilant and rigorous in identifying and disciplining profession members found to be engaging in unethical or illegal conduct.

  As a part of this latter effort, a National Disciplinary Information System (NDIS) was established within the Clearinghouse (later, Council) on Licensure Enforcement and Regulation (CLEAR), an affiliate of the Council of State Governments. NDIS lists disciplinary action taken against individuals in a sizable number of separately licensed professions and occupations, including health care. The list is carried in a bimonthly report and is available to participating state and professional enforcement and disciplinary agencies.[28]

- In the late 1980s and early 1990s, a third wave of state regulation ensued, instigated by providers and other special interests to counteract federal and state movements toward managed care and other ways to contain the rapid rise in health care costs. The Hospital Insurance Association of America (HIAA) alleged that nearly 200 state legislative bills had been introduced and some already enacted in 1991 alone. They were directed primarily at utilization measures being undertaken by insurers, HMOs, and others to curb or eliminate unnecessary health care costs (such as those discussed in succeeding sections).[29]

In the early 1990s, the principal foci of federal and state action on the regulatory side were directed toward (1) shifting the emphasis in health services toward preventive care and the encouragement of managed care; (2) attacking the remaining barriers to effective and equitable delivery and pricing of health care; and (3) initiating new legislation and regulations in the area of cost containment and to deal with various problems of waste, abuse, and fraud. Policy options in these areas are examined in the following sections.

RETILTING THE SYSTEM TOWARD PREVENTIVE CARE AND COST CONTAINMENT

The unfavorable consequences, both in health outcomes and in financial cost, of preventive care neglect and lack of incentives for efficiency have become obvious. A number of public and private policies were being advanced in the early 1990s to achieve a shift in priorities toward more cost-effective procedures.

Greater Priority to Preventive Care

Concerned with the large numbers of disadvantaged children, the Children's Defense Fund (CDF) argued, "Most children and their parents need child care, not foster care; a checkup, not a hospital bed."[30] Steps toward greater emphasis on preventive, in contrast to acute, care include cessation of the "hospital centering" of many insurance reimbursement procedures, a continuing public education campaign to urge preventive care, and removing access barriers to such care. A 1992 *Business Week* editorial declared:

Public health needs constant attention. [When a problem is dealt with] fickle politicians turn to the next problem. . . . The budget for . . . Centers for Disease Control got flattened out, so the agency pared spending for preventive-care programs such as immunization and infectious-disease tracking. . . . The result has been a startling increase in . . . measles, sexually transmitted diseases, AIDS, and infant mortality.[31]

Repeal of Prior Hospitalization Requirements. Certain laws and regulations and insurance policy provisions required hospital admission on an inpatient status as a prior step for reimbursable preventive or diagnostic services for mothers and children. Some of these instances were cited earlier in connection with prenatal and postnatal care reimbursement under the Medicaid program. They represented a hangover from the early days of health insurance that tended to center protection around hospital care. (Some of the prior hospitalization requirements were initiated in connection with the Medicare program, which is not relevant here except for the Medicare category applying to total disability.)

Except for possible objections by some hospitals and physicians whose practices are largely hospital-based and the widespread inconvenience to third-party payers on the occasion of almost *any* legislative or regulatory change, no substantial opposition should arise to a careful purging of the rules to facilitate this maximization of opportunity for preventive care and diagnostic services.

An Energetic and Continuing Educational Campaign. With public and private organizations and the media using their communication skills and resources, such a campaign would be for the purpose of encouraging citizens to promote good health and prevent disease in themselves, their families, and their communities. (The campaign of successive surgeons general of the U.S. Public Health Service (USPHS) and countless public and private efforts to reduce the incidence of smoking have been an outstanding example, as have educational programs directed toward exercise and healthy food habits.) This public/private policy aimed at preventive care meets with widespread acceptance, with opposition generally limited to affected interest groups.

In the same vein, federal and state policy initiatives toward significant investments, as well as public education efforts, appeared needed in environmental health, accident prevention programs, early detection and treatment of disease, timely immunizations, and vaccine development.[32] (The Southern Legislative

Conference adopted a policy statement dealing with infant mortality to "document the scope of infant mortality and factors related to its prevalence throughout the South [and] to raise the level of public awareness of the problem.")[33]

Increasing Scope and Availability of Preventive Care Services. Reed Tuckson stated the case thus:

Universal access to comprehensive, coordinated health care that emphasizes prevention, early diagnosis, and appropriate medical intervention . . . must be at the heart of any cost-reduction effort . . . ensure that providers and clinical facilities are available in urban and rural areas now underserved. To this end, the National Health Service Corps and the public health system should be expanded at both the national and state levels.[34]

The first part of this type of prescription has been widely subscribed to and cited earlier from diverse sources such as the Children's Defense Fund, National Commission on Children, and former surgeon general Koop. However, as Carolyn Davis, former head of the federal Health Care Financing Administration, pointed out, after stating the need for increased preventive care services, "because, at least initially, these services represent added costs, any expansion must be slow and incremental. . . . To play on the old adage, we must 'spend money to save money.' "[35]

The fiscal/political problem in expanding preventive care services and facilities—as well as nearly any other service of a noncrisis or daily use nature for large numbers of the same people—was being exacerbated in state and local governments in the early nineties, due to recessionary and tax-revolt pressures. Coupled with the increase in scope and availability of preventive care and diagnostic services, particularly relevant to perinatal care for mothers, infants, and young children, was the need for intensive outreach services by maternal and child health (MCH) and Medicaid administrators to inform and persuade the women involved to visit the available facilities. Intensified outreach, however, faces the same hesitation in a climate of fiscal austerity as proposals for expanded services. There are also the behavioral aspects of reluctance to go to preventive care facilities. Policy options regarding persuasive actions that might be taken by state legislation and regulation in regard to behavioral impediments are discussed subsequently. Immediately related to the whole issue of availability and utilization of preventive services is the issue of "managed care."

Cost Reductions Through Managed Care

The term *managed health care* as used in the health insurance and other health-related businesses and professions refers "to any system that manages the delivery of health care *in such a way that the cost is controlled.*" The traditional combination of health insurance and unlimited patient choice-of-physician/fee-for-service structure requires various kinds of management of health care.[36] The key objective of managed care, as used here, is to control costs while assuring quality. The term also embraces utilization management and health care delivery systems that are alternatives to the traditional structure mentioned above.

Utilization Management. Utilization management consists of a set of *administrative* programs for reducing resources consumed in health care.[37] A wide variety of utilization management techniques, structures, and approaches have evolved in the United States. Some are built into one or more of the alternative delivery systems discussed later. The major ones include (1) hospital preadmission certification programs, (2) hospital discharge planning, (3) second surgical opinion, and (4) audits and retrospective reviews.

Two important conditions, among others, accompany the introduction of utilization management. First, the particular measures undertaken *need to be acceptable both to the primary physician and to the patient.* Traditionally, the doctor-patient relationship was considered sacrosanct, and the imposition of such procedural control as second opinion and prehospital admission review, were considered intrusive and unacceptable by many in the medical profession. However, once the insurers began to require them, that official opposition largely dissipated, given the economic attraction to a physician of an insured, as opposed to an uninsured, patient and the fact that other physicians were doing the reviewing in most cases.

A second condition, much more difficult to meet, has been *confidence in the cost-effectiveness* of the utilization measure. It is difficult to meet for two reasons: (1) the relatively high cost of a number of the measures, such as second opinion (unless of a useless, "old boy," accommodative nature) and preadmission certification, and (2) data adequate to determine cost-effectiveness *over time* are extremely hard to establish, in the absence of carefully controlled experiments, which in themselves are quite expensive. Consequently, many self-insuring employers and insurance companies tend to experiment—instituting a measure for a specified period, with continuance dependent upon whether it appears to be a money-saver.[38]

Alternative Delivery Systems. In its 1991 health insurance data compilation, the HIAA observed:

During the past 5 to 10 years, the health care delivery and financing system has evolved at a pace that few expected, largely in response to the acute concern about the ever-rising cost of care. The most visible change has been the explosion of what are becoming known as managed care delivery systems of which HMO's [health maintenance organizations] and PPO's [preferred provider organizations] are the best known examples.[39]

The *HMO concept* appeared as early as 1929 when a rural farmers' cooperative health plan was established by an Elk City, Oklahoma, physician, as well as the formation of a group practice plan by Los Angeles physicians who entered into a prepaid contract to provide health services to around 2,000 water company employees.

In the mid- to late 1930s, the Group Health Association of Washington, D.C.

(GHAW), was formed, and its existence was confirmed by judicial opinion over the organized opposition of the local medical society, and by 1960 it was operating with a coverage of around 100,000; the Kaiser-Permanente (KP) Medical Programs was formed in California in 1947 and in 1992 was the largest and most widely distributed HMO in the country (17 states and the District of Columbia), with 6.5 million members.[40]

HMOs continued to expand slowly until after 1973, when Congress enacted the HMO Act (PL 93–222), which authorized federal funds to help establish and develop HMOs. It *required most employers to offer an HMO option to employees* where federally qualified HMOs were available.[41] Due to the favorable cost record of HMOs, Medicare and Medicaid also turned to them.[42] However, the CDF in a 1988 report contended that the HMOs "are far less prevalent among firms that employ primarily low-income workers. Indeed, health maintenance organizations traditionally have avoided marketing their services to less affluent populations whose members may be more likely to have pre-existing health problems."[43]

By 1990, 569 HMOs were serving 36.5 million people. Between January 1986 and December 1990, HMOs added 15.3 million new members, 1.7 million in calendar year 1990.[44] In 1990, only three states were without a single HMO— Alaska, Mississippi, and Wyoming. States and territories where HMOs served 20 percent or more of the population in 1990 were D.C. (72.9); California (30.7); Massachusetts (26.5); Oregon (24.7); Hawaii (21.6); Wisconsin (21.7); Rhode Island (20.6); and Colorado (20.0).[45]

As of the early 1990s there were four principal models of HMOs.[46] The first was the *staff model* in which the physicians, including nurses and supporting staff, are on the HMO payroll on a salaried basis, sometimes augmented by other cash or noncash incentives, such as retirement, health, and other benefits. Depending on the organization's size, many or few of the services of medical subspecialists are handled through outside referrals. Some of the earlier HMOs, including the Puget Sound group health cooperative in Seattle, were still following the staff model in 1993. In 1991, of the 569 HMOs, 61 were of this type and covered between 4 and 5 million enrollees.

A major advantage of this model is its single-tier nature, with the primary care physicians on top of the cost situation at most points and in a competitive mode vis-à-vis other providers, including other HMOs. A disadvantage often cited is the relatively limited patient choice among primary physicians, often limited to one in the case of a subspecialty, but in the larger HMOs, the range of choice of one's primary physicians may run to a half dozen or more at any one branch clinic location. A major disadvantage besetting new HMOs just getting established lies in the high capital and operational start-up costs.

Second, the *group model*, typified by Kaiser, involves a physician medical group, contracting with the entity that is financially responsible for covering enrollees. In the *captive group* category of this model, the medical group exists solely to provide services to the HMO's beneficiaries/members and is encouraged or formed by the HMO for that purpose. In the *independent group* category, the HMO contracts with an independent group to provide physician services to its members, with that group also providing services to nonmembers of the HMO health plan and engaging in other "non-HMO business." The cost control advantage is not as direct or strong as in the staff or captive group models. The two group models totaled 77 out of 569 in 1990, with 10.4 million enrollees.[47]

Third, in the *network model*, like the Health Insurance Plan (HIP) of the New York metropolitan area, the HMO contracts with two or more independent group practices to provide the physician services. These independent group practices may be broad and multispecialty or may be groups of primary care physicians. A physician in the network may have arrangements with one or more HMOs. The patient has greater flexibility in choice of physician, but the cost control function becomes more diffused. There were 82 network plans in 1990, with 5.1 million enrollees.[48]

Fourth, the *independent practice association (IPA) model* is an association of individual, independent physicians or small groups of physicians formed for the purpose of contracting with one or more managed health care organizations— HMOs, PPOs, and others. The GHAA annual count of those IPAs that are tied to HMOs numbered 333 in 1990–91 and had about 43 percent of the total HMO enrollment that year (14.7 million).[49] These IPAs provide a mechanism for translating capitation payments from an HMO into another form of payment— often fee for service to individual participating physicians. They also provide a mechanism for HMOs to recruit leaders and panel members of participating physicians. From the HMO's perspective there are two major disadvantages of this model. First, the formation of an IPA enables the participating physicians to bargain as a group with the HMO. Second, and more important, the whole concept of utilization management is watered down, since the physicians remain individual private practitioners and feel more loyalty to their IPA fellows than to the HMO.

Preferred Provider Organizations (PPOs) comprise the second major category of managed care institutions. The PPOs give patients greater freedom in choosing providers, but simultaneously they try to guide patients to cost-conscious and cost-effective providers. The PPOs are often organized by insurers. A final type, combining HMO and PPO functions, is *point of service (POS)* plans, which use a network of selected participating providers. Covered consumers select a primary care physician, who controls referrals to medical specialists. If the consumer receives care from a provider in the network, he or she pays no appreciable amount and does not file a claim. If the service is rendered by a nonplan provider, the consumer is responsible for a higher copayment and/or deductible. At the end of 1990, PPOs numbered 798, with 48 million persons having access, in comparison with 34.5 million enrolled in HMOs.[50]

Appropriate Mixes in Medical Skills. Closely associated with alternative delivery systems is the "skill mix," or suboccupational composition of physician services. Often the mix of primary care and general practitioners, on one hand,

and specialists and subspecialists, on the other, is tied closely to the type of delivery system. Frequently cited in overall assessments of the U.S. health care system was a general observation that there were too many specialists in relation to general practitioners and that this imbalance drives up costs. Many HMOs, especially of the staff and group models, exercise careful review over referrals to outside specialists and subspecialists as a cost control mechanism.

The objective of a $12 million Medical Outcomes Study conducted out of the New England Medical Center was "to examine whether specialty and system-of-care exert independent effects on resource utilization." The study comprised cross-sectional analyses of about 20,000 patients who visited providers' offices during 9-day periods in 1986. The setting consisted of 349 physicians' offices practicing (1) family medicine, (2) internal medicine, (3) endocrinology, and (4) cardiology, within HMOs; large, multispecialty groups; and solo practice or small single-specialty group practices in three major cities. The measures of utilization were (1) hospitalizations, (2) annual office visits, (3) prescription drugs, and (4) common tests and procedures, with rates estimated on both a per visit and per year basis. The outcomes were that higher utilization was related to (1) specialty and (2) fee-for-service plan and solo practice or single-specialty group practice. The latter had 41 percent more hospitalizations than HMOs.[51]

Comments accompanying the published report were (from a lead author of one of the reports): "A lot of patients in those [subspecialists'] offices aren't that sick and shouldn't be there" and (from an outside editorial comment in the same issue of the journal in which the reports appeared): as to a way to gain cost control we need "to pay attention to the mix of physicians providing health care and the way in which they are organized."[52] (As noted subsequently in this chapter, the ACSS report took note of the skill mix issue in relation to the future of the National Health Service Corps.)

The Congressional Budget Office (CBO) conducted an

illustrative exercise designed to provide a sense of the order of magnitude of . . . reductions in national health expenditures (NHEs) that might result from universal adoption of two specific forms of managed care. One is staff- and group-model HMOs, the forms of managed care for which demonstrated cost savings are greatest. The other is "effective" forms of utilization review [UR] which the CBO interprets to mean utilization review that incorporates precertification and concurrent review of inpatient care. . . . The illustrative analyses suggests that [for staff or group model HMOs] NHEs might be lower by about 10 percent. Alternatively if all . . . health care services . . . were delivered through . . . effective forms of UR, the resulting reduction in NHEs might be no more than 1 percent.[53]

Public Policy Considerations in Managed Care. At the beginning of the 1990s, the apparent health, economic, and other consequences of the increased use of managed care included:

- A major advantage, especially in the case of staff and group types of HMOs, producing savings in both employer-provided and governmental health programs, achieved partly through federal mandating of an HMO option and partly through consumer attraction to lower costs, compared with the fee-for-service approach.

- An appreciable increase in emphasis on preventive care in most of the alternative delivery systems, especially those based on a capitation rate, because of its demonstrated cost-effectiveness; this emphasis was especially important for those population and income categories not otherwise motivated to seek preventive care, whereby HMO or other organization personnel *take the initiative* to schedule members for examinations, vaccinations, and other precautionary measures.

- On the other hand, U.S. comptroller general Charles Bowsher in 1991 testimony before the House Committee on Ways and Means stated that

  businesses' use of managed care is unlikely to contain overall health care spending in the future for three reasons: First, managed care has sometimes achieved one-time savings, but whether it moderates the upward trend of spending is debatable. Second, managed care seems unlikely to cover a large enough proportion of Americans during the next decade to moderate the upward trend. . . . Currently, HMOs cover only 8 percent of Americans (actually, 35 million in 1991 was about 14 percent of the total population). . . . Third, managed care does not seem to restrain those forces that increase overall . . . spending but that originate outside the managed care population—medical "arms races" [e.g., unnecessary use or expansion of expensive equipment by neighboring hospitals where use volume is low].[54]

- Additionally, a decrease in consumer choice and flexibility in obtaining health services, causing restiveness among the "people being managed" and the criticism from some that the general evolution in private and public sector policies was pointing toward "forcing many millions of people into HMOs, while the well-heeled stay free to pick and choose their medical care."[55]

Striking a balance between freedom of choice and cost containment considerations seemed to be a major challenge to national and state governments in formulating health care delivery and financing policies in 1993. The national government could move rapidly toward adopting a universal coverage, single-payer system and in effect preempt further state experimentation with alternate health care delivery and insurance approaches. Conversely, it might take an incremental approach, revising and reforming the Medicaid and Medicare programs, while further searches for improvement went on in the private sector and by state and local governments. Some of those experiences and possibilities are examined next.

Curbing Unnecessary Use or Expansion of Medical Facilities, Technology, and Equipment

Dr. Everett Koop, in a 1992 newspaper column, commented:

In health care, more is not always better. . . . The amount of health care consumed by Americans differs remarkably, depending on where they live. Bostonians receive almost twice as much hospital care and at twice the cost per capita as do New Havenites [with no evidence of better health]. A $300 million annual savings could result if the Boston figures were reduced to the New Haven level.[56]

In his testimony cited previously, Comptroller General Bowsher stated:

A recent example of high-tech escalation has been reported in the county containing Altoona, Pennsylvania: a hospital and a group of radiologists each have acquired MRI machines. Another MRI also serving Altoona residents is nearby in the next county. . . . With these machines, physicians apparently performed more MRI scans per resident than were done in Philadelphia and many other hospitals in the state.[57]

In international comparative terms, Henry Aaron pointed out that the United States was making far greater use of high technology than Canada and Germany; in 1987, the United States had 7.4 times as many radiation therapy and 8 times as many MRI units as Canada and 4.4 times as many open heart surgery units as Germany, clearly making U.S. hospital treatment more intricate, specialized, and costly than elsewhere. However, part of the result of this was faster release from hospitals, and to that extent some partially offsetting savings resulted.[58]

Certificate of Need Concept. The Health Planning and Resource Development Act of 1974 required that all states receiving federal health resources enact certificate of need (CON) laws or regulations providing for state review and approval of planned capital investments of health care institutions. By 1980, all states except Louisiana had put such programs into place. Some states extended such controls to physicians' offices as well as hospitals, but this was very limited and controversial. Subsequent research on the effectiveness of CON controls consistently found that they did not restrain hospital spending, and in 1986, CON requirements for states were dropped. Those who support health planning and CON requirements suggest, however, that CON in most states, at times, was applied in an inconsistent and politically motivated way that was not compatible with cost-consciousness and the orderly adoption of new technologies. On the other hand, a few states, including Maryland, retained and strengthened their CON programs.[59]

By the late 1980s, sentiment was developing in several states to revive or strengthen their earlier CON statutes, while a number of others believed that those laws should be discarded. In a handful of states, CON laws had been followed by companion legislation imposing state agency control over not only capital expenditures but also hospital operational rates and charges.

If the CON concept is reinvigorated at federal or state levels or both, note needs to be taken of the strengths and weaknesses growing out of the earlier experience. CON legislation had both good and bad results in metropolitan areas, where duplication of facilities was most often encountered. It forced a greater sense of community responsibility upon hospital administrators; by requirements for consumer representation on health planning advisory committees, it opened the door to the consumer voice as to where and how facilities were located and operated. Such consumer opinion was often at odds with health technicians' views on optimal placement. The public hearing process in connection with certificate or license application began to enable the public as a whole to have its say.

On the other hand, the process was accompanied in a number of states by much bickering between health planning and overall planning agencies of the state government, between state and local authorities, and between government and the private sector. Considerable sentiment developed in several quarters for placing health facility planning in nonprofit, rather than strictly governmental, organizations, and enabling legislation made this course of action optional in the mid-1970s.

The oversupply of physicians, especially specialists, and resulting increases in physician costs and treatment rates, have also become a major issue. Some have called for adoption of national policies—supported by appropriate changes in funding—to control both the overall number of physicians being trained and the mix of specialties. In terms of possible state and federal legislation strengthening, modifying, or eliminating the CON provisions, there seem to be several considerations.

- For state legislation, some kind of CON provisions appears appropriate in at least some states. The examples cited by Koop and Bowsher speak for themselves. The overuse and duplication problems tend to be more severe in metropolitan areas, with the result that meeting costs of new technology requires a higher level of testing and referrals than would otherwise be necessary. In rural areas or in urban places where a structure for cooperative use of facilities and equipment is already in place, further regulatory mechanisms might not be required.

- The prior difficulties of complex processes and turf battles would need to be avoided in framing legislation and regulations; otherwise, more harm than good probably would result.

- Whether or not federal legislation requiring CON or other means of controlling technology overuse or duplication avoidance should be adopted would depend on how it fitted in with other federal cost controls. Additionally, federal preemption of state regulatory authority in a substantive area as diverse as this is always questionable, due to widely varying conditions among and within states.

- If federal legislation were considered, it probably would be highly desirable that flexibility be provided for further state experimentation and innovation.

- A separate issue, but closely linked with CON legislation, is the question of including operational services and supply of physicians.

Hospital Pooling, Mergers, and Joint Ventures. Although pooling of scarce equipment makes economic sense, it is done less frequently than would be possible in a reinvigoration of the CON concept. However, when complete facilities are merged or mergers are attempted, real difficulties arise. The ACSS

1991 report pointed out that communities develop a strong sense of identity with their local hospitals and are reluctant to see one facility close in favor of another. It stated:

Communities have proposed mergers of two hospitals in order to maintain their sense of community identity while pooling services, personnel and expensive equipment. However, current antitrust laws prevent such mergers because of the anticompetitive impact. Alternatively other communities have proposed joint ventures using two hospital facilities for a hospital and a different purpose such as a nursing home, but their proposals have been inhibited because of antitrust laws as well as Medicare fraud and abuse considerations.[60]

The council proposed that legislation be enacted to permit mergers of two hospitals in the same community in limited cases and that "the proposed legislation should include criteria relating to the length of time each hospital has served the community, the occupancy rates and relative financial condition of each . . . and the willingness of each . . . to engage in the merger." It further urged that

the Attorney General and the Secretary of Health and Human Services jointly develop proposals for legislation to amend the antitrust laws to permit two hospitals in the same community [in limited cases], to enter into a joint venture for the provision of hospital services at one facility and health-related services . . . at the other. . . . The . . . legislation should include criteria [rather similar to those for mergers].[61]

Dealing with Malpractice and Tort Liability. In late 1990, the U.S. General Accounting Office (GAO) stated to the Congress that "the present methods for resolving medical malpractice claims in the United States are neither efficient or equitable. Claims take a long time to be resolved; awards and settlements are unpredictable; and legal costs are high."[62] Medical malpractice was cited as a major factor in nearly every report, article, or other review of the U.S. health care delivery system from the late 1980s onward. Former surgeon general Koop, in listing the major ills in the health care system, said: "We need to reform the malpractice mess that spends more on legal overhead than on injury compensation and passes the bill along to us. . . . If doctors were no longer forced to practice defensive medicine, the savings would be incalculable."[63]

Malpractice insurance premiums for some specialties, especially obstetrics, were running up to $100,000 per year, leading to both (1) excessive prescribing of unnecessary tests and procedures as defense against potential litigation and (2) shortages of physicians willing to enter the high-risk areas or types of practice depending upon governing state laws regarding insurance and malpractice awards. Consequently, in terms of policy action by state legislatures or by federal preemptive legislation, the major thrust of most proposals has been toward capping amounts of, and opportunities for, malpractice awards. These include:

- "Enactment of meaningful tort reform to diminish the practice of defensive medicine."[64]
- "Encourage states to enact reforms to reduce malpractice liability. . . . The example of our Canadian neighbors shows that we can significantly reduce malpractice costs by, for example, limiting lawyers' acceptance of contingency fees, conducting [malpractice] trials by judge rather than by jury, and setting caps on awards for 'pain and suffering.' "[65]

Malpractice suits are brought and tried within the framework of "tort liability" as it has evolved within the U.S. legal system. Movements for reform of state tort liability statutes began to occur in the late 1970s and increased through the 1980s.

The Rand Corporation's Institute for Civil Justice conducted research on a number of tort liability issues, with mixed conclusions. On the impact of fee arrangement of lawyer effort (contingency or hourly basis), one study found no significant difference on smaller cases. On the severity and frequency of medical malpractice claims, caps on awards significantly reduced severity, and shorter statutes of limitation reduced frequency, but some researchers cautioned that the tort reform goal should not be to reduce claims costs but to deter medical negligence and assure timely compensation of victims.[66] But over time, a distinct shift away from fault as the basis of liability occurred, and more and more juries searched for "deep pockets" that could be used for compensation, and as one of the consequences malpractice insurance, as well as other insurance premiums, ascended steeply.

In addition to encouraging the practice of "defensive medicine," the medical malpractice environment makes it more difficult for physicians to initiate, or collaborate in, cost containment strategies, because *consideration of costs* in a practice decision can make the decision more susceptible to liability in the event of a lawsuit. However, as the CBO report on health costs pointed out, the development of clinical practice guidelines (as discussed later) and results from research on the health outcomes of different treatments may provide a sounder foundation of knowledge that will enable physicians to make more cost-effective, as well as more appropriate, decisions.[67]

Another adverse impact of the malpractice environment upon efforts to improve the health care system lies in the threat to community health centers, the functions of which were described in chapter 3. The malpractice insurance costs to these clinics rose at a much greater rate than the federal grants upon which many of them were depending. Because such a large proportion of center clientele were in the low-income category, one policy option was to extend the protections of the Federal Tort Claims Act, under which medical professionals in federal hospitals were already excluded, to cover health professionals working in the centers.[68]

Two state malpractice reform laws, both enacted in 1975, proved to be moderately effective in braking (1) the escalation of malpractice awards and (2) rising costs of malpractice insurance. The Indiana law was passed at the initiative of then-physician-governor Otis Bowen. The Indiana components were (1) a cap on *all* damages, set initially at $500,000; this subsequently was revised to $750,000 for claims arising after January 1, 1990, (2) mandatory pretrial review by a three-provider panel (one selected by claimant, one by defense, and one jointly by the first two) to make an informal determination of liability, (3) a Patient Compensation Fund to pay out claims in excess of $100,000, administered by the state insurance department and financed by a surcharge on individual providers and institutions, and (4) a cap on attorney fees at 15 percent of awards. The initial cap of $500,000 on damages kept Indiana out of the "lottery size" settlements in various other states (with the national average malpractice verdict going to $1.1 million in 1989). California's law, the Medical Injury Compensation Recovery Act (MICRA), likewise capped pain and suffering awards at $250,000, encouraged arbitration, shortened the statute of limitations on claims, and limited lawyer contingency fees to 40 percent of awards up to $50,000 and 10 percent for those over $200,000.[69] A GAO report on the California experience concluded that the law had been effective in holding down the cost of malpractice claims.[70]

Illustrative of other state legislation initiated or enacted to deal with medical malpractice reform as of 1990 were the following:

• Florida and Virginia "no-fault" liability coverage was being provided for newborn birth-related injuries through a voluntary workers' compensation-type system under which physicians and hospitals were paying fees to support the compensation fund.[71]

• The West Virginia legislature directed the State Board of Risk and Insurance Management to provide malpractice insurance for all medical practitioner participants in a primary professional malpractice insurance program.[72]

• Missouri adopted a program to cover malpractice claims made against physicians who were under contract with local health departments, using the state's general liability fund for its own employees.[73] Similarly, under local legislation, Montgomery County, Maryland, established a public-private partnership whereby obstetricians were employed at market rates to provide delivery services to health department-referred patients in order to cover them by the county's self-insurance program.[74]

In its 1991 report the ACSS put forward a two-part proposal to change the medical malpractice environment in several respects. The first part was a suggested Federal Beneficiary Malpractice Adjudication Act, and the second was a Model State Malpractice Adjudication Act. The proposed federal legislation would establish a national administrative tribunal to hear malpractice claims arising from the medical care of federal beneficiaries, that is, individuals entitled to receive or be reimbursed for health care from the federal government. Using expeditious procedures, the tribunal would award a prevailing claimant compensation for economic losses resulting from physical harm caused by negligent treatment plus reasonable attorney fees. By enabling an individual to obtain prompt resolution of a claim against a health professional or other provider, the proposed act would also be expected to encourage prompt and effective pre-hearing mediation and settlement.

The model state malpractice act would be developed by the HHS secretary in consultation with the states. Its purpose would be to restrain further growth in malpractice insurance costs. The award to a prevailing claimant would consist of compensation for economic losses resulting from physical harm caused by negligent treatment plus reasonable attorney fees and would be the exclusive remedy to a claimant. The award could not exceed $200,000 per claimant; derivative damages, pain and suffering, and such items as loss of spousal consortium would be out of bounds. A state Advisory Council on Standards of Health Care would be created to develop guidelines for use in evaluating claims of malpractice.[75]

Rather than attacking the malpractice award and insurance system through the avenue of conventional reform of the tort liability system, some would protect the patients' interests by mitigating the extent of injuries and simultaneously eliminate a substantial portion of the necessity for defensive medicine, thus reducing costs. This approach would identify types of *avoidable injuries in advance*. If a listed injury occurred, it would be promptly compensable under standard payment rules. Such an occurrence would constitute an "accelerated compensation event" (ACE), a class of medical injuries normally preventable but easily identifiable, the listing of which would be unlikely to distort clinical decisions. Randall Bovbjerg summarized the case for such an approach thus:

ACEs are preferable to traditional tort reforms. They are intended to avoid problems rather than find fault; to focus on the results of care rather than on the process; and to judge responsibility dispassionately in advance rather than during emotion-laden court cases. . . . ACEs look forward to encourage early rehabilitation and promote prevention of future injuries. The law instead looks backwards. It seeks to prove liability retrospectively, emphasizing restitution and, often, retribution.[76]

An important link connecting the ACE approach with the ACSS model state law proposal, the Indiana law, and some other state laws comprises a preliminary determination as to whether or not malpractice occurred. This link has arbitration aspects, and in late 1991, 15 states had specific statutes on malpractice arbitration, but very few claims had been filed under them. No-fault programs were another alternative to litigation being tried; under this approach, compensable injuries and compensation amounts are specified. After an injury has been established, it is not necessary to identify the cause.[77] The arbitration, no-fault, and ACE approaches, in turn, are linked to the broad reform in diagnostic and treatment procedures generally—developing through research and experience a *listing of appropriate procedures and treatment*—as proposed by Drs. Koop, Lundberg, and many others in the medical profession. Such a listing not only would provide a basis for judging malpractice claims, but also would reduce unnecessary procedures driven by economic or legal defense motivation or both.

Major opposition to most aspects of general tort liability reform, including medical malpractice, traditionally came from trial attorneys (Association of Trial Lawyers of America) and consumer groups (Ralph Nader, Sidney Wolfe, and others). Labor unions occupied a middle position. AFL-CIO president Lane Kirkland was quoted as saying that "the crucial matter of malpractice reform" should be handled in a broad, labor-favored overhaul of the health care system. A spokesperson for the U.S. Chamber of Commerce perceived a growing consensus for malpractice reform.[78]

Policies to Curb Waste, Abuse, and Fraud

A combination of unique conditions in the U.S. medical and health system produced a high volume of unnecessary expenditure. These conditions included a multiplicity of providers and insurers; the noncompetitive nature of major parts of the system (e.g., a surplus of physicians in an area may lead to higher, rather than lower, costs as prescribed services expand to maintain or enhance existing incomes); granting of hospital privileges; interlocking physician ownership of testing and diagnostic facilities; overbilling of some patients or insurers to compensate for inadequate or no payments by others; and mountains of paperwork to meet requirements of insurers, managed care operators, and governmental agencies.

Standardization and Computerization of Records, Forms, and Reporting. Possible annual savings in this area have been estimated at tens of billions of dollars. This would require collaborative action among insurers and federal and state governments, facilitated by enabling or ratifying legislative action in several respects, or alternatively mandated and prescribed in a universal, single-payer national insurance system.

The 1991 Advisory Council on Social Security (ACSS) proposed, as a part of its health care reforms, a drastic reduction in paperwork associated with health claims. It recommended the convening of an Advisory Council on Health Claim Standardization to consist of representatives of the American Hospital Association, American Medical Association, HIAA, Blue Cross–Blue Shield, consumer groups, individual hospitals and health insurers, and the federal Health Care Financing Administration. This body would be charged with developing a uniform health claim reimbursement form that would include the information needed to determine a patient's health insurance coverage and eligibility to participate in federal, state, or private health care programs. When promulgated, the form would be the sole form required by claims processors for making payment on a reimbursement for hospital inpatient and/or physician's services.[79]

Policing of Abuse and Fraud. Conflicts of interest, such as physician ownership of diagnostic and testing facilities, were described in chapter 2 and illustrated by a near monopoly situation in Florida. To deal with this problem, New Jersey and Michigan enacted laws banning physician referrals to "same physician-owned" clinical laboratories, and Florida in 1992 was considering such legislation. A federal law, effective in 1992 placed restrictions on such practices in the referral of Medicare patients. In December 1991, the American Medical Association adopted a new policy stating that, in general, doctors should not make referrals to facilities or other health care businesses in which they had invested.[80] Additionally, the top antitrust official of the Federal Trade Commission (FIC) announced that the FTC was "aggressively pursuing several investigations" of the various self-referral complaints that had been brought to the commission.[81]

As much as $70 billion of annual U.S. health care outlays was being lost through fraud and abuse by unscrupulous health care providers within the health insurance system, according to an estimate by the U.S. General Accounting Office.[82] Furthermore, auditors for government agencies and private insurers indicated that questionable bills had been most frequently submitted by surgeons and other specialists, in contrast to general practitioners. Auditors and claims examiners also indicated that the most common techniques was the fragmentation or "unbundling" of bills, whereby the sum of the parts was more than the whole (e.g., collection of bills for a particular operation that is supposed to be reported as a single overall procedure). Part of the manipulation of codes under federal reimbursement procedures reflected a response to new Medicare fee schedules, one of the purposes of which was to shift reimbursement income from specialists to general practitioners and family physicians.[83]

The principal policy and administrative response from governments and insurers to problems of abuse, waste, and fraud naturally has been to close loopholes and to tighten restrictions, while respecting the fact that a sizable share of the country's health care is delivered by self-employed practitioners, who are beset with numerous problems associated with the growing complexity of the health care system, including the paperwork requirements of public and private insurers. Another response from public agencies, insurance companies, and other third-party payers has been to urge consumers to check carefully their hospital, drug, and other medical bills and to bring errors to the attention of the insurers. However, one of the side effects of the earlier described sharp declines in the consumer share of health expenditures and the full front-end coverage features in many plans was to decrease or eliminate the consumer's interest in, or vigilance about, the corrections of medical bills, because it mattered not to him or her, since it was being *completely* borne by another party.

Another effect of the declining consumer share was to decrease the political concern and self-interest of the insured citizen about public policy efforts to tighten up on unnecessary health care expenditures, so long as such reform efforts did not harm the consumer. The very high influence of the health industry in Washington and state capitals has been attributable, in considerable measure, to the active financial participation of the industry in political campaigns via "MedPacs" and many similar organizations.[84]

Guidelines for Appropriate Medical Procedures

In the early 1990s a consensus was developing within the medical profession, health insurance industry, government, and many other quarters that (1) many unnecessary medical procedures were being performed and (2) there was a need for agreed-upon clinical guidelines as to appropriate levels and types of procedures that, when disseminated and followed, could result in multibillion-dollar reductions in health care costs, while at the same time maintaining or improving the level of health outcomes. The following comments from a former surgeon general, the editor of the *JAMA*, the vice chairman of Metropolitan Life, the former head of the federal Health Care Financing Administration (HCFA), and a report from the Congressional Budget Office (CBO) have been illustrative of the emerging consensus.

- "The scientific basis of medicine is much weaker than most patients or even physicians realize, and this leads to treatment based on uncertainty. We need to undertake a systematic, well-funded program of 'outcomes research' to enable patients and physicians to know the [probable] outcomes of all medical treatments."[85]
- "The causes of this runaway trend [in health care costs] range from inflation in general to specific aspects of the nation's health and health care systems. Among these are . . . inappropriate use of diagnostic and therapeutic procedures; an increased number of health care professionals. . . . Here are some of the options: Educate physicians and the public as to when various procedures for diagnosis are—and are not—appropriate. A related stronger move would be to link insurance payments to adherence by providers and patients to recognized clinical guidelines."[86]
- "We must deal with the problem of unnecessary and potentially harmful health-care treatment that costs the U.S. billions of dollars each year. Some of this treatment is given because physicians do not know what works and what does not. Accordingly, we should pursue research on outcomes associated with particular treatments and disseminate that information to physicians. We should also eliminate financial incentives that might encourage the provision of inappropriate care."[87]
- "We must finance and promote further research into the effectiveness of standard medical tests and treatments. If we know which . . . bring about the best medical results we can establish specific guidelines for practice. Many studies have demonstrated that at least one-third of many procedures and tests performed today are unnecessary. The establishment of clear-cut, acceptable protocols could save billions of dollars."[88]
- "Other countries . . . monitor and review providers, rather than individual patients and procedures. . . . They apply this process uniformly and comprehensively to all physicians in large geographic areas. . . . All Canadian provinces have systems to monitor physicians' practice patterns. These systems identify physicians who bring patients back when not clearly medically necessary, who order more laboratory work than other physi-

cians. . . . In British Columbia . . . physicians with statistical profiles more than two standard deviations from the average for the physicians' peer group (defined by specialty and geographic area) are reviewed by a committee that can recommend penalties for cause.''[89]

The foregoing options and/or proposals from eminent sources seemed to produce a range between Lundberg (AMA) and CBO (British Columbia example)— a range broad in implementation detail but remarkably narrow in general thrust with clinical guidelines based on health outcomes research and experience. To achieve this goal of a set of widely applicable guidelines for appropriate clinical procedures would require extensive collaboration among the medical profession (including its numerous specialties, where most of the philosophical and technical controversies would likely arise); the health insurance industry; providers, including hospitals, HMOs, and various health care institutional categories, as well as federal and state health and health financing agencies; and, last but not least, public and private health research enterprises. On its face this would appear to be an extremely ambitious endeavor, with a successful conclusion much in doubt.

On the other hand, a number of partial components were in place or in the process of development in 1991, some of which were being driven by requirements attached to Medicare and other federal financing (e.g., reimbursement fees for each of around 500 diagnostic related groups—DRGs), others initiated by the medical profession, and others by state governments, many trying to husband financial resources (e.g., Oregon "health rationing" legislation, in cataloging and cost-effectiveness prioritizing several hundred discrete diagnostic and treatment procedures).

The increasing use of stored databases on symptoms, diagnoses, treatment procedures, and outcomes makes the research and guideline development task somewhat less awesome than it would have been in earlier years. The existence and use of such databases and accompanying software can also play a role in reducing defensive medicine through improved defense of malpractice suits.[90]

The structure for a combined outcomes research/guideline development/administration could come into being through numerous negotiation/adoption approaches, such as (1) incorporation within a national health insurance or other omnibus health care legislation enacted by the Congress, (2) initiation through national legislation of an evolutionary structure, focusing on an initial research program to fill in gaps in existing scientific findings and experience on outcomes, with provision for staged expansions and/or pilot implementation of statewide guidelines in some states, with subsequent revisions and eventual incorporations into a national pattern, (3) creation of a national representative body charged with guideline development, and (4) congressional encouragement and assistance to a small number of states to develop and apply guidelines, with further national action dependent on subsequent evaluations of such programs, including the gains of probable savings against accompanying factors of regimentation, professional and public reactions, and other factors.

The experiences in former West Germany, Canada, and other countries apparently produced "quasi-successful" administration of some or many nationwide standards. Growing convictions expressed from the various health care authorities cited earlier seemed to indicate that many billions of dollars were being wasted on unnecessary diagnostic and treatment procedures.[91] Therefore it appears imperative to many that various private and public policy initiatives be undertaken on this large and complex task.

AVAILABILITY OF, AND ACCESS TO, ADEQUATE HEALTH CARE

Policy options on financial access via insurance and other financial means were examined earlier. Here we are concerned with policies on the health care personnel, physical, and other resources that should be made available and with physical access to them, especially in underserved rural and inner-city areas.

Infinite Demand, Finite Resources

To the litany of causes of escalating health care costs already discussed or noted (aging, overuse, and unnecessary expansion in medical technology and its physical and human investment components, growing demand and decreasing cost-consciousness by many insured consumers, tax system perversities, and medical malpractice-defensive medicine), former Colorado governor Richard Lamm added and emphasized one more: *the refusal to recognize that infinite needs have collided with finite resources.* He challenged:

The medical model that assumes we can deliver to every patient all possible health care. America must eventually admit to its collective self that some limits must be set. Our medical genius has outpaced our ability to pay for all we are capable of doing. Once we admit this we will, at last, be able to address the issue of buying the most health care with our limited resources. *Any other alternative to facing the new reality of exploding technology will be fiscal suicide.* . . . The best building in almost every town in America is the hospital (35 percent vacant) and the worst . . . is usually the school (overcrowded). . . . We will not remain a great nation by overtreating the sick and undereducating our children.[92]

A related step called for by George Lundberg in his proposals for health care reform was to "stop providing futile care that merely prolongs dying."[93]

In the 1980s public opinion and both national and state legislators became increasingly concerned about two health care issues that became more interrelated: (1) roles of next of kin, physicians, and others in the continuation of life-sustaining treatments (LSTs) for the terminally ill and (2) the increasing numbers and costs of long-term care (LTC) of the very old in nursing homes, a growing proportion of which was being financed by Medicaid. The first—decisions about LSTs—opened up possibilities and legislative proposals, intermingled with judicial decisions, to (1) authorize and give legal precedence to "living wills," whereby the individual could order in advance the discontinuance of such treatments when an illness became terminal, and/or (2) give similar precedence to "durable powers of attorney" to designated next of kin or other person for decisions, binding on attending physicians, as to such discontinuance. A number of states and subsequently the Congress enacted legislation along these lines. The federal law—the Patient Self-Determination Act[94] (November 1990)—directs physicians and hospital staff to explain the options of living will, power of attorney, and others to newly admitted patients.

Life-Sustaining Treatments. The issue of these treatments had led the congressional Office of Technology Assessment (OTA) to conduct a 1987 assessment of life-sustaining technologies and the elderly.[95] The continuing developments led to another study, examining the problems and processes of clinical decision making about LSTs, recognizing that such decisions often were made on an ad hoc basis resulting in differing considerations within a single hospital or other institution, pointing to the need for decision-making protocols therein. The resulting OTA report to the Congress listed several options:[96] (1) no action; (2) seek more information via research and hearings; (3) encourage and facilitate state and private efforts to address problems in clinical decision making; (4) encourage states and voluntary agencies to adopt protocols; and (5) instruct federal agencies operating or regulating health care facilities to require those facilities to adopt such protocols.

Already noted was an emerging consensus in the early 1990s for clinical guidelines on the appropriateness of various procedures, based on a combination of medical and cost effectiveness. A convergence of ethical, legal, medical, and economic views was occurring, leading state legislatures to consider alternate approaches to what became known as "health care rationing." Earlier, in connection with LTC, the focus had been on the elderly and LSTs, that too much money and health care resources were being directed toward the old, while not nearly enough was being allocated to the young. There were calls for American society to review its social, as well as economic policies in the light of newer medical, technological, and ethical realities.[97]

Others felt it more desirable to focus on a combination of age and procedure. For example, scholars at Britain's York University developed a concept of quality-adjusted life-years, or QALYs. This would start with the extra years of life that a procedure offered, combined with a disability-distress matrix and a financial cost computed (e.g., home renal dialysis had a cost, on a scale of zero to 10, of 17.3, compared with 8 for a heart transplant, 4 for a kidney transplant, and a fraction of 1 for an antismoking campaign).[98]

"Health Rationing." In the late 1980s the Oregon legislature initiated a plan of rationing medical services financed by Medicaid in such a way as to rule out

highly expensive procedures judged to be of low cost-effectiveness in terms of being the *least likely* to improve life or to provide a reasonable chance of medical success and concurrently to extend Medicaid to a large number of lower-income, medically needy, and uninsured persons and families. A Health Services Commission was established under the legislation and directed to produce a priority list of health conditions. The list was drafted, released in early 1991, and ratified by the legislature in early 1992, subject to federal approval under the Medicaid waiver procedure. Despite much internal federal support, the waiver request was denied by the Bush administration, largely due to compliance problems with the Americans with Disabilities Act. In March 1993, however, the Clinton administration approved Oregon's waiver requests. Under the Oregon initial list, high-priority conditions included pneumococcal pneumonia; tuberculosis; foreign body in pharynx, trachea, or esophagus; peritonitis; ruptured intestine; hernia; and ectopic pregnancy. Bottom priority and extremely unlikely to be treated included chronic pancreatitis; extremely low birth weight babies (under 1.3 pounds and under 23 weeks gestation); and anencephaly and similar conditions in which a child is born without a brain. For many conditions the place on the priority list depended on how far the condition had progressed and how much could be done to improve the quality of life (e.g., HIV was on the list three times—near the top, middle, and end stage at bottom, where only comfort is provided).[99]

The policy options regarding limitation of availability, or "rationing," founded on any of the alternate bases described above—cost-effectiveness only, cost combined with age and/or quality of life—or other criteria were considered in several states in 1992–93. The principal argument for moving in those directions was to enable more public and other resources to be available to education and other pressing domestic problems. Two principal arguments against were (1) using the low-income population represented by Medicaid recipients as the testing ground, since lower cost-effectiveness or other priority measures could be disregarded by those able and willing to pay for them and (2) perceived ethical mores and professional responsibilities of health care personnel to protect and preserve life. The latter of these was also an argument against the clinical protocol approach examined earlier.

Regarding the more specific approach represented by the Oregon legislation, the two foregoing arguments against still apply, as well as the advantage cited. However, it also represented a major step forward for the uninsured "working poor" and their families—a sizable proportion of the entire uninsured population—through their absorption into Medicaid and given basic medical coverage. A collateral benefit of this step would be the further distancing of Medicaid from welfare by adding a sizable *employed* segment to its beneficiary population. A second major positive aspect of the Oregon legislation was to lay the groundwork for a modest payroll tax, combined with a state risk pool, to reduce to near zero the uninsured population, arriving at the "Hawaii condition" with a considerably smaller health insurance tax burden on small business. (A GAO report on the

Oregon proposal, though generally supportive, did not take a position on the rationing aspects; it recommended that if the plan were approved, the state strengthen its assurances that adequate physician capacity be in place before the sizable increase in Medicaid enrollment.)[100]

Improving Physical and Informational Access to Health Care

Major policy and management steps are required in order to meet the weaknesses and other problems of physical access to health care facilities and services that were identified earlier. These were (1) rural and urban areas not adequately covered by medical facilities, including the crucial needs of public hospitals, community health centers, and mobile clinics; (2) insufficient doctors and other health personnel in the underserved areas; and (3) transportation needs incurred by scattered sites of health care facilities and services, requiring needless travel from one site to another by patients with more than one medical eligibility, or other administrative or "process" requirement.

Of the estimated 26 million medically underserved Americans in rural, inner-city, and other areas, the segment with which we are most directly concerned here are those low-income households containing expectant mothers, mothers, and infants or young children. For a considerable part of the overall unmet need, a substantial expansion in capacity of community and migrant worker health centers was recommended by a variety of sources. The high priority attached by state and local governments to these needs and experimental approaches for their remediation was illustrated by the fact that of the ten Ford Foundation Innovation Awards for 1991, three were in this category.

Access Via the Schools. At the outset, a resource neglected until the 1990s and with possibilities continuing but barely touched, *public school buildings and facilities* must be examined, especially in connection with meeting the severe need for health care *informational outreach* described earlier and for a variety of other young children and adolescent health and associated social services.

Public and private school personnel constitute an often untapped source of information as to health and other nonacademic problems of students *and of their siblings, parent(s), and other household members.* As already emphasized, inner-city infants and young children, especially blacks and Hispanics, have been in increasingly desperate straits regarding health care; the waiting periods at public hospitals and at clinics lengthen as the number to be served grows and the clinic capacities remain stagnant or lessen. Much early preventive child care is needed before age three, but as an expanded Head Start and other preschool programs come on line, public school facilities and personnel represent an early point of access.

Through appropriate arrangements for interchange of information among school, public health, social work, and other personnel, at-risk families can be identified and their problems confronted at an early stage. The principle of early preventive care can be implemented more easily. Also the school site may at times be a more convenient or safer meeting place for child, parent, and health or other personnel.

Preventive health care such as immunizations, eye checks, and other similar services by nurses or other professional personnel can also be delivered at schools, since ''in many cases helping high-risk pregnant women and children gain access to health care means taking the services to them.''[101] This may be at the home, a health van visiting the neighborhood, or the school grounds.

The NCC stated in its 1991 report:

Health education programs in schools are an important avenue for teaching children about the risks and consequences of unhealthful behaviors, such as smoking, alcohol and other drug use, and violence. And they can help children learn how to promote their own health through proper nutrition, hygiene, pregnancy prevention (including abstinence), and physical fitness. A growing number of schools across the country are initiating comprehensive school health programs that combine health education with health services designed to prevent or identify and treat students' physical and mental health problems. These programs are also aimed at creating a healthful environment in the school, for example by banning smoking for students and adults, promoting physical fitness, serving nutritious food, and eliminating hazards to physical safety.[102]

Quite often the bunching of school-linked health, social services, and other noneducational services needed by children at or near a school can result in significant savings while expanding services, because of its one-stop nature. Michael Kirst, a longtime expert on educational and related matters, defines school-linked services as the linking of the school to at least two or more other children's services in a continuing, collaborative relationship:

Collaboration is a joint venture between schools and other agencies to deal specifically with a set of families and their children. . . . [This involves merging] children's policy, *children's finance*, and traditional school finance. . . . The way to fund school-linked services is to divert existing funding streams like Medicaid and drug prevention money to schools or nearby facilities, i.e., to the one-stop shopping location.[103]

A Florida school-based *financial* access innovation might be noted here. A demonstration program called Healthy Kids in selected districts was enabling school children up to age 19 without health insurance and eligible for the National School Lunch Program to be policyholders of free or low-cost health insurance. The premium subsidies would be 100 percent or less, depending on whether the child was in the free or discounted school lunch category.[104]

Two of the 10 annual Ford Foundation Awards for innovations in state and local governments in 1991 went to school-based social service programs, as did 1 of the 15 finalist (runner-up) recognitions.[105] They were:

Award: New Jersey, School-Based Youth Services. In 1987 New Jersey [began offering troubled teenages] comprehensive social services at a place where they already go almost every day—their schools. By 1991 school-based youth service centers were operating in 29 high schools across the state [serving] more than 18,000 teenagers. The governor increased the program's budget, allowing seven new centers in elementary and middle schools to open . . . Iowa and Kentucky are [interested] states that have copied New Jersey's model. . . . New Jersey officials, meanwhile, would like to apply the model to other social service programs.[106]

Award: K-SIX Early Intervention Partnership, Fresno, California. In 1984 Fresno launched [this program] in two pilot schools and by 1991 the program had expanded to ten elementary schools, all of them in distressed urban neighborhoods and rural areas where many poor Hispanics, African Americans, Southeast Asians, and Native Americans live . . . school officials report that unexcused absences have fallen by an annual average of 40 percent for children enrolled in the K-SIX program, and serious misbehavior problems have declined by 70 percent. Of the 66 K-SIX children who had reached high school age last year, none had dropped out or become teenage parents. *The latter is noteworthy because Fresno County has one of California's highest rates of teenage pregnancy.*[107]

Finalist: Independence Public Schools, Independence, Missouri, School of the 21st Century. [This program] expands the [school district] mission to include affordable child care and family services that are integrated into each neighborhood elementary school. . . . All year round, all-day child care for preschoolers and before- and after-school care for youngsters six to twelve [are provided]; home [prenatal] visits and continuing until [age] five; training for child-care providers; and information for parents about resources available. The program's annual budget, some $1.5 million, is supported by parent fees, private foundations, and public funds.[108]

Julia Lear and Philip Porter, codirectors of the privately supported School-Based Adolescent Health Care Program, pointed out that given changing family structure and increased labor force participation by mothers:

Schools are feeling the pressure to redefine their mission, including playing roles that traditionally have been allotted to the family. This is especially true of schools serving poor families, where teachers are confronted daily by social and health problems they were not trained to solve. In the past, students with problems beyond the scope and competence of education were either "referred out" to experts in the community or ignored. But now a new vision of schools is being considered, the expansion of resources and services provided to students and their families *inside* the school.[109]

In 1991 a number of cities, such as Birmingham, Los Angeles, Memphis, New Orleans, New York, and Washington, were utilizing some of their schools in the foregoing way. Also, Kentucky mandated a health center in those junior and senior high schools in which 20 percent of the children were eligible for federal support funds for the educationally disadvantaged. In 1990 Seattle passed a tax levy supporting a school-based health center in every high school. Lear and Porter commented further that though school-linked health services at an away-from-school site appear to offer adequate services, "students don't travel well and they don't carry appointment books . . . especially true of boys, who seldom show up at community-based clinics but who appear in much larger numbers at the high school health centers."[110]

The congressional Office of Technology Assessment in its 1991 study of adolescent health observed that in overcoming major access barriers:

Comprehensive school-linked or community-based services can potentially meet several needs. . . . These include early intervention services that may not be covered by health insurance, free or low-fee care, confidentiality of services, evening and weekend hours of operation, adolescent involvement in [service design/management]. . . . Few studies have been conducted on the effectiveness of such centers in adolescents' access to . . . health and related services.[111]

In contrast to the foregoing cited advantages of school-based health clinics, three obstacles are often encountered—opposition of traditional public school establishments to having programmatic relations with the city or county government; reluctance of school professionals to get into "parenting" of children or anything having to do with the teaching of "values"; and opposition of parents who object to their children's being exposed or having access to a school health clinic that does counseling on sex relations, AIDS, or sexually transmitted diseases, contending that moral values should be taught at home.

However, an official of the Council of Great City Schools, an organization representing the 50 or so largest city school systems, commented that "there was a time when schools wanted to be islands unto themselves [concerned solely with education]. . . . Nowadays, kids are arriving at the schoolhouse door with so many problems, coming from families and communities in such disarray, schools have to do more for them or they won't have much chance of educating them."[112] Also, from other sources: "The children [seen] in their school nurses office here [in Pittsburgh] can neither breathe nor hear well and cannot calm themselves when they are upset. They are part of a silent plague in America's schools: children whose ailments are not life-threatening, but learning-threatening."[113]

To meet the third obstacle—values teaching—state laws or regulations or those of local boards of education began in the late 1960s to accompany authorizations or mandates for inclusion of sex education in the curriculum with provisos requiring parental approval for the children to attend. A modified approach to the issue was reflected in a 1987 report of the Committee for Economic Development (CED):

In-school health services are an appropriate mechanism through which to provide sex education, pregnancy prevention programs and follow-up services, and substance abuse programs. In the area of birth control information and services, each school should work with parents and others in the community to design a health services program that conforms to specific community needs, values, and standards.[114]

With the increasing public alarm at the growing incidence of AIDS, sexually transmitted diseases, and teenage pregnancies, these types of community strictures were encountering substantial legal and other opposition in the early 1990s. This related to growing public debate about objectionable language and censorship.[115]

Public Hospitals, Community Health Centers, Mobile Clinics

Noted earlier were repeated instances of failures of federal and state programs to deliver what was promised, in Medicaid and other health care areas. The president of the American Public Health Association complained about this gap in these terms: "We have been plagued too often by entitlement without availability as illustrated by providers who refuse Medicaid patients, and by availability without entitlement as illustrated by hospitals that turn away the uninsured."[116] Hospitals, centers, and clinics are where this gap most often appears.

Public Hospitals. In the early 1990s, government-financed hospitals (e.g., those operated by city and county governments) were rapidly becoming the major, and often the only, facilities available to uninsured patients needing emergency care. A report of the National Association of Public Hospitals (NAPH) detailed the increasingly critical position of the country's public hospitals. The average wait for a bed in the emergency rooms of these hospitals had reached more than five hours. This had several causes, not the least of which was the inevitable result of more and more people neglecting to get preventive care and a high level of cocaine and other drug-driven emergency room visits. "Many hospitals now are literally functioning daily and nightly as if there were a disaster or combat [zone] in the cities," commented Dr. Arthur Kellerman, head of the Emergency Department of the Memphis Regional Medical Center.[117]

The NAPH report declared:

A small group of metropolitan area hospitals makes up our nation's institutional health safety net today. We do not believe . . . it inappropriate to refer to them as the very foundation of the nation's health system. . . . [These 100 large urban hospitals] may seem like a small number in a country that boasts over 6,000 acute care hospitals. But . . . with combined gross revenues of over $10 billion, these major, tertiary hospitals truly serve as "national health insurance" by default, in most of our nation's metropolitan areas.[118]

In rural areas as well, public hospitals serve an underserved segment of the population. Regarding hospital closings, such hospitals "are particularly at risk . . . as many are located in rural areas, and they serve poor patients who often have inadequate insurance. . . . While public hospitals . . . constitute approximately 14% of hospital beds, they serve a disproportionate number of the poor and disadvantaged."[119] On this point, the NAPH report also noted the growing seriousness of economically driven "patient transfers and dumping" of patients upon public hospitals, with many of the transfers coming from private nonprofit hospitals enjoying tax exemption.[120] A 1990 GAO report on nonprofit hospitals raised a similar question, concluding that "if Congress wishes to encourage nonprofit hospitals to provide charity care and other community services, it should consider revising [tax exemption criteria]."[121]

In contrast to the economic squeeze suffered by many public hospitals, a few of them were beginning to assemble sufficient resources to establish relatively scarce specialized services, such a high-level trauma care, burn treatment, and diagnostic testing. Where this occurs, the hospital is then in a much stronger revenue position. Parkland Memorial and Jackson Memorial in Dallas and Miami, respectively, along with Harborview Medical Center in Seattle, were in this relatively favorable position in early 1992 and apparently were able to accommodate the sizable number of additional paying patients without appreciable effect upon their basic safety net mission. However, this tendency to stray from the mission was a recognized danger in the widening search for expanded roles in order to achieve stronger budgetary positions.[122]

In summarizing the policy dilemma facing a city or county government in considering how to keep its hospital open in the face of fiscal pressures. Andrew Bindman and others stated:

In deciding to close a hospital, policy-makers must consider the negative impact that such a step will have on patients and assess the adequacy and effectiveness of the remaining health care services. Equitable social policy dictates that when hospitals close, compensatory services must be made available for displaced patients. As the excesses in the health care system are dismantled, cohesive state and national policies are needed to ensure that access to essential services that impact on patients' health are not simultaneously eliminated.[123]

Community Health Centers and Mobile Clinics. The neighborhood and community health centers were also facing growing problems in the early 1990s, as described earlier. They were playing an ever-stronger role in serving young adolescents and young adults, as well as expectant mothers, infants, and small children.[124] Strong action to stabilize and expand their number and scope were coming from the Advisory Council on Social Security (ACSS), the National Commission on Children, and other sources. They coincided in thrust, differing only in a few specifics. Three representative policy recommendations were:

To improve access to primary care for children and pregnant women in underserved communities, funding for Community and Migrant Health Centers should be substantially increased. New funds should be used to expand both sites and capacity. . . . We urge that funding be increased by approximately $150 million (from $530 to $680 million) as the first step in a $1 billion increase over the next five years to double the number of centers and substantially increase the capacity of existing centers. In FY 1992 this expansion would add approximately 160 new centers and 1.5 million new patients. . . . By FY 1996 the program would extend services to an additional 7 million new patients altogether. In the final year of this proposed expansion, the Secretary of Health and Human Services [should] reassess the level of unmet need and review plans for further program expansion (National Commission on Children).[125]

The Council recommends that new Federal funding be provided to establish an additional 250 community and migrant health centers. . . . [in areas of] high concentrations of underserved populations such as high-risk pregnant women or the homeless. . . . [Also] that there be established 20 "R.E.A.C.H." (Rural Emergency Access to Community Health) centers to provide emergency access to community health services in rural areas (Advisory Council on Social Security).[126]

More specifically, the council proposed that $25 million in federal funding be made available to establish the new centers ($1 million per center), accompanied by $290 million in *annual* operating funds. The secretary of HHS would be authorized to establish, as a demonstration project, 20 centers to provide rural emergency access to community health centers. "These could be free-standing centers, could be consolidated with existing community or migrant health centers currently serving these areas, or could be incorporated in the design of new community or migrant health centers."[127]

In addition to increased federal support, the Children's Defense Fund proposed that state governments consider making contributions from their general funds to support community health centers and local MCH programs and that private and nonprofit groups support the establishment and maintenance of projects that help families and children obtain access to health services.[128]

Mobile clinics comprise a highly valuable resource in many urban areas—another means of bringing health services to the poor rather than requiring the poor to appear at one or more clinics or offices. As Gretchen Buchenholtz, president of the Association to Benefit Children in New York City, emphasized, "The people aren't getting health care even though it's available because it's very difficult for them to access those services. Lugging three kids, waiting six hours . . . those logistics are time-consuming and paralyzing. This [van] brings the services on site."[129]

One-Stop-Shopping Access Arrangements. In addition to mobile vans that bring medical and other health services directly to neighborhoods and homes, location of health, and sometimes associated, services, as at school buildings, at a single site can improve greatly the physical access situation. This is obvious both in efficiency and in convenience to patients and often, but not always, represents a decrease in rental costs. However, significant barriers exist to the adoption and execution of such a policy. The following points are drawn from a study of maternal and child health services but are applicable to young child, adolescent, and other health services. Barriers and possible means to surmount them include the following:[130]

- Conflicting regulations on eligibility for closely associated programs—change regulations to provide a combination of consistency in policy and flexibility in execution.

- Lack of adequate resources for onetime start-up costs—provide discretionary funds for this purpose.
- Staff resistance to change (e.g., loss of personnel in Mississippi when staff moved from single-purpose clinics to a comprehensive delivery site; Michigan union contracts delineating specific jobs in specific bargaining units)—develop staff training program in advance to help community interest and increase public awareness, thereby helping create an interested and vocal constituency.

Bringing Adequate Physician and Other Medical Staff to Underserved Areas.
As in the case of expanding the number of, and increasing the fiscal resources for, community health centers, there was growing urgency in the early 1990s about the shortage of health care staff in many rural and inner-city areas, concurrent with an oversupply of medical specialists.

The ACSS, in its 1991 report, stated that "the National Health Service Corps (NHSC), which encourages the diffusion of primary care physicians as well as dentists and other health care professionals into medically underserved areas (known as 'Health Professional Shortage Areas') has not effectively fulfilled this mission in recent years."[131] Between 1981 and 1991 the Reagan and Bush administrations and successive HHS secretaries had been endeavoring to phase out the NHSC. The number of professionals had shrunk to 1,500 by 1989, then increased to 1,751 in 1990. Beginning in the 1991 fiscal year, appropriations for loans and scholarships grew to $49 million from a 1990 level of $11 million and to $59 million for FY 1992.

The council strongly recommended that:

legislation be enacted to permit the Secretary of Health and Human Services and the Assistant Secretary for Health to revise the priorities of the National Health Service Corps so as to focus more attention on demonstrated unmet need. Specifically, the NHSC should be authorized to increase the access of target populations to primary medical care, that is, the urban and inner-city poor especially infants and children; high-risk pregnant women; migrant workers and their families; drug and alcohol abusers; and the homeless.

The NHSC should be authorized to encourage primary care physicians to serve in community and migrant health centers or in related health programs, or in underserved rural areas and offer them incentives for efficient private practice in the areas in which they locate. The Council recommends an increase of $100 million for the budget of the NHSC to fund these activities. . . . In awarding [NHSC] scholarships, the Corps should, more actively than at present, seek to recruit individuals *from* the medically underserved areas in which they will be asked to serve upon graduation.[132]

The proviso regarding residential location of applicants is very important—a new physician formerly from a rural or suburban area may find a crime- and drug-ridden and poverty-stricken inner-city neighborhood so new, alien, and frightening that he or she will be unwilling to locate or remain there. Conversely, a new physician from a central city or suburb may find a small town or rural village to be slow-paced, lacking in social/cultural amenities, or having a too homogenous population.[133] The ACSS also described, as a possible reform prototype, an arrangement whereby Medicaid physician payment rates would be increased in rural underserved areas in order to attract physicians in nearby urban areas to establish part-time offices in the rural areas.[134]

The Children's Defense Fund, in addition to urging the continued revitalization of the NHSC and bringing the loan and loan repayment programs back up to the 1980 level, called on the state governments to "use state funds for support of graduate education in ways that encourage physicians and other health professionals to practice in medically underserved areas."[135]

The NCC proposed an increase of $80 million per year to support 700 professionals with scholarships and 400 with loan repayments each year. At the rate of increase, the corps would reach an adequate pool of health providers to serve all medically underserved areas by the year 2000.[136]

How to Get Hospitals, Physicians, and Clinics to Carry Their Share of Caring for the Poor and Underserved. The access problems described earlier and their possible remediation through measures just discussed have dealt mostly with the needed expansion of facilities and services. However, some of these problems have been exacerbated by various factors, both external and internal to the health care delivery system. Demographic change, rural-to-urban and city-to-suburb population migration, and growing specialization within the medical profession have caused numerous cities, counties, and towns, formerly adequately served, to become underserved. Medicaid payment maxima and other factors have caused physicians, clinics, and hospitals to lessen service to the uninsured. (Noted earlier was the extent to which nonprofit, tax-exempt hospitals are carrying their share.)

The 1991 report of the ACSS called attention to the need to utilize more fully the structure of public-private partnerships to cope with some of these problems.[137] Additionally, there has been a growing need for increased professional, community, and media attention to the selfless energy with which some health care professionals provide volunteer service without pay to clinics, community, and migrant health centers and in individual practice to serve the uninsured. In an area where the numbers of uninsured, low-income patients considerably outnumber the available health care workers and facilities, such recognition may need to be handled in low key, lest the volunteers become even more inundated. In other cases, corporations, foundations, HMOs, and others lend a hand either through financing or in carrying part of the responsibility of meeting at least a minimal portion of low-income, uninsured patients. For example, in one Maryland county, the local government and an HMO entered into such a sharing arrangement for pediatric care for low-income patients.[138]

Improved Access for Minorities. In 1990, the Intergovernmental Health Policy Project (IHPP) of George Washington University inventoried state health departments to determine how many had established offices to deal specifically with the health needs of minority residents. Despite a modest gain in life expectancy rates for blacks and Hispanics in recent years, there remains a significant gap in the health status of white and minority populations—particularly blacks—

in the United States. Although disparities are long-standing, intensified media interest in the issue had increased pressure for a more focused government response.

The IHPP survey found five states (Ohio, Michigan, Missouri, South Carolina, and New Jersey), plus a handful of other state-sanctioned entities, addressing those needs. By late 1991, three more state minority health offices had come into being (Massachusetts, Arkansas, and Georgia). Though the dollars necessary to put teeth into the efforts were scarce, the enthusiasm of the officials running them was found to be quite high. The Massachusetts health commissioner had carved out an office of minority health within the department. The Arkansas legislature had approved a minority health office and commission. Georgia's minority health office had resulted from a governmentwide reorganization effort. Located in the Department of Human Resources, it had a director, epidemiologist, and secretary. In addition, minority health initiatives had been undertaken in six other states (Alabama, Indiana, Mississippi, Louisiana, Delaware, and Illinois). The duties and responsibilities of the foregoing minority health units ranged from data collection/dissemination to development of new policy initiatives, but with modest financing.[139]

These recommendations, calling for expanded federal-state outlays for community/migrant health centers and clinics and for increased federal aid for the NHSC, while addressing indisputable needs, still encountered important barriers that tend to delay, rather than defeat, the proposals. The severe fiscal pressures at all three levels of government that existed in the early nineties tended to make it necessary or desirable that the then-existing health center and NHSC programs be revised to remove any substantial weaknesses in structure or management. For example:

- Federal requirements for health center governance through boards independent of outside control were not being met or enforced in a number of cases. For instance, in New York City 4 community centers were failing to meet such requirements in the mid-1980s; by 1990, 3 had complied, but 1 dropped out of the program rather than comply. In New York State 16 centers were terminated during the 1980s for (1) poor fiscal and/ or clinical management, (2) failure to comply with governing board requirements, or (3) a statutory 5 percent national limit on the amount of federal funds that could go to public centers whose governing board powers did not include the establishment of policy.[140] Were the governing board standards ill-advised, or was state/federal enforcement uncertain or ambiguous?

- Language barriers increasingly face migrant workers seeking care in the migrant centers; many of the applicants speak little or no English.[141]

INCENTIVES AND SANCTIONS INFLUENCING CLIENT HEALTH BEHAVIOR

In chapter 3 numerous problems were identified of adverse health behavior on the part of individual patients; these stemmed both from neglect and from irresponsibility in *initiation* of the particular behavior and/or lack of will to halt its *continuance*.

The groups in which adverse behavior bears the most irreversible consequences appear to be expectant mothers, parent(s) of young children, and adolescent youth. The 1970s and 1980s saw relatively successful use of both incentives and sanctions in one major health area—smoking. This effort, along with policy actions taken by private employers and by public authorities at all three levels of government, resulted in a marked decreased in smoking and future onset of diseases associated with the habit. The anti-smoking campaign involved three major elements: (1) *education* and public information campaigns; (2) *incentives*, such as discounts for nonsmokers in health insurance premiums; and conversely, (3) *sanctions* in the forms of continually increasing cigarette taxes, prohibition against smoking in selected public places, and segregation of smokers in travel, eating, and other public accommodations. The latter two—public accommodations and travel segregation—were intended to convey the message that smoking was antisocial as well as unhealthy; it was also being recognized as dangerous to others (inhalation of others' smoke). Public information and specific educational programs to alter life-style traits adverse to the individual and/or the public health comprise an initial step toward altering behavior, with incentives and sanctions a second phase. Sex, AIDS, and pregnancy education programs are examined first, followed by incentives and sanctions. Drug education, substance abuse, and violent behavior are reviewed subsequently.

Adolescent Health and Sex, AIDS Education, and Pregnancy Prevention

The spread of HIV/AIDS during the latter 1980s convinced most school systems that early information about sexual activity, if not already included in the instructional program, needed to be instituted. In early 1991, the Congressional Office of Technology Assessment (OTA) issued a report outlining major issues in adolescent health and policy options for consideration by the Congress.[142] The report summarized the concept of a comprehensive school health program, developed and defined by the USPHS Centers for Disease Control, steps one through eight comprising:[143]

1. A documented, planned, and sequential program of health education for students in grades kindergarten through 12.

2. A curriculum that addresses and integrates education about a range of categorical health problems and issues (e.g., human immunodeficiency virus (HIV) infection, drug abuse, drinking and driving, emotional health, environmental pollution) at developmentally appropriate ages.

3. Activities to help young people develop the skills they will need to avoid behaviors that result in unintentional and intentional injuries; drug and alcohol abuse; tobacco use; sexual behaviors that result in HIV infection, other sexually transmitted diseases,

and unintended pregnancies; imprudent dietary patterns; and inadequate physical activity.

4. Instruction provided for a prescribed amount of time at each grade level.
5. Management and coordination in each school by an education professional trained to implement the program.
6. Instruction from teachers who have been trained to teach the subject.
7. Instruction of parents, health professionals, and other community members.
8. Periodic evaluations, updating, and improvement.

The National Commission on the Role of the School and Community in Improving Adolescent Health, a joint project of the National Association of State Boards of Education and the American Medical Association, recommended that young people receive a "new kind of health education—a sophisticated, multifaceted program that goes light years beyond present lectures on 'personal hygiene' or the four food groups and . . . [should] provide honest relevant information about . . . family life and sex education . . . begins before students are pressured to experiment with risky behaviors and continues throughout adolescence."[144]

The OTA report presented specific education and health service options related to *AIDS/HIV infection and other sexually transmitted diseases*, including the following:[145]

- Improve adolescents' access to health and related services.
- Encourage school districts to make condoms and condom-related education easily available to the adolescents who are most likely to be sexually active (e.g., older adolescents).
- Support active and flexible approaches to the provision of treatment for STDs to encourage adolescents to seek treatment and return for follow-up care.
- Target AIDS/HIV prevention (e.g., condom distribution) and education efforts to adolescents living on their own.
- Support outreach efforts to bring adolescents who are not in contact with the mainstream health care system into clinical trials for AIDS drugs.
- Support the provision of information to adolescents on the prevention and treatment of AIDS and STDs.
- Support the provision of information relevant to obtaining access to services for the prevention and treatment of AIDS and STDs.
- Support training and dissemination of information on the specific needs of adolescents for health care workers in STD clinics.
- Support the dissemination of prevention and education efforts into nonmetropolitan areas, to younger adolescents, to adolescents who are intravenous drug users, and to homosexual or bisexual adolescents.

Illustrative of state legislative initiatives to implement AIDS and related sex education programs were the following 1991 enactments.[146]

Arizona (SB 1396, Chapter 269, 1991 Laws). Requires each common, high, and unified school district to provide HIV/AIDS instruction to students in kindergarten through grade 12. Instruction must be appropriate to grade level; be medically accurate; promote abstinence, discourage drug abuse; and dispel myths regarding AIDS transmission. Prohibits districts from including instruction that promotes a homosexual life-style; portrays homosexuality as a positive alternative life-style; and suggests that some methods of sex are safe methods of homosexual sex. State departments of Health Services and of Education must review materials on request of school district. Parents must be notified that they can withdraw child from AIDS instruction.

California (AB 11, Ch. 818, 1991 Laws). Amends the law related to AIDS prevention instruction and instruction materials. Changes provisions for AIDS instruction for pupils in junior high or middle school to pupils "in grades 7 to 12 inclusive." Requires emphasis that abstinence from sexual intercourse and IV drug use is most effective means of prevention. Instruction must also include medical statistics on failure and success rates of condoms and other contraceptives in preventing HIV infection.

Nevada (ACR 30, File 153, 1991 Laws). Directs state department of education and each local school board to submit progress report on the implementation of required AIDS and sex education, with any recommended policies, programs, and proposed legislation to next state legislative session in 1993.

Virginia (HJR 437, 1991 Laws). Directs state board of education to strive aggressively to increase the adequacy of AIDS education in K–12 schools. School divisions that are not complying with prior guidelines will be encouraged to revise their approaches more realistically to reflect current issues related to HIV and other STDs.

Abortion, abstinence, contraception, and other aspects of sex education seem to be as controversial in the nineties as in the seventies despite numerous polls showing a large majority of Americans to be in favor of sex education in the schools. In a late 1991 editorial, the *New York Times* commented as follows regarding the rapidly growing number of crack-addicted and other premature and extremely low-weight infants being born to mothers who were still children themselves: "How much better it would be if such suffering could be headed off at the start. By contraception, for example . . . yet . . . after discounting for inflation Federal funding for contraceptive services has fallen by almost two-thirds since 1980."[147] The Sex Information and Education Council of the United States, noting that as of 1991, 22 states were requiring all their high school districts to include sex education in their curriculum and 24 others were officially encouraging it, had concluded that fewer than 10 percent of American children were receiving sex education in school. Consequently, the council had formed a panel of 20 educators and health care experts to draw up plans and guidelines for a comprehensive treatment of the subject, covering 36 topics, such as reproduction, puberty, masturbation, dating, love, sexual abuse, and parenting, as well as abortion, abstinence, and contraception. These guidelines were released in mid-October 1991.[148]

Dr. Roy Schwarz, the vice president for medical education and science of the AMA, welcomed the report, as did a representative of the National School Boards Association (NSBA) who had served on the drafting panel. Some organizations and individuals were highly critical. Phyllis Schafly, president of the Eagle Forum, was quoted as calling the idea of such guidelines "outrageous" and saying that teaching about contraception would undoubtedly encourage sexual activity. Dr. Schwarz contended that what it might do was result in abstinence, caution, and selectivity and give an informed basis for making decisions.[149]

An official of the Alan Guttmacher Institute, a nonprofit research organization in New York, commented that the federal government's primary prevention policy was placing practically exclusive emphasis on abstinence, contending that "one answer for all teenagers was unrealistic." USPHS data presented earlier would seem to bear that out, since repeated Centers for Disease Control surveys found that a majority of teenagers of both sexes had become sexually active by their senior year in high school. An HHS deputy assistant secretary for population affairs contended that the importance of abstinence was not being overstated— "Abstinence is 100 percent effective."[150] A high school teacher in Westport, Connecticut, commented, "Vows of abstinence break more frequently than contraceptives."[151]

The director of the Adolescent Pregnancy Prevention Clearinghouse at the Children's Defense Fund summed up the decades-old dilemma about sex education and school health clinics with the following comment:

While there is still no consensus about whether society should encourage abstinence versus contraception as our primary prevention method, there can be little debate that the success of any pregnancy prevention effort ultimately lies in impressing upon teens the absolute necessity and logic of doing *one of these two things*. The question is, of course, how? One important answer has been the need to provide more sexuality-specific information, guidance, and services. The greater the barriers to receiving this kind of information and the necessary services, the greater the risk of early sexual activity or pregnancy.[152]

Irresponsibility of young males who decline to take precautions and take pride in fathering a child but who then do not endeavor to provide child financial or other support was coming under increasing criticism and condemnation in the early 1990s, fueled by disappointing child support enforcement data such as those presented in chapter 2. The seriousness and complexity of this problem, especially as it related to African Americans, were voiced in a series of articles edited by Dionne Jones and Stanley Battle. In an overview introduction to the articles, Jones stated:[153]

These racial/ethnic differences may be a reflection of the decisions of these groups regarding marriage, sexual activity, contraceptive use and abortion. Moreover, [they] may be related to higher poverty rates and lower academic skills among young [minority] females, as well as unemployment and low wages among young African-American males. . . . Contrary to popular belief, teenage pregnancy and childbearing are stressful events not only for teenage mothers, but also for the teenage males who become fathers . . . the socioeconomic, health, emotional and psychological well-being of many of these youth tend to be below standard. Their knowledge of, and access to health care appear to be limited, if [existing at all]. . . . A multidisciplinary approach must be taken by professionals to attack this problem. . . . Just as the problem [is multidimensional] so too, the strategies used for remediation [must be likewise].

[The dimensions should include education/basic skills, work skills, and also social support to help] build and enhance self-esteem. . . . Sexuality and parenting skills should be another component of comprehensive health care. In 1985, [the National Urban League] launched the Adolescent Male Responsibility Program to provide services and programs to adolescents who are fathers as well as to those who are not. [As a part of this program,] a successful public awareness campaign was launched via the media: radio, newspapers and posters. Nearly half of the 113 Urban League affiliates have participated in these three projects. [Also] all affiliates are involved in [these] youth-directed activities.

While significant reductions in teenage pregnancy have occurred in a number of urban areas where school-based or near-school clinics have been established, the OTA study referred to earlier reported less conclusive results from surveys undertaken in the later 1980s.[154]

During that same period the National Governors' Association (NGA) established a Task Force on Teenage Pregnancy, chaired by then Illinois governor James Thompson. It reported a few substantial before-and-after results (e.g., St. Paul clinic—teenage fertility rate decline of 40 percent over 10 years and a reduction of repeat pregnancies to 2 out of 143 in two Arkansas counties). The task force recommended the establishment by communities of comprehensive health clinics in or near schools in high-risk areas. It noted:

Such clinics offer a wide range of services, only some of which are directed at pregnancy prevention. Services include comprehensive laboratory screening; diagnosis of health disorders; physical examinations; treatment of minor injuries; tests and treatment for sexually transmitted diseases; counseling about sexuality; gynecological exams; birth control referrals; and follow-up exams for birth control users. A few clinics offer birth control prescriptions. Often these clinics provide the first comprehensive and diagnostic health care youth have received in years and treat injuries that would otherwise go untreated. . . . These clinics generally are not financed by the school board, nor are they staffed by school personnel. Rather they use the school's physical plant or they locate close to the school to offer teenagers ready access to health services. Clinics have been planned and operated by local hospitals, medical schools, public health departments, community clinics and Planned Parenthood affiliates. Financing is obtained from federal, state, and local funds, as well as private foundations and corporate grants.[155]

The abortion option for pregnant teenagers, along with abortion in general, has been even more controversial than the issue of sex education in the schools. Somewhat less than half of all high school student pregnancies are terminated by abortion, going to well over half for the lower teens. Public and parental opinion about a woman's right to abortion varies from region to region, state to state, and so on down to the neighborhood and household level, dependent on education, religious beliefs, and a variety of other personal, social, economic, and political factors. The key issue regarding teenage abortion, especially below 18, has been (1) the degree of parental involvement that is desirable and (2) whether it should be required by law.

As of 1991, according to combined data from Congressional Quarterly, Inc., American Civil Liberties Union, and the Alan Guttmacher Institute, consent of both parents was being *required and enforced* by two states (North Dakota and Massachusetts) and consent of one parent by eight (Alabama, Indiana, Louisiana, Michigan, Missouri, Rhode Island, South Carolina, and Wyoming). Notification, but not consent, of at least one parent was being enforced by seven states (Arkansas, Maryland, Minnesota, Nebraska, Ohio, Utah, and West Virginia). The remaining states having notification/consent requirements were either not enforcing or in judicial enjoinment status. Ten states had no such statutory requirements (Washington, DC, Hawaii, Iowa, Kansas, New Hampshire, New Jersey, New York, Oklahoma, Texas, and Vermont).[156]

The legal situation on abortion in general was becoming a state-by-state choice, with some flexibility for restrictions but not universal prohibition, following the U.S. Supreme Court decision in *Webster v Reproductive Health Services* (109 S. Ct. 3040, 1989) and was likely to remain so, even if *Roe v Wade* (which essentially made abortion in most circumstances a basic constitutional right) were later overturned. Leaving the issue to the states would permit adjustment to varying cultures and traditions pursuant to the federalism concept.[157] It would leave many women deeply disappointed, even though in many or most cases, relatively unrestricted abortion choice would be the rule, except for parental notification; the latter raises difficult issues of law, values, psychology, and other considerations.

For example, in a survey of 2,400 adolescents by the Guttmacher Institute, it was found that "most" teenagers would rather seek illegal abortion, self-induce abortion, give birth, or leave home than involve their parent(s) in their pregnancy decisions. A St. Paul obstetrician termed parental involvement as "ideal, but sometimes impossible. . . . A teen may encounter violent abuse if she is forced to bring an estranged parent into the process." Others argue that "your daughter needs your permission to get her ears pierced, but can have an abortion without your knowledge." However, a number of states recognize the need for seeking treatment without parental consultation, such as in birth control, STDs, and drug/alcohol abuse.[158]

Of course, there are no easy answers to the foregoing pro and con arguments. A large part of the problem appears to be the rapidly changing and often disintegrating nature of the American family structure, as reviewed in the preceding chapter. The challenge was stated thus by William Raspberry, a black male and long time columnist for the *Washington Post*:

Whether the measure is teen pregnancy or teen violence, adolescent rootlessness or adolescent suicide, the indications are that our children are less happy, less healthy and less secure than we were and that things aren't getting better. And they won't get better, I fear, until we learn once again to honor, preserve and strengthen the one arrangement that seems to offer the best chance for producing healthy, happy and competent children: *the child-centered marriage.*[159]

Financial Incentives/Sanctions to Influence Behavior

In the late 1980s and early 1990s, an incentive/sanction combination began to be applied to behavior. A major step in this direction was taken by Congress in the enactment of the Family Support Act of 1988, requiring, with some exceptions, adult welfare recipients to be available and qualified for employment. By the early 1990s, driven by rising welfare rolls already at record levels (over 4.5 million families on AFDC), on one hand, and critical budgetary pressures due to recession-induced falling revenues, on the other, state governments began to adopt, experiment with, or consider incentives and sanctions directed toward serious behavioral shortcomings of welfare recipients and others. Information on these types of changes, along with other state budget and legislative proposals, was collected by the American Public Welfare Association from state human service directors and summarized in its monthly report in early 1992.[160] These requirements and sanctions included:

- Denial of additional AFDC benefits to women receiving such benefits when and if she gives birth to more children. (New Jersey)[161]
- Reduce AFDC payments by 20 percent, with recipients being able to get them back by enrolling in preventive health care and keeping their school-age children in school, and require as a condition of Medicaid eligibility, the selection of a family physician by the client. (Maryland)[162]
- Require that minor parents live with one of their parents or guardian or in an adult-supervised living arrangement in order to be eligible for their own separate welfare grant. (Connecticut)[163]
- Teens with two or more unexcused absences from school to have their welfare grant reduced. (Ohio)[164]
- AFDC benefits reduced by up to $200 per month per child not attending school. Enacted by legislature in 1987; mixed evaluations. Governor seeking expansion of original pilot project to four counties for children 6 through 12. (Wisconsin)[165]
- On initiative ballot to confine AFDC benefits for new state residents to that of state of previous residency; provides a $50 each monthly incentive to parenting and pregnant teenagers under 19 if they remain in school; grant reduced by equal amount for those who drop out. (California)[166]

However, major controversies surrounded practically all of these incentives and sanctions. On the incentive side, there was growing support among private and public employers for bonuses or penalties in connection with "wellness" programs. Not smoking, agreeing to wear seat belts, and meeting weight, cholesterol, and other "healthy indicators" were examples. Nevertheless, there were some skeptics, alleging that good health bonuses were illogical and unfair (e.g., the genetic nature of obesity, risk factors not spread evenly among socioeconomic and income groups, and questions of privacy). Also several states in mid-1992 were considering, and two (West Virginia and Wyoming) had passed, "rights of privacy" laws prohibiting employers from firing, demoting, or refusing to employ people who smoked regularly off the job.[167]

An assessment of a California public health campaign *financed by a tax increase of 25¢ a pack* by ballot initiative in 1988 found that the incidence of adult smoking by Califorians declined by 17 percent over three years—from 28.8 percent in 1987 to 22.2 percent in 1990. There were differences of opinion as to whether the tax increase or education campaigns were mainly responsible. The Tobacco Institute claimed the former. The target of the campaign was to decrease the rate of smoking from 22 percent in 1990 to 6 percent by 2000.[168]

Objections to the five state initiatives listed above were based on (1) unfairness of singling out welfare and Medicaid recipients for incentives and sanctions (i.e., "punishing the poor") and (2) the initiatives' questionable effectiveness or other substantive reasons. On the fairness issue, the stronger objections were directed at the California initiative, particularly cuts as high as 25 percent. Proposals in the plan would also have limited for one year newcomers to the state to the level that they were receiving in their former state (designed to deter potential migrants from coming in because of high California benefits). Isabel Sawhill of the Urban Institute commented: "This is in keeping with the whole tenor of the times. There is a strong feeling out there . . . that too much money is going to people who don't play by middle-class rules and this is an attempt by the Governor to tap into those feelings."[169] "A punitive and Draconian package," said the Center on Budget and Policy Priorities.[170]

On the other hand, Charles Murray of the American Enterprise Institute, in criticizing the New Jersey provision limiting the benefits for women on welfare if they have additional children, said, "The New Jersey plan would neither help nor hurt. It just will not make much difference. . . . The problem is not that single mothers are on welfare, but that there are so many single mothers concentrated in poor communities. . . . We do not know how—*no matter how much money we spend*—to substitute social programs for competent parents."[171]

Other poverty researchers, regardless of philosophical differences, tended to agree with Sawhill, in expressing skepticism about behavioral incentives/sanctions. Conversely, Gerald Miller, director of Michigan's Department of Social Services, strongly supported Wisconsin's "Learnfare" and its adoption in Michigan: "I'm so supportive . . . because I know now what doesn't work," meaning the then status quo.[172] Lawrence Mead of New York University, although supportive of some of the state initiatives, conceded that ''it is difficult enough to force changes in behavior like study and work. . . . It is much harder when you get into private behaviors such as marriage and childbearing.'' He felt, however, that demoralized poor people would be helped by hearing government express strong approval or disapproval for different kinds of behaviors.[173]

Columnist Robert J. Samuelson also emphasized the behavioral base for the growing societal ills of suicide, divorce, one-parent families, and unmarried births:

Government didn't cause these trends. Personal behavior is what matters most. . . . There's less time for children: to love them, play with them, help with homework, and discipline them. . . . But children are not the only victims of this process. They're participants . . . they absorb society's conflicting values. . . . The more of the man-made world that children experience, the more they assume they know . . . the less they think they need adults. . . . Should welfare rules be tightened to deter out-of-wedlock births or to compel work? . . . Liberals want more ''support systems.'' Conservatives want to promote stay-at-home motherhood with tax breaks. Both sides exaggerate the impact of government policies on families. . . . No one will raise our children for us. . . . This is the most important work of our lives. . . . The responsibilities and choices are ours.[174]

On the substantive side of the incentive/sanction issue, Douglas Besharov, another American Enterprise Institute scholar, proposed some guidelines for incentives and penalties attached to welfare payments—a ''new paternalism'' with support from both ends of the political spectrum, after observing that it made sense to endeavor to obtain more responsible behavior from welfare recipients, a central underpinning of 1988's Family Support Act.

The suggested guidelines were:[175]

- The incentive/sanction combination should not be dominated by budget considerations, but rather toward behavioral change.
- The behavioral change(s) sought should be within reach of the recipient (requiring a teenage parent to attend school—as in Wisconsin and Ohio—but not penalizing adult parents for child's refusal to attend school).
- Behavioral changes should have broad public support (e.g., preventive health care for child).
- Legislators should recognize and be reconciled to varied consequences (reducing or eliminating welfare benefit to mothers having additional children likely to result not only in contraceptive precautions or abstinence but also in substantial increases in abortions).
- Compliance determination process should be easy and fair.
- Rewarding positive behavior often may be more productive than imposing penalties.
- Incentive or sanction should encourage long-term changes by built-in incremental approach (small annual bonuses rather than one-shot rewards).
- Prudent use of incentives/sanctions and approached with both caution and humility—step by step and avoidance of overreacting or overpromising.

Nonfinancial Sanctions Against, and New Remedies for, Irresponsible Parental Behavior

Child abuse and other illegal activity by parent(s) against children were reviewed in the preceding chapter. These prenatal and postnatal irresponsibility/misbehavior cases grew so rapidly in the 1980s that public policy issues of a new order began to arise. These included:

- Regarding repeated pregnancies by drug-/alcohol-addicted women; if in the first trimester, should abortion be counseled by attending physician or ordered by court? Should temporary (implant or contraceptive) or permanent sterilization ever be a legal remedy?
- Should prosecution under the criminal justice code be initiated where maternal drug addiction or other similar illegal action deforms, seriously injures, or destroys a fetus?

Prosecution for fetal injury or other abuse has been undertaken in a number of states. Bauer and King of the National Conference of State Legislatures (NCSL) reported several examples.

At least 60 women had been prosecuted for exposing their unborn children to drugs.

In Florida, a woman was convicted of "delivering" drugs to her twins through their umbilical cords. In Kansas, a woman was sent to jail for eight years—convicted of criminal abuse and drug possession—for risking death or serious injury to her unborn child. In Texas, the mother of a stillborn baby whose liver was filled with enough cocaine to kill an adult was sentenced to 12 years in prison, convicted of cocaine possession.

In Wyoming, a pregnant woman was arrested and jailed, charged with child abuse by excessive alcohol, a legal drug. The case was dismissed because of insufficient evidence that the fetus was being damaged.[176] In mid-1992, the State Supreme Court of Connecticut ruled unanimously that a pregnant woman who injected cocaine into one of her veins before going into labor had not abused her baby, even though the baby, when born, was severely traumatized. The ruling was based on the lack of authority under state law for punitive action.[177]

These kinds of cases pose several questions: Is jail the answer to protecting the unborn, or will the prosecution threat cause the woman to forgo prenatal care? Should drug-exposed infants be removed from parental custody? Should legislative solutions deal with legal, as well as illegal, drugs? Examined in the succeeding section is the question of mandatory drug testing where use is suspected; one of the most crucial questions where drug use is involved is whether a treatment slot is promptly available. Usually not, unfortunately.

Bauer and King reported that legislators across the country were struggling to find ways to prevent problems such as those cited in Florida and Wyoming. Several states, rather than imposing criminal penalties, had added prenatal drug exposure to child protection laws (Florida, Illinois, Indiana, Massachusetts,

Minnesota, Nevada, New Jersey, Oklahoma, and Utah). Several states intensified education efforts, and a member of the Georgia House stated: "Legislators need to be educated—I promise you they are ignorant. I guarantee that with eduction there would be less incarceration and more 'rehabilitation.' " Bauer and King summarized the dilemma facing the legislatures as "preventing the problems . . . while striking a balance between the mother's rights and those of her child."[178]

POLICY OPTIONS IN CURBING SUBSTANCE ABUSE AND VIOLENT BEHAVIOR

Like health care in general, the drug-violence-crime-recidivism cycle in the 1970–90 period was (1) moving increasingly to the forefront of U.S. domestic policy, (2) comprising an inextricably related set of major interacting elements, and (3) possessed of many problems, but very few evident or logical avenues of pursuit for public-policy makers. Public outrage and resulting "zero tolerance" approaches in criminal justice quickly overloaded the judicial and correctional segments of that system with steeply escalating detention facility and prison populations, comprising increasingly significant proportions of juvenile and young adult offenders. Increasing proportions of violent crimes were attributable to drug use and addiction, as also was the case for repeat offenders; likewise, a majority of those convicted of violent crime had suffered physical or sexual abuse as young children. A high percentage of child abusers were parent(s), who in turn were more and more frequently under the influence of alcohol or other drugs at the time the abuse was committed.

Despite the seemingly inseparable relationship between drug abuse and violent behavior, our examination of policy options in this section is directed first at alcohol/drug issues, because *in so many instances, drugs cause violence to happen.*

Drug Abuse: Policy Issues in Education, Prevention, Law Enforcement, and Treatment

The pervasiveness and serious consequences of adolescent drug abuse among American youth were succinctly summarized by the NCC:

More than half of all young people report that they have tried an illicit drug by the time they complete high school, and rates of crack cocaine use remain disturbingly high among some youths. Young people who abuse drugs are very likely to drop out of school, to engage in premature and unprotected sexual activity, and to commit crimes. They are at very high risk of contracting sexually transmitted diseases, including AIDS, of experiencing accidents and injuries, and of ending up in jail. As one young man Commission members met who was serving time in a maximum-security prison put it, "Kids who do drugs are killing themselves slowly."[179]

The 1980s saw a spate of federal and state crime control legislation, much of it focused on the drug problem and much of that centered on the "get tough" enforcement and mandatory sentencing aspects.

By the late 1980s, however, some states were shifting their legislative intiatives to more comprehensive approaches, as illustrated in the Washington legislature by an "Omnibus Alcohol and Controlled Substance Act of 1989," which included sections to (1) increase mandatory minimum sentences for drug offenders; (2) establish two experimental "adult regimented inmate disciplinary" projects or "boot camps" and a similar project for juveniles 12 to 18; (3) broaden authority for communication interception between or among suspected drug offenders; (4) broaden asset forfeiture laws to include real property; (5) establish "off-limits areas" and court enjoinment of suspected drug traffickers from entry thereto; (6) create a state grant program for community mobilization efforts; (7) authorize involuntary treatment of drug offenders; (8) begin a state grant program for joint local government, nonprofit, school district, and other agencies and organizations for "early intervention" efforts in grades K–9; (9) establish a priority treatment program to serve pregnant and postbirth women and their infants and children; (10) increase taxes on alcohol and tobacco, with revenues going initially to finance a drug enforcement and education account; and (11) initially appropriate about $60 million.[190]

In the 1991 sessions, state legislatures enacted more than 350 drug-related laws and debated several hundred others, and in 1992, 42 states enacted over 300. In both years states were moving away from punitive sanctions and toward reducing the barriers to treatment and improving community-based programs for those needing help. The new laws ranged from strict enforcement measures to drug treatment for criminals in correctional facilities and for drug-abusing pregnant women and their families. The "get tough" approach was still present, giving attention not only to treatment but to prevention measures such as drug-free schools and neighborhoods and to use in the workplace or otherwise connected with employment.[181]

In its analysis of the 1991 laws, the Intergovernmental Health Policy Project reported that of 10 issue areas, the states legislating on them numbered as follows: enforcement (26), workplace (24), treatment (23), drunk driving license revocation (21), prevention (20), schools (19), maternal and child health (18), youth/family (13), corrections (11), and administration (11).[182]

Drug Abuse Education and Prevention. As in other health care areas, education and prevention were proving to be the most cost-effective, in contrast to either enforcement or treatment. A 1984 Rand research report commented:

Programs to control [drug use] have employed three principal methods: (1) *enforcement* of drug laws; (2) *treatment* of chronic abusers; and (3) *prevention* of initial drug use. We find that while intensified law enforcement is not likely to reduce adolescent drug use, and the benefits of expanded treatment remain uncertain, prevention programs hold more promise. The most encouraging evidence comes from the success of school-based programs to prevent cigarette smoking, which offer a strategy that may be adaptable to other drugs.[183]

A subsequent 1990 Rand study developed and tested a prevention curriculum procedure based on the "social influence model," tested it on 7th and 8th graders at 30 schools in Oregon and California between 1984 and 1986, and assessed the effects over 15 subsequent months. It was aimed at preventing or reducing adolescents' use of alcohol, cigarettes, and marijuana. The social influence approach tries (1) to help identify the pressure to smoke or use alocohol or drugs, (2) to counter pro-use arguments, and (3) to teach children to say no when directly offered a smoke, drink or drug. To provide motivation for saying no, the program emphasizes the negative effect the use has on teens *now*, in their daily life and social relationships. "This has more relevance for most teens than long-time health effects, which seem as unreal to teenagers as growing old."[184]

In terms of final results, the curriculum was more effective against marijuana and cigarettes than alcohol. Rand researcher conclusions from the project included: (1) the social influence model merits implementation in the nation's middle and junior high schools; (2) social influence programs are most effective when the prevailing social context reinforces their messages; (3) legalizing marijuana and other drugs could undermine prevention efforts; (4) adolescents who are confirmed cigarette users need a more aggressive program than the social influence model alone provides; and (5) booster programs are critical for extending the effects of social influence programs.[185]

The seriousness of the alcohol problem and its connection with societal tolerance, relevant to Rand's second conclusion, was highlighted subsequently in the 1991 national surveys of high school seniors and college students, under the sponsorship of the U.S. Department of Health and Human Services. In 1991, cocaine use among seniors had fallen from 5.3 percent in 1990 to 3.5 percent and from a peak of 13.1 in 1985, and among college students it had fallen to 3.6 percent from 17.0 in 1986. LSD use had not declined since the early 1980s, with some upward drift among college students. However, use of alcohol, particularly binge drinking (five or more drinks in a row during the preceding two weeks), was at 30 percent in 1991 among seniors and 43 percent among college students.[186]

On the other hand, the national household survey by the National Institute on Drug Abuse showed use any time in the preceding month to be at 20.3 percent among youths age 12–17 and 63.6 percent among young adults age 18–25, compared with respective highs for the young and older groups of 37.2 percent and 75.9 percent, both in 1979.[187] Considerable blame for the persistent use of alcohol in society, especially among adolescent youth, was pointing toward the advertising media for its ads for alcoholic products presented in a highly attractive way to young people.[188] The National Governors' Association in its 1991 policy statements reaffirmed an earlier adoption of the following position on health promotion and prevention measures:

The federal government [should] expand its health promotion activities and encourage critical state preventive health initiatives and programs. Most health care professionals believe that personal behavior and habits such as smoking, exercise, diet, and alcohol and drug abuse are major determinants of morbidity and mortality. [Often] health education and promotion programs can play an important role in modifying unhealthful practices.[189]

The initiative taken by the surgeon general on alcohol advertising targeted to young people seemed to fit precisely the thrust of the NGA policy statement.

On the state legislative front, 1991 and 1992 sessions saw the enactment of a variety of measures on drug education and prevention in 20 states, concentrated on drug-free zones, eradicating drug-related nuisances from neighborhoods, and establishing community substance prevention programs. Drug-free zones were expanded, for example, to public housing in Minnesota; New Hampshire established a committee to examine the feasibility of expanding such zones not only to public housing but to public parks and playgrounds; and Utah expanded the zones to include shopping malls, theaters, sports and other facilities, and any parking lot near any of the specified types of facilities. Seven states expanded these zones in 1992 (California, Colorado, Connecticut, Georgia, New Hamsphire, Oklahoma, and Tennessee). Four states initiated or strengthened nuisance abatement laws regarding drug use or distribution (Minnesota, Michigan, Florida, and Maryland). Five others (Texas, Pennsylvania, Ohio, Alaska, and Virginia) acted in the education, advertising, and promotion areas. Alaska, one of the heavy alcohol-use states, designated 1991 as Take Pride in Sobriety Year. Minnesota established grants for community prevention programs on alcohol/drug abuse and related health behaviors.[190]

Nationally, the OTA adolescent health study proposed, as one of several policy options related to alcohol, tobacco, and drug abuse, that for health education, the federal government "support the provision to adolescents of information relevant to obtaining access to a range of substance abuse treatment options" and also education and other programs that would foster changes in adolescents' environment—the social influence aspect discussed earlier. Specifically, the option involved "a range of changes in the social environment that have been *associated* with lower rates of problem use of alcohol, tobacco, and illicit drugs, and may have other beneficial effects on adolescent health and well-being (e.g., reductions in parental drug use, higher levels of adult supervision, less contact with drug-using peers, perceptions of socially acceptable life options)."[191]

Also on the national level, the GAO conducted two studies of drug prevention efforts: (1) two programs operating concurrently by the Department of Education's (DE) Drug-Free School Recognition Program and the Exemplary Program Study by the Department of Health and Human Services (HHS) and (2) a group of 16 community-based drug abuse education programs regardless of funding source.

On the DE and HHS programs, the GAO commented:

The policies underlying both recognition efforts limited eligible programs to those with a "no-use" approach to drug abuse prevention for youths. In the strictest sense, no-use programs are those with a consistent message that any use of drugs, alcohol, or tobacco is always wrong and harmful. Responsible-use approaches, on the other hand, while *not condoning* the use of drugs, alcohol, or tobacco, may attempt to prevent or delay the onset of substance use by stressing informed decision making, or may aim to reduce the riskiest forms of use (such as drinking and driving) and encourage reduction in use *for those who are already involved* [with these substances].

GAO further noted that "current research evidence has not demonstrated the general superiority of one prevention approach over any other, nor have any evaluations isolated the effects of a no-use approach. Further, responsible-use approaches are widespread, as shown by the continued presence of Students Against Driving Drunk (SADD) chapters in 25,000 middle and high schools."

On the second study, GAO emphasized that the community-based programs took a comprehensive approach toward youths as opposed to combating drug use alone. Features were identified in the programs evoking the most enthusiastic participation: (1) comprehensive strategy; (2) an indirect approach, emphasizing a range of healthy habits; (3) participation of students in shaping the program; (4) a culturally sensitive orientation; and (5) highly structured activities. GAO found evlauation data collection under way but nothing in outcomes research on a longitudinal basis. It urged Congress to consider funding long-term, national, independent evaluation of community-based prevention programs.[192]

In the foregoing review of drug education and prevention approaches, very few existing or potential objections were noted. There has been one latent controversy over both antismoking and antialcohol measures: the right of privacy to engage in a legal activity *off the job* and freedom of speech, as applied to curbing alcohol advertising so as to make it less appealing to adolescent youth. In the latter case, an industrywide voluntary standard would be a possibility. Or, if public opinion were aroused sufficiently, the alcohol-associated companies might bow to the popular will. It would appear that a school curriculum of the kind used in the Rand project, as modified or elaborated by future research and experience, could not help but ameliorate, to varying, but significant degrees, the temptations facing adolescents. Public information campaigns directed to parents and to societal leaders to set appropriate examples—as have occurred in the case of smoking—also appeared to hold substantial promise.

Alcohol/Drug Issues in the Workplace. Alcohol/drug issues within the context of employer "wellness" programs and financial disincentives or positive incentives for being tobacco-, alcohol-, and drug-free were discussed earlier. As these incentives and penalties began coming into use, so did the question of drug testing for a variety of purposes. Dramatic air and railroad disasters when the pilot or engineer was under the influence of drugs or alcohol led to demands that individuals in public safety occupations be tested—on preemployment basis and thereafter, routinely or randomly without notice.

A less strict approach was to test only when there was admission or suspicion of use or to initiate the testing subsequent to, and continuing after, an instance of work hindrance through drug use. Testing without consent and/or without the knowledge of the individual being tested became contentions issues in a number of quarters. Some national and much state legislation was enacted. Rights of privacy and protection against self-incrimination were, and continued to be, argued between law enforcement personnel and civil libertarians. Those aspects of drug testing related primarily to the criminal justice system are examined subsequently. Some issues relate primarily to fair and unfair employment practices, and those are examined here.

State legislation in 1991 on drug testing *in the workplace* included comprehensive treatment of the issue in Mississippi; safeguards for such testing by three other states (Louisiana, North Carolina, and Texas); and mandatory testing for intrastate truck drivers (Connecticut and Montana). The Mississippi legislation (S 2172, Ch 610, '91 Laws) laid down procedures and guidelines for mandatory use by public employers and voluntary use for private ones; for the latter, those adopting the procedures are protected by the state government against any resultant legal action. The guidelines include (1) a required employer policy statement containing the policy on drug use, ensuring confidentiality for employees, circumstances under which testing may occur, consequences of refusal to be tested, opportunities for treatment if tested positive, and tie-in or other reference to the relevant bargaining agreement; (2) listing of positions requiring testing; (3) collection and documentation of specimens; (4) confirmation of test results; and (5) *prohibition* of requiring abstention from tobacco during nonworking hours.[193]

Sixteen states enacted 1992 treatment legislation, including treatment for minors and regulatory requirements for treatment professionals and facilities. Laws in 1991 and 1992 provided for treatment and other assistance to pharmacists, physicians, nurses, dentists, and other health professionals with substance abuse problems and for monitoring such dependence through oral queries, testing, and other appropriate measures. Texas amended its laws to provide for probationary licenses to practice law under the same types of arrangements. Health care professionals, because their actions, if impaired by alcohol or other drugs, can threaten the health and lives of those being treated, come under surveillance and assistance by a variety of procedures specified in legislation or embodied in standards adopted by state professional organizations. Also, as in Oregon (SB 759 Ch 774 '91 Laws), patient confidentiality may be set aside by the health care provider if the patient is in a condition as to endanger others, such as driving, and public safety or other authorities may be notified, with immunity to the person so doing.

While occasionally applicable to workplace issues, but not primarily so, sweeping 1991 legislation was enacted in Louisiana, calling upon the larger parishes, mainly in the New Orleans area, to install a pretrial drug testing program *for all persons arrested for state offenses*. No person would be released by the court without agreeing to submit to further random testing and agreeing to refrain from possession or use of drugs while under custody of the court, including probation. (The legislation might be called deficient in (1) precluding use of state funds for the testing program, leaving financing up to local, federal, or other financial sources and (2) not linking drug treatment into the probationary or other restraint period.)[194]

From the standpoint of the young adolescent, the continued expansion of alcohol and drug testing in the workplace and elsewhere signaled (1) the increasing societal disapproval of drug/alcohol abuse and (2) the growing possibility of encountering testing and/or monitoring when he or she enters the labor force.

Drug Law Enforcement. In the early 1990s, a growing body of public opinion, as well as opinion of experts in the legal, economic, and social aspects of America's drug problems, was that (1) much more needed to be done on the demand side of illicit drugs—restoring drug-ridden neighborhoods and making drug dealing much more difficult—and (2) law enforcement had to take a new turn with increased emphasis on a nonprison type of punishments, penalties, and restitutions. Some of the state legislation mentioned already, such as drug-free zones, was illustrative of new approaches to enforcement. Attention is given here to asset forfeiture; neighborhood reclamation; and solicitation of minors for drug distribution tasks.

Drug-Ridden Neighborhood Environments. Drug-plagued neighborhoods create a devastatingly negative effect upon young children and adolescents growing up and going to school in the area. In addition to exposure to drugs and the lucrative nature of the drug trade, violence increases, and the lives and property of the area children and adults are ever more threatened. Syndicated columnist Neal Peirce, an extensive commentator on state and local governmental and civic affairs, stated that in these neighborhoods, "kids get exposed to the drug trade's most alarming values—lawlessness, violence, sex-for-sale, instant gratification, ostentatious displays of gold jewelry, and expensive cars. Elderly people become fearful, stop socializing in the parks. Property values plummet; physical degradation spreads."[195]

An organization known as the American Alliance for Rights and Responsibilities outlined in a 1992 article steps that communities and citizens could take to rid themselves of flagrant drug markets. Tactical objectives included:[196]

- Broadcasting community intolerance—(1) confronting drug customers and dealers, organizing citizen patrols, picketing of businesses and landlords hospitable to the drug trade and (2) cleaning up the neighborhood—removing trash, enforcing city codes, increasing street lighting.

- Denying access to space—(1) abolishing site-specific sites, getting public housing and private rental leases changed, rehabilitating or razing abandoned properties; (2) discouraging entrance—ID procedures, fences/barriers, (3) widening drug-free zones.

• Destroying dealer sense of impunity—(1) increasing police presence, (2) enacting driver license revocation laws, (3) asset seizure and forfeiture.

On the other hand, the 10th anniversary report of the Milton S. Eisenhower Foundation took a much less optimistic view of the potential of neighborhood block patrols and similar activities, especially for poverty-stricken *inner-city* neighorhoods, where the drug market influences are so strong, even when combined with community-based policing and its foot patrols. The report commented:

There is little evidence that community-based policing in the form of foot patrols reduces crime *per se*. Evaluations in [Flint, Michigan; Kansas City, Missouri; Newark, New Jersey; Houston, Texas; and New York City] all point to this conclusion. . . . The tactical model that frequently underlies block organizing efforts in particular seems to rest on a set of presumptions about residents' energy and stability that is more appropriate to a stable middle-class or working-class neighborhood than to poorer communities with higher transiency, lower resources and fewer social networks. But it is precisely those communities that most suffer from urban violence.[197]

The foundation report listed the following "street lessons": (1) inner-city non-profits can be efficient as lead institutions; (2) technical assistance increases the odds for success; (3) it is folly to expect success without adequate resources; (4) voluntarism is being oversold in the inner city; (5) public sector agencies, including the police have a crucial role; (6) block watch, neighborhood watch, and other conventional tactics are sharply limited; and (7) higher standards of evaluation are needed.[198]

Drug enforcement among adolescents attending school had a continuing weakness dating from the late 1960s and was only beginning to abate in the early 1990s—the unwillingness of school principals and teachers to report students suspected of using drugs and similar reluctance of many parent(s), especially from suburbia, to believe, or even hear, that their children might be using drugs. A *Washington Post* editorial about large-scale marketing of LSD in two Fairfax County (Virginia) high schools illustrated the problem.

The case prompts many conclusions. One is that teachers and other school-based personnel are too cautious or unwilling to seek out or report students suspected of abusing drugs. [The school superintendent] describes a thoroughly unacceptable situation, particularly given the fact that Virigina law provides immunity for teachers accused of making false allegations in such cases. . . . What of the seemingly thorough nine years of drug-abuse education that is offered? . . . Students have suggested that they have been taught far more about the dangers of other illegal drugs . . . but that they have heard relatively little about the consequences of using LSD.[199]

Asset Forfeiture. Laws to strengthen asset forfeiture were enacted in five states in 1991 (Georgia, Arkansas, Washington, Maine, and Oregon). Oregon specified that claimant would have acquiesced in the prohibited conduct if he or she knowingly failed to take reasonable action to preclude, avoid, or negate use of the property for the prohibited conduct. Georgia enacted the usual provision that any real or personal property acquired with proceeds from the manufacture, distribution, or sale or prohibited substances would be forfeited.[200]

Using Minors for Drug Violations. In 1991 four states (Idaho, Nebraska, Oregon, and Louisiana) increased penalties for using minors to distribute illicit drugs or for any other task that involved violation of laws concerning them. The Louisiana law provided that any adult so using a minor would be imprisoned for not less than 20 years without parole or probation. Oregon and Idaho made involvement of a minor in the manufacture or delivery of any illegal drug, including more than five grams of marijuna, a felony. Nebraska provided that in delivery of drugs to minors or otherwise involving them in the drug trade, not knowing the age of the minor would not be a defense.[201]

In other drug enforcement legislation enacted in 1991, 15 states increased or expanded penalties. Mandatory penalties (which automatically expand the prison population) were enacted in Alabama, Louisiana, Maryland, Montana, and Washington. Three of the 15 states increased fines (California, Rhode Island, and Virginia). Four states (North Dakota, California, Maryland, and Florida) enacted or strengthened penalties for using drugs while hunting or otherwise carrying arms; Maryland provided that anyone convicted of a drug-related felony would be prohibited thereafter from owning a firearm.[202]

Ownership and use of firearms by juveniles were noted earlier, especially the joint *JAMA* editorial by Koop and Lundberg. In the special *JAMA* issue in which the "Bite the Bullet Back" editorial appeared, several articles detailing the handgun threat to American society were presented.[203] Gun control as a policy issue has been prominent in public opinion since the 1960s, especially after the Reagan assassination attempt. State legislatures have been acting cautiously, in the face of strong political pressure from the National Rifle Association, hunters, and others seeing constitutional significance in the "right to bear arms." It appeared in 1993 that the time for definitive federal action had arrived, given the homicide epidemic and the interstate nature of the gun trade.

Drug Treatment

Many shortcomings in the nation's drug treatment programs were detailed in chapter 3. Most of the weaknesses appeared to center around the following, not in any order: (1) extreme shortage of treatment slots, (2) for various reasons, the unavailability of treatment for pregnant women in numerous treatment facilities, often attributed to fears of legal liability, (3) the relative lack of causality research, (4) a similar lack of research on effectiveness of various treatment modes, (5) practically no knowledge of the relative effective treatment approaches for crack cocaine, (6) political antipathy to the concept of "treatment on demand" and assertions that addicts must prove their intention to abstain before being admitted to treatment—an attitude that a sizable body of opinion deplored, (7) financial barriers in the Medicaid program with a heavy tilt toward inpatient treatment and unavailability of Medicaid coverage for less expensive residential treatment centers.[204]

The 10th anniversary report of the Milton S. Eisenhower Foundation dealing with "street lessons on drugs and crime for the nineties," commented as follows on drug treatment:

The surface has barely been scratched when it comes to treatment innovations in the United States. There are a total of 5,000 existing treatment centers of all kinds. Most are short term and outpatient. There is as yet little scientific proof of their cost-effectiveness. Too much of what passes for drug treatment today is overly expensive, insufficiently evaluated, poorly staffed and too little oriented toward integrating the drug abuser into a productive life in a functioning community. . . . There is poor coordination in terms of channeling the estimated 4 million addicts into [treatment]. A majority of treatment slots are still for heroin users. Yet they now are far outnumbered by cocaine addicts and multiple abusers—who require different treatment strategies.

We do know this: Something close to a consensus has emerged that significantly more funding is required to close the gap between treatment need and availability among the disadvantaged. Without it, hard drugs will continue to ravage families and communties in the inner city; drug-related violence will continue at levels that place many neighborhoods in a state of siege. . . . As a high official at the National Institute on Drug Abuse has observed, "for many addicts, it's not rehabilitation; it's habilitation. They don't know how to read or look for work, let alone beat their addictions." . . . Community-based facilities may need placement in more neighborhood police substations to encourage acceptance by . . . residents, who otherwise would fear for their safety.[205]

Causality and Treatment Research Needed. Regarding crack cocaine, a 1991 GAO report found:

No state-of-the-art treatment method for crack abusers exists. Traditional drug treatment programs designed primarily for heroin addicts are being used to treat many crack addicts. Meanwhile, drug treatment researchers are experimenting with new strategies. . . . It will be several years before any reliable drug is available to treat crack addiction.[206]

An earlier GAO report dealing with research needs in drug treatment recommended that "the Secretary of Health and Human Services direct NIDA [National Institute on Drug Abuse] to implement its strategic planning process and develop a plan that sets forth its long-term overall treatment research objectives and the relative priorities assigned to the different categories of treatment research. This plan should consider (1) current and anticipated trends of drug abuse and (2) the needs of treatment practitioners, who have a key stake in the results of NIDA's research. . . . Funding for the training of drug abuse researchers has not kept up with increases in funding for drug abuse research. This . . . has slowed progress in . . . treatment research.[207]

In testimony before a subcommittee of the House Committee on Government Operations, the assistant comptroller general for Program Evaluation and Methodology reported on an extended inquiry into drug abuse research, one part of

which had involved consultation with 30 experts across the country—both pro-
ducers and users of research—to suggest needed work, and stated to the
subcommittee:

We did find particularly high consensus on the need for causality research in the suggestions from [the experts]. . . . Understanding the causes of drug abuse could be a highly
useful basis for developing prevention and treatment ideas. Without such understanding,
interventions are often pure guesswork and cumulative learning then depends on after-
the-fact evaluations that must compete for funds with service programs and are methodologically challenging to perform.

Concerning prevention and treatment, the interviews showed more variability in the
expert views on . . . research topics. The effectiveness of different prevention approaches
remains an area of major uncertainty, with special emphasis on learning more about early
interventions, family involvement, and community-wide efforts. Further, the experts
urged research on positive and negative features of U.S. media approaches such as shock
advertisements and study of alternative policy approaches to drug prevention in other
countries such as those of Western Europe. Familiar issues surfaced concerning treatment
research, including evaluation studies to sort out which elements of complex programs
are most useful and for whom at different stages of the treatment process, a global concern
for continued study of the effectiveness of all current treatments, and finding new approaches to treating drug problems, including medications development.[208]

Methadone Maintenance. The use of methadone as a stabilizing and gradual
withdrawal agent proved moderately effective for heroin over an extended period
dating from the 1970s. A comparable agent has not existed for cocaine, but
methadone maintenance continues to serve hundreds of thousands of heroin
addicts on the way to ultimate abstention. However, a study released in early
1992 reviewed dosages and other practices at 172 methadone clinics (over half
of all such clinics nationwide) and found differences in (1) the amount of methadone administered, (2) the willingness of clinics to let patients have some voice
in how to manage their addiction problem, and (3) the average length of treatment. Earlier studies had shown the higher dosages had helped keep patients in
the program longer. Of the nearly 3,400 patients treated in the preceding year,
over half had had no input on their treatment, and 7,000 others were taking
doses that were too small. The authors of the study, Thomas D'Aunno and
Thomas Vaughn, argued that improving the treatment program would help ensure
the addiction would be fully overcome, which would be greatly beneficial in
stemming the spread of AIDS in light of the sizable proportion of transmission
via IV drug use. In an editorial comment in the same *JAMA* issue, James Cooper
noted that psychoactive drugs often were ineffectively used, and methadone was
no exception. He called for further study and argued that "more than ever before,
we need to remove the remaining arbitrary state or program policy restrictions
on methadone dose and duration of treatment."[209]

"Crack Babies" an Urgent Problem. Among the unmet needs stated at the
outset, to fill the demand for treatment slots to accommodate expectant mothers

probably was the most urgent short-term action required in the early 1990s. The health and financial cost of crack babies is very high, and drug treatment beginning early in pregnancy would ease this tragic situation greatly. In 1990 public health authorities were estimating the number of babies so affected at 30,000 to 100,000, and this range increased in 1991 to 91,000 to 240,000. Based on an estimate of 158,400 cocaine-exposed infants, the additional hospital and medical costs were placed at $504 million for 1990, not counting "boarder" costs incurred by extended hospital stays. In the *JAMA* article carrying these estimates, it was stated that the "free-base (crack) cocaine advent has resulted in an epidemic of fetal cocaine exposure . . . particularly in large cities. . . . Fetal exposure to cocaine has been associated with . . . a variety of neuro-behavioral and circulatory complications. . . . Some complications . . . may be catastrophic."[210]

Abuse, Depression, and Mental Health Issues

It is clear from material presented in chapter 3 and just elaborated that indisputable linkages exist between alcohol/drug abuse, on one hand, and child abuse, emotional instability, adolescent violent behavior, and often juvenile crime, on the other. Less marked, but still frequent, linkage often exists between child abuse early in life and subsequent emotional instability and a resort to substance abuse and similar behavior patterns. By the early 1990s, abuse, neglect, and abandonment of one's children were placing increasing burdens upon child welfare agencies and upon the foster care and adoption systems.

Traditionally, public policy to protect the overall well-being, health, and general interests of children had been vested in child welfare agencies in state and local governments and in the federal departments of Labor, HEW, and HHS. Generally, the foci of child welfare agencies comprised orphaned children, infants born out of wedlock and available for adoption, and children endangered within, or dislodged from, their homes and requiring subsequent protection until adoption or other permanent placement could be arranged. The use of illicit drugs, the incidence of family breakups, and the extent of child abuse by one or both parents began to grow in the late 1960s, increased further in the 1970s, and accelerated in the 1980s. The child welfare system became overloaded—in numbers and in the diversity and complexity of problems demanding immediate attention and action.

Curbing Child Abuse. The NCC stated in 1991 that reports of child abuse and neglect had risen 259 percent between 1976 and 1989 and that more than 50 percent of all out-of-home placements were for children needing protection from adults in their own homes. Several factors had contributed to the increases in the number of children in out-of-home placements—family poverty and homelessness; number of single-parent families; births to teenagers remaining at a high level; and continued flourishing drug use in large cities and small communities nationwide. The commission reported, however, that an analysis of the factors placing children at risk of maltreatment had suggested that only family income was consistently related to all categories of abuse and neglect. When other factors, such as single parenthood and race, were controlled for income, there was no positive correlation with heightened risk of abuse or neglect.[211]

A 1987 report of the National Governors' Association (NGA), a joint product of its Committee on Human Resources and its Center for Policy Research, noted that "The U.S. Department of Justice has reported an increase in the U.S. prison population from 195,000 in 1972 to 547,000 in 1986. According to the American Humane Association, 80 percent of these inmates *were abused as children.*"[212]

However, for understandable, but unjustifiable, reasons, the accuracy of child abuse data, although having improved from earlier years, was still leaving much to be desired by 1990. Urban Institute researchers examined the nature and prevalence of cases reported to child protective agencies between 1980 and 1986 as to reporting methods, extent of underreporting, and types of cases most underreported. (In 1980 the child protective agencies were aware of only 33 percent of those known to community professionals.) Major findings of the study were:[213]

- Overall, the reporting practices of agencies had improved post-1980, but substantial underreporting still existed.

- Older victims were less likely to be known to the child protective agencies, contradicting the assumption that younger children were more overlooked due to evidential/legal aspects. The nature of the abuse determined which cases would be reported most often, with sexual abuse most likely to be reported, neglect least likely (though, if chronic, it is more harmful), and physical/emotional in the middle.

- Sex, race, and income were not determinants in reporting of cases.

The Child Welfare League of America (CWLA) in a 1992 report ascribed the principal cause of child abuse to drug and alcohol abuse. Based on a 10-state survey of children served by public child protective service workers in 1990, 37 percent of reports were from families in which there was an alcohol- or drug-abusing caregiver or in which the children themselves were alcohol or drug abusers. A similar survey of nonprofit child welfare agencies found the drug-child abuse connection to be over 55 percent. The public-private difference was attributable to a higher percent use of drug-alcohol screening—42 percent of state agencies and 71 percent of the not-for-profits.[214]

Child abuse had become a major, if not the principal, cause of child welfare agency assumption of jurisdiction over children. The extent to which primary or predominant reliance is placed on retention in the home, combined with drug treatment, counseling, or other measures, is a policy issue involving the entire child welfare system and is examined later. Child abuse policy issues addressed here are preventive measures and comprise (1) early identification of at-risk mothers in the prenatal period or soon after the infant's birth and of home conditions that may place the infant at risk and (2) parenting counseling and education of the parent(s), actual or expecting.

On parent education, the NCC commented that in recent years several states had begun to invest in prevention-oriented programs designed to strengthen and support families and enhance parents' child-rearing abilities. These included parenting education (Minnesota and Missouri); pilot family support programs for families with children (Connecticut and Maryland); and an Ounce of Prevention Fund—combining state and private funds to sponsor family support, parent education, and early child development programs in more than 45 locations (Illinois).[215] The commission recommended that "federal, state, and local governments, in partnership with private community organizations, develop and expand community-based family support programs to provide parents with the knowledge, skills, and support they need to raise their children."

However, a 1992 GAO report found the following: "Available information indicates that federal funding for [child abuse] prevention—which is provided primarily by [HHS]—is relatively low, often taking the form of short-term grants for demonstration projects. In contrast the federal government provides billions of dollars annually to states to provide foster care and other assistance for children who have been abused."[216]

The House Select Committee on Children, Youth, and Families endorsed parenting education as a part of home visiting programs in "reducing the incidence of child abuse and neglect."[217]

Such programs (1) help ensure that expectant mothers seek and obtain prenatal care; (2) establish a link with child welfare and health care systems; and (3) help the expectant or new mother understand and accept the obligations of responsible motherhood. On the other hand, parenting programs are labor-intensive and could be more expensive than similar counseling and persuasion obtained coincidentally with prenatal visits to an OB/GYN and later to a pediatric nurse or physician. It could be argued that in the case of mothers on Medicaid, once a regular contact is established with a doctor or clinic, being tied into the health care chain might comprise a continuing deterrent to irresponsible behavior of a force equal to, or greater than, a parenting outreach effort operating out of a child welfare or other agency. However, the case overload and other problems facing those agencies make a fairly strong case for parenting programs, offering clear short-term benefits—in curbing child abuse and providing other health/educational advantages.

Emotional Instability and Other Mental Health Issues. Emotional and other mental health problems in infants, young children, and adolescents stem from a variety of causes; prominent among them are (1) drug/alcohol effects upon fetus; (2) child abuse; (3) diagnosable mental disorders; and (4) mental suffering and disability from external factors, such as household poverty, inadequate care, parental hostility, or other environmental conditions. OTA and PHS studies had estimated that 12 percent of children were suffering from a mental health disorder severe enough to require treatment, and far less than half of those were getting adequate attention, in contrast to a national health goal to reduce the proportion to 10 percent in 2000. There was agreement among a variety of sources (e.g., NCC, CDF, National Mental Health Association) that (1) services were deficient; (2) services were overly tilted toward inpatient services, often in out-of-area facilities; and (3) home- or community-based treatment was highly preferable to the late 1980–early 1990 mix.[218]

As noted earlier in relation to homelessness, the transition from inpatient care of the mentally ill of all ages from state mental hospitals to community-based facilities was a very difficult and faulty one. When the plight of emotionally disturbed children and youth reached the point that "exposure to violence [was] a normal part of life," the policy choices between institutionalization, on one hand, and home care, on the other, became an increasingly difficult one.

State legislation concerning mental health facilities and services for children in 1991 and 1992 included the following types:[219]

- Community-based services (as in Arkansas, 1991) that included a single point of entry; screening and assessment; case management and review; evaluation and an array of mental health services; and the amendment to state's children's mental health services law, clarifying implementation responsibilities between the state and the county governments (California, 1992).
- Establishment of a state psychiatric 20-bed residential facility for the treatment of seriously emotionally disturbed children (Montana, 1991) and emphasizing need to utilize outpatient, instead of inpatient, treatment for children whenever appropriate (Oklahoma, 1992).
- Designation of severely emotionally disturbed children as a priority population for receiving mental health services financed by the state (Washington, 1991).
- Licensing of school psychologists (West Virginia, 1991).
- Requiring culturally relevant mental health assessment, case management, and treatment services to be available to minors who are, or about to be, placed out of home by court and/or child welfare agency (California, 1991).
- A school-based early mental health intervention and prevention services grant program under the state director of mental health (California, 1991).
- Separating mental health commitment procedures as between adults and minors (South Carolina, 1991).
- Strengthening and improving access to community-based mental health facilities (several states, 1991 and 1992).

The search for intermediate placement between foster care and institutionalization for those children for whom home care is not feasible or desirable is explored subsequently as a part of child welfare system reform.

Adolescent Violent Behavior and the Juvenile Justice and Correctional Systems

Violence among adolescents and young adults was increasing at an alarming rate at the close of the 1980s. Violence and other antisocial behavior had been a growing problem over the two preceding decades, largely centered in inner-city public schools, public housing projects, and city streets. Homicide rates among high school–age youths rose steadily, as did violence within schools, touching teachers as well as students, as noted in chapter 3. In subsequent years, however, largely coincident with the spread of crack cocaine (which often induces violent behavior) and "drug turf wars," the use of firearms among youth became more common, not only in large cities but in suburban and nonmetropolitan areas as well. Policy options are examined in the respective contexts of (1) youth violence in general; (2) juvenile justice, sentencing, and incarceration patterns; and (3) drug treatment for juvenile offenders held in jails or prisons.

Dealing with Violent Behavior Tendencies. Deborah Prothrow-Stith, a specialist in adolescent medicine, emphasized the negative effect upon offspring of becoming a teenage unwed mother, one of the bases being that becoming a teenager and becoming a mother required exactly the opposite skills.[220]

In terms of remediation, a few actions, after preliminary, but not thorough, long-term evaluations, were being found productive. Principally they comprised various forms of early home and school intervention. First, children in the intermediate and upper grades found to be at risk due to being violence-prone or having other negative behavioral traits are being home-visited and counseled, along with family members and friends; and public and private social agencies endeavor to help allay the major irritants that seem to drive the behavioral tendencies.

Second, where the situation as a whole is found intractable, temporary or longer-term steps are taken, including drug treatment for a parent or the child, moving the child to a more secure environment such as a group home, and/or, if other measures fail, child welfare agency assumption of custody. The use of volunteers and caring neighbors is a frequent resource. Also new pacifying and stabilization efforts within the schools are undertaken, including special courses in "emotional literacy" and visiting lecturers and counselors, including role models listened to and "semirespected" by discouraged and disaffected youth.

The Juvenile Justice System. For lawbreaking behavior subject to prosecution, the youth becomes involved with the juvenile court and correctional systems, a long-standing arrangement in the state court systems for adjudicating and endeavoring to correct—through custody change, probationary supervision, detention, or other means—the offending behavior and to set the offender on a law-abiding path. However, like the child welfare system and many state court systems in general, the juvenile justice system became overloaded with cases, partially attributed to harsher punishments meted out by state legislative bodies and, on occasion, by the Congress.

In a 1988 article, "Juvenile Justice in Turmoil," Barry Krisberg, president of the National Council on Crime and Delinquency and a member of the California attorney general's advisory council on criminal justice policy, stated:[221]

Unless Californians act quickly and decisively, our system of dealing with troubled and troublesome youngsters will crumble into disarray.... The California Youth Authority is severely overcrowded operating at 140 percent of its design capacity. For lack of bed space, hundreds of children are sleeping on floor mats in Los Angeles County juvenile detention centers. A recent . . . report found chronic overcrowding in the juvenile facilities of eleven counties serving the most populated regions of the state. Probation caseloads have crept up to unacceptable levels.

Krisberg examined several policy options for the state and endorsed a general juvenile correctional policy, in use in Utah and Massachusetts and under consideration elsewhere, of "abandoning the large-scale congregate training schools in favor of small specialized programs for the dangerous few and community-based programs for most juvenile offenders [thereby offering] much greater hope of protecting public safety, reducing wasteful correctional operations and providing individualized quality care for troubled youngsters." He also speculated on the possible value, where there is a fragmentation of responsibility at the state level, for creation of a State Department for Children and Families that could set goals and expectations for governmental programs that promote the well-being of young people. An important objective "should be the reallocation of scarce public resources from *existing remedial programs to more cost-effective preventive efforts* [such as Head Start and a Homebuilder's Program offering] and intensive home-based services to troubled families."[222]

Sentencing of Juvenile Offenders. The general wave of "get tough on crime" legislation produced a sharp increase in juvenile, as well as adult, incarcerations, especially for drug-related offenses. The CDF contended that inappropriate and unwise placements were increasingly frequent in the juvenile justice system. It noted that states and local governments were overusing secure facilities despite evidence from states like Utah, which had demonstrated that "home-based care and community-based placements can serve many youths effectively." Tennessee had concluded that for nearly two-thirds of the children being presently placed in institutional and other secure residential programs, less secure and expensive placements would have been more appropriate.[223]

In connection with sentencing, Krisberg observed:

Many of the immediate reform steps that must be taken involve careful studies of strategic points in the juvenile justice process. . . . Many states are developing objective risk assessment instruments for use in assigning youthful offenders to appropriate placements. Juvenile corrections traditionally has relied on psychological testing and clinical judgments to make custody assignments. . . . The results of more objective offender classification have consistently shown that many offenders can be safely housed in lower levels of custody.[224]

If more offenders were placed in lower custody levels, a significant variance in types of facilities would be possible with a lower per capita cost. The comparative costs between maintaining a juvenile in a detention facility and placing him or her under supervised probation are striking, often a ratio of three, four, or more to one. A *New York Times* editorial commented:

As separate agencies, jails and probation compete for scarce criminal justice resources. Jails tend to come out ahead: the public and politicians like the sound of concrete and steel for criminals, despite the massive costs. Yet powerful arguments support the need for greater spending on probation, where current funding levels require single officers to monitor so many convicts that effective help and supervision may be impossible. Most who wind up on probation are young first and second offenders whose greatest needs are drug treatment, education or a more structured life. . . . Many judges still order probation for offenders who seem too vulnerable for chaotic jails. . . . Developing probation to the point that it could dependably provide services along with meaningful supervision could rescue young lives and make a real dent in petty crime.[225]

Chester Newland, then editor of *Public Administration Review*, decried California's correction policy, "which currently relies largely on a . . . system of costly incarceration and minimally supervised probation." He argued that experience in other states "had demonstrated a constructive strategy [that] calls for a . . . policy based on balanced use of prisons and jails, fines and victim restitution, programs for substance abusers, and work furloughs and electronic surveillance in a matrix with other intermediate sanctions." He went on to cite various advantages of such a strategy, including cost savings.[226]

On the other hand, it would be a mistake to base sentencing changes strictly on fiscal grounds, argued Penelope Lemov:

For the most part such sanctions which range from boot camps, house arrest and day reporting centers to community service . . . have been sold to state legislators and county councils on the grounds of fiscal savings. . . . Once the prisons are set up—the guards are in place . . . it doesn't cost $44 a day for each additional prisoner. . . . Real money is saved [only] when enough inmates are diverted so that a prison wing or entire facility is closed down. And that's a tall order. [But noting that some states were starting to divert enough prisoners at least to put off the need to build a new prison:] "If intermediate sanctions aren't the cure they're at least the start."[227]

Intermediate levels of custody short of state prisons began to attract favorable attention in the late 1980s. "Boot camps" were the most prevalent of these, and by mid-1991, 17 states and some localities were operating such camps, which were being considered in several other states, with some camps emphasizing rehabilitation and others stressing punishment. The camps were designed to inculcate discipline and strengthen character in first-time offenders who would have gone to jail or state prison, depending on age, the offense category, and other factors. Evaluators of some of the camp programs found little, if any, reduction in recidivism. Others felt that "the experience" and changes in personal demeanor and attitude were valid objectives in themselves.[228]

An important political factor on the opposing side of shifting from incarceration to supervised probation has been "the growing clout of prison guards." Robert Gurwitt, citing data from the American Correctional Association, pointed out:

The number of state-level corrections officers around the country grew some 62 percent between 1985 and 1990 [99,000 to 159,000]. . . . Nowhere are the guards more active . . . than in California, where the California Correctional Peace Officers Association has emerged as one of the state's most forceful political presences . . . the organization has been one of the more forceful advocates for meeting the state's prison crunch by building more prisons and increasing the number of guards. . . . The Michigan Corrections Organization has opposed proposals to make prisoners already serving time eligible for boot camps.[229]

As Jerome Miller, director of the National Center on Institutions and Corrections, commented: "Jails are run by sheriffs. Getting a constantly bigger share of the budget enhances their political power."[230]

Another option in sentencing is conditionality, whereby the offender is given a suspended sentence to incarceration, conditional upon performance of certain tasks or acts, such as victim restitution or, as practiced for drug offenses, entering and completing specified treatment, followed by a period of supervised probation during which he or she is subject to random testing and concluding with lifting the original sentence after a significant period of drug freedom, obtaining and holding a job, or meeting other conditions. The major cause of the prison explosion was the *statutory* imposition of fixed mandatory sentences for drug-related offenses. Sentences based on successful completion of drug treatment were appearing to hold promise in reducing the inflow to prisons of persons arrested or detained for possession, intent to distribute, or other nonviolent offenses.

An example of conditional sentencing was in Oakland, California, where the municipal court judge and the Alameda County probation department tracked 100 cases diverted to treatment and other supervision compared with 100 prior undiverted cases. Arrests for new offenses dropped from 69 in the earlier 100 cases to 36 in the diverted group. A senior drug researcher with the Rand Corporation commented: "Diversion in most cases means neglect. Here they're actually doing something with the cases."[231] In approaches similar to Oakland's, "drug courts" were established in Portland, Oregon and Miami; in the latter case, drug abuse defendants were given a clear choice—one-year treatment under court supervision or going to trial. The results were greatly reduced recidivism rates among prior offenders.[232]

But worthwhile as these experimental endeavors may be, a universal or substantial reversal of public opinion and of policy and practice cannot be expected in the absence of (1) a wide range of controlled experiments over longer time periods, (2) considerable further research to ascertain effectiveness of various treatment modes, and (3) intensified causality research on drug addiction.

Drug Treatment for Juvenile Offenders. A realtively overlooked, but politically unattractive, element of the criminal justice system in the early 1990s was long-term treatment of addicted inmates in detention centers and prisons. This was a very severe situation for juvenile offenders in particular. The high correlation between drug use and crime commission was well established in the 1980s, as were (1) proportions of the prison inmates that were incarcerated because of drug-related offenses and/or were substance abusers themselves and (2) proportions of repeat offenders returning to prison after discharge, a growing proportion of whom were, or became, substance abusers during their first term and continued use until entry for a second. This pointed toward a top priority, if not an absolute necessity, for administering drug treatment, including aftercare follow-up, to all inmates having committed drug-related offenses or having been under the influence of drugs at time of offense and to all other inmates found by random testing to be addicted anytime during their initial term.

In 1990, of the nation's 680,000 state prison inmates, more than 500,000 seemed to have substance abuse problems, but fewer than 20 percent were receiving any type of drug treatment in prison.[233] In five states (New York, Louisiana, Michigan, Washington, and Wisconsin) visited by GAO researchers in 1990, no more than 10 percent of inmates were in any type of drug treatment, although estimates of the percentage of inmates with substance abuse problems ranged from 70 to 85 percent in each state. The percent receiving treatment in each were New York, 10; Louisiana and Michigan, 6; Washington and Wisconsin, 4.[234]

The treatment situation was equally bleak in the federal prison system. A 1991 GAO report found that the federal Bureau of Prisons (BOP)

estimates that 27,000 of its 62,000 inmates (44 percent of the [federal] prison population) have moderate to severe substance abuse problems. . . . Most inmates with histories of significant substance abuse are not in treatment despite BOP's initiatives to provide them with an intensive treatment program. Only 364 of the estimated 27,000 federal inmates with . . . substance abuse problems are receiving treatment within these programs.[235]

The report noted further that:[236]

- "Since the escalation of the war against drugs in 1986, the federal inmate population has risen by more than 50 percent, with a 139 percent increase in the proportion of incoming inmates convicted of drug-related offenses."
- "Drug treatment experts agree that incarcerated inmates often need more extensive treatment [than education/counseling] to overcome their addiction. . . . Critical elements [of treatment] have been identified. . . . These include separating inmates enrolled in treatment from the general prison population and providing for aftercare or services after release."
- "During fiscal year 1989 BOP developed its new treatment strategy and began to implement it in October 1989."
- "A key feature . . . was . . . providing intensive treatment . . . in a separate setting."
- "Few inmates have volunteered to enroll. . . . An inmate at one prison . . . told us that drug treatment would not work in prison because inmates have no motivation to seek treatment. . . . In the absence of self-motivation, outreach to inmates is especially important."

The report concluded with a recommendation to the attorney general that he "direct the Director of the Bureau of Prisons to

• undertake an aggressive outreach effort to encourage inmates with moderate to severe substance abuse problems to enroll in BOP's intensive treatment programs, and

• assure that provision is made for both aftercare treatment services for released inmates who participated in the intensive programs as well as for education and counseling services in all prisons."[237]

Barriers to the establishment and implementation in state and federal prisons noted in the foregoing two GAO reports, besides competition for funds, were (1) the BOP relied upon inmates volunteering for treatment rather than using active recruiting, pressure, incentives, and indirect or direct compulsion methods; and (2) in the state prisons dealing with the "difficulty of balancing correctional concerns with treatment goals. . . . Correctional staff often view the basic purpose of incarceration as punishment; treatment staff may view incarceration as an opportunity for rehabilitation. Prison inmates told us that correctional staff often view them as individuals incapable of change. On the other hand, treatment staff may not fully recognize the importance of security concerns."[238]

One approach to the above problem might be a separation of responsibility, as well as facilities, at the individual institution level for the conduct of inmate drug treatment programs, with the assignment of specialized personnel security staff to the treatment area to maintain safety and with professional drug treatment, mental health, and associated professional staff supplied by state health authorities. An opposite approach—integrated staffing (i.e., cooperation between treatment and correctional staff)—was proposed by a National Task Force on Correctional Substance Abuse Strategies in the early 1990s. [239]

In contrast to the poor treatment records noted in the GAO reports was growing evidence of substantial success where effective programs were mounted. In a treatment program called Stay 'N Out operating in the Arthur Kill Correction Facility on Staten Island, New York, and at a women's prison in Manhattan, more than 77 percent of the men who remained in the program for 9–12 months were not rearrested and stopped abusing drugs during the three years after their release. Only 50 percent of a group of comparable parolees who did not participate did as well. Programs with a similar format were operating in 1991 at the Pima County jail in Tucson, Arizona, and the Oregon state prison system. Obstacles to replicating the Stay 'N Out format included the punitive mind-set of state prison officials and the scarcity of evaluation reports on successful programs.[240]

Behind the difficulties just cited was underlying sentiment in public opinion and state legislator/congressional attitudes—low opinion of drug addicts, even lower for addicts who get into criminal behavior of any type, and still lower for those committing violent crimes. Until legislators and the general public become convinced, through careful evaluations, of the cost-effectiveness of prison drug treatment, fund authorization, appropriation, and allocation for this purpose appear to face an uphill struggle.

Despite the foregoing difficulties in giving higher priority to drug treatment in correctional institutions, for those arrested and awaiting trial and for those on parole, 1991 saw considerable state legislative activity pointed toward relieving the abysmal numbers and problems just described. Eleven states enacted laws regarding drug issues in state correctional systems.

Most of the new laws focused on treatment issues, particularly within correctional facilities, but also on treatment in lieu of incarceration, on release programs to gain access to treatment, and on treatment programs for parolees and probationers. One of the more comprehensive was in Texas, which established an extensive treatment alternative to incarceration programs in each county with a population of a half million or more—Bexar (San Antonio), Dallas, Harris (Houston), and Tarrant (Fort Worth). (Travis County, in which Austin is located, fell a few thousand short of the threshold number in 1991). In addition a program was established to confine and treat inmates with a history of drug/alcohol abuse, with the inmates in treatment housed in discrete units and separated from the general prison population. By 1997 about 2,000 beds are projected. Participation in an aftercare program was to be a condition of parole after release from prison.[241]

Mandatory participation, in contrast to self-motivated volunteers in the federal program, was enacted in several states, including:[242]

- Court of jurisdiction required to recommend that a defendant committing a crime when under drug/alcohol influence participate in drug-counseling/education program while imprisoned (1991, California: AB 170, Ch. 552).

- A person convicted of a first time drug offense *may be required* to enter a screening, evaluation, and education program (1991, Viriginia: SB 772, Ch. 482) (1992, Kentucky).

- Enhancement of substance abuse care in local detention facilities (North Carolina: HB 428, Ch. 237).

- Intensive residential treatment for juvenile offenders 10–13, followed by minimum 9 months aftercare (1992, Florida).

- Department of Corrections *mandated* to establish a drug treatment program for persons imprisoned, which must include mental and physical rehabilitation in a facility of the department (Nevada: HB 305, Ch. 297).

- *State health agency* must establish standards for correctional agency screening for drug abuse (Oregon: HB 2199, Ch. 808).

- Alternative sentencing authority for felony drug-related offenses; offender may be committed to a residential or community-based treatment program (Montana: SB 310, Act 89) (1992, South Carolina).

- Offering treatment as a condition of parole (1992, California, Louisiana, Virginia, Ohio).

- Drug testing to identify inmate abusers and determine appropriate treatment (1992, Florida, Georgia, Hawaii, North Carolina).

Foster Care and the Child Welfare System

The number of children in foster care was approaching or exceeding a half million in 1992, and a growing backlog of abused, neglected, or abandoned children were in child welfare custody awaiting placement in foster care, group homes, or other arrangements. Public and legislative concerns were being increasingly expressed, ranging from the need for less hesitance on the part of child welfare agencies and courts in either keeping children with their parent(s) or quickly returning them there, to a reinstitution of a late twentieth-century version of the traditional orphanage. Regarding the last option, a basic question would appear to be, Under what circumstances or criteria would a public orphanage, staffed with qualified professional and paraprofessional personnel, offer a better chance for successful child development than other placements, from the standpoint of health, education, and future qualifications for labor force entry and the pursuit of a normal life-style? Policy perspectives presented here include studies and analyses from the GAO, Children's Defense Fund, National Commission on Children, Child Welfare League of America, American Public Welfare Association, and an article by Senator Patrick Moynihan of New York.

Lack of a nationwide database on foster care was highlighted in a 1991 GAO report: "Although the 1986 Omnibus Budget Reconciliation Act called for an improved foster care information system by October 1991, little progress has been made. HHS is behind schedule in developing related regulations, statutory deadlines are out-dated, and there is uncertainty over how the system should be financed."[243]

More children needing to reenter foster care was a changing and disturbing factor. The GAO report stated:

Of children reunited with their families in 1986, up to 27 percent subsequently reentered foster care. The median length of stay for children entering or leaving care in 1986 in the states and localities reviewed varied from 8 to 19 months. . . . If a similar analysis were done [in 1991], it might show even longer periods of care and increased reentry . . . social conditions affecting children and their families, such as parental substance abuse have worsened. More families have severe problems, treatment services for children are more difficult to obtain, and caseworkers face the threat of legal liability if an abused child is returned home and abuse recurs.[244]

Children were spending more time in child welfare custody or foster care awaiting services, reunification, or adoption. This was due to such factors as too few caseworkers, shortages of treatment facilities and services for children and their families, and caseworkers' fears that abused children released from foster care may be abused again.[245] The CDF expressed the view that severe staff problems deter the child welfare services from giving an adequate response to needs of children and their families. These staff problems included poor supervision and training; low salaries; poor working conditions, and not infrequent threats to personal safety. This results in high staff turnover and consequent high vacancy rates. In 1989 nearly all child welfare agencies were reporting recruiting difficulties, most seriously in the child protective services.[246]

The NCC recommended a comprehensive community-level approach to strengthen families:

We believe that early family support and the availability of preventive services will ultimately lessen the need for children to be removed from their homes. We therefore urge that programs and services for vulnerable children and their families be restructured to include . . . protecting abused and neglected children through more comprehensive child protective services, with a strong emphasis on efforts to keep children with their families or to provide *permanent placement* for those removed from their homes.[247]

But trends in the early 1990s seemed to be running contrary to "permanent placement," as noted in the GAO report.

The commission described a series of options for children for whom remaining at, or returning, home was not possible. These included, for children who cannot be placed with relatives,

well-trained and properly supported foster families [which] typically provide the most intimate environment. . . . Group homes that are properly staffed and supervised and that offer counseling, supervision, and discipline in small family-like settings can also provide supportive environments [especially suitable for older children and adolescents]. Children's centers that provide a home-like environment for small groups of children, are staffed by skilled professionals, and offer a complete range of services—or coordinate with other providers to meet children's needs—are another option. . . . Their visibility can create opportunities for community support and involvement and heighten children's chances of adoption.[248]

In 1990, the Child Welfare League of America (CWLA) convened a North American Commission on Chemical Dependency and Child Welfare. The commission recommended that federal and state governments take a number of steps toward making children and families higher priorities in drug control policies, including a proper balancing of the rights of chemically dependent parents with the needs of children when placement decisions are made. It called upon the research community to:[249]

- More accurately identify and describe the numbers and characteristics of alcohol- or drug-involved children and families . . . served by the child welfare system.
- Evaluate the effectiveness of child welfare interventions in preventing and responding to alcohol and drug issues that impact upon children and their families.
- Improve screening, assessment, and decision making for alcohol- or drug-involved children or families.
- Develop and evaluate model collaborative child welfare and alcohol and drug treatment approaches for children, adolescents, and families in the child welfare system.

In 1991 the National Association of Child Welfare Administrators issued a set of guiding principles for working with substance-abusing families and drug-exposed children. The principal points therein were:[250]

- The mission of child welfare is to protect children and help assure their healthy development . . . when families refuse or are unable to safely care for a child . . . child protective services [CPS] will intervene and provide a safe living environment.

- A comprehensive child and family service system, not CPS alone should be established to take the lead in collaboration with health, mental health and substance abuse systems . . . in providing services to drug dependent infants . . . siblings and parents.

- Substance abuse treatment programs [tailored to] families and pregnant women must be made available . . . be community-based, culturally appropriate, and family-focused.

- If a jurisdiction . . . mandates drug testing pregnant women and newborns, such testing must be universal . . . not targeted to specific populations [i.e., all pregnant women and newborns at all medical facilities]. . . . Test results should be used only to identify families in need of treatment and make referrals. [They] should not be used for punitive action.

- A positive drug test . . . should precipitate a report to the public CPS agency for an investigation to determine if a risk exists. It should not be the sole basis for court action or removal of the child.

- Families/children are best served when treatment and family preservation services are central and when medical, social work, and other supporting services are provided. Laws and rules should strengthen, not hinder families needing help.

- The family's prognosis should determine length of treatment. Laws/regulations setting time frames on parental custody should not be based solely on the drug abuse factor.

- When children must be removed from their birth parent(s), kinship care should be used if possible, unless child welfare agency finds it an unsuitable caregiver.

- Social agencies and juvenile justice system should make special provisions to serve this drug-affected population.

- Court, human service, and law enforcement staff should be jointly trained in identification of substance-affected families/children and the appropriate interventions.

In a comprehensive speech to the Senate in the spring of 1992, Senator Bill Bradley of New Jersey listed two major steps of a child welfare system nature to ameliorate the ills besetting children's lives in urban America.

The first concrete step is to bring an end to violence, intervene early in a child's life, reduce child abuse, establish some rules, remain unintimidated, and involve the community in its own salvation. . . . Our schools can no longer allow the 5 to 10 percent of kids who don't want to learn to destroy the possibility of learning for the 90 to 95 percent who do want to learn.[251]

The second step is to bolster families. . . . That effort begins with the recognition that the most important year in a child's life is the first. Fifteen-month houses must be established for women seven months pregnant who want to live the first year of their life as a mother in a residential setting. . . . Fifteen-month houses would reduce parental neglect and violence by teaching teenage mothers how to parent. . . . But there is also a hard truth here. No institution can replace the nurturing of a loving family. The most important example in a child's life is the parent, not celebrities, however virtuous or talented they may be.[252]

The National Governors' Association policy positions for 1991–92 on the child welfare system included the following points:[253]

- The present child welfare system is ill-equipped to effectively respond to the rising number of troubled children and families in need of help. The system all too frequently operates on a crisis mode.

- The nation needs to create a child welfare system that reaches parents and children before crises occur and that will better assist families in handling crisis situations when they do occur. Program priorities should be better focused on prevention, early intervention, and family preservation activities.

- An effective child welfare system is critical. . . . Improvements are needed to reduce the danger of abuse and neglect, family disruption, and unnecessary out-of-home placements, enhance adoption opportunities and facilitate family unification.

- Comprehensive, multidisciplinary, family-centered program approaches are critical. National reforms will be required to enhance intersystem linkages, help eliminate artificial boundaries created by categorical requirements, and alter investment patterns to encourage creative, flexible financing.

The National Commission on Child Welfare and Family Preservation was formed in 1988 by the American Public Welfare Association (APWA) to examine the then-existing child welfare situation and propose reforms that would promote the healthy development of children and empower families to protect, nurture, and support that development. The commission comprised 25 members, mostly state, district, and county directors of departments of human resources and social services and a few directors of child services, but including a number of others. In a major report, the commission summarized the dilemma of child welfare and human service administrators as follows:[254]

- Absence of adequate public policies and programs in employment assistance and income support (e.g., AFDC and general assistance), educational opportunities, access to medical care, affordable housing, wholesome and crime-free communities, and social services to troubled families.

- Priority of crisis over long-term needs—"current service systems almost exclusively serve families/children in acute difficulties, teenage pregnancy and AIDS."

- Growth in abuse/neglect reports require immediate resource allocation to investigative efforts. Consequently in many communities the only alternative available is removal and placement of children in foster care. For many poor and/or minority children, society is predisposed to removal and placement as the social service of choice.

As a tripartite policy, the commission proposed (1) broad support of all families; (2) assistance to families in need; and (3) protection of children from serious familial abuse and neglect. For the third—child protective services—the commission proposed the following: (1) child welfare protective services should protect children from serious maltreatment, make *reasonable* efforts to keep children *safely* in their own homes, and provide *permanency* for children removed from their families, (2) state governments should provide leadership, program coordination, and technical assistance to communities; provide financial and other incentives to community initiatives; and clearly define family well-being outcomes and the measures of the achievement of such outcomes for monitoring and accountability purposes; and (3) the federal government should provide national leadership and establish national programs, uniform data definitions and collection, and publish periodic "State of the Family and Child" assessments.[255]

In a 1989 article on "Post-Industrial Social Policy," U.S. senator Patrick Moynihan observed that with "a great shift in industrial production had come an emergent form of dependency . . . and a new form of social distress, associated with the 'post-marital' family." He further observed that one of the products of this, along with poverty and other ills, was the inexorably growing proportion of "no-parent children," and

We are likely to respond to this development by re-establishing orphanages. Most orphanages in the United States were founded in response to epidemics . . . or wars (primarily the Civil War). Orphanages were a humane development in their day, but they are now mostly gone, replaced by foster care. . . . But now that drug addiction has become epidemic in certain portions of the population, present arrangements may not suffice to get us through the emerging crisis.[256]

Moynihan subsequently referred to the orphanage issue as a "high voltage subject. You get an awful shock if you go near it, so people avoid it. *But custodial institutions are on their way.*"[257]

Several crucial considerations arise in connection with out-of-home placements. First is the extent to which retention in the home or reunification with the parent(s) is to be favored over other courses in the face of varying estimates such as (1) small or modest odds against permanence of such retention or reunification, (2) modest odds at the outset but heavier after first failed reuinification, and (3) heavy odds at the outset.

Second, if out-of-home placement is to be made at the outset or later, the following considerations, among others, are crucial: (1) permanence; (2) quality of care, including environmental and emotional stability of the caregivers and of associates in the household or group home; (3) degree, quality, and appropriateness of supervision and protection afforded to the child or children in the potential household or caring establishment; and (4) extent of concentration, with minimal preoccupation, upon providing a continuing and caring effort toward the healthy development of the child and his or her intellectual progression toward adulthood.

Essentially, the continuing overall policy issue here is what criteria should be employed as general guidance for determining where, among the out-of-home placement options, a particular child should be placed. The range begins with relatives, proceeds to foster home with possible subsequent adoption, to a group home, childrens' center, or other group arrangement where the adult supervision is continuing and health care and other human services brought in as needed. Many child welfare administrators believe that as the foster care placement process is improved, such a family environment will and should serve most out-of-home placement needs. Moynihan and others believe that the effect of hard drugs and their effects on infants and young children is such that a stronger supervisory regimen than the typical foster home situation provides may be required to a considerably greater degree than contemplated in the public policies of the early 1990s. The volatility of the national drug abuse situation makes the setting of firm policies for the future extremely difficult and often highly speculative.

IMPROVING HEALTH DATA: CAUSALITY AND OUTCOMES RESEARCH; POLICY EXPERIMENTATION AND PROGRAM EVALUATION

For several of the major health policy issues discussed in this and the preceding chapter, both public and private sector decision makers have been operating without sufficient data, analysis, and evaluative breadth and depth, drawing upon a sufficient range of evaluative skills and approaches. Advancing technology, social change, and economic influences have combined to force policy reactions of a short-term and ameliorative nature designed to pacify public worry and anger. Few of the policy options examined have seemed to inspire a combination of solid and widespread confidence as to what the odds might be for successful outcomes or, in some substantive areas, whether the right questions have yet been asked. The latter concern appears most pronounced in approaches to diagnostic and treatment criteria and guidelines; causes of drug addiction and for its successful and cost-effective treatment; and the influencing of health-connected behaviors. These include both private and public sets, such as employer-driven wellness programs and public-policy–driven incentives against, and penalties for, irresponsible actions and practices.

This points to the need for (1) information, both episodic and trend-setting, and databases from which such gathered information can be drawn; (2) use of scientific sampling techniques and control groups and the following of particular sets and samples over extended periods; and (3) in some cases, obtaining comparable information across a balance of sites. The role of state health and child welfare agencies and of improved uniform national reporting schedules for use by physicians and other individuals, agencies, and organizations is especially crucial in drug addiction, AIDS, and child abuse.

A second area of need is long-term research and analyses of such types as those conducted by (1) the Manpower Demonstration Research Corporation (MDRC) on the efficacy of work-related requirements for welfare recipients, including implementation of the Family Support Act of 1988, and on the efficacy of changing welfare from a dependency to a program of economic assistance in transitional periods of hardship,[258] (2) the Institute for Research on Poverty at Madison, Wisconsin, on poverty causes and remedial approaches, and (3) the Rand Corporation, Institute of Justice, and others on drug addiction, imprisonment, and recidivism.

A third area of need lies in increased flexibility in federal waiver policy under certain grant-in-aid programs so as to permit a wider range of experimentation by state and local governments to ascertain or develop possible new avenues in health and social policy, such as incentives and penalties related to behavior patterns and in regulatory policy on private sector experimentation in relation to employer-provided insurance, wellness programs, drug testing, and other health issue areas, to be supplanted by national policies when and if conclusive evaluations isolate the more effective and equitable endeavors.

SUMMARY OBSERVATIONS

At the outset of this book, the growing disparity between labor force skill needs in the next century and the quality of available U.S. workers was described. The major remediation alternatives boiled down to (1) lengthening use of older workers; (2) increasing immigration quotas for the highly skilled; and (3) reclaiming the present and future at-risk youth populations. In addition to the urgent needs in research and program evaluation just discussed, the principal policy issues and options in health care needs of mothers, infants, children, and adolescents in the U.S. population in the early 1990s centered on the following.

Considerably hindering the realization of the reclamation alternative are inadequate health care services for the economically disadvantaged and the destructive social and health behavior of American youth, with particular harm to those also most affected by economic deprivation. This chapter has been concerned with both the health access and behavioral problems, the latter being disastrous not only to health but to educational attainment and quality-of-life opportunity.

The health care access (informational, financial, and physical) part of the policy challenge to public and private sectors is one of financial and personnel resource organization, deployment, reallocation, and a strong, stable, and equitable safety net of basic health care coverage of a sort that encourages economical utilization and productive competition between and among private providers and underwriters.

The behavior part increasingly threatens the physiological and social fabric of U.S. society, with drugs, AIDS, child abuse, violence, crime, and correctional system recidivism, combining to erode the health/education base of all, and the physical survival of many, American adolescents and young adults. Dealing with health-threatening and antisocial behavior brings into conflict two basic rights guaranteed to all Americans, young and old, under the Constitution—public safety and individual freedom, because to protect one it appears necessary to encroach further upon the other.

This encroachment goes beyond prohibition and punishment of criminal conduct—actual or suspected—and embraces persuasive and coerceive action to discourage behavior that can and does lead to criminal or other antisocial conduct and to ensure compliance by restraint and coercion through measures that invade what previously were considered rights of privacy (as through mandatory, random drug testing). The encroachment also embraces through a "new paternalism," incentives and penalties (clean needle and condom distribution, bonuses for marriages of unwed mothers and penalties for not seeing a doctor or for teenage unwed motherhood), designed to avoid or strongly discourage those actions that so often lead to disastrous outcomes.

A crucial policy stage in the restructuring of the U.S. health care system was reached in mid-1993. The Clinton administration was completing its formulation of a comprehensive health reform program, embracing a system of managed competition, cost control, and expanded insurance coverage. A number of members of Congress manifested another body of opinion favoring a less broad approach.[259] The overriding issue for Congress and the country was one of *comprehensive* national action versus *incremental* national legislation, based upon experience with state health reform programs that had been enacted in the 1990–93 period. The CBO pointed out in a May 1993 report that the managed competition approach "has not been tried anywhere in the world." As noted earlier, states recently had enacted various laws to (1) install various forms of such competition (Florida); (2) try out a single-payer approach (Vermont); (3) regulate health care costs (Maryland); (4) delineate appropriate from inappropriate medical procedures (Oregon); and (5) expand health insurance coverage (Washington). These initiatives, as modified by state experience, could provide a moderately solid base for deciding whether and how to mandate them through federal legislation for nation-wide application.[260]

In any event, as President Clinton and the 102nd Congress in 1993–94 work toward a national approach to insurance coverage and cost containment, many new approaches to critical health problems facing our youth will continue to be tried in the states; many representative examples have been presented in the preceding sections and pages. Courage to experiment, but prudence, restraint, and, above all, rigorous, objective, and competent evaluations prior to adoption for wider application are among the necessities facing the president, Congress, governors, state legislators, local governments, and the business and civic communities, as the decade of the nineties proceeds.

NOTES

1. Yankelovich, D., "A Missing Concept," *Kettering Review*, Fall 1991, 58.

2. "Ten Legislative Issues to Watch," *Governing*, January 1992, 38; "1993 Preview: No Surprises on States' Health Care Wish Lists," *State Health Notes* 13, no. 146, December 14, 1992, 1.

3. Eckholm, E., "Health Benefits Found to Deter Job Switching," *New York Times*, September 26, 1992, B1, B12.

4. Koop, C.E.K., *The Memoirs of America's Family Doctor* (New York: Random House, 1991); comments on the "McNeil-Lehrer News Hour," February 14, 1991.

5. CBO, *Universal Health Insurance Coverage Using Medicare's Payment Rates*, December 1991, x, xi. See also Osborne, D., and Gaebler, T., "Creating an Effective Health Care System" (in which some features of the German system are noted, including requirements for employer-provided insurance but limiting government subsidization to the unemployed and self-employed). *Reinventing Government* (Boston: Houghton-Mifflin, 1992), 312–14.

6. "Highlights of AARP's Health Care America Proposal," *AARP Bulletin*, March 1992, 33, no. 3, 1, 7–8. See also Fein, R., "Prescription for Change," *Modern Maturity*, August-September 1992, 22–35.

7. U.S. Advisory Commission on Intergovernmental Relations (ACIR), "Overview of the U.S. Health Care Industry and Analysis of Major Reform Proposals" (staff memorandum), November 15, 1991, 2 of attachment. See also Meyer, J., Silow-Carroll, S., and Sullivan, S., *A National Health Plan in the U.S.: The Long-Term Impact on Business and the Economy* (Washington, DC: Economic and Social Research Institute, 1991); Wolfe, B., "Changing the U.S. Health Care System: How Difficult Will It Be?" *Focus* 14, no. 2, Summer 1992, 16–20; "Special Section on Health System Reform," *Urban Institute Policy and Research Report*, Summer 1992, 10–20.

8. Lamm, R., *The Brave New World of Health Care* (Denver: University of Denver, May 1990), 15; Thurow, L., "Medicine and Economics," *New England Journal of Medicine* 313, 1985, 611–14.

9. Biemesderfer, S., "Running for Coverage," *State Legislatures*, July 1992, 54, 57–59. On ERISA issue, see U.S. General Accounting Office (GAO), *Access to Health Care: States Respond to Growing Crisis*, GAO/HRD–92–70, June 1992, 5–6, 81–82. See also "Focus on Universal Access: A Comparison of Three Plans," *State Health Notes*, June 1, 1992; Cooper, H., "States Take the Lead in Insurance Reform," Health Costs, *Wall Street Journal*, June 30, 1992, B–1, quoting HIAA report that 18 states, 11 in 1992, had enacted laws helping small businesses provide employee health benefits.

10. Butler, S., " 'Play or Pay' Health Care Plan Is Bound to Be a Loser," *Wall Street Journal*, January 3, 1992, A–6. Conversely, "Choice #3, Mandated Coverage—Fixing the System by Filling the Gap," *The Health Care Crisis: Containing Costs, Expanding Coverage. National Issues Forums* (New York: McGraw-Hill, 1992), 33–39.

11. Koop, C.E.K., "McNeil-Lehrer." For employment impacts within the health insurance industry, see Smith, L., "The Coming Health Care Shakeout," *Fortune*, May 17, 1993, 70–75.

12. Morrisey, M., "Mandates: What Most Proposals Would Do," *The American Enterprise*, January-February 1992, 63–66; quote appears on 66.

13. Hutter, A., Jr., "Escaping America's Health Care Maze: By Shifting—and Hid-

ing—Medical Costs, We're Wasting Billions of Dollars," *Washington Post*, February 23, 1992, C–4.

14. Fuchs, V., "Don't Look for Better Health from National Health Insurance," *Wall Street Journal*, December 11, 1991, A16.

15. Pauly, M., "Why Is American Health Care So Hard to Reform?" *The American Enterprise*, 60–63.

16. GAO, *Comptroller General's 1991 Annual Report*, 6.

17. 1991 Advisory Council on Social Security (ACSS), *Commitment to Change: Foundations for Reform* (Washington, DC: ACSS, 1991), 12. See also, mirroring the minority view on the council, "Choice # 2, Radical Surgery: Universal Rights and Public Responsibilities," *The Health Care Crisis*, 23–32.

18. Health Insurance Association of America (HIAA), *Source Book of Health Insurance Data 1991* (Washington, DC: HIAA, 1991), 5–6.

19. Rabkin, M., in Ratner, J. (ed.), "The High Cost of Health," *GAO Journal*, Summer/Fall 1991, 16.

20. Matula, B., in "The High Cost of Health," 19.

21. Hey, R., and Carlson, E., "Health Reform Gridlock? Americans Still Want It Both Ways," *AARP Bulletin* 33, no. 1, January 1992, 1, 13.

22. National Commission on Children (NCC), *Beyond Rhetoric: A New American Agenda for Children and Families* (Washington, DC: National Commission on Children, May 1991), 144–45.

23. Brook, R., et al., "The Effect of Coinsurance on the Health of Adults: Results of the Rand Health Experiment," Project R–3055-HHS, as reported in *Rand Checklist*, March 1985, no. 336, 1.

24. *Beyond Rhetoric*, 145.

25. Enthoven, A., "Reforming Tax Treatment of Health Insurance," *Proceedings of the Eighty-Third Annual Conference 1990* (Columbus, OH: National Tax Association-Tax Institute of America, 1991), 145–46.

26. Butler, S., in "The High Cost of Health," 13.

27. Enthoven, A., "Reforming Tax Treatment," 146–47.

28. National Governors' Association, *Policy Positions 1990–1991*, B–18, 49. See also Lemov, P., "Health Care Reform: The State Get Serious," *Governing*, October 1992, 27–29.

29. Tuckson, R., and Matula, B., in "The High Cost of Health," 9, 19.

30. Children's Defense Fund (CDF), *An Opinion Maker's Guide to Children in Election Year 1992: Leave No Children Behind* (Washington, DC: CDF, 1992). See also Koop, C. E., "Health Care Figuring Out What Works and What Doesn't: No Health Care Reform Proposal Will Succeed If It Does Not Encourage and Reward Prevention," *Washington Post*, August 23, 1992, C–7.

31. "More Ounces of Prevention" (editorial), *Business Week*, August 17, 1992, 118.

32. Matula, B., 19. See also *National Civic Review* 81, no. 2, featuring "Promoting Community Health," Spring-Summer 1992, 105–54.

33. Southern Legislative Conference, "Proposed Policy Position: SLC Financial Commitment to the Southern Regional Project on Infant Mortality" (adopted August 10, 1992) (Lexington, KY: Southern Legislative Conference of the Council of State Governments).

34. Tuckson, R., 9.

35. Davis, C., "The High Cost of Health," 12.

36. Kongstvedt, P. (ed.), *The Managed Health Care Handbook* (Rockville, MD: Aspen, 1989), xiii. See also *Implementing Managed Care*, Report no. 968 (New York: Conference Board, 1991), GAO, *Utilization Review: Information on External Review Organizations*, GAO/HRD 93–22 FS, November 1992.

37. Ginsburg, P., and Sunshine, J., *Cost Management in Employee Health Plans* (Santa Monica, CA: Rand Corporation, supported by Robert Wood Johnson Foundation, 1987), 19.

38. Ibid., 19–26.

39. HIAA, *Source Book*, 18.

40. McCleod, G., "An Overview of Managed Medical Care," in Kongstvedt, P. (ed.), *The Managed Health Care Handbook*, 4–5. See also Foster, L., *Emerging Issues: Medicaid Managed Care* (Lombard, IL: Midwestern Legislative Conference of the Council of State Governments, October 1992).

41. HIAA, *Source Book*, 19.

42. Among the most comprehensive cost comparison studies by governmental and nonprofit research organizations was Manning et al., *A Controlled Trial of the Effect of Prepaid Group Practice in the Utilization of Medical Services*, R3029-HHS (Santa Monica, CA: Rand Corporation, 1985). See also GAO, *Medicaid: States Turn to Managed Care to Improve Access and Control Costs*, GAO/HRD–93–46, March 1993.

43. CDF, *A Children's Defense Budget 1989: An Analysis of Our Nation's Investment in Children*, 1988, 73.

44. Group Health Association of America (GHAA), "HMO Fact Sheet" (Washington, DC: GHAA, April 1991), 1; HIAA, *Source Book*, 19, reported 34 million in 1990.

45. HIAA, *Source Book*, 32; data source reported: Inter Study, *The Inter Study Edge*, 1991, vol. 5.

46. Wagner, E., "Types of Managed Health Care Organizations," *Managed Care Handbook*, 14–18; GHAA, "HMO Fact Sheet;" HIAA, *Source Book*, 19, 33.

47. HIAA, *Source Book*, 33.

48. Ibid.

49. Ibid.

50. Ibid.

51. Greenfield, S., et al., "Variations in Resource Utilization Among Medical Specialties and Systems of Care," *Journal of the American Medical Association (JAMA)*, 267, no. 12, March 25, 1992, 1624–30, 1617, 1665; Winslow, R., "Study Shows System of Family Doctors, Not Specialists, Would Be Less Costly," *Wall Street Journal*, March 25, 1992, B–2.

52. *JAMA*, ibid.

53. CBO, *CBO Staff Memorandum: The Potential Impact of Certain Forms of Managed Care on Health Care Expenditures* (Washington, DC: CBO, August 1992, revised), 1–2. See also Freudenheim, M., "Managed Care: Is It Effective?" Business and Health, *New York Times*, September 1, 1992, D–2.

54. Bowsher, C., "U.S. Health Care Spending: Trends, Contributing Factors, and Proposals for Reform," GAO/T-HRD–91–16, April 17, 1991, 17–18.

55. Cohen, T., "Health Care and the Class Struggle," *New York Times*, op-ed, November 17, 1991, Sec. 4, 17. Conversely, Rivers, R., "Prudential Urges Public and Private Health Care Reforms," *Council of State Governments*, 4–5.

56. Koop, C., Laszewski, R., and Wennberg, W., "Health Care: Tinkering Won't Help," *Washington Post*, February 19, 1992, A–19.

57. Bowsher, C., 15.

58. Aaron, H., *Financing America's Health Care: Serious and Unstable Condition* (Washington, DC: Brookings Institution, 1991), 85–86. Data references cited: Rublee, D., "Medical Technology in Canada, Germany, and the United States," *Health Affairs* 8, Fall 1989, 178–81; Jonsson, B., "What Can Americans Learn from Europeans?" *Health Care Financing Review, 1989 Annual Supplement*, 89.

59. *Rising Health Care Costs*, xvii. See also Lee, P., and Legnini, M., in "The High Cost of Health," 23; Wagar, L., "Rebirth of a Good Idea," *State Government News*, June 1992, 20–22 (on restoration of CONs); Rich, S., "Cost Cutting in Maryland Paves the Way: Rate Setting System for Hospitals May Be a Model," *Washington Post*, Health, December 8, 1992, 7.

60. *Commitment to Change*, 371–72. See also Tomsho, R., "Limited Service Hospitals Find a Market," Health, *Wall Street Journal*, July 23, 1992, B–1, McAllister, B., "Health Care Plan Seen Cutting VA Hospital Use," *Washington Post*, May 8, 1992, A–21.

61. *Commitment to Change*, 371–72.

62. GAO, *Medical Malpractice: Few Claims Resolved Through Michigan's Voluntary Arbitration Program*, GAO/HRD–87–73, May 20, 1987, *Medical Malpractice: A Continuing Problem with Far-Reaching Implications*, GAO/T-HRD–90–24, April 26, 1990.

63. Koop, Laszewski, and Wennberg.

64. Lundberg, G., in "The High Cost of Health," 8.

65. Davis, C., in "The High Cost of Health," 11.

66. Kritzer, H., et al., *The Impact of Fee Arrangement on Lawyer Effort*, P–7180–ICJ, January 1986; Danzon, P., et al., *The Effects of Tort Reforms on the Frequency and Severity of Medical Malpractice Claims*, P–7211-ICJ, March 1986 (Santa Monica, CA: Rand Corporation).

67. *Rising Health Care Costs*, 23. See also U.S. Congress, House Committee on Ways and Means, *Medical Malpractice*, Committee Print, April 26, 1990.

68. As reported in Pear, R., "Community Health Clinics Cut Back as Malpractice Insurance Costs Soar," *New York Times*, August 21, 1991, A–18.

69. "State of the Art: Indiana Insurance Law Withstands the Test of Time," *State Health Notes*, November 1991, 4; California data from Intergovernment Health Project files. See also Devlin, K., "Missouri's Medical Care Legal Expense Fund," *Innovations* (Council of State Governments, 1992).

70. GAO, *Medical Malpractice: Case Study on California*, GAO HRD–87–21 S–2, December 1986, 10.

71. Hill, I., "Improving State Medicaid Programs for Pregnant Women and Children," *Health Care Financing Review 1990 Annual Supplement*, December 1990, 83.

72. Ibid.

73. Ibid.

74. Montgomery County, MD, County Council, *Resolution* 11–1012, September 20, 1988.

75. ACSS, *Commitment to Change*, 299–314. See also NGA, *National Meeting on Health Care Cost Containment and Federal Deficit Reduction*, December 15, 1992, 12.

76. Bovbjerg, R., "Better Medicine for Medical Malpractice" (personal views), Urban Institute, *Policy and Research Report*, Winter/Spring 1992, 28.

77. GAO, *Medical Malpractice: Alternatives to Litigation*, GAO/HRD–92–98, Jan-

uary 1992, 2. See also GAO, *Practitioner Data Bank: Information on Small Malpractice Claims*, GAO/IMTEC–92–56, July 1992, 1–5.

78. Solloway, M., and Wessner, C., in *Major Changes in State Medicaid Programs 1990* (Washington, DC: Intergovernmental Health Policy Project, August 1991), 17. See also Chase, M., "Consumer Crusader Sidney Wolfe M.D. Causes Pain to FDA, AMA and the Health Industry," *Wall Street Journal*, April 7, 1992, A–18.

79. *Commitment to Change*, 354–55. See also GAO, *Automated Medical Records: Leadership Needed to Expedite Standards Development*, GAO/IMTEC–93–17, April 1993.

80. As reported in Grossman, L., "Florida May Curb Doctors' Referrals to Linked Clinics," *Wall Street Journal*, October 28, 1991, B–5b.

81. As reported in Pear, R., "AMA Acts to Curb Profits from Referrals," *New York Times*, December 12, 1991, A–26. See also Hillman, B., et al., "Physicians' Utilization and Charges for Outpatient Diagnostic Imaging in a Medicare Population" (a research project concluding that "nonradiologist physicians who operate diagnostic imaging equipment in their offices perform . . . examinations more frequently, resulting in higher imaging charges per episode of medical care") *JAMA* 268, no. 15, October 12, 1992, 2050–59.

82. GAO, *Health Insurance: Vulnerable Payers Lose Billions to Fraud and Abuse*, GAO/HED–92–60, May 1992, 1.

83. As reported in Pear, R., "Federal Auditors Report Rises in Abuses in Medical Billing," *New York Times*, December 20, 1991, A–1. See also GAO, *Medicare: Millions of Dollars in Mistaken Payments Not Recovered*, GAO/HRD–92–26, October 1991, 1–7, Castro, J., "Condition Critical: Millions of Americans Have No Medical Coverage and Costs Are Out of Control," *Time*, November 25, 1991, 38; Meier, B., "A Growing U.S. Affliction: Worthless Health Policies," *New York Times*, January 4, 1992, A1.

84. Kemper, V., and Novak, V., "What's Blocking Health Care Reform? The Real Culprit May Be the Medical Industry Money That Helps Keep Politicians in Office," *Common Cause Magazine* 18, no. 1, January-March 1992, 8–13, 25.

85. Koop, D. E., et al., "Health Care: Tinkering Won't Help."

86. Lundberg, George, D., in "The High Cost of Health," 7.

87. Briggs, Philip, in ibid. 10–11.

88. Davis, Carolyn K., in ibid., 11.

89. CBO, *Rising Health Care Costs*, 39–40.

90. Ruffenbach, G., "Health Costs: Doctors Turn to Software to Avoid Malpractice Suits," *Wall Street Journal*, March 3, 1992, B–1.

91. Estimates by medical and other "experts" of the combined annual savings in curbing fraud and unnecessary practices ranged downward from $200 billion—Castro, J., in "Condition Critical," 42.

92. Lamm, R., *The Brave New World of Health Care*, 2.

93. "The High Cost of Health," 7.

94. 42 USC 1395 cc (f). See also Cate, F., and Gill, B., *The Patient Self-Determination Act: Implementation Opportunities*, a White Paper (Washington, DC: Annenberg Washington Program, Communications Policy Studies of Northwestern University, 1991); National Center for State Courts (NCSC), *Guidelines for State Court Decision Making in Authorizing or Withholding Life-Sustaining Medical Treatment* (Williamsburg, VA: NCSC, 1992).

95. OTA, *Life-Sustaining Technologies and the Elderly*, 1987.

96. OTA, "Institutional Protocols of Decisions About Life-Sustaining Treatments," *OTA Report Brief*, August 1988, 2.

97. Callahan, D., *Setting Limits: Medical Goals in an Aging Society* (New York: Simon and Schuster, 1987). See also Abram, M., "Restricting Medical Access: How Much Personal Health Care Can Society Afford?" *Washington Post*, June 22, 1992, A–17. Conversely, Otten, A., "Ethicist Draws Fire with Proposal for Limiting Health Care to Aged," *Wall Street Journal*, January 22, 1988, 29.

98. As reported in "Healthy Results," *The Economist*, October 26, 1991, 83, referring to Maynard, A., "Developing the Health Care Market," *Economic Journal*, September 1991.

99. "Oregon Releases Revised Priorities List," *State Health Notes*, March 1991, 5.

100. GAO, *Medicaid: Oregon's Managed Care Program and Implications for Expansions*, GAO/HRD–92–90, June 1992, 5, 57–61. See also Weiner, S., and Hanley, R., "Winners and Losers: Primary and High-Tech Health Care Under Health Care Rationing," *Brookings Review*, Fall 1992, 46–49.

101. *Beyond Rhetoric*, 154.

102. Ibid., 132. See also USPHS, *Healthy People 2000*, 253–54.

103. Kirst, M., "Financing School-Linked Services," *Policy Brief*, no. 7 (Los Angeles: USC Center for Research in Education Finance [CREF], University of Southern California, January 1992), 1–2. See also Sachar, S., et al., *From Homes to Classrooms to Workrooms: State Initiatives to Meet the Needs of the Changing American Family* (Washington, DC: National Governors' Association, Committee on Human Resources, 1992), 29–35.

104. "Florida Offers Health Insurance to Children." *State Legislatures*, August 1991, 9.

105. Ford Foundation in collaboration with the John F. Kennedy School of Government, Harvard University, *Innovations in State and Local Government 1991* (New York: Ford Foundation, 1992), 2, 26–30.

106. Ibid., 19. For further examples from New Jersey, Illinois, and Missouri school-based local programs centered on family problems, see Collis, C., "Strengthening Family Ties," *State Government News*, September 1991, 24–26. See also Taylor, P., "Bringing Social Services into Schools—Holistic Approach Offers Health and Child Care, Family Counseling," *Washington Post*, May 2, 1991, A–1.

107. Ford Foundation, 7 (emphasis added).

108. Ibid., 29.

109. Lear, J., and Porter, P., "Help Our Children: Bring Health Care into the Schools," *Washington Post*, December 1, 1991, C5. See also "Health, Social Services to Families: Can Schools Provide the Crucial Link?" *The Link* 11, no. 2 (special issue) (Charleston, WV: Appalachian Education Laboratory covering KY, TN, VA, WV, Summer 1992), 1–13.

110. Lear and Porter.

111. OTA, "U.S. Adolescents Face Barriers to Appropriate Health Care," Press Advisory, April 22, 1991, 1–2.

112. Taylor, P., "Bringing Social Services into the Schools."

113. Chira, S., "Poverty's Toll on Health Is Plague of U.S. Schools, *New York Times*, October 5, 1991, A–1.

114. Committee for Economic Development (CED), *Children in Need* (New York: Committee for Economic Development, 1987), 52.

115. *The Boundaries of Free Speech: How Free Is Too Free?*, National Issues Forums (New York: McGraw-Hill, 1992).

116. Roemer, R., "The Right to Health Care—Gains and Gaps," *American Journal of Public Health* 78, no. 3, March 1988, 242.

117. As reported by Rowan, C., "Public Hospitals: Situation Critical," *Washington Post*, February 19, 1991, A–17.

118. National Association of Public Hospitals, *America's Safety Net: Foundation of Our Nation's Health System* (Washington, DC: NAPH, 1991), 1.

119. Bindman, A., Keane, D., and Lurie, N., "A Public Hospital Closes: Impact on Patients' Access to Care and Health Status," *JAMA* 264, no. 22, December 12, 1990, 2899.

120. *America's Safety Net*, 63–64. See also Ansberry, C., "Dumping the Poor: Despite Federal Law, Hospitals Still Reject Sick Who Can't Pay," *Wall Street Journal*, November 29, 1988.

121. GAO, *Nonprofit Hospitals: Better Standards Needed for Tax Exemption*, GAO/HRD–90–84, May 1990, 3.

122. Enos, G., "Government Centers of Excellence: Special Services Breathe Life into Public Hospitals," Special Report—Health Care, *City and State*, March 9, 1992, 16–17.

123. Bindman, 2904.

124. Gross, J., "Afraid and Hurt, Young Turn to Clinics," *New York Times*, January 28, 1992, A–1.

125. *Beyond Rhetoric*, 149–50.

126. ACSS, *Commitment to Change*, 114.

127. Ibid., 261.

128. CDF, *State of America's Children 1991*, 1991, 72–73.

129. As reported by Gross, J., "Healing on Wheels: Van for Welfare Children," *New York Times*, January 27, 1988, A–1. See also Hays, C., "Free Care for the Poor and Pregnant Comes on Wheels" (in New Haven, CT), *New York Times*, January 21, 1992, B–5.

130. Macro Systems Inc., *One-Stop Shopping for Perinatal Services: Identification and Assessment of Implementation and Methodologies* (Washington, DC: National Center for Education in Maternal and Child Health, 1990), 25–28. See also *One-Stop Shopping: The Road to Healthy Mothers and Children* (Washington, DC: National Commission to Prevent Infant Mortality, 1991).

131. *Commitment to Change*, 260.

132. Ibid., 262. See also "Is There a Family Doctor in the House? More GPs May Be the Answer to America's Crisis" (Cites director of Health Resources and Services Administration of HHS as source for reported drop from a 50–50 generalist-specialist mix in 1960s to 30–70 in 1990), *Business Week*, Science and Technology, November 2, 1992, 124–25.

133. Brown, D., "Recruiters Offer Doctors a Small Town 'Option': Aggressive Approach Taken Amid Shortages," *Washington Post*, October 6, 1991, A–3.

134. *Commitment to Change*, 146.

135. CDF, *State of America's Children*, 72.

136. *Beyond Rhetoric*, 148.

137. *Commitment to Change*, 18–19.

138. Goldstein, A., "County Enlists Physicians to Aid Children," *Washington Post Montgomery Weekly*, March 5, 1992, MD 1.

139. "Update on Minority Health: Little Money, Abundant Optimism," *State Health Notes*, October 7, 1991, 1–2.

140. GAO, *Health Care: Public Health Service Funding of Community Health Centers in New York City*, GAO/HRD–90–121.

141. Ibid., 6. See also GAO, *Hispanic Access to Health Care: Significant Gaps Exist*, GAO/T-PEMD–91–13, September 19, 1991, 40–42.

142. OTA, *Adolescent Health: Summary and Policy Options*, vol. 1, OT A–H–468 (Washington, DC: U.S. Government Printing Office, April 1991). See also OTA, "New AIDS Definition Will Significantly Increase Number of Cases Reported But May Still Fail to Adequately Capture Some Major Risk Groups," Press Advisory August 13, 1992. Also GAO, *Needle Exchange Programs: Research Suggests Promise as an AIDS Prevention Strategy*, GAO/HRD–93–60, March 1993.

143. OTA, *Adolescent Health*, 26–27.

144. Ibid., 27.

145. Ibid., 94.

146. Bowleg, L., *A Summary of HIV/AIDS Laws from the 1991 State Legislative Sessions* (AIDS Policy Center, Intergovernmental Health Policy Project, January 1992), 8–9. See also from IHPP, Leeds, H., "1992 Funding Survey: Cases Up, Money Thinned: New More Detailed Data" (9-state survey—California, Florida, Georgia, Hawaii, Maryland, Nevada, New Jersey, New York, Texas—showing 1992 funding comparisons with 1991), *Intergovernmental AIDS Reports* 5, no. 6, November 1992, 1–2.

147. *New York Times* (editorial), October 21, 1991.

148. *Guidelines for Comprehensive Sexuality Education at Kindergarten Through 12th Grade* (New York: Sex Information and Education Council of the U.S. 1991).

149. As reported by Lawson, D., "Guide Charts Path for Sex Education," *New York Times*, October 17, 1991, C–1. See also Nazario, B., "Schools Teach the Virtues of Virginity" and "Sex Education Classes Can Be Extremely Explicit," *Wall Street Journal*, February 20, 1992, B–1, B–3.

150. Vobejda, B., "Teen Birthrates Reach Highs Last Seen in '70s: U.S. Pregnancy-Prevention Strategy Faulted," *Washington Post*, January 19, 1992, A–3.

151. Nazario, B–1.

152. Pittman, K., Adams-Taylor, S., and Morich, M., "Adolescent Pregnancy Prevention," in Kyle, J. (ed.), *Children, Families & Cities: Programs That Work at the Local Level* (Washington, DC: National League of Cities, 1987), 159–60 (emphasis added).

153. Jones, D., and Battle, S. (eds.), *Teenage Pregnancy: Developing Strategies for Change in the 21st Century* (New Brunswick, NJ: Transaction, 1990), 5–7. See also "Educating Teenage Males About Sex and AIDS," *Urban Institute Policy and Research Report*, Fall 1992, 4–5; Noah, T., "Support Group Helps Neglectful Inner-City Dads to Shoulder the Responsibilities of Fatherhood," *Wall Street Journal*, February 19, 1992, A–16.

154. OTA, *Adolescent Health*, 95.

155. "Task Force on Teenage Pregnancy," *Making America Work: Bringing Down the Barriers* (Washington, DC: Center for Policy Research, National Governors' Association, 1987), 65.

156. Gleeson, K., "Legislating Family Relationships," *ZPG Reporter*, September

1991, 7. See also Sylvester, K., "Making Families Talk About Abortion," *Governing*, April 1993, 22–23.

157. Halva-Neubauer, G., "Abortion Policy in the Post *Webster* Age," *Publius: The Journal of Federalism*, Summer 1990, 27–44.

158. Gleeson, 7.

159. Raspberry, W., "Rescuing Marriage Before It's Too Late—It Isn't Primarily About Individual Men and Women, It's About Families and Rearing Children," *Washington Post*, January 3, 1992, A–23 (emphasis added).

160. *W Memo* 4, no. 4, April 1992 (Washington, DC: American Public Welfare Association [APWA]).

161. Ibid., 9.

162. Ibid., 8. See also " 'Ounce of Prevention' Plan on the Fast Track in Maryland," *State Health Notes*, October 7, 1991, 1.

163. *W Memo*, 5–6.

164. Ibid., 10.

165. Ibid., 12. See also DeParle, J., "Workfare, Learnfare, Wedfare: Why Marginal Changes Don't Rescue the Welfare System," *New York Times*, March 1, 1992; Also DeParle, "Fueled by Social Trends, Welfare Cases Are Rising, *New York Times*, January 10, 1992, A1, A16.

166. *W Memo*, 5.

167. Stout, H., "Paying Workers for Good Health Habits Catches On as a Way to Cut Medical Costs," *Wall Street Journal*, November 26, 1991. Conversely, Walters, J., "More Mind-Your-Own-Business Laws," *Governing*, June 1992, 20.

168. Winslow, R., "California Push to Cut Smoking Seen as Success," *Wall Street Journal*, January 15, 1992, B–1, B–5.

169. As reported in Gross, J., "California Proposes Cutting Aid to Poor," *New York Times*, December 11, 1991, A–25.

170. As reported in Faludi, S., and Chase, M., "Surging Welfare Costs, Struggle to Control Them Join Health Care Expense as Hot Political Issue," *Wall Street Journal*, December 11, 1991, A–18.

171. Murray, C., "Stop Favoring Unwed Mothers," *New York Times*, January 16, 1992, A–23.

172. As quoted in Chargot, P., "Cut Class, Get a Smaller Check," *State Legislatures*, October 1991, 12–13.

173. Taylor, P., "The Welfare Beast—Can the Program Ever Be Tamed?" *Washington Post*, February 9, 1992; Eberstadt, N., "America's Infant Mortality Problem: Parents," *Wall Street Journal*, January 20, 1992, op-ed.

174. Samuelson, R. J., "Government and the Family—What Matters for Families Can't be Bought with Government Subsidies or Tax Breaks," *Washington Post*, January 30, 1992, A–23.

175. Besharov, D., "Cautions for the New Paternalism," *Washington Post*, January 5, 1992, C–7.

176. Bauer, L., and King, M., "When Drugs Are the Ties That Bind," *State Legislatures*, September 1991, 12–13.

177. As reported in Johnson, K. "Child Abuse Is Ruled Out in Birth Case," *New York Times*, August 18, 1992, B–1.

178. Bauer and King, 14–18.

179. *Beyond Rhetoric*, 34.

180. State of Washington, Senate Bill 5832, later enacted as HB 1793.

181. *State Substance Abuse Laws 1991* (Washington, DC: IHPP, George Washington University, January 1992), 1 and "1992 State Substance Abuse Laws," *State ADM Report IHPP*, December 1992, 5–6, 12–16.

182. Ibid., "1991 State Substance Abuse Laws" in chart form preceding page 1.

183. Polich, J. M., Ellickson, P., Reuter, P., and Kahan, J., *Strategies for Controlling Adolescent Drug Use* (Santa Monica, CA: Rand Corporation, February 1984), v.

184. Ellickson, P., and Bell, R., *Prospects for Preventing Drug Use Among Young Adolescents* (Santa Monica, CA: Rand Corporation, 1990), 8.

185. Ibid., 18–41.

186. University of Michigan (IHIS contractor for the annual student surveys) News and Information Service, "Most Forms of Drug Use Decline Among American High School and College Students," January 27, 1992 release, 2–5.

187. National Institute on Drug Abuse, HHS, *NIDA Capsules*, December 1991, 4.

188. Stout, H., "Surgeon General Wants to Age Alcohol Ads," *Wall Street Journal*, November 5, 1991, B–7.

189. National Governors' Association, *Policy Positions 1991–92*, Sec. 5.4.6 on Health and Medical Care (Washington, DC: National Governors' Association, 1992), 70.

190. *State Substance Abuse Laws 1991*, 57–64; "1992 Substance Abuse Laws," *State ADM Report*, 13. See also IHPP, *Major Health Legislation in the States: '92*, January 1993; Ebener, P., Feldman, E., and Fitzgerald, N., *Federal Data Bases for Use in Drug Policy Research: A Catalogue for Data Users* (Santa Monica, CA: Rand Corporation, 1993).

191. OTA, *Adolescent Health*, 102.

192. GAO, (1) *Drug Use Prevention: Federal Efforts to Identify Exemplary Programs Need Stronger Design*, GAO/PEMD–91–15, August 1991, 2; (2) *Adolescent Drug Use Prevention: Common Features of Promising Community Programs*, GAO/PEMD–92–2, January 1991, 1–4, 44–45.

193. *State Substance Abuse Laws 1991*, 89, 93; "1992 Substance Abuse Laws," 15.

194. *State Substance Abuse Laws 1991*, 89, 96–97.

195. Peirce, N., "Fighting Drugs on the Home Turf, Block by Block," (Baltimore) *Sun* (and other newspapers), July 1, 1991.

196. Conner, R., and Burns, P., "The Winnable War: How Communities Are Eradicating Local Drug Markets," *Brookings Review*, Summer 1992, 27–29. See also Conner and Burns, *The Winnable War: A Community Guide to Eradicating Street Drug Markets* (Washington, DC: American Alliance for Rights and Responsibilities, July 1991).

197. *Youth Investment and Community Reconstruction: Street Lessons on Drugs and Crimes for the Nineties* (Washington, DC: Milton S. Eisenhower Foundation, 1990), 43, 45.

198. Ibid., Contents. See also Reuter, P., "Hawks Ascendant: Punitive Trend on Anti-Drug Policy," *Rand Reprints* (Santa Monica, CA: Rand Corporation, 1992).

199. "A Not-So-Drug-Free Zone," *Washington Post* (editorial), September 21, 1992, A–22.

200. *State Substance Abuse Laws 1991*, 31–32.

201. Ibid., 32–41.

202. Ibid., 31–32.

203. The scientific articles in the June 10, 1992, special issue of *JAMA* 267, no. 22 referenced in chapter 3 were: Well, D., and Hemenway, D., "Loaded Guns in the Home:

272 America's Future Work Force

Analysis of a National Survey of Gun Owners," 3033–37; Callahan, C., and Rivara, F., "Urban High School Youth and Handguns: A School-Based Survey," 3038–42; Saltzman, L., et al., "Weapon Involvement and Injury Outcomes in Family and Intimate Assaults," 3043–47; Fingerhut, L., et al., "Firearm and Nonfirearm Homicide Among Persons 15 Through 19 Years of Age 1979 Through 1989," 3048–53; Fingerhut, L., et al., "Firearm Homicide Among Black Teenage Males in Metropolitan Counties 1983–85 and 1987–89," 3054–58; "Assault Weapons as a Public Hazard in the United States," Committee on Scientific Affairs, American Medical Association, 3067–70.

204. GAO, *Substance Abuse Treatment: Medicaid Allows Some Services But Generally Limits Coverage*, GAO/HRD–91–92, June 1991, 3–4, 7–8.

205. *Youth Investment and Community Reconstruction*, 79–80. See also "Fighting the Right Drug War" (editorial), *U.S. News and World Report*, April 26, 1993, 74.

206. GAO, *Drug Abuse: The Crack Cocaine Epidemic: Health Consequences and Treatment*, GAO/HRD–91–55FS, January 1991, 4.

207. GAO, *Drug Abuse: Research on Treatment May Not Address Current Needs* GAO/HRD–90–114, September 1990, 4.

208. GAO, *Drug Abuse Research: Federal Funding and Future Needs* (Statement of Eleanor Chalimsky, assistant comptroller general for Program and Methodology Division before the Subcommittee on Legislation and National Security, House Committee on Government Operations), GAO/T-PEMD–91–14, September 25, 1991, 13–15.

209. D'Aunno, T., and Vaughn, T., "Variations in Methadone Treatment Practices: Results from a National Study." See also Cooper, J., "Ineffective Use of Psychoactive Drugs: Methadone Treatment Is No Exception," *JAMA* 267, no. 2, 253–58, 281–82, respectively.

210. Phibbs, C., "Neonatal Costs of Maternal Cocaine Use," *JAMA* 206, no. 11, September 18, 1991, 1521–26. See also Winslow, R., "Cocaine Babies Lift Hospital Costs, Researchers Find," *Wall Street Journal*, September 18, 1991, B–4.

211. *Beyond Rhetoric*, 284.

212. *The First Sixty Months: A Handbook of Promising Prevention Programs for Children Zero to Five Years of Age*, Joint report of the National Governor's Association Committee on Human Resources and the NGA Center for Policy Research (Washington, DC: National Governor's Association, 1987), 2 (emphasis added).

213. As reported in *Policy and Research Report* (Washington, DC: Urban Institute, Winter/Spring 1992), 25. Full report contained in Institute Research Paper "Reporting of Child Maltreatment: A Secondary Analysis of Child Abuse and Neglect," May 1991.

214. Child Welfare League of America (CWLA), *Children at the Front: A Different View of the War on Drugs and Alcohol* (Washington, DC: CWLA, 1992), 175.

215. *Beyond Rhetoric*, 276.

216. GAO, *Child Abuse: Prevention Programs Need Greater Emphasis*, GAO/HRD, 92–89, August 1992, 3.

217. House Select Committee, *Opportunities for Success*, 141. See also Newman, L., and Buka, S., *Every Child a Learner: Reducing Risks of Learning Impairment During Pregnancy and Infancy* (Denver: Education Commission of the States, 1990).

218. OTA news release, January 15, 1987; USPHS, *Healthy People 2000*, 564; CDF, *State of America's Children 1991*, 126; *Beyond Rhetoric*, xxxxi, 125, 200. See also Shuchman, M., a "Psychological Help for Children in Urban Combat," *New York Times*, Health, February 21, 1991, B–9.

219. *1991 State Mental Health Laws*, 83–89; "1992 Mental Health Laws," *State ADM*

Report, 7, 8. See also Ruffenack, G., "Slashes in Mental Health Benefits Start to Hurt Patients, Medical Officials Say," *Wall Street Journal*, March 19, 1991, B–1.

220. Prothrow-Stith, D., with Weissmann, M., *Deadly Consequences: How Violence Is Destroying Our Teenage Population and a Plan to Begin Solving the Problem* (New York: HarperCollins, 1991).

221. Krisberg, B., "Juvenile Justice In Turmoil," in Kirlin, J., and Winkler, D. (eds.), *California Policy Choices*, vol. 4. (Sacramento, CA: Sacramento Public Affairs Center, University of Southern California, 1988), 119.

222. Ibid., 140–41 (emphasis added).

223. CDF, *State of America's Children 1991*, 126.

224. Krisberg, 136–37.

225. "Get Creative on Corrections," *New York Times* (editorial), January 20, 1992, A–18.

226. Newland, C., "Refocusing California Corrections," in *California Policy Choices*, vol. 6, 1990, 119, 211. See also Thome, J., "State Associations Work to Let Juveniles Out of County Jails," *County News*, November 11, 1991, 6.

227. Lemov, P., "The Next Best Thing to Prisons," *Governing*, December 1991, 34, 36.

228. Mahtesian, C., "The March of Boot Camps," *Governing*, June 1991, 21. See also Peirce, N., "Youth Service Is on the March; It Can Provide Work and Discipline," *Philadelphia Inquirer*, June 15, 1992 (and other newspapers).

229. Gurwitt, R., "The Growing Clout of Prison Guards," *Governing*, December 1991, 37.

230. Peirce, N., "The Jails Are Full Because It Is Good for the Jail Business to Fill Them," (Baltimore) *Sun*, January 22, 1992, 9A; "Filling Our Prisons Isn't Deterring Crimes," *Philadelphia Inquirer* January 13, 1992, 7A.

231. As reported in Gross, J., "Stressing Therapy, Court Gains with Drug Users," *New York Times*, June 21, 1991, A–14.

232. As reported in Raspberry, W., "Common Sense About Drugs," *Washington Post*, March 27, 1992.

233. As reported in GAO, *Drug Treatment: State Prisons Face Challenges in Providing Services*, GAO/HRD/91–128, September 1991, 6. Data source cited was Criminal Justice Institute, *The Corrections Yearbook, Adult Prisons and Jails–1990*, 2, 3, 48.

234. GAO, *Drug Treatment*, 6.

235. GAO, *Drug Treatment: Despite New Strategy, Few Federal Inmates Receive Treatment*, GAO/HRD–91–116, September 1991, 1–3, 5.

236. Ibid., 2.

237. Ibid., 12.

238. GAO, *Drug Treatment: State Prisons*, 9. See also DiIulio, J., Jr., "A Limited War on Crime That We Can Win: Two Lost Wars Later," *Brookings Review*, Fall 1992, 7–11; Oberdorfer, L. (Judge, U.S. District Court for District of Columbia), "A Safety Valve for U.S. Prisons" (conditional sentencing), *Washington Post*, op-ed, June 23, 1992, A–21.

239. U.S. Department of Justice, National Institute of Corrections, *Executive Summary—Intervening with Substance-Abusing Offenders: A Framework for Action*, Report of the National Task Force on Correctional Substance Abuse Strategies (Washington, D.C.: U.S. Department of Justice, National Institute of Corrections, June 1991), 9, 14.

240. As reported by Barret, P., "Prison Drug Treatment Attracts Interest As Evidence Mounts That It's Successful," *Wall Street Journal*, Politics, May 20, 1991.

241. *State Substance Abuse Laws 1991*, 13.

242. Ibid. 13, 14; "1992 State Substance Abuse Laws," 14–16.

243. GAO, *Foster Care: Children's Experiences Linked to Various Factors; Better Data Needed*, GAO/HRD–91–64, September 1991, 1.

244. Ibid., 2–3.

245. Ibid., 9.

246. CDF, *State of America's Children*, 124.

247. *Beyond Rhetoric*, 295–97.

248. Ibid., 299.

249. Child Welfare League of America, *Children at the Front: A Different View of the War on Alcohol and Drugs*, Executive Summary (Washington, DC: Child Welfare League of America, 1992), 6, 19.

250. Joint issuance of National Association of Public Child Welfare Administrators and National Council of Human Services Administrators, "Guiding Principles for Working with Substance-Abusing Families and Drug-Exposed Children: The Child Welfare Response," (Washington, DC: American Public Welfare Association, 1991), 2–3.

251. *Congressional Record*, March 26, 1992, 4243.

252. Ibid., 4244.

253. National Governors' Association, *Policy Positions*, 127. See also "Family Preservation Programs," *From Homes to Classrooms to Workrooms*, 55–64.

254. National Commission on Child Welfare and Family Preservation, *A Commitment to Change* (Washington, DC: American Public Welfare Association, 1991), 4.

255. Ibid., vii (emphasis added).

256. Moynihan, D. P., "Toward a Post-Industrial Social Policy," *Public Interest*, no. 96, Summer 1989, 17, 25.

257. Gross, J., "Collapse of Inner City Families Creates America's 'New Orphans,' " *New York Times*, March 29, 1992 (emphasis added).

258. "Research Sheds New Light on Reforms," summarized in *Ford Foundation Letter*, Fall 1991, 10–11. Full report in Gueron, J., and Pauly, E., *From Welfare to Work* (New York: Russell Sage Foundation, 1991). See also De Parle, J., "To Moynihan, Welfare Dependency Signals New Ill," *New York Times*, December 9, 1991, A–13, Spalter-Roth, R., et al., *Combining Work and Welfare: An Alternative Anti-Poverty Strategy* (Washington, DC: Institute for Women's Policy Research, 1992), Kirkland, R., "What We Can Do Now," *Fortune* June 1, 1992, 41.

259. Speech by Senator John H. Chafee (R–RI) to "Health Care Policy Makers," June 25, 1993. Endorsed health reform of 8 increments: (1) insurance market reform— no discriminatory selection; (2) small group purchasing organizations; (3) medical liability reform; (4) federal preemption of state-mandated benefits and state anti-managed care laws; (5) making health insurance costs of individuals 100 percent tax deductible; (6) paperwork reduction; (7) expansion of community health centers in underserved areas; and (8) greater emphasis on preventive care. No play or pay and no national budget caps on health costs.

260. CBO, *Managed Competition and Its Potential to Reduce Health Spending*, May 1993, x. See also Crock, S., "Radical Surgery for Medicine? Hold that Scalpel," *Business Week*, July 12, 1993; Lemov, P., "States and Medicaid: Ahead of the Feds," *Governing*, July 1993, 27.

Chapter 5 ⸻⸻⸻

Deterrents to Adequate Education

The previous chapters of this book suggest that the nation's public education system is greatly affected by the social, economic, and demographic changes that are taking place in society. After the family, the schools are the most significant influence on the values, behavior, and learning of children and youth. Yet, the problems experienced by students, teachers, administrators, and parents in elementary and secondary schools and the prospects for effective remedial actions are often conditioned by factors that have little direct relevance to public education and often occur before the formal education process begins.

Perhaps the best illustration of the above point is the changing nature of the discipline problems experienced in public schools. In the 1950s and early 1960s, when one of the authors was enrolled in elementary and secondary schools, the chief problems included talking in class, running in the halls, speeding in the parking lot, getting out of turn in line in the cafeteria, wearing improper clothing, cheating on tests, and rivalry between vocational and college-bound students. By the 1980s and 1990s, the greatest problems in schools included substance abuse, pregnancy, absenteeism, assault, poor nutrition, robbery, murder, vandalism, and gang warfare. To this list could be added AIDS, racism, and multicultural tensions.

In this context, the public schools of our nation face a terrible dilemma. On one hand, expectations are high on the part of parents, employers, and public officials as far as the capacity of the elementary and secondary education systems to produce graduates who are employable and able to compete in a global economy is concerned. On the other, despite massive infusions of funding since the early 1980s, the educational mission and performance of public schools are compromised and complicated by the need to overcome social disadvantages and learning disabilities that originated and are reinforced outside the classroom.

Moreover, at a time when President Bill Clinton and many state and local officials are advocating the "reinventing" of government in terms of the roles, relationships, and responsibilities of public agencies vis-à-vis the private sector and citizens-customers, several school systems remain bastions of organization status quo and inertia. Although the number and types of course offerings have changed over the years, few fundamental changes have occurred in such areas as the structure of the typical school day, class schedule, lecture-based approach to learning, dynamics of superintendent-principal-teacher interactions, teacher training and qualifications, and parental roles. As the chief proponents of "reinventing government," David Osborne and Ted Gaebler, have pointed out:

Traditional public education is a classic example of the bureaucratic model. It is centralized, top-down, and rule-driven; each school is a monopoly; customers have little choice; and no one's job depends on their performance. It is a system that guarantees stability, not change.

Public education's customers—children, families, and employers—have changed dramatically over the past 50 years. Yet most schools look just like they did 50 years ago.[1]

By way of background, it is essential to grasp the basic problems and needs experienced by elementary and secondary schools across the country and the deterrents to their effective resolution. This chapter reviews the weaknesses of the public education system in preparing the youth of our nation for employability. To place this discussion in context at the outset, a selective overview of significant trends in elementary and secondary education is provided.

ENROLLMENT AND INSTRUCTIONAL TRENDS

During the post–World War II "baby boom," enrollments in elementary and secondary schools grew at a rapid pace. As indicated in Table 5.1, from 1949–50 until fall 1971 the total student population in public schools grew 84 percent, from 25.1 million to 46.1 million. Beginning in the early 1970s, however, enrollments began to decline, as the "baby boomers" opted for smaller families for economic and professional reasons, more women preferred careers to motherhood, and the effects of rising divorce rates took their toll on childbearing. As a consequence, public elementary and secondary enrollments dropped steadily from 45.7 million in fall 1972 to 39.8 million in 1986. Since that time enrollments have rebounded, rising gradually to a projected 43 million in 1993 and 47 million by 2002, with nearly all of this growth occurring in the kindergarten through eighth grades.[2]

Table 5.1 also reveals that of the 62.7 million total elementary and secondary school population in fall 1993, 5.4 million or about 9 percent were projected to be enrolled in private institutions, including both religiously affiliated and nonsectarian schools. In contrast with public school trends, private school enrollments remained steady from 1971 to 1979, after declining from their 6.3 million peak seven years previously. Beginning in fall 1980, private enrollments began to rise, from 5.3 million to 5.7 million students four years later, then gradually

Table 5.1

Enrollment in Educational Institutions, by Level and Control of Institutions, 1940–50 to Fall 2002 (in thousands)

Year	Total Enrollm't All Levels	Elementary & Secondary Total	Public elementary & Secondary Schools			Private Elementary and Secondary Schools[1]		
			Total	Kindergarten through Grade 8	Grades 9-12	Total	Kindergarten through Grade 8	Grades 9-12
1	2	3	4	5	6	7	8	9
1949-50	31,151	28,492	25,111	19,387	5,725	3,380	2,708	672
Fall 1959	44,497	40,857	35,182	26,911	8,271	5,675	4,640	1,035
Fall 1964	52,996	47,716	41,416	30,025	11,391	[2]6,300	[2]5,000	1,300
Fall 1965	54,394	48,473	42,173	30,563	11,610	6,300	4,900	1,400
Fall 1966	55,629	49,239	43,039	31,145	11,894	[2]6,200	[2]4,800	[2]1,400
Fall 1967	56,803	49,891	43,891	31,641	12,250	[2]6,000	[2]4,600	[2]1,400
Fall 1968	58,257	50,744	44,944	32,226	12,718	5,800	4,400	1,400
Fall 1969	59,055	51,050	45,550	32,513	13,037	[2]5,500	[2]4,200	[2]1,300
Fall 1970	59,838	51,257	45,894	32,558	13,336	5,363	4,052	1,311
Fall 1971	60,220	51,271	46,071	32,318	13,753	[2]5,200	[2]3,900	[2]1,300
Fall 1972	59,941	50,726	45,726	31,879	13,848	[2]5,000	[2]3,700	[2]1,300
Fall 1973	60,046	50,444	45,444	31,401	14,044	[2]5,000	[2]3,700	[2]1,300
Fall 1974	60,297	50,073	45,073	30,971	14,103	[2]5,000	[2]3,700	[2]1,300
Fall 1975	61.004	49,819	44,819	30,515	14,304	[2]5,000	[2]3,700	[2]1,300
Fall 1976	60,490	49,478	44,311	29,997	14,314	5,167	3,825	1,342
Fall 1977	60,003	48,717	43,577	29,375	14,203	5,140	3,797	1,343
Fall 1978	58,897	47,637	42,551	28,463	14,088	5,086	3,732	1,353
Fall 1979	58,221	46,651	41,651	28,034	13,616	[2]5,000	[2]3,700	[2]1,300
Fall 1980	58,305	46,208	40,877	27,647	13,231	5,331	3,992	1,339
Fall 1981	57,916	45,544	40,044	27,280	12,764	[2]5,500	[2]4,100	[2]1,400
Fall 1982	57,591	45,166	39,566	27,161	12,405	[2]5,600	[2]4,200	[2]1,400
Fall 1983	57,432	44,967	39,252	26,981	12,271	5,715	4,315	1,400
Fall 1984	57,150	44,908	39,208	26,905	12,304	[2]5,700	[2]4,300	[2]1,400
Fall 1985	57,226	44,979	39,422	27,034	12,388	5,557	4,195	1,362
Fall 1986	57,709	45,205	39,753	27,420	12,333	[2]5,452	[2]4,116	[2]1,336
Fall 1987	58,254	45,488	40,008	27,933	12,076	5,479	4,232	1,247
Fall 1988	58,485	45,430	40,189	28,501	11,687	5,241	4,036	1,206

Table 5.1 (continued)

Year	Total Enrollm't All Levels	Elementary & Secondary Total	Public elementary & Secondary Schools			Private Elementary and Secondary Schools[1]		
			Total	Kindergarten through Grade 8	Grades 9-12	Total	Kindergarten through Grade 8	Grades 9-12
1	2	3	4	5	6	7	8	9
Fall 1989 [3]	59,436	45,898	40,543	29,152	11,390	5,355	4,162	1,193
Fall 1990 [4]	60,160	46,450	41,224	29,888	11,336	5,226	4,090	1,136
Fall 1991 [5]	61,189	47,032	41,839	30,353	11,486	5,193	4,069	1,124
Fall 1992 [5]	61,836	47,601	42,250	30,663	11,587	5,351	4,192	1,159
Fall 1993 [5]	62,776	48,410	42,971	31,091	11,880	5,439	4,250	1,189
Fall 1994 [5]	63,791	49,279	43,749	31,451	12,298	5,530	4,300	1,230
Fall 1995 [5]	64,675	50,054	44,442	31,782	12,660	5,612	4,345	1,267
Fall 1996 [5]	65,561	50,759	45,074	32,068	13,006	5,685	4,384	1,301
Fall 1997 [5]	66,309	51,331	45,585	32,343	13,242	5,746	4,422	1,325
Fall 1998 [5]	66,977	51,750	45,955	32,661	13,294	5,795	4,465	1,330
Fall 1999 [5]	67,572	52,110	46,276	32,843	13,433	5,834	4,490	1,344
Fall 2000 [5]	68,098	52,406	46,539	33,032	13,507	5,867	4,516	1,351
Fall 2001 [5]	68,544	52,679	46,782	33,172	13,610	5,897	4,535	1,362
Fall 2002 [5]	69,026	52,996	47,068	33,245	13,823	5,928	4,545	1,383

[1] Beginning in fall 1980, data include estimates for an expanded universe of private schools. Therefore, these totals may differ from figures shown in other tables, and direct comparisons with earlier years should be avoided.

[2] Estimated.

[3] Preliminary data.

[4] Based on "Early Estimates" surveys.

[5] Projected.

— Indicates data not available.

Source: U.S. Department of Education, National Center for Education Statistics, *Statistics of State School Systems; Statistics of Public Elementary and Secondary School Systems; Statistics of Nonpublic Elementary and Secondary Schools; Projections of Education Statistics to 2002;* Common Core of Data, "Fall Enrollment in Institutions of Higher Education"; and Integrated Postsecondary Education Data Systems (IPEDS). "Fall Enrollment" surveys. Cited in U.S. Department of Education, National Center for Education Statistics, *Digest of Education Statistics: 1992,* (Washington, D.C.: U.S. Government Printing Office, October 1992), p. 12.

slipping back to 5.2 million by 1990. Again in fall 1991 enrollments rebounded, growing to a projected 5.9 million by 2002.

For the 1980–90 decade, between 11 and 12 percent of the total elementary and secondary student body went to private schools. This growth-decline trend reflects, among other factors, the preference of some parents to pay for private education as an alternative to sending their children to mediocre or poor public schools, which often were both uncaring and unsafe, as well as the inability of most family budgets to absorb this expense.

It should be noted that nursery schools—operating predominantly under non-profit auspices but with increased governmental involvement—have continued to expand. In 1991, 996,000 children were enrolled in public nursery schools, and 1.83 million were in similar private schools. This 2.82 million nursery school enrollment represented a 62 percent increase from 1975. In 1984, over 70 percent of white nursery school students were in private schools, compared with one-third of black nursery school children.[3]

With respect to kindergarten, the opposite enrollment pattern is evident. In 1991, 2.97 million 3- to 5-year-olds were enrolled in public programs, while 543,000 participated in private programs. As in the case of public nursery schools, both public and private kindergarten enrollments fluctuated during the 1980s, but the overall trend was growth in both programs, increasing 11 percent for public and 3 percent for private kindergartens over the 1975 levels.

These figures reflect an important trend that began in the 1970s. While total student enrollments in both public and private elementary and secondary schools were declining, preprimary enrollments of children aged three to five were on the rise. The proportion of the population in this age group enrolled in preprimary programs grew 19 percent between 1970 and 1980, from 37.5 percent to 52.5 percent, and an additional 37 percent between 1980 and 1990, the peak year, when 59.4 percent of the 3- to 5-year-old population were enrolled. In 1991, this figure dropped to 55.7 percent, due to a decline in both public and private nursery school enrollments.[4]

Turning to the amount of time 3- to 5-year-olds spend in preprimary programs, in 1991, 38 percent of the children were enrolled for the full school day. This figure reflects an increase from 31.8 percent in 1980 and 17 percent in 1970 (see Table 5.2).

With respect to the future, by the year 2002 the total number of students enrolled in public elementary and secondary schools is projected by the U.S. Department of Education (DOE) to increase by 9 percent over the 1992 level, to 47 million. At the same time, private enrollments will also grow by about 9 percent over this time period, to 5.9 million.[5] These enrollment increases are due to rising birthrates since 1977—the so-called baby echo—which were reflected in elementary school enrollments in the early 1980s and in secondary school enrollments in the early 1990s and beyond. For many school districts, these figures mean that new buildings will need to be constructed and older ones renovated.

Table 5.2

Enrollment of Children Age 3–5 in Preprimary Programs, by Level and Control of Program and by Attendance Status, October 1965 to October 1991 (in thousands)

Year and Age	Total Population, 3-5 yrs.	Total	% Enrolled	Enrollment by Level and Control Nursery School Public	Nursery School Private	Kindergarten Public	Kindergarten Private	Enrollment by Attendance Full-day	Part-day	% Full-day
1	2	3	4	5	6	7	8	9	10	11
1965	12,549	3,407	27.1	127	393	2,291	596	—	—	—
1970	10,949	4,104	37.5	332	762	2,498	511	698	3,405	17.0
1975	10,185	4,955	48.7	570	1,174	2,682	528	1,295	3,659	26.1
1979	9,119	4,664	51.1	633	1,228	2,381	421	1,454	3,210	31.2
1980	9,284	4,878	52.5	628	1,353	2,438	459	1,551	3,327	31.8
1981	9,421	4,937	52.4	—	—	—	—	1,472	3,465	29.8
1982	9,873	5,105	51.7	729	1,423	2,459	494	1,574	3,531	30.8
1983	10,254	5,384	52.5	809	1,538	2,416	623	1,686	3,700	31.3
1984	10,612	5,480	51.6	742	1,593	2,668	476	1,929	3,550	35.2
1985	10,733	5,865	54.6	846	1,631	2,847	541	2,144	3,722	36.6
1986	10,866	5,971	55.0	829	1,715	2,859	567	2,241	3,730	37.5
1987	10,872	5,931	54.6	819	1,736	2,842	534	2,090	3,841	35.2
1988	10,993	5,978	54.4	851	1,770	2,875	481	2,044	3,935	34.2
1989	11,039	6,026	54.6	930	1,894	2,704	497	2,238	3,789	37.1
1990	11,207	6,659	59.4	1,199	2,180	2,772	509	2,577	4,082	38.7
1991	11,370	6,334	55.7	996	1,828	2,967	543	2,408	3,926	38.0

— Indicates data not available

Source: U.S. Department of Education, National Center for Education Statistics, *Preprimary Enrollment*, various years; and U.S. Department of Commerce, Bureau of the Census. Current Population Survey, unpublished data. Cited in U.S. Department of Education, National Center for Education Statistics, *Digest of Education Statistics: 1992* (Washington, D.C., U.S. Government Printing Office, 1992) p. 61.

The changing demographics of the public school population will have varying impacts across the nation, with the sharpest growth between 1990 and 2002 occurring in the Northeast (22%) and West (18%), compared with more modest growth in the South (15%) and the Midwest (7%). With respect to enrollment levels, between 1990 and 2002, kindergarten through 8th grade will experience a 12 percent overall rise, with the greatest growth at the secondary level. The geographic distribution is as follows: Northeast, 17 percent; West, 14 percent; South, 13 percent; and Midwest, 5 percent. For 15 states, the enrollments in this category will decrease.[6]

By the mid-1990s high school enrollments are expected to rebound from their decline during the latter half of the 1980s, and they will continue to surge through 2002, with an overall increase of 23 percent during this period. The regional growth rates for public institutions are projected at: Northeast, 33 percent; West, 29 percent; South, 21 percent; and Midwest, 11 percent.[7] These increases will produce an 11 percent rise in the number of public high school graduates between 1989 and 2002. Increases will occur in at least 37 states, especially in the West.[8]

Student Body Composition

Turning to the racial composition of public elementary and secondary schools, figures compiled by the DOE indicate that K–12 minority enrollments are growing, while the white student population is shrinking. The national averages in 1986 and 1988 are:[9]

	1986	1988
White	70.4%	61.4%
Black	16.1%	21.4%
Hispanic	9.9%	12.7%
Asian or Pacific Islander	2.8%	3.5%
American Indian/Alaskan Native	0.9%	1.0%

The age group composition of those attending public or private elementary and secondary schools has not changed markedly in recent years, with one exception. In 1991, the enrollment rates were as follows:[10]

3 and 4 years	40.5%
5 and 6 years	95.4%
7 to 13 years	99.6%
14 to 17 years	96.0%

18 and 19 years	59.6%
20 to 24 years	30.2%

The youngest age group has experienced the greatest long-term growth in enrollments. As indicated in Table 5.3, in 1965, 10.6 percent of the children in the three- and four-year-old age category were enrolled in public and private schools, and this proportion has climbed nearly fourfold in subsequent years. This trend reflects the increasing recognition among parents and educators of the need for students to get an early exposure to structured learning, as well as the key role of federal programs like Head Start in providing nutritional services, as well as social and educational experiences, to poor and disadvantaged children.

As shown in Table 5.4, from 1975 until 1989 the enrollment rates of black children aged three and four years exceeded those for whites and Hispanics; in 1989–91, however, the white enrollment proportions for these age groups exceeded the rates of other races. Although the table reveals a few exceptions, in general the proportion of the white population aged 3–19 enrolled in school was greater than that of black and Hispanic children.

Teachers

In 1992, 2.8 million classroom teachers were projected by DOE to be employed in elementary and secondary schools, of whom 2.4 million were public school teachers. They accounted for 16.3 percent of the total state and local work force. About 1.6 million were elementary teachers, and 1.2 million were in secondary schools. By the year 2002, DOE projects that the total number of K–12 public school teachers will grow to 2.76 million, 2.84 million, or 2.9 million, depending on how the growth assumptions for personal income and local education revenue receipts from states are affected by economic realities. During this time the number of private school teachers will increase from approximately 358,000 in 1992 to 405,000, 417,000, or 430,000 in 2002, depending on the economy.[11]

Teacher-student ratios in public schools have narrowed as enrollments have declined in many places. In 1977, for example, there were 21.1 pupils per teacher in elementary schools and 18.2 in secondary schools; the figures for private schools were 20.0 and 15.1, respectively. By 1989, these ratios had declined to 17.7 for public elementary and 16.4 for public secondary schools, while the private school figures were 15.1 and 11.7, respectively. As enrollments increased, ratios also began to grow, and by 1992 they had reached 18.9 for public elementary and 15.3 for public secondary, with the respective private figures being 16.4 and 11.2 (using DOE's middle alternative projections). By 2002, the ratios are projected to be 17.6 for public elementary, 15.3 for public secondary, 15.4 for private elementary, and 11.4 for private secondary.[12]

The average salaries of public elementary and secondary teachers reached an all-time high level of $34,413 in 1991–92, as indicated in Table 5.5. In part

Table 5.3

Percentage of the Population Age 3–19 Enrolled in School,[1] by Age, 1965–91

Year	Total 3 to 34 years	3 and 4 years	5 and 6 years	7 to 13 years	14 to 17 years	18 and 19 years
1	2	3	4	5	6	7
1965	55.5	10.6	84.9	99.4	93.2	46.3
1966	56.1	12.5	85.8	99.3	93.7	47.2
1967	56.6	14.2	87.4	99.3	93.7	47.6
1968	56.7	15.7	87.6	99.1	94.2	50.4
1969	57.0	16.1	88.4	99.2	94.0	50.2
1970	56.4	20.5	89.5	99.2	94.1	47.7
1971	56.2	21.2	91.6	99.1	94.5	49.2
1972	54.9	24.4	91.9	99.2	93.3	46.3
1973	53.5	24.2	92.5	99.2	92.9	42.9
1974	53.6	28.8	94.2	99.3	92.9	43.1
1975	53.7	31.5	94.7	99.3	93.6	46.9
1976	53.1	31.3	95.5	99.2	93.7	46.2
1977	52.5	32.0	95.8	99.4	93.6	46.2
1978	51.2	34.2	95.3	99.1	93.7	45.4
1979	50.3	35.1	95.8	99.2	93.6	45.0
1980	49.7	36.7	95.7	99.3	93.4	46.4
1981	48.9	36.0	94.0	99.2	94.1	49.0
1982	48.6	36.4	95.0	99.2	94.4	47.8
1983	48.4	37.5	95.4	99.2	95.0	50.4
1984	47.9	36.3	94.5	99.2	94.7	50.1
1985	48.3	38.9	96.1	99.2	94.9	51.6
1986	48.2	38.9	95.3	99.2	94.9	54.6
1987	48.6	38.3	95.1	99.5	95.0	55.6
1988	48.7	38.2	96.0	99.7	95.1	55.6
1989	49.1	39.1	95.2	99.3	95.7	56.0
1990	50.2	44.4	96.5	99.6	95.8	57.2
1991	50.7	40.5	95.4	99.6	96.0	59.6

[1] Includes enrollment in any type of graded public, parochial, or other private school in regular school systems. Includes nursery schools, kindergartens, elementary schools, colleges, universities, and professional schools. Attendance may be on either a full-time or part-time basis and during the day or night. Enrollments in "special" schools, such as trade schools, business colleges, or correspondence schools, are not included.

Source: U.S. Department of Commerce, Bureau of the Census, *Historical Statistics of the United States, Colonial Times to 1970; Current Population Reports*, Series P-20, various years; and unpublished data. Cited in U.S. Department of Education, National Center for Education Statistics, *Digest of Education Statistics: 1992* (Washington, D.C.: U.S. Government Printing Office, 1992), 15.

Table 5.4

Percentage of the Population Age 3–19 Enrolled in School, by Race/Ethnicity and Age, October 1975 to October 1991

Year and age	All Races	White, non-Hispanic	Black, non-Hispanic	Hispanic Origin
1	2	3	4	5
1975				
3 and 4 years	31.5	31.0	34.4	27.3
5 and 6 years	94.7	95.1	94.4	92.1
7 to 9 years	99.3	99.4	99.3	99.6
10 to 13 years	99.3	99.3	99.1	99.2
14 and 15 yrs.	98.2	98.5	97.4	95.6
16 and 17 yrs.	89.0	89.5	86.8	86.2
18 and 19 yrs.	46.9	46.8	46.9	44.0
1980				
3 and 4 years	36.7	37.4	38.2	28.5
5 and 6 years	95.7	95.9	95.5	94.5
7 to 9 years	99.1	99.1	99.4	98.4
10 to 13 years	99.4	99.4	99.4	99.7
14 and 15 yrs.	98.2	98.7	97.9	94.3
16 and 17 yrs.	89.0	89.2	90.7	81.8
18 and 19 yrs.	46.4	47.0	45.8	37.8
1985				
3 and 4 years	38.9	40.3	42.8	27.0
5 and 6 years	96.1	96.6	95.7	94.5
7 to 9 years	99.1	99.4	98.6	98.4
10 to 13 years	99.3	99.3	99.5	99.4
14 and 15 yrs.	98.1	98.3	98.1	96.1
16 and 17 yrs.	91.7	92.5	91.8	84.5
18 and 19 yrs.	51.6	53.7	43.5	41.8
1989				
3 and 4 years	39.1	42.2	39.0	22.3
5 and 6 years	95.2	95.7	94.6	93.3
7 to 9 years	99.2	99.4	99.0	98.1
10 to 13 years	99.4	99.5	99.3	99.1
14 and 15 yrs.	98.8	99.1	99.4	96.4
16 and 17 yrs.	92.7	93.1	93.8	86.4
18 and 19 yrs.	56.0	58.0	49.8	44.6

Table 5.4 (continued)

Year and age	All Races	White, non-Hispanic	Black, non-Hispanic	Hispanic Origin
1	2	3	4	5
1990				
3 and 4 years	44.4	47.2	41.8	30.7
5 and 6 years	96.5	96.7	96.5	94.9
7 to 9 years	99.7	99.7	99.8	99.5
10 to 13 years	99.6	99.7	99.9	99.1
14 and 15 yrs.	99.0	99.0	99.4	99.0
16 and 17 yrs.	92.5	93.5	91.7	85.4
18 and 19 yrs.	57.2	59.1	55.0	44.0
1991				
3 and 4 years	40.5	43.4	36.8	30.1
5 and 6 years	95.4	95.8	95.6	93.0
7 to 9 years	99.6	99.6	99.6	99.5
10 to 13 years	99.7	99.7	100.0	99.3
14 and 15 yrs.	98.8	98.9	99.1	97.3
16 and 17 yrs.	93.3	94.8	91.8	82.6
18 and 19 yrs.	59.6	61.8	55.5	47.9

1 Includes enrollment in any type of graded public, parochial, or other private school in regular schools. Includes nursery schools, kindergartens, elementary schools, high schools, colleges, universities, and professional schools. Attendance may be on either a full-time or part-time basis and during the day or night. Enrollments in "special" schools, such as trade schools, business colleges, or correspondence schools, are not included.

Source: U.S. Department of Commerce, Bureau of the Census, Current Population Survey, and unpublished data. Cited in U.S. Department of Education, National Center for Education Statistics, *Digest of Education Statistics: 1992* (Washington, D.C.: U.S. Government Printing Office, 1991, 1992), p. 16.

due to the education reform movement launched in the early 1980s, during the last decade the average salary, adjusted for inflation, increased 21.6 percent in constant dollars.

A comparison of the salaries of full-time teachers in public and private schools in 1987–88 revealed a number of differences and similarities:[13]

• In both systems, the total earned income of male teachers exceeded that of female teachers, with the average salaries being $32,436 and $26,345 for men and women in public schools, respectively (a 23% difference), and $23,237 and $16,924 for their private counterparts (a 37% difference).

• From the above figures, clearly public school teachers earn more than private school teachers.

• With respect to race, in both public and private schools white teachers earned more than black and Hispanic teachers, while Asian or Pacific Islander teachers earned more than their colleagues of other races. The average salary figures for public and private

Table 5.5

Estimated Average Annual Salary of Teachers in Public Elementary and Secondary Schools, 1959–60 to 1991–92

| School Year | Current Dollars | | | Constant 1990-91 Dollars [1] | | |
	All Teachers	Elementary Teachers	Secondary Teachers	All Teachers	Elementary Teachers	Secondary Teachers
1	2	3	4	5	6	7
1959-60	$4,995	$4,815	$5,276	$23,495	$22,648	$24,817
1961-62	$5,515	$5,340	$5,775	$25,358	$24,554	$26,554
1963-64	$5,995	$5,805	$6,266	$26,865	$26,013	$28,079
1965-66	$6,485	$6,279	$6,761	$28,089	$27,197	$29,285
1967-68	$7,423	$7,208	$7,692	$30,167	$29,293	$31,260
1969-70	$8,626	$8,412	$8,891	$31,560	$30,777	$32,530
1970-71	$9,268	$9,021	$9,568	$32,244	$31,385	$33,288
1971-72	$9,705	$9,424	$10,031	$32,596	$31,652	$33,691
1972-73	$10,174	$9,893	$10,507	$32,847	$31,940	$33,922
1973-74	$10,770	$10,507	$11,077	$31,925	$31,145	$32,835
1974-75	$11,641	$11,334	$12,000	$31,064	$30,245	$32,022
1975-76	$12,600	$12,280	$12,937	$31,401	$30,603	$32,241
1976-77	$13,354	$12,989	$13,776	$31,446	$30,587	$32,440
1977-78	$14,198	$13,845	$14,602	$31,330	$30,551	$32,221
1978-79	$15,032	$14,681	$15,450	$30,329	$29,621	$31,172
1979-80	$15,970	$15,569	$16,459	$28,431	$27,717	$29,302
1980-81	$17,644	$17,230	$18,142	$28,151	$27,490	$28,945
1981-82	$19,274	$18,853	$19,805	$28,306	$27,688	$29,086
1982-83	$20,695	$20,227	$21,291	$29,141	$28,482	$29,981
1983-84	$21,935	$21,487	$22,554	$29,785	$29,177	$30,625
1984-85	$23,600	$23,200	$24,187	$30,839	$30,316	$31,606
1985-86	$25,199	$24,718	$25,846	$32,005	$31,394	$32,827
1986-87	$26,569	$26,051	$27,244	$33,012	$32,369	$33,851
1987-88	$28,034	$27,518	$28,799	$33,447	$32,831	$34,359
1988-89	$29,568	$29,023	$30,229	$33,720	$33,098	$34,473
1989-90	$31,350	$30,806	$32,036	$34,123	$33,531	$34,870
1990-91	$32,977	$32,389	$33,780	$34,034	$33,427	$34,862
1991-92	$34,413	$33,822	$35,217	$34,413	$33,822	$35,217

[1] Based on the Consumer Price Index, prepared by the Bureau of Labor Statistics, U.S. Department of Labor.

Source: National Education Association, *Estimates of School Statistics:* and unpublished data. (Latest edition 1991-92. Copyright 1992 by the National Education Association. All rights reserved.) Cited in U.S. Department of Education, National Center for Education Statistics, *Digest of Education Statistics: 1992,* (Washington, D.C.: U.S. Government Printing Office, 1992), p. 83.

Figure 5.1
Percent Distribution of Public Elementary–Secondary Education Revenue,
1989–90

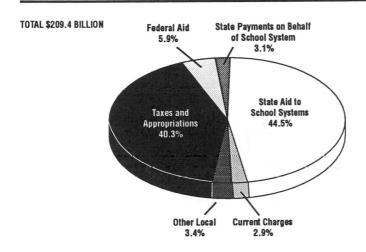

TOTAL $209.4 BILLION

Federal Aid
5.9%

State Payments on Behalf
of School System
3.1%

State Aid to
School Systems
44.5%

Taxes and
Appropriations
40.3%

Other Local
3.4%

Current Charges
2.9%

teachers, respectively, were: white, $28,226 and $18,244; black, $27,786 and $16,774; Hispanic, $27,234 and $18,360; and Asian/Pacific Islander, $30,262 and $24,475.

INTERGOVERNMENTAL TRENDS IN EDUCATION

Public education is the largest function of state and local government and one of the biggest challenges to public officials. In 1989–90, a total of $211.7 billion was spent by the public sector on elementary and secondary education (including current and capital outlays and debt payments), a 9.7 percent increase over the 1988–89 figures.[14] Figures 5.1 and 5.2 depict the division of responsibility for elementary and secondary education, together with a breakdown of the major areas of expenditure by school systems.

The Local Role

Public education has long been considered the most basic local function in all states except Hawaii, where it is a state function. Historically, the system is highly decentralized, with local school districts assuming significant responsibilities for educating America's youth pursuant to broad goals and guidelines dealing with curriculum, achievement standards, and personnel policy, which are established by state government. These local duties include (1) hiring of most teachers and principals; (2) selecting textbooks and teaching materials; (3) advising students on career and personal matters; (4) providing extracurricular activities; (5) maintaining relationships with parents; (6) furnishing nutritional,

Figure 5.2
Percent Distribution of Public Elementary–Secondary Education Expenditures, 1989–90

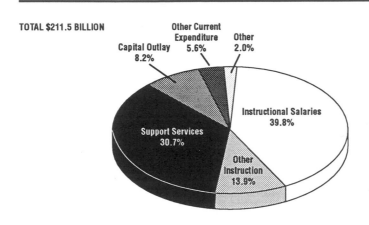

TOTAL $211.5 BILLION

Other Current Expenditure 5.6%

Other 2.0%

Capital Outlay 8.2%

Instructional Salaries 39.8%

Support Services 30.7%

Other Instruction 13.9%

SOURCE: U. S. Department of Commerce, Bureau of the Census, *Public Education Finances:1989–90* (Washington, D.C.: U. S. Government Printing Office, June 1992), p. 8.

health care, and social services; and (7) determining afterschool uses of buildings and facilities.

For many years local property taxes accounted for the lion's share of the revenues needed to sustain and strengthen elementary and secondary education. According to the U.S. Census Bureau, 91 percent of these schools were operated by districts that are administratively and fiscally independent of general-purpose local governments, which has been a reflection of the desire to insulate public education from partisanship and patronage historically associated with local politics. The remainder of these districts are classified as "dependent" systems, since they lack autonomy from county, municipal, town, or township governing bodies.[15]

The twentieth century has witnessed a steady centralization in public education, both horizontally and vertically. At the local level, as shown in Table 5.6, the most significant structural change has been the reduction in the number of school districts, mainly in rural areas, through consolidation. Mergers took place for a variety of reasons, such as rising personnel and administrative costs, declining local tax bases, increased opportunities for economies of scale, transportation improvements, and growing concerns about inequities in per pupil expenditures. In 1937–38, for example, 119,001 school districts were in existence; nearly 60 years later, the number had decreased to 15,358.[16] Some 84,538 public schools were served by these districts, 76 percent of which were elementary and 28

Table 5.6
Public School Districts and Public Elementary and Secondary Schools, 1929–30 to 1990–91

School Year	Public School Districts [1]	Public Schools [2] Total, All Schools [3]	Total, Reg. Schools [4]	Elementary Schools Total	Elementary Schools One-teacher	Secondary Schools
1	2	3	4	5	6	7
1929-30	-	-	-	238,306	149,282	23,930
1937-38	119,001	-	-	221,660	121,178	25,467
1939-40	117,108	-	-	-	113,600	-
1945-46	101,382	-	-	160,027	86,563	24,314
1947-48	94,926	-	-	146,760	75,096	25,484
1949-50	83,718	-	-	128,225	59,652	24,542
1951-52	71,094	-	-	123,763	50,742	23,746
1953-54	63,057	-	-	110,875	42,865	25,637
1955-56	54,859	-	-	104,427	34,964	26,046
1957-58	47,594	-	-	95,446	25,341	25,507
1959-60	40,520	-	-	91,853	20,213	25,784
1961-62	35,676	-	-	81,910	13,333	25,350
1963-64	31,705	-	-	77,584	9,895	26,431
1965-66	26,983	-	-	73,216	6,491	26,597
1967-68	22,010	-	94,197	70,879	4,146	27,011
1970-71	17,995	-	89,372	65,800	1,815	25,352
1973-74	16,730	-	88,655	65,070	1,365	25,906
1975-76	16,376	88,597	87,034	63,242	1,166	25,330
1976-77	16,271	-	86,501	62,644	1,111	25,378
1978-79	16,014	-	84,816	61,982	1,056	24,504
1980-81	15,912	85,982	83,608	61,069	921	24,362
1982-83	15,824	84,740	82,039	59,656	798	23,988
1983-84	15,747	84,178	81,418	59,082	838	23,947
1984-85	-	84,007	81,147	58,827	825	23,916
1985-86	-	-	-	-	-	-
1986-87	[5] 15,713	83,455	82,190	60,784	763	23,389
1987-88	[5] 15,577	83,248	82,248	61,490	729	22,937
1988-89	[5] 15,376	83,165	82,081	61,531	583	22,785
1989-90	[5] 15,367	83,425	82,396	62,037	630	22,639
1990-91	[5] 15,358	84,538	81,746	61,340	617	22,731

[1] Includes operating and nonoperating districts.
[2] Schools with both elementary and secondary programs are included under elementary schools and also under secondary schools.
[3] Includes regular schools and special schools not classified by grade span.
[4] Includes elementary, secondary, and combined elementary/secondary schools.
[5] These data are from sample surveys and should not be compared directly with the data for earlier years.
- Indicates data not available.

Source: U.S. Department of Education, National Center for Education Statistics, *Statistics of State School Systems; Statistics of Public Elementary and Secondary School Systems; Statistics of Nonpublic Elementary and Secondary Schools; Private Schools in American Education,* and Common Core of Data survey. Cited in U.S. Department of Education, National Center for Education Statistics, *Digest of Education Statistics: 1992* (Washington, D.C.: U.S. Printing Office, 1992), 95.

percent were secondary (some were combined schools). The numbers of schools have begun to climb from their historic low of 83,165 in 1988–89.

The State Role

Vertically, the states have gradually assumed a more prominent and pronounced role in education policy and funding. They are now considered the "education watchdogs of our time."[17]

In the colonial period, none of the constitutions of the original 13 states even mentioned education. The Northwest Ordinance of 1787 required territories seeking statehood to provide constitutonally for public education of their citizens. As a result, nowadays virtually all state constitutions guarantee free public education to their citizens. State constitutions specify a "uniform," "thorough," "efficient," or "adequate" system.

Governors and legislators view education as a function critical to the employability of their citizens, to the overall quality of life afforded by their state, and to the ability to attract foreign investment. The states' educational activism grew during the post–World War II period in response to a variety of problems at the local level, including the rapid suburbanization of many areas and need for constructing schools to accommodate the "baby boom" generation. Later, state activism responded to the growth and influence of public employee organizations, concerns about inadequate teacher qualifications, and pressures for desegregation. State policy gradually became more prescriptive and preemptive in virtually all areas of public education.

Fiscal Disparities. Complaints and subsequent litigation over funding inequities inherent in the local property tax–based approach have proved a powerful force behind greater state intervention in recent years. The ability of certain districts to generate substantial revenues for school purposes from taxing residential and commercial property meant that children in other districts were shortchanged, despite frequently higher tax rates in these areas. Other sources of potential inequities besides state aid formulas are contributions to teachers' pension and Social Security funds, which are matched by the state without regard to local district ability to pay, and funding arrangements for capital projects, which are more likely to be undertaken by wealthier systems.

The inequities in spending attributable to variations in taxable wealth were first found unconstitutional by the California Supreme Court in the 1971 *Serrano v. Priest* case, in which plaintiffs argued that the California approach of financing public schools through the property tax system violated the equal protection clause of the Fourteenth Amendment. The court agreed that, despite often higher rates, the low tax bases of poorer districts made it impossible for them to fund public schools at levels comparable to richer districts. Therefore, the state must ensure that education expenditures, and presumably quality, should not be determined by the tax wealth of the school district. Two years later, in *San Antonio Independent School District v. Rodriquez*, the U.S. Supreme Court, in reversing the federal district court's decision and finding that education was not a fundamental right protected by the U.S. Constitution, put the challenge of equalization of fiscal disparities in the constitutional and political realms of the states.

Since that time, the states have risen to the challenge by substantially increasing spending for foundation programs, in order to guarantee a minimum level of educational expenditure for each pupil. In addition, power equalization programs were expanded that "guarantee that each district will have the ability to generate the same revenue per pupil from a given tax rate, regardless of the size of the district's tax base. Each district then determines the local tax rate. If the revenues raised locally from this levy do not amount to the program's guaranteed level, the state provides the difference."[18]

Between 1971 and 1988, 18 state supreme courts decided cases on education fiscal inequities. These cases focused on whether education was a "fundamental right" protected by the Constitution and, if so, whether "absolute equality" of funding was required. Seven state systems were found unconstitutional (California, New Jersey, Connecticut, Washington, Wyoming, West Virginia, and Arkansas). In 1989, three state school financing systems were struck down by the highest court (Montana, Texas, and Kentucky), while Wisconsin's was upheld. In 1990 New Jersey's system was again declared unconstitutional while Oregon's was upheld a year later. In 1992 cases were dismissed in four states— New Hampshire (appealed in 1993), Virginia, Washington, and West Virginia— and one was settled out of court (Indiana). The following year two systems (Tennessee and Massachusetts) were declared unconstitutional. According to the Education Commission of the States, as of June 1993 suits were pending in another 23 states (see Table 5.7).[19]

These recent cases reflect growing dissatisfaction with the actions by legislatures to recognize need in state education spending determinations by taking property values and tax effort into account in establishing foundation programs, rather than simply distributing aid on the basis of number of students in a school district. They also underscore the recognition by plaintiffs that the judicial process is sometimes a more successful way to achieve remedial action than the political process.

Not surprisingly, striking an acceptable balance has proven to be a three-dimensional challenge for state officials. Proponents of local control, many of whom represent wealthier districts, argue that their school systems should be free to spend as much as they wish on the education of their children and not be forced to "level-down" their spending to reduce intrastate disparities in fiscal capacity or effort. At the same time, representatives from poorer districts, which often have relatively more at-risk, educationally disadvantaged, and low-income students, demand to be "leveled-up" by substantial infusions of state funds. In a recession-constrained, antitax environment, governors and legislators have often responded by diverting funds from wealthier to poorer districts, under the watchful eyes of the courts as well as representatives from the affected jurisdictions. In addition, they have sought to ensure that local districts do not use

Table 5.7
Status of School Finance Court Cases, 1973-93

Action by State's Highest Court		Under Court Challenge
Declared Unconstitutional	System Upheld*	
California (1971)	Arizona (1973)	Alaska (1986)
New Jersey (1973, 1990)	Michigan (1973)	Minnesota (1988)
Connecticut (1977)	Idaho (1975)	Alabama (1990, 1991)
Washington (1978)	Oregon (1976,1991)	California (1990)
West Virginia (1979)	Ohio (1979)	Idaho (1990)
Wyoming (1980)	Pennsylvania (1979)	Illinois (1990)
Arkansas (1983)	Georgia (1981)	Missouri (1990)
Kentucky (1989)	Colorado (1982)	Nebraska (1990)
Montana (1989)	New York (1982)	Oklahoma (1990)
Texas (1989)	Maryland (1983)	Arizona (1991)
Tennessee (1993)	Oklahoma (1987)	Kansas (1991, 1992)
Massachusetts (1993)	Wisconsin (1989)	Michigan (1991)
Tennessee (1993)		Montana (1991)
		New Jersey (1991)
		Ohio (1991)
		Pennsylvania (1991)
		Rhode Island (1991)
		South Dakota (1991)
		Louisiana (1992)
		Maine (1992)
		Wyoming (1992)
		New Hampshire (1993)
		North Dakota (1993)

* Case dismissed: Virginia (1992), Washington (1992), West Virginia (1992). Case settled out of court: Indiana (1992).

Source: Elam, S.M., Rose, L.C., Gallup, A.M., "The 23rd Annual Gallup Poll of the Public's Attitudes Toward the Public Schools," *Phi Delta Kappan*, September 1991, p. 52; updated by authors using data from Fulton, M., "States in Which the School Finance System is Currently Being Challenged (and year filed)," Education Commission of the States, June 1993.

state aid increases to reduce their financial commitments to education by imposing local maintenance of effort requirements.

While state actions to promote equality of opportunity through greater horizontal equity in school finance have been significant, albeit prodded by the courts, the impacts in terms of equality of outcomes have not been analyzed until recently. In a paper examining California's experience published in 1992, Professor Thomas A. Downes concluded, "There is no sign that relative increases in funding translated into improved relative performance or that the constraints inherent in the finance reforms altered the relative standing of high wealth districts."[20]

The "Adequacy" Factor. An April 1993 decision by an Alabama state court ruling that the school system was unconstitutional because it failed to give students an "adequate" education may lead to additional judicial challenges on this ground as well as on inequities stemming from fiscal disparities. School systems with high dropout and violence rates, insufficient instructional materials and low quality teachers, physical facilities that are in disrepair or dangerous, students who perform poorly on academic competency or skill achievement tests, and other demonstrated indicators of inadequate performance may, depending on the severity of these conditions, be in violation of students' constitutional or statutory rights.[21]

Expenditure Trends. As a consequence of these trends, the states' financial involvement in elementary and secondary education has greatly expanded. As indicated in Table 5.8, over the 30-year period from 1959–60 to 1989–90, the states' share of public school district funds increased from 39.1 percent to 47.2 percent, while the local portion decreased from 56.5 percent to 46.6 percent (see also Appendix 5.A). In dollar terms, in 1989–90, state expenditures for elementary and secondary education amounted to $98.1 billion, compared with $96.8 billion from local sources. Beginning in the late 1980s the state proportion of total school funding decreased slightly, while that of local jurisdictions increased.[22]

Public education is the largest component of state and local budgets with per pupil expenditures, adjusted for inflation, averaging 4 percent growth a year from 1959–60 to 1986 87.[23] As shown in Table 5.9, in 1992–93, an estimated $6,285 was spent on each student in average daily attendance in public elementary and secondary schools.

Spending varies greatly from state to state and within districts in a state in different ways (Appendix 5.B reveals the interstate differences). Per pupil expenditures in 1989–90 ranged from highs in the District of Columbia ($8,904), Alaska ($8,374), New York ($8,062), New Jersey ($7,991), and Connecticut ($7,604) to lows in Utah ($2,730), Idaho ($3,078), Mississippi ($3,096), Alabama ($3,327), and Arkansas ($3,485). Research by some school finance experts, such as Deborah Verstegen, has found a strong linkage between the amounts of federal aid received and state own-source school expenditures, raising concerns that existing formulas exacerbate disparities between wealthy and poor states. States with relatively large low-income and minority student populations may be adversely affected.[24]

The Federal Role

National involvement in public education is more than 200 years old. As noted earlier, the Northwest Ordinance of 1787 made federally-held land available to states for public schools. In percentage and dollar terms, the federal role in elementary and secondary education has been relatively small—accounting for $14.1 billion or about 6 percent of total revenues in 1993. Federal spending in this area has grown about 11 percent since 1980, adjusted for inflation, but the total share from this source has not exceeded 10 percent.[25]

According to the U.S. Advisory Commission on Intergovernmental Relations

Table 5.8
Revenues for Public Elementary and Secondary Schools, by Source of Funds, 1919–20 to 1989–90

| School Year | Total | In Thousands | | | Percentage Distribution | | | |
| | | Federal | State | Local [1] | Total | Federal | State | Local [1] |
1	2	3	4	5	6	7	8	9
1919-20	$970,121	$2,475	$160,085	$807,561	100.0	0.3	16.5	83.2
1929-30	$2,088,557	$7,334	$353,670	$1,727,553	100.0	0.4	16.9	82.7
1939-40	$2,260,527	$39,810	$684,354	$1,536,363	100.0	1.8	30.3	68.0
1941-42	$2,416,580	$34,305	$759,993	$1,622,281	100.0	1.4	31.4	67.1
1943-44	$2,604,322	$35,886	$859,183	$1,709,253	100.0	1.4	33.0	65.6
1945-46	$3,059,845	$41,378	$1,062,057	$1,956,409	100.0	1.4	34.7	63.9
1947-48	$4,311,534	$120,270	$1,676,362	$2,514,902	100.0	2.8	38.9	58.3
1949-50	$5,437,044	$155,848	$2,165,689	$3,115,507	100.0	2.9	39.8	57.3
1951-52	$6,423,816	$227,711	$2,478,596	$3,717,507	100.0	3.5	38.6	57.9
1953-54	$7,866,852	$335,237	$2,944,103	$4,567,512	100.0	4.5	37.4	58.1
1955-56	$9,686,677	$441,442	$3,828,886	$5,416,350	100.0	4.6	39.5	55.9
1957-58	$12,181,513	$486,484	$4,800,368	$6,894,661	100.0	4.0	39.4	56.6
1959-60	$14,746,618	$651,639	$5,768,047	$8,326,932	100.0	4.4	39.1	56.5
1961-62	$17,527,707	$760,975	$6,789,190	$9,977,542	100.0	4.3	38.7	56.9
1963-64	$20,544,182	$896,956	$8,078,014	$11,569,213	100.0	4.4	39.3	56.3
1965-66	$25,356,858	$1,996,954	$9,920,219	$13,439,686	100.0	7.9	39.1	53.0
1967-68	$31,903,064	$2,806,469	$12,275,536	$16,821,063	100.0	8.8	38.5	52.7
1969-70	$40,266,923	$3,219,557	$16,062,776	$20,984,589	100.0	8.0	39.9	52.1
1970-71	$44,511,292	$3,753,461	$17,409,086	$23,348,745	100.0	8.4	39.1	52.5
1971-72	$50,003,645	$4,467,969	$19,133,256	$26,402,420	100.0	8.9	38.3	52.8

1972-73	$52,117,930	$20,843,520	$4,525,000	$26,749,412	100.0	8.7	40.0	51.3
1973-74	$58,230,892	$24,113,409	$4,930,351	$29,187,132	100.0	8.5	41.4	50.1
1974-75	$64,445,239	$27,211,116	$5,811,595	$31,422,528	100.0	9.0	42.2	48.8
1975-76	$71,206,073	$31,776,101	$6,318,345	$33,111,627	100.0	8.9	44.6	46.5
1976-77	$75,322,532	$32,688,903	$6,629,498	$36,004,134	100.0	8.8	43.4	47.8
1977-78	$81,443,160	$35,013,266	$7,694,194	$38,735,700	100.0	9.4	43.0	47.6
1978-79	$87,994,143	$40,132,136	$8,600,116	$39,261,891	100.0	9.8	45.6	44.6
1979-80	$96,881,165	$45,348,814	$9,503,537	$42,028,813	100.0	9.8	46.8	43.4
1980-81	$105,949,087	$50,182,659	$9,768,262	$45,998,166	100.0	9.2	47.4	43.4
1981-82	$110,191,257	$52,436,435	$8,186,466	$49,568,356	100.0	7.4	47.6	45.0
1982-83	$117,497,502	$56,282,157	$8,339,990	$52,875,354	100.0	7.1	47.9	45.0
1983-84	$126,055,419	$60,232,981	$8,576,547	$57,245,892	100.0	6.8	47.8	45.4
1984-85	$137,294,678	$67,168,684	$9,105,569	$61,020,425	100.0	6.6	48.9	44.4
1985-86	$149,127,779	$73,619,575	$9,975,622	$65,532,582	100.0	6.7	49.4	43.9
1986-87	$158,523,693	$78,830,437	$10,146,013	$69,547,243	100.0	6.4	49.7	43.9
1987-88 [2]	$169,561,974	$84,004,415	$10,716,687	$74,840,873	100.0	6.3	49.5	44.1
1988-89	$192,016,374	$91,768,911	$11,902,001	$88,345,462	100.0	6.2	47.8	46.0
1989-90	$207,583,910	$98,059,659	$12,750,530	$96,773,720	100.0	6.1	47.2	46.6

[1] (including intermediate) Includes a relatively small amount from nongovernmental sources (gifts and tuition and transportation fees from patrons). These sources accounted for 0.4 percent of total revenues in 1967-68.

[2] Revised from previously published figures.

Source: U.S. Department of Education, National Center for Education Statistics: *Statistics of State School Systems; Revenues and Expenditures for Public Elementary and Secondary Education*; and Common Core of Data survey. Cited in U.S. Department of Education, National Center for Education Statistics, *Digest of Education Statistics: 1992* (Washington, D.C.: U.S. Government Printing Office, 1992), p. 150.

Table 5.9
Total and Current Expenditures per Pupil in Public Elementary and Secondary Schools, 1959–60 to 1992–93

| | Expenditures Per Pupil in Average Daily Attendance | | | |
| | Unadjusted Dollars | | Constant 1990-1991 Dollars [1] | |
School Year	Total Expenditure	Current Expenditure	Total Expenditure	Current Expenditure
1959-60	471	375	2,216	1,765
1961-62	517	419	2,387	1,927
1963-64	559	460	2,504	2,063
1965-66	654	538	2,832	2,329
1967-68	786	658	3,196	2,675
1969-70	955	816	3,494	2,985
1970-71	1,049	911	3,651	3,170
1971-72	1,128	990	3,788	3,324
1972-73	1,211	1,077	3,908	3,477
1973-74	1,364	1,207	4,043	3,578
1974-75	1,545	1,365	4,122	3,641
1975-76	1,697	1,504	4,230	3,747
1976-77	1,816	1,638	4,277	3,856
1977-78	2,002	1,823	4,419	4,022
1978-79	2,210	2,020	4,459	4,077
1979-80	2,491	2,272	4,434	4,044
1980-81	2,742[2]	2,502	4,375[2]	3,991
1981-82	2,973[2]	2,726	4,367[2]	4,003
1982-83	3,203[2]	2,955	4,511[2]	4,161
1983-84	3,471[2]	3,173	4,714[2]	4,309
1984-85	3,722[2]	3,470	4,863[2]	4,535
1985-86	4,020[2]	3,756	5,106[2]	4,770
1986-87	4,308[2]	3,970	5,353[2]	4,933
1987-88	4,654[2]	4,240	5,553[2]	5,059
1988-89	5,109	4,645	5,827	5,297
1989-90	5,526	4,960	6,015	5,399
1990-91	5,841[2]	5,243[2]	6,028[2]	5,411[2]
1991-92	6,094[2]	5,470[2]	6,094[2]	5,470[2]
1992-93	6,285[2]	5,641[2]	6,043[2]	5,424[2]

[1] Based on the Consumer Price Index, prepared by the Bureau of Labor Statistics, U.S. Department of Labor, adjusted to a school year basis.
[2] Estimated.

Source: U.S. Department of Education, National Center for Education Statistics, *Statistics of State School Systems; Revenues and Expenditures for Public Elementary and Secondary Education:* and Common Core of Data survey. Cited in U.S. Department of EducationNational Center for Education Statistics, *Digest of Education Statistics: 1992,* (Washington, D.C.: U.S. Government Printing Office, 1992), p. 159.

(ACIR), in 1991 there were 125 categorical grants serving a wide range of education purposes and clienteles and administered by a number of agencies including the Departments of Education, Health and Human Services, Agriculture, Defense, Labor, Energy, Veteran Affairs, the National Science Foundation, and the National Aeronautics and Space Administration. The U.S. Congressional

Budget Office (CBO) estimates that the main purpose of 70 percent of federal educational aid is promotion of equal opportunity, even though there has never been "an overall plan or a consistent philosophy" linking the various federal programs.[26]

The national government's financial contribution to public education is expected not to grow substantially despite the commitment of the Clinton administration and members of Congress to many existing federal programs as well as to new initiatives to attain the national educational goals and improve the skills and employability of the current work force and student body. Significant long-term constraints are imposed by the need to reduce the budget deficit while at the same time respond to pressures for increased assistance on other domestic fronts such as health care, AIDS, drug abuse prevention, homelessness, infrastructure, natural disaster relief, and the environment. Chapter 7 reviews options for refining the national government's role in view of both federal budget constraints and the states' record on the school reform front.

Despite its relatively modest financial contribution, the federal government's impact has been significant, in at least six ways:

1. The federal government has funded a number of programs designed to help overcome some of the deterrents to learning experienced by low-income, minority, and handicapped children. Many of these educationally disadvantaged students attend central city school systems. The Head Start preschool program, which was launched in the 1960s as part of President Lyndon B. Johnson's "War on Poverty," has been a popular and somewhat effective instrument. Head Start has become an established and expanding enterprise under subsequent Republican and Democratic presidents, amounting to $2.8 billion in 1993. About 700,000 3- to 5-year-old children were enrolled in 36,000 Head Start classrooms by the early 1990s, only one of three who were eligible. Over 90 percent of the children come from families living below the poverty level, and 10 percent are handicapped. In addition to classroom instruction, children receive breakfast and lunch, health need assessments, eye examinations, and immunizations.[27] A second Great Society program is the Job Corps, in which 62,000 students from poor families are enrolled (about 5% of the 16- to 21-year-olds who are eligible). Participants receive education and training to help prepare them for employment.

The major federal initiative to provide remedial education to disadvantaged children has been Title I of the 1965 Elementary and Secondary Education Act (now Chapter 1 of the Augustus F. Hawkins–Robert T. Stafford Elementary and Secondary School Improvement Amendments of 1988), with annual appropriations over $6.8 billion. Grants are made based on a formula that recognizes the number of low-income children in an area. Funds may be used to provide compensatory or supplemental services to eligible children like teachers' aides, remedial or specialized classes in reading, mathematics, and other subjects in which students are performing significantly below grade level, and individualized instruction opportunities. CBO estimates that over 5 million educationally deprived, disabled, neglected, delinquent, or migrant children received Chapter 1–supported services in 1992.[28]

Other noteworthy federal programs designed to promote equal educational opportunity include special education, bilingual education, and Indian education. According to the National Center for Education Statistics, in 1989–90, 384,204 children 3- to 5-years-old were served by the 1975 Education of the Handicapped Act (now the Individuals with Disabilities Education Act). Since the act was amended by Congress in 1986 to give the right of a "free and appropriate" education to handicapped children in this age group, the number of participants nationally has increased almost 21 percent. Moreover, in 1989–90, some 4.6 million children aged 0 to 21 years were served by federally aided special education programs. Of these students, 44 percent were learning disabled, 21 percent were speech impaired, 12 percent were mentally retarded, and 8 percent were seriously emotionally disturbed.[29]

A listing of 12 federal children's programs—ranging from Women, Infants, and Children (WIC), Prenatal Care, and Medicaid to Lead Screening, Smoking Cessation for Pregnant Women, and Home Visiting—appears in Appendix 5.C. In the judgment of the Democratic majority of the Select Committee on Children, Youth, and Families of the U.S. Congress, these programs have proven cost-effective. (The 11-member Republican minority, it should be noted, issued a statement contending that the committee's study had not evaluated the effectiveness and efficiency of these programs or the "nonsystem" of public child health and welfare of which they are a part. According to the minority members, in oversimplifying and overstating the benefits, "this Report is a goal-line defense of the programmatic status quo. It fails to objectively identify the deficiencies of the programs as they relate to the overall social welfare system."[30]

2. Federal judicial decisions, beginning with the 1954 landmark case *Brown v. Board of Education of Topeka*, in which the Supreme Court struck down racial segregation in public schools as violating the 14th amendment's equal protection clause, and the 1971 *Swann v. Charlotte-Mecklenberg County Schools* (North Carolina), which approved court-ordered busing of students in order to achieve school desegregation, have extended the national government's "presence" in the policies and practices of school systems across the country, especially as they relate to the rights of ethnic minorities. Congressional enactments like the Civil Rights Act of 1964 also have had a significant impact on state and local education authorities. These judicial and legislative decisions have dealt with issues of equity in education, such as the rights of the handicapped, student discipline policy, spending on students enrolled in poor school districts, female athletes, and limited English–speaking students.

3. Federal regulations attached to grant-in-aid programs have produced a considerable effect on local schools. Many of these mandates deal with environmental, health, and safety matters, and include exposure to lead contamination, radon, asbestos, poor indoor air quality, hazardous waste, and leaking

underground storage tanks. Other requirements cover such diverse matters as handicapped access to school facilities, bilingual education offerings, and women's athletics programs. These and other "social regulations" attached to the receipt of federal educational aid, have altered school district priorities and often imposed uncompensated costs.[31]

4. In addition to the key roles the federal government has played in promoting equal opportunity and leveraging compliance with national social policy and minimum standards through grant-in-aid and regulatory policy, since the 1950s it has stimulated and supported state and local reform efforts and special emphasis programs. Chapter 2 of Title 1 of ESEA, for example, consolidated more than 30 categorical programs into a block grant, the 1982 Federal, State, and Local Partnership for Educational Improvement. In 1993 state and local education authorities received $474 million to undertake a broad spectrum of elementary and secondary school improvements such as curriculum updating, increased student support services, and instructional enhancements. Consistent with the block grant philosophy, recipients are accorded considerable latitude as to determining priorities and designing programs to carry them out. With respect to special emphasis programs, the Drug-Free Schools and Communities Act of 1986 supports school-based drug education and prevention programs and personnel, which in 1993 reached 95 percent of the public elementary and secondary students. Funding for that year was $598 million.[32]

5. A fifth major area of federal involvement has been funding programs to promote educational preparation for employability. These efforts include adult and vocational education programs totaling $1.48 billion in 1993, which is about 10 percent of federal elementary and secondary education related spending. Chief among these are the Carl D. Perkins Vocational and Applied Technology Education Act, which provides funds to support state efforts to enhance occupationally specific instruction and to develop marketable skills, especially for those who have experienced difficulty entering the workplace, and the Adult Education Act, which provides funds to promote adult literacy, high school completion, and employment-related training.[33]

6. The sixth important federal role is presidential leadership, what President Theodore Roosevelt called the "bully pulpit." Most presidents since Washington have had strong views on public education and in modern times proposed programs to carry them out. President Ronald Reagan's secretary of Education, Terrel Bell, established the National Commission on Excellence in Education, and when its report attracted critical acclaim, President Reagan embraced some of its thrust. The 1983 report, which will be considered later in this chapter, launched three significant waves of education reform efforts led by the states. More recently, President George Bush campaigned as the "Education President." His historic September 1989 summit with the nation's governors at the University of Virginia in Charlottesville led to a joint agreement to pursue vigorously six national educational goals and to develop a strategy, "America 2000," to facilitate their implementation. While neither the Reagan nor Bush

administrations provided much new money, a national debate was triggered over how the quality of the nation's public schools could be raised so as to prepare students better for entry into the work force.

President Clinton's education agenda includes calls for a $9 billion funding increase for Head Start over five years to allow all eligible underprivileged children to participate, extend the program from a half-day to a full day and from 9 to 12 months, raise teachers' and teachers' aides' salaries, and improve facilities. As discussed later, the administration has also encouraged employers to spend 1.5 percent of their payroll on worker training and education, supported public school choice and national goals and assessment standards for public education, called for increased federal funding for school security devices, and proposed creation of a national community service program.

In summary, the preceding discussion reveals four significant recent trends: growth in the number of students enrolled in public elementary and secondary schools in the 1990s; continued variation and diversity in per pupil spending on both interstate and substate bases; greater centralization of financial and policy responsibility at the state level; and increased federal leadership (and rhetoric) despite diminished funding. The next section addresses the impact of these trends in the delivery and financing of education in terms of concerns about the output of public elementary and secondary schools during the past two decades.

A NATION AT RISK

The significance of state and local educational spending and size of the public sector work force involved in elementary and secondary teaching, advising, and administration have raised public awareness concerning the return on this substantial investment. Unfortunately, the results have not been impressive; in fact, for some time a consensus has existed among a large and diverse group of educators, employers, elected officials, students, and parents that the public schools are failing in their responsibility for preparing our nation's youth to enter the work force. For example:

- From *Fortune* magazine: "The main challenge confronting state school administrators in the Nineties is still the need to prepare students for jobs. By that measure, virtually all are flunking."[34]

- From the Committee for Economic Development: "One of the weak links in the American system of human capital investment is the connection between school and work. In contrast with their peers abroad, American high school students frequently do not have good job skills and are left to fend for themselves in the job market."[35]

- From former New Mexico governor Garrey Carruthers, 1989–90 chairman of the Education Commission of the States: "How far behind are we? If education had progressed like the computer industry, kindergarten through college would take 10 minutes and cost five cents."[36]

- From Jack Foster, Kentucky's former secretary of Education: "Unless we make fundamental changes, we as a nation are not going to make it. We don't have time to tinker around the edges anymore."[37]

- From a February 1990 ABC News poll: "Eighty-one percent of a nationally polled sample agreed the United States must do something radical to improve education or the nation will turn into a second-rate power. Almost 90% agreed that America's children will have to be educated in new and very different ways to succeed in the next century. Only 6% believed their local schools were excellent, while nearly three times as many said their schools were poor. The rest thought they were just adequate. And yet, these same people did not think education was in crisis. They pointed to many other social problems, such as hunger, drugs, and the budget deficit, as more important."[38]

A significant crossroad in the debate over to what extent the nation's public elementary and secondary schools needed revamping and what the nature of restructuring should be was the landmark report *A Nation at Risk: The Imperative for Educational Reform*, by the National Commission on Excellence in Education. The nonpartisan, 18-member "blue-ribbon" body included representatives from the education community, public officials, and the private sector. It was chaired by David P. Gardner, president of the University of California. Interestingly, only one teacher—Jay M. Sommer, a 25-year foreign language instructor at New Rochelle High School in New York and 1981 National Teacher of the Year—was included among the membership. Created in August 1981 by President Reagan's secretary of Education, Terrel H. Bell, in response to "the widespread public perception that something is seriously remiss in our educational system,"[39] the commission's charge included:

- assessing the quality of teaching and learning in our Nation's public and private schools, colleges, and universities;
- comparing American schools and colleges with those of other advanced nations;
- studying the relationship between college admissions requirements and student achievement in high school;
- identifying educational programs which result in notable student success in college;
- assessing the degree to which major social and educational changes in the last quarter century have affected student achievement; and
- defining problems which must be faced and overcome if we are successfully to pursue the course of excellence in education.[40]

Previous Reform Efforts

The National Commission was not the first, nor would it be the last, significant effort to examine the public elementary and secondary education system and recommend improvements. The post–World War II general mood of confidence and complacency about the caliber and output of public schools ended dramatically with the launching of Sputnik in 1957. Prominent public officials like Admiral Hyman Rickover claimed that America had fallen badly behind the Russians in educating students in science, mathematics, foreign languages, and engineering and in preparing them to contribute to the cold war and to bolster the nation's international economic competitiveness. As Professor Diane Ravitch observed, "For the first time since the end of World War II, people of all political backgrounds agreed that the national interest depended on improving the quality of America's schools. . . . Sputnik came to be a symbol of the consequences of indifference to high standards."[41]

Not surprisingly, the initial responses to Sputnik were establishment of a federal aid program and release of an avalanche of reports funded by foundations and the federal government. The year after Sputnik, for example, Congress passed the National Defense Education Act, which authorized fellowships and low interest loans to able students for graduate and undergraduate studies. The act also provided funds for colleges and secondary schools to strengthen curricula and instruction in subject areas deemed essential to the nation's defense, such as science, mathematics, and foreign language.

With respect to research, in 1958 the Rockefeller Brothers Fund issued *The Pursuit of Excellence*, authored by John Gardner, president of the Carnegie Foundation for the Advancement of Teaching. The report "made nothing happen, but it accurately reflected hopes for the renewal of American society through the infusion of higher educational aspirations."[42] A year later, James B. Conant's *The American High School Today* was released by the Carnegie Corporation. The report called for establishment of "comprehensive" high schools to serve the general educational needs of all youth, to offer nonacademic courses such as vocational education to those who were not going on to college, and to provide advanced courses in science, languages, and mathematics. The Ford Foundation and National Science Foundation also joined the debate over educational quality, funding curriculum revision efforts aimed at substituting "discovery" for "lecturing," model school district reforms in central cities, innovative teaching techniques, and special programs for gifted and talented students as well as those in need of compensatory and remedial programs.

The pursuit of educational improvement along these lines was stalled by the social and racial upheavals of the 1960s. Public schools were engulfed by the turbulent reactions to the assassinations of President John F. Kennedy, Rev. Martin Luther King, and Senator Robert Kennedy; the Vietnam War; the urban crisis; unrest on college campuses; and the advent of protest politics. The response to the cold war was displaced by the response to racial and economic injustice.

The urgency and volatility of these social and political trends placed considerable stress on the education system. Instead of focusing on curriculum improvements geared to the college-bound, public schools in many communities were confronted by demands for citizen control of school boards and neighborhood decentralization of school districts, use of nonracially biased tests, hiring of teachers and principals who reflected the ethnic composition of the community served by the school, establishment of courses aimed at instilling greater awareness of cultural history and racial identity, and adoption of open admissions policies and "alternative schools" approaches to foster experimentation in instructional methods and goals. (As discussed in the next chapter, three decades later similar demands were voiced, particularly with respect to inner-city and urban school systems.) Ravitch has explained the perceptions of public schools at the time that gave rise to these and other demands:

The indictment of the school was overwhelming. In the eyes of the critics, the school destroyed the souls of children, whether black or white, middle-class or poor. It coerced unwilling youths to sit through hours of stultifying classes, breaking their spirits before turning them out as either rebellious misfits or conforming cogs in the great industrial machine. It neglected the needs of individuals while slighting the history and culture of diverse minorities. It clung to a boring, irrelevant curriculum and to methods that obliterated whatever curiosity children brought with them. It drove away creative teachers and gave tenure to petty martinets. For those who agreed with the critics, there was no alternative other than to change the schools or to abandon them.[43]

Like the response to Sputnik, the challenges confronting society and schools in the 1960s were met by a multitude of reports and experimental programs, many of which were sponsored by foundations and the federal government.

The underlying assumptions in the various approaches were, first, that there was little in the schools worth preserving; second, that anything innovative was bound to be better than whatever it replaced; third, that the pathology of the schools was so grave that the only change worth attempting must be of a fundamental, institutional, systemic kind; and fourth, that the way to change society and to turn it against war and racism was to change (or abandon) the schools.[44]

While there was considerable rhetoric associated with the remedial efforts, there also were concrete actions taken, largely by the Johnson administration and the courts. In 1965 alone, Congress enacted the Elementary and Secondary Education Act, which targeted federal aid on poor children and inner-city schools (Title I) and provided funds to school districts for undertaking innovative projects (Title III), established the Teacher Corps to encourage careers in teaching, and created Operation Head Start, noted earlier, to provide preschool educational, nutritional, and health assistance to disadvantaged children. At the same time, the federal courts began ordering busing of students to help break down economic barriers to quality education stemming from central city-suburban fiscal disparities and to promote racial integration of schools, at the risk of accelerating white flight to the suburbs and severance of neighborhood-school linkages.

This federal leadership role continued well past the Great Society. The Nixon administration, for instance, proposed an Experimental Schools Program, National Institute of Education, and Better Schools block grant which sought, respectively, to encourage innovations in curriculum design, increase research and dissemination of results, and give greater program flexibility to local school districts. Congress passed the Bilingual Education Act of 1968, the Rehabilitation Act of 1973, and the Education for All Handicapped Children Act of 1975. The growing federal financial role was accompanied by a stronger regulatory presence, especially as a result of Title VI of the Civil Rights Act of 1964, which authorized federal officials to withhold or withdraw funds if they were being used by recipients for discriminatory purposes.

The cumulative indicators of these developments in terms of the federal government's role in public education have been pointed out by Ravitch:[45]

- the number of pages of federal legislation relating to education grew from 80 to 360 between 1964 and 1976;
- the number of federal regulations concerning education grew from 92 to nearly 1,000 between 1965 and 1977; and
- the number of federal court decisions impacting on education grew from 729 to over 1,200 between 1966 and 1970.

Yet, despite the activism at the national level, few would disagree that the quality of public education was mainly a state and local responsibility. The 1972 report by the President's Commission on School Finance, which was appointed by President Richard Nixon to assess revenue needs and resources of both public and private elementary and secondary schools, underscored the preeminent state role in raising and allocating funds and evaluating results and the preeminent local board of education role in running school systems. At the same time, the commission recognized the federal government's key facilitative role:

The commission recommends that the Federal role in elementary and secondary education embrace the following major functions: (a) providing leadership in educational reform through research, evaluation and demonstration activities; (b) stimulating State and local public and private activity to meet national concerns and interest and, where necessary, providing continuing financial support; (c) providing incentives and mechanisms designed to more nearly equalize resources among the States for elementary and secondary education and (d) serving as a center for collection, evaluation and publication of educational data. In brief, the Commission sees the Federal Government performing a leadership and pioneering role in long-range educational policy, but only a supplementary role to the States in the financing of school capital and operating costs.[46]

With respect to the effects of these trends on the public schools, by the end of the 1970s teachers, principals, administrators, curriculum planners, and students were struggling to design and implement educational programs at the elementary and secondary levels amid a variety of divergent and sometimes conflicting forces, such as:

- curricula that included a "smorgasbord" of college preparatory, general studies, and vocational education courses together with special-emphasis classes in black and women's history and remedial or compensatory learning and such electives as sex, consumer, career, driver, or drug education;

- school boards on which parents played an aggressive and sometimes accusatory role vis-à-vis teachers and principals over volatile issues such as busing;

- instructional programs geared to bilingual considerations;

- classrooms where students having learning, physical, and mental disabilities were "mainstreamed" with other students;

- schools where racial and economic tensions created volatile environments demanding discipline rather than nurturing learning; and

- teachers who felt they were unappreciated and underpaid and who were often unqualified or unprepared to deal with the nontraditional school learning environment and expectations as to their growing noninstructional roles.

The interplay of the racial, political, and economic forces that dominated and divided American society during the 1960s and 1970s with school systems that had been largely impervious to significant change produced frustrations over performance and calls for reform that came to a head in the early 1980s. With the establishment of the National Commission on Excellence in Education, the stage was set for another campaign in what Diane Ravitch called "the troubled crusade," launched by mounting concerns about the nation's international economic competitiveness. Although some two dozen committees or task forces were already at work at that time, Secretary Bell succeeded through the commission's work (and despite the Reagan administration's threats to abolish the Department of Education) to focus national attention on education.

The Commission's Findings

In 1983, the commission released its report to the secretary, the president, and the nation. Concluding that "our nation is at risk" and America's once-preeminent position in commerce, industry, science, and technology was being challenged and overtaken by other nations, the commission pinpointed the educational system as a major cause of this decline:

We report to the American people that while we can take justifiable pride in what our schools and colleges have historically accomplished and contributed to the United States and the well-being of its people, the educational foundations of our society are presently being eroded by a rising tide of mediocrity that threatens our very future as a Nation and a people. What was unimaginable a generation ago has begun to occur—others are matching and surpassing our educational attainments.

If an unfriendly foreign power had attempted to impose on America the mediocre educational performance that exists today, we might well have viewed it as an act of war. As it stands, we have allowed this to happen to ourselves. We have even squandered the gains in student achievement made in the wake of the Sputnik challenge. Moreover, we have dismantled essential support systems which helped make those gains possible.

We have, in effect, been committing an act of unthinking, unilateral educational disarmament.

Our society and its educational institutions seem to have lost sight of the basic purposes of schooling, and of the high expectations and disciplined effort needed to attain them.[47]

The commission's research and public hearings across the country found ample evidence of the "rising tide of mediocrity." For example:[48]

- On 19 academic tests American students were never first or second and were last seven times compared with their counterparts in other industrialized countries.
- Some 23 million American adults were functionally illiterate in reading, writing, and comprehension skills, including about 13 percent of all 17-year-olds and as many as 40 percent of minority youth.
- Average high school student achievement scores on most standardized tests were lower than when Sputnik was launched.
- The tested ability of over half of gifted students fell below their actual achievement.
- Many 17-year-olds lacked "higher-order" intellectual skills, such as drawing inferences from written material (40% could not do so); writing a persuasive essay (80% could not do so); and solving a mathematics problem requiring several steps (two-thirds could not do so).
- Remedial mathematics courses in public four-year-colleges increased by 72 percent and comprised 25 percent of all mathematics courses taught in such institutions.
- The Department of the Navy reported that one-quarter of its recruits could not read at the ninth grade level, the minimum needed to comprehend written safety instructions.

SAT Scores. A major area of dismay to members of the commission was declining student performance on the College Board's Scholastic Aptitude Tests (SAT). As discussed in chapter 6, SAT scores continue to be cause for concern, if not alarm.

As shown in Table 5.10, from 1969–70 until the early 1980s, the verbal and mathematical scores of college-bound male and female seniors steadily dropped. With only two exceptions (verbal scores in 1969–70 and 1970–71), the scores of females on these tests fell below those of males every year from 1969 to 1983. The gap is particularly noticeable for mathematics scores, averaging 47 points over that 14-year period.

The scores of white students in particular had remained basically flat since 1979. On the other hand, the average scores registered by black youth had increased by nine points for both verbal and mathematics by 1982–83. For Mexican-American (Hispanic) students, the score increases were three points and four points, respectively. Despite these increases, the minority averages were still well below the national figures for each year (see Table 5.11).

The scores in mathematics and science were of particular concern to the commission members and others, since these had been considered since Sputnik as subjects warranting greater emphasis. Yet, the SAT averages were far from

Table 5.10
Scholastic Aptitude Test Score Averages for U.S. College-Bound High School Seniors, by Sex, 1969–70 to 1990–91

School Year	Verbal Score				Mathematical Score			
	Total	Male	Female	Diff.	Total	Male	Female	Diff.
1	2	3	4	5	6	7	8	9
1969-70	460	459	461	-2	488	509	465	44
1970-71	455	454	457	-3	488	507	466	41
1971-72	453	454	452	2	484	505	461	44
1972-73	445	446	443	3	481	502	460	42
1973-74	444	447	442	5	480	501	459	42
1974-75	434	437	431	6	472	495	449	46
1975-76	431	433	430	3	472	497	446	51
1976-77	429	431	427	4	470	497	445	52
1977-78	429	433	425	8	468	494	444	50
1978-79	427	431	423	8	467	493	443	50
1979-80	424	428	420	8	466	491	443	48
1980-81	424	430	418	12	466	492	443	49
1981-82	426	431	421	10	467	493	443	50
1982-83	425	430	420	10	468	493	445	48
1983-84	426	433	420	13	471	495	449	46
1984-85	431	437	425	12	475	499	452	47
1985-86	431	437	426	11	475	501	451	50
1986-87	430	435	425	10	476	500	453	47
1987-88	428	435	422	13	476	498	455	43
1988-89	427	434	421	13	476	500	454	46
1989-90	424	429	419	+10	476	499	455	+44
1990-91	422	426	418	+8	474	497	453	+44

Source: College Entrance Examination Board, *National Report on College-Bound Seniors*, various years. (Copyright 1991 by the College Entrance Examination Board. All rights reserved.) Cited in U.S. Department of Education, National Center for Education Statistics, *Digest of Education Statistics: 1992* (Washington, D.C.: U.S. Government Printing Office, October, 1992), p. 125. Statistics on male-female score differences calculated by authors.

encouraging. With respect to mathematics questions, the averages of participants correctly answering questions had increased by 1 percent (to 56.4%) for 9-year-olds and nearly 4 percent (to 60.5%) for 13-year-olds between 1977–78 and 1981–82 but had decreased slightly (0.2%) for 17-year-olds (to 60.2%). Again, while their scores in these areas had improved somewhat over the years, the performance of blacks and Hispanics lagged significantly behind that of white students in all age categories.[49]

With respect to science proficiency, similar results were evident. The average scores for 17-year-olds had declined in each of the three assessment areas—content; inquiry; science, technology, and society (−0.5%)—between 1976–77 and 1981–82. A smaller decrease was evident for 13-year-olds—(−0.4%, −0.5%, and 0.6%, respectively)—while 9-year-olds had registered improve-

Table 5.11
U.S. Scholastic Aptitude Test Score Averages, by Race/Ethnicity, 1979–80 to 1990–91

Racial/Ethnic Background	1979-80	1980-81	1981-82	1982-83	1983-84	1984-85	1986-87	1987-88	1988-89	1989-90	1990-91
SAT - Verbal											
All Students	424	424	426	425	426	431	430	428	427	424	422
White	442	442	444	443	445	449	447	445	446	442	441
Black	330	332	341	339	342	346	351	353	351	352	351
Mexican-American	372	373	377	375	376	382	379	382	381	380	377
Puerto Rican	350	353	360	358	358	368	360	355	360	359	361
Asian-American	396	397	398	395	398	404	405	408	409	410	411
American Indian	390	391	388	388	390	392	393	393	384	388	393
Other	394	388	392	386	388	391	405	410	414	410	411
SAT - Mathematical											
All Students	466	466	467	468	471	475	476	476	476	476	474
White	482	483	483	484	487	490	489	490	491	491	489
Black	360	362	366	369	373	376	377	384	386	385	385
Mexican-American	413	415	416	417	420	426	424	428	430	429	427
Puerto Rican	394	398	403	403	405	409	400	402	406	405	406
Asian-American	509	513	513	514	519	518	521	522	525	528	530
American Indian	426	425	424	425	427	428	432	435	428	437	437
Other	449	447	446	446	450	448	455	460	467	467	466

Source: College Entrance Examination Board, *National Report on College-Bound Seniors*, various years. (Copyright 1991 by the College Entrance Examination Board. All rights reserved.) Cited in U.S. Department of Education, National Center for Education Statistics, *Digest of Education Statistics: 1992*, (Washington, D.C.: U.S. Government Printing Office, 1992), p. 125.

ment of almost 3 percent in the last category. As with the mathematics scores, black students performed significantly below their white contemporaries in all assessment areas.[50]

Overall, the commission concluded that historically the SAT scores had consistently declined since 1963, with mathematics scores dropping almost 40 points and verbal scores dropping over 50 points. In addition, the number of students performing at superior levels (scoring 650 or higher) fell during this period.[51]

SAT scores, however, are not a complete or even accurate measure of the performance of either students or schools, in the judgment of some educators and researchers. Diane Ravitch explained their views prior to the release of *A Nation at Risk*:

Not everyone saw the SAT score decline as a catastrophe. There were those who said that the falling scores meant nothing at all because the drop in the mean was caused by the increased numbers of poor, black, and female students taking the tests. And then there were those critics of testing who said that the test itself meant nothing at all, so it scarcely mattered whether national scores went up or down.[52]

Nevertheless, as the cries of alarm about the condition of America's public elementary and secondary system were sounded in response to the commission's report, SAT scores became a litmus test of the results of various reforms.

Besides SAT scores, the commission was concerned about other aspects of public education. It focused attention on four key components of the education process: curriculum content, knowledge and skill expectations, time, and teaching. The major conclusions and concerns are summarized.

Curriculum Content. The "smorgasbord"-style curriculum that was part of the school's response to the 1960s was found lacking in focus, relevance, and utility by the early 1980s. The availability of "soft" electives and "general studies" programs provided a less-than-challenging way for many students to earn a high school diploma, resulting in many graduates' lacking both relevant skills and proper attitudes to enter the work force or college. To illustrate its point that in the educational curriculum cafeteria, "appetizers and desserts can easily be mistaken for the main courses," the commission noted the following:[53]

- Students have shifted from vocational and college preparatory programs to "general track" courses in large numbers, with the proportion of students taking a general program of study growing from 12 percent in 1964 to 42 percent in 1979.

- With respect to more intellectually challenging courses, 31 percent of recent high school graduates had completed intermediate algebra, 13 percent had taken French 1, 16 percent had taken geography, and 6 percent had completed calculus.

- One-quarter of the credits earned by general track high school students were "soft courses" in physical and health education, work experience outside the school, remedial English and mathematics, and training for adulthood and marriage.

Knowledge, Ability, and Skill Expectations. In the commission's judgment, the diversification of public elementary and secondary curricula reflected a lowering of expectations by educators, school board members, and elected officials concerning student performance. In most of the 37 states requiring competency examinations, for example, the tendency was for "minimum" to become "maximum" standards.[54] This phenomenon was revealed in several indicators cited in the final report:[55]

• Even though average student achievement had dropped, the amount of homework for high school seniors had decreased (two-thirds reported less than one hour a night), and grades had risen.

• Students in many other industrialized nations spent about three times more class hours taking courses in mathematics (other than arithmetic or general mathematics), biology, chemistry, physics, and geography than their science-oriented American counterparts, who took four years of science and mathematics in secondary school.

• In 1980 only eight states required high schools to offer foreign language instruction, and none required students to take the courses. Thirty-five states required only one year of mathematics, and 36 required only one year of science to meet graduation requirements.

• In 13 states, student electives could comprise half or more of the units required for high school graduation.

• Many textbooks were unchallenging and uninteresting, with a majority of students reporting being able to master about 80 percent of the subject-matter texts before even opening the books.

• Expenditures for textbooks and other instructional materials had dropped by 50 percent since the mid-1960s.

Use of Time. As indicated in Table 5.12, in 1984–85, students were required to spend an average of 178 days a year in public high school. They took six classes totaling 5.14 hours a day. In contrast, high school students in England attended 8 hours a day, 220 days a year.[56]

These U.S. figures, which were generally accurate for the time period examined by the commission, mask another concern, the amount of time actually spent in instruction as opposed to study halls, driver education, choir, home economics, athletics, and other non-academic pursuits. In many schools, courses of this kind received the same valuation in terms of graduation credits as mathematics, chemistry, history, or English. The commission found some schools that offered students only 17 hours of academic instruction during the week, with the average school providing only about 22 hours.[57]

Teachers. Finally, the commission expressed great concern about the caliber and motivation of public elementary and secondary teachers, as well as their treatment by school administrators. In general, it was found that teachers were poorly paid (the average salary in 1981–82 was $19,274, according to DOE's National Center for Education Statistics) in light of their responsibilities, that

Table 5.12
Average Number of Days per School Year, Classes per Day, Hours of Class per Day, and Minutes per Class in Public High Schools, by Selected School Characteristics, 1984–85

School Characteristic	Days per School Year	Credit Classes per Day	Hours of Class per Day	Minutes per Day
1	2	3	4	5
United States Average	178.0	6.1	5.14	51.1
District Enrollment Size				
Less than 2,500	177.5	6.1	5.22	51.0
2,500 to 9,999	179.0	5.8	4.92	50.9
10,000 or more	179.1	5.9	5.19	53.2
Metropolitan Status				
In SMSA,[1] inside central city	179.0	5.9	4.98	51.2
In SMSA,[1] outside central city	179.0	5.9	4.92	49.7
Outside SMSA[1]	177.4	6.1	5.26	51.8
Region				
North Atlantic	180.2	6.0	4.45	44.8
Great Lakes and Plains	177.8	6.0	5.10	51.2
Southeast	177.9	5.8	5.33	54.9
West and Southwest	176.7	6.3	5.61	53.2

[1] Standard Metropolitan Statistical Area.

Source: U.S. Department of Education, National Center for Education Statistics, Fast Response Survey System, "Public High School Graduation Requirements." Cited in U.S. Department of Education, National Center for Education Statistics, *Digest of Education Statistics: 1992* (Washington, D.C.: U.S. Government Printing Office, 1992), p. 142.

many had to supplement their income with part-time and summer jobs, which diminished their ability to keep abreast of developments in their fields or to obtain additional professional training, and that there were few financial incentives for instructional excellence or even longevity.

With regard to their qualifications, the commission concluded that:

• Too many teachers are being drawn from the bottom quarter of graduating high school and college students.

• The teacher preparation curriculum is weighted heavily with courses in "educational methods" at the expense of courses in subjects to be taught.

• Half of the newly employed mathematics, science, and English teachers are not qualified to teach these subjects; fewer than one-third of U.S. high schools offer physics taught by qualified teachers.[58]

The commission also found considerable frustration experienced beyond pay and parental expectations. In particular, many teachers did not feel they had a

voice in important instructional matters like the selection of textbooks and revision of the curriculum. This inadequate consultation made some feel like
unappreciated and undervalued partners in the educational process.

To sum up, the commission's report placed the problems of public elementary
and secondary education under a harsh spotlight. No one was immune from
some blame—students, teachers, principals, administrators, parents, and public
officials all were found culpable for the malaise that had affected public schools.
In fairness, the commission recognized that much progress had been made in
educating the average citizen, compared with attainment levels in mathematics,
science, literature, and other subjects a generation ago. But, with respect to the
average high school or college graduate, they had lost ground compared with
their peers 25 or 35 years ago.[59] The "bottom line" assessment was dramatically
stated by Paul Copperman: "For the first time in the history of our country, the
educational skills of one generation will not surpass, will not equal, will not
even approach, those of their parents."[60]

Recommendations

The commission's final report contained a series of recommendations for
immediate and long-range improvements in the nation's schools. They rested on
the assumptions that "everyone can learn, that everyone is born with an urge
to learn which can be nurtured, that a solid high school education is within the
reach of virtually all, and that life-long learning will equip people with the skills
required for new careers and for citizenship."[61]

The general recommendations and specific implementing recommendations
were organized in terms of the four key areas in which the commission's findings
were presented earlier (content, standards and expectations, time, and teaching),
together with a fifth series of prescriptions dealing with "leadership and fiscal
support." With respect to the first three, the commission called for the following:

- We recommend that State and local high school graduation requirements be strengthened
  and that, at a minimum, all students seeking a diploma be required to lay the foundations
  in the Five New Basics by taking the following curriculum during their 4 years of high
  school: (a) 4 years of English; (b) 3 years of mathematics; (c) 3 years of science; (d)
  3 years of social studies; and (e) one-half year of computer science. For the college-
  bound, 2 years of foreign language in high school are strongly recommended in addition
  to those taken earlier.

- We recommend that schools, colleges, and universities adopt more rigorous and measurable standards, and higher expectations, for academic performance and student conduct, and that 4-year colleges and universities raise their requirements for admission. . . .

- We recommend that significantly more time be devoted to learning the New Basics.
  This will require more effective use of the existing school day, a longer school day,
  or a lengthened school year.[62]

In the fourth area, teaching, the commission recommended a sevenfold action agenda designed to "improve the preparation of teachers or to make teaching a more rewarding and respected profession."[63] The components were:

1. Persons preparing to teach should be required to meet high educational standards, to demonstrate an aptitude for teaching, and to demonstrate competence in an academic discipline. Colleges and universities offering teacher preparation programs should be judged by how well their graduates meet these criteria.

2. Salaries for the teaching profession should be increased and should be professionally competitive, market-sensitive, and performance-based. Salary, promotion, tenure, and retention decisions should be tied to an effective evaluation system that includes peer review so that superior teachers can be rewarded, average ones encouraged, and poor ones either improved or terminated.

3. School boards should adopt an 11-month contract for teachers. This would ensure time for curriculum and professional development, programs for students with special needs, and a more adequate level of teacher compensation.

4. School boards, administrators, and teachers should cooperate to develop career ladders for teachers that distinguish among the beginning instructor, the experienced teacher, and the master teacher.

5. Substantial nonschool personnel resources should be employed to help solve the immediate problem of the shortage of mathematics and science teachers. . . . Other areas of critical teacher needs, such as English, must also be addressed.

6. Incentives, such as grants and loans, should be made available to attract outstanding students to the teaching profession, particularly in those areas of critical shortage.

7. Master teachers should be involved in designing teacher preparation programs and in supervising teachers during their probationary years.[64]

Turning to the final recommendation—leadership and fiscal support—the commission urged a wide range of parties, especially the federal government, to take steps to implement its recommendations. Principals and superintendents were encouraged to build community and school support, and school boards were called upon to acquire greater leadership skills. State and local elected officials were urged to assume primary responsibility for school policy, financing, and governance. The federal government was looked to for agenda setting; for stimulating research, data gathering, and demonstration projects; for supporting programs targeted to special groups (minorities, handicapped, gifted, and talented); for helping train teachers in areas of critical need; for protecting constitutional and civil rights; and for furnishing student financial aid.[65]

In summing up its case for timely and effective citizen and public official action, the commission pointed out: "Excellence costs. But in the long run mediocrity costs more."[66]

INITIAL RESPONSES TO *A NATION AT RISK*

The response to *A Nation at Risk* was multifaceted and mixed. Overall, the reactions were positive. Most observers believed the National Commission deserved credit for "telling it like it is" in terms of the state of American elementary and secondary public education and for offering prescriptions that charted a path to reform. Moreover, supporters and skeptics alike agreed that its report—6 million copies of which had been distributed within a year following its release, according to the Department of Education—had put education improvement on the public policy "front burner."[67] In the judgment of Ernest L. Boyer, president of the Carnegie Foundation for the Advancement of Teaching and former U.S. commissioner of Education, it "struck with megaton force" and launched the "Great Debate of '83."[68]

Bouquets and Brickbats

The initial response by political leaders seemed to confirm Dr. Boyer's assessment. Some 30 governors organized task forces on schools, and thousands of bills were introduced in state legislatures, especially in the South.[69] By the first anniversary of the commission's report,

There have been, at last count, 30 other national reports on education, 290 state commission and blue ribbon task force reports, at least two widely acclaimed television documentaries, extensive newspaper and magazine coverage of education and now even a motion picture about teachers, all purporting to know what is wrong with the nation's schools and what will make them right.[70]

In support of their observation that the states' response to the stimulus from the commission's report was substantial and even surprising, Denis Doyle and Terry Hartle pointed out:

In Arkansas, the legislature passed 122 separate measures concerning the public schools between September 1983 and September 1984. The Texas legislature met in a special session, passed a comprehensive school reform package, and enacted a finance reform bill to pay for it. Florida has enacted so much legislation that the state senate was asked to put a moratorium on new education measures until those already approved had been implemented. South Carolina adopted a series of sweeping education reforms and raised taxes to pay for them.[71]

In reviewing these responses Education secretary Terrel H. Bell observed in the fall of 1984, "We have so many reforms on the platter that we may have indigestion."[72]

Indeed, a considerable amount of activity on the education reform front was already under way at the state level before release of *A Nation at Risk*. In 1983–84 the Council of State Governments (CSG) surveyed the chief state school officers in each state, together with the District of Columbia and Puerto Rico, to determine the extent to which the National Commission's recommendations had been, or would be, adopted. Of the 43 who responded, approximately half reported that their state had already adopted 25 of the 50 reforms included in the CSG survey. When those indicating their state was currently working on implementation were added to this base, 35 of the 50 recommendations had been adopted by half of the states.[73] The council concluded: "Policy-makers were taking the matter of reform for educational excellence to heart *well before* the Commission's report was finalized."[74]

The report also altered President Reagan's agenda. Before the commission completed its work, the president's approach to education reform focused on tuition tax credits, higher graduation standards, merit pay for teachers, and school prayer. Afterward, the president quickly climbed on the bandwagon and embraced the broader recommendations, even though they did not include his agenda.[75] However, President Reagan was critical of the motives and methods of the "federal education bureaucrats" in the department established by his predecessor, Jimmy Carter. In fact, "in his weekly radio announcement following the release of *A Nation at Risk*, the president specifically blamed previous federal involvement for current educational problems mentioned in the report, and highlighted his educational policy agenda, including the tax credit and voucher proposals."[76] Interestingly, although at the ceremony in which he received the report the president commended the members for their "call for an end to Federal intrusion," the National Commission did not criticize the federal government.[77] On the contrary, as indicated in the previous section, it recommended several significant national policy and financial leadership roles.

Under secretaries Bell and, later, William Bennett, the Department of Education gained a reprieve from abolition by taking the lead in shaping the federal government's response to *A Nation at Risk*. Yet, the parameters of this response were defined by the president in a December 1983 speech to 2,300 educators and elected officials at a National Forum on Excellence in Education held in Indianapolis to discuss the report, where he declared, "American schools don't need vast new sums of money as much as they need a few fundamental reforms . . . we need to restore good old-fashioned discipline."[78]

On the other hand, some believed that while the report unleashed a flurry of activity by other commissions, task forces, and researchers across the country, as well as policy initiatives at the state and local levels, "it fell in at the head of a parade that had already begun to take shape."[79] To these observers, the states' vigorous response to the National Commission was no surprise since state-led education reform had begun more than a decade earlier. As a result of the challenges public schools confronted in the turbulent sixties, states emphasized greater accountability on the part of teachers and students in the form of more rigorous academic standards, greater use of minimum competency tests, and initiation of assessment programs.[80] "Policy makers had a straight-forward view; they wanted to raise educational standards and to hold educators responsible for the quality of schools."[81] The states' response to the school finance equity court cases in the early seventies also was a significant backdrop to the National Commission's work, for it accelerated fiscal centralization to accompany the policy centralization trend.

A second line of criticism maintained that the recommendations in *A Nation at Risk* were, for the most part, conventional wisdom and that the report was yet another classic example of a missed opportunity to build support for what was really needed to improve public schools—radical reorganization. Those who argued this point felt that the modest results of the effort were predictable from the outset due to the decision to use the "reform by commission" approach. Paul Peterson of the Brookings Institution, for example, contended that it is the nature of most commissions that they "do not address the most difficult conceptual or political issues. Instead, they reassert what is well-known, make exaggerated claims on flimsy evidence, pontificate on matters about which there could scarcely be disagreement, and make recommendations that either cost too much, cannot be implemented, or are too general to have any meaning."[82]

From this perspective, at best the National Commission's report rode the crest of the wave of school reform and helped build public support for ongoing state and local efforts. At worst, the effort was an instrument for the Reagan administration to further its own policy agenda, especially to slow the growth of the federal government's financial and programmatic roles in public education, which had been building since the Great Society, and to promote local flexibility and discretion in meeting elementary and secondary educational needs.[83]

A third source of criticism and the most serious was the education community. Some educators argued not that the recommendations lacked boldness and innovativeness but that they missed the mark entirely. Mary Hatwood Futrell, former president of the National Education Association, delivered one of the most stinging criticisms. In her judgment, the report was "deeply flawed" by its focus on the instrumental, rather than intrinsic values of education, underscored by the commission's reference to the nation's committing "unthinking, unilateral educational disarmament."[84] Education, therefore, became a vehicle for promoting the national interest and democratic values: "The destiny of American democracy, it was argued, demanded what revitalized education alone could deliver: technological might in the service of military security, a rejuvenated economy in the service of reclaimed dominance in the international marketplace, and the social and political integration of waves of new immigrants in the service of national harmony."[85] Lost in the rush to respond to the commission's challenge were an appreciation for teachers and sensitivity to the teaching and learning processes, as well as recognition of the special needs of disadvantaged and at-risk students.

At the same time, some critics of the teaching profession noted that teachers and their unions had rarely been proponents of bold, radical, or innovative changes in schools and curricula and historically had often been opponents of reform. In an article questioning whether the teacher's call for "empowerment" went beyond improving their personal benefits, Fred M. Hechinger noted, "There has been no serious departure from the way the American school has been organized for more than 100 years: teachers and students confined for 50 minutes at a time to cubicles called classrooms; a teacher lecturing and students (sometimes) listening, and tests asking students to regurgitate recently acquired knowledge."[86]

POST-1983 SCHOOL REFORMS

If 1983 is considered a watershed year in the "great debate" over education reform, subsequent years have witnessed considerable activity at all levels of government and in the business community to implement school reforms recommended by the National Commission and other study groups established in the second half of the 1980s. Looking back on these efforts, it is possible to identify three major "waves" of school reform set in motion by *A Nation at Risk*, which are summarized in this section. The major components of each wave are identified in Table 5.13.

The First Wave: Standards from the Statehouse

As Mary Hatwood Futrell has put it, the first wave of education reform was top-down, from the statehouse to the schoolhouse, wherein governors and legislators sought to make improvements by passing preemptive statutes and imposing stringent regulations: "Their battle cry was 'more!': more tests for students and teachers, more credits for graduation, more hours in the school day, more days in the school year, more regimentation, more routinization, more regulation."[87] According to Dr. Futrell, between 1983 and 1985, state legislatures passed over 700 laws "stipulating what would be taught, when it should be taught, how it should be taught, and by whom it should be taught."[88] The emphasis here was basically on the education needs and performance of the majority of students, especially those who were college-bound. Less concern was apparent in connection with at-risk children and youth, with those enrolled in vocational education programs, or with those who were educationally, physically, or emotionally handicapped.

Chief state school officers also favored the standard-setting approach. In the Council of State Governments' 1983 survey, these respondents were asked to rank the three most important recommendations made by the National Commission. Their top choices were:

- Schools have adopted measurable standards and higher expectations for academic performance and student conduct (selected by 50 percent).
- State has strengthened state and local high school graduation requirements (31 percent).
- Persons preparing to teach in own state are required to meet high educational standards (21 percent).

Table 5.13
Responses to A *Nation at Risk*: Three Waves of 1980s Educational Reform

I Standards	II Schools	III Students
• Require more academic courses for high school graduation (English, science, mathematics, foreign language).	• Raise teacher salaries. • Reduce class size and teacher-student ratios. • Use performance-based teacher incentives (merit pay, career ladders, master teachers).	• Raise per pupil expenditures. • Establish and enforce disciplinary codes. • Provide incentives to reduce dropout rates and assist those who have left school to complete graduation requirements.
• Use higher caliber more challenging textbooks. • Raise SAT scores. • Lengthen school day and school year. • Use assessment procedures to report school progress in achieving educational goals.	• Establish mentoring programs to assist new teachers. • Allow teachers more time for preparing lessons, grading, and reviewing homework. • Give teachers time off and financial support for professional development and in-service education.	• Early identification of those at-risk and home intervention and counseling of students and parents. • Counseling and support for pregnant students. • More health, drug, alcohol, and sex education programs and related counseling.
• Require competency tests and certification of new teachers. • Reduce "general studies" tracks, and increase vocational education offerings. • Require English, mathematics and writing proficiency tests. • Mandatory kindergarten.	• Offer incentives to attract science and mathematics teachers. • Adopt school-based management practices, and community-elected school boards.	

Source: Authors' compilation.

• Curriculum in the first eight grades is designed to provide a sound base for study in these and later years (17 percent).[89]

An important aspect of the first-wave response is the question, Education for what? As more and more attention was devoted to the globalization phenomenon and to the world economy, successful school-to-work transitions were considered essential to bolstering the nation's competitiveness at home and abroad. As Japanese automobile manufacturers toured the United States in search of suitable locations for Honda, Nissan, and Toyota assembly plants, for instance, the quality of a state's educational system was viewed as a significant asset—or liability. Similarly, as American companies sought to open markets abroad for exportation of their products, the ability of their work force to "read, write, and reason" became important considerations in the pricing and quality control of goods and services. The ability of corporate representatives to understand the culture, speak the language, and be familiar with the history and geography of their counterparts from other countries became increasingly significant conditioners of successful negotiations.

The Second Wave: The Schoolhouse

The states' political and bureaucratic actions during the first wave were often greeted by concern and criticism on the part of educators, teacher union representatives, school board members, and school administrators. In response to growing realizations that "if education were to serve as an instrument for social and economic revitalization, the instrument ought to be wielded by educators, not legislators,"[90] the arena shifted from the statehouse to the schoolhouse. The second wave of education reform, therefore, sought both to empower and to improve the nation's teachers. Merit pay plans, career ladders, and across-the-board salary increases were called for as supplements to competency tests to recognize and encourage teacher excellence.

These efforts were supported by a growing number of reports from a wide range of sources urging a more bottom-up approach to school improvement. Among the most important contributions were the following four studies and projects:

1. The Carnegie Foundation's 1983 report on the American high school developed a vision of what secondary schools should strive to accomplish. The study proposed four goals comprising the mission of high schools and identified ways for them to be achieved, particularly through redesigning rather than tinkering with the curriculum:

   First, the high school should help all students develop the capacity to think critically and communicate effectively through a mastery of language. Second, the high school should help all students learn about themselves, the human heritage, and the interdependent world in which they live through a core curriculum based upon consequential human experiences common to all people. Third, the high school should prepare all students for work and further education through a program of electives that develop individual aptitudes and interests. Fourth, the high school should help all students fulfill their social and civic obligations through school and community service.[91]

   The foundation subsequently awarded $800,000 to 200 high schools that were pursuing excellence in curriculum, teachers, technology, and other areas covered in its report.

2. Theodore R. Sizer, a former high school teacher and dean of the Harvard Graduate School of Education, published an assessment of the nation's high schools entitled *Horace's Compromise*. Cosponsored by the National Association of Secondary School Principals and the National Association of Independent Schools, the report also focused on the problems with high school curricula and recommended restructuring to achieve

five "imperatives" for improved secondary schools: (1) allow teachers and students flexibility to work and learn in their own ways, (2) insist that students demonstrate mastery of schoolwork, (3) ensure incentives are appropriate, (4) encourage students to use their minds, and (5) provide structural flexibility and simplicity.[92]

3. In 1986 the Carnegie Corporation released a major report dealing with the status of public school teachers. In *A Nation Prepared: Teachers for the 21st Century*, the authors called for teachers to be given greater discretion and authority:

> Within the context of a limited set of clear goals for students set by state and local policymakers, teachers, working together, must be free to exercise their professional judgment as to the best way to achieve these goals. This means the ability to make—or at least to strongly influence—decisions concerning such things as the materials and instructional methods to be used, the staffing structure to be employed, the organization of the school day, the assignment of students, the consultants to be used, and the allocation of resources available to the school.[93]

4. In 1985 the National Education Association (NEA) established a Mastery in Learning Project, in which 26 schools were selected to develop a bottom-up needs assessment and local options to meet them. Four years later, NEA created the National Center for Innovation, which included this project, a Learning Labs Initiative (district-based change), the Mastery in Learning Consortium (school-based change), the Teacher Education Initiative (improved professional practice), and the Excellence in Action programs. Over 60 community sites—school districts, individual and clustered schools, and teacher preparation institutions—and hundreds of teachers and administrators have been involved in "laboratories" for experimenting with education change and developing a research-based "theory of action for school transformation." The National Center designates programs that have successfully overcome problems and disseminates information about these models.[94]

As an alternative to across-the-board solutions, the second wave also emphasized decentralized, differentiated responses. While teachers were the focal point, it was recognized that superintendents and principals, school boards, and the private sector all had a stake and should work together to achieve desirable outcomes. An example of this emphasis was the work of the Committee for Economic Development, a national group of business leaders interested in the public service. The committee published two reports during the 1980s (*Investing in Our Children: Business and the Public Schools* and *Children in Need: Investment Strategies for the Educationally Disadvantaged*) calling for comprehensive reform of elementary and secondary schools and improvement of both teachers and teaching in order to bolster the skills and employability of students and especially to prepare disadvantaged children for productive careers.[95] In *Children in Need*, for example, the committee recommended strategies for the public and private sectors to implement its action agenda:

We believe that any plan to restructure public schools that serve the disadvantaged should include the following elements:

• School based management that involves principals, teachers, parents, students, and other school personnel in shared decision making and accountability for results. School management should encourage flexibility and innovation in the school curriculum, teaching methods, and organization.

Table 5.14
Some Services Provided by Public Schools

- Basic education
- Career preparation
- Advancement of analytical, critical, and synthesizing skills
- Personality development
- Physical and athletic skill development
- Artistic and esthetic expression
- Human interpersonal skills
- Motivation (desire to learn and grow)
- Cooperative attitudes (obedience to authority, and so on)
- Understanding of self, improved self-concept
- Chemical dependency prevention and treatment
- Hot breakfasts and lunches for the poor
- Hot breakfasts and lunches for all
- Parent effectiveness training
- A full range of opportunities for the handicapped
- Baby sitting services
- Bicultural education for those from family backgrounds from other cultures
- Community education
- Preschool programs
- Individualized special education programs allowing students to be "mainstreamed" where possible
- Band, orchestra, choir, drama, and a whole range of "cocurricular" programs

Source: Mauriel, J.J., *Strategic Leadership for Schools: Creating and Sustaining Productive Change* (San Francisco: Jossey-Bass Publishers, 1989), p. 23.

- Teachers who have made a commitment to working with the disadvantaged and who have expertise in dealing with children with multiple problems. Special support for those teachers' needs to be made available by school districts and schools of education.
- Smaller schools and smaller classes that are designed not only to raise achievement levels but to increase quality contact with teachers and other adults.
- Support for preschool and child-care programs by the school system where appropriate for the community.
- Up-to-date educational technology integrated into the curriculum to provide new learning opportunities for students and additional pedagogical support for teachers.
- Support systems within the schools that include health services, nutritional guidance, and psychological, career, and family counseling.
- Increased emphasis on extracurricular activities that help build academic, social, or physical skills.[96]

A critical component of the second-wave response was recognition that the schoolhouse had undergone substantial transformation as a consequence of the societal changes that have been discussed earlier in this book. Schools were responsible for far more than providing a conducive learning environment, and the duties of teachers went well beyond teaching. Table 5.14 illustrates the multifaceted services performed by public schools.

The Third Wave: Students

One criticism of the National Commission's report was its cursory treatment of student needs and challenges, especially in light of the changing demographics of the elementary and secondary school population. In 1984 Ernest Boyer predicted that by the 1990s black and Hispanic youth will comprise almost one-third of the nation's total school enrollment and a considerably greater proportion of central city schools. Yet, "the truth is that, more and more, the students who are going to populate our schools will be precisely those students who have historically been least well served there."[97]

The third wave of school reform, therefore, dealt with the twin goals of equality of opportunity and excellence in achievement.[98] In other words, it was expected that every student—despite race, sex, socioeconomic status, place of residence, family status, physical condition, or other factors—should be able to attain his or her full potential in the classroom and ultimately in the workplace and in society. While schools still have an instrumental value, education also has intrinsic value.

How schools and the educational experience needed to be changed to attain these equity and excellence goals was not readily apparent. Yet, most agreed that this was a worthy challenge and that much could be gained from experiments at the grass roots.[99] Of particular concern were the needs of at-risk children and youth.

Students at Risk. One year after the release of *A Nation at Risk*, a Gallup Poll was conducted probing the attitudes of teachers and the general public toward schools. The results appear in Table 5.15. It is interesting to note that while some of the previously noted systemic problems identified by the National Commission were raised, they generally received relatively low ratings. The public seemed more concerned about them than did the teachers. At the same time, problems such as lack of parental and pupil interest and inadequate financial support were given high ratings by teachers. Both parents and teachers were very concerned about the lack of discipline.

This survey and others like it conducted in subsequent years underscore a major point running throughout this chapter: adequate preparation of the current and next generation of America's work force is a responsibility that transcends the educational system. While governmental intervention and business involvement are essential ingredients of the employability formula, the achievement of desired results will be conditioned by factors and forces in the larger society.

In the educational context, these limitations were first recognized in research by sociologist James S. Coleman in 1966. The "Coleman Report" to Congress found basically that "more dollars do not produce better scholars."[100] Professor Coleman's research found no statistically significant correlations between student achievement and outlays, curriculum, facilities, class size, teacher experience, and other variables. However, he did find that performance was affected by family background and socioeconomic characteristics. Black students, for ex-

Table 5.15
Attitudes Toward Public Schools: Teachers and the General Public, 1984

	Percentage	
Problem	Teachers	Public
1	2	3
Parents' Lack of Interest/Support	31	5
Lack of Proper Financial Support	21	14
Pupils' Lack of Interest/Truancy	20	4
Lack of Discipline	19	27
Problems with Administration	10	3
Poor Curriculum/Poor Standards	7	15
Use of Drugs	5	18
Low Teacher Salaries	5	4
Difficulty Getting Good Teachers	4	5
Large schools/overcrowding	4	4
Teachers' Lack of Interest	4	5
Integration/Busing	2	6

Note: Fewer than 5 percent listed any other problem as major.

Source: "The Gallup Poll of Teachers' Attitudes Toward the Public Schools," *Phi Delta Kappan*, October 1984.

ample, did better at predominantly white, rather than at predominantly black, schools, a finding that was used to support busing of pupils to overcome school segregation in many central cities. The "Coleman Report" has been followed by more than 150 studies that have sought to replicate its findings; in only 18 of 120 of these analyses was a statistically significant correlation found between spending and performance.[101]

A 1990 report by the National Conference of State Legislatures (NCSL) identified several persistent barriers to learning that both students and teachers must overcome. The report cited a 1990 study by the Children's Defense Fund, which raised a number of troubling statistics about children and youth in contemporary society that are often carried into the classroom:

Every day, 2,989 American children see their parents divorced.

Every 26 seconds, a child runs away from home.

Every 47 seconds, a child is abused or neglected.

Every seven minutes, a child is killed or injured by guns.

Every 53 minutes, a child dies because of poverty.

Every day, 100,000 children are homeless.

Every school day, 135,000 children bring guns to school.

Every eight seconds of the school day, a child drops out.

Every day, six teenagers commit suicide.[102]

These and other influences create formidable barriers for the schools to overcome. As indicated earlier in this book, family dissolution, parental disinterest,
negative peer pressure, exposure to drugs and violence, and other unfortunate
societal trends and influences create insecurity and low self-worth images that
pose severe challenges for the normal educational process. In this context, for
example, raising academic standards for graduation and other components of the
"get tough and get better" approach to education reform may simply frustrate
at-risk students, many of whom are poor and nonwhite, and cause them to drop
out of school.[103] As the Committee for Economic Development put it:

Often the public schools operate much like factories, with an assembly-line approach to
turning out students. For some students, this approach can be disastrous: ... too many
schools that serve disadvantaged populations are opting for control rather than education,
magnifying the alienation often experienced by the poor and minorities. . . . Too many
schools offer a large, impersonal environment that more closely resembles a factory than
a haven for learning.[104]

The committee also said: "Beleaguered by powerful social forces swirling
around them, the schools are ill equipped to respond to the multidimensional
problems of poor and minority youngsters. The discrimination their students face
and the alienation these children feel are often compounded by an archaic school
structure and an unresponsive bureaucracy."[105]

In the final analysis, as the previously cited Gallup Poll reveals, parents are
a crucial conditioner of the success of efforts to achieve educational excellence
and equity. Yet, too often, as former Illinois governor James R. Thompson has
observed: "Some people spend more time taking care of their lawns than they
do taking care of their children's education. Well, I guess grass grows easier
than kids."[106] Or, as David Pierpont Gardner, chairman of the National Commission, stated: "It is not easy for teachers to motivate students to learn if
learning is not respected in the home. If at home or in the community the work
of the school is regarded with indifference, then whatever the level of dedication,
commitment and ability possessed by the teachers, the salvage rate will be
low."[107]

In view of these factors, the sequel to *A Nation at Risk* perhaps should have
been titled "Students at Risk." For as the educational reform movement reached
the third wave, it had become apparent that the availability of preschool programs
like Head Start and various home interventions were key to the success of children
and youth in the classroom. Of particular significance here was the 1985 report
of the National Coalition of Advocates for Students, entitled *Barriers to Excellence: Our Children at Risk*, which both popularized use of the term "*at-risk*"
children and pointed out that they were the most serious problem confronting
the public schools: "Policymakers at many different levels talk of bringing
excellence to schools and ignore the fact that hundreds of thousands of youngsters
are not receiving even minimal educational opportunities guaranteed under

law. . . . From the minute they walk into school, any low-income students get the message that society does not really care about their education, that schools expect little from them.''[108] Two years later, in assessing the educational reform record since *A Nation at Risk*, Fred Hechinger concluded that policymakers had gotten the message that focusing on standards and schoolhouse issues were incomplete and even inaccurate responses:

A ray of hope: public and professional attention has begun to shift from the high schools to the elementary schools, kindergartens and early child care and education. Slowly there appeared to be an awakening this year to the fact that what happens in the early years determines much of the children's and the schools' later success or failure.

The year's overall progress may deserve little better than a C +. But the grade could improve in the years ahead if policy makers move from worry about ''A Nation at Risk'' to action on behalf of children at risk.[109]

RESPONSES FROM THE STATEHOUSES AND THE WHITE HOUSE

The three waves of education reform occurred simultaneously in many states and communities throughout the nation during the latter half of the 1980s and continuing into the 1990s. While the emphasis, approaches, and timing differed, standards, schooling, and students were in the forefront of educational reform. Their prominence was undoubtedly a result of the proliferation of national studies, task forces, and state legislative initiatives that called attention to the problems highlighted by the National Commission, as well as the possible remedial actions. Before turning to an assessment of the reform record, the contributions of the nation's governors and former president George Bush to these efforts are discussed, for they reflect an important recent shift in policy and philosophical emphasis, as described by Ernest L. Boyer:

Something quite remarkable is going on. Today, the citizens of this country are increasingly dissatisfied with a piecemeal approach to education. For the first time in our history, Americans appear to be more concerned about national outcomes than about local school control. And they're demanding evidence that our huge, 180 billion dollar annual investment in public education is paying off. . . .

The message—it seems to me—is absolutely clear. After years of vigorously defending local school control, the nation is now supporting—indeed almost demanding—national leadership in education, while still maintaining vitality at the local level. It's a new challenge, something we've never faced before, and how we respond surely will shape public education and the nation for years to come.[110]

Toward a National Curriculum

Education secretary William Bennett was largely responsible for the growth in the federal government's leadership role in education reform during the mid-

1980s. Especially significant were two volumes—*James Madison High School* and *James Madison Elementary School*—that were released in 1987 and 1988, respectively. These reports contained suggested core curricula for secondary and elementary students, including subject descriptions and reading titles, as well as profiles of schools demonstrating ''curricular excellence.''[111] Although Secretary Bennett indicated that the suggestions reflected his views, rather than federal policy, and the curricula ''is not a monolithic program to be uniformly imposed or slavishly followed,''[112] the fact that it emanated from Washington, D.C., was troublesome to some observers, who were concerned about the erosion of local control of public schools. Others, however, have pointed out that the United States is the only industrial country lacking a national curriculum and that a common core of knowledge taught in schools was long overdue and essential to ''cultural literacy'' and economic competitiveness.[113]

The Education Summit

A second significant example of this shift occurred in September 1989, when President Bush and the nation's governors convened a historic ''education summit'' in Charlottesville at the University of Virginia to discuss the major problems confronting elementary and secondary education and to develop an action agenda. At the February 1990 meeting of the National Governors' Association (NGA), the six ''National Education Goals'' that had been identified at the summit and targeted for attainment by the year 2000 were formally adopted. They were:

1. All children in America will start school ready to learn.
2. The high school graduation rate will increase to at least 90 percent.
3. American students will leave grades four, eight, and twelve having demonstrated competency in challenging subject matter including English, mathematics, science, history and geography; and every school in America will ensure that all students learn to use their minds well, so they may be prepared for responsible citizenship, further learning, and productive employment in our modern economy.
4. U.S. students will be first in the world in science and mathematics achievement.
5. Every adult American will be literate and will possess the knowledge and skills necessary to compete in a global economy and exercise the rights and responsibilities of citizenship.
6. Every school in America will be free of drugs and violence and will offer a disciplined environment conducive to learning.[114]

Appendix 5.D indicates the objectives the president and governors agreed on to help achieve these goals.

For some three years preceding the summit, governors, through NGA, had been tracking education reform progress. In 1986, under then Tennessee governor Lamar Alexander, who was serving as NGA's chairman, the association defined a five-year agenda for improving public schools and committed itself to monitoring and reporting annually on state implementation initiatives and outcomes. Seven areas were considered key components of the "Time for Results" project:

- creating a more highly professional teaching force;
- strengthening school leadership and management;
- promoting greater parent involvement and choice in their youngsters' education;
- helping at-risk children and youth meet higher educational standards;
- making better use of the resources invested in school facilities; and
- strengthening the mission and effectiveness of colleges and universities.[115]

Opinion polls conducted in 1990 and 1991 by the Gallup organization asked respondents to assign a priority to each goal and to indicate their view as to the likelihood of its attainment by the year 2000. Over the two years sampled, the public's assessment of the importance of all six goals increased, with half or more assigning "very high" priority status to five goals and two-fifths rating the sixth (world mathematics and science achievement) in this category (see Table 5.16). With respect to implementation, however, the public was most doubtful about the possibility of attaining drug- and violence-free schools that offer disciplined learning environments (77% responded "very unlikely" or "unlikely" in 1991), followed by world mathematics and science achievement (68%) and adult literacy and skill competence (64%). The goal most likely to be attained was readiness to learn, in the opinion of 47 percent of those surveyed. For the remaining two goals, approximately half of the respondents felt implementation was unlikely. Overall, the public seems quite skeptical of attaining the national education goals by the turn of the century.

America 2000

The third major example of the shift in education reform leadership took place in April 1991, when the Bush administration unveiled a four-part education strategy intended to help communities across the country achieve the six national education goals. Described as "four big trains, moving simultaneously down four parallel tracks," the America 2000 strategy envisioned:

For today's students, we must radically improve today's schools by making all 110,000 of them better and more accountable for results.

For tomorrow's students, we must invent new schools to meet the demands of a new century with a New Generation of American Schools, bringing at least 535 of them into existence by 1996 and thousands by decade's end.

For those of us already out of school and in the work force, we must keep learning if we are to live and work successfully in today's world. A "Nation at Risk" must become a "Nation of Students." For schools to succeed, we must look beyond our classrooms to our communities and families. Schools will never be much better than the commitment

Table 5.16
Priority Assigned and Likelihood of Attainment of the National Goals for Education, 1991

National Goals by the Year 2000	Priority assigned to each goal (percent distribution)					Likelihood of goal attainment (percent distribution)				
	Very High 1991	High 1991	Low 1991	Very Low 1991	Don't Know 1991	Very Likely 1991	Likely 1991	Unlikely 1991	Very Unlikely 1991	Don't Know 1991
	2	3	4	5	6	7	8	9	10	11
All children in America start school ready to learn	52	38	6	1	3	10	37	33	14	6
The high school graduation rate will increase to at least 90%	54	37	5	1	3	6	36	39	14	5
American students will leave grades 4, 8, and 12 having demonstrated competency in challenging subject matter[1]	55	35	6	1	3	6	36	36	15	7
American students will be first in the world in mathematics and science achievement	43	41	11	2	3	4	22	45	23	6
Every adult American will be literate and will possess the skills necessary to compete in a global economy and to exercise the rights and responsibilities of citizenship	50	36	9	2	3	6	25	41	23	5
Every school in America will be free of drugs and violence and will offer a disciplined environment conducive to learning	63	23	6	5	3	4	14	38	39	5

1 Subject matter includes English, mathematics, science, history, and geography. In addition, every school in America will insure that all students learn to use their minds in order to prepare them for responsible citizenship, further learning, and productive employment in a modern economy.

Source: *Phi Delta Kappan,* "The Annual Gallup Poll of the Public's Attitudes Toward the Public Schools," September 1991. (This table was prepared February 1992.) Cited in U.S. Department of Education, National Center for Education Statistics *Digest of Education Statistics: 1992* (Washington, D.C.: U.S. Government Printing Office, 1992), 29.

of their communities. Each of our communities must become a place where learning can happen.[116]

America 2000 reflected, among other things, impatience with the pace and extent of school reform during the 1980s. While the NGA and others had encouraged state initiatives and reported on their impact, local follow-through on the national goals had been characterized by slow pace, modest scope, and insignificant impact. While public education spending, in real terms, had increased 33 percent per pupil since *A Nation at Risk*, "the results have not improved, and we're not coming close to our potential on what is needed."[117] President Bush's second Education secretary, Lamar Alexander, sought more radical reforms and more rapid action—"a crusade, not a program."[118] In a speech at the 1991 annual meeting of the National Conference of State Legislatures, he explained: "We're trying to create a populist revolt, a sense of dissatisfaction with the status quo. . . . The best thing we could do is to start over, school-by-school, with clear, high standards and community support and objectives that would help us move rapidly toward the national education goals."[119]

Secretary Alexander sought to accelerate changes through four strategies. Communities would be encouraged (1) formally to adopt the national goals; (2) to develop their own approaches for accomplishing them; (3) continuously to assess progress, especially through achievement tests of 4th, 8th, and 12th grade students and issue "report cards"; and (4) to commit to setting up at least one "break-the-mold" school. As an incentive for the latter, a nonprofit New American Schools Development Corporation was created, chaired initially by former New Jersey governor Thomas Kean and then by David T. Kearns, to provide funds for one "new American school" in each congressional district. Some $150–200 million raised in private funds would be accompanied by congressional appropriations for onetime awards of $1 million to help launch each school and support the developmental work of public-private design teams. More flexible federal aid would also be provided to the "America 2000 Communities," which would be designated by governors. Basically these communities were those that had agreed to implement Secretary Alexander's four strategies. With respect to the first group of 535 new American schools, governors and the secretary of Education would determine their location. To fund the new American school grants, as well as other related America 2000 initiatives, President Bush requested $690 million in the 1992 federal budget, and in May 1991 he sent the Congress a proposed "America 2000 Excellence in Education Act" to implement the other aspects of the reform agenda, which included a "choice" proposal giving parents vouchers to use to send their children to private or parochial schools as alternatives to public schools.

In response, Congress formulated a "Neighborhood Schools Improvement Act" (S.2), which did not provide for choice arrangements or new American schools. Instead, the bill established policies and action plans that sought to expand the federal government's commitment to achievement of the national

education goals. The bill also authorized establishment of a National Education
Goals Panel and National Education Standards and Assessments Council, which
would develop voluntary national education content and voluntary school delivery
standards and monitor progress in implementing the national education goals.
S.2 authorized local education agencies to request waivers of certain statutory
or regulatory requirements—such as social, health, and nutritional services to
disadvantaged children—that impeded their reform efforts. Beginning in fiscal
year 1993, $800 million was authorized for block grants to state educational
agencies to support efforts by state and local districts to improve the quality of
education in neighborhood public schools.[120] In late September 1992 Senate and
House of Representatives conferees agreed on a compromise version, but it was
killed on October 2, when supporters failed by one vote to invoke cloture on a
Republican-backed Senate filibuster. Although Secretary Alexander reportedly
called the bill "worse than awful," and a presidential veto was threatened, a
Washington Post editorial assessed the importance of the bill as follows:

Congress didn't—still doesn't—know how to assist schools. Education legislation is
usually aimed at helping particular categories of kids, not particular schools. This bill is
a little different. That's why educators and lobbyists are referring to it as a "break-
through," even a "landmark"—a bit hyperbolic when compared with family leave and
other legislation, but perhaps true. It looks like a mouse compared with the much weightier
elementary and secondary act Congress must renew and amend next year. But it does
manage to squeak, ending a congressional silence on reform. Until now, the only other
federal voice was the Bush administration's. This bill isn't what the president asked for,
but it's something for an education president to sign.[121]

The reactions to the America 2000 "crusade" ran the gamut from "simplistic
educational ideology run rampant,"[122] to "another chapter in a crucial struggle
in American Society, one that pits 'our children' against 'those other children.' "[123] to "the first serious policy initiative in the nation's history to address
that issue [of whether, how, and for whom the federal role in education should
be enlarged]."[124] The unconventional thrust of America 2000, founded on parental choice of schools for their children to attend (even though the report
included only an 85-word paragraph on the subject)[125] led one observer to note:
"The enthusiastic reception that America 2000 has received beyond the beltway
is matched only by the disdain heaped on it by what may best be thought of as
'the educational policy analysts in exile,' the educators who have not had a home
in the executive branch since Carter."[126]

While America 2000 put public education reform approaches and progress
under a harsh spotlight, it also politicized the issue at the national level. As
Harold Howe II, former U.S. commissioner of Education, pointed out:

My main concern about this new growth in federal influence in education stems in part
from the vigor and prominence of statements in the document averring that no such thing
is intended. . . . As I compare these disclaimers with some of the specific ideas and

proposals of America 2000—new national tests, new national standards, vigorous federal encouragement of choice, new federally appointed agencies to oversee research, and a nationwide emphasis on five academic subjects (English, mathematics, science, history, and geography) that leave out major areas of learning—I am reminded of Hamlet's musing: "The lady doth protest too much, methinks."[127]

ASSESSING THE RESULTS

In the wake of the 1983 report of the National Commission on Excellence in Education, the 1989 presidential-gubernatorial goal setting at the Education Summit, and the 1991 strategic planning initiative of "America 2000," a number of steps were taken to assess the results of education reforms through a variety of monitoring and reporting efforts. Chief among these were:

1. The National Assessment of Educational Progress (NAEP), a measurement of academic achievement levels of 4th, 8th, and 12th grade students attending public and private schools in reading, writing, mathematics, science, history, civics, and geography. The results are reported as "The Nation's Report Card." The NAEP tests have been conducted since 1969, with financial support from the National Center for Education Statistics of the U.S. Department of Education. The Educational Testing Service prepares the reports.[128]

2. The National Education Goals Panel (NEGP), established by NGA and comprised of eight governors (one of whom served as chair), two senior federal executive branch officials, and four congressional leaders. The panel's responsibilities include determining indicators for measuring national education goal achievements and reporting on the federal government's follow-through on funding, flexibility, and mandate restraint commitments made at the Charlottesville education summit. Of particular importance to the America 2000 project was the panel's roles in developing "world-class standards" for each of five core subjects students need to know in order to succeed in contemporary society (English, history, mathematics, science, geography) and in implementing a voluntary nationwide examination system to monitor implementation of these standards.[129]

3. The National Council on Education Standards and Testing, established by Congress and the president in June 1991 and consisting of 32 members, including educators and researchers, members of Congress and the federal executive branch, governors and state legislators, and business representatives, with Colorado governor Roy Romer serving as cochairman. The council's basic purpose was to advise on the desirability and feasibility of national standards and testing. In January 1992 it recommended establishment of "world-class" minimum national standards of what students should know in mathematics, science, history, and other subjects at particular junctures of their education and use of essay and problem-solving tests to gauge progress. The use of voluntary standards and performance-based assessment measures for both students and school systems also were recommended by the Council.[130]

4. As noted in chapter 1, the Secretary's Commission on Achieving Necessary Skills (SCANS), established by the secretary of Labor in 1990 and chaired by former Labor secretary William E. Brock, was charged with the task of identifying standards essential

for successful job performance. The 30 SCANS members—representing for-profit and nonprofit organizations, labor, commerce, educators, and school administrators—determined five generic competencies (resources, interpersonal skills, information, systems, and technology), which, together with basic skills (reading, writing, arithmetic, speaking, and listening), thinking skills, and personal qualities (self-esteem, integrity), were key ingredients to preparing a world-class work force.[131] These SCANS competencies and skills were intended to be a major part of President Bush's "break-the-mold-schools" component of America 2000. The committee will promote development and utilization of assessments of student achievement, as well as examine the implications for curriculum, teaching materials, teacher training, and school organization. It estimated that "less than half of young adults can demonstrate the SCANS reading and writing minimums, even fewer can handle the mathematics."[132]

The "Goals 2000: Educate America Act"

In April 1993, the tenth anniversary of the release of *A Nation At Risk*, President Bill Clinton transmitted to the U.S. Congress for consideration the "Goals 2000: Educate America Act." If enacted, the bill (H.R. 1804) would codify into law the six national education goals and make Congress a full partner with the administration, the nation's governors, and others in efforts to reform education to ensure economic competitiveness and promote lifelong learning.

Five other major titles of the act would:

• Establish in law the bipartisan National Education Goals Panel (NEGP) which would report annually on progress in implementing the national goals and work to build public support for reforms to help attain them. In addition, the NEGP would be responsible for approving the criteria for voluntary national content, student performance, and opportunity-to-learn standards, as well as the standards themselves, and for approving criteria for certifying state assessment systems.

• Create a National Education Standards and Improvement Council (NESIC) composed of 20 members appointed by the president which would work with national organizations of educators and other concerned officials and citizens to develop criteria for certifying voluntary national curriculum content standards (of what all students should know and be able to do) and opportunity-to-learn standards (to ensure students have access to curriculum, instructional materials, teachers, technologies, and other means to enable them to gain the knowledge and skills specified in the content standards). The latter would be voluntary and general in nature, and would serve as qualitative benchmarks for states to use in formulating their own opportunity-to-learn standards. The council also would develop criteria for certification of state assessment systems over a four-year period; on a voluntary basis, states could submit their standards and assessment system to the council to certify as to their consistency with the national standards and criteria.

• Challenge states to develop through a broad-based, gubernatorially appointed panel, a comprehensive improvement plan and strategies for: preparing content standards, student assessments and performance standards, and teacher training; developing school-based opportunity-to-learn standards; giving educators tools and incentives to create better outcomes for students; and involving local education agencies, schools, parents, and the community in the design and implementation of reforms.

*   Authorize grants to school districts and individual schools to facilitate preparation and execution of local education improvement plans.

*   Set up a National Skill Standards Board, composed of 28 members, to design a voluntary national system of skill standards needed in broad clusters of major occupations and systems to assess, update, and disseminate information about the standards. The act would authorize $15 million for fiscal year 1994 for the board.

Reflecting the fiscal constraints imposed by the federal budget deficit, as well as the historically small federal share of K–12 education funding relative to local and state governments, the bill would authorize $393 million for fiscal 1994. As pointed out earlier in this chapter, this amount would be less than the 1993 appropriations for ESEA Chapter 2 block grants ($474 million), drug-free schools ($598 million), and adult education ($305 million). Nearly all of these funds would be allocated to states on a formula basis.

Two substantive amendments approved by the House Subcommittee on Elementary, Secondary and Vocational Education added a seventh national goal— improving school staff development—and a requirement that states specify "corrective actions" they would take if local schools or districts fail to attain the state's opportunity-to-learn or performance standards.

The Reform Record: Administrator, Teacher, and Public Appraisals

In view of the considerable rhetoric and not insignificant action at all levels of government and in the private sector during the "education decade" of the 1980s, the 10th anniversary of *A Nation at Risk* is a particularly appropriate time to examine the reform record. At the outset, it must be recognized that the architects of these reforms recognized that in view of the various factors cited earlier as affecting the educational process, it would take several years for improvements to be registered. The National Commission, for example, had initially set a 5-year time horizon, which was lengthened to 10 years by Reagan administration officials. Both the NGA and Bush administration reforms targeted the year 2000 for attainment, a timetable that public opinion polls found unrealistic. In the meantime, however, it is possible, using data from the assessments noted earlier in this section and other survey research, to obtain a reading on the implementation record.

This review is conducted in two ways. First, some general assessments of school reform by teachers, administrators, and the public are reported. Second, the empirical results of the three waves of education reform—standards, schools, and students—are examined.

As indicated in Table 5.17 the United States spends more per pupil than any

Table 5.17

Enrollment and Expenditures for K–12 Education in OECD Member Countries, 1985

Country	Enrollment, Percent of Total Population K-12	Expenditures, Percent of Gross Domestic Product [1] K-12	Expenditures per Pupil, K-12 Based on 1985 OECD PPPI [2]
1	2	3	4
United States [3]	19.7	3.8	3,314
Australia	18.9	3.1	1,983
Austria	15.8	3.6	2,497
Belgium	19.7	4.1	2,234
Canada	19.4	4.0	3,192
Denmark [4]	18.3	4.3	3,123
France	21.8	3.9	2,032
Ireland	25.6	4.4	1,161
Italy [5]	19.5	3.3	n/a
Japan [3]	20.0	3.1	1,805
Netherlands	[6] 20.2	3.5	1,956
New Zealand	22.9	2.8	1,262
Norway	19.8	4.1	2,900
Sweden	18.0	4.9	3,214
Switzerland	14.2	3.6	3,683
United Kingdom	16.8	2.3	2,251
West Germany	18.0	2.2	2,253

n/a indicates data not available.

[1] Gross domestic product data from Statistical Office of the United Nations, New York, New York, *Statistical Yearbook* (copyright).

[2] U.S. data from U.S. National Center for Education Statistics, *Digest of Education Statistics, 1989*. Based on OECDs 1985 Purchasing Power Parities Index.

[3] Data for public and private expenditures.

[4] 1986 data.

[5] 1983 data.

[6] 1984 data.

Source: Except where noted, United Nations Educational, Scientific, and Cultural Organization, Paris, France, *Statistical Yearbook* (copyright). Cited in U.S. Department of Commerce, *Statistical Abstract of the United States: 1991 Edition* (Washington, D.C.: U.S. Government Printing Office, 1991), 840.

other country, except Switzerland. Yet, as will be seen, in international test comparisons American students clearly fare much worse than their foreign counterparts. It should be recognized that such comparisons may be misleading due to the techniques used to convert different currencies into dollars and to the differing features of the educational systems. In the United States, for example, expenditures include certain noninstructional outlays, such as for student transportation, that are not made by other countries.

According to the National Center for Education Statistics, expenditures for public elementary and secondary schools increased 28.5 percent in constant dollars between 1975–76 and 1989–90. Overall spending is projected to grow 36.3 percent between 1989–90 and 2000–2001. On a basis of per pupil in average daily attendance, constant dollar outlays rose 41.1 percent between 1975–76 and 1989–90 and will increase 25.3 percent between 1989–90 and 2000–2001.[133]

The growth of public funding has not been accompanied by significant improvements in the output of the educational process or in perceptions about the overall quality of public schools. At best, the gains have been modest, and they have been confined to already high-achieving students from schools located in relatively affluent suburbs and to some minority students. Many of those who are at risk or who attend inner-city systems have been left behind in the movement to reform public education. This general assessment has been shared by a wide range of observers, as illustrated by the following studies, surveys, and statements.

On the fifth anniversary of the publication of *A Nation at Risk*, the U.S. Department of Education released *American Education: Making It Work*. The report's "good news" was a small (16 points out of 1,000) increase in SAT scores, a 10 percent rise in high school senior scores on history exams, and an improvement in homework policies in one-quarter of the high schools. The "bad news," however, commanded greatest media and official attention, especially the continued high dropout rates among black and Hispanic youth, unevenness in curriculum content, inadequate student skill preparation, and outmoded teacher hiring and promotion practices. Then Education secretary William Bennett blamed the "educational establishment," particularly teachers' unions: "You're standing in the doorways, you're blocking up the halls of education reform," he said.[134] In response to Secretary Bennett's charges, Albert Shanker, president of the American Federation of Teachers, asserted: "The constant criticism is demoralizing. . . . If the Secretary of Commerce disliked businessmen as much as Bennett dislikes teachers, the President would throw him out of the Cabinet."[135]

In 1988, the Carnegie Foundation for the Advancement of Teaching issued *Report Card on School Reform*. Of the 13,500 teachers surveyed, 70 percent gave the reform movement a "C" grade or less, with 20 percent giving reform a "D" or "F." Even though the report noted that at the five-year mark progress had been made in such areas as education mission and goals, principal leadership roles, business-school partnerships, curriculum improvements, student achievement levels, and teacher compensation, teachers remained quite skeptical. The report concluded that teachers were discouraged because they had not been genuine partners in the reform effort and had been made more responsible but not more empowered: "Almost forgotten is the fact that, when the renewal movement first began, teachers were sharply criticized in several states that quickly introduced teacher tests. There was a clear signal that teachers were the problem, rather than the solution, and the focus was on failure, not success."[136]

More recently, a 1990 survey of "The Condition of Teaching" by the Carnegie Foundation for the Advancement of Teaching reported that 18 percent of teachers gave a grade of "A" or "B" to the national school reform movement, while 54 percent gave it a "C," and 38 percent gave it a "D" or "F." As indicated

Table 5.18
Teachers Give Lower Grades to School Reform, 1987–90

Place and Date	"A"	"B"	Grades "C"	"D"	"F"
1	2	3	4	5	6
In the nation:					
1990	1%	17%	54%	19%	9%
1987	2%	29%	50%	13%	6%
In your state:					
1990	2%	26%	44%	20%	8%
1987	4%	31%	41%	16%	8%
At your school:					
1990	7%	37%	38%	13%	5%
1987	8%	36%	36%	13%	7%

Question: "If you were to give a grade to the national educational reform movement, what would it be?"

Source: The Carnegie Foundation for the Advancement of Teaching. Cited in Walters, L. S., "A Report Card on School Reform," *The Chrisitian Science Monitor,* October 3, 1990, p. 12.

in Table 5.18, these grades were lower than those given three years previously. However, teachers were much more favorable about the results of efforts to make improvements at their school and in their state. Among the troubling findings of the survey were that about 40 percent of the teachers said if they could "turn back the clock," they would not enter the profession; 61 percent reported morale at their school was "fair" or "poor"; student apathy and absenteeism were reported to be problems by 65 percent and 41 percent of the elementary and secondary teachers, respectively; and 71 percent felt their students would do only enough work to get by, while 58 percent believed students would cheat to get good grades.[137] In response to the survey results, Professor Theodore Sizer of Brown University stated: "The reform movement simply hasn't affected, in any consequential way, the way that schools work. We have the same vehicle being asked to drive at about the same speed with pretty much the same equipment."[138] In fact, Frank Newman, president of the Education Commission of the states, estimated that only 1 percent of all public schools in the country were undergoing restructuring.[139]

The 23d annual Gallup Poll on public attitudes toward public schools, released in the fall of 1991, revealed much higher grades for local schools than the teachers' ratings. As shown in Table 5.19, in recent years about two-fifths of the poll respondents gave schools in their community an "A" or "B" while only 15–17 percent gave them a "D" or failing grade. At the same time, these ratings have remained essentially stable since the release of *A Nation at Risk* despite the infusion of substantial new monies into the educational system. The

Table 5.19
Grading the Local Public Schools, 1982–92

Ratings Given the Local Public Schools (in percents)

Grade(s)	1992	1991	1990	1989	1988	1987	1986	1985	1984	1983	1982
1	2	3	4	5	6	7	8	9	10	11	12
A & B	40	42	41	43	40	43	41	43	42	31	37
A	9	10	8	8	9	12	11	9	10	6	8
B	31	32	33	35	31	31	30	34	32	25	29
C	33	33	34	33	34	30	28	30	35	32	33
D	12	10	12	11	10	9	11	10	11	13	14
FAIL	5	5	5	4	4	4	5	4	4	7	5
Don't Know	10	10	8	9	12	14	15	13	8	17	11

Question: "Students are often given the grades 'A', 'B', 'C', 'D' and 'FAIL' to denote the quality of their work. Suppose the public schools themselves, in this community, were graded in the same way. What grade would you give the public schools here - A, B, C, D, or Fail?"

Source: Elam, S.M., Rose, L. C., and Gallup, A.M., "The 24th Annual Gallup Poll of the Public's Attitudes Toward the Public Schools," *Phi Delta Kappan*, September 1992, p. 45.

Gallup Polls have also revealed some interesting, but not surprising, findings: schools across the nation receive lower grades than those in the respondent's community; teachers receive higher grades that principals and other administrators; and elementary school teachers, principals, and administrators are graded higher than their high school counterparts. More than half gave "C" or "D" grades to community school boards and to the parents who raised students.[140] The survey also reported the general finding that "familiarity with the public schools builds respect."[141] However, of particular significance to those concerned about "children at risk," blacks and inner-city residents were both far more critical of public schools and supportive of radical changes than the other poll respondents.[142] (see Table 5.20).

In summary, the preceding data indicate that the overall results of the education reform movement during the 1980s have not been impressive in terms of international comparisons or in the judgment of elementary and secondary school teachers and the parents of children who have the greatest educational needs and learning constraints. While the general public is much more favorably disposed toward the improvements made in their community's school system, their perception of national progress is much less positive. Public opinion experts like Daniel Yankelovich, president of the Public Agenda Foundation, have noted similar contradictions in the results of polls of public attitudes toward health care and the Congress. In the next section, the results of the three waves of educational reform are examined.

Standards

As explained earlier, the initial response to *A Nation at Risk* from the statehouse was "more and higher" standards aimed at the majority of students. In 1991 the Council of State Governments issued a report comparing the status of the states' actions on the recommendations of the National Commission on Excellence in Education in 1989 with the 1984 survey results covered earlier in this chapter. Forty-five chief state school officers replied to the former questionnaire.[143] With respect to instructional content, CSG's survey found that in 1989:[144]

- 38 states had acted to strengthen graduation requirements, compared with 30 in 1984;
- 21 states had adopted measurable standards and higher expectations for student academic performance and conduct, compared with 23 in 1984;
- 16 states had updated college preparatory course standards, compared with 17 in 1984, while 9 had done so for science courses not geared to the college-bound, compared with 13 in 1984;
- 28 states in both 1989 and 1984 had made high school fine and performing arts curricula more rigorous;
- 32 states had strengthened curriculum for the first eight grades, in order to provide a foundation for subsequent study, compared with 38 in 1984.

Table 5.20
Grading the Public Schools, by National Sample and Public School Parents, 1991

1	A&B	A	B	C	D	F	Don't Know
	2	3	4	5	6	7	8
By National Sample							
Public schools nationally	21	2	19	47	13	5	14
Public schools in this community	42	10	32	33	10	5	10
Public school teachers in this community	53	16	37	27	6	3	11
Public school principals and other administrators in this community	43	13	30	28	11	5	13
Public elementary school teachers in this community	57	19	38	22	5	2	14
Public elementary school principals and other administrators in this community	47	15	32	25	8	3	17
Public high school teachers in this community	40	10	30	28	9	4	19
High school principals and other administrators in this community	37	10	27	26	11	5	21
The school board in this community	30	8	22	30	12	8	20
Parents of students in the local schools for bringing up their children	30	5	25	37	16	7	10
By Public School Parents Only							
The school your oldest child attends	73	29	44	21	2	4	•
Teachers in the school your oldest child attends	72	31	41	21	4	2	1
Principals/administrators in the school your oldest child attends	61	29	32	24	6	4	5

Grades Assigned (in percents) (column header spanning A&B through Don't Know)

• Indicates less than one-half of 1%.

Source: Elam, S.M., Rose, L.C., and Gallup, A.M., "The 23rd Annual Gallup Poll of the Public's Attitudes Toward the Public Schools, " *Phi Delta Kappan*, September 1991, p. 54.

On the other hand, only 10 states had required high school students to have 4 years of English, 3 years of mathematics, science, and social studies, and a half year of computer science in order to graduate (compared with 5 states in 1984). Thirteen required foreign language in the elementary grades, down from 18 in 1984. Thirteen states also required two years of language instruction for college-bound students, up from 6 in 1984.

CSG also probed state actions on the standards and expectations fronts. It found that in 1989:[145]

• 32 states were using standardized achievement tests at major student transition points to higher levels, compared with 33 in 1984;

- 22 states were using tests to certify student credentials, identify needs for remedial intervention, or identify capabilities for advanced work, compared with 31 in 1984;
- 17 states reported making textbooks and other learning materials more rigorous, compared with 23 in 1984.

In explaining the decreases in state adoptions of certain standards, CSG concluded that some of the chief state school officers had indicated that the standards were no longer "relevant" or "appropriate" to their circumstances. Others, however, were "taking a more realistic view of what they have in place and can implement."[146]

These and other standard-setting and raising actions led by governors and legislators had not yielded significant positive results by the 1990s. The pace of reform was painstakingly slow, and neither lofty expectations nor even more funds could alter student performance. In fact, sometimes these efforts were counterproductive as they simply raised the frustration level and subsequent dropout rates of at-risk students who often were left behind in the rush to achieve "world-class" status or develop "high-performing" schools.

Even for the majority of students, by the mid-1980s it was becoming clear that achievement was more than a matter of money or even state-imposed standards. Especially since 1983, the sharp escalation in per pupil spending has not been accompanied by rising Scholastic Aptitude Test (SAT) or American College Testing (ACT) assessment scores. Graphic illustration of this point is found in Figure 5.3. While the downward spiral in SAT performance was halted by 1980–81, the scores have risen only slightly above this low point and are nowhere near their 1970–76 highs.

A related concern has been the drop in the number of students scoring above the 600 level on the verbal SATs, even though grade point averages were higher compared with previous test-takers. Between 1972 and 1992 the number of high-achieving students declined by 35 percent, while the mathematics section score proportions remained about flat (18.1% in 1992; 17.9% in 1972).[147] The reading scores of 9-, 13-, and 17-year-old students recorded by the National Assessment of Educational Progress remained static during the 1980s despite a sharp upswing in spending.

The release of these data reopened the debate triggered by publication of the Coleman Report in 1966 over why the scores had not gotten better. Some contended that the inclusion among the test-taking pool of greater numbers of minority youth, who tend to score lower than white students, was the key factor. While the percent of participating minorities climbed from 16 to 28 percent between 1977 and 1991, their scores also improved—by 19 points on SAT verbal and 31 points on math—while those of white youth dropped. Others explained away the lower scores of American children compared with their foreign counterparts on the grounds of cultural differences, including greater parental expectations in other countries about the education process and their children's achievement, the pressure on students to succeed in school beginning at an early

Figure 5.3

Total Expenditure per Pupil in Average Daily Attendance (ADA)[1] and Scholastic Aptitude Test (SAT) Scores, School Years, 1970–89

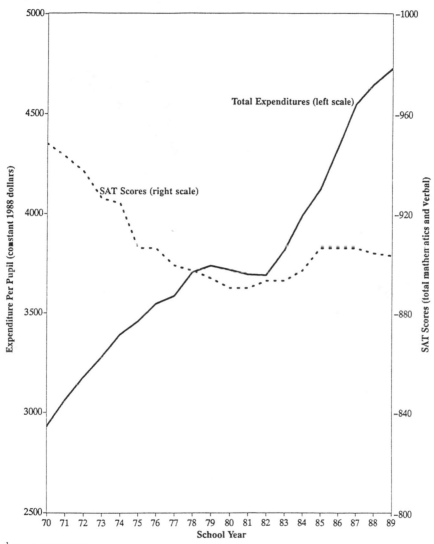

[1] Constant 1988 dollars.

Sources: U. S. Department of Education, National Center for Education Statistics, *Digest of Education Statistics 1969*, and *The Condition of Education 1990* (Washington, D.C., 1969 and 1990). Cited in U. S. Advisory Commission on Intergovernmental Relations, *The Structure of State Aid to Elementary and Secondary Education* (Washington, D.C.: U. S. Government Printing Office, M-175, December 1990), p. 4.

time, and the support for longer school days and school year. Still others pointed to the growth in the number of students for whom English was not their first language, the decline in special classes and curricula for high-achieving students, and grade inflation. Most observers, however, placed major responsibility on the public educational system in the United States and the deficiencies in it identified by the National Commission.[148]

As noted earlier, a particularly disturbing aspect of the scores on various educational attainment measures is the gap between white and minority students. The findings in the 1990 National Assessment of Educational Progress, for instance, revealed little progress in achieving a major goal of the educational reform movement during the two preceding decades—strengthening the performance of minority students—as measured by average scores by 9-, 13-, and 17-year-olds on reading, mathematics, science, civics, and geography proficiency tests.[149]

As shown in Table 5.21, the average reading, mathematics, and science proficiencies of black students reported by the Educational Testing Service were comparable with those of Hispanic students. Yet, the minority student proficiency levels were well below those of white students on each measure. While these averages mask significant educational needs some white students have, such as those living in rural communities, as well as high educational attainment by some blacks and Hispanics, the data are cause for considerable concern.

Table 5.21 also reveals that student performance has improved since the 1970s. Except for reading scores of 9- and 13-year-olds, proficiency increases were attained in the subject areas examined by all age groups. Moreover, the performance differentials between white and minority students have been gradually narrowing. Contrary to the findings in some earlier studies, by the late 1980s available data indicated that as students progressed through the educational system, proficiency gaps decreased rather than increased for 9-, 13-, and 17-year-olds. However, this trend has been influenced by lack of significant attainment increase by white students: "The progress made in reducing the disparities between these groups has primarily been a result of improved performance by minority students. The levels of performance shown by white students have remained quite stagnant across time."[150]

These results are especially frustrating to those who are concerned about international competition, from the standpoints of the United States' shrinking share of world high school enrollees as well as the costs and constraints resulting from inadequately skilled high school graduates entering the work force.[151] A 1992 survey of 175,000 students worldwide conducted by the Educational Testing Service (ETS) illustrates this point. Nine-year-olds in 14 countries and 13-year-olds in 20 countries were tested. The ETS found that among the latter group, American students scored 55 percent out of 100 on mathematics tests, while Korean and Tiawanese students topped the United States with scores of 73. In science, American students scored 67, about 11 points below the Koreans and Tiawanese. The spread was less substantial for 9-year-olds, particularly in sci-

Table 5.21

Average Proficiency in Various Subject Areas by Race/Ethnicity, 1976–80 and 1989–90

Race/Ethnicity	Age 9		Age 13		Age 17	
1	2		3		4	
Reading	1979-80	1989-90	1979-80	1989-90	1979-80	1989-90
Nation	215.0	209.2	258.5	256.8	285.5	290.2
White	221.3	217.0	264.4	262.3	292.8	296.6
Black	189.3	181.8	232.8	241.5	243.1	267.3
Hispanic	190.2	189.4	237.2	237.8	261.4	274.8
Mathematics	1977-78	1989-90	1977-78	1989-90	1977-78	1989-90
Nation	218.6	229.6	264.1	270.4	300.4	304.6
White	224.1	235.2	271.6	276.3	305.9	309.5
Black	192.4	208.4	229.6	249.1	268.4	288.5
Hispanic	202.9	213.8	238.0	254.6	276.3	283.5
Science	1976-77	1989-90	1976-77	1989-90	1976-77	1989-90
Nation	219.9	228.7	247.4	255.2	289.5	290.4
White	229.6	237.5	256.1	264.1	297.7	300.9
Black	174.8	196.4	208.1	225.7	240.2	253.0
Hispanic	191.9	206.2	213.4	231.6	262.3	261.5

Column header caption: *Proficiency*

Source: U.S. Department of Education, National Center for Educational Statistics, National Assessment of Educational Progress, *Trends in Academic Progress*. Prepared by Educational Testing Service. Cited in U.S. Department of Education, National Center for Educational Statistics, *Digest of Educational Statistics: 1992* (Washington, D.C.: U.S. Government Printing Office, October 1992), pp. 112, 118, 123.

ence, where the United States came in third of 10 countries with 63 percent. Interestingly, the survey found no correlation between performance and class size, length of school year, and spending levels for books, computers, and teachers. It did find, however, a strong inverse relationship between achievement and time spent watching television. Students in most of the countries surveyed spent far less time watching television and far more time doing homework and reading than their American counterparts.[152]

Table 5.22 provides international comparative data on proficiency test scores and factors affecting educational achievement. In 1991 American students fared very poorly on mathematics and science proficiency tests; 13-year-olds in the United States were ranked 14th in the former and 13th in the latter among 15 countries. The percentages of American students who reported spending two hours

Table 5.22
Proficiency Test Scores in Mathematics and Science for 13-Year-Old Students, by Selected Countries, 1991

Area	Average days of instruction in year	Mathematics Rank	Percent correct	Average minutes of mathematics instruction each week	% Students who spend 2 hrs. or more on homework per day	% Students who watch television 5 hours or more per day	Science Rank	Percent correct	Averagew minutes of science instruction each week	% Students who spend 2 hrs. or more on homework per day	% Students who watch television 5 hours or more per day
1	2	3	4	5	6	7	8	9	10	11	12
Canada	188	9	62	225	27	14	9	69	156	26	15
France	174	6	64	230	55	5	10	69	174	55	4
Hungary	177	5	68	186	58	13	4	73	207	61	16
Ireland	173	11	61	189	63	9	14	63	159	66	9
Israel	215	8	63	205	50	20	8	70	181	49	20
Italy	204	7	64	219	79	5	7	70	138	78	7
Jordan	191	15	40	180	56	7	15	57	180	54	10
Scotland	191	10	61	210	14	24	11	68	179	15	23
Slovenia	190	12	57	188	28	4	6	70	283	27	5
South Korea	222	1	73	179	41	11	1	78	144	38	10
Soviet republics	198	4	70	258	52	17	5	71	387	52	19
Spain	188	13	55	235	64	10	12	68	189	62	11
Switzerland	207	3	71	251	20	7	3	74	152	21	7
Taiwan	222	2	73	204	41	10	2	76	245	44	7
United States	178	14	55	228	29	20	13	67	233	31	22

Source: National Center of Education Statistics, U.S. Department of Education, and the National Science Foundation, *Learning Mathematics and Learning Science*, February 1992. Cited in U.S. Department of Commerce, *Statistical Abstract of the United States: 1992* (Washington, D.C.: U.S. Government Printing Office, 1992), p. 830.

or more per day on homework in these subjects also were well below those for most other countries, while the percentages of American students who reported watching television five hours or more a day were substantially higher than those for most other countries. Interestingly, American 13-year-olds received about as much or more average minutes of weekly mathematics and science instruction than their foreign counterparts, yet their proficiency scores did not appear to reflect the greater classroom time devoted to these subjects. Only three other countries required fewer than the United States' 178 instructional days.

One consequence of the insufficient time many American high school students spend in school or at homework is the need for remedial education in the workplace or college. A survey of the 1991 college freshman class conducted by the *Chronicle of Higher Education* revealed that 28.7 percent believed they will need remedial work in mathematics, 12.5 percent in English, 11.7 percent in science, and 11.1 percent in foreign language.[153]

Finally, it should be noted that the "more and higher" standards approach to education suffers from incomplete and inaccurate measures of performance. As Chester E. Finn has charged, "When it comes to consumer information, the American education system has been engaged in a massive cover-up."[154] For example, according to Finn, at the Charlottesville education summit, the governors and federal education officials identified some 90 possible indicators to use to monitor progress toward the national education goals. Yet, in 1990, state-by-state data were available for only 16 of these measures, and the reliability of these varied. Not only did this situation make it difficult to track the states' implementation record and dim prospects for successful goal achievement, but "as for wanting trustworthy information about where one's child or the school down the road stands vis-à-vis these national goals, one must be ingesting something illicit even to conjure such a fantasy."[155]

Unreliable or incomparable test results can produce false readings of performance—"the 'Lake Wobegon' effect, in which practically everyone scores above average."[156] This tendency is exacerbated by the actions of many school systems to water down course content in order to facilitate compliance with state-imposed graduation requirement hikes. After visiting some 60 public schools across the country, Thomas Toch found that juniors and seniors were taking freshman-level courses and that not many so-called advanced courses were truly advanced.[157]

The Schoolhouse: Teachers and Teaching

The previous sections reported data showing that teachers and the general public had different views regarding the problems confronting the public schools and the overall assessment of the educational reform record. Moreover, while some (such as the National Commission and the Carnegie Foundation) believe teachers to be at the forefront of efforts to change public schools, others (such as former DOE secretary Bennett) consider teachers and their unions to be among the most formidable obstacles to change. This section reviews how these and other differing perspectives affected the second wave of the reform movement.

Teachers were the beneficiaries of the increase in spending for elementary and secondary education during the 1980s. The 1989 CSG survey respondents indicated that 35 states had increased teacher salaries in the previous 12 months alone.[158] In terms of trends, while teacher salaries declined 10.4 percent in constant dollars between 1975–76 and 1980–81, they have risen consistently since then. Salaries grew about 22 percent in constant dollars between 1981–82 and 1989–90 and are projected to increase nearly 18 percent between 1989–90 and 2000–2001.[159]

With respect to the characteristics of the 2.32 million teachers in public elementary and secondary schools in the late 1980s:[160]

- They were evenly divided between the elementary and secondary levels;
- 70 percent were women;
- 86 percent were white, 8 percent were black, and 3 percent were Hispanic;
- 35 percent were between ages 30 and 39, 32 percent were between 40 and 49, 18 percent were over 50, and 13 percent were under 30;
- 52 percent had a bachelor's degree, 40 percent had a master's degree, 6 percent had an education specialist degree, and 1 percent had a doctorate;
- 45 percent had 10 to 20 years' teaching experience, 26 percent had 3 to 9 years' experience, 21 percent had more than 20 years' experience, and 8 percent had less than 3 years' experience;
- 22 percent of the secondary school teachers taught English, 19 percent taught mathematics, 14 percent taught social studies, and 11 percent taught science.

Table 5.23 provides data on the expectations and ideals of new teachers. Most respondents were positive before and after their first year that all children could learn, that they could make a difference in their students' learning despite what happened elsewhere in the school, and that they had been prepared to teach a diverse student body. Opinions were more evenly divided over whether teachers could reach more than two-thirds of the students and the desirability of more prior practical teaching training experience. Finally, nearly 90 percent agreed with the statement that "many children come to school with so many problems that it's very difficult for them to be good students."

Survey data reveal teachers' initial optimism did not produce long-term job satisfaction or willingness to remain in the profession. Similarly, salary increases seem to have produced no significant improvements along these lines. As Table 5.24 indicates, the responses to surveys by the U.S. Department of Education revealed no significant attitudinal changes between 1984 and 1989.

This response pattern may reflect in part the impact of implementation of certain National Commission recommendations on teacher morale. For example, according to CSG:[161]

Table 5.23
New Teachers' Expectations and Ideals Before and After Their First Year of Teaching, 1990 and 1991

	Percent of Teachers							
Item	Agree strongly		Somewhat agree		Somewhat	disagree	Disagree	strongly
	Before 1st year	After 1st year	Before 1st year	After 1st year	Before 1st year	After 1st year	Before 1st year	After 1st year
1	2	3	4	5	6	7	8	9
Attitudes about teachers and students								
All children can learn	93	88	6	10	(1)	1	(1)	(1)
I can really make a difference in the lives of my children	83	68	16	30	1	1	(1)	(1)
If I do my job well, my students will benefit regardless of how the rest of the school functions	42	43	47	46	10	9	1	2
Many children come to school with so many problems that it's very difficult for them to be good students	28	47	47	42	18	8	6	3
Even the best teachers will find it difficult to really teach more than two-thirds of their students	8	14	38	44	39	30	15	11
Attitudes about teacher preparation								
My training has prepared me to teach students from a variety of ethnic backgrounds	42	30	39	40	15	21	5	9
All teachers should take a national standardized test to demonstrate their qualifications	31	24	35	34	19	23	15	19
I wish I had more practical training to be a teacher before I begin teaching in my own classroom	26	28	32	33	23	25	18	14

1 Less than 0.5 percent.

Source: Metropolitan Life/Louis Harris Associates, Inc., *The American Teacher, 1991*, copyrighted. Cited in U.S. Department of Education, National Center for Education Statistics, *Digest of Education Statistics: 1992* (Washington, D.C.: U.S. Government Printing Office, 1992), p. 82.

Table 5.24
Percentage and Level of Job Satisfaction of Public School Teachers, 1984–89

Item	Percent of Teachers					
	1984	1985	1986	1987	1988	1989
1	2	3	4	5	6	7
Satisfaction With Job as a Teacher in Public Schools:						
All Teachers	100	—	100	100	100	100
Very Satisfied	40	—	33	40	50	44
Somewhat Satisfied	41	—	48	45	37	42
Somewhat Dissatisfied	16	—	15	12	11	11
Very Dissatisfied	2	—	4	2	2	3
Seriously Considered Leaving Teaching To Go Into Some Other Occupation	—	51	55	52	—	—
Likely To Leave the Teaching Profession To Go Into Some Other Occupation Within the Next 5 Years	—	26	27	22	26	26

— Indicates data not available.

Source: Metropolitan Life/Louis Harris Associates, Inc., *The American Teacher, 1989*,
copyrighted. (This table was prepared January 1990.) Cited in U.S. Department of
Education, National Center for Education Statistics, *Digest of Education Statistics:
1991* (Washington, D.C.: U.S. Government Printing Office, 1991), p. 81.

- In 1989, 37 states required persons preparing to teach to meet high educational standards, compared with 29 in 1984, while 30 states required them to demonstrate an aptitude for teaching, 1 more than in the earlier survey;

- 33 states required teachers to demonstrate competence in an academic discipline in 1989, 11 more than five years previously;

- With respect to pay issues, 10 states reported that teacher salaries were professionally competitive, adjusted to marketplace conditions, and based on performance, compared with 9 in 1984;

- Only 1 state tied salary increases to an evaluation system that rewarded superior performance and penalized inferior performance and included peer review (down from 8 in 1984), while 4 states reported using such a system for tenure decisions (down from 10 in 1984), and 6 states used it for retention decisions (down from 9 in 1984);

- With respect to the frequently recommended "career ladder" system to distinguish among beginning, experienced, and master teachers, only five states had adopted this approach by 1989, the same number as in 1984;

- Master teachers were involved in designing teacher preparation programs and supervising beginning teachers in 24 states in 1989, an increase of 10 since 1984.

As in the case of standards, certain recommendations were deemed "inappropriate" by chief state school officers as well as teachers. These included the use of 11-month contracts for teachers, career ladders, evaluation-based promotions, and establishment of a 200- to 220-day school year.

An Arkansas Example. Arkansas is a good example of the approach many states took to reform. Following hearings during 1983 in each of Arkansas's 75 counties, a committee chaired by Hillary Rodham Clinton recommended and Governor Bill Clinton supported legislation to raise and toughen education standards and to remove incompetent teachers. These reforms included smaller classes; a longer school day and year; mandatory kindergarten; special courses for "gifted and talented" children; required offerings in chemistry, physics, computer science, advanced mathematics, foreign language, and other subjects; and higher high school graduation requirements. The legal dropout age was raised from 15 to 16. Any third, sixth, or eighth grader who failed to pass a standardized examination could not be promoted, and he or she would receive remedial help. An eighth grader failing the test twice would be given an alternative high school education. Accompanying a proposed sales tax hike to pay for salary increases and the addition of new teachers was a requirement for existing teachers to pass a competency test, geared to the eighth grade level. The latter was strongly opposed by the Arkansas Education Association, as well as the National Education Association, but it was approved by the legislature, together with the other components of the package, due in large part to the governor's vigorous lobbying effort. Ten percent of the teachers who took the competency test failed, and 3.5 percent of the state's teacher population (1,315) subsequently left their profession. Union-backed efforts to repeal the competency test have not been successful.[162]

Teaching Conditions. Statistics prepared by the U.S. Department of Education shed greater light on the comparative state actions reported by CSG. Two areas of particular interest are teaching assignments and involvement in decision making.

With respect to the former, as indicated in Table 5.25, typical class sizes were still fairly large by the late 1980s, with the average being 23 students nationally, and over one-third of the teachers were concerned about this situation. As reported earlier, one proxy for class size in public elementary and secondary schools, pupil-teacher ratios, had begun to decline from 17.9 pupils per teacher in the fall of 1985 to 17.2 in the fall of 1991.[163] Nearly four-fifths of the teachers reported spending 40–59 hours per week on the job. Yet one in five felt they were not qualified to teach subjects they were assigned.

Turning to what might be called "teacher empowerment" issues, it appears that little progress had been made nationally by 1987 in expanding teacher participation in personnel and budgetary matters. For the most part, as shown in Table 5.26, a teacher's decision-making role was confined to instructional matters.

Other useful indicators of progress in the "schoolhouse" component of the

Table 5.25
Selected Characteristics of Public School Teachers' Current Teaching Assignments, 1987

Characteristic	Percent of Teachers
1	2
Number of Students per typical class:	
19 or less	20%
20 to 29	64%
30 or more	16%
Feelings about most typical class size:	
Too large	36%
About right	62%
Too small	1%
Average number of hours per week spent on job:	
Less than 40	11%
40 to 59	78%
60 or more	11%
Teaching subjects unqualified to teach:	20%

Source: U. S. Department of Education, National Center for Education Statistics, *Digest of Education Statistics: 1991* (Washington, DC: U. S. Government Printing Office), p. 77

Table 5.26
Percentage of Teachers Involved in Making Selected Decisions, 1987

Decision	Percent Involved
1	2
Choosing Textbooks	79
Shaping the Curriculum	63
Tracking Students into Special Classes	45
Setting Promotion and Retention Policies	34
Deciding School Budgets	20
Evaluating Teacher Performance	10
Selecting New Teachers	7
Selecting New Administrators	7

Source: U. S. Department of Education, National Center for Education Statistics, *Digest of Education Statistics: 1991* (Washington, DC: U. S. Government Printing Office), p. 78.

educational reform movement have been compiled by the National Governors' Association. Its National Education Goals Panel monitored results for five years. Two key areas were teaching and school leadership.

Turning to the former, NGA established a Task Force on Teaching in the belief that while nearly all states had raised teacher salaries and standards, more comprehensive steps needed to be taken, including:[164]

- Create a national board to define teacher standards;
- Recruit able teacher candidates;
- Rebuild teacher education;
- Improve teacher compensation, both at entry and throughout the career;
- Redesign the structure of the teaching career;
- Align teacher incentives with schoolwide student performance; and
- Redesign schools to create more productive working and learning environments.

In assessing progress on these seven fronts since 1986, the task force found:[165]

1. While a National Board for Professional Teaching Standards had been created in 1987 to develop "high and rigorous" standards for the teaching profession and to issue certificates to experienced teachers who apply for certification in 1993, the states were mired in debates over whether their boards for issuing entry-level teaching licenses should be autonomous and dominated (numerically) by teachers. Fifteen states required applicants to attain a minimum grade point average, 21 required them to pass a state-prescribed standardized test prior to entry into a teacher education program, and 15 required evaluation of classroom performance before issuing a regular license.

2. A wide array of efforts were under way to heighten the attractiveness of the teaching profession and increase the pool of prospective qualified teachers, such as providing scholarships and forgivable loans, identifying alternative career routes to teacher licensure for retired military personnel and other adults who lacked formal training in professional education (33 states), creating special programs geared to recruiting minority candidates (11 states), and establishing regional credentials for licensure to facilitate interstate mobility of candidates (9 states).

3. Slow progress was reported in teacher education, with relatively few states raising standards for teacher education programs or requiring teachers to have significant course work and even a major in an academic area in addition to education.

4. As pointed out previously in this section, considerable progress was evident on increasing teacher compensation on an across-the-board basis, boosting the average beginning salary in 1990–91 to $21,542 and overall salary to $32,880. However, these salaries still lagged behind those of other professions and in fact declined 0.5 percent from the preceding academic year. In addition, state attempts

to hike mathematics and science teacher pay and to differentiate raises on the basis of performance had met with political resistance by teachers' unions.

5. Regarding teacher incentive plans such as career ladders and linking salary increases to evaluations of classroom performance, while a few successful experiments were reported in states like Missouri, Tennessee, Arizona, California, and Utah, NGA concluded, "For the most part, the teaching career is still flat; for the vast majority of teachers, performance has little or no impact on their roles, responsibilities, or compensation, and job expectations change little from their first day of teaching to the day they retire."[166]

6. Although teacher incentive programs had not proven very popular, school performance programs were under development in at least eight states, where increases in test scores, decreases in dropout rates, and other factors would be used as a basis for rewarding teachers within a school context rather than on the basis of their individual performance.

7. The task force had little to report on school restructuring aimed at improving teaching and learning.

The NGA's monitoring agenda also included "school leadership," since the role of principals and superintendents was considered critical to the "schoolhouse" wave of educational reform. Its Task Force on Leadership and Management called upon states to:

- Revise preparation programs for administrators so that new principals are trained to be effective school leaders;
- Ensure that administrator selection and licensure practices reflect the skills and knowledge needed by effective principals;
- Develop an evaluation system for principals;
- Provide ongoing training for school administrators; and
- Reward principals and schools for improved student achievement.[167]

NGA found some examples of solid state efforts to improve school leadership through tightening licensure requirements, offering internships and mentoring to prospective or beginning principals, revamping administrator preparation curricula, and increasing principal assessments. However, in general it concluded: "Few states have developed comprehensive strategies to improve the caliber of principals or have made administrative improvement part of the state's larger education reform agenda. And unfortunately, a heterogeneous leader corps remains elusive; principals and superintendents still are primarily white and male."[168]

In summary, the results of state actions on school-related components of the educational reform agenda, from the perspective of the nation's governors, were mixed. While substantial progress was registered in improving teacher salaries and raising standards, little fundamental change was evident in the structure of schools, the approach to teaching and rewarding teachers, and the role of teachers.

Teacher morale also did not improve significantly during the 1980s. As Donald J. Senese, former U.S. assistant secretary for Educational Research and Improvement, stated in a 1985 speech, the notions of the "shopping mall high school," where value-neutral schools offer courses of varying degrees of difficulty and usefulness (from algebra to bachelor living) was too firmly ingrained in American education.[169]

Moreover, the " 'treaty of mediocrity,' where the students and teachers say in effect to each other, 'If you don't bother me, I won't bother you!' " was too prevalent.[170] Both conditions continued to confront elementary and secondary schools in the 1990s. As a result, as a Heritage Foundation critic of the Bush administration's education initiative put it: "We don't need America 2000 schools. . . . What we need is America 1950 schools."[171]

Students

The third wave of educational reform focused on students, especially those who were not helped by the earlier efforts to raise SAT scores, strengthen the curricula for the college bound, and offer specialized and advanced courses. As discussed earlier in this chapter, the goals here were excellence and equity. Available data, however, indicate that much remains to be accomplished in both areas.

The review of the first wave of educational reform covered the emphasis placed upon more rigorous curriculum content, higher student promotion and graduation standards, and longer school daily schedules and annual calendars as key ways to improve learning, as measured by SAT scores. The third wave of reform reflected a broader vision of educational attainment, in terms of both substance and audience. It was well expressed in the first national goal developed at the Charlottesville education summit:

By the year 2000, American students will leave grades four, eight, and twelve having demonstrated competency in challenging subject matter including English, mathematics, science, history, and geography; and every school in America will ensure that all students learn to use their minds well so they may be prepared for responsible citizenship, further learning, and productive employment in our modern economy.[172]

As indicated in the previous section, in 1990 the National Assessment of Educational Progress (NAEP) issued its annual edition of "The Nation's Report Card," which summarized 20 years of assessment of student achievement. The overall NAEP results were "a bleak portrait of the current status of student achievement in the United States."[173] Clearly, public elementary and secondary schools had to make significant and swift strides if the national goal was to be achieved by the end of the century. The findings were summarized as follows:

• Students' current achievement levels are far below those that might indicate competency in challenging subject matter in English, mathematics, science, history and geography.

—Students can read at a surface level, getting the gist of material, but they do not read analytically or perform well on challenging reading assignments.

—Small proportions of students write well enough to accomplish the purposes of different writing tasks; most do not communicate effectively.

—Students' grasp of the four basic arithmetic operations and beginning problem-solving is far from universal in elementary and junior high school; by the time that students near high-school graduation, half cannot handle moderately challenging material.

—Only small proportions of students appear to develop specialized knowledge needed to address science-based problems, and the pattern of falling behind begins in elementary school.

—Students are familiar with events that have shaped American history, but they do not appear to understand the significance and connections of those events. . . .

• Trends across the past 20 years suggest that, although some ground lost in the 1970s may have been regained in the 1980s, overall achievement levels are little different entering the 1990s than they were two decades earlier.

• Very few students demonstrate that they can use their minds well. In recent assessments, more students appear to be gaining basic skills, yet fewer are demonstrating a grasp of higher-level applications of those skills.

• Despite progress in narrowing the gaps, the differences in performance between White students and their minority counterparts remain unacceptably large. Little progress has been made in reducing gender performance gaps favoring males in mathematics and science and females in writing.

• Large proportions of students, even including those in academic high-school programs, are not enrolled in challenging mathematics and science coursework. Instructional time is particularly low for science in elementary schools, writing in middle schools, and geography in high schools.

• Across the past 20 years, little seems to have changed in how students are taught. Despite much research suggesting better alternatives, classrooms still appear to be dominated by textbooks, teacher lectures, and short-answer activity sheets.[174]

Dropouts. A NAEP finding of particular concern was the differential in the persistence, as well as the performance, of white, black, and Hispanic students, As indicated earlier, while test scores for black and Hispanic youth have improved incrementally, they still fall well below those of their white counterparts.

With respect to the persistence factor, or high school completion, between 1975 and 1991 the rates for 19- to 20-year-old blacks improved 9 percent (from 71% to 80%), compared with 3 percent for whites (from 86% to 89%), and 2 percent overall (from 83% to 85%). Hispanic youth, however, registered a 5 percent drop (from 66% to 61%), and their completion rates were 24 points below those of all 19- to 20-year-old students. For the 16- to 24-year-old group, over this period black student dropout rates also improved 9 percent (from 23% to 14%), compared with 2 percent for whites and 1 percent overall, while Hispanic dropouts increased 6 percent. The gap between white and black students

Figure 5.4
High School Completion Status: Percentage of Young Adults[1] with High School Credentials, 1991

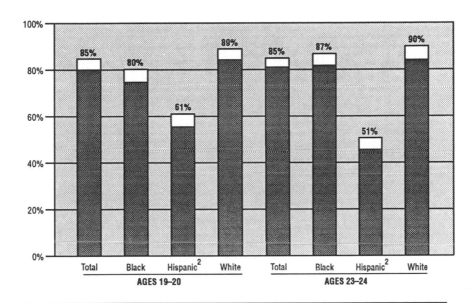

SOURCE: National Education Goals Panel, *The National Education Goals Report: Building a Nation of Learners* (Washington, D.C.: U.S. Government Printing Office, 1992), p. 22.

NOTES: [1] Does not include those still enrolled in high school.
[2] Hispanic rates may vary more than rates for other groups because of a small sample size.

decreased from 15 to 9 percentage points for 19- and 20-year-olds and from 12 to 5 for 16- to 24-year-old youth.[175]

In 1991, as shown in Figure 5.4, the high school graduation rate was 85 percent for all 19- and 20-year-old students, compared with 80 percent for blacks and 61 percent for Hispanics. Similar or somewhat higher rates are evident for the 23- and 24-year-old group, except for Hispanics. It should be noted that the overall high school completion rates are at an all-time high for the United States.

About 90 percent of these graduates earned a high school diploma, while the remainder received an alternative credential such as the General Educational Development (GED) certificate. As shown in Table 5.27, in 1990, 410,000 persons received a GED, 41 percent of whom were over 25 years of age and two-thirds of whom were over 20 years. In addition to appealing to older students, the certificate—which can be attained after passing a 7-hour, 35-minute test— also is a means for former dropouts to achieve high school graduation equivalency status. As can be seen in the table, the number of persons receiving GED credentials has decreased from the 1981–82 peak levels.

Table 5.27
General Educational Development (GED) Credentials Issued and Age of Test Takers, 1974 to 1990

		Percentage distribution of GED test takers, by age				
Year	Total, in thousands	19 yrs. old or less	20-24 years old	24-29 years old	30-34 years old	35 yrs. old or over
1	2	3	4	5	6	7
1974	294	35	27	13	9	17
1975	340	33	26	14	9	18
1976	333	31	28	14	10	17
1977	332	40	24	13	8	14
1978	381	31	27	13	10	18
1979	426	37	28	12	13	11
1980	479	37	27	13	8	15
1981	489	37	27	13	8	14
1982	486	37	28	13	8	15
1983	465	34	29	14	8	15
1984	427	32	28	15	9	16
1985	413	32	26	15	10	16
1986	428	32	26	15	10	17
1987	444	33	24	15	10	18
1988	410	35	22	14	10	18
1989	357	36	22	14	10	17
1990	410	35	25	14	10	17

1 Number of persons receiving high school equivalency certificates based on the GED test.

Source: American Council on Education, General Educational Development Testing Service, *GED Statistical Report*, various years. Cited in U.S. Department of Education, National Center for Education Statistics, *Digest of Education Statistics: 1992* (Washington, D.C.: U.S. Government Printing Office, 1992), p. 109.

Another perspective on dropouts is provided by Table 5.28, which shows the change in the rate by sex as well as by race/ethnicity from 1975 to 1991. While the percentage of dropouts among 16- to 24-year-olds in the population has declined for non-Hispanic whites and blacks, it has grown for both Hispanic men and women. White non-Hispanic dropout rates are well below those of both black and Hispanic men and women.

With respect to the reasons 8th and 10th graders gave for dropping out, "did not like school" was the major education-related factor cited by white, black, and Hispanic students, and pregnancy was the major family/job-related reason. As shown in Table 5.29, white students were most likely to cite school-related factors.

According to the National Center for Education Statistics, 47 percent of the sophomores who dropped out of school in 1980 had returned and completed school by 1986. In terms of race/ethnicity, 49 percent were black, 48 percent were white, and 36 percent were Hispanic.[176] Data reported in 1990 by students who had dropped out between 8th and 10th grades found that a sizable proportion

Table 5.28
Percentage of High School Dropouts Among Persons 16 to 24 Years Old,[1] by Sex and Race/Ethnicity, October 1975 to October 1991

Year	Total				Men				Women			
	All Races	White non-Hisp.	Black non-Hisp.	Hispanic Origin	All Races	White non-Hisp.	Black non-Hisp.	Hispanic Origin	All Races	White non-Hisp.	Black non-Hisp.	Hispanic Origin
1975	13.9	11.4	22.9	29.2	13.3	11.0	23.0	26.7	14.5	11.8	22.9	31.6
1976	14.1	12.0	20.5	31.4	14.1	12.1	21.2	30.3	14.2	11.8	19.9	32.3
1977	14.1	11.9	19.8	33.0	14.5	12.6	19.5	31.6	13.8	11.2	20.0	34.3
1978	14.2	11.9	20.2	33.3	14.6	12.2	22.5	33.6	13.9	11.6	18.3	33.1
1979	14.6	12.0	21.1	33.8	15.0	12.6	22.4	33.0	14.2	11.5	20.0	34.5
1980	14.1	11.4	19.1	35.2	15.1	12.3	20.8	37.2	13.1	10.5	17.7	33.2
1981	13.9	11.4	18.4	33.2	15.1	12.5	19.9	36.0	12.8	10.2	17.1	30.4
1982	13.9	11.4	18.4	31.7	14.5	12.1	21.2	30.5	13.3	10.9	15.9	32.8
1983	13.7	11.2	18.0	31.6	14.9	12.2	19.9	34.3	12.5	10.1	16.2	29.1
1984	13.1	11.0	15.5	29.8	14.0	12.0	16.8	30.6	12.3	10.1	14.3	29.0
1985	12.6	10.4	15.2	27.6	13.4	11.1	16.1	29.9	11.8	9.8	14.3	25.2
1986	12.2	9.7	14.2	30.1	13.1	10.3	15.0	32.8	11.4	9.1	13.5	27.2
1987	12.7	10.4	14.4	28.6	13.3	10.8	15.5	29.1	12.2	10.0	13.4	28.1
1988	12.9	9.6	14.5	35.8	13.5	10.3	15.0	36.0	12.2	8.9	14.0	35.5
1989	12.6	9.4	13.9	33.0	13.6	10.3	14.9	34.4	11.7	8.5	13.0	31.6
1990	12.1	9.0	13.2	32.4	12.3	9.3	13.9	34.3	11.8	8.7	14.4	30.3
1991	12.5	8.9	13.6	35.3	13.0	8.9	13.5	39.2	11.9	8.9	13.7	31.1

[1] "Status" dropouts.

Note.—"Status" dropouts are persons who are not enrolled in school and who are not high school graduates. People who have received GED credentials are counted as graduates. Data are based upon sample surveys of the civilian noninstitutional population.

Source: U.S. Department of Commerce, Bureau of the Census, *Current Population Survey,* unpublished tabulations; and U.S. Department of Education, National Center for Education Statistics, *Dropout Rates in the United States.* Cited in U.S. Department of Education, National Center for Education Statistics, *Digest of Education Statistics: 1992* (Washington, D.C.: U.S. Government Printing Office, 1992), 109.

Table 5.29

Reasons Given by Students between the 8th and 10th Grades for Dropping Out of School, by Race/Ethnicity, 1990

Reason	Black	Percents Hispanic	White
School-related reasons			
Did not like school	45	42	58
Felt I didn't belong	8	19	31
Could not keep up with schoolwork	30	20	36
Was failing school	30	39	45
Did not feel safe at school	20	13	10
Family/Job-related reasons			
Could not work and go to school at same time	9	14	16
Had to support family	8	13	9
Was pregnant	41	21	32
Became a parent	19	10	13

Source: National Education Goals Panel, *The National Education Goals Report: Building A Nation of Learners* (Washington, D.C.: U.S. Government Printing Office, 1992), p. 80.

would be likely to return to school, especially if they felt they could obtain a good job after graduation or if they felt they could graduate. Table 5.30 shows the responses by race/ethnicity.

The School and Home Environments. There are several possible explanations for these findings. One is that the schools many blacks and Hispanics attend do not provide environments that are conducive to learning. Another is that the homes of some of these youth similarly are not supportive of the education process. With respect to the former, a 1988 survey found that teachers in inner-city and urban schools were much more likely to report disciplinary, learning, social, and behavioral problems than their colleagues in suburban, rural, or small town schools (see Table 5.31). The extent of basic learning skill deficiencies, alcohol and drug abuse, teenage pregnancies, and disciplinary problems identified by inner-city teachers, with the exception of alcohol consumption, was more than twice the rates for other school systems.

The public generally agrees with teacher assessments of problem areas. Since the early 1980s, the top two problems reported in the annual Gallup Poll on the public's attitudes toward public schools have been use of drugs and lack of discipline. Lack of financial support has been a distant third. In the 1991 survey 22 percent of the respondents identified drug abuse and 20 percent identified disciplinary problems, compared with 38 percent and 19 percent, respectively, in 1990.[177]

Data collected by the National Educational Goals Panel reveal few encouraging and several disturbing trends with respect to the school environment. On the

Table 5.30
Reasons Given by Dropouts between the 8th and 10th Grades for Returning to School, by Race/Ethnicity, 1990

Reason	Black	*Percents* Hispanic	White
School-related reasons			
If I felt sure I could get a good job after graduation	85	67	56
If I could participate in sports or other activities	28	30	28
If I felt I could graduate	85	57	53
If I felt sure I could get tutoring help	53	58	43
If there were no gangs at school	11	23	10
Family/Job-related reasons			
If I could attend classes at night or on weekends	47	48	48
If I didn't have to work to support self or family	26	18	29
If child care were available at school	29	19	10

Source: National Education Goals Panel, *The National Education Goals Report: Building A Nation of Learners* (Washington, D.C.: U.S. Government Printing Office, 1992), p. 81.

encouraging side, it appears that in-school drug use is declining, at least among 12th graders. From 1980 to 1991, student use of alcohol, marijuana, and cocaine on school grounds declined sharply. Over this period the percentages of these students reporting using drugs at school during the previous year went from 21 percent to 5 percent for marijuana, from 14 percent to 7 percent for alcohol, and from 3 percent to 1 percent for cocaine.[178] Yet a 1989 survey found that 31 percent of high school seniors believed alcohol and marijuana were easy to obtain at their school.[179]

NAEP found that even though drugs were rarely used in schools, overall drug use reported by high school seniors was considerable, even though declining. In 1991, 54 percent of these students reported using alcohol during the previous 30 days, compared with 72 percent in 1980, while 16 percent reported using marijuana, compared with 34 percent previously.[180] Drug use by white students exceeded that by minority students. The rates for alcohol were: white, 58 percent; Hispanic, 54 percent; and black, 34 percent. For marijuana, they were: white, 15 percent; Hispanic, 14 percent; and black, 7 percent. As indicated in earlier chapters, substance abuse—whether at school or another place—impairs performance and poses health risks.

In part because of drug dealing, school is far from a "safe haven," especially for black students. In 1991, 20 percent of black 12th graders reported being threatened with a weapon during the preceding year, compared with 15 percent of Hispanic students and 13 percent of white students. Ten percent of the black seniors reported being injured by a weapon while at school, compared with 7

Table 5.31

Rating of School Problems by Teachers and Students, 1988

Selected problems	Total	Inner city	Urban	Sub-urban	Small town	Rural	% of Students who say they know 10 or more students involved in each problem
1	2	3	4	5	6	7	8
The number of students requiring constant discipline	14	27	19	11	12	10	30
The number of students who lack basic skills (Student's item: can't read)	16	38	16	12	14	13	5
The number of teenage pregnancies [1]	12	28	9	5	13	12	9
The number of students drinking alcohol [2]	33	32	20	24	38	38	47
The number of students using drugs [2]	14	26	11	14	12	15	25
The number of incidents involving violence in school [2]	4	10	4	3	5	(3)	(3)
Have threatened or become violent with other students	—	—	—	—	—	—	23
Have threatened or become violent with teachers	—	—	—	—	—	—	5
The number of dropouts [1]	9	30	11	6	6	9	9

1 Asked of junior high and high school students and teachers only.
2 Asked of all students and junior high and high school teachers.
3 Less than 0.5 percent.
— Data not available.

Source: Metropolitan Life/Louis Harris and Associates, Inc., *The American Teacher, 1988.* Cited in U.S. Department of Education, National Center for Education Statistics, *Digest of Education Statistics: 1992* (Washington, D.C.: U.S. Government Printing Office, 1992), p. 31.

percent of Hispanic students and 5 percent of white students.[181] Overall, student victimization has been on the rise since 1980. In 1991, 42 percent of the 12th graders reported property thefts during the previous year, 28 percent reported vandalism of their property, 26 percent were threatened without a weapon, and 15 percent were injured without a weapon.[182]

These findings suggest that learning often becomes secondary to surviving in many schools. This is especially the case in inner-city systems. While in 1991 teachers generally felt safe in school during the day, 15 percent of those in city schools reported feeling unsafe after hours, compared with 6 percent in town schools and 5 percent in suburban or urban fringe schools. Overall, 8 percent of the teachers reported feeling unsafe after school hours, compared with 1 percent during school hours.[183]

The rates of teacher victimization in the forms of verbal abuse and threats are also higher in city schools. In 1991, 28 percent of the teachers in these schools reported verbal abuse within the preceding four weeks, 15 percent reported being threatened with injury during the preceding 12 months, and 3 percent reported being physically attacked during the preceding 12 months. For comparative purposes, the overall reporting rates for the above kinds of teacher victimization in all types of schools were 19 percent, 8 percent, and 2 percent, respectively.[184]

From a teacher's standpoint, this situation can be very frustrating. Concerns over lawsuits have caused teachers to avoid physical contact with students, even to escort them to the principal's office. While states like Michigan have taken action recently to give teachers more authority to use physical force, it is still difficult for many teachers to bring discipline to the classroom and to protect themselves in this manner.[185]

The serious learning and personal safety problems confronting students and teachers in many inner city schools were vividly described in Jonathan Kozol's 1991 book, *Savage Inequalities: Children in America's Schools*. His examination of conditions in six school systems—East St. Louis; the south side of Chicago; New York City; Camden, New Jersey; Washington, D.C.; and San Antonio—revealed persistent racial segregation, where "social policy has been turned back almost one hundred years." The schools were filthy, rundown, and violent. In the author's judgment, they were "extraordinarily unhappy places" characterized by despair, disrepair, and danger. They reminded him of " 'garrisons' or 'outposts' in a foreign nation."[186]

All in all, these findings lead to the conclusion that for both students and teachers, the learning process often is disrupted or displaced by fears for personal or property safety. It is increasingly common for school hallways to be patrolled by police or uniformed security guards, for students to enter school through metal detectors to reveal guns, knives, or other hidden weapons, and for gang-related violence to make schools battlegrounds. In this environment, it is small wonder that students who need the most help—those considered at risk—receive the least attention.

It also is not surprising that many of the best teachers avoid inner-city systems.

While these systems have sought to attract good teachers through salary incentives ("combat pay"), college tuition reductions and favorable educational and loan repayment schedules, free parking, extra service credits toward retirement, and guaranteed summer employment, the response has not been overwhelming. As a result, other steps have been proposed, such as busing teachers from central locations to troubled schools (Houston and New York City).[187]

Turning to the home environment, the 1966 Coleman report discussed earlier raised the crucial importance of family background and socioeconomic factors, as opposed to public spending, on educational attainment. The growing incidences of single-parent families, working mothers, and latchkey children, among other demographic trends discussed in earlier chapters, pose severe challenges to the at-home learning process and for parental involvement in school activities. As noted previously, American elementary and secondary students spend significantly more time watching television and less time doing homework than their counterparts in foreign countries. In part this pattern is a reflection of parental absenteeism or inadequate supervision.

A 1988 survey of eighth grader parental involvement found that family rules had been established for doing homework (92%), maintaining a certain grade average (73%), and the number of hours of television watched on school days (62%). Twenty-nine percent reported never or seldom helping with homework, while 35 percent had contacted the school about their child's academic program, and 53 percent about academic performance. Only 32 percent belonged to a parent-teacher organization (PTO), and 36 percent had attended a PTO meeting.[188]

With respect to younger children, in a 1991 survey of the home activities of 3- to 8-year-olds, these children watched from 2.2 to 2.6 hours of television a day, with nursery school and kindergarten students reporting higher rates. Fourteen percent of the third grade or higher students were read to every day, compared with 22 percent of the second graders, 33 percent of the first graders, 40 percent of the kindergarten attendees, and 47 percent of the nursery schoolers. The percentages of the above students being read to several times per month or week were: 62, 67, 62, 56, and 51, respectively. Twenty-four percent of the third graders or higher were never read to or were read to several times a year; the figures for other categories were 11 percent for second grade, 5 percent for first grade, 4 percent for kindergarten, and 2 percent for nursery school.[189]

Early Intervention Strategies. Especially since the publication of *A Nation at Risk*, educators and public officials have increasingly recognized the inability of the traditional educational process to prepare today's youth for challenging careers and productive lives. While much attention is still devoted to the K–12 years, most experts agree that formal education should begin well before age six and last a lifetime through continuing and adult education programs. Our interest, for purposes of this book, is with the former group and the early intervention strategies that can help ameliorate the effects of the social deterrents on students.

Table 5.32
Percentage of Kindergarten Students Who, in the Opinion of Their Teacher,
Were Not Ready to Begin School, 1991

State	Percentage	State	Percentage
1	2	3	4
United States Overall	35%		
Alabama	36	Montana	28
Alaska	34	Nebraska	29
Arizona	35	Nevada	39
Arkansas	42	New Hampshire	29
California	38	New Jersey	27
Colorado	32	New Mexico	40
Connecticut	24	New York	36
Delaware	42	North Carolina	39
Florida	38	North Dakota	23
Georgia	41	Ohio	33
Hawaii	47	Oklahoma	40
Idaho	26	Oregon	32
Illinois	31	Pennsylvania	29
Indiana	32	Rhode Island	40
Iowa	25	South Carolina	40
Kansas	27	South Dakota	29
Kentucky	40	Tennessee	39
Louisiana	39	Texas	37
Maine	30	Utah	26
Maryland	31	Vermont	28
Massachusetts	26	Virginia	34
Michigan	27	Washington	33
Minnesota	24	West Virginia	34
Mississippi	41	Wisconsin	32
Missouri	33	Wyoming	26

Source: Carnegie Foundation for the Advancement of Teaching, survey of 7,000 kindergarten
teachers in 1991. Cited in *New York Times*, December 8, 1991, p. 34.

The magnitude of this problem is revealed by a 1991 study by the Carnegie
Foundation for the Advancement of Teaching. In its report, *Ready to Learn: A
Mandate for the Nation*, the results of a survey of school readiness were reported.
Increased school readiness was a key component of both the national education
goals and America 2000 efforts. As shown in Table 5.32, the 7,000 kindergarten
teachers participating in the survey believed that, overall, nationally over one-
third of their students were not prepared to begin school. Forty-two percent of
the teachers indicated that their students were less ready to learn than those
entering their classroom five years ago.[190]

A 1987 study by James Coleman and Thomas Hoffer provided another important perspective on these challenges. The authors compared public, religious,
private sector, and independent private high schools on a number of measures.
While the latter schools accounted for approximately 6 and 4 percent of the total

K–12 school population, respectively, their qualitative impact was substantial. In particular, the Catholic schools were found to be more effective in raising academic achievement in verbal and mathematical skills and in reducing dropout levels. Especially significant was the finding that black and Hispanic children and students from low-income and single-parent families were positively affected by the Catholic school system, in comparison with their counterparts in public and independent private schools. In the authors' judgment these performance differentials were attributable to the academic demands placed on students by Catholic schools, as well as the effects of the religious community approach in overcoming family deficiencies. It should be noted that the performance of students in other private schools was greatly below that of students in the Catholic schools but generally above that of students in public schools.[191]

The health care and educational challenges discussed throughout this book converge when the so-called nontraditional approaches to education are discussed. Particularly important here are a variety of preschool programs aimed at children prior to entering elementary school, including maternal and child health, Head Start, home counseling, day-care preschools, and other compensatory education efforts. The most recent addition is free preschool programs for handicapped children, which 48 states had established with federal financial support by 1991; about 10 percent of the eligible 3- to 5-year-olds participate.[192]

Supporters contend that, although sometimes expensive, as in the case of handicapped children, such intervention can be easier than at a later time, in terms of the receptivity and adaptability of the child, as well as more cost-effective in the long run than counseling, remedial education and training, unemployment compensation, and welfare.[193] For example, a study of Head Start participants in the Perry Preschool Project in Ypsilanti, Michigan, revealed that for every $1 invested, $6 was saved in potential spending for corrections, welfare, teen pregnancy, and special education.[194] This saving is slightly higher than the average return ($4.75) other studies have reported on the Head Start investment.

Yet, there is considerable room for progress; and some skeptics question the long-term effects of these initiatives. For example, a review of evaluations of 210 Head Start programs over the past 25 years revealed a "fade-out" phenomenon, in which the social and academic gains of poor children disappeared after about two years.

The most carefully conceptualized and rigorously designed, implemented, and assessed of these efforts have decreased the educational deficiencies of disadvantaged children in the short term. However, the compensatory education movement has yet to document an appreciable cognitive impact that carries through well into the elementary years.[195]

In view of the fact that Head Start participants spend about four hours a day for eight months a year in the program, may have had poor prenatal experiences, low birth weight, and drug-abusing mothers, and live in a dysfunctional family and community environment, it is not surprising that the long-term effects of the program have not been more substantial or sustained. Even though Head Start is a "two-generational" program in many places—where parents are involved on policy councils or as staff members—or, on a more limited experimental basis, receive counseling and referral services in job training, literacy, and substance abuse, it will take considerable time for positive effects to be evident. In the final analysis, many observers would agree with Isabel Sawhill's assessment of the results of most children's programs: "We simply do not know whether they work."[196]

Nevertheless, Head Start remains politically popular; real dollar outlays doubled between 1989 and 1992. In 1992, Senator Edward M. Kennedy introduced a bill to increase annual spending to $8 billion from its $2.8 billion 1993 level, which would make Head Start available to all eligible 3- to 5-year-olds. The Clinton administration has sought congressional approval of a $9 billion expansion of the program over a 5 year period.

A 1991 special report on education in *Fortune* magazine began with the statement: "When it comes to early childhood education, the U.S. ranks near the bottom of the class."[197] Indicative of this low rating was a finding by the Committee for Economic Development that in 1986, $264 billion was spent on educating children six years and older, while only $1 billion was spent on those five and younger.[198] According to the National Educational Goals Panel, in 1991, 41 percent of all 3- to 5-year-old children in families with an annual income of $30,000 or less were enrolled in preschool.[199] Another indicator is the fact that Head Start programs currently serve only 28 percent of the eligible children. In comparison, more than 80 percent of French children between three and six attend preschool, while about 95 percent of Japanese children in this age group are enrolled. In China, children two months to three years attend nurseries while older children go to kindergarten. The basic intent of these and other preschool programs is to help ensure that children are healthy, properly supervised, exposed to positive learning experiences, and ready to enter elementary school. The tuition costs are generally low and adjusted for income.

The addition of programs to assist handicapped children has been viewed by experts like Ernest L. Boyer as having an impact beyond serving their immediate clientele. In his view, the handicapped programs were "a dramatic advance and the final step in a national education strategy that has been developing for over two decades," leading to free preschool education for all 3- to 5-year-olds.[200] These advances have been largely due to federal law, regulations, and grants-in-aid.

In its 1990 assessment of *Results in Education*, the National Governors' Association Task Force on Readiness reported on progress in five key recommended state action agenda items for helping ensure educational achievement for at-risk children. These were:[201]

- Increase access to quality early childhood development programs;
- Provide parent training;

- Encourage consideration of services to children;
- Improve schooling for all youngsters, including these at risk; and
- Create alternative programs for potential dropouts.

The task force commended the states for adopting innovative and important programs to implement these recommendations, such as:[202]

- 11 states had provided additional financial aid to expand children's access to Head Start, and others had enlarged preschool programs;
- 30 states had sponsored programs teaching parenting skills, and eight states had established programs targeted to teen parents;
- Most states had adopted programs aimed at preventing students from dropping out of school, and many had set up "drop-in" or "second-chance" programs to encourage reenrollment of dropouts;
- 27 states were participating in a program supported by the Carnegie Corporation to target remedial education, health, and social assistance on middle school youth in order to encourage them to stay in school.
- As will be discussed in chapters 6 and 7, several states had taken steps to use the school site as the place for integrating social service programs to help better focus and coordinate assistance to students and parents, as well as for making available literacy, job training, and parenting skills to parents.

Despite this progress, NGA concluded that much more needed to be done to expand and institutionalize successful state experimental and model programs:

Existing programs to improve the achievement of at-risk students and prevent students from dropping out promote marginal rather than systematic improvement. Even the best programs have not been institutionalized. And states still have not found an effective way to disseminate information about model and exemplary programs from one school district to another so that their use can become widespread. Instead, schools and districts often develop good programs individually. As states move into the 1990s, they must move beyond this isolated approach to one involving more comprehensive reform of the education system.[203]

In its 1991 report, *Beyond Rhetoric*, the National Commission on Children stressed the need for educational excellence: "Every child must enter school ready to learn, every school must be able to meet the needs of its students, and every American must value education and impart that value to children."[204] To accomplish this goal, the commission recommended five interrelated strategies, which are considered among the policy issues and options discussed in the next chapter:

- First, children must be born healthy and have access to high-quality early childhood experiences during their first five years so that they start school ready to learn.

- Second, all schools must reach basic standards of excellence through adoption of a rigorous and challenging curriculum, fundamental restructuring to achieve school-based management, creation of accountability measures and means of recruiting and retaining skilled teachers and effective principals, improvements in the school environment, and equitable financing across school districts.

- Third, an important aspect of school restructuring is school choice. While choice is not an end in itself nor a substitute for high quality, it can be effective in promoting many of the necessary improvements in schools.

- Fourth, schools and communities should create multidisciplinary initiatives to help children with serious and multiple needs reach their academic potential.

- Fifth, parents, communities, employers, and the media should take mutually reinforcing steps to emphasize to young people the personal rewards and long-term benefits of high academic and intellectual achievement, hard work, and perseverance.[205]

SUMMARY OF EDUCATIONAL DETERRENTS

The preceding summary indicates that the rhetoric of educational reform has exceeded the reality of actual accomplishment. To their credit, nearly all states responded to the challenges to the nation posed by the National Commission on Educational Excellence in *A Nation at Risk* with significant increases in financial aid for elementary and secondary schools. Many of these monies were used to increase teachers' salaries. The states also acted decisively to raise academic standards for students and competency standards for teachers and administrators. The states, therefore, cannot be faulted for failure to respond during the 1980s.

Table 5.33 presents a rating by *Fortune* magazine of the top five and bottom five achieving states on seven key indicators of educational improvement. Although few generalizations are possible when comparing only these factors, some interesting findings are evident. Clearly, the South as a region continues to lag behind the rest of the country in achievement; all five of the low performers were southern states. No regional pattern is shown by the high performers, although two are midwestern states. The average teacher's salary and per pupil expenditure were much higher in the top five states than the bottom five, even with cost-of-living differentials taken into account, and their teacher-pupil ratios were lower. The differentials across the nation revealed in the other 40 states' performance accurately reflect the considerable diversity that continues to characterize our nation's educational system despite the centralizing trends since the 1950s.

A 10th anniversary assessment of the post–*A Nation at Risk* reform record by Terrel Bell concluded: ''It hasn't left a legacy in that it has dramatically improved education, but it has left a legacy in that it has caused education to remain among the top four or five items on the American agenda.''[206] Indeed, after three waves of education reforms over nearly 10 years, addressed to standards, teachers and teaching, and student performance and persistence, the results are disheartening and disillusioning. Students, parents, teachers, school administrators, and public

Table 5.33
The Nation's Report Card: High and Low Achievers

State	High School Graduate Rate; 1989	SAT-'91/ ACT-'89 Scores *	Average Teacher Salary; 1990	Pupil/ Teacher Ratio; 1989	Expenditure per Pupil; 1989	Teacher Salaries as % of Total School Expenditure	Competency Test Required for Grad'n
1	2	3	4	5	6	7	8
The National Average							
	74.1%	833/18.0	$29,773	16.9	$4,606	36.5%	
The Top Five							
Connecticut	83.2%	897	$40,768	13.1	$6,857	39.4%	No
Wisconsin	81.8%	20.1	$32,600	15.9	$5,266	37.3%	No
Minnesota	88.6%	19.7	$32,190	17.2	$4,755	33.1%	No
Virginia	74.7%	890	$30,926	15.9	$4,352	35.8%	No
Iowa	86.4%	20.1	$26,747	15.7	$4,285	36.6%	No
The Bottom Five							
North Carolina	68.8%	844	$27,814	17.1	$3,874	36.3%	Yes
South Carolina	65.0%	832	$26,638	17.0	$3,736	40.6%	Yes
Georgia	62.1%	844	$28,013	18.3	$3,852	33.6%	Yes
Louisiana	56.9%	17.1	$24,300	18.0	$3,317	35.5%	Yes
Mississippi	60.1%	15.9	$24,365	18.2	$2,874	41.5%	Yes

* SAT scores range from 400 to 1600; ACT scores 1 to 36.

Source: Adapted from *Fortune*, October 21, 1991, pp. 138-39.

officials all seem to agree that, at best, more time will be needed to attain the lofty goals established at the Charlottesville education summit and most recently embodied in the Clinton administration's proposed "Goals 2000: Educate America Act." At worst, the reform agenda may simply be off base. The latter skeptics would agree with the Coleman report finding that "more dollars do not necessarily produce better scholars" and conclude that genuine education reform begins in the living room and dining room—not in the classroom.

The indicators of education reform failures are widespread:

- Low student competency ratings in key subjects like English, mathematics, science, history, and geography;
- Poor performance by American students on SAT examinations relative to their foreign counterparts;

- Lack of significant improvement in teacher job satisfaction;

- Resistance by teachers, principals, and unions to efforts to restructure teaching, reward superior teachers, and replace the concept of the "shopping mall high school";

- A significant and alarming gap between the academic achievement of white, compared with black and Hispanic, students;

- Continued high dropout rates, especially for minority and other at-risk students; and

- Increasing crime and violence at the school site, especially in inner cities, affecting both students and teachers.

From this chapter it is clear that the nation's public school systems have a long way to go to respond adequately to challenges posed by the needs and deterrents. The issues involved are complex, and many of the options for dealing with them are costly, sometimes controversial, or both. There are no panaceas, "quick fixes," or "one best way" here. The next chapter covers these issues, experiments, and policy options that the public and private sectors could address in order to support and strengthen the efforts by schools to prepare our work force better for the workplace of the future.

NOTES

1. Osborne, D., and Gaebler, T., *Reinventing Government: How the Entrepreneurial Spirit Is Transforming the Public Sector* (Reading, MA: Addison-Wesley, 1992), 314.

2. U.S. Department of Education, Office of Educational Research and Improvement, National Center for Education Statistics, *Digest of Education Statistics: 1991* (Washington, DC: U.S. Government Printing Office, 1991), 12.

3. U.S. Department of Labor, Commission on Workforce Quality and Labor Market Efficiency, *Investing in People* (Washington, DC: U.S. Government Printing Office, September 1989), 22, 28–32; Johnson, W., and Packer, A., *Workforce 2000: Work and Workers for the 21st Century* (Indianapolis: Hudson Institute, June 1987), 113.

4. U.S. Department of Commerce, *Statistical Abstract of the United States 1991* (Washington, DC: U.S. Government Printing Office, 1991), 134.

5. U.S. Department of Education, Office of Educational Research and Improvement, *Projections of Education Statistics to 2002* (Washington, DC: U.S. Government Printing Office, December 1991), 5. For detailed information on private schools see U.S. Department of Education, Office of Educational Research and Improvement, *Private Schools in the United States: A Statistical Profile, with Comparisons to Public Schools* (Washington, DC: U.S. Government Printing Office, February 1991).

6. U.S. Department of Education, *Projections of Education Statistics to 2002*, 95.

7. Ibid., 97.

8. Ibid., 123.

9. Ibid., 58; U.S. Department of Education, Office of Civil Rights, *1988 Elementary and Secondary School Civil Rights Survey* (Washington, DC: U.S. Government Printing Office, 1988).

10. U.S. Department of Education, Office of Educational Research and Improvement, National Center for Education Statistics, *Digest of Education Statistics: 1992* (Washington, DC: U.S. Government Printing Office, 1992), 15.

11. Ibid., 13.

12. Ibid.

13. Ibid., 81.

14. Ibid., 153; U.S. Department of Education, *Digest of Education Statistics: 1991*, 117.

15. U.S. Department of Commerce, Bureau of the Census, *Public Education Finances: 1988–89* (Washington, DC: U.S. Government Printing Office, June 1992), 2.

16. U.S. Department of Education, *Digest of Education Statistics: 1991*, 93. See also National Education Association (NEA), *Estimates of School Statistics 1989–90* (Washington, DC: NEA), 9.

17. Committee for Economic Development (CED), *Children in Need: Investment Strategies for the Educationally Disadvantaged* (New York: CED, 1987), 18.

18. See U.S. Advisory Commission on Intergovernmental Relations, *The Structure of State Aid to Elementary and Secondary Education* (Washington, DC: U.S. Government Printing Office, M–175, December 1990); Katz, J., "The Search for Equity in School Funding," *Governing*, August 1991, 20–22; U.S. Advisory Commission on Intergovernmental Regions, *State Aid to Local Government* (Washington, DC: U.S. Government Printing Office, A–34, April 1969), 14–19, 31–60.

19. Elam, S. M., Rose, L. C., and Gallup, A. M., "The 23rd Annual Gallup Poll of the Public's Attitudes Toward the Public Schools," *Phi Delta Kappan*, September 1991, 52. See also Haman, F., *School Daze: Education Finance in the Midwest* (Chicago: Midwestern Legislative Conference, Council of State Governments, January 1993); Hickrod, G. A., "Flunking on School Funding," *State Government News*, June 1993, 10–11.

20. Downes, T. A., "Evaluating the Impact of School Finance Reform on the Provision of Public Education: The California Case," *National Tax Journal* XLV (1992), 405–19.

21. Felsenthal, E., "School System in Alabama Gets 'F' from Court," *Wall Street Journal*, April 6, 1993, B–1, 6.

22. See also U.S. Department of Commerce, Bureau of the Census, *Public Education Finances: 1989–90* (Washington, DC: U.S. Government Printing Office, 1993), 12–13.

23. U.S. Advisory Commission on Intergovernmental Relations, *The Structure of State Aid to Elementary and Secondary Education*, iv.

24. Department of Education, *Digest of Education Statistics: 1992*, 161; *State Legislatures*, March 1993, 13. See also Verstegen, D. A., *The Impacts of Litigation and Legislation on Public School Finance: Adequacy, Equity, and Excellence* (New York: Ballinger, 1990); Verstegen, D. A., "International Comparisons of Education Spending: A Review and Analysis of Reports," *Journal of Education Finance*, Spring 1992, 257–76; Verstegen, D. A., *Closing the Gap? An Equity Analysis of Funding for Education in the Commonwealth of Virginia* (Richmond: Virginia Education Association, 1990).

25. U.S. Congressional Budget Office, *The Federal Role in Improving Elementary and Secondary Education* (Washington, DC: U.S. Government Printing Office, May 1993), 1–3. See also U.S. Department of Education, National Center for Education Statistics, *Federal Support for Education: Fiscal Years 1980 to 1992* (Washington, DC: U.S. Government Printing Office, February 1993). For a review of the growth of the federal government's role in elementary and secondary schools since 1785, see U.S. Advisory Commission on Intergovernmental Relations, *Intergovernmentalizing the Classroom: Federal Involvement in Elementary and Secondary Education* (Washington, DC:

U.S. Government Printing Office, March 1981). For a discussion of the role of presidents in shaping public education policy, see Thompson, K. W., *The Presidency and Education* (Lanham, MD: University Press of America, vol. 1, 1990).

26. U.S. Advisory Commission on Intergovernmental Relations, *Characteristics of Federal Grant-in-Aid Programs to State and Local Governments: Grants Funded FY 1991* (Washington, DC: U.S. Government Printing Office, March 1992), 12; CBO, *The Federal Role in Improving Elementary and Secondary Education*, 1.

27. See Zigler, E., and Valentine, J. (eds.), *Project Head Start: A Legacy of the War on Poverty* (New York: Free Press, 1979); Jordan, M., "Shalala Pledges Major Changes in Head Start Program," *Washington Post*, May 7, 1993, A8.

28. CBO, *The Federal Role in Improving Elementary and Secondary Education*, 2.

29. U.S. Department of Education, *Digest of Education Statistics: 1992*, 64–65. See also Birman, B., "Visibility and Leadership: The Changing Federal Role in Education," *The GAO Journal*, Fall/Winter 1992, 3–11; National Education Goals Panel, *The National Education Goals Report: 1992, Building a Nation of Learners* (Washington, DC: U.S. Government Printing Office, 1992), 266–78.

30. U.S. Congress, Select Committee on Children, Youth, and Families, *Opportunities for Success: Cost-Effective Programs for Children Update, 1990* (Washington, DC: U.S. Government Printing Office, October 1990), 157. See also Sawhill, I. V., "Young Children and Families," in Aaron, H. J., and Schultze, C. L. (eds.), *Setting Domestic Priorities: What Can Government Do?* (Washington, DC: Brookings Institution, 1992), 166–68.

31. See Kirp, D. L., and Jensen, D. N. (eds.), *School Days, Rule Days: The Legalization and Regulation of Education* (Philadelphia: The Falmer Press, 1986).

32. CBO, *The Federal Role in Improving Elementary and Secondary Education*, 3–4.

33. Ibid.

34. Herkoff, R., "For States: Reform Turns Radical," *Fortune*, October 21, 1991, 144.

35. Committee for Economic Development, *An America That Works: The Life-Cycle Approach to a Competitive Work Force* (New York: CED, 1990), 10.

36. Education Commission of the States (ECS), *Sharing Responsibility for Success* (Denver: ECS, July 1990), 5.

37. Herkoff, 137.

38. Education Commission of the States, *Sharing Responsibility for Success*, 8.

39. National Commission on Excellence in Education, *A Nation at Risk: The Imperative for Educational Reform* (Washington, DC: U.S. Government Printing Office, April 1983), 1.

40. Ibid., 1–2.

41. Ravitch, D., *The Troubled Crusade: American Education, 1945–1980* (New York: Basic Books, 1983), 228–29.

42. Ibid., 230. For an examination of subsequent reform efforts, see 228–66.

43. Ibid., 237.

44. Ibid., 237–38.

45. Ibid., 312.

46. The President's Commission on School Finance, *Schools, People, & Money: The Need for Educational Reform* (Washington, DC: U.S. Government Printing Office, 1972), xii.

47. National Commission on Excellence in Education, 5–6.

48. Ibid., 8–9.

49. U.S. Department of Education, *Digest of Education Statistics: 1987* (Washington, DC: U.S. Government Printing Office, 1987), 89.

50. Ibid., 90.

51. Ibid.

52. Ravitch, D., *The Schools We Deserve: Reflections on the Educational Crises of Our Times* (New York: Basic Books, 1985), 60.

53. National Commission on Educational Excellence, 18–19.

54. Ibid., 20.

55. Ibid., 19–21.

56. Ibid., 21.

57. Ibid., 22.

58. Ibid., 22–23.

59. Ibid., 11.

60. Ibid.

61. Ibid., 24.

62. Ibid., 24, 27, 29.

63. Ibid., 30.

64. Ibid., 30–31.

65. Ibid., 32–33.

66. Ibid., 33.

67. Doyle, D. P., and Hartle, T. W., *Excellence in Education: The States Take Charge* (Washington, DC: American Enterprise Institute, 1985), 14. See also Lewis, A. C., "A Nation at Risk: One Year Later," *Phi Delta Kappan*, April 1984, 515.

68. Boyer, E., "Reflections on the Great Debate of '83," *Phi Delta Kappan*, April 1984, 525.

69. Ibid.

70. Reed., S., "The Reform Movement Still Surging, *New York Times*, November 11, 1984, 33.

71. Doyle and Hartle, 17.

72. Donohue, J., "Notes and Quotes on School Reform," *America*, October 27, 1984, 241.

73. Sims, E. N., *The Recommendations of the National Commission on Excellence in Education: Reviewing the State Response* (Lexington, KY: Council of State Governments, 1984), 54.

74. Ibid.

75. Lewis, 515.

76. Wimpelberg, R. K., and Ginsberg, R., "Are School Districts Responding to a Nation at Risk?" *Education and Urban Society*, February 1985, 200.

77. Fiske, E. G., "35 Pages That Shook the U.S. Education World," *New York Times*, April 27, 1988, B10.

78. Donohue, 243.

79. Pepho, C., "States Move Reform Closer to Reality," *Phi Delta Kappan*, December 1986, K1. See also Wimpelberg and Ginsberg.

80. Ibid., K2.

81. Doyle and Hartle, 14.

82. Cited in Lewis, 517.

83. Wimpelberg and Ginsberg, 199.

84. Futrell, M. H., "Mission Not Accomplished: Education Reform in Retrospect," *Phi Delta Kappan*, September 1989, 11.

85. Ibid.

86. Hechinger, F. M., "1985: A Year of Talk But Little Action," *New York Times*, December 31, 1985, C7.

87. Futrell, 11.

88. Ibid.

89. Sims, 8.

90. Futrell, 11.

91. Boyer, E. L., *High School: A Report on Secondary Education in America* (New York: Harper and Row, 1983), 66–67. See also Reed; Perrone, V., and associates, *Portraits of High Schools* (Princeton, NJ: Princeton University Press, 1985); Coleman, J. S., Hoffer, T., and Kilgore, S., *High School Achievement: Public, Catholic, and Private Schools Compared* (New York: Basic Books, 1982).

92. Sizer, T. R., *Horace's Compromise: The Dilemma of the American High School* (Boston: Houghton Mifflin, 1984), 214.

93. Cited in Hill, D., "What Has the 1980s Reform Movement Accomplished?" *The Education Digest*, February 1990, 5.

94. See Watts, G. D., and Castle, S., "Electronic Networking and the Construction of Professional Knowledge," *Phi Delta Kappan*, May 1992, 684–89.

95. CED, *Children in Need: Investment Strategies for the Educationally Disadvantaged* (New York: CED, 1987); CED *Investing in Our Children: Business and the Public Schools* (Washington, DC: CED, 1985).

96. CED, *Children in Need*, 12–13.

97. Boyer, "Reflections on the Great Debate of '83," 528.

98. Ibid., 527. See also Futrell, 13–14; Verstegen, D. A., and Ward, J. G. (eds.), *The 1990 American Finance Association Yearbook: Spheres of Justice in Education* (New York: HarperCollins Publishers, 1991).

99. Futrell, 13–14.

100. Coleman, J. S., *Equality of Educational Opportunity* (Washington, DC: U.S. Government Printing Office, 1966).

101. Hanusck, E. A., "Throwing Money at Schools," *Journal of Policy Analysis and Management*, Fall 1981, 19–41.

102. Glosoff, H. L., and Koprowicz, C. L., *Children Achieving Potential: An Introduction to Elementary School Counseling and State-Level Policies* (Denver: National Conference of State Legislatures, 1990), 3.

103. Berger, J., "Educators Call Bennett Too Negative," *New York Times*, April 26, 1988, A23. See also Hechinger, F. M., "After a Year of Criticism, Whither the Schools?" *New York Times*, December 27, 1983, C16.

104. Committee for Economic Development, *Children in Need*, 12.

105. Ibid., 2.

106. National Governors' Association (NGA), *Results in Education: 1990* (Washington, DC: NGA, 1990), 23.

107. Gardner, D. P., "A Nation of Underachievers," *New Perspectives Quarterly*, Fall 1990, 6.

108. Cited in Hill, D., "What Has the 1980s Reform Movement Accomplished?" *Education Digest*, February 1990, 4.

109. Hechinger, F. M., "Final Grade: Modest Gains," *New York Times*, June 16, 1987, C8.

110. Boyer, E. L., "The National Education Index: A Framework for State Accountability," speech delivered at the Fortune Education Summit, Washington, DC, October 29, 1990, *Vital Speeches of the Day*, 190.

111. Bennett, W. J., *James Madison High School: A Curriculum for American Students* (Washington, DC: U.S. Department of Education, 1987); *James Madison Elementary School: A Curriculum for American Students* (Washington, DC: U.S. Department of Education, August 1988). For more recent examples of state efforts along these lines, see Honig, B., *It's Elementary: Elementary Grades Task Force Report* (Sacramento: California Department of Education, 1992).

112. Bennett, *James Madison Elementary School*, 7.

113. See Hirsch, E. D., *Cultural Literacy*, 1987; CBO, *The Federal Role in Improving Elementary and Secondary Education*, 6–12.

114. U.S. Department of Education, *America 2000: An Education Strategy* (Washington, DC: U.S. Government Printing Office, 1991), 3. See also Silver, H., and Silver, P., *An Educational War on Poverty* (New York: Cambridge University Press, 1991).

115. NGA, *The Governor's 1991 Report on Education: Results in Education: 1987* (Washington, DC: NGA, 1987), 1. See also the annual reports under the same title issued in 1988, 1989, 1990, and 1991 for descriptions of state initiatives in each of the seven reform areas, as well as *Educating America: State Strategies for Achieving National Education Goals* (Washington, DC: NGA, 1990).

116. Department of Education, *America 2000*, 6–7.

117. Ibid., 9.

118. Kaplan, G. R., "Watch Out for America 2000: It Really IS a Crusade," *Education Digest*, September 1991, 8.

119. *State Legislatures*, October 1991, 6.

120. U.S. Congress, House of Representatives, "Neighborhood Schools Improvement Act," *Conference Report*, 102D Congress, 2d Session, Report 102–916, September 25, 1992, 3–4.

121. "School Reform: Congress Squeaks," *Washington Post*, September 29, 1992, A20.

122. Kaplan, 9.

123. Lewis, A. C., "America 2000: What Kind of Nation?" *Phi Delta Kappan*, June 1991, 735.

124. Doyle, D. P., "America 2000," *Phi Delta Kappan*, November 1991, 186.

125. Howe, H., "A Bumpy Ride on Four Trains," *Phi Delta Kappan*, November 1991, 194.

126. Doyle, 186.

127. Howe, 193.

128. Mullis, I.V.S., Owen, E. H., and Philips, G. W., *America's Challenge: Accelerating Academic Achievement* (Washington, DC: U.S. Department of Education, September 1990).

129. National Education Goals Panel (NEGP), *The National Education Goals Report: 1991, Building a Nation of Learners* (Washington, DC: NEGP, 1991).

130. National Council on Education Standards and Testing, *Raising Standards for American Education* (Washington, DC: U.S. Government Printing Office, January 24, 1992). See also Jordan, M., "Nationwide Tests Urged for Schools," *Washington Post*, January 25, 1992, A1, A3–A4.

131. U.S. Department of Labor, the Secretary's Commission on Achieving Necessary Skills, *What Work Requires of Schools: A SCANS Report for America 2000* (Washington, DC: U.S. Government Printing Office, June 1991), 11–17.

132. Ibid., 27.

133. Gerald, D. E., and Husar, W. J., *Projections of Education Statistics to 2001: An Update*, ix.

134. "A New Battle over School Reform," *Time*, May 9, 1988, 60.

135. Ibid., 61.

136. Boyer, E. L., *Report Card on School Reform: The Teachers Speak* (Princeton, NJ: Carnegie Foundation for the Advancement of Teaching, 1988), 10.

137. Boyer, E. L., *The Condition of Teaching: A State-by-State Analysis, 1990* (Princeton, NJ: Carnegie Foundation for the Advancement of Teaching, 1990).

138. Walters, L. S., "A Report Card on School Reform," *Christian Science Monitor*, October 3, 1990, 12.

139. Ibid.

140. Elam, S. M., Rose, L. C., and Gallup, A. M., "The 23rd Annual Gallup Poll of the Public's Attitudes Toward the Public Schools," *Phi Delta Kappan*, September 1991, 54.

141. Ibid.

142. Ibid., 55.

143. Sims, E. N., *Excellence in Education: Reviewing the State Response* (Lexington, KY: Council of State Governments, 1991).

144. Ibid., 6.

145. Ibid., 12.

146. Ibid.

147. Shea, C., "Fewer Test Takers Get Top Scores on the Verbal SAT," *Chronicle of Higher Education*, January 13, 1993, A29–A33.

148. Ravitch, D., "U.S. Schools: The Bad News Is Right," *Washington Post*, November 17, 1991, C7. For a more optimistic assessment, see Bracey, G. W., "The Greatly Exaggerated Death of Our Schools," *Washington Post*, May 5, 1991, K1, 5. See also Ravitch, D., and Finn, C. E., Jr., *What Do Our 17-Year-Olds Know? A Report on the First National Assessment of History and Literature* (New York: Harper and Row, 1987).

149. Mullis et al., *America's Challenge: Accelerating Academic Achievement*, 38–47. See also Carnegie Commission on Science, Technology, and Government, *In the National Interest: The Federal Government in the Reform of K–12 Math and Science Education* (New York: Carnegie Commission on Science, Technology, and Government, September 1991).

150. Mullis et al., 47.

151. Johnston, W. B., "Global Work Force 2000: The New World Labor Market," *Harvard Business Review*, March–April 1991, 121–22.

152. "Students Test Below Average," *Washington Post*, February 6, 1992, A1, A4; "American Children Trail in Math and Science," *New York Times*, February 6, 1992, A14.

153. "This Year's College Freshmen: Attitudes and Characteristics," *Chronicle of Higher Education*, January 22, 1992, A34.

154. Finn, C. E., Jr., "The Case for National Testing," *GAO Journal*, Summer/Fall 1991, 38. See also Special Study Panel on Education Indicators, *Education Counts: An*

Indicator System to Monitor the Nation's Educational Health (Washington, DC: U.S. Government Printing Office, September 1991).

155. Finn, "The Case for National Testing," 40.

156. Finn, C. E., Jr., and Neill, M., "Debate: To Test or Not to Test, That Is the Question," *Washington Post Education Review*, April 5, 1993, 4.

157. See Toch, T., *In the Name of Excellence* (New York: Oxford University Press, 1991); Toch, T., "Diplomas and Dunces," *Washington Post*, August 18, 1991, C1.

158. Sims, 22.

159. Gerald and Hussar, ix.

160. Department of Education, *Digest of Education Statistics: 1992*, 76, 79.

161. Sims, 22–23.

162. Osborne, D., *Laboratories of Democracy* (Boston: Harvard Business School Press, 1988), 92–96.

163. Department of Education, *Digest of Education Statistics: 1992*, 73.

164. NGA, *Results in Education: 1990* (Washington, DC: NGA, 1990), 12. For earlier recommendations for improved teacher education programs, see the following reports by the Holmes Group: *Tomorrow's Teachers* (East Lansing, MI: The Holmes Group, 1986); *Tomorrow's Schools: Principles for the Design of Professional Development Schools* (East Lansing, MI: The Holmes Group, 1990).

165. NGA, *Results in Education*, 12–17.

166. Ibid., 16.

167. Ibid., 6.

168. Ibid., 7.

169. Senese, D. J., "Capturing the Spirit of Educational Quality," *Vital Speeches of the Day*, February 26, 1985, 423.

170. Ibid.

171. McGurn, W., "Lamar's Choice, *National Review*, August 26, 1991, 21.

172. See Appendix 5.D.

173. Educational Testing Service, *Accelerating Academic Achievement*, 9–10.

174. Ibid.

175. National Education Goals Panel, *The National Education Goals Report: 1992*, 76.

176. Ibid., 23.

177. U.S. Department of Education, *Digest of Education Statistics: 1992*, 28.

178. National Education Goals Panel, *The National Education Goals Report: 1992*, 50.

179. Ibid., 46.

180. Ibid., 49–50.

181. Ibid., 52.

182. Ibid., 51.

183. Ibid., 53.

184. Ibid., 54.

185. *State Legislatures*, June 1992, 12.

186. Kozol, J., *Savage Inequalities: Children in America's Schools* (New York: Crown Publishers, 1991), 4–5.

187. See Colman, W. G., "Schools, Housing, Jobs, Transportation: Interlocking Metropolitan Problems," in U.S. Department of Health, Education, and Welfare, National Institute of Education, *School Desegregation in Metropolitan Areas: Choices and Pros-*

pects (Washington, DC: U.S. Government Printing Office, October 1977), 34–36; Berger, J., "Incentive Plan by Fernandez for Teachers," *New York Times*, August 4, 1992, B1.

188. U.S. Department of Education, *Digest of Education Statistics: 1992*, 30.

189. Ibid., 135. See also Barton, P. E., and Coley, R. J., *America's Smallest School: The Family* (Princeton: Educational Testing Service, 1992).

190. Chira, S., "Report Says Too Many Aren't Ready for School," *New York Times*, December 8, 1991, 34.

191. Coleman, J. S., and Hoffer, T., *Public and Private High Schools: The Impact of Communities* (New York: Basic Books, 1987), 1467–68.

192. de Courcy Hinds, M., "Nationwide Revolution in Education Is Giving Handicapped a Headstart," *New York Times*, July 17, 1991, A19.

193. Natriello, G., McDill, E. L., and Pallas, A. M., *Schooling Disadvantaged Children: Racing Against Catastrophe* (New York: Teachers College Press, Columbia University, 1990), 46–138.

194. Richman, L. S., "Struggling to Save Our Kids," *Fortune*, August 10, 1992, 37.

195. Natriello, 68. See also Schweinhart, L. J., and Weikart, D. P., "What Do We Know So Far? A Review of the Head Start Synthesis Project," *Young Children*, January 1986, 49–55; Besharov, D. J., "Why Head Start Needs a Re-Start," *Washington Post*, February 2, 1992, C1, C3; Lombardi, J., *Head Start: The Nation's Pride, A Nation's Challenge. Recommendations for Head Start in the 1990s* (Washington, DC: National Head Start Association, 1990).

196. Sawhill, 169; Taylor, P., "A Fresh Start in Heading Off Family Crisis," *Washington Post*, April 18, 1992, A1, A6.

197. Camenita, S. "Preschool Around the Globe," *Fortune*, October 21, 1991, 148–58.

198. Committee for Economic Development, *Children in Need*, 21.

199. National Education Goals Panel, *The National Education Goals Report: 1992*, 69.

200. de Courcy, A19.

201. National Governors' Association, *Results in Education: 1990*, 28. For an update see National Governors' Association (NGA), *Every Child Ready for School: Report of the Action Team on School Readiness* (Washington, DC: NGA, 1992).

202. Ibid., 28–34.

203. Ibid., 28.

204. National Commission on Children, *Beyond Rhetoric: A New American Agenda for Children and Families* (Washington, DC: U.S. Government Printing Office, 1991), 177.

205. Ibid., 178–79.

206. Zook, J., "10 Years Later, Many Educators See Little Progress for the 'Nation at Risk,' " *The Chronicle of Higher Education*, April 21, 1993, A–19, A–24–25; Koprowicz, C. L., "From Statehouse to Schoolhouse," *State Legislatures*, February 1993, 24–26; Asayesh; G. "Ten Years After 'A Nation at Risk,' " and Goldberg, M., and Renton, A. M., "Heeding the Call in a 'Nation at Risk,' " *The Social Administrator*, 50, no. 4, April 1993, 9–14, 16–18, 20–23.

Chapter 6 ⸻⸻⸻⸻⸻

Policy Issues and Alternatives for Restructuring the U.S. Public Education System

The preceding chapter described and analyzed the history of the education reform "movement" during the past 35 years and highlighted current efforts to identify and overcome the deterrents to achieving the high-quality elementary and secondary education so vital to a competitive economy and healthy society. In this chapter, the major issues on the public education policy agenda that relate to work force preparation and employability are presented and discussed in terms of the pro and con arguments that have accompanied their consideration. National policy initiatives and implementing actions, as well as experiments and innovations at the state and local levels, are also examined.

SHIFTING THE FOCUS OF EDUCATION REFORM

The review of recent educational reform activities in chapter 5 revealed a rather mixed "report card." If public and private sector policymakers were to be graded on *effort*—that is, steps taken to raise the visibility of K–12 education needs, to identify and undertake possible remedial measures, and to spend public monies to take action—they would receive an "A." President George Bush and Education secretaries Terrel Bell and William Bennett would be praised for national leadership in calling attention to the need for establishing national goals and recognizing innovative efforts. Former state governors such as President Bill Clinton, secretary of Education Richard Riley and his predecessor, Lamar Alexander, and many current and former legislators would be recognized for their courage in raising taxes or diverting state funds from other programs to bolster appropriations for local school systems and in attempting to improve teacher quality and raise attainment standards. Many local education administrators, school boards, and teachers would be cited for raising concerns about instructional quality, school safety, and the special needs of at-risk children, as well as for their leadership in pursuing innovative solutions to their student and systemic problems.

By the early 1990s, the result of what Dennis Doyle and Terry Hartle called "the greatest and most concentrated surge of educational reform in the nation's history"[1] were readily apparent:

- state and federal spending for elementary and secondary schools had increased;
- teachers' pay had risen in every state;
- most states tested teachers for competency;
- graduation requirements had been stiffened;
- scores of black and Hispanic youth on proficiency tests had increased;
- required mathematics and science courses were on the upswing; and
- teacher-student ratios had decreased.

Despite these gains in "Educating Eddie," the results have been barely passing—perhaps a "D" for most states.[2] As indicated previously, by most measures—SAT scores, reading and comprehension, analytic capabilities, foreign language and geography competence, and reasoning ability—most students are not better off as a result of a decade of emphasis on standards, schools, and students. Indeed, many are worse off! John E. Chubb and Terry M. Moe described the dilemma as follows:

For America's public schools, the last decade has been the worst of times and the best of times. Never before in recent history have the public schools been subjected to such savage criticism for failing to meet the nation's educational needs—yet never before have governments been so aggressively dedicated to studying the schools' problems and finding the resources for solving them.

Whether the criticisms have come from average citizens, business leaders, public officials, or educators themselves, they have had a common thrust: the schools are failing in their core academic mission, particularly in the more rigorous areas of study—math, science, foreign languages. . . . America's children are not learning enough, they are not learning the right things, and, most debilitating of all, they are not learning how to learn.[3]

As a result, "the hard fact is that as the 1990s begin our schools look more like those of the early 1980s than unlike them."[4] At least seven factors have impeded the pace of educational reform.

First, a good case can be made that during the 1980s educational reformers correctly determined that a key way to improve outputs was to increase inputs. Higher standards, more money, better teachers, and other steps would, over time, produce desired results. These commitments should not be underestimated, despite their failure to make a significant difference in the performance of most schools and students. Yet, these traditional responses were fairly easy to take, and they did little to challenge, let alone threaten, the well-ingrained institutional status quo of public elementary and secondary education:

Schools are conservative institutions, slow to change in the best of times. They do not lead, they follow, and they follow long-term secular trends. Schools respond to demographic, legal, economic, and cultural changes that are themselves slow to evolve. Unlike the best colleges and universities, where new ideas are generated, schools are mainly repositories of information that they attempt to transmit to students. Thus, schools stick to what they have long known: standard day-to-day practices, schools organized around state and local regulation, and systems that are best described as insulated, even isolated, from changes around them.[5]

A second inhibiting factor is the politics of the nation's public schools. During the 1980s, a large and diverse coalition formed to support the education reformer's crusade. Elected and appointed officials, the business community, civic and minority group leaders, and parents seemingly had been united in their desire for schools to produce better-educated, more highly skilled, more readily employable graduates. They demonstrated a willingness to play a role in helping achieve these goals. Yet, in most school systems powerful vested interests—superintendents, teachers' and custodial unions, and education bureaucracies—have excluded them from decision making on significant matters. The reluctance of the education "establishment" to share power or relinquish its monopolistic control and the inability of the reform coalition to unite and overcome the forces of institutional resistance have produced marginal and incremental changes, at best.

Third, despite evidence that overall elementary and secondary schools are in trouble, as indicated by the survey results presented in chapter 5, many parents seem to feel their child's school is an exception. Therefore, a strong and sustained "grass-roots" movement to push for improvement has not been forthcoming in many communities. Many parents have not been willing to become partners in school reform because, as Chester E. Finn puts it: "Most Americans don't know how bad it really is because they believe the part that touches them and their children is pretty good. . . . Americans have been seduced into thinking their own kid is doing O.K."[6]

The fourth factor has been the ability of many parents to "vote with their feet," or their pocketbook, on educational matters. If public schools in their community deteriorate physically or instructionally or become security risks, many parents have the option to move to another neighborhood or locality or to enroll their children in private schools. Often these parents are affluent leaders in their community. Their preference for "flight rather than fight," when it comes to school reform, sends a depressing and disturbing message to those who are unable or unwilling to follow suit.

Fifth, many educators have been reluctant to become stakeholders of the reform movement. They have been on the sidelines, rather than the front lines, for a variety of reasons, including preoccupation with pay; lack of support for teachers from principals and superintendents; fears of firing, demotion, or reassignments; defensiveness of teacher unions; and resistance to new methods and ideas. Conflicts between the National Education Association (NEA) and American Federation of Teachers (AFT) over policies and priorities relating to school reform have further exacerbated the situation.

America's educators act as though they have no stake in the movement for educational excellence. It is a supreme irony that educators and their professional associations are, by and large, in the rear guard of academic improvement. They are not pushing the cause of higher standards; on the contrary, they often object both to the changes and to the people who want to make them.[7]

Sixth, demographic, economic, social, and political changes described in preceding chapters—including the breakdown of the traditional family unit; growth in the number of single-parent households, women in the work force, and latchkey children; persistent high rates of substance abuse and violence in neighborhoods; emergence of a two-tier labor force where both college- and high school–educated youth experience difficulty finding appropriate employment opportunities; and increased cultural diversity exemplified by the number of children for whom English is a second language—pose enormous obstacles for school reformers to overcome. Their challenge is exacerbated by the expectations of parents and politicians for quick results and their unwillingness to raise taxes to pay for the costs of public education improvements.

Finally, the reform movement has become crowded and confused over the years. Politicians at all levels of government have been eager to get on the education reform bandwagon and to offer their plan for remedial action. Professional associations, interest groups, researchers, and consultants have unleashed an avalanche of findings, recommendations, and case studies. As yet, little effort has been devoted to evaluating the results and distilling the lessons from the myriad experiences across the country or to promoting the approaches that seem to hold promise of success. Just as reformers have been criticized for prescribing the "one best way" to achieve a desired outcome, by the early 1990s the concern was that there were too many prescriptions with unknown long-term effects. According to the Education Commission of the States (ECS), "school and policy leaders are confused by the growing number of reform efforts and question how these efforts fit with one another and pertain to their schools."[8]

Looking ahead, the foregoing suggest that if educational reform is to continue at even a modest pace, it will be necessary to adapt to a different environment. During the 1980s, efforts to improve public schools took place in a favorable fiscal climate, especially at the state level. Nationally, during the Reagan and Bush presidencies, deregulation was emphasized, as was decentralization. The 1990s presented a different picture to the Clinton administration and to state and local leaders. At least 10 key influencing factors can be identified.

1. Economic prosperity was halted for an extended period by a severe national recession, which made it especially difficult for state and local policymakers to launch new education initiatives, let alone continue past commitments. Because education is such

a significant component of state and local finances, it has been a target for budget cutters.

2. Substantial growth in interest payments on the federal deficit, as well as for entitlement programs, constrained the ability of the federal government to establish new or increase existing grants-in-aid for elementary and secondary education. A renewed interest in federal "load-shedding" further diminished prospects for significant assistance from Washington, D.C.

3. Fiscal austerity at the state and local levels has had mixed effects on educational innovation. In some places fiscal crises provided impetus for change, while in others new activities were cut back. "Last-in first-out" layoff policies, coupled with hiring freezes, deprived school systems of much-needed "new blood."

4. Mounting evidence indicated that the deregulatory trend has been replaced by national reregulation.[9] Moreover, the actions by Congress (and state legislatures) to impose mandates on lower governmental levels or units increased, despite an inability or unwillingness to provide compensatory financial assistance. Educational policy and programs have been prime candidates for increased and more stringent mandates, and schools have had fewer resources and less flexibility to implement them.[10]

5. Depressed economic conditions have been accompanied by efforts to recentralize authority that states devolved to local school systems. As states are expected to play the roles of fiscal "Robin Hood" as a result of school finance disparity court suits, as well as to compensate for the effects of fiscal stringency, federal aid reductions, and local property tax constraints, there have been less tolerance for diversity and more pressure for statewide uniformity. The 1991 Gallup Poll on public attitudes toward schools found that 80 percent of the respondents believed state education should be the same for all students regardless of whether they reside in wealthy or poor districts, while 62 percent favored court action to equalize per pupil expenditures.[11]

6. Even where states have taken action to comply with court-ordered equalization, the effort has often been complicated and controversial. In Texas, for example, in January 1992 the state Supreme Court for the third time since 1989 struck down the legislature's equalization plan as being contrary to the state constitution's guarantee of an efficient and equitable system of public education. The plan for the second largest school system in the nation would have created countrywide education districts that would pool property tax collections and redistribute funds among rich and poor districts. The court held that since the state mandated the rates and determined the distribution and use, it had in effect imposed a state property tax in violation of the Texas constitution. State District Judge F. Scott McCown ordered the legislature to develop a fourth plan by June 1993 or state aid to local districts would be cut off, forcing many districts to close. The state legislature did so, passing a law that was signed by Governor Ann Richards on May 31, 1993. Under the latest version, a maximum level of $280,000 in property wealth per average student was established for each school district. The 98 of the state's 1,048 districts that exceeded that figure have a range of options to take in order to achieve compliance with the statute, including merging with another district, consolidating tax bases with poorer districts, shifting property to another district's tax rolls, sending students to schools in other districts under contractual arrangements, and giving funds to the state to redistribute.

If these districts fail to comply, the state commissioner of education is authorized by law to order commercial taxable property to be moved from one district's rolls to another's and to consolidate districts. Attorneys for poorer districts, however, have indicated that they will challenge the constitutionality of the 1993 plan since, among other deficiencies in their judgment, it still leaves an approximate $600 gap per student between poorer and wealthier districts. In December 1993 Judge McCown ruled the plan constitutional; however, an appeal to the state supreme court is likely.[12]

7. For some politicians, schools are no longer "in." Many state legislators already believe that they have "fixed" public schools with higher standards and more funds from general appropriations or earmarking of lottery proceeds and that progress, while slow, will eventually be forthcoming. Others have been unwilling to take on the "education establishment" to hasten the pace of reforms because the voting strength of school employees could shorten their political careers. Still others are willing to mandate school districts to set up programs for "parenting education" (35 states) and other worthy purposes but are unwilling to provide additional funds to compensate for the costs.[13]

8. Education leaders have been dismayed by the politicization of school reform through national goals, America 2000, and numerous gubernatorial initiatives and often declined to be associated. For example, based on interviews with governors' education policy advisers, legislative staff, state and district school superintendents, principals, and business leaders in six states in 1991, ECS found: "People working in schools continue to question whether there is real, long-term commitment and sustained leadership for systemic reform. Many question whether national efforts are more than rhetoric or affect reform in the school. . . . While educators are generally familiar with the National Education Goals and America 2000, many question how they relate to their schools."[14]

9. The anti-incumbent mood of the public will probably produce greater turnover of offices at the local and state levels and on school boards. If education reform leaders are retired by the electorate, the pace of improvement will likely slow as newcomers must be "brought up to speed." As ECS has noted, "Systemic reform suffers from a lack of continuity because people are constantly 'starting over.' "[15]

10. The antitax mood of the public has made it difficult to raise new monies to implement education reforms, equalize expenditures, or reduce the dependence of local schools on property taxes. In Michigan, for example, in March 1993 national attention was focused on the public schools in the rural community of Kalkaska, which closed more than 2 months before the end of the school year because voters rejected a property tax increase to close a budget deficit; spending cuts and service reductions were the alternative. Three months later, state voters went to the polls and rejected a proposal that had been approved by large bipartisan majorities in the legislature, endorsed by Governor John Engler, and supported by teachers' unions, local elected officials, and automobile industry representatives, among others. Proposal A would have increased the state's sales tax by 50 percent (from 4 to 6 percent), which would have enabled local property taxes to be cut and annual increases to be limited. Voters could still approve higher property taxes in order to boost per pupil school spending, provided the new rate was consistent with the maximum statewide figure. A $4,800 per pupil spending minimum was guaranteed by Proposal A, which would have been a substantial increase for many poorer districts. Nevertheless, the proposal failed to win voter support, the third time in four years that a sales tax hike for education

purposes was rejected. Before the vote, Governor Engler described the greatest hurdle to be overcome by proponents: "A general feeling that government can't be trusted and that, even though there is a very impressive coalition of support for this proposal, it must be a trick." In July 1993 the legislature approved and Governor Engler signed a bill to eliminate local property taxes as the primary source of public school funding beginning with the 1994–95 school year; however, by the end of the year lawmakers had not reached agreement on a replacement.[16]

To sum up, the results of the 1980s efforts and the challenges of the 1990s and beyond are shifting the focus of education reform from higher standards to process and structure issues, from more resources to measurable results and better outcomes. As John Chubb and Eve Hanushek have put it, "Improving the achievement of American school children requires the more difficult and radical step of reforming the entire organization of American schools."[17]

RESTRUCTURING SCHOOLS

The road to public education reform is long and difficult, and successful ending of the journey will take considerable time. As indicated earlier, there have been, and will be, many obstacles to overcome. Yet, despite frustrations with the pace and results of efforts taken during the 1980s, the "crusade" continues in search of what the Education Commission of the States calls "systemic reform": "Fundamental, innovative, coordinated changes in the financing, governance, management, content and conduct of education, focused on producing *major* gains in the learning of *all* students."[18]

Several steps that states and local districts have taken to attain these changes through restructuring schools are reviewed here. *Restructuring* covers a wide variety of approaches. When asked by ECS to define this term, educator and business leader responses "ranged from demanding more from schools regarding student learning to reconfiguring decision making for schools to detailing changes in instructional practice." In these terms, the survey participants reported that 50–60 percent of the schools were "exploring" restructuring. Another 10–25 percent were "making significant progress." ECS estimated that in 1991, 3–5 percent of the schools were "seriously engaged" in restructuring, as indicated by their willingness to make "significant changes in school and classroom practice," compared with 1–2 percent in 1990.[19]

National, regional, and local coalitions and consortia of educators, business leaders, and experts have been established to serve as a force for restructuring. The National Alliance for Restructuring Education was established by Marc Tucker, director of the National Center on Education and the Economy, and David Hornbeck, chief architect of Kentucky's education reform plan. Five states—Arkansas, Kentucky, Vermont, New York, and Washington—and four cities—Pittsburgh, Rochester, San Diego, and White Plains, New York—have been involved. This network involves exchanging information on a wide range of restructuring approaches and experiences. The group's goal is, by 1995, "to have 243 redesigned schools in seven states to serve not simply as models for replication but rather as models for the process of redesigning schools."[20]

A second example is the Coalition of Essential Schools, founded by Brown University professor Theodore Sizer in 1990. Some 700 public and private middle and high schools have joined the network, 130 of which are labeled "essential schools" in that they are implementing nine common reform principles espoused by the founder, aimed at helping adolescents use their minds well.[21]

In the view of some observers, broad public and private sector support for restructuring education has occurred on account of, rather than in spite of, this definitional vagueness. According to Professor Richard Elmore, for example, the motives behind restructuring have been threefold: (1) increasing the nation's international competitiveness through investing in human capital to produce a better-educated and more readily employable work force; (2) achieving greater equity and social justice by giving poor, minority, at-risk children the educational tools and values they will need to hold jobs and avoid dependency; and (3) dealing with the qualitative and quantitative "crises" of the teaching force, by providing economic and other incentives for the current generation of elementary and secondary school teachers to remain in the public school system and enhance their skills, while making teaching an attractive long-term career option for college graduates.[22]

Likewise, restructuring efforts have generally encompassed one or more of four components: (1) empowerment of teachers, parents, and students vis-à-vis the school bureaucracy; (2) accountability on the part of school systems for the results of student performance; (3) academic content upgrading to instill higher-order knowledge and understanding; and (4) involvement of the private for-profit and nonprofit sectors in public education delivery.[23] According to a report prepared for the National Conference of State Legislatures (NCSL), two major policy themes link the differing interpretations of, and approaches to, "restructuring":

We cannot achieve significantly improved student knowledge and skill with a centralized, bureaucratic system that focuses attention on rules and procedures rather than on results. Each learning environment is a unique combination of personalities, relationships, and physical circumstances that requires frequent adjustment specific to that environment; these are most effective when made by those on-site.[24]

As a result of this diversity of motives and themes, efforts to achieve "systemic reform" through restructuring are like the proverbial double-edged sword:

School restructuring has many of the characteristics of what political and organizational theorists call a "garbage can"; that is, the theme of restructuring schools can accommodate a variety of conceptions of what is problematical about American education, as well as a variety of solutions favored by certain interest groups in search of problems. As long as the theme of school restructuring is fluid and unspecified, it functions well as a rallying point for reformers. But once the theme is defined, it may begin to divide rather than unite diverse political interests. A major policy question in the debate over restructured schools, to paraphrase Gertrude Stein's famous line about Oakland, California, is "when you get there, is there any there there?'' That is, is there enough substance behind restructuring proposals to constitute a reform agenda, and if there is, what political and practical problems does the agenda raise?[25]

The remainder of this chapter addresses this fundamental question by reviewing the range of remedial policy options generally embraced or proposed by restructuring advocates, beginning with more modest approaches to changing the school year and day and then focusing on governance issues and market-oriented reforms. The review covers components of two of the three waves of school reform identified in chapter 5: (1) standards, or the ''more and higher'' approach that characterized late 1970s and early 1980s efforts; and (2) schools, involving actions, taken mainly after release of *A Nation at Risk*, to improve teaching, teachers, and educational governance. The third and most recent wave— students—especially steps to identify and respond to the needs of at-risk children, is addressed later in the chapter.

Expanding the School Year

Long before education reformers began advocating a longer school year to emulate the approach taken in other countries, the traditional school calendar had been under reconsideration and revision for other reasons. Allowing schools to remain unused and students to be off for an extended vacation was considered anachronistic and costly carryovers from an agrarian society, where youth were needed for farm work during the summer months. In particular, overcrowded conditions in large urban school systems compelled school administrators to utilize classroom space that would otherwise be vacant during the 2½-month summer break.

California has been a leader in this ''assault on tradition.'' Twenty percent of its 5 million elementary and secondary school children are on a year-round schedule. Most are enrolled in Los Angeles's 646 schools, which operate on a multitrack calendar. Basically, the student body is divided into groups, or tracks, and one group is on vacation at any given time. The school is open all year, and the staggered schedule allows more students to be accommodated.[26]

In recent years, school systems that have changed the traditional calendar have adopted a single-track schedule. In other words, all students are on the same school-vacation schedule. According to the National Association for Year-Round Education, approximately 1.3 million K–12 students (about 2.5% of the national total) in 1,600 schools found in 23 states attended year-round schools in 1991— approximately twice as many students and schools than 2 years previously. In the early 1980s, 278,000 students were enrolled in 349 year-round schools.[27]

The most common year-round schedules provide for nine weeks of school, followed by three weeks of vacation, much like a quarter system in higher education. Other quarterly variations feature 60 days in school, with either 15 or 20 days of vacation, and 90 days in school with 30 days of vacation.[28] For example, in 1991 the Carlisle Elementary School in Plano, Texas, embarked on a pilot project for the school district in which the summer break was shortened by one month, a two-week October break was added, and one week was added to the winter and spring breaks.[29]

As can be seen from these examples, year-round schools may or may not be used to extend the amount of time students spend in the classroom. Due to international comparisons, such as in Japan and Korea, where students are in school 243 and 222 days, respectively, there is increasing interest in adding at least 20 or 30 days to the typical 180-day school year. Former Governor Jim Florio of New Jersey, for instance, has proposed extending the school year to 200 and then to 210 days, as well as lengthening the school day, pursuant to recommendations of a Quality Education Commission. Former Governor L. Douglas Wilder of Virginia has advocated adding 20 days to the public school calendar year by 2000; similar action was taken in Maryland in September 1990, effective with the 1992–93 school year.[30]

In September 1992 Japan's Education Ministry agreed to a "major reform," giving students one Saturday a month off from school. Normally students spend an average of 243 days a year in school (240 is the minimum requirement), attending five days a week and Saturday morning. The school year begins in April and ends in March, with a one-month summer vacation and two weeks over New Year. Normally, after the regular school day, students go to private *juikee*, or cram schools, to prepare for entrance exams to prestigious junior high schools, high schools, and universities. The reform was intended to reduce some of the pressure on students and give them opportunities for varied experiences. In fact, the ministry published a 225-page book suggesting appropriate activities.[31]

While a 1992 Gallup Poll found that 55 percent of Americans supported extending the 9-month school year by 30 days, to about 210 days, compared with 44 percent in 1984, year-round schools and a longer school year are still controversial reforms. Many parents are opposed even to lengthening the school day by one hour.[32]

Proponents cite the following advantages of expanding the school year:

- Year-round schools are an appropriate response to changing K–12 education demographics, which indicate a resurgence of school enrollments that could possibly lead to overcrowding of systems operating on a traditional schedule or to costly construction of new buildings at a time of fiscal constraint;
- Since it is easier for children to retain information over shorter, rather than longer, breaks, year-round schedules facilitate learning;
- The continuity afforded by the year-round schedule provides a more supportive learning environment for students with learning disabilities, emotional problems, or English comprehension difficulties;
- Teachers support the nontraditional calendar because they have more quality teaching time and less need to "retool" after a long summer break;
- School buildings are fully utilized throughout the year;

- At-risk children, especially teenagers in high crime areas, are kept off the streets and occupied productively during the summer;
- By departing from the traditional summer vacation, a year-round schedule paves the way for adoption of a longer school year, which enhances the prospects for higher educational attainment.

On the other hand, critics cite the following disadvantages of the year-round approach, with or without an increase in the number of days in the school year:

- It is contrary to the American culture and disrupts family vacation schedules;
- It poses economic threats to summer camps, which are dependent on long vacation periods;
- It creates child-care difficulties for single parents who must work when their child is on break;
- It creates scheduling difficulties with children at different schools operating on different breaks. (As one third-grade youngster reported: "I get real mad because I have to go to bed, and my brothers and sisters get to stay up late and watch movies and in the morning they get to sleep in and I'm like, 'I don't want to go to school,' and I have to go downstairs and get my hair brushed and my little sister gets to be on the couch and watch TV."),[33]
- It places additional stress on aging and deteriorating school buildings, requiring acceleration of repair or replacement schedules, and greater expenditures for maintenance, security, and air-conditioning.
- It will be costly for systems to pay salaries, pensions, and health insurance for teachers, school bus drivers, cafeteria and custodial employees, and others usually off for the summer (the costs of an extra month of schooling are estimated to total between $11 and $20 billion across the country);[34] and
- It does nothing to change the traditional and outmoded teacher-student learning relationship.

Reorganizing the School Day

A second "assault on tradition" in a growing number of school systems is reorganizing the school day to allow for longer, but fewer, classes, Typically, a student moves from class to class at 45- to 50-minute intervals. While students are exposed to a variety of subjects each day, there is often insufficient time for solid learning to take place. With six or seven classes, homeroom, study hall, lunch, and physical education, students might change rooms as many as 9 or 10 times a day—and change clothes once. This frantic schedule is stressful and promotes hyperactivity and short attention spans. At the same time, teachers must "package" lectures and discussion time to fit this narrow format, as well as rotate from classroom to study hall supervision to cafeteria duty. After taking attendance and collecting homework, there may be only 25–30 minutes left for learning.[35]

A major experiment with a different format was launched in 1988 by the Masconomet Regional School District in Topsfield, Massachusetts. In addition to its traditional daily structure ("Trad Pro"), a "Renaissance Program" ("Ren Pro") was set up as a pilot. The 105 students in 9th and 10th grade volunteering to participate in Ren Pro took two "macroclasses" each day lasting 118 minutes. Only two subjects were studied for each 60-day trimester. They also attended two 46-minute Trad Pro sessions each day (an elective and physical education). The teachers instructed 6 classes each year (5 for Trad Pro teachers), and class size averaged about 13 students, compared with 20 in Trad Pro. Unfortunately, despite a favorable evaluation by a team of Harvard University researchers, which concluded that Ren Pro students were performing academically at levels similar to, or higher than, those of their Trad Pro counterparts, the program was discontinued by the school board in October 1991 due to controversy over its costs and benefits. The arguments raised by its supporters and critics are relevant to other efforts to reorganize the typical school day.

Those favoring fewer, longer classes argued that:

- Both students and teachers benefit from having a less "nomadic" daily routine and more opportunity to concentrate on substance. Especially beneficial was having sufficient time to present information, discuss ideas in-depth, debate issues, and digest knowledge;
- Longer classes will give teachers a better opportunity to get to know students and give them more individualized attention;
- Class sizes and teacher-student ratios are decreased as a result of "macroclasses," which are conducive to the learning process.

Critics of the approach raised the following concerns:

- Learning may be impeded, rather than improved, since the length of class is well beyond student attention spans, and retention of knowledge may suffer from only a 60-day exposure to subjects;
- A "school within a school" may have divisive effects on the student body and impair friendships that would normally be nurtured during the school day;
- Honor students will have their academic standing jeopardized and prospects for admission to top colleges diminished by participating in a nontraditional program;
- Teachers who must participate in both traditional and nontraditional classes will be overburdened.

Despite the fate of the Masconomet experiment, it is likely that the severe limitations of the typical school day will lead to similar restructuring efforts. Indeed, more than 500 educators from over 35 states and 4 countries visited or made inquiries to the regional school district![36]

In addition, it should be noted that a less drastic, controversial, and costly alternative to reorganizing class structure is simply to add an hour to the normal school day. The National Commission on Educational Excellence recommended that the school day last for seven, rather than five or six hours. A number of states—including Florida, California, Illinois, and Ohio—have added a seventh or eighth period, although budget constraints have slowed implementation. While providing 45–50 minutes more daily contact time may well be desirable, the critical consideration from the standpoint of performance is how it is used, given the limitations of the traditional format. Teachers' unions have opposed lengthening the school day, asserting that there are no guarantees that the additional time will actually improve results and that their contracts would be violated unless boards of education provided additional compensation. For example, in March 1993 the Montgomery County, Maryland, Board of Education approved the superintendent's proposal to add 15 minutes to the elementary school day in order to save an estimated $1 million a year in reduced bus transportation costs, despite bitter opposition from teachers who contended that the schedule change would reduce their time for lesson preparation and contribute to further demoralization (due to no cost-of-living increases since 1990).[37]

Still other systems are reorganizing the school day by instituting longer classes that meet two or three times a week instead of daily. While the same amount of instructional time is involved, the courses are yearlong. This approach gives the teacher more opportunity to get to know students and gives students an opportunity to absorb substantive material better.

Increasing School-Based Noneducational Services

A third "assault on tradition" has challenged the long-standing view that the sole purpose of schools is to educate. Students who have other needs must go outside the school to agencies in the social services system for assistance. This type of fragmented, piecemeal response runs contrary to the growing sentiment favoring integrated, unified approaches, especially for at-risk children and youth and those from poor families, many of whom lack health insurance. As noted earlier, the school site has become a major operational base for the delivery of health care and other social services.

For some time, schools have required students to take classes in health and hygiene and more recently in sex education, AIDS prevention, and family living. They provide children's breakfasts, day care, and counseling regarding drug/alcohol abuse and birth control. Most schools had a resident nurse or physician on-call arrangement for students needing medical attention during the day. Immunizations, screening for vision and hearing problems, and physical examinations have been customarily provided during school hours.

What sets the current efforts apart are both the severity of the problems confronting some students and the recognition that sound health goes hand in hand with receptivity to learning. Therefore, several urban school districts—including Birmingham, Memphis, St. Paul, New Orleans, New York, Los Angeles, Seattle, and Washington, D.C.—have set up school-based health care and social service centers. Kentucky mandates family resource centers and youth service centers in all junior and senior high schools in which 20 percent of the students are eligible for federal educationally disadvantaged children funding and free school meals. The names of these centers—such as "New Beginnings" (San Diego), "Family Net" (New Jersey), and "Family Connection" (Georgia)—symbolize that these schools are assuming a role once played by the family, which divorce, desertion, and poverty have all too often rendered moot.[38] As the National Governors' Association (NGA) observed in its 1992 report *From Homes to Classrooms to Workrooms*: "As outside forces change the structure of the American family, it is not surprising that schools—and educators—are being called upon to relieve some of these pressures by providing a wide variety of services that go far beyond simply educating students. . . . The success of a wide array of school-based programs demonstrates that schools can be effective providers of more than educational services."[39] In NGA's judgment, the keys to success of school-based initiatives are delegation of decision-making authority and significant discretion to the local level and community involvement.

In 1985 Oregon became the first state to fund health clinics in public high schools. Starting as a pilot program involving 5 clinics, by 1989–90, 12 were in operation. Students in junior and senior high schools receive free health care in a nonthreatening environment from nurses and nurse-practitioners, social workers, and physicians. The average clinic budget is $120,000. Parental consent for services provided to students under 15 years of age is required in the majority of clinics, and parents are encouraged to participate on advisory boards. This program has spread to 150 clinics funded by 30 states.[40]

What these centers have in common is the up-front recognition that certain students have serious needs for nutritional, medical, and mental health care and counseling that might otherwise be unmet if not attended to by the schools or referred by them to appropriate clinics or hospitals with which they are closely associated. School-based health personnel do not spend time merely arranging management of cases by outside agencies. Instead,

by being on campus, the health center staff can not only assist in health education classes, it can also organize sports clinics or health fairs, serve as crisis-response committees, work with guidance counselors on drop-out prevention, form student committees to develop health promoting activities, offer clinical back-up to school-based child care centers, and provide faculty training on adolescent health issues.[41]

As part of a larger health or social service care system—like county health departments, community health agencies, or university medical centers—the school-based unit has ready access to resources and expertise. Their services are normally funded by third-party reimbursements, private grants, and local and state agencies.

Typically, school-based health centers spend most of their time handling acute illness and injury cases. Psychosocial services, physical examinations, immunizations, and screenings are other major areas of activity.[42]

Opponents of school-based health care and social services argue that using schools as the base for these efforts dilutes their education mission. Moreover, students might well receive better attention if they went directly to the agency capable of providing it instead of relying on a middleman. Some also object to the amount of time spent on reproductive health care (about 15%), contending that these units are really "sex clinics," giving advice on abortions and family planning issues that are better left to parents.

Supporters of school-based health care argue that they are effective "one-stop shops" for youths to get assistance they might not otherwise request or receive if they had to go outside the school. The convenience of the school site, the compassion of personnel, the familiarity with the student, and the ability of the center to develop a coordinated response to the student's health problems and to connect with larger systems at no significant increase in the school budget have seemed to be compelling justifications of this approach. A 1992 Gallup Poll reported that 77 percent of the respondents favored using public school buildings to administer and coordinate health and welfare services provided to youth by various governmental agencies.[43] (This issue is addressed in chapter 7 in the context of services integration.)

DECENTRALIZING AUTHORITY AND RESPONSIBILITY

The preceding three examples focused on organizational changes designed to enhance the instructional mission of public schools as well as their capacity to remedy health care and social service needs to affect student learning capabilities. Even though they are relatively modest approaches, they have not been widely acclaimed or embraced by school systems across the country. Now we turn to two more controversial school governance issues.

As noted at the outset of this chapter, for the most part, parents have not been significant partners in educational reform. In fact, in the judgment of John Chubb and Terry Moe, "despite all the grumbling, no powerful political groups with a stake in public education—business groups, civil rights groups, civic groups, religious groups—have dedicated themselves to reforming the institutions of educational governance."[44] The reason for this reluctance is what they call the "one best system" by which public schools are governed. Despite considerable interstate diversity in the approaches to K–12 public education and the outcomes, the current education system has certain common characteristics. Those with vested interests—school board members, teachers' unions and principals' associations, superintendents, administrators, other professionals, custodial workers, textbook publishers, testing services, and college and university education schools—cling to the status quo and resist fundamental change. While they compete among themselves for power, influence, and resources, "current arrangements put them in charge of the system, and their jobs, revenues, and economic security depend on keeping the basic governance structure pretty much as it is."[45] Neither the education "bureaucracy" nor state and local officials, it is charged, have powerful economic or political incentives to push for fundamental change in the "one best system" of governing schools.

This system is reinforced by myriad rules and regulations issued by local, state, and federal authorities. These directives covering curriculum content, class size, daily schedule, teacher qualifications, hiring policies, and the like seek centralization, standardization, and conformity—they deter decentralization, flexibility, and experimentation necessary to discovering, testing, and replicating alternative approaches to school governance and instruction.

School Governance

The principal vehicles for citizen control of public education, school boards, it is alleged, have become more obstacles to, than spearheads of, fundamental education reform. In a 1992 report, *Facing the Challenge*, the Twentieth Century Fund Task Force on School Governance concluded that the tendency to micromanage had caused boards to become too involved in the day-to-day running of schools—a task for professional administrators—leaving too little time or interest for policy. In the task force's judgment:

School boards must become policy boards instead of collective management committees. This will require granting them the policymaking latitude that would allow them to function as bodies responsible for governance; they will be responsible for setting broad policy guidelines, establishing oversight procedures, defining standards of accountability, and ensuring adequate planning for future needs.[46]

The task force urged the states to change their relationships with school boards by "repealing all current laws and regulations specifying the duties, functions, selection, and role of school boards."[47] At the same time, states should establish performance criteria and hold local boards accountable for student results and for financial and managerial effectiveness.

The political and bureaucratic obstacles to reform are formidable. As Chris Pipho, director of the ECS education clearinghouse, put it: "School systems are like huge amoebas . . . they have great capacity for absorbing any attempts at change and then moving on."[48] School board "empowerment," in a policy, rather than procedural, sense, will be an important test case of this proposition.

School-Based Management

The first wave of school reform, with its emphasis on standards, actually strengthened the bureaucratic rigidities associated with educational governance. Some of the second-wave initiatives, however, were intended to promote institutional change. One of them has involved decentralization of authority through school-based management.

According to Chubb and Moe, school-based management plans usually entail the establishment of general policies by the state legislature and education agency and by local districts, with individual schools delegated significant budget, program, and operational authority to implement them. Principals make decisions with input from councils composed of teachers, parents, students, and other "stakeholders" in the school system. The councils may be advisory or possess decision-making authority. A reporting, monitoring, and evaluation system generates data to enable district and state educational decision makers to hold principals accountable.[49]

School-based management approaches were pioneered in the 1970s and could be considered the antithesis of the "one best system" concept. Hawaii was the first to set up a statewide system. Chicago; Columbus, Ohio; Dade County, Florida; Jefferson County (Louisville), Kentucky; Rochester, New York; and Prince William County, Virginia, have been leaders in the continental United States.

Two factors have kindled interest in school-based management: (1) as a response to the significant growth in state K–12 spending and accompanying bureaucratic control during the 1980s, reformers have sought to decentralize decisions over certain issues to the district level and (2) as a reaction to fiscal and managerial crisis in the local schools and breakdown in institutional capacity to provide quality education in safe schools, school-based management has been embraced "with the enthusiasm of a drowning man for a life preserver."[50]

More recently, school-based councils have been proposed as components of plans to overhaul elementary and secondary school bureaucracies as a result of state and local fiscal problems. In October 1991, for instance, Massachusetts governor William Weld proposed creation of school governance councils composed of parents, teachers, and principals to formulate policy, make hiring recommendations, and establish curriculum requirements. These actions were formerly the domain of popularly elected local school committees, which would remain in place to set goals and oversee implementation, much like corporate boards of directors.[51] Massachusetts' Education Reform Act of 1993, described later in this chapter, requires all schools to establish school councils, composed of parents, teachers, and community volunteers, to meet regularly with the principal to formulate plans for making school improvements and for enhancing parental involvement. A student representative serves on high school councils.

The Kentucky and Chicago Approaches. Recent experiments with school-based management in Kentucky and Chicago illustrate some of the advantages and limitations of this approach. In Kentucky, decentralization was a component of a statewide effort to make fundamental reforms prompted by a 1989 declaration by its Supreme Court: "Lest there be any doubt, the result of our decision is that Kentucky's entire system of common schools is unconstitutional."[52] As in other states, the Kentucky Supreme Court had found that the local property-based system for financing much of K–12 education was inequitable because it permitted rich districts to spend more on students than could poorer ones. But the court's declaration had gone well beyond education finance: "It was a surprise to everyone, a chilling experience," said Representative Roger Noe, chair of the House Education Committee.[53] More than likely, the court was influenced by Kentucky's low ranking among the states in high school diplomas awarded, college attendance and graduation rates, and other indicators of educational achievement.

In 1990, the legislature responded by enacting what was at the time considered America's most radical education reform act, which went well beyond equalizing educational expenditures. AFT president Albert Shanker hailed it as "the smartest statewide proposal that exists anywhere. It's the most exciting, and if the state would stick with it long enough and fine-tune it, it could be a model for the rest of the country."[54]

The 940-page, 20-pound bill had five major components:

1. The Department of Education was abolished, all of its staff were fired, the position of elected school superintendent was eliminated, and many state regulations were scrapped. An education commissioner appointed by the governor was to set up a new departmental structure designed to "serve as helpmate to the individual schools, rather than dictator."[55]

2. A Council on School Performance Standards was created to develop a long-term plan for educational improvement, together with performance targets and assessment measures. If a school consistently fails to meet these goals it will be declared "in crisis," outside managers will be sent in, personnel may be fired, parents may take their children elsewhere, and the school could be closed. On the other hand, high-performing schools would be eligible for additional state funds.

3. Each district was required to set up at least one school site–based council, and by June 30, 1996, every school in the state has to have such a body. Councils are to be composed of two parents, three teachers, and the principal. Their functions include formulating curricula, overseeing the budget, hiring and firing teachers, paying staff, and determining school hours. Each council receives $75 per student and may use these funds at its discretion.

4. Teacher training was reorganized, and outsiders were permitted to enter the profession.

5. To fund the new system, the legislature hiked business and sales taxes, which were expected to yield more than $1 billion over a two-year period.

In Chicago, citizens, rather than the courts, were the change agents. Fiscally, the effort has been labeled "reform-on-a-shoestring."[56] A broad-based coalition, the Alliance for Better Chicago Schools (ABC), in the words of Chester Finn, "declared war" on the city's 540 schools, which were performing poorly in terms of such measures as national test scores, graduation rates, dropouts, and violence. The guiding principles of the coalition were sixfold: (1) school-based decision making; (2) greater authority for principals; (3) more teacher accountability; (4) equitable funding for all children regardless of race or income; (5) decentralization and downsizing of central administration; and (6) strengthening of the School Finance Authority's role to intervene as "court of last resort" if school administrators failed to comply with the reforms.[57]

The ABC lobbied the state legislature to approve legislation, the Illinois School Reform Act, that would implement its principles and, in particular, dismantle the large, centralized bureaucracy and decentralize decisions to 10-member councils.[58] The councils are composed of six parents, two teachers, and two community leaders, elected for two-year terms. Each council is authorized to hire and fire principals (who lost their tenure under the legislation), develop school improvement goals and plans to achieve them, and oversee budgets. Councils also have received some discretionary funds from local businesses, foundations, and the state which have been used to hire teacher aides.

In the first elections for the school councils, some 17,000 candidates ran for 5,400 seats, and 317,000 citizens voted. According to Joe Reed, president of Leadership for Quality Education, which was formed to ensure a business presence in the coalition. "It was assumed that if 1½ candidates ran for every one of the 5,400 positions to be filled on the school councils, it could be counted as a success."[59] Over twice that number ran.

While both the Kentucky and Chicago plans are quite different and are in their early stages of implementation, some common obstacles to school-based management have been revealed by their experiences:

- Funding has been limited by state and local educational budget cutbacks and by taxpayer resistance to new or higher levies.
- The "bureaucratic swamp" has not been drained by new structures, new personnel, or new goals. Particularly in Chicago, the Board of Education has been unwilling to relinquish the reins of power. There has been no evidence that a lean central office bureaucracy is more responsive than a bloated one.
- The ability of councils to hire and fire teachers has been constrained by contractual commitments and by union pressures.
- The method for electing council members has proven more controversial and complex than originally intended. In Chicago, the Illinois Supreme Court ruled that the system violated "one person, one vote" requirements because it gave parents too much representation and a "special interest."[60]
- The start-up of councils has been uneven, especially because citizen members have needed time and training to be "brought up to speed" in order to make decisions on complicated and sometimes confusing educational matters.
- Parental interest in councils, both as observers and participants, has not been strong.

The early lessons from the Kentucky and Chicago experiments were replicated in a research report by RAND's Institute for Education and Training issued in 1991. The research team studied school-based management in five school systems during the 1989–90 and 1990–91 school years. Studies of experiences in other communities were also reviewed. The researchers arrived at five conclusions:

1. Though site-based management focuses on individual schools, it is in fact a reform of the entire school system.

2. Site-based management will lead to real changes at the school level only if it is a school system's basic reform strategy, not just one among several reform projects.

3. Site-managed schools are likely to evolve over time and to develop distinctive characters, goals, and operating styles.

4. A system of distinctive, site-managed schools requires a rethinking of accountability.

5. The ultimate accountability mechanism for a system of distinctive self-managed schools is parental choice.[61]

The RAND researchers emphasized the crucial role of the central office, superintendents, and school boards. They must send schools clear and consistent messages in support of school-based management and demonstrate a willingness to refrain from micromanaging operations and engaging in "projectitis," as well as restraint in mandating curriculum, textbooks, instruction priorities, and teacher responsibilities. A "central office 'hands off' policy is key to success."[62]

In its review of the literature on experiences with restructuring, the NCSL identified a number of common obstacles to school-based management. These included: (1) contractual and regulatory roadblocks, such as union agreements and state accreditation standards; (2) vagueness of "boundary lines" for the exercising of authority by principals, teachers, and advisory councils; (3) teacher reluctance to be involved in administrative decisions; (4) cumbersome and excessively formal and rigid decision-making processes and too much emphasis on consensus as a condition for action; and (5) excessive amounts of time required for implementation.[63]

From the above findings and conclusions, it is clear that school-based management approaches require major commitments from key participants in the education process if decentralization is to have a chance to succeed. The RAND researchers summarized the implications of their work as follows:

- Businesses, civic leaders, and other lay supporters of the schools must understand that site-based management represents a profound change in the ways that schools do business. It will not always work smoothly or produce quick results.

- The school board must commit itself to site-based management as its basic strategy of reform, and the superintendent must promote it as a primary test.

- The teachers' union must agree to collaborate with the superintendent, preparing teachers to accept greater responsibility and intervening in schools frozen by internal conflicts.

- The traditional control mechanisms of the school system's central office must relax and its responsiveness to schools requesting help must increase.

- Teachers and principals in each school must move beyond normal short-term preoccupations with their working conditions to issues of climate, curriculum, and pedagogy that fit the needs of the neighborhood and the student body.

- Teachers and principals must develop a new culture of accountability in which they take the initiative to inform parents and the general public about what they intend to provide students and how they will ensure that students succeed.[64]

In an editorial commenting on the RAND study, the *Washington Post* observed that the message to educational reformers was clear: "Districts interested in decentralizing won't succeed unless school boards, administrators and state legislators devote themselves to the task, which can take several years. Teachers, so accustomed to responding to central office dictates and state regulations, won't seize the initiative otherwise."[65]

At the same time, it must be recognized that school-based management systems shift some power but, if the ingredients to success identified by RAND are not included, may not fundamentally alter the institutional framework of public education—the "one best system." According to Chubb and Moe, it

is another way of controlling the schools within an essentially bureaucratic system. Its very name, in fact, is wonderfully appropriate, for what it suggests is that principals, teachers, and others at the lower reaches are fundamentally engaged in the "management" of schools—a bureaucratic conception, if there ever was one, of what effective education is all about.[66]

Adopting and Implementing Market-Oriented Reforms

The RAND report on site-based management concluded that parental choice was a powerful way to hold schools accountable:

Choice underlines the need for each school to offer a coherent social and instructional climate and to prove that it can deliver on promises. For a decentralized school system, choice creates a decentralized accountability process in which the individual school carries the burden of product differentiation and proof of performance. Even school systems that cannot move all the way to full parental choice can make individual schools the focus of accountability by basing performance goals on each school's mission and strategy.[67]

Choice is a term that embraces a variety of approaches—principally magnet schools, open-enrollment plans, tuition tax credits, and vouchers—that are intended to introduce a marketplace orientation to the public education system. Both conservatives and liberals have endorsed the concept of allowing parents greater latitude to select the public school that best matches the interests and abilities of the student. The implicit competition among schools is considered beneficial to effective and efficient performance. According to Chubb and Hanushek, the case for market control has three chief components:

First, if public education is governed more by markets than by politics, the relationship between schools and democratic authorities will become much less bureaucratic and much less prone to the problems of excessive regulation and inadequate accountability that now plague our school systems. Second, freed from bureaucratic constraint but subject to competition and choice, schools should organize themselves more effectively. Third, competition and choice should promote closer and more cooperative relationships among schools, students, and parents. The overall effect of these developments should, in turn, be greater student achievement.[68]

Therefore, while school-based management and market-oriented reforms are not incompatible, they rest on fundamentally different assessments of the problems confronting public schools and offer different prescriptions and priorities for treatment. Choice plans are essentially "customer"-focused and seek to address a variety of needs, including students who are not being served well by the present system, dropout prevention and the noneducational needs of at-risk children and youth, alternatives to forced busing, and parental pressures for higher levels of educational attainment and business pressures for better skills and attitude development. School governance and management reforms are means to the end of responding effectively to diverse student needs and expectations. School-based management focuses mainly on teacher, principal, and school board empowerment resulting from decentralization of state authority. The proposals are geared to education professionals initially and students secondarily. Choice proponents believe better education will come about as a result of competition within the public school system and between public and private schools, while school-based management advocates would give individual schools more control over curriculum, personnel, budget, and other policies but not encourage competition.[69]

School choice was pioneered by Minnesota (which is discussed later), and during the 1980s several districts implemented market-oriented programs. Basically, this system has three "building blocks": (1) the right of parents and students to select the school of their choice; (2) the availability of options in terms of the types of schools and curricula; and (3) the granting of considerable decision-making flexibility and autonomy to each school.[70] The four approaches most commonly adopted are discussed below.

Magnet Schools. Many of the 5,000 magnet schools across the country were initially established in response to court-ordered busing, and many were set up in minority neighborhoods. They have successfully furthered desegregation and racial balance through voluntary action. With the U.S. Supreme Court's March 1992 ruling in a case involving a De Kalb County (Georgia) school district, that districts have no obligation to remedy racial imbalances attributable to demographic conditions, public schools were given greater legal latitude to redesign and reorganize themselves. It is likely that the number of magnet schools will continue to grow for reasons other than promoting desegregation.[71]

The concept of the magnet school also has been quite popular with parents, students, and educators in districts not having integration issues. It has been estimated that in urban districts, some 20 percent of high school students are enrolled in magnets.[72] Basically, these schools offer specialized curricula, such as for gifted and talented youth, dropouts, or those needing remedial education. Courses are taught by faculty who are expert in the subject matter, and student enrollment is based on interest and ability rather than attendance zone. Admission may be competitive selection, via a lottery system, or "first come, first served."

Supporters of magnet schools argue that they have been especially successful in promoting racial diversity in inner-city school systems. Their specialized curricula have helped keep white, middle-class students in urban public schools and slowed the flight of taxpaying parents and high-achieving students to suburbia. The above-average scores of magnet students on standardized proficiency tests have helped bolster the overall standing of districts. Furthermore, magnet schools are "cradles of change," and the experiments with new teaching techniques, curricula, and instructional materials can have spillover benefits to the entire district.

The positive effects of magnet-voluntary schools on desegregation, compared with busing and mandatory reassignment to magnet schools, have been demonstrated in research by Professor Christine Rossell. Based on a review of 119 school districts, 20 in-depth, the voluntary plan was called "the new civil rights alternative": It is "the most efficient type of plan because the ratio of students assigned to students enrolled is the highest of all the plans. It is the most equitable because it empowers both black and white parents and is preferred by both races."[73]

On the other hand, magnet school critics contend that these institutions are elitist, in that they enroll only relatively small percentages of the student body. About one-fourth to one-third of the magnet schools select their students based on grades. These "public prep schools" are accused of consuming a larger share of educational funds than other schools in their district and skimming off the most talented students and teachers, leaving a mediocre student body behind.[74] As a result, the task of improving traditional public schools is made even more difficult, especially in central cities. While recognizing that magnet schools have facilitated desegregation, skeptics point out that the level of federal funding for such purposes has been too low and that the requirement for magnets to attain close to 50 percent white enrollment in order to be eligible for federal support excludes minority students. The higher performance of magnet school students should not be a surprise, some observers say, because they attract the best students and give them greater attention and more resources. For example, in Houston, magnet schools spend from $400 to $1,300 more per pupil than traditional schools; the national average has been estimated at $200 more per pupil.[75] Despite innovative spinoffs, magnet schools do little to improve the learning of students left behind and do nothing to change the culture of the educational bureaucracy. These factors may increase tensions between administrators of traditional public schools and magnets. As Tom Gaul, former principal of Woodbridge High School in northern Virginia, put it: "As principal of a school sending 60-some of its best academicians [to Thomas Jefferson] . . . I saw it as someone raiding my student body."[76]

One response to these concerns about interschool competitive advantage is to make each school in the district a magnet. In Montclair, New Jersey, for example, since 1970 each of the district's eight elementary schools and two middle schools has had a specialized theme, such as information and technology, and parents are able to select the school that best matches their child's interests and abilities. Each school is also racially balanced, with a 51 percent white and 49 percent minority composition. In September 1990 the district opened the first family magnet, the Rand Early Childhood School, for preschool through second graders, and requires regular participation by an adult family member in school activities.[77]

Open Enrollment Plans. Magnet schools offer several advantages from racial, instructional, and learning standpoints—the demand side of public education. As Chubb and Moe have pointed out:

Broadly speaking, schools of choice tend to be more informal, professional, and unified around a common mission than regular schools of assignment are. Their teachers are more autonomous, more excited about their work, more influential in decision-making, and happier with their overall situations. Students are more satisfied with their chosen schools; dropout and absenteeism rates are down; achievement scores are up. Parents are better informed, more supportive, and participate more actively.[78]

Magnet schools also may offer greater flexibility and appeal by allowing parents and students from outside the traditional school attendance zone and even outside the district to participate. While intradistrict and interdistrict open enrollment plans are on the upswing, the latter are an especially attractive way to increase the market orientation of public schools.

Following are several examples of both types of open enrollment magnets. These plans, which are generally regarded as being innovative or "cutting edge," illustrate the variety of approaches that are available to state and local governments.

Minnesota. As indicated earlier, Minnesota pioneered school choice in 1987 with an Open Enrollment Program, where students were permitted to attend any public schools anywhere in the state, provided their parents could pay transportation and tuition charges above the state and locally funded minimum or foundation levels. At least 15 other states—including Arkansas, Idaho, Iowa, Nebraska, Ohio, Oregon, and Utah—subsequently adopted statewide choice systems.

In 1991, the Minnesota legislature went a step further and enacted a "chartered schools" bill, under which teachers who are certified by the state and community leaders are authorized to create their own schools. They must define the type and focus of schools—such as for at-risk children or those interested in science and mathematics—and then seek a local public school board sponsor. A contract or charter with performance objectives is then executed and approved by the state board of education. The chartered school must be nonsectarian, free, in compliance with antidiscrimination laws, and open to all. It has a great degree of autonomy from bureaucratic influence by being exempt from federal and state rules and regulations, except for health and safety and antidiscrimination. State and local funds are allocated on a per pupil basis, and chartered schools are also eligible to receive federal aid. The number of chartered schools is limited to two per district and eight statewide. If after three years, the chartered school does not meet its contractual obligations, the local board can terminate the arrangement.[79] While some skeptics have asserted that this approach merely gives parents with hockey-playing children more options to strengthen team lineups, or that it is symbolic politics, the flexibility of intrapublic sector choice is attractive.

California. In September 1992, California became the second state to authorize charter schools. Under the Charter Schools Act, up to 100 such public schools may be established by districts. Per pupil funding of $4,800 would follow the student to the school of his or her choice. The charter schools are also eligible to receive compensatory and special education funding, like Minnesota's approach. Most state regulations would be waived in return for the independently operated charter schools' specifying educational outcomes to be achieved and measuring student progress. According to *Education Week*, despite teachers' union opposition the bill was supported by the legislature and Governor Pete Wilson, in part to counteract political forces pushing a 1994 ballot initiative that, if approved, would give parents vouchers to use to send their children to private and parochial, as well as public, schools. The initiative, proposition 174, was turned down by the voters in a November 2 special election.

At the end of 1992, charter school proposals were under consideration in Colorado, Connecticut, Florida, Georgia, Massachusetts, New Jersey, Pennsylvania, and Tennessee.[80] Opponents of charter schools have argued that existing schools could provide the same opportunities as the proposed alternative, if they too were given relief from regulations, received more parental interest and involvement, and attracted highly motivated teachers. Supporters have replied that districts have had their chance to perform, and their response has been inadequate. They point to this approach to choice as providing a "self-improving" stimulus to existing schools as well as a limited-risk opportunity for experimentation. Moreover, "they let an innovation appear without having to secure the prior approval of those who will be threatened if it succeeds."[81]

Massachusetts. In June 1993 the Massachusetts legislature passed and Governor William Weld signed a comprehensive Education Reform Act which revamped the existing choice program and embodied a number of other significant improvements in finance, management, and teaching. Massachusetts also became the fourth state to authorize charter schools (Georgia had done so in April 1993).

Under the new statewide choice program parents may send their children to any participating public school having space available at no cost. State funding follows the student to his or her school, and transportation is provided to encourage involvement of low-income students in the program. Participation is capped at 1 percent of total students enrolled in public schools in fiscal 1994; this limit will be 2 percent by 1997. The act authorized creation of not more than 25 charter schools across the state, and limited both the number that could be set up in cities (5 in Boston and Springfield and no more than 2 in other cities) and the number of students that could enroll (not more than .75% of total annual public school enrollment). Districts are to be reimbursed for the tuition of students attending a charter school. As in Minnesota, the charter schools are to be set up by teachers, parents, business and community leaders, and others and operate independently of school committees. They are to be free and serve as "laboratories" for creating innovative and experimental educational programs. Among the other major reforms included in the act are:

- Establishment of higher and more relevant academic standards for students, better core subject curriculum frameworks for educators, tougher disciplinary requirements, and more performance-based assessments. Students can receive a determination of competency (10th grade), a certificate of mastery (for superior performance), or a certificate of occupational proficiency (for a trade or skill).
- Creation of school councils.
- Abolition of teacher tenure and replacement by "just cause" review standards and third party arbitration procedures.
- Increased funding for teachers' professional development.
- Provision of alternative certification paths to encourage college graduates and professionals in other fields to enter teaching, and student loan repayment deferrals or forgiveness for teachers who have demonstrated excellence in the classroom.
- Elimination of the role of school committees in hiring and firing teachers, principals, instructional and administrative aides, and deputy and assistant superintendents.
- Granting of greater managerial, personnel, and operational authority to principals, together with increased accountability.
- Provision for under-performing schools to be given a probationary period to improve. If remedial actions prove ineffective, the principal may be removed and, in chronic cases, the school placed in educational receivership.
- Directing the Board of Education to set standards for vocational education, school-to-work transition, and adult basic education and literacy services programs. The board also must establish minimum nutritional standards for schools, and ensure that lunches are made available to all students and that breakfasts are provided for all low-income children.
- Setting a goal to make early educational opportunities available to all at-risk three- and four-year-old children.
- Requiring the departments of Mental Health, Mental Retardation, Social Services, and Youth Services to prepare a plan by December 1993 for spending between 1 and 2 percent of their budgets in school-based centers.
- Mandating a study of regional boarding schools and other educational alternatives for handling dropouts and chronically disruptive students.

With respect to funding, to reduce property tax–induced disparities the act raised the demographically determined foundation budget to an average of approximately $5550 per student over a 7-year period, which represented about a doubling of the state's contribution. A uniform statewide minimum standard of effort, based on property wealth and income, also was established for local school appropriations. State foundation, tax equity, and overburden (for jurisdictions with disproportionate non-educational outlays) aid would be provided to close a gap between this figure and the foundation budget amount. Overall, the act projects a $1.27 billion increase in state educational spending over 7 years. Some observers are skeptical about the state's ability to meet this commitment in view of the effects of the national recession on Massachusetts' economy, the governor's anti-tax stance, legislator reluctance to raise taxes, and the public's general aversion to higher taxes unless they can be linked to an important need.

Dade County. In 1989 Dade County, Florida, adopted a plan similar to Minnesota's charter schools called "Saturn Schools." The emphasis has been on teams of educators, union representatives, and administrators designing "new schools that embody a coherent approach to learning with staff committed to that approach."[82] This effort builds on Dade County's earlier pioneering work in school-based management that commenced in 1986.

Cambridge. In Cambridge, Massachusetts, since 1981 there have been no neighborhood schools or attendance zone barriers. Parents of the 7,700 students in the school system can send their children to any of the 14 schools within the district. A variety of educational programs is offered, including remedial reading, teenage parenting, and courses for the gifted. An assignment officer matches student priorities with school openings and monitors racial balance. Nearly all students receive one of their top four selections, and many receive their first priority. Teacher and student satisfaction levels are high, as are reading and math achievement scores, and the performance gap between the best and worst schools has narrowed. The dropout rate has also decreased. Overall public school enrollments have grown from 78 percent of kindergarten-aged children entering in 1979 to 89 percent by 1987.[83]

Manhattan. In Manhattan's District No. 4 school in East Harlem, New York, the 14,000 prekindergarten through ninth grade students are able to participate in "school within a school" programs. Rather than the traditional approach where a building is dedicated to one type of school, a number of different schools are housed under one roof. Some 20 buildings house 52 separately run schools like the East Harlem Career Academy, the Creative Learning Community, the Academy of Environmental Science, the Jose Feliciano Performing Arts School, and the Isaac Newton School for Math and Science. Each school has its own "director" (a teacher who also performs principal duties), staff, and student body. Schools, not central administration, control their own admissions, and teachers have considerable latitude as to curricula, programs, methods, and the like. "Teachers, parents, and students are all encouraged to think of themselves as their schools' 'owners' and to take the responsibilities—and the pride and involvement—that real ownership entails."[84] After two decades of experience, District 4 has succeeded in attracting poor and minority students reasonably proportionate to their share of the city's population and providing useful and desirable curriculum alternatives. Classes are relatively small and student performance has been generally impressive in recent years. In 1991 the district was second in reading in Manhattan, and attendance averaged 90 percent. The District 4 student body ranks between 16th and 18th on city reading tests, and those reading at or above grade level grew from 16 percent in 1973 to 65 percent in 1992.[85] However, critics have charged that the results of the District 4 experiment have been skewed by talented students having been "creamed" from other schools, by federal funding for innovative programs, and by the growth in the number of students from the middle-class.[86]

Kansas City. In Kansas City, a different variation is being attempted, involving infrastructure combined with instructional improvements. In a 1984 desegregation case, instead of forced busing, a U.S. judge ordered the state to pay for any new schools and equipment in the inner city that the Kansas City school district was unable to fund, as a way to make the system attractive to both blacks and whites. The school population is three-quarters nonwhite, even though the city population is heavily white. The judge prescribed a 40 percent white–60 percent minority enrollment goal, with no deadline. Some $500 million in construction funds have been spent thus far of an estimated $1.2 billion in commitments. Examples include the $32 million Central High School, with state-of-the-art athletic facilities, and the Computers Unlimited School, which has $4.5 million worth of hardware and software. These are 2 of some 56 magnet schools in the city from which pupils are free to select an education program that matches their interests.

Parents who favor an old-fashioned, no-frills education can choose a Latin grammar magnet—something like a Catholic school without the nuns. If they want discipline, there's the Military Science magnet, where high schoolers wear uniforms and train for armed-services careers. If they want flexibility and individual creativity, they can send their kids to a Montessori magnet, a total-immersion foreign-language magnet, or a Computers Unlimited magnet. If they don't like magnet schools at all, there remain a score of traditional schools.[87]

Parents may have to pay tuition costs for their children to attend school in another district, and transportation is a special challenge since if students live more than a mile from school, the district must transport them: "Some 4,000 students make it to school under their own power, but in a logistical nightmare, a fleet of buses and chartered taxi cabs drives 90,000 miles—each day—hauling some 32,000 other thither and yon over the sprawling district."[88]

The Record. It should be noted that while choice plans such as the above have had beneficial effects, the jury is still out. For example, in October 1992 the Carnegie Foundation for the Advancement of Teaching released a study of 13 states having some form of choice arrangements. The report's main conclusions, that some 70 percent of parents did not want to send their children to another school and that existing programs were expensive, widened the gap between rich and poor districts, and did not produce significant educational gains, have been criticized on methodological and substantive grounds.[89] As indicated in chapter 5, the effects of education reform efforts require several years to come to fruition and for the results to be properly evaluated. Most of the choice plans are still in their infancy.

Choice has failed as well as succeeded in the short term. In 1988 the Richmond, California, unified school system adopted a plan whereby each of its 47 schools offered specialized courses like computer science and video production, together with the core elementary and secondary curriculum. While choice reduced drop-out rates and increased daily attendance, the effects on student test scores were negligible. Moreover, the costs of hiring new teachers and purchasing equipment put the system $29 million in debt, bankruptcy was declared, and schools remain open under court order.[90]

The advantages and disadvantages of open enrollment plans are similar to those associated with the magnet school. In particular, choice has helped keep white, middle-class taxpayers in urban school districts, promoted racial balance, and offered students attractive, quality educational and skill development programs. Still, some students are left behind, if their parents cannot afford tuition or transportation, if parents select schools close to their work, or if the student is not accepted at his or her top-choice school. Moreover, choices are confined to the public sector and are still subject to bureaucratic and political forces that have undercut both school performance and educational reform over the years. When parochial and private schools are included among parental choice options, teachers' unions object to the diversion of taxpayer dollars from supporting public schools and constitutional issues may be raised. As will be seen, these negative reactions and legal concerns undercut the choice component of the Bush administration's America 2000 proposal. As the Richmond case illustrates, choice can be hazardous to school system budgets.

Tuition Tax Credits. For those advocating increasing the supply side of elementary and secondary education, tuition tax credits offer some promise. Under this proposed arrangement, the federal or state government would give parents a credit against their income taxes for a portion of the school tuition bill. The amount of the credit suggested by proponents ranges from $500 to $1,000 per child each year.

Supporters of this approach argue that by making private schools more affordable to families, competitive pressure would be placed on public schools as well. The monopoly that education bureaucracies have on supply would be ended. Since studies have shown that private schools generally provide a better educational experience at lower cost and lesser bureaucracy, student performance and preparation for higher education and work force entry would be enhanced.[91]

For example, church-supported schools have become increasingly popular with black parents, who see them as the only viable alternative to urban public schools.[92] In fact, these schools also are popular with white parents. Top officials of the Bush administration were criticized for sending their children to private sectarian, as well as nonsectarian, schools instead of the District of Columbia public schools.[93] Despite urging from the superintendent of the District of Columbia public schools, President Clinton and his wife, Hillary, decided to send their daughter to Sidwell Friends, a prestigious school founded by the Quakers, in Washington, D.C.

In any event, even though blacks are usually Protestant, enrollments in Catholic schools have soared in some cities, while these schools have had to close in other localities. Supreme Court justice Clarence Thomas's nationally televised statements during the Senate confirmation hearings in 1991, attesting to the values instilled in him by nuns while he was enrolled in parochial school in Savannah, Georgia, may have spurred some interest in parochial school education.[94] However, while tuition tax credits would probably be an effective complement to charitable contributions, their impact in terms of the number of eligible minority parents would probably be limited.

Critics of tuition tax credits also counter these propositions by pointing out that the amounts of tuition tax credit usually proposed are relatively small in comparison with the costs of private schools, so competition would be limited to affluent and upper middle-class families, many of whom have already chosen the private school option. For those who have small tax liabilities, a credit may be irrelevant, unless coupled with additional federal or state aid for disadvantaged, learning disabled, or physically handicapped children. Therefore, tuition tax credits do little to help at-risk students and may even promote racial imbalance in public schools.

At this point, the assertions of the critics have apparently been persuasive. No state has adopted the tax credit approach, nor has it been seriously considered by the U.S. Congress.

Vouchers. The fourth and most ambitious market-oriented approach is a plan under which government would provide funding for education directly to students in the form of a voucher. Students could then use their voucher to buy education from the school of their choice. Vouchers could be restricted to public schools, or there could be no limits on their use. The size of the school budgets would depend on the number of students enrolled, rather than on traditional incremental budgeting practices.

Voucher proposals have been debated since the idea was first raised by conservative economist Milton Friedman in 1955. Three recent presidents (Nixon, Reagan, and Bush) endorsed voucher experiments for education and housing. Yet, experience has been limited, largely due to the strong and sustained opposition from educational associations, members of Congress, and public education advocates.

The logic of the voucher plan is as follows: opening up the educational system to other suppliers, particularly high-performing private schools, would increase competition; competition would force public schools to become leaner administratively, more flexible programmatically, and more client-oriented; and decision making would be decentralized, with teachers being empowered. These effects would lead to higher-quality programs more responsive to student needs and interests, as well as to greater teacher satisfaction.

At the same time, government would retain a vital "umpire" role, through the regulatory process. For example:

The government could give parents information about schools and ensure the accuracy of information provided by schools. It could minimize inequality by providing the educationally disadvantaged with larger-than-average vouchers, which would make these students attractive candidates to schools that might otherwise not want them. It could require all participating private schools to accept vouchers as full payment, in other words to become completely publicly funded. The government could also set desegregation goals and regulate admissions consistent with them. Finally, the government would have final authority to set eligibility rules, graduation requirements, teacher certification requirements, admission rules, financial constraints, and anything else it believes important for participating private as well as public schools.

Obviously, the more government regulation, the further the plan deviates from the concept of an educational market. Nevertheless, the government has the authority to create any kind of market it likes and to pursue whatever mix of quality and equality goals it likes.[95]

The sole current experiment with vouchers is in Milwaukee, Wisconsin. It began as a 1989 budget compromise between Republican governor Tommy Thompson and Democratic representative Polly Williams, a black leader from Milwaukee. With their support legislation was enacted and went into effect in September 1990 to allow 1,000 inner-city students to attend private schools using vouchers worth $2,900. Only 258 of the eligible children participated, however, and the experiment has not been fully evaluated. Initial findings by the Wisconsin Department of Public Instruction revealed that some choice students who were initially lagging behind their peers academically have now caught up. While test scores had improved somewhat, parental involvement in their children's education had increased considerably because of choice.[96] The evaluator recommended continuation for several more years. The plan is being challenged in the courts, largely over the issue of First Amendment church-state separation—a major hurdle for both voucher plans and tuition tax credits.

Partly due to the Wisconsin experiment, in 1991 the Pennsylvania senate narrowly voted to give parents a grant of up to $900 a year to help them send their children to a public school outside their neighborhood or to a private school. Scholarships also were made available regardless of family income.[97] In a related development, in 1991 the New York Board of Regents narrowly defeated a proposal to provide tuition vouchers to some 5,000 students in New York City schools due to concerns about what would happen to the students left behind in underachieving schools and objections to the use of public monies to support gifted and talented students' attendance at private schools in the city. According to *Governing* magazine, by mid-1993 over 12 state legislatures had debated a voucher plan like Milwaukee's, but none had passed a bill along these lines. The voters also have been reluctant, defeating in 1992 a Colorado ballot initiative which would have established a statewide voucher plan, and in 1993 California's Propositon 174 and a Wisconsin state education superintendent candidate who endorsed vouchers.[98]

Popularity and Acceptance. To sum up, with the exception of vouchers, choice plans are gaining popularity with the public-policy makers, and as experience grows, they are becoming more accepted by educators. The 1991 annual Gallup Poll of Public Attitudes Toward the Public Schools found that 62 percent favored allowing parents and students to choose the schools in their community that they will attend. Yet, few parents of students in public schools indicated a willingness to change their schools even if given the option to do so—further evidence of the "my child's school is doing OK" syndrome. Fifty percent supported a voucher plan; this approach was especially popular among minorities and urban residents. However, 68 percent opposed allowing public monies to be spent for private schools that parents or students might select.[99]

The high-water mark to supporters of market-oriented approaches was President George Bush's willingness to include parental choice in his America 2000 proposal. The president's plan was sweeping—states would pay for students to attend the school of their choice, including private and parochial schools, while the federal government would:

- Provide $30 million to facilitate state efforts to design choice plans;
- Provide $200 million to assist disadvantaged children who wanted to participate; and
- Change federal laws so educationally disadvantaged children would not lose federal Chapter I aid if they changed schools under a choice plan (worth approximately $5.5 billion). In other words, funds would follow the child, regardless of the school attended.[100]

Time magazine reported that the president's proposal had implications well beyond the choice proposal: "For the first time, a President has made it a priority to question the monopoly power of America's public schools. In a few years, Choice has moved from the intellectual fringe to the bully pulpit of the White House."[101]

The congressional response to both choice and America 2000, however, has been cool, partly due to the opposition from teachers' unions, among other things, to providing public funds to support private schools when so much remains undone in the effort to reform public educational institutions. The Clinton administration has endorsed introducing competition in K–12 education through the choice approach but within public school systems.

At the state level, pressure is also building on governors and legislators to revoke what has been called the "exclusive franchise" that states have historically given to public school systems. As U.S. senator David Durenberger has asked:

As long as local school boards have an "exclusive franchise" on starting and running new public schools, we'll never see a substantial increase in the number of school choices that can be made. Few Americans would accept a situation in which A&P insisted on an "exclusive franchise" to operate every grocery store in Washington. So why do we insist that only the local school board be allowed to start and operate public schools inside the boundaries of its district?[102]

The implications of franchise removal are as follows, according to Ted Kolderie:

- It means the state agrees the district will have the final decision about improvement. Governors and legislators like to talk as if they control improvement. They do not. They can propose and promise, plead and threaten. They can give money. They can issue orders. And often the districts do respond. But whether they do or not, in the end, is up to them. If the district does not give the kids a good education the state does not send in another organization that will. It accepts the pace of improvement at which the district is able or willing to move.

- The state also agrees to accept whatever reasons the district has for its decision to change or not to change, even if those reasons have to do mainly with the private or personal interests of the adults involved, as they sometimes do.

- And the state agrees to accept those decisions, and the reasons for them, whether or not the students learn. Within very broad limits the state assures the districts their existence, their students, their revenues, their security, their annual funding increases— *their* material success—independent of the level of *student* success.[103]

It should be noted that these conditions run contrary to traditional state-district relations, as well as to public expectations, and therefore may prove difficult to incorporate.

Looking Ahead—and Abroad. The preceding discussion of school restructuring in general and choice approaches in particular suggests that this traditional relationship will change in the years ahead, as impatience with the pace and results of educational reform grows. Yet, while the traditional public school may no longer adequately serve the best interests of students, parents, educators, and elected officials, the most desirable and feasible alternatives are neither clear nor noncontroversial. As an illustration of the difficulty policymakers experience separating the reality from the rhetoric of school reform, excerpts from a *Backgrounder* report by the Heritage Foundation entitled "Nine Phoney Assertions About School Choice: Answering the Critics!" appear in Appendix 6.A.

The arguments in support of, or opposed to, choice are controversial. Moreover, additional time will be needed for ongoing experiments in districts across the country to produce results amenable to evaluation before empirically based assessments of choice experience can be made. Much attention will be focused on Minnesota's pioneering choice plans for open enrollments between public school districts and for chartered schools, an approach Richard Elmore has called "the managed competition of the education reform movement." As of mid-1993, there was some debate over the state's 5-year choice record. A June *Governing* magazine assessment concluded "solid evidence about how it is working is scant. One thing that is known is that only a small number of students have crossed district lines in Minnesota, about 1.8 percent in the 1991–92 school year." An April *Wall Street Journal* article by Joe Nathan, director of the Center for Social Change at the Hubert H. Humphrey Institute of Public Affairs, University of Minnesota, sought to dispell myths about the state's experience and concluded that while school choice works in Minnesota: "Choice is a powerful tool, like electricity, which must be handled carefully. Some choice programs, including some public school plans, create more problems than they solve. Minnesota's plan isn't right for every state."[104]

A British Example. Some lessons from the British experience with choice are instructive. In June 1988, the Thatcher government's landmark Education Reform Act was passed by Parliament, which sought to improve Britain's 26,000 public schools, many of which were performing poorly on the basis of international standards and scores, through a threefold approach: national curriculum standards, national tests, and school-based management. The latter featured a voucher-type plan, under which parents could enroll students in any public school within or outside traditional local education authority boundaries. Funds (80% of which are provided by the national government) would follow the students. The major effects of this choice approach have included:

• Enrollments at good schools grew at a rapid rate;

• Few poor schools have been closed and instead have slowly withered;

• Failing schools have had little money or incentive to improve themselves;

• Parents have complained about the limited number of choices at their disposal, in view of waiting lists and transportation constraints;

• Because of a loophole in the law, where under local education agencies (LEAs) did not have to honor parent requests when efficient education or use of resources would be jeopardized, local authorities had considerable leverage in assigning students, even when this meant sending them to unpopular schools in order to maintain their economic and operational viability;

• The establishment of new schools has been restricted by the national government's concern about vacant places in existing ones serving the same population; and

• Some schools have screened out at-risk or potentially troublesome students, as well as those having special educational needs (who must be placed in regular classrooms, under the law).

The British law did generate interschool competition to the extent that many schools printed brochures describing their programs, academic performance, and admission requirements. Some even hired marketing consultants! Most districts distributed pamphlets to parents covering appeal procedures if their children were not admitted to the school of their choice.

Interestingly, the two "antisystem" features of the Thatcher reform package have encountered the greatest resistance. The act authorized schools to opt out of the local educational authority if they became dissatisfied with the LEA's responsiveness and effectiveness and believed they would perform better on their own and become "grant-maintained," or accountable to only their governing boards and the national government. In addition, the creation of 20 "city technology colleges" (CTCs) was authorized, funded in part by business contributions, to offer combined academic-vocational training. (The CTC experience is described in the next section.) Both the LEAs and the technology colleges have been opposed by the Labour Party and the educational "establishment."[105]

On balance, for choice plans to spread beyond the experimental and rhetorical stages, for the public's enthusiasm to be translated into meaningful action, and for the "franchise" to be replaced by an approach that education stakeholders support, at least two political and practical factors will have to be overcome:

Politically, choice has come to be seen as a movement against public schools, and teachers' unions and administrators oppose it. Choice can, in the long run, become a liberating force for all parties in public education, but educators will understandably approach it with caution.

As a practical matter, choice presupposes the existence of a selection of schools, each of which has sufficiently high quality and definitive enough character to attract parents and students. Such schools will take time to develop in many places, and the grounds for choice will therefore be established only over a period of several school years.[106]

Dealing with School System Failure

The example of the bankruptcy of the Richmond, California, system underscores the reality that school reform may well be risky business. Political, bureaucratic, and fiscal "land mines" lie in the path of reformers. While efforts to restructure schools are receiving increasing attention as an extension of the movement by governors and legislators during the 1980s to, as Chester Finn has put it, take "civilian control" of schools,[107] the day-to-day management of elementary and secondary education cannot be ignored.

Three recent illustrations of school system failure underscore this point:

• In 1989, the Chelsea, Massachusetts, school system turned over management responsibility to Boston University for a 10-year period. Although the teachers' union objected that this shift was an unwelcome step toward privatization, local and state authorities approved the experiment. University president John Silber promised "new priorities, added resources, basic changes in school operations and much brighter results."[108]

• In New Jersey, in 1989 former governor Thomas Kean and the state education commissioner put the Jersey City school board in "educational receivership" as a result of fiscal improprieties and poor performance and installed their own management team. Similar actions were taken against Patterson in 1991 by Governor Jim Florio. At least 15 other states have declared that they will take over the management of local schools in the event of "education malpractice."[109]

• In Harlan, Kentucky, on January 31, 1992, three of the five-member school board were ousted by the state education commissioner after a hearing before a panel of state education officials. The hearing revealed alleged infractions, including receiving kickbacks from businesses awarded school contracts, giving school contracts to relatives, violating state competitive bidding laws, and accepting credit from local stores.[110]

These and other less dramatic efforts illustrate the consequences of poor management. At the same time, as indicated in the discussion of the Twentieth

Century Fund's school governance task force report in a previous section, politicization of school boards and centralization of rule making and regulatory authority provide an occasionally hostile environment for effective administration. Even though only 341 of the nation's approximately 15,000 school superintendents are now elected, removing the superintendent's name from the ballot has not removed him or her from politics. It is not surprising, therefore, that as of January 1991 some 19 inner-city school systems were recruiting superintendents, and the average tenure had slipped from five years in the 1970s to three years. According to the Council of the Great City Schools, in early 1993 superintendents in 40 of the nation's 45 largest urban school districts had not been in their office before 1990. A hypothetical advertisement in a *Governing* magazine story ran as follows: "HELP WANTED: Thick-skinned administrator to run troubled big-city school system. Political hassles endless. Micro-management by employer a way of life. Responsibilities include solving all of society's problems."[111]

For teachers, the local school environment was not much better. As described earlier in this chapter, narrowly segmented time blocks, state-mandated courses, outmoded curricula and teaching aids, noninstructional duties, and the like contributed to low morale and high frustration. When coupled with relatively low pay, despite catch-up actions taken by the 1980s, there were strong disincentives to pursuing a career in K–12 teaching or remaining in the profession.

In light of these factors, some observers would argue that recognizing restructuring efforts may require considerable time to implement more immediate steps need to be taken to ensure that schools are well managed, that curricula are relevant, and that teachers are motivated. Issues associated with the last two areas are considered in the next sections.

Revamping Curricula

In 1985, the Committee for Economic Development warned that "schools cannot be all things to all people; if they try, they will invariably fail."[112] In CED's judgment, schools needed clearly to identify their goals and objectives and deploy resources accordingly. Their curriculum is the means to these ends.

CED stressed two types of curriculum.

- The *invisible* curriculum, including traits of self-discipline, reliability, perseverance, honesty, and cooperativeness that are instilled in students; and
- The *common* curriculum, "that balances the teaching of the basics of what should be mastered in a modern technological society with the need for desirable regional or local variations."[113] The core of this curriculum is English language proficiency.

Since that time a considerable amount of attention has been devoted to desirable curriculum improvements at the elementary and secondary levels, in the context of overall restructuring efforts. A 1990 report published by the National Governors' Association as part of its "Results in Education" project highlighted some of the major challenges inherent in efforts to improve curriculum and instruction.

Curriculum and instruction must be modified to promote the acquisition of higher-order— not just basic—skills by all students. Subject matter and teaching that is now superficial, fragmented, and repetitious needs to change to emphasize applying skills, deep understanding, and cohesive knowledge. School goals and assessment tools must reflect these higher-order skills. Teaching strategies must actively engage students in thinking rather than relegating them to passive roles and rote learning. This requires increased flexibility in the use of instructional time, learning activities that are substantially more challenging and engaging, and more varied grouping arrangements that go beyond conventional age-based groups and promote student interaction and cooperative efforts.[114]

A review of the myriad actions states and districts have taken to reassess and realign their curricula in order to facilitate the development of intrinsic, basic, and higher-order skills by their students is beyond our scope. The focus here is on the skills considered to be most relevant to employability and how, through revamping curricula, they can be taught and acquired.

A key concern running throughout the literature on educational reform has been the diminished rigor and relevance of courses aimed at the non–college-bound. "Unless he's going to college there's no need for a student to take geometry," a Florida high school principal observed. The National Association of Secondary School Principals has concluded that two years of mathematics and science are sufficient for job-bound students.[115]

Moreover, with the exception of the 2 percent of students enrolled in advanced placement programs, courses aimed at the college-bound have also been diluted. Despite substantial efforts during the 1980s to raise standards and emphasize courses such as science, mathematics, and foreign language, the curriculum of too many high schools has been watered down by:[116]

- A plethora of "remedial" courses;
- Allowing juniors and seniors to take courses for graduation credit that were designed for freshmen or sophomores;
- Misassignments of teachers to subjects for which they are not qualified, leading to instruction "from the book";
- Dull, superficial, outdated, incomplete, and inaccurate textbooks (a review of 10 history books for 7th to 12th graders in Texas public schools by a Christian group revealed 5,200 mistakes, many of which had not been discovered in prior reviews by a panel selected by the state education board or by staff of the Texas Education Agency);[117]
- Authorization for students to fulfill graduation requirements with nonacademic courses like vocational offerings; and
- Allowing students to study only basic aspects of certain subjects, in "general" courses on science and math, and not challenging them to enroll in courses of progressively

greater difficulty, making it possible for some students to go graduate and go on to college without having experienced chemistry, biology, physics, algebra, or geometry.

In this context, one recent indication of requisites for effective job performance, from the Secretary's Commission on Achieving Necessary Skills (SCANS), chaired by former U.S. labor secretary William E. Brock is quite sobering. This effort was part of President Bush's America 2000 initiative. As indicated in chapters 1 and 5, the SCANS "workplace know-how" included five competencies effective workers should possess (resources, interpersonal skills, information, systems, technology) and three foundation skills workers in high-performance workplaces need (basic skills, thinking skills, personal qualities).

In its April 1992 final report the commission recommended the implementation of a five-part "reinventing schools" agenda by the year 2000:

- Workplace know-how (the SCANS foundation and workplace competencies) should be taught along the entire continuum of education, from kindergarten through college.
- Every student should complete middle school (about age 14) with an introduction to workplace know-how.
- Every student by about age 16 should attain initial mastery of the SCANS know-how.
- Every student should complete high school sufficiently proficient in the SCANS know-how to earn a decent living.
- All federally funded programs for youths and adults, including vocational education programs, should teach the SCANS know-how at appropriate levels.[118]

In addition, the commission recommended that private firms identify individual learning needs and offer training programs to bring their current employees to higher proficiency levels. It called for establishment of a national system that would enable educational institutions to certify to prospective employers that their graduates have achieved SCANS competencies. As indicated in chapter 5, the Clinton administration's proposed "Goals 2000: Educate America Act" would create a National Skill Standards Board to design a voluntary national system of skill standards needed in major occupational clusters.

A wide variety of actions has been taken by school systems to achieve the curriculum changes illustrated in the CED, NGA, and SCANS recommendations. In the next sections, the most commonly utilized steps to enhance learning basic skills and facilitating the transition from school to workplace are examined.

Classroom Improvements. Part of the effort to restructure schools has involved changes in the organization of classes and instructional techniques. In too many school systems too many teachers still must rely on the chalk-and-blackboard approach. The objectives of these efforts have included removing artificial learning barriers that are age-determined, bolstering the academic rigor of college preparatory programs, introducing teaching innovations, and utilizing modern technology. Examples of recent efforts include:

- Elimination of the grade separations for students in elementary schools, so that progress can be determined by ability rather than ages.[119]

- Widespread utilization of computer technology to enable high school students to communicate with college professors and fellow students in other schools or even other countries and to tap statistical databases of government agencies, libraries, and electronic bulletin boards. Particularly promising is increased use of key-pad technology to make computer-assisted teaching more interactive by connecting students with distant teachers through instant feedback.[120]

- Changes in the traditional role of teachers as a result of technology, moving away from "presenter and knowledge provider to act as collaborators, researchers, mentors, facilitators and long-range planners."[121]

- Using multimedia programming to make science, math, history, and other subjects "come alive" through talking encyclopedias and interactive audiovideo textbooks.[122]

- Introducing multicultural education into the curriculum to offset "Eurocentric" view points on histories and cultures of minority groups.

The National Education Association and the Learning Channel have coproduced "Teacher TV," which offers advice and strategies to teachers on new ways to teach learning skills, to inspire students, and to involve parents and the community. Innovative approaches to school reform are highlighted, and controversial issues are debated. While the primary audience is teachers, the Learning Channel has 15 million cable subscribers, so a sizable number of other viewers are potentially made aware of developments in public education.

A controversial proposal involves expansion of "Channel One," an advertising-supported daily news program launched in March 1990 and 3 years later viewed by 8 million students at 11,000 junior high and high schools. Co-owned by Whittle Communications and Time Warner, Inc., Channel One's annual revenues exceed $90 million. Whittle gives participating schools television sets, videotape players, and other equipment. The programs last 12 minutes, including 2 minutes of advertising. The response from educators has been mixed, with the public affairs learning benefits offset by concerns about the undue influence of advertising from cosmetics, athletic shoe, and "junk food" manufacturers. Whittle Communications is planning to offer an elementary school version of its news programs, while education officials in states such as Texas, New York, and California have banned the program or are considering doing so.[123]

The above innovations are merely illustrative of the bold steps that many local districts and states have been taking on the curriculum front. While it is still too early to discern their impact upon competency and skill levels, what is known is that school administrators have been criticized for making major expenditures required to implement these changes, for computer hardware and software, new manuals or textbooks, and the like during a period when public education budgets are thinly stretched. Furthermore, it could be argued that these advances are of interest and benefit only to relatively few students—given the fact that only about 30 percent of the high school graduates go on to a 4-year college.

What about the remainder of the student body who do not enroll in or complete college? How have they benefited from curriculum revamping?

Assisting Non–College-Bound Students. In 1988 the William T. Grant Foundation Commission on Work, Family and Citizenship released a report entitled *The Forgotten Half: Non–College-Bound Youth in America.*[124] The report pointed out that about 20 million people between 16 and 24 would probably not go to college and that most were in considerable need of school-to-work transition programs. Yet, such programs were in short supply at the time. Unfortunately, that continues to be the case. Vocational education and apprenticeship programs have not reached sufficient numbers of people, nor have those programs that are available provided participants with marketable skills. The commission recommended expansion of several "added choice" opportunities for those who are without skills and unemployed—including the Job Corps, state and local youth corps, and the armed forces—and offering more preemployment training, lifelong learning, and community service alternatives to those who are not college-bound.

In a 1990 report the U.S. General Accounting Office (GAO) found that the United States invested heavily in college education, but about half as much was spent for educating and training noncollege youth. Foreign countries invested more than the United States in noncollege education and training and did more to guide the transition from school to work. According to GAO, foreign schools expect all students to perform well, while American schools tolerate (and promote) laggards; foreign schools certify student competency, while American schools certify completion; and foreign schools provide (and often guarantee) remedial education and training and other directed assistance to jobless out-of-school youth, while American training programs reach only a modest number of those eligible.[125]

In a December 1992 "transition series" report to the Clinton administration and Congress, GAO estimated that 1 out of 3 youths 16- to 24-years of age will not possess the skills needed to meet employer requirements for entry-level, semi-skilled, or high-wage occupations. These youth include 5.5 million high school dropouts and 3.8 million graduates with inadequate competencies. Echoing conclusions reached by the Educational Testing Service in its 1990 report, *From School To Work*, that "the United States does very little to smooth the transition from school to work for high school graduates, while it spends large sums on those who continue their educations," and that "for the non–college-bound, the road to employment is, and long has been, a bumpy one," two years later GAO found, compared to other nations, the United States still lacked a coherent strategy for preparing youth for employability.[126]

For many high school graduates, jobs in the secondary labor market—such as retail sales and food service—are the most likely option. Because the skill requirements are not substantial, employers often ignore high school grades, which further weakens the connection between educational attainment and employability. Often these youth flounder for some time after graduation, moving from job to job, seeking (but not finding) rewarding opportunities. Frustrated and believing themselves to be failures, they go on the unemployment rolls.

Three major remedial approaches have been proposed: vocational education and "tech prep," apprenticeships, and community service.

From Vocational Education to "Tech Prep." In its 1990 report, *An America That Works*, CED observed that "vocational education is the neglected stepchild of the American public education system and is frequently dismissed by critics as irrelevant to the needs of students and employers alike."[127] In its 1985 study, cited earlier, the committee had argued that:

- Much vocational curricula did not relate to the work force and required substantial reform.

- Students graduating from vocational education programs needed to demonstrate a higher level of academic competence.

- Employees needed to become more actively involved in curriculum assessment and review and in program evaluation.

- A vocational education degree needed to do more than signify a second-rate student.[128]

In CED's judgment, while there had been notable progress in some school systems during the five-year interval, much remained to be done. Particularly important has been the need to teach both basic and vocational skills, coupled with relevant work attitudes and experience through apprenticeship programs and alternative schools or academies within high schools that specialize in vocational programs such as auto repair, food services, child and geriatric care, building trades, business occupations, and equipment maintenance.

Since publication of CED's report there has been growing interest in technical preparatory ("tech prep") programs. According to the December 1992 issue of the National Education Association's *NEA Today*, tech prep's popularity has grown rapidly following its introduction in 1987–88. More than 1,000 high schools in the nation have established such a curriculum, and over 40 percent of all students are enrolled (compared with one-third who are enrolled in college prep curricula).

Tech prep runs in tandem with college preparation courses and provides students with a sequence or cluster of courses of vocational, as well as academic, content, such as computers and electronics. Graduates then go on to obtain two-year associates or technical degrees at community colleges.

Tech prep curricula are more difficult and demanding than the traditional vocational education or general studies tracks that they replace. For example, students take algebra and chemistry rather than general mathematics and sciences courses. However, they offer relevance as well as rigor. Graduates not only have skills that enhance their employability but also have a two-year postsecondary degree, which enhances their mobility in the job market. These advantages, it is anticipated, will also help give students incentives to stay in school and thereby reduce dropout rates.[129]

Tech prep programs are one of the important ways to facilitate school-to-work transitions, a critical need identified in the June 1990 report by the National Center on Education and the Economy's Commission on the Skills of the American Workforce, entitled *America's Choice: High Skills or Low Wages!* which influenced the Clinton presidential campaign proposals on education and training. The commission was chaired by Ira Magaziner, who now serves as senior advisor for policy development in the Clinton administration, and co-chaired by former U.S. labor secretaries William Brock and Ray Marshall. It recommended:[130]

- A national performance standard, benchmarked to the highest world standards, should be established for all students to attain by age 16. After passing a series of assessments related to the standard, students would receive a Certificate of Initial Mastery, which would qualify them for work, a college preparatory program, or pursuit of a Technical and Professional Certificate or an associate's degree. The latter certificates would require completion of a 2- to 4-year work-study program, and would qualify the student for entry into various service or manufacturing occupations. Advanced certificates also could be sought for occupations requiring higher orders of technical skills.

- In addition to assuming much of the responsibility for the above, states should establish and finance alternative learning environments for those who fail to attain the certificate. Youth centers should be set up for dropouts, and youth should not be permitted to work before the age of 18 unless they possess a Certificate of Initial Mastery.

- Federal, state, and local authorities should work together to create a system of Employment and Training Boards to manage, oversee, and coordinate school-to-work transition programs in their jurisdiction.

Efforts by public school systems to move in the directions suggested by CED and the commission, among others, have been slowed by the difficulty of freeing up additional local or state funds for curriculum development and teacher retraining at a time when district budgets and state educational aid are constrained by the national recession and antitax public sentiments. Another concern is equity: will all interested students be allowed to enter the tech prep curriculum or certificate programs, especially those who require the greatest amount of remedial course work and other attention, and, if so, how will the special needs of these youth be met? Despite these limiting factors, it is likely that the number of schools offering tech prep and other school-to-work transition programs will continue to increase in response to both support from the Clinton administration and dissatisfaction with traditional curricula of the non–college-bound.

Apprenticeships. The U.S. General Accounting Office shared CED's concerns about the often difficult transition from school to work for those who were not college-bound. In a 1991 report, GAO noted that apprenticeship programs—where youth "learn by doing" under the tutelege of a mentor or master craftsperson—were not widely used (less than 0.3% of the U.S. labor force are apprentices) and in practice, the participants were well beyond the high school level, with an average age of 29 years. GAO observed that cooperative education programs in high schools and two- and four-year colleges did offer promise, since they combined classroom instruction with work experience and on-the-job training, sometimes leading to permanent employment. About 8 percent of high school juniors and seniors were enrolled in these apprentice-type programs, of whom 77 percent were white and 52 percent were female. GAO concluded that while cooperative education appeared beneficial, it had to overcome two formidable obstacles: lack of student and employer awareness about the programs and how to get involved in them; and a negative reputation of the programs as being "dumping grounds" for academically weak students.[131] At the same time, GAO recognized that the federal government had a leadership role in this area and recommended that the Department of Education:

• Develop national data and conduct evaluations of high school cooperative education programs to help refine and improve program structure as well as seek opportunities to promote and expand high-quality cooperative education in our nation's schools.

• Request states to encourage schools to provide students with completed training plans together with school and employer assessments, as a form of certification of students' skill attainment. Schools should consider the applicability to training plans of common skill standards being developed under the leadership of the Departments of Education and Labor.[132]

A year later, GAO issued a second report on apprenticeships. It found further evidence that American employers rarely use apprenticeships, that apprenticeships play a declining role in worker training, and that participation patterns raised equal employment opportunity concerns. In 1990, approximately 283,000 workers were registered in 43,000 apprenticeship programs—equivalent to about 2 percent of the college student population—which represents an 11 percent decline since 1980. The number of apprenticeship programs also dropped over the decade, and most of those remaining are concentrated in construction, metal trades, and corrections. Half of the programs had no active apprentices in early 1991. Minority and women apprentices were underrepresented in higher-paying occupations and overrepresented in lower-paying ones. GAO recommended that the secretary of labor, Bureau of Apprenticeship and Training, and Women's Bureau work to increase recruitment of women into apprentice programs.[133]

Adoption of the CED and GAO recommendations, while beneficial, would still place the United States well behind some of its economic competitors. In Germany, which has the most well-established system, nearly two-thirds of all youth participate in some 600,000 apprenticeships. At the age of 15 or 16, compulsory school graduates seek an employer from among 480 trades for whom they can serve as an apprentice. After three years work, their achievement is tested in accordance with nationally established skill standards. Those who pass become journeymen, and their credentials are recognized throughout the country. Three more years of work—and completion of additional courses on law, business management, and technology—qualify the journeyman to take a test to become a master, which is a prerequisite for opening a business.[134] In Japan, there are very close high school–employer linkages, which greatly facilitate student placements. Employers rely heavily on recommendations from schoolteachers and administrators in making their hiring decisions.

In a 1992 report, *Mandate for Change*, published by the Progressive Policy Institute, Ted Kolderie, Robert Lerman, and Charles Moskos proposed a school-based apprenticeship program having five components. Among other advantages, this system would establish close connections between classwork and the world of work, give students incentives to remain in school, and put noncollege youth on a positive path to employment.

1. Change school curricula to expose students in the seventh through tenth grades to information about various occupations, including visits to and short internships at work sites.

2. Offer tenth-grade students a choice between pursuing a job apprenticeship or remaining on a purely academic track. Those choosing the former option would sign formal contracts with specific employers.

3. Create a range of three-year apprenticeships that begin in the eleventh grade. Students could earn skill certifications and academic credit as they combine workplace training with school courses.

4. Give apprentices a comprehensive test at the end of the twelfth grade to ensure educational and job proficiency.

5. Develop a combined work-based and school-based curriculum that involves spending increasing amounts of time at the work site. Their third year (thirteenth grade) would involve material advanced enough to permit the apprentices to earn one year of credit toward an Associate's degree.[135]

In the United States, 24 states had youth apprenticeship programs in various stages of development by mid-1993.[136] Oregon's approach to curriculum revamping is the most ambitious and comprehensive to date. In 1991, the legislature passed the Oregon Educational Act for the 21st Century in response to concerns about a 25 percent dropout rate and desires to give students more and better options and ultimately improve the quality of the work force. The measure:

• Expanded Head Start to cover half of all eligible low-income children by 1996 and all such children by 1998 to help ensure they will be ready to learn when they enter public school.

• Students from kindergarten through the third grade will be grouped by abilities rather than age levels.

• Students must demonstrate their academic progress in grades 3, 5, 8, and 10, and schools must assist those having difficulty keeping up.

• At age 16 or 10th grade, a student would acquire a Certificate of Initial Mastery, based on his or her performance, which attests to having accomplished a basic level of understanding and competency and is the "union card" for further education or employment. If they fail to do so, they will receive extra attention until they attain their certificate. "The primary benefit of this certificate lies in what it would signify to any employer or college in the state: that the holder, regardless of the school he or she attended, possesses certain fundamental knowledge and skills and is prepared for further academic study, technical training or employment."[137]

- At age 18, students would seek a Certificate of Advanced Mastery of either college preparatory material or applied skill courses.
- School-site councils will be established.
- Parents will be permitted to move their children to any other school in the state if dissatisfied with their progress, while 11th and 12th grade students can make this decision if they possess certificates of mastery.
- Learning centers will be set up to advise and assist dropouts.
- Business would be involved in setting curricula for vocational courses.
- The school day will be lengthened from 175 days to 220 by 2010.[138]

The act also established a Youth Apprenticeship Pilot Program, under which interested 11th and 12th grade students would be placed in apprenticeships by teachers, school administrators, or regional technical coordinators. Students may not work more than 20 hours a week. Employers receive tax credits to help cover student wages. By 1993, 30 high school students were enrolled.[139]

Oregon's approach to certification and apprenticeships is consistent with many of the previously described recommendations by SCANS, CED, and the Commission on the Skills of the American Workforce. Moreover, it goes a long way toward putting vocational education on a par with college preparatory courses, at some possible risk of "tracking" poor and minority students into vocational pursuits and having inadequate funding (only $2 million in start-up funds were provided).

Wisconsin also has taken significant steps to better prepare students for the world of work. Its 1991 School-to-Work Transition Initiative included a technical preparation curriculum combining the last two years of high school with the first two years of college, a Gateway Assessment administered to 10th graders to evaluate their academic progress, and youth apprenticeships. Participants in the latter program spend the summer between the 11th and 12th grades in an apprenticeship, for which they receive credits for high school as well as for technical colleges or universities. Along with their high school diploma, graduates receive a Certificate of Occupational Proficiency from the State Department of Labor, Industry and Human Relations.[140]

While offering youth valuable practical experience in the workplace, as well as building self-confidence, social skills, and a work ethic, as GAO reported apprenticeships have not proven as popular or as widespread in the United States in comparison with other countries. As a result, often there are more interested students than available slots. In part, this situation is due to the prohibitive costs of apprenticeships to some employers, in terms of both student wages and supervisory time. Businesses also have been reluctant to pay for the training that is needed to facilitate participation by many at-risk youth. The difficulty of developing agreed-upon standards or credentials for certifying competency in a number of occupations has halted progress as well.

To help accelerate the pace of apprentice program development at the state and local levels, the Clinton administration has proposed establishment of a national apprenticeship program that would combine classroom instruction with skill training for high school dropouts and graduates as well as community college and vocational school students. The president's proposal would build on 1991–92 efforts by senators Sam Nunn and John Breaux to seek congressional approval of $50 million for grants for apprenticeship demonstration grants and by the Bush administration to seek $100 million for such purposes. President Clinton has indicated that he will request two or three times the amount sought by his predecessor.[141]

Community Service. In addition to vocational education programs and apprenticeships, community and neighborhood service programs have been advocated as means of instilling youth with the obligations of citizenship, in addition to providing them with job experience, work discipline, self-esteem building, and interpersonal skill development opportunities. In 1983 the Carnegie Foundation for the Advancement of Teaching recommended the inclusion of community service as part of the mandatory middle school curriculum, "to help students discover that they are not only autonomous individuals, but also members of the larger community to which they are accountable," and two years later 70 percent of 1,100 public and private high schools surveyed nationwide reported having such a program. In 1993 as estimated 1 million or more high school students participated in voluntary school-based community service programs through clubs, course electives, and classroom-integrated service activities.[142]

In 1992 the Maryland Board of Education was the first to mandate that in order to graduate from high school, all public school students in the state must spend 75 hours on community service. Twenty-two of the state's 24 school systems opposed the requirement. Teachers, administrators, and legislators have expressed fears about the capacity of already overloaded curricula and overworked teachers to absorb these new programs, as well as about the availability of appropriate community service projects. Some parents have raised first amendment rights concerns and involuntary servitude objections, which have been rejected by the courts.[143]

Despite these efforts, most observers agree that more needs to be done as a matter of national policy to overcome "the nasty habit in this country of expecting our teenagers to either go to college or wander around aimlessly from job to job until they find something that fits them."[144] As President Bill Clinton has put it during his last term as governor, "We are failing our young people, because we don't have a real school-to-work system in America."[145]

In 1990 Congress enacted the National and Community Service Act, which authorized $22 million for 8 national youth service pilot projects. Participants were to receive $5,000 vouchers for 1 or 2 year's service. A Commission on National and Community Service was created to administer the program. Subsequently, the Clinton administration proposed a major voluntary national service program. In its first year $389 million would be provided for loan forgiveness to 25,000 college-bound, college, or post-college students, growing to $7.4 billion and 100,000 students by 1997. Students would work at minimum-wage community service jobs for 2 years and also receive a voucher for $13,000 which could be used to pay college loans. In response to concerns expressed by veterans' groups that the national service benefits would be more generous than those provided under the GI bill, in May 1993 the administration scaled back the amount of the voucher to $10,000 ($5,000 per year of service). Congress further reduced the amount available to $4,725 a year for grants and loan-forgiveness to college students for tuition, health care, and living expenses in return for 2 years of community service. It authorized $1.5 billion over 3 years, beginning with $300 million for fiscal 1994. In September 1993, Congress passed and President Clinton signed the national service legislation.

Critics of the national service initiative argued that the federal budget deficit precludes establishing a new social program of this nature, which raises expectations but fails to achieve the financial magnitude necessary to make much impact in terms of either participation or public service contribution. Some alleged that service-for-tuition arrangements are a form of bribery! Others expressed concerns that allowing students to serve for 2 years as teachers' aides, auxiliary police, park maintenance personnel, disaster relief workers, or in other minimum-wage occupations or capacities would at best be "make-work" opportunities and, at worst, displace current employees with students who were willing to work for lower pay and fewer benefits. Some education officials voiced objections to the plan because they believed it would be funded by existing appropriations that would otherwise be available for higher education purposes, rather than with new monies. And students complained that the amount of the voucher is small relative to tuition costs, and that only middle-class or wealthy students could afford to participate.[146]

Supporters pointed to the altruistic value of such a program, in terms of the democratic citizenship and public-spirited values first identified in 1910 by William James in his influential essay "The Moral Equivalent of War." They further rebutted by noting Reserve Officer Training Programs, which pay students to train for military service, as well as the U.S. Army's offer to pay as much as $20,000 toward college tuition for its recruits. They asserted that national service would be a "civilian GI bill," which would guarantee college or postsecondary education to those who participate; this program would be an especially important way to deal with unemployment resulting from Defense Department downsizing and to help reduce welfare rolls, while at the same time performing valuable public service.[147]

Reinvigorating Principals and Teachers

Thus far the discussion of restructuring elementary and secondary education has focused on organization, governance, administration, and curriculum matters. It is now time to address the "people dimension," the role of principals and teachers, followed by a critical segment of the student population, those in the "third wave" of reform—at-risk youth.

Principals have not received as much attention from education reformers as they probably deserve. After all, they are the leaders of their school, "the managers of the vision," the responsible administrators. Most studies have concluded that the key ingredients to the formula for successful principals are the ability to identify important tasks to be accomplished, to delegate and communicate, to assess performance—and to put in long hours. In recent years, however, more and more emphasis has been placed on retooling the skills of current principals to enable them to manage schools like small corporations. In addition, attention has been given to removing some of the obstacles to the recruitment of the next generation of school leaders and developing incentives to help ensure that the best principals remain in the profession.

The National Governors' Association Task Force on Leadership and Management recommended in 1986 a fivefold agenda that has current relevance:

- Revise preparation programs for administrators so that new principals are trained to be effective school leaders;
- Ensure that administrator selection and licensure practices reflect the skills and knowledge needed by effective principals;
- Develop an evaluation system for principals;
- Provide ongoing training for school administrators; and
- Reward principals and schools for improved student achievement.[148]

New Jersey has pioneered in revamping the principal's post, as well as developing alternate route programs enabling people who have not taken teaching courses to become teachers. The former program rests on the assumptions that schools operate much like businesses and that principals can learn what they need to know about their schools while on the job. Alternate-route principals must have a master's degree in business administration or a "leadership field" and during their first two years report to an experienced principal. Only about a dozen principals have entered the alternate program, so its effects are not known.

While not questioning the need to manage schools in a businesslike way, critics have asserted that for principals to be effective in dealing with teachers and unions on salary, curriculum, and other matters, previous classroom experience or service as vice principal is essential.[149] These experiences also are a critical part of the socialization of principals to the culture of public schools.

A sensitive issue in the effort to upgrade school administration is the desirability of giving principals tenure in either the district or their school. Job security, rather than academic freedom, is at the core of this debate. Proponents argue that if principals are to be encouraged to implement reforms that may prove controversial with unions, teachers, or parents, their jobs and careers should not be jeopardized. In the absence of tenure, principals might be more inclined not to "make waves" and to make incremental changes when broad vision and bold steps are really needed. Skeptics, however, assert that much like what has happened in higher education, tenure may protect ineffective and incompetent principals from removal and thereby slow progress in improving school administration. The kind of school leaders the reform movement truly needs, it is argued, is in high demand in the education marketplace, so tenure should not be a significant factor. A long-term (i.e., 3- to 5-year) contract with the school board would give principals sufficient protection from arbitrary removal, as well as cover severance arrangements in the event of firing for cause.

Turning to teachers, the NGA task force also recommended several actions to improve both teachers and teaching. These included:

- Create a national board to define teacher standards;
- Recruit able teacher candidates;
- Rebuild teacher education;
- Improve teacher compensation, both at entry and throughout the career;
- Redesign the structure of the teaching career;
- Align teacher incentives with schoolwide student performance; and
- Redesign schools to create more productive working and learning environments.[150]

After the governors' recommendations were offered, there was considerable activity in state legislatures and school districts to attempt to make teaching a more attractive and remunerative career. As reported in chapter 5, much effort was directed to increasing salaries, which on average doubled during the 1980s. While this was a significant first step, as indicated in the NGA policy, much more needed to be done. These improvements are particularly timely in light of projections by the American Federation of Teachers (AFT) of a shortage of some 310,000 teachers by the year 2001. In 1993, 51.6 percent of public-school teachers were over 40 years of age; unless poor working conditions, relatively low salaries, school violence, and other disincentives are overcome, in AFT's judgment it will be very difficult for districts to find qualified replacements.[151] The following sections review recent actions on related fronts.

Career Ladders and Master Teachers. Career ladders, or "differentiated staffing patterns," are a response to the criticism that the egalitarian teaching profession offers horizontal, but not vertical, advancement opportunities. This is especially a concern to women, who comprise about two-thirds of the public-school teacher population yet only 5 percent of the nation's superintendents.[152]

Basically, to move up, a teacher must move out of the school or the teaching profession. However, by supplementing classroom work with other related responsibilities—research, curriculum development, and administration—the groundwork for promotion can be laid.

Proponents of career ladders argue that such differentiation of responsibilities helps avoid teachers' getting substantively "stale" or organizationally "tunnel-visioned." A varied assignment provides them with opportunities to learn more about other aspects of the school system they would not likely have encountered during the normal course of their teaching work. Particularly promising is coupling differentiated roles with career professional teacher plans, so the teacher can move up the rungs of the professional ladder from associate to mentor or master teacher, gaining professional recognition, responsibilities for leadership and supervision, and financial rewards. A key feature (and concern) is "the career ladder with its hierarchical promotions and pay is a permanent structure; decisions are irreversible."[153]

On the other hand, career ladders have been criticized because in some systems they have become more like routine rotating job assignments than career advancement programs. There is little growth potential in performing mundane duties and few guarantees that participating teachers would be rewarded for taking on new responsibilities and heavier work loads. One teacher in a Utah study "characterized the career ladder as a 'stepladder'; you step up and you step down."[154] Teachers' support for career ladders—always at a minimum level of enthusiasm—has also been diminished by distrust of peer evaluation mechanisms, concerns about "deadwood" teachers getting onto the ladder, and suspicions about patronage appointments.

Merit Pay. One of the more popular responses to the criticisms of classroom teaching and teachers that were made during the first and second waves of education reform was the establishment of merit pay plans. Under this arrangement teachers' salaries are based on the academic performance of their students and school. Southern governors like Lamar Alexander of Tennessee were in the forefront of merit pay, contending that if the public schools were to retain the "best and the brightest" teachers, more had to be done than simply raise overall salary levels. Good teachers needed to be encouraged and rewarded for their efforts, while poor teachers needed to be discouraged and unrewarded. Unfortunately, most educational systems do not operate this way—before or since the advent of merit pay—and most merit pay plans have been of limited duration.

The major arguments against this approach are: (1) flaws in evaluating student performance will lead to arbitrary and unfair teacher salary determinations; (2) if the most important influences on educational attainment are the family structure, home environment, and income level, then teachers will be paid based on conditions over which they have no control; (3) teachers will be inclined to "teach to the test" rather than use innovative or more effective instructional techniques, since the test results directly influence their salary; (4) due to budget restrictions, merit pay awards may be limited to only a few teachers who "walk upon water"; [155] (5) teachers in inner-city or urban systems, who may be the most dedicated to helping at-risk students, would consequently be penalized in comparison with their colleagues in suburban schools; (6) local and state politicians and school board members have been willing to reduce or eliminate merit pay when confronted by budget deficits, raising questions as to their commitment to this approach; and (7) teamwork is a key factor in schools, and merit pay would force teachers to compete with one another, which would undermine cooperation, communication, and coordination. In light of these concerns "merit school" plans, where teachers receive bonuses for the performance of the entire student body, determined in national competition, have been proposed by American Federation of Teachers president Albert Shanker and others as desirable alternatives to merit pay for individual teachers. [156]

Some of the concerns and frustrations about merit pay are revealed in the following commentary by Arlene Hoebel, a teacher at Woodson High School in Fairfax County, Virginia. In her "teacher's view," the program should be buried:

My perception is that most teachers who tried out for merit pay were already strong teachers. Many other equally competent teachers did not apply, because they didn't want to bother with the Mickey Mouse stuff that was involved in qualifying for it.

It took a teacher's time away from classroom preparation. For each of six observations (some announced, some unannounced), there was an hour pre-conference with the would-be evaluator. On the day of the observation, the evaluator took down all that was said and done in a classroom, then typed the notes up in a report, followed by a post-conference with the teacher who had been observed. At the post-conference, the evaluators would make "constructive" suggestions even though they often admitted that they had to fish for things to recommend.

One evaluator's suggestion to a particular teacher was that the teacher put the desks in his room in a circle for a more "spontaneous" environment. The next evaluator told the same teacher to put his desks in rows for a more "structured" effect. The teacher had to write a rebuttal to each suggestion. More time was taken later to discuss these addenda with the principal. Multiply the above process by six observations, and you see the time and expense that accrued. [157]

On the positive side, even though experience with merit pay is limited, researchers have found that teacher salary determinations by principals do not rest entirely on their students' test scores. These studies also suggest that it is possible to separate the effects of families and the performance of teachers. Under a variation of the plan—"merit schools"—schoolwide performance would be emphasized, which would build teamwork and lessen competition among teachers. [158]

The fundamental flaw of merit pay is the difficulty of relating performance to pay in the face of doubts and resistance by the education bureaucracy and teachers' unions. Personnel regulations, contracts, and detailed rules on such matters as preparation time, hall and cafeteria duty, and participation in extracurricular activities tend to protect teachers, principals, and administrators who are performing poorly or at mediocre levels—some of whom may have tenure—and to reduce principals' discretionary authority. Until these inhibiting factors are removed, there seems to be little hope for widespread adoption of merit pay.

Tenure. Another approach to providing teachers with incentives to stay in their classrooms rather than seek higher-paying opportunities is tenure. Proponents of giving teachers such status after a required probationary period, years in service, certification, and other qualifications are met argue that such teachers deserve protection from arbitrary action by principals or politicians. While lifetime job security may not be possible, especially during tight budget times, tenure guarantees due process. In the classroom, tenure also provides academic freedom, which enables teachers to raise sensitive issues, challenge speakers, and provide controversial materials. Although there is always the possibility of "deadwood" being tenured, this is lessened to the degree that evaluations are conducted by peers rather than principals.

Tenure opponents assert that lifetime employment guarantees are rare in other professions, that such "contracts" reduce administrators' flexibility in dealing with fiscal crises, and that teacher accountability would be diminished. As an alternative to tenure, multiyear renewable contracts can be used and teachers given time off for participation in professional development programs to improve their performance and remain current in their professional substantive field.[159]

Other Incentives. Career ladders and merit pay plans have had limited impact on improving teachers and teaching, due to resistance from virtually all sectors of the educational profession, and tenure has been a hotly debated topic. At the same time, it should be recognized that one of the goals of these incentive plans—attracting and retaining the "best and the brightest"—already has been achieved. Despite union concerns about shortages, more and better teachers are entering the public schools, a December 1991 article in the *Wall Street Journal* reported, because of "higher pay and concern for schools."[160]

Some skeptics might argue that in light of these trends, "tinkering" with instructional innovations or administrative reforms like the above is unnecessary. Nevertheless, a number of other incentives that have been suggested beyond these recommended by the National Governors' Association should be noted.[161] These include:

- Giving teacher training more prestige and greater status within colleges and universities by emphasizing higher-quality programs and producing higher-quality graduates in "centers of pedagogy" and "practice schools" akin to teaching hospitals.[162]

- Requiring all teachers to hold a master's degree in education, arts and sciences, or a specialized subject area to enhance the prestige of the profession, provide an additional rationale for pay increases, and improve teaching success (although there is no research evidence to support the latter claim).[163]

- Broadening of alternative career paths to teaching, so that people making midcareer changes or holding degrees in substantive areas rather than education administration could enter the field.

- Reducing emphasis education schools place on educational courses and increasing emphasis on subject matter preparation for new teachers or even requiring all high school teachers to have experience or a college minor in the subject matter area for which they were hired.

- Giving prospective elementary and secondary teachers tuition waivers and deferred loan repayment schedules, especially to induce more men to enter elementary school teaching.

- Upgrading the training of principals to give them strong administrative, human relations, and motivational skills, to make principals both the top manager and the educational leader of public schools.

National Standards. Another area of reform that would have beneficial effects on teachers, teaching, and outcomes is establishment of national standards as to what students need to know and be able to do to succeed in work and in life and utilization of assessments of progress. As discussed earlier, this approach builds on the more than two decades of work of the National Assessment of Educational Progress and more recently, the recommendations by the National Council on Education Standards and Testing to create a voluntary system. A survey of 100 national education, business, civil rights, and other leaders by Mary Hatwood Futrell found general agreement that a national core curriculum would eventually be implemented (together with the National Education Goals, a national system of student examinations, and a national certification process for teachers) and lead to a more centralized public education system in the United States. However, they opposed required use of standardized national curriculum and tests; the majority supported making their use by public schools optional.[164]

Critics of national standards argue that it is contrary to the tradition of local control of public schools, that national standards will lead to a national curriculum, that schools would focus exclusively on courses relating to the standards and ignore other important subjects like music and art, that teacher creativity would be stifled, and that at-risk children and students of inner-city schools would be discriminated against. Supporters, including the Clinton administration, assert that it will be difficult, if not impossible, to achieve the National Education Goals without a system of national standards, as provided for in the "Goals 2000: Educate America Act." They differentiate standards, which are general, from a nationally prescribed curriculum for local schools, which specifies in detail the topics to be taught. They point to foreign countries like Germany, Japan, France, and Korea, which have used this approach successfully to raise student achievement. But perhaps most importantly, from a teacher's perspective, agreement on what high school graduates should know and be able to do provides clarity and challenge that are currently lacking, which causes frustration. As AFT president Albert Shanker has noted in supporting national standards:

In countries that have such standards, educators work backward from that picture to decide what kids need to learn and when, and what constitutes excellent, adequate, and failing levels of performance. Youngsters and their parents understand that there are certain expectations about what students will achieve. Teachers know what to teach and—with help from parents—pressure the kids to meet the standards. Textbooks and other materials are tightly focused on giving students the content they need.

Exams go hand in hand with these standards, and unlike our standardized tests, they are based on the curricula students have been taught. Students are carefully prepared for these exams and study hard for them. And when they pass, they have a credential that certifies to all concerned—parents, institutions of higher education, future employers—what they know and can do. This contrasts sharply with most of our high school diplomas, which certify primarily that recipients have spent the required amount of time in school.[165]

Empowerment. In the final analysis, perhaps the most significant nonmonetary incentive is the most difficult to achieve—sharing of authority and decision-making responsibilities between teachers and principals. Much has been written about the virtues of teacher "empowerment," yet little progress has been made. As noted in chapter 5, there have been promising efforts to make teachers full partners in school improvement within the context of collective bargaining agreements such as NEA's Mastery in Learning (MIL) Project. For decentralized school management to succeed, with or without national standards, both principals and teachers must change the ways they do business:

Many principals are not prepared for such roles, having been expected in recent years to be aggressive and efficient school managers. . . . However, unless principals accept shared leadership and collegial policymaking with teachers as legitimate goals, they are likely to interpret all teacher activity as encroachment and all faculty successes as failures of their own, to clutch their formal powers more tightly, and to assert their superior positions more forcefully.

Teachers, too, as participants in decision making, must adopt new attitudes. Teachers are inclined to withdraw from policymaking in their schools; they have implicitly negotiated a treaty that protects their classroom autonomy in exchange for knowing their place and leaving school management to administrators. But if collegial decision making is to thrive, interaction between teachers and administrators must be ongoing and teachers must be willing to leave the protection of their classrooms. A solitary individual or two cannot be expected to redirect a school that is set in its ways; a certain substantial number of able teachers will have to emerge who, together with the principal, can initiate, sustain, and institutionalize new school norms and practices.[166]

To sum up, thus far this chapter has reviewed a range of issues that are associated with efforts to restructure schools. Assuming that some of these initiatives are successful, what would the restructured school do, and how would it operate? Table 6.1 indicates a range of possible responses to these questions.

RESPONDING TO AT-RISK YOUTH

Much of this book has been devoted to describing and analyzing approaches the public and private sectors can take to provide more opportunities for at-risk

Table 6.1
What Restructuring School Districts Do

Provide Leadership

Make long-term commitment to comprehensive change:
- Guided by goals not prescriptions
- Characterized by many reinforcing strategies and steps

Communicate goals, guiding images, and information:
- Create a language for change and a focus on student learning
- Have direct communication between schools and district leaders

Encourage experimentation and risk taking:
- Begin with schools that volunteer
- Support experimentation with waivers from constraining rules

Demonstrate and promote shared decision making:
- Involve all staff in developing educational goals and values
- Limit faculty meetings to items that require immediate action

Create New Organizational Structures

Participate actively in building new alliances:
- Make cooperative agreements with teachers' unions
- Create new joint ventures with foundations, advocacy groups, businesses, and universities

Devolve authority to schools and to teachers:
- Give schools authority over staffing and materials budgets
- Provide incentives for principals to involve teachers in school-site decisions

Promote creation of new roles, for example:
- Teachers as leaders, evaluators, curriculum developers, and facilitators of student learning
- Administrators as facilitators of teachers and as instructional leaders

Develop and demonstrate during the summer new models of:
- Restructured programs for staff and students
- Support for teachers to develop curriculum and educational materials

Create new forms of accountability that:
- Match the comprehensive nature and time line of restructuring
- Use many measures, including those defined by schools

Table 6.1 (continued)

Provide Support and Assistance

Provide a broad range of opportunities for professional development • • •
- On- and off-site assistance for teachers and administrators
- Development sessions that include techniques in management, clinical supervision, instruction, and content

Provide time for staff to assume new roles and responsibilities:
- Time for planning, working with colleagues, and school decision making
- Release time for professional development activities

Seek supplementary sources of funding and assistance from:
- State and federal governments
- Local businesses, private foundations, and individuals

Source: David, J.L., "Restructuring in Progress: Lessons from Pioneering Districts," in R.F. Elmore, and Associates, *Restructuring Schools: The Next Generation of Educational Reform* (San Francisco: Jossey-Bass Publishers, 1990), pp. 244-5

children and youth to lead productive, rewarding life-styles and to contribute to society. This section reviews some of the pros and cons associated with the schools' response to a challenge issued by NGA, based on its assessment of progress between 1986 and 1990:

Despite the development of many model and exemplary programs, states still have far to go in attaining success and higher achievement for all students. Existing programs to improve the achievement of at-risk students and prevent students from dropping out promote marginal rather than systemic improvement. Even the best programs have not been institutionalized. And states still have not found an effective way to disseminate information about model and exemplary programs from one school district to another so that their use can become widespread. Instead, schools and districts often develop good programs individually. As states move into the 1990s, they must move beyond this isolated approach to one involving more comprehensive reform of the education system.[167]

To underscore this concern, in 1991 a study by the Carnegie Foundation for the Advancement of Teaching, entitled *Ready to Learn: A Mandate for the Nation* was released. Some 7,000 kindergarten teachers across the country participated. On average, they reported that 35 percent of their students started school unprepared to learn, and 42 percent said their students were less prepared than five years ago, particularly in their vocabulary and sentence structure skills.[168]

In response to these and similar findings, as well as to the first National Education Goal (by the year 2000 all children will start school ready to learn), the National Governors' Association has established an action team on school readiness, cochaired by Ohio governor George Voinovich and New Mexico governor Bruce King. In 1992 NGA published a report, *Every Child Ready for School*, covering state experiences and benchmarks for successful implementation.[169]

Part of the difficulty is the absence of commonly shared definitions for "at-risk" youth as well as for the factors, such as "chronically or excessively absent," that indicate potential dropouts. For example, a 1990 survey of 15 states by the Southern Regional Education Board revealed three major shortcomings:

• Most states do not have basic information on who drops out, when, and why.

• Strategies for focusing and maintaining the attention of public and professional educators on the problem for a decade do not exist in most states.

• Comprehensive plans are not in place in most states for implementing school-level practices to encourage students to stay in school and to eliminate practices that contribute to students dropping out.[170]

Parent Intervention Strategies

Much of the education literature holds that where at-risk children are concerned, the sooner schools and social agencies can intervene with parents or otherwise provide whatever remedial actions are needed—nutrition, health care, education, safety—the better, as far as immediate and long-term results are concerned. As the education reform movement progressed, it became more apparent that the prospects for a child's successful learning experience and a youth's successful completion of high school were greatly affected by facilitative steps taken in and out of the school.

Yet, for a long time, low-income children have not received the attention they deserve. In 1972, for example, the President's Commission on School Finance found that only 47 percent of 5-year-olds and 20 percent of 4-year-olds from these families received preschool training.[171] According to NGA, almost 20 years later, nearly two-thirds of the states had developed early childhood education and parenting programs, although the majority were of a pilot nature, did not operate statewide, and were limited to four-year-olds.[172]

One key way to increase the "readiness" of at-risk children is to expand preschool education, and proposals have been made to do so for several years. Illustrative of these steps are the following:

(1) group preschool participation for all four- and five-year-old children with families whose incomes are below the poverty level; (2) planned educational components built into day care programs for children with working mothers; (3) parent education programs for parents of children from birth through age three; (4) provision by all secondary schools and colleges of child development programs to give students the understanding and skills necessary to be good parents; (5) development and broadcast of television and other media programs such as "Sesame Street" as supplements to home or school-based programs, serving both children and parents.[173]

For many of these children, however, school-based initiatives are insufficient. Similarly, efforts to provide preschool education at day-care facilities and multiservice centers have had limited impact and duration, and by 1992 only 11 states had appropriated funds to expand Head Start. Therefore, in recent years, more direct intervention strategies have become increasingly popular. Examples of these strategies include parent training, parent remedial education, and home visitations.

Parent Training. As of 1992, 30 states supported programs that teach parenting skills, eight of which are targeted to teen parents. One of the best known is Arkansas's Home Instruction Program for Preschool Youngsters (HIPPY), where some 2,400 welfare mothers spend 20 minutes each day teaching their children from workbooks. Others are Minnesota's Early Childhood Family Education and Missouri's Parents as Teachers (PAT) programs. The early effects of these efforts suggest that preschoolers are better prepared to enter kindergarten and that parents have improved their literacy and occupational skills.[174]

Parent Remedial Education. Bringing parents back to high schools to complete diploma requirements, together with their children, is also gaining popularity. In Louisville, Kentucky, for example, mothers working to improve their literacy skills (only 1% are fathers) sit in classes next to their preschoolers three days a week, ride the school bus together, and eat lunch in the cafeteria together. Toyota Motor Corporation has given $2 million to expand the program and set up new ones in the cities of Atlanta, Rochester, Tucson, Pittsburgh, and Richmond. The skills and attitudes instilled in parents in this environment are brought back to the home, where more time is spent reading to children and helping get them ready for school.[175]

Home Visitations. Home visiting has proven to be a valuable health care tool for at-risk families with young children—especially for women risking poor birth outcomes, premature or low-birth weight infants, and teenage mothers. This approach also has positive effects on preschool education. According to the General Accounting Office, every one dollar spent on preschool education saves three to six dollars later in remedial education, welfare payments, and crime costs.[176] GAO concluded that home-visited children had improved in their intellectual development.

In August 1992 the National Governors' Association endorsed a bipartisan national strategy for improving children's readiness for school. Aimed particularly at disadvantaged and at-risk students, the strategy called for improvement of preschool programs, health and nutrition, and social services for parents.[177]

Prevention Programs for Potential Dropouts

While some important pilot projects have been developed by states and local districts indirectly to help preschool children develop important learning skills and habits, of greater interest and concern to educators and policymakers are programs targeted to children and youth at risk of failure. Persisting high dropout rates for minority and white students and the subsequent expense to society of providing income assistance and health maintenance, the loss of tax revenues and productivity, and the social and economic costs of apprehending, incarcerating, and rehabilitating those who turn to crime and drugs make dropout prevention a high-priority item on the education reform agenda.

In its 1992 Education Survey *The Economist* observed, in a section entitled "The drop-out society?": "The most dramatic problem is the collapse of inner-city education. Ghetto schools are churning out children whose lack of mental skills and surfeit of emotional problems would render them unemployable in the third world, let alone the first."[178] Data reported in chapter 5 underscore the severe challenges confronting inner-city schools, especially compared with suburban systems. While a report by the Council of the Great City Schools, "National Urban Education Goals: Baseline Indicators, 1990–91," found a number of encouraging trends, such as rising reading and mathematics scores, declining dropout rates, and overall student achievement levels comparable with many suburban and rural schools, observers would agree that *The Economist*'s assessment is still applicable to public schools in most American central cities.[179]

According to the Southern Regional Education Board, states need to develop early warning systems to identify potential dropouts, work closely with local school districts on intervention strategies that will keep these students in school, and closely monitor the effects. Key indicators of dropout potential include:

- Retained in the same grade one or more years
- Chronic absenteeism
- Failing grades or low grade point average
- Difficulties with reading and school work in general
- Extenuating circumstances, such as pregnancy, drug or alcohol dependency
- School discipline problems
- From economically disadvantaged families
- Parent who failed to complete high school
- Older siblings who have dropped out
- From broken homes/single parent families[180]

Most states have established such programs, albeit many are of piecemeal, pilot, demonstration, or otherwise short-term nature. Some are more negative than incentive-based in nature. Examples of positive approaches include the following:[181]

- Identifying youngsters at an early age who have characteristics associated with dropouts and providing counseling, tutoring, and mentoring for remaining in school (Rochester's Home-Based Guidance program, for example, assigns 20 students to each mentor-teacher, who monitors their progress and works closely with their parents).
- Establishing choice options enabling potential dropouts to transfer to a school that offers

a curriculum that is more appealing to the students and more compatible with their abilities.

- Establishing alternative public schools, such as Detroit's school for inner-city boys, the nation's first, to try to overcome hard-core problems with specially trained teachers and curricula designed to restore dignity and offer hope.[182]

- Expanding remedial education programs intended to bring potential dropouts up to grade level and reduce frustrations accompanying failure to keep pace.

- Offering to provide state funding to cover the costs of a college education if the youth stays in school and attains good grades (Hawaii, Louisiana, and Rhode Island).

- Revising the curriculum to ensure that all students learn higher-order or critical thinking.

- Easing residency requirements, providing transportation, in-school social services and counseling, and tutoring for homeless children.

- Giving each high school graduate a written warranty assuring prospective employers that he or she has the basic skills needed to enter the work force and committing to offer remedial education if the employer is not satisfied (a program pioneered by the Los Angeles Unified School District, commencing with the class of 1994).[183]

- Setting up state interagency task forces, involving health, education, and social service agencies, to design and coordinate programs aimed at preventing dropouts and providing incentive funds to districts that develop innovative collaborative approaches.

- Establishing high schools modeled on Albuquerque's "Recovery High," dedicated to providing therapy to former substance abusers in addition to the regular curricula. Students volunteer to go to the school and may transfer credits and return to regular high school. In June, 20 students were admitted, with the program to grow to 150. It has been supported by the Robert Wood Johnson Foundation.[184]

- Establishing master's degree programs, such as pioneered by New Mexico's College of Santa Fe, to train future teachers as well as school nurses and social workers to deal with at-risk children and their families.[185]

In the view of many observers, penalty-oriented approaches are fortunately on the decline. The most commonly used sanction was to revoke the driver's license of dropouts, a step that may have had more negative than positive effects since it narrowed the job options of these former students and may even have kindled antisocial feelings and even further alienated the at-risk youngster. A related approach taken by Michigan in 1992 is to allow school districts to prohibit students with poor grades from taking driver education classes.

Homeless Children. A growing concern is the children of the homeless, many of whom live nomadic life-styles and are high dropout risks. The National Law Center on Homelessness and Poverty estimates there are 250,000 school-age homeless children in the country, and one in four are not attending school. Scorn from fellow students and disdain by some teachers are powerful disincentives to the homeless student. Homeless children also tend to score well below grade level on standardized tests and are more likely to have to repeat a grade. Moreover, until recently, when transportation, counseling services, and tutors were provided, the educational progress of homeless children and their special needs were not being addressed by inner-city and urban school systems.[186] In 1990, Congress appropriated $7.2 million for the education of homeless children. Examples of innovative school district responses include:[187]

- In Orange County, California, the Board of Education purchased two motor homes, equipped them as classrooms, and sent them to welfare hotels, fast-food restaurants, parking lots, and public parks in search of homeless children, who then receive instruction two or three times a week;
- Several Maryland counties send teachers to shelters for the homeless at night to help children with homework;
- The city of Baltimore uses taxis to transport homeless children to and from school;
- In New York City, some principals go to welfare hotels in the morning to get children up for school.

A 1990 report by the National Foundation for the Improvement of Education described the common elements of successful dropout prevention programs, based on the results of 47 programs funded by the foundation in 22 states, involving over 3,300 students and more than 500 teachers and counselors. The underlying themes of success were:

- Teachers have been encouraged and empowered to help students set goals and tackle problems;
- A learning environment exists that encourages students to develop positive self-images;
- High, yet realistic expectations for students have been established;
- The business and governmental communities, as well as principals, teachers, and school boards have been mobilized in support of at-risk children's programs.
- Early interventions to target children at risk have occurred and those identified have been linked with motivated teachers;
- Parents have been enlisted as genuine partners through nurturing home-school connections.[188]

According to *Fortune* magazine, "One reason for the nation's 29% high school dropout rate is that young people don't see a clear connection between what they're supposed to learn in class and what they'll need to succeed in a career. Why should a kid struggle through math if he doesn't have a clue as to how he'll use it?"[189] In addition to the above remedial actions, efforts to ensure smoother school-to-work transitions, such as apprenticeships, should prove welcome.

Reentry Programs

State and school system experience with drop-in programs is growing, but it is still insufficient as a basis for generalization as to which approaches offer the most promise. State-funded second-chance programs are on the rise, and many are targeted to young mothers and are coupled with school-to-work transition programs.

These programs seek to provide encouragement and support for completion of the high school degree. In several states, however, the General Educational Development (GED) certificate is offered as an alternative. As indicated in chapter 5, more than 400,000 students, many of whom are former dropouts, receive such a certificate each year, and some 10 percent of those who possess a high school degree as their terminal certificate received it through the GED. Recent research, however, has questioned the value of the certificate. A study by Professor James Heckman and Stephen Cameron concluded that the rise of popularity of the GED was due to its being a prerequisite for many federal programs, rather than its value in the marketplace. In fact, "wages paid GED holders are substantially lower than those paid to high school graduates," they found.[190] While these research results have been challenged, more than likely they will trigger concern about this alternative for encouraging dropout reentry.

Like dropout programs, drop-in programs have their "carrot and stick" components. In part due to the federal Family Support Act of 1988, states have greater discretionary authority to move welfare clients into training, employment, and education. In Ohio, for example, the Learning, Earning, and Parenting (LEAP) program penalizes teenage mothers $62, or 20 percent of their welfare check, if they fail to regularly attend school or a program leading to a GED certificate or high school diploma. On the other hand, a $62 bonus is given to those who miss fewer than four days a month. A May 1993 interim evaluation by the Manpower Demonstration Research Corporation found that LEAP had operated relatively well since 1989 and that it had succeeded in increasing school retention and inducing dropouts to return to school.[191] Other experiments are Minnesota's "Learnfare" program, which requires teenage mothers to attend school as a condition for receiving welfare checks, and Wisconsin's "Learn-fare," which penalizes parents on welfare if their children have three days of unexcused school absences.[192]

Service Coordination. Drop-in programs are especially dependent on inter-agency cooperation for their success. Without day care, transportation, and other support, young mothers would find it especially difficult to reenter school and ultimately the workplace.

As indicated earlier, using schools as "one-stop shops" for the provision of social services has shown promise as a means of helping prevent dropouts and facilitate drop-ins, by bringing the services to them. Three examples of the types of innovative "holistic" programs being utilized follow.[193]

In New Jersey, 30 high schools have established centers offering family and individual counseling, physical and mental health services, drug abuse counseling, employment assistance, and teen parenting. Centers also offer room for youth to talk, "decompress," and play games. In Plainfield High School, for instance, the program has worked in this way, as described by Roberta Knowlton, director of the New Jersey School-Based Services Program:

Not long ago, a student told a counselor that her girlfriend was planning to run away from home. The counselor then discovered that the girl had been raped by her sister's boyfriend and that she was afraid to tell her parents because her stepfather was sexually abusing her. The counselor convinced the parents to enter counseling and the stepfather to sign a contract promising to stop the abuse.

"Talk about prevention. If that young woman had run away, she would have been at risk for pregnancy, substance abuse and criminality," said Knowlton. The young woman graduated from high school and went to college.[194]

In Illinois, the Urban Education Partnership Grant Network enrolls about half of the school-age population in 43 schools, many located in poorer neighborhoods, with students coming from housing projects and female-headed families. Each school receives not more than $60,000 over a 2-year period to develop partnerships with businesses, universities, and public agencies to support creative ways to attract and retain the interest of at-risk children and youth.

In the St. Louis, Missouri, school district under a $569,000, 2-year grant from the state, the Caring Communities program arranges for the provision of social service needs to students referred by teachers because of academic or behavioral problems. Their services are provided by a variety of local agencies at school with follow-up at home.

In assessing the pros and cons of the wide variety of actions being taken by states and local districts in response to concerns about at-risk youth, it is very difficult to be critical of the intentions of those involved. Perhaps here more than in any other area of educational reform, there are no "one best ways." Not surprisingly, there has been considerable experimentation, and most of the programs are of too recent origin to have produced results that can be adequately evaluated. (Chapter 7 deals further with services integration at the school site.)

On the other hand, while these efforts are commendable, as the NGA has pointed out, it is unfortunate that most are being conducted at the demonstration or pilot level—in terms of both their funding support and duration. It is also unfortunate that so few states have mustered statewide efforts. Possibly this reluctance is due to the effects of the recession and politicians' frustration at the lack of "quick fixes" or "easy answers." In any event, in an area where comprehensive, coordinated approaches are needed on an interagency and intergovernmental basis to deal with problems that ignore the boundaries of the school system, there seems to be considerable fragmentation of effort.

SCHOOL SECURITY AND VIOLENCE

In chapter 5, data were presented showing the significant increases in school violence in recent years and the consequent concerns on the part of students, teachers, and parents about safety and security. It is estimated that the costs of school violence and vandalism amount to $200 million each year.[195]

A number of steps have been taken to help minimize violence including drug- and gun-free school zones, hall patrols, and metal detectors. In early 1993 the National Education Association called on the Clinton administration to enforce a federal law making carrying firearms onto school property a crime.[196]

As we conclude the chapter, it is appropriate to review one of the emerging controversial issues on the public education horizon relating to violence—the use of alternative schools. While weapon searches and security devices and personnel may or may not deter violent behavior, major student disciplinary problems will not be affected by these actions. Students who are habitually disruptive and disrespectful in the classroom can quickly upset the learning environment for all students. Restrictions on corporal punishment make it difficult for teachers and principals to respond effectively. Chronic truants are another case, who come to school, wander the halls, visit with friends, play sports, buy or sell drugs, or attack foes—but rarely attend class. Marginal dropouts are a third category, who, because teachers fear they will leave school, are often excused from homework, regular attendance, and orderly behavior.[197]

These three types of students intimidate teachers and fellow students. They are abundant in inner-city schools but are present to some extent in all systems. How to handle them effectively and equitably has been a perplexing problem.

One school of thought argues that these incorrigible students, after proper warning, be banned from the class they disrupted for an entire semester. A more extreme approach is to pull troublemakers from public school and send them to an alternative institution where, in a boot camp environment, they would be under strict discipline to shape up. Removing these chronic discipline problems, it is argued, is a less costly alternative than continuing to condone behavior that disrupts the learning process and threatens personal safety.

On the other hand, segregation of hard-core troublemakers raises due process concerns among civil libertarians. Moreover, the likelihood that many of those involved would be minority youth raises racial discrimination and justice concerns among others.

In 1993 the Virginia legislature passed and Governor L. Douglas Wilder signed a School Crime and Violence Prevention Act requiring parents, when they register their son or daughter for school, to disclose whether the student has been previously expelled. School boards may refuse to accept such students. Juvenile court judges must notify school superintendents of alcohol, drug, or weapons offense convictions and may deny a drivers license to guilty students. Under other related laws enacted during the 1993 session, discipline records must follow a student who transfers to another school, and 4 pilot programs were authorized for students who are expelled from school to be enrolled in separate alternative schools.[198]

Instead of isolating troublemakers in separate rooms or schools, some systems have relied on peer pressure and positive reinforcement to deal with disruptive students. For example:

- In Columbus, Ohio, a "Youth to Youth" program has made the Eastmoor Middle School drug-free and significantly reduced violence and vandalism. Modeled on a peer-pressure organization founded in the 1980s by Comp-Drug Corporation, the program features students meeting together daily to share concerns, feelings, and experiences about drug and alcohol abuse and to receive positive feedback from their peers.[199]
- In Anacostia High School, Washington, D.C., a Public Service Academy was established in 1990, one of 80 across the country financially supported by the National Academy Foundation. Students are encouraged to pursue public service careers by teachers and role models in the community instilling a sense of pride in their academic accomplishments, discipline in their conduct, and accountability for their actions. Students in the academy work closely with the same teachers for three years and develop a strong sense of comradery and positive outlook, which reduces behavioral problems often resulting from student's feelings of frustration and hopelessness about their future. (Academies are covered in chapter 7.)[200]

Clearly, something must be done to restore order to many public schools if education reform is to have a chance to succeed. It is likely that the alternative school approach will receive considerable discussion and debate in the years ahead.

IMPROVING EDUCATION DATA, OUTCOMES RESEARCH, AND PROGRAM EVALUATION

As rising costs of public education, coupled with the continued poor or mediocre performance of many public school students, lead to demands for more outcomes-oriented approaches, there will also be a need for clearer definitions of terms like *at-risk* and *dropout*, crisper statements of educational mission, measurable goals and objectives, and better data on which to make decisions. These needs will be especially apparent for public school systems, where, unlike their private counterparts, there is no marketplace mechanism despite the growing number of choice arrangements across the country.

As Chester E. Finn has contended, despite the fact that "American education is drowning in certain kinds of data about itself," the system operates in an information vacuum:[201]

- Outcomes are measured in terms of time and money spent, courses offered, degrees conferred, and students taught; little is known about learning outcomes on an interstate, intrastate, and international comparative basis.
- Parents cannot compare their child's school with others in the district or state or with national goals.

- Only a relatively few schools give their "building report cards" to parents and the press.

- State test results are not meaningful as measures of a graduate's skills in the workplace; sufficient data on student knowledge levels in various subjects are not available on a state or local basis.

- While there is an abundance of national and state education goals, most oriented to the year 2000, specific indicators that could be used to measure the extent of their attainment are too often lacking.

The National Center for Education Statistics Special Study Panel on Education Indicators cited the following examples of problems with data on dropouts as illustrative of fundamental weaknesses in the design, reporting, and analysis of educational indicators being used by the states:

According to some national statistics, Georgia's school drop out rate is 37–39%. A recent study completed by researchers at the University of Georgia concludes that it is closer to 18%. How reliable is either statistic? Which is correct?

The answer is probably both but they cannot be compared. Most dropout numbers are accurate within the context of the definition and time frame used and how data are collected and computed. These vary greatly from state to state, district to district, and organization to organization. Three researchers used 25 different computations taken from cities, districts and states around the country to calculate the Austin, Texas school district's dropout rate. The study yielded 15 different statistics ranging from 10.1 percent to 57 percent.[202]

The problems of inaccurate and misleading information are compounded by the manipulation of data for political and financial purposes. For example, according to Aaron Pallas of Michigan State University, counting dropouts "is a social and political process." In some of the nation's large cities "there are phantom kids carried on the books long after they have dropped out because schools want to maintain their numbers; they don't want to be called into question."[203]

A number of remedial actions have been taken by governmental agencies, not-for-profit organizations, associations of educators and other public officials, and the private sector. They include:[204]

- The National Center for Education Statistics is conducting a Dropout Statistics Field Test to use a common set of definitions as a basis for collecting comparable data on dropouts. Twenty-seven states are participating.

- The National Assessment of Educational Progress is carrying out a Trial State Assessment of 8th-grade mathematics, in which 37 states are involved.

- The Council of Chief State School Officers has launched a Science and Math Indicators Project and an Education Data Improvement Project to develop common information bases and reporting formats.

- The National Center for Education Statistics has been working to provide comparable and timely data on public school enrollments, staffing, funding, and other areas. In July 1991 its Special Study Panel on Education Indicators released a report that defined recommended indicators of the "health" of education, identified research and data collection needs and how they could be addressed, and proposed an indicator development plan.[205] The panel believed that information needs were especially critical with respect to learning outcomes, quality of institutions, three-year-old profiles, first grade assessment, and young adult assessment.[206]

- The National Educational Statistics Agenda Committee of the National Forum on Educational Statistics has recommended steps for improving data on educational resources, staffing, and student performance and progression.

- Both NGA and the National Conference of State Legislatures (NCSL) have urged the nation's governors and legislators to work with state education agencies and local districts to develop indicators of performance quality and effectiveness. NCSL, for instance, has called upon the states to establish a three-part accountability system consisting of "clear and measurable goals that describe intended outcomes; assessment tools that measure progress toward the goals, [and] incentives that reward goal-achievement and ensure adjustments in case of failure."[207] While no state had taken such a comprehensive approach as of 1993, Vermont, California, South Carolina, and Kentucky among others were moving in that direction.

- In 1992 the U.S. Office of Technology Assessment published a report, *Testing in American Schools: Asking the Right Questions*, which described new and innovative approaches to testing as a means for policymakers and administrators accurately to monitor and evaluate the effects of education improvement programs.[208]

- Since 1988 the Organization for Economic Cooperation and Development's Center for Educational Research and Innovation has supported research on comparable international education system indicators.[209]

A serious effort to fill the above and other aspects of the information vacuum must be made in the years ahead if education goals are to be taken seriously, if progress is to be charted, and ultimately if taxpayer confidence in public schools is to be restored.

SUMMARY

The preceding review of major education reform issues has in several places raised more questions than it has provided answers about "what works." In part, this is due to the relative recency of many of the approaches reported on and the considerable extent to which they are of a demonstration or pilot nature.

Clearly, a substantial amount of experimentation and innovation is under way in search of ways to prepare students for successful careers and lives.[210] Relevant foreign experiences are being closely examined as to their applicability to the American education system and workplace. Exciting partnerships have been developed among educators, parents, government officials, and the business community. The next chapter explores the nature and impact of these intergovernmental, interagency, and public-private partnerships.

NOTES

1. Doyle, D. P., and Hartle, T. W., *Excellence in Education: The States Take Charge* (Washington, DC: American Enterprise Institute for Public Policy Research, 1985), 1.

2. Lays, J., "Educating Eddie," *State Legislatures*, April 1991, 20–21.

3. Chubb, J. E., and Moe, T. M., *Politics, Markets, and America's Schools* (Washington, DC: Brookings Institution, 1990), 1.

4. Doyle, D. P., Cooper, B. S., and Trachtman, R., "Education Ideas & Strategies for the 1990s," *American Enterprise*, March/April 1991, 26.

5. Ibid.

6. Lays, 20.

7. Doyle, Cooper, and Trachtman, 26.

8. Education Commission of the States (ECS), "Keeping the Promises of Reform: A State Strategy" (Denver: ECS, 1991). See also ECS, *School Reform in 10 States* (Denver: ECS, December 1988).

9. See U.S. Advisory Commission in Intergovernmental Relations, *Federal Regulation of State and Local Governments: The Mixed Record of the 1980s* (Washington, D.C.: U.S. Government Printing Office, July 1993).

10. Doyle, Cooper, and Trachtman, 26.

11. Elam, S. M., Rose, L. C., and Gallup, A. M., "The 23rd Annual Gallup Poll of the Public's Attitudes Toward the Public Schools," *Phi Delta Kappan*, September 1991, 52.

12. *State Legislatures*, April 1992, 10; "New Texas School Plan Faces Challenge," *Washington Post*, June 2, 1993; Jones, T., "Public Schools All Over Strive to Stay Afloat," *Chicago Tribune*, June 6, 1993, 1, 5; "Court Ruling Leaves Texas School Finance Dispute Far from Resolved, *Washington Post*, December 11, 1993, A6.

13. Herbers, J., "The Real Obstacle to Education Reform," *Governing*, June 1991, 74.

14. Education Commission of the States (ECS), "Status of Reform 1991: A Report to the Business-Education Policy Forum" (Denver: ECS, 1991), 2–3.

15. Ibid., 6.

16. Walsh, E., "Michigan Voters to Weigh Sharp Rise in Sales Tax," *Washington Post*, May 31, 1993, A13; Walsh, E., "After Killing Property Taxes for Schools, Michigan Deadlocks on Funding." *Washington Post*, December 18, 1993. A6.

17. Chubb, J. E., and Hanushek, E. A., "Reforming Educational Reform," in Aaron, H. J. (ed.), *Setting National Priorities: Policy for the Nineties* (Washington, DC: Brookings Institution, 1990), 213. See also National Academy of Public Administration, *The Public Management Challenge in K to 12 Education: New Partnerships and New Approaches* (Washington, DC: National Academy of Public Administration, May 1991).

18. Education Commission of the States, "Status of Reform 1991," 1.

19. Ibid. See also the following ECS reports: *Introduction to Systemic Education Reform: Restructuring the Education System* (1992); *Exploring Policy Options to Restructure Education* (1991).

20. Sylvester, K., "Business and the Schools: The Failure and Promise," *Governing*, September 1992, 25.

21. Graham, E., "Digging for Knowledge," *Wall Street Journal*, September 11, 1992, 81.

22. Elmore, R. F., "Introduction: On Changing the Structure of Public Schools,"

in Elmore, R. F. and associates, *Restructuring Schools: The Next Generation of Educational Reform* (San Francisco: Jossey-Bass, 1990), 1–3.

23. Ibid., 5–10.

24. Rebarber, T., *State Policies for School Restructuring* (Denver: National Conference of State Legislatures, April 1992), 3.

25. Elmore, 4.

26. Mydans, S., "In an Assault on Tradition, More Schools Last All Year," *New York Times*, August 18, 1991, A–1, 22.

27. Ibid., A22.

28. Ibid.

29. Ibid., A–1.

30. King, W., "Longer Year Is Advocated for Schools," *New York Times*, January 6, 1992, B–1, 5; Tousignant, M., "Virginia Education Secretary Pushes 20-Day Extension of School Year," *Washington Post*, June 27, 1992, B3.

31. Reid, T. R., "Japan Plans a Day Off," *Washington Post*, September 12, 1992, A1–A12. See also Feiler, B. S., "Why Japan's Schools Succeed," *Washington Post*, February 17, 1993, A19; Brown, D. L., "Students Say Yes to Stress," *Washington Post*, April 13, 1993, A1, A12.

32. Elam, S. M., Rose L. C., and Gallup, A. M., "The 24th Annual Gallup Phi Delta Kappa Poll of the Public's Attitudes Toward the Public Schools," *Phi Delta Kappan*, September 1992, 49

33. Mydans, 22.

34. Cooper, K. J., "Majority in Poll Favor Extending School Year," *Washington Post*, August 23, 1991, A3.

35. Walters, L. S., "Longer Classes, But Fewer of Them," *Christian Science Monitor*, October 24, 1990, 12–13.

36. "Test of Longer Classes Wins Praise and Criticism," *New York Times*, March 27, 1991, A–2.

37. Buckley, S., "Montgomery Teachers See 15 Minutes as Too Much," *Washington Post*, March 13, 1993, B1.

38. Lear, J. G., and Porter, P. J., "Help Our Children: Bring Health Care into the Schools," *Washington Post*, December 1, 1991, C5–6.

39. Sachar, S. F., *From Homes to Classrooms to Workrooms: State Initiatives to Meet the Needs of the Changing American Family* (Washington, DC: National Governors' Association, 1992), 29.

40. Albert, K. M., "School-Based Adolescent Health Programs: The Oregon Approach," Council of State Governments, *Innovations*, October 1989.

41. Lear and Porter, C5–6.

42. Ibid. For examples of school-based services programs, see Sachar, 30–36.

43. Elam, Rose, and Gallup, "The 24th Annual Gallup Phi Delta Kappa Poll of the Public's Attitudes Toward the Public Schools," 51.

44. Chubb and Moe, 12–13.

45. Ibid., 12.

46. Twentieth Century Fund, *Facing the Challenge* (New York: Twentieth Century Fund, 1992), 5. See also Raywid, M. A., "Rethinking School Governance," in Elmore, 152–205; and the report by a joint study group of federal education officials and state school boards association representatives: U.S. Department of Education, *National Education Goals: America's School Boards Respond* (Washington, DC: U.S. Government Printing Office, April 1992).

47. Twentieth Century Fund, 9–10.

48. Walter, J., "The Most Radical Idea in Education: Let the Schools Run It," *Governing*, January 1991, 42.

49. Chubb and Moe, 200.

50. Ibid., 199.

51. Walser, N., "Plan to Overhaul a School System," *New York Times*, A20.

52. "American Survey: Unaccountable, Ineducable, Unmanageable, Unreformable," *The Economist*, March 16, 1991, 19.

53. Walters, 44. See also Chi, K., "From Reform to Dropout Cures," *State Government News*, September 1991, 30.

54. Walters, 45. For a report on implementation progress of the Education Reform Act, see National Governors' Association (NGA), *Redesigning an Education System: Early Observations from Kentucky* (Washington, DC: NGA, 1993).

55. Ibid., 44.

56. Ibid., 45.

57. Reed, J. "Grass Roots School Governance in Chicago," *National Civic Review*, Winter 1991, 42–43.

58. Walters, 42–43.

59. Reed, 44.

60. Peirce, N. R., "Crib Death for School Reform?" *State Government News*, February 1991, 9.

61. Hill, P. T., and Bonan, J., *Decentralization and Accountability in Public Education* (Santa Monica: RAND Institute for Education and Training, 1991), v–vi.

62. "When Schools Chart Their Own Course," *RAND Research Review*, Fall 1991, 7–9.

63. Rebarber, 6–7.

64. Hill and Bonan, vii.

65. "When Schools Take Charge," *Washington Post*, June 21, 1991, A16.

66. Chubb and Moe, 201.

67. Hill and Bonan, 69.

68. Chubb and Hanushek, 230.

69. For a comparison of school-based management and choice concepts see Raywid, 156–59. See also Education Commission of the States (ECS), *A State Policy-Maker's Guide to Public-School Choice* (Denver: ECS, 1989); "Free Market Education: The Choice for the 21st Century?" *Business Week*, December 7, 1992, 4–32. For examples of successful market-oriented reforms, see Osborne, D., and Gaebler, T., *Reinventing Government: How the Entrepreneurial Spirit Is Transforming the Public Sector* (Reading, MA: Addison-Wesley, 1992), 5–8, 54–56, 93–104, 155–56. See also "A Primer on Choice in Education: Part 1, How Choice Works," the Heritage Foundation *Backgrounder*, March 21, 1990; "Choice In Education: Part II, Legal Perils and Legal Opportunities," the Heritage Foundation *Backgrounder*, February 18, 1991.

70. Chubb, J. E., and Moe, T. M., *A Lesson in School Reform from Great Britain* (Washington, DC: Brookings Institution, 1992), 9–11.

71. Gurwith, R., "Getting off the Bus," *Governing*, May 1992, 30–36.

72. Chubb and Hanushek, 235.

73. Rossell, C. H., *The Carrot or the Stick for School Desegregation Policy: Magnet Schools or Forced Busing* (Philadelphia: Temple University Press, 1990), 210–11.

74. See "Schools That Work," *U.S. News and World Report*, May 27, 1991, 59–66.

75. Wells, A. S., "Once a Desegregation Tool, Magnet School Becoming School of Choice," *New York Times*, January 9, 1991, B6.

76. Marcus, E., "Area's Magnets Showing Their Merits," *Washington Post*, September 11, 1991, A1, A8.

77. Wells.

78. Chubb and Moe, 209.

79. Durenberger, D., "Minnesota's Choice," *Washington Post*, September 9, 1991, A19; Pipho, C., "School Reform: The Beat Goes On," *State Government News*, September 1991, 20–21. For a thorough review of choice options, issues, and policy considerations see Virginia Department of Education, *School Choice in Virginia and the Nation* (Richmond: Virginia Department of Education, October 24, 1991). For a detailed account of the background and implementation of the charter schools, see Kolderie, T., "The Charter Schools Idea," a paper prepared by the Public Services Redesign Project, Center for Policy Studies, St. Paul, MN, n.d.

80. Olson, L., "California Is Second State to Allow Charter Schools," *Education Week*, September 30, 1992, 1, 23.

81. Kolderie, T., Lerman, R., and Moskos, C., "Educating America: A New Compact for Opportunity and Citizenship," in Marshall, W., and Schram, M., *Mandate for Change* (New York: Berkley Books, 1992), 134.

82. See Rebarber, 7–9.

83. Chubb and Moe, 210–11.

84. Ibid., 212–13.

85. Shapiro, W., "Tough Choice," *Time*, September 16, 1991, 58; Rebarber, 7.

86. Sylvester, K., "School Choice and Reality," *Governing*, June 1993, 40–41.

87. Farney, D., "Can Big Money Fix Urban School Systems? A Test Is Under Way," *Wall Street Journal*, January 7, 1992, A1, A4.

88. Ibid., A4.

89. See Chira, S., "Research Questions Effectiveness of Most School-Choice Programs, *New York Times*, October 26, 1992, A–1; MacGuire, I., "The Carnegie Assault on School Choice," *Wall Street Journal*, November 25, 1992, A12.

90. Shapiro, 57.

91. For a comparison of public with private systems, see Chubb and Moe, 69–184; "The Private vs. Public School Debate," *Wall Street Journal*, July 26, 1991, A8.

92. Miller, K., "Church-Backed Schools Inspire Detroiters," *Wall Street Journal*, August 29, 1991, B1.

93. "Schools as Symbols: Where Policymakers Send Their Children," *Washington Post*, May 5, 1992, A23.

94. Lachman, S. P., and Kosmin, B. A., "Black Catholics Get Ahead," *New York Times*, September 14, 1991, A–19.

95. Chubb and Hanushek, 240.

96. Shapiro, 54, 57–58. See also Toulmin, C., and Bukolt, M., *School Choice* (Madison: Wisconsin Legislative Fiscal Bureau, Information Paper #31, January 1993).

97. *Wall Street Journal*, December 2, 1991.

98. Shapiro, 58; Sylvester, 37. See also Odden, A., "Financing Public Schools," in Kirlin, J. J., and Winkler, D. R. (eds.), *California Policy Choices* (Los Angeles: University of Southern California, 1991), 93–124.

99. "Parents Support Choice for Schools, Poll Finds," *New York Times*, August 23, 1991, D–18.

100. Shapiro, 55. See also Rapp, D., "The Intensely Local Question of School Choice," *Governing*, July 1991, 63.

101. Shapiro, 56.

102. Durenberger, D., "Minnesota's Choice," *Washington Post*, September 10, 1991, A19.

103. Kolderie, T., "The States Must Withdraw the Exclusive Franchise," *National Civic Review*, Winter 1991, 52.

104. Sylvester, 39–40; Nathan, J., "School Choice Works in Minnesota," *Wall Street Journal*, April 22, 1993, A14. Chira, S., "Schools Vie in a Marketplace: More 'Choice' Can Mean Less," *New York Times*, January 7, 1992, A–1, A–10.

105. Chubb and Moe, *A Lesson in School Reform*, 20–41.

106. Hill and Bonar, 71.

107. Finn, C. E., Jr., "The Radicalization of School Reform," *Wall Street Journal*, February 2, 1990, A14.

108. Ibid.

109. Ibid.

110. Celis, W., "In Test of Kentucky Education Law, State Takes Over Harlan District," *New York Times*, February 5, 1992, B–7.

111. Olson, L., "Do School Boards Make Bad Bosses?" *Governing*, March 1991, 25. See also Wilson, B. L., "Polls Close for the Superintendent," *Governing*, October 1992, 30; Jordan, M., "Big City School Chiefs Learn Reform Is Not 1 of the 3 Rs," *Washington Post*, February 13, 1993, A1, A7.

112. Committee for Economic Development, *Investing in Our Children*, 20.

113. Ibid., 21.

114. David, J. L., Cohen, M., Honetachlager, D., and Traiman, S., *State Actions to Restructure Schools: First Steps* (Washington, DC: National Governors' Association, 1990), 1–2. See also Cohen, M., *Restructuring the Education System: Agenda for the 1990s* (Washington, DC: National Governors' Association, 1988); Elmore, R. F., *Early Experience in Restructuring Schools: Voices from the Field* (Washington, DC: National Governors' Association, 1988).

115. Toch, T., "Diplomas and Dunces," *Washington Post*, August 18, 1991, C1.

116. Ibid.

117. Putka, G., "Readers of Latest U.S. History Textbooks Discover a Storehouse of Misinformation," *Wall Street Journal*, February 12, 1992, B13.

118. The Secretary's Commission on Achieving Necessary Skills, *Learning a Living: A Blueprint for High Performance* (Washington, DC: U.S. Department of Labor, April 1992), 90. For a critique of the SCANS effort, see Samuelson, R. J., "Gibberish on Job Skills," *Washington Post*, July 11, 1991, A15; Brock, W., Marshall, R., and Tucker, M., "What America Needs: A License to Skill," *Washington Post*, July 4, 1993, C5.

119. Alexander, S., "Trailing in Education for Years, Kentucky Tries Radical Reforms," *Wall Street Journal*, January 5, 1993, A1, A6.

120. Teltsch, K., "To Teach Distant Pupils, Educators in Kentucky Turn on Interactive T.V.," *New York Times*, October 30, 1991, B7.

121. National Foundation for the Improvement of Education, *Images in Action* (Washington, DC: National Foundation for the Improvement of Education, n.d.). See also Johnson, S. M., *Teachers at Work: Achieving Success in Our Schools* (New York: Basic

Books, 1990); Pauly E., *The Classroom Crucible: What Really Works, What Doesn't, and Why* (New York: Basic Books, 1991).

122. See "Finally, an A+ for Computers in Class?" *Business Week*, November 11, 1991, 158–62.

123. Elliott, S., "Channel One May Provide Program for Grade Schools," *New York Times*, November 20, 1991, D22, and *State Legislatures*, February 1993, 13.

124. William T. Grant Foundation Commission on Work, Family and Citizenship, *The Forgotten Half: Pathways to Success for America's Youth and Young Families* (Washington, DC: The Foundation, November 1988).

125. U.S. General Accounting Office, *Training Strategies: Preparing Noncollege Youth for Employment in the U.S. and Foreign Countries* (Washington, DC: U.S. Government Printing Office), 3. See also Nilsen, S. R., and Sehgal, E. B., "From School to Work," *GAO Journal*, Fall/Winter 1992, 27–32.

126. U.S. General Accounting Office, *Education Issues* (Washington, DC: U.S. Government Printing Office, December 1992), 18–19.

127. Committee for Economic Development, *An America That Works*, 71.

128. Ibid.

129. *NEA Today*, December 1992, 4–5.

130. National Center on Education and the Economy, *America's Choice: High Skills or Low Wages!* (Rochester, NY: The Center, June 1990), 1–9; Educational Testing Service (ETS), *From School to Work* (Princeton, NJ: ETS, 1990), 27.

131. U.S. General Accounting Office, *Transition from School to Work: Linking Education and Worksite Training* (Washington, DC: U.S. Government Printing Office, August 1991), 27–39. See also U.S. General Accounting Office, *Transition From School to Work: States Are Developing New Strategies to Prepare Students for Jobs* (Washington, DC: U.S. Government Printing Office, September 1993).

132. Ibid., 41.

133. U.S. General Accounting Office, *Apprenticeship Training: Administration, Use, and Equal Opportunity* (Washington, DC: U.S. Government Printing Office, March 1992), 2–5. See also De Parle, J., "Teaching High School Students How to Work," *New York Times*, November 26, 1992, A1, D15; Hamilton, S. F., *Apprenticeship for Adulthood* (New York: Free Press, 1990).

134. U.S. General Accounting Office, *Apprenticeship Training*, 2, 5. See also Nothdurft, W. E., *School Works: Reinventing Public Schools to Create the Workforce of the Future* (Washington, DC: Brookings Institution, 1989).

135. Marshall and Schram, 140.

136. Liddell, S. A., "Putting the Future on the High (Skills) Road," *State Legislatures*, May 1993, 20.

137. Shreve, D., and Liddell, S., "Reading, Writing, and Job Training," *State Legislatures*, November 1991, 31.

138. Ibid., 30–33. See also Celis, W., "Oregon to Stress Job Training in Restructuring High School," *New York Times*, July 24, 1991, A1, A18; Pipho, C., "School Reform: The Beat Goes On," *State Government News*, September 1991, 18–19; Olson, L., "Oregon's Choice: World-Class Education," *State Government News*, October 1992, 18–21.

139. Liddell, 20.

140. Ibid. See also DePerle, J., "Teaching High School Students How to Work," *New York Times*, November 26, 1992, A1, D15.

141. *Business Week*, February 22, 1993, 77.

142. Boyer, E. L., *Report Card on School Reform: The Teachers Speak* (Princeton,

NJ: The Carnegie Foundation for the Advancement of Teaching, 1988), 3; Zinser, J., "Mandating Community Service: Service or Servitude?" *State Legislatures*, March 1993, 31, 33; Alexander, S., "Middle Schools Add Community Service to Curriculum to Teach Responsibility," *Wall Street Journal*, April 21, 1992, B1–2; Leff, L., "Service Requirement for Students Attached," *Washington Post*, January 28, 1993, B3.

143. *State Legislatures*, June 1993, 9.

144. Derby, S., "What Students Want," *Vocational Education Journal*, October 1991, 24.

145. Clinton, B., "Apprenticeship American Style," *Vocational Education Journal*, October 1991, 23.

146. McCarthy, C., "Clinton's Call to Service," *Washington Post*, March 13, 1993, A21; Chira, S., "National Service: Ideal vs. Reality," *New York Times*, March 3, 1993, B13; Jaschik, S., "Clinton's National-Service Plan Disappoints Students and Colleges," *Chronicle of Higher Education*, May 12, 1993, A27, A32–33.

147. Marshall and Schram, 148–49.

148. National Governors' Association, *Results in Education: 1990*, 11.

149. De Palma, A., "Principals of Success," *New York Times*, November 3, 1991, A4, 21. See also McNeil, L. M., "Contradictions of Control, Part 1: Administrators and Teachers," *Phi Delta Kappan*, January 1988, 333–485.

150. De Palma, 12.

151. *Fortune*, March 8, 1993, 10–11.

152. Hicks, J., "Women in Waiting," *New York Times*, November 3, 1991, A4, 19.

153. Johnson, S. M., "Redesigning Teachers' Work," in Elmore, R. F., and associates, *Restructuring Schools*, 129–33.

154. Ibid., 131.

155. Hoebel, A., "Merit Pay: The Boom That Went Bust," *Washington Post*, March 29, 1992, C8.

156. For a review of the pros and cons of merit pay, see Chubb and Hanushek, 225–27; Chubb and Moe, 196–97. For arguments supporting school competition and "merit schools," see Osborne and Gaebler, 156–59.

157. Hoebel.

158. Chubb and Hanushek, 226.

159. "Should We Get Rid of Teacher Tenure?" *State Government News*, June 1992, 12–13.

160. Putka, G., "Teacher Quality Rise with Improved Pay, Concern for Schools," *Wall Street Journal*, December 5, 1991, A1, A8.

161. See also the following reports by the Holmes Group, *Tomorrow's Teachers* (East Lansing, MI: The Holmes Group, 1986); *Tomorrow's Schools: Principles for the Design of Professional Development Schools* (East Lansing, MI: The Holmes Group, 1990).

162. Goodlad, J. I., *Teachers for Our Nation's Schools* (San Francisco: Jossey-Bass, 1990).

163. Knapp, J. L., McNergney, R. F., Herbert, J. M., and York, H. L., "Should Master's Degree Be Required of All Teachers?" *Journal of Teacher Education*, March–April 1990, 27–37.

164. For an examination of the likely consequences of the National Education Goals, a national system of teacher examinations and certification process, and a national core curriculum, see Mary Alice Franklin Hatwood Futrell, Analysis of National Leaders' Perception of Major Education Reform Policies Centralizing Effects on Public Education

(Ph.D. dissertation submitted to George Washington University, September 30, 1992). See also Finn, C. E., "Fear of Standards Threatens Education Reform," *Wall Street Journal*, March 23, 1992, A10; American Association of School Administrators, *America 2000: Where School Leaders Stand* (Arlington, VA: American Association of School Administrators, 1991).

165. Shanker, A., "The First Step Toward Reform," *GAO Journal*, Fall/Winter 1992, 37.

166. Johnson, 343. For examples of MIL Projects, see Watts, G. D., and McClure, R. M., "Expanding the Contract to Revolutionize School Renewal," *Phi Delta Kappan*, June 1990, 765–74.

167. National Governors' Association, *Results in Education: 1990*, 28.

168. Boyer, E. L., *Ready to Learn: A Mandate for the Nation* (Princeton, NJ: Carnegie Foundation for the Advancement of Teaching, 1991); Chira, S., "Report Says Too Many Aren't Ready for School," *New York Times*, December 8, 1991, A1, 34.

169. National Governors' Association (NGA), *Every Child Ready for School* (Washington, DC: NGA, 1992). See also Southern Regional Education Board, *Readiness for School: The Early Childhood Challenge* (Atlanta: Southern Regional Education Board, 1992). For a digest of publications and policy positions of organizations concerned with child care issues, see Child Care Action Campaign, *Where They Stand: Policies on Child Care and Education* (Washington, DC: Child Care Action Campaign, March 1993).

170. Bottoms, G., and Presson, A., *Reaching the Goal to Reduce the Dropout Rate* (Atlanta: Southern Regional Education Board, 1991), 3.

171. Presidents' Commission on School Finance, *Schools, People, and Money—The Need for Educational Reform*, xv.

172. Nation Governors' Association, *Results in Education: 1990*, 28. See also Council of Chief State School Officers, *Family Support: Education and Involvement, A Guide for State Action* (Washington, DC: Council of Chief State School Officers, 1989).

173. Colman, W. G., *Cities, Suburbs, and States: Governing and Financing Urban America* (New York: Free Press, 1975), 171.

174. National Governors' Association, *Results in Education: 1990*, 28. See also Brody, J. E., "Better Discipline? Train Parents, Then Children," *New York Times*, December 3, 1991, C1, C13; Tousignant, M., "A Chance at Starting Even: Family Literacy Program Blossoms in Va.," *Washington Post*, January 22, 1992, A1, A16; Ensign, D., "Missouri's Parents as Teachers," Council of State Governments, *Innovations*, July 1989; Knapp, E. S., "A Family Affair," *State Government News*, August 1992, 16–19, 26; Osborne and Gaebler, 55–56; Jordan, F., *Innovating America* (New York: Ford Foundation, July 1990), 16–27.

175. Marriott, M., "When Parents and Children Go to School Together," *New York Times*, August 21, 1991, B7. See Devlin, K. M., "Kentucky's Parent and Child Education Program," Council of State Governments, *Innovations*, June 1991.

176. U.S. General Accounting Office, *Home Visiting: A Promising Strategy for At-Risk Families* (Washington, DC: U.S. Government Printing Office, July 1990), 14, 59.

177. National Governors' Association, *Every Child Ready for School*.

178. *The Economist*, November 21–27, 1992, 8.

179. Smith, F., and Casserly, M., "City School Myths," *Washington Post*, November 24, 1992, A21. See also the following reports by the Council of Great City Schools: *Strategies for Success: Achieving the National Urban Education Goals* (Washington, DC:

Council of Great City Schools, 1990); *Results 2000: Progress in Meeting Urban Education Goals* (Washington, DC: Council of Great City Schools, 1990).

180. Bottoms and Presson, 13. See also Southern Regional Education Board, *Readiness for School: The Early Childhood Challenge* (Atlanta: Southern Regional Education Board, 1992).

181. See National Governors' Association, *Results in Education: 1990*, 28–31; Osborne and Gaebler, 149, 171.

182. Wilkerson, I., "To Save Its Men, Detroit Plans Boys-Only Schools," *New York Times*, August 14, 1991, A17.

183. "Productivity Assured—or We'll Fix Them Free," *Business Week*, November 25, 1991, 34.

184. *Governing*, May 1992, 20.

185. *Governing*, July 1992, 21.

186. Richardson, L., "New York Schools Following Behind Homeless," *New York Times*, January 2, 1992, B1–2.

187. Pear, R., "Homeless Children Challenge Schools," *New York Times*, September 9, 1991, A10.

188. National Foundation for the Improvement of Education, *A Blueprint for Success—Lessons Learned: NFIE's Dropout Prevention Initiative* (Washington, DC: The Foundation, 1990).

189. Deutachman, A., "Why Kids Should Learn About Work," *Fortune*, August 10, 1992, 86.

190. Mathews, J., "Study: GED's Fall Short of Diplomas for Jobs," *Washington Post*, January 12, 1992, A10. See also Peterson, I., "As More Earn Equivalency Diploma, Its Value is Debated," *New York Times*, October 21, 1992, B10.

191. Bloom, D., Fellerath, V., Long, D., and Wood, R. G., *LEAP Interim Findings on a Welfare Initiative to Improve School Attendance Among Teenage Parents* (New York: Manpower Demonstration Research Corporation, May 1993).

192. "The ABCs of Coaxing Teen Mothers Back to School," *Business Week*, October 21, 1991, 96; Osborne and Gaebler, 150.

193. Collis, Cheri, "Strengthening Family Ties," *State Government News*, September 1991, 24–26.

194. Ibid., 25.

195. DeWitt, K., "Teachers Ask Government to Battle School Violence," *New York Times*, January 15, 1993, A10. See also Bennett, W. J., "The Moral Origins of the Urban Crisis," *Hudson Opinion*, June 1992.

196. De Witt.

197. Toby, J., "To Get Rid of Guns in Schools, Get Rid of Some Students," *Wall Street Journal*, March 3, 1992, A14.

198. Harris, J. F., "State Gives Schools Access to Records of Juvenile Crimes, *Washington Post*, April 8, 1993, 3.

199. Stout, H., "Determined Principal and Faculty Use Discipline and Peer Pressure to Make a School 'Drug Free,' *Wall Street Journal*, October 1, 1991, A22.

200. Welsh, P., "Raising Grades, Not Hell," *Washington Post*, December 29, 1991, C1, C4.

201. Finn, C. E., Jr., "The Case for National Testing," *GAO Journal*, Summer/Fall

1991, 30–42. See also Murnane, R. J., and Levy, F., "Education and Training," in Aaron, H. J., and Schultze, C. L. (eds.), *Setting Domestic Priorities: What Can Government Do?* (Washington, DC: Brookings Institution, 1992), 201–7.

202. Georgia Alliance for Public Education, "Critical Issues in Education," cited in National Center for Education Statistics, *Education Counts* (Washington, DC: U.S. Government Printing Office, September 1991), 15.

203. Sylvester, K., "The Many-Sided Dropout Problem," *Governing*, March 1992, 27.

204. See Creech, J. D., *Educational Benchmarks 1990* (Atlanta: Southern Regional Education Board, 1990), 3; *Educational Benchmarks 1992* (Atlanta: Southern Regional Education Board, 1992).

205. National Center for Education Statistics, *Education Counts*.

206. Ibid., 49.

207. Rebarber, T., *Accountability in Education* (Denver: National Conference of State Legislatures, July 1991), ix.

208. U.S. Congress, Office of Technology Assessment, *Testing in American Schools: Asking the Right Questions* (Washington, DC: U.S. Government Printing Office, 1992). See also Fuhrman, S. H., and Malen, B. (eds.), *The Politics of Curriculum and Testing* (Philadelphia: Falmer Press, 1991).

209. Organization for Economic Cooperation and Development (OECD), Center for Educational Research and Innovation, *The OECD International Education Indicators: A Framework for Analysis* (Paris: OECD, 1992).

210. For an example of fresh thinking, involving a proposed national system of experimental schools, see Allen, D. W., *Schools for a New Century: A Conservative Approach to Radical School Reform* (New York: Praeger, 1992).

Chapter 7 _____

Public and Private Sector Roles in Preparing America's Future Work Force

The previous chapters of this book have examined the changing demographics of the nation's work force, described the health care and education deterrents to meeting future employability needs, and analyzed issues and options associated with removal or remediation of these deterrents. The purpose of this chapter is to identify the roles of, and relationships between, the public and private sectors in the preparation of America's future work force.

The first section reviews the historical and current patterns of governmental responsibility and discusses proposals for "sorting out" financial, administrative, regulatory, and other aspects of service delivery within the public sector. This examination builds on material presented in chapter 1. The second section discusses intergovernmental and interagency efforts to coordinate and integrate the delivery of services. The third section considers community and business responses to the challenges of work force preparation through educational and health care reform, including "contracting out" and privatization options as well as "partnership" arrangements between the public and private sectors.

DOMESTIC ROLES IN TRANSITION

In *Federalist* No. 45 James Madison argued:

The State governments will have the advantage of the Federal Government, whether we compare them in respect to the immediate dependence of the one on the other; to the weight of personal influence which each side will possess; to the powers respectively vested in them; to the predilection and probable support of the people; to the disposition and faculty of resisting and frustrating the measures of each other.

Many state and local officials believe that Madison's assessment was wrong. Over 200 years of congressional enactments and Supreme Court decisions have significantly reduced the authority and independence of subnational units and bolstered the role of the federal government.[1]

The Growing Federal Role: Conflicting Signals

The federal government's expanding domestic leadership position beginning in the 1930s was reflected in its steadily growing involvement through conditional grants-in-aid for functions that were once exclusively or predominantly performed by states and localities, such as transportation, housing, education, health, and welfare. The accompanying regulations became focal points of intergovernmental interaction.

Conditional grants were instrumental in supporting ongoing subnational activities, stimulating new efforts, improving comprehensive planning, financial management, and reporting capabilities, enhancing the caliber of personnel, and encouraging research.[2] As indicated in chapter 1, during the 1960s and 1970s there was an explosion of these programs under both Democratic and Republican presidents: the number of programs grew from 130 in 1960 to over 500 in 1980; the amounts of aid increased from $7 billion in FY 1960 to $88.9 billion in FY 1980; and the portion of state and local budgets accounted for by federal funds went from 14.7 to 23.2 percent.[3]

During the latter half of the twentieth century, social regulation became a major area of national interest—and controversy—as the federal government's involvement in state and local activities expanded. These social regulations of the 1960s and 1970s were different from their predecessors in a number of ways. Instead of curbing abuse or compensating for marketplace deficiencies, regulatory policy became "political" in the sense of serving as a vehicle for transmitting national values to subnational units and the private sector. In addition to the commerce clause, the Fourteenth Amendment, which provides that "no State shall make or enforce any law which shall abridge the privileges or immunities of the citizens of the United States; nor shall any State deprive any person of life, liberty, or property, without due process of law; nor deny to any person within its jurisdiction the equal protection of the laws," was applied by the U.S. Supreme Court to extend the federal regulatory presence in such areas as anti-discrimination, affirmative action, citizen participation, and public facility access. State and local governments were relied upon as implementers of national policy. New actors were brought into the regulatory process as well, including citizen groups and public lobbies.

The broadening of the federal role, from regulation of private sector economic activities under the interstate commerce clause to encompass further the implementation of important public programs supported by conditional, or categorical, grants was a reaction to a number of political factors. These included a programmatic and regulatory "green light" signal to Congress and federal agencies by the Supreme Court; public opinion that was supportive of a strong national role in such areas as civil rights, environmental quality, public health protection, higher education, and occupational safety; growth in the number of "public interest" lobbies that advocated federal involvement and often opposed business as well as state and local government "special interests"; and national domestic budgetary constraints that sometimes precluded offering of federal financial "carrots" but permitted the use of regulatory "sticks" to accomplish national goals.[4] It was also a response to concerns about the capacity and commitment of subnational governmental units not only efficiently and effectively to plan and manage programs but to ensure that desirable social benefits would be attained. From the standpoint of the dynamics of the federal-state-local program partnership, the significance of these changes has been explained:

The most important factor establishing a favorable climate for intergovernmental regulation . . . was the elaboration and expansion of the federal grant system. The pervasive growth of federal grants-in-aid accustomed both federal policymakers and state and local officials to engage in combined operations wherever possible. Once this pattern was established and made familiar in assistance programs, it was only a short conceptual leap to think of placing federal regulations in this mold as well—especially in the many areas where states possessed distinctive competence and experience.[5]

By the early 1980s there was mounting evidence of dissatisfaction with the "partnership." For example, reporting on the 1980 annual meeting of the National Governors' Association, journalist David Broder quoted a number of state chief executives who, in his judgment, were "feeling burned" about their relationship with Washington.[6]

- Otis Bowen, Republican governor of Indiana, said, "It is clear that Washington has changed the terms of the partnership [in ways that] demand a new response from the states, a response that is more aggressive, more independent, more skeptical of federal power."
- George Bushee, Democratic governor of Georgia, said, "To me, there is no doubt that the federal umbilical cord is beginning to strangle us. . . . If something isn't done . . . then I fear that my successors and yours ultimately will be relegated to mere clerks of the federal establishment."
- Richard Snelling, Republican governor of Vermont, said, "The federal system has reached a crossroads. The role of the states has been eroded to the point that the authors of the Constitution would not recognize the intergovernmental relationships they crafted so carefully in 1789."
- Bruce Babbitt, Democratic governor of Arizona, said, "The federal system is in complete disarray. Congress has lost all sense of restraint. . . . The 10th Amendment, reserving powers to the states, is a hollow shell."

Similarly, in his first State of the Union message in 1982, President Ronald Reagan echoed the conclusion of the U.S. Advisory Commission on Intergovernmental Relations (ACIR), noting that "contemporary intergovernmental relations . . . have become more pervasive, more intrusive, more unmanageable, more ineffective, more costly, and above all, more unaccountable.''[7]

The focal points of much of this anti-Washington sentiment were federal programs and regulations. As the ACIR put it, the system was "out of control":

The federal government has taken over policy leadership in virtually every functional field in which it offers aid . . . a condition of overload has arisen from: (1) the seemingly endless proliferation of aid programs into areas wholly national (like social welfare programs) or wholly local or even private, as well as into activities that are legitimately of a national interest; (2) the expansion of eligibility to reach directly almost all of the categories of subnational governmental activity; (3) the advent of more conditions and more national policy requirements; (4) the mounting difficulty of any level or unit within a level to keep track of, not to mention oversee, the system; and (5) the public's growing disenchantment with a system that seems out of control.[8]

Business leaders were also skeptical. During the 1970s, while the amount of economic regulatory activity had decreased, the number and costs of "social regulations" had steadily risen. The consequences of, and reactions to, these developments have been explained:

The business community [has] come to perceive increases in social regulation as the most important contemporary threat to its wealth and power. If executives were asked, at any time throughout the seventies, to cite the changes in business-government relations that had most disturbed them, the newer social regulations would probably be near the top of the list. By the early seventies, executives had begun to resent both the arrogance and ignorance of regulatory officials. Business executives and those sympathetic to them publicly blamed government regulation for a wide variety of ills ranging from increasing the price of consumer products to reducing the incentive for innovation and risk taking, from impairing productivity to retarding the rate of investment in new plants and facilities. Companies, business associations and conservative foundations began to invest considerable sums in the preparation and dissemination of articles, books, studies and reports documenting the problems created by the federal government's efforts to better protect consumers, employees, and the environment.[9]

In response to these criticisms, President Ronald Reagan's New Federalism initiative, launched in 1982, reopened the debate about the proper balance of power and allocation of responsibilities between the national and state governments and between the public and private sectors. For the first time since Franklin D. Roosevelt, a national administration advocated a fundamental realignment of the federal government's role. But the Reagan proposals had the opposite intent. In contrast with previous administrations during the 1970s, instead of expanding the national financial, programmatic, and regulatory presence, the emphasis was placed on contracting it and relying more on the free market allocation of revenues and services.

Despite their distress with the seemingly unmanaged growth of the central government's regulatory bureaucracy, Nixon, Ford, and Carter never exhibited the fundamental skepticism and philosophical antipathy toward federal regulation that characterized the Reagan period. They essentially kept the faith with the New Deal principle that federal programs were an appropriate response to socioeconomic problems; their main concern was getting the biggest bang for the federal buck.[10]

With these initiatives, the intergovernmental pendulum swung to the "laboratories of democracy" and "grass-roots governments"—to the states, localities, and individual citizens. The private sector was looked to for joint ventures with governments in delivering services and for responsible exercise of economic power in the absence of regulatory interventions.

The New Federalism of the 1980s had four chief components:[11]

1. *Decrementalism*, or cutting into the base of grant-in-aid programs to state and local government. This "cut and cap" strategy resulted in a sharp slowdown in the overall growth rate of grants and in a real decline in the share of the gross national product, state and local expenditures, and the federal domestic budget accounted for by federal aid.

2. *Decentralization*, featuring the consolidation of financially smaller and programmatically narrower conditional grant programs into 10 broad-purpose "block grants," which reduced the total number of federal programs by almost 25 percent. Within the block grant framework, restrictions on the purposes of expenditures were lessened, reporting requirements and cross-cutting regulations were relieved, and recipient discretion in targeting monies for priority areas was increased. Included among the successful Reagan initiatives were the Improving School Programs State Block Grant, the Job Training Partnership Act, the Community Services Block Grant, the Preventive Health and Health Services Block Grant, the Alcohol, Drug Abuse, and Mental Health Services Block Grant, the Mental Health Services for the Homeless Block Grant, the Community Youth Activity Block Grant, and the Maternal and Child Health Services Block Grant.

   Title V of the 1981 Omnibus Budget Reconciliation Act (the Education Consolidation and Improvement Act) is an example of both decrementalism and decentralization. It replaced Title 1 of the 1965 Elementary and Secondary Education Act (Chapter 1) and merged some 38 education categoricals (Chapter 2). The latter sought to reduce recipient paperwork burdens, give states greater administrative responsibility, and provide more flexibility to local education agencies (LEAs) in tailoring federal funds to their needs. Chapter 2 block grant funding was $440 million in 1982 and $450 million in 1983, compared with a $510 million preconsolidation level, approximately 12 percent less. These funds accounted for only 5 percent of total federal education spending during the early 1980s. In 1984, the General Accounting Office examined 13 state experiences and reported that LEAs favored the block grant approach, state officials had mixed views of its desirability compared with categorical grants, and interest groups preferred the latter mechanism.[12]

3. *Devolution*, a 1982 "swap/turnback" proposal, under which the federal government would have gradually assumed full responsibility for Medicaid and food stamps. At the same time, the states would have taken over welfare and shared responsibilities with local governments for a variety of transportation, community, and economic development programs. This was the most ambitious intergovernmental "sorting out"

initiative ever taken by a president. However, while it stimulated discussion and debate, by 1983 the proposal was dead due to (1) the failure of the Reagan administration to have implementing legislation introduced in Congress; (2) concerns on the part of members of Congress and special interest groups that devolution would leave national interests unmet or inadequately addressed; (3) insufficient consultation of local elected officials and state legislators; (4) skepticism on the part of state and local government representatives that the federal government would keep its commitments gradually to phase out affected programs over a 10-year period and adequately to finance the "Federalism Trust Fund" that would be set up for purposes of this transition; (5) fears that "devolution" was merely an administration code word for domestic budget cutting to reduce the federal deficit; (6) disagreements among governors about whether states should take over welfare and, if so, how the financial and political costs of leveling benefits upward or downward to achieve greater nationwide uniformity would be handled; and (7) strong doubts on the part of big city mayors and urban county executives that, in the absence of federal guarantees, states would pass through their "fair share" of funding.

4. *Deregulation*, through lifting federal requirements on states and localities and the private sector—in such areas as bilingual education, prevailing wage rates, and transportation of the handicapped. This was done to encourage competition, reduce implementation delays, attract investment, and lower compliance costs.

While these New Federalism initiatives had laudable objectives, their implementation sent mixed signals to state and local governments and the private sector. Although considerable rhetoric was devoted to regulatory relief, the principal beneficiaries were those in the private sector—the transportation industry, telephone and cable television companies, and savings and loan associations. By comparison, state and local "victories" (e.g., block grants, alleviation of certain programmatic and cross-cutting requirements) were not considered to be significant from administrative cost and efficiency standpoints.

Wherever private interests clashed with New Federalism principles—such as trucking deregulation in which state restrictions on the length, width, and weight of trailer trucks were partially preempted in return for states' sharing in a gasoline excise tax increase—private interest prevailed, and the states were preempted by Congress with the administration's support. Moreover, whenever special interests or national concerns (e.g., incidences of drinking alcoholic beverages and driving) clashed with New Federalism principles (e.g., state authority to regulate minimum drinking ages), again states and localities were the losers.

Despite the emphasis on decentralization and deregulation objectives during the Reagan era, Congress proceeded to enact laws containing direct orders, cross-cutting requirements, crossover sanctions, and partial preemptions. A study of the history of preemption statutes by Professor Joseph F. Zimmerman for the ACIR found that 350 bills had been enacted since 1787, most of which dealt with health and safety or business matters. Of the total, 26 percent (91) had been enacted during 1980–88 and another 27 percent (95) had been enacted since 1970.[13] Clearly, for state and local governments as well as industry, social regulations increased rather than diminished during the 1980s, despite an avowed presidential effort to reverse course.

Fiscally, although by the early 1990s federal aid accounted for about 17 percent of state and local budgets, reflecting a steady decrease from the 1978 peak of approximately 25 percent, the opposite occurred with respect to the number of programs. From a low point of 392 categorical and 12 block grant programs in 1981 in the wake of the "decrementalism" effects of the Omnibus Budget Reconciliation Act, the number of grants-in-aid climbed steadily to an all-time high of 543 ten years later. Only 14 of these were block grants (see Appendix 7.A). Between 1989 and 1991, 13 new education- and 28 new health and human services–related categoricals were enacted by Congress.[14] ACIR concluded in 1992, "While the grant system was simplified in the 1970s and early 1980s, giving states and localities more discretion in the use of funds, there has been an inclination recently to return to categorical grants in promoting federal policies through the financial assistance system."[15]

The States' Resurgence: Local and Private Sector Impacts

At the same time the federal government was sending conflicting signals to state and local officials and the private sector, the states were flexing their muscles. In fact, the New Federalism initiative focused national attention on the role and activities of state governments and highlighted their resurgence, even though a "silent revolution" had been taking place in state capitols across the country for more than two decades, featuring the modernization and strengthening of most executive, legislative, and judicial branches.[16] As Professors Richard Nathan and Fred Doolittle have concluded, "The most important federalism change brought about by Reagan's policies—one that was probably unanticipated by Reagan and his advisors—was the way in which the social program retrenchment goals and his block grant and related devolutionary policy initiatives activated state governments and enhanced their role in the nation's governmental system."[17]

Local governments were the first to experience the state's transition, in the form of increased activism as funders, administrators, and regulators. The states' evolving role in domestic programs was greeted with mixed reaction. While local officials were not pleased with the termination of their direct ties with Washington, they generally welcomed state compensatory funding for programs that were "cut, capped, and consolidated" by the Reagan administration and Congress. In addition to financial support for block grants, according to the National Association of State Budget Officers, direct state aid to local governments increased some $57 billion between 1981 and 1988, from $90.2 billion to $145.6 billion. During the same period, federal aid to local governments declined by $5 billion, from approximately $22 billion to $17 billion. While 53 percent of state aid went to school districts for elementary and secondary education, nevertheless, the overall amount and the rate of growth of state aid were substantial.[18]

Local officials soon recognized that the "golden rule" (he or she who has the gold makes the rules) was skillfully practiced by state officials. For many years, state administrators had been "watchdogs" over local officials. An important part of their stewardship responsibility in grant programs involved ensuring that performance standards were met and the purposes of federal-state programs were achieved through a variety of planning, administrative, auditing, and reporting requirements. Even when the federal government simplified and streamlined these standards, such as through management circulars promulgated by the Office of Management and Budget, state administrators often added their own fiscal, program, information, and record-keeping requirements. These additional state regulations are intended to ascertain that their oversight obligations to federal funding agencies have been satisfied, to provide additional documentation of recipient activities, to establish "audit trails," and to reconcile federal guidance with state administrative procedures and fiscal rules.[19] Usually the states have not provided additional funds to compensate for the increased administrative costs resulting from exercise of their multifaceted regulatory roles in grant programs.

"SORTING-OUT" RESPONSIBILITIES

The evolution of the American federal system during the twentieth century, particularly developments on the intergovernmental relations front since 1960, has followed no "grand design" or systematic pattern. The intergovernmental pendulum has swung during conservative periods from a national to a state-oriented system and back again during liberal periods.[20] But as the preceding analysis demonstrates, the cyclical nature of these trends conceals inconsistencies, irregularities, and ironies. Education and health care policies are prime examples of the contradictions and crosscurrents accompanying transition in the focal points of domestic governance, especially during the last decade of the twentieth century.

The upward shift of responsibility for education, health care, and other services once performed predominantly at the local level has occurred for a variety of reasons, including to (1) increase public sector funding levels by tapping the wealthier and more progressive tax bases of states and the federal government; (2) better equalize per capita spending across jurisdictions and assure greater equity in service delivery; (3) take advantage of economics of scale inherent in larger geographic bases for program administration; (4) overcome the unwillingness or inability of some states and localities to perform at acceptable levels; and (5) achieve statewide or national minimum standards.

While these purposes are commendable, the relatively rapid escalation of state and federal involvement and the associated "marbleization" or mixing of responsibilities have had some dysfunctional effects. In a comprehensive examination of the causes and consequences of the growth in the federal government's role between 1960 and 1980, the ACIR concluded:

The federal government has overused the grant-in-aid mechanism, sometimes giving the state and local governments roles in certain programs that could be handled best by the federal government itself, while at other times establishing a federal role in programs better left to state and local governments. In these cases, the grant mechanism often unnecessarily complicates the administration of the program, confuses political and program accountability, reduces effectiveness, interferes with economic efficiency, and rarely achieves equity goals.[21]

The commission called for a "decongesting" of the federal grant system.

More recently, a 1992 article by then ACIR executive director John Kincaid questioned, "Is education too intergovernmental?"[22] While yielding some benefits—such as higher spending levels and greater equalization—"intergovernmentalization" of public education, where one level of government raises funds and another spends them, has created and exacerbated systemic problems, such as (1) increases in mandates imposed on recipient units; (2) growth of bureaucracy and administrative costs; (3) reduction of school accountability to communities and parents and insulation of school boards and superintendents from citizen influence and control; (4) institutional "bigness," in terms of the size of school districts, and remoteness from neighborhoods or "grass-roots" involvement; and (5) horizontal and vertical fragmentation of the delivery system within, across, and between governmental levels, which fosters policy confusion and inconsistency.

The above concerns about public education have been repeated with respect to other program areas, where a myriad of local, state, and federal executive, legislative, and judicial agencies exercise varying degrees of authority. One response to this dilemma has been to seek to rationalize the nonsystem by "sorting out," "reassigning," or "realigning" program responsibilities.

While the evolution of intergovernmental relationships in domestic affairs has been a reactive, rather than a rational, phenomenon, over the past half century attempts have been made to arrive at some generalizations about what seems to work as far as the allocation of functional responsibilities is concerned. Pioneering theoretical work on "sorting out" has been performed by at least three national intergovernmental bodies—the "Kestnbaum" Commission on Intergovernmental Relations (1953–55),[23] the Joint Federal-State Action Committee (1957–60),[24] and the ACIR.[25] Several state intergovernmental organizations—beginning with the California Council on Intergovernmental Relations (1970)—also made important contributions here.[26] Probably the most interesting work in terms of principles of federalism was done by the oldest body—the Commission on Intergovernmental Relations—even though its study preceded two dramatic shifts in the intergovernmental pendulum (1960–80; 1980–89).

Emphasizing that "in the federal system action should be proportionate to need,''[27] the commission favored a limited federal role in service delivery and regulatory affairs. National intervention would be appropriate only:

(a) When the National Government is the only agency that can summon the resources needed for an activity . . .

(b) When the activity cannot be handled within the geographic and jurisdictional limits of smaller governmental units, including those that could be created by compact . . .

(c) When the activity requires a nationwide uniformity of policy that cannot be achieved by interstate action . . .

(d) When a State through action or inaction does injury to the people of other States . . .

(e) When States fail to respect or to protect basic political and civil rights that apply throughout the United States.[28]

In the case of education, the commission expressed concern about possible national interference and recommended that "responsibility . . . continue to rest squarely upon the states and their political subdivisions" and that "the states act vigorously and promptly to discharge their responsibility." It recommended against federal aid for elementary and secondary education, except for temporary assistance in financing capital construction of school facilities in financially hard-pressed states.[29] With respect to public health, a similarly restricted federal role was envisioned. Federal aid was to supplement, not supplant, state and local expenditures and to be used to encourage the adoption of new approaches and establish national minimum standards, developed by representatives of all three levels of government and nongovernmental health groups.[30] The commission further recommended that welfare and general assistance programs be financed and administered by states and localities but that federal aid for dependent children, child welfare services, and foster care be continued.[31]

Twenty-six years later, in its landmark 1981 review of "The Federal Role in the Federal System," ACIR urged Congress and the president to:

(1) reexamine federal, state, and local roles in and contributions to the principal functional areas of public policy, including assessments of the desirability of fully nationalizing some functions while reducing, eliminating or forestalling federal involvement in others; (2) assess the interrelationships among the full range of programs in each policy field; and (3) consider the possible use of instruments other than grants-in-aid to realize national objectives.[32]

The commission reaffirmed its previous recommendations, made in 1969, that the federal government assume full responsibility for provision of Aid to Families with Dependent Children, Medicaid, and General Assistance. In that report, *State Aid to Local Government*, ACIR also recommended that states assume substantially all responsibility for financing local public education, with assurance of retention of local policy control, "in order to create a financial environment more conducive to attainment of equality of educational opportunity and to remove the massive and growing pressure of the school tax on owners of local property."[33]

In its 1981 volume, the commission expanded its recommended federal role to include moving

more toward the assumption of full financial responsibility for those existing governmental programs which are aimed at meeting basic human needs for employment security, housing assistance, medical benefits, and basic nutrition. In assuming full financial responsibility, the federal government should take steps to ensure uniform levels of benefits, adjusted for cost of living variations, and consistent nationwide administration.[34]

Accompanying this nationally oriented sorting out of responsibility would be a decongestion strategy aimed at reducing the number of federal categorical grants through consolidation of programs that are closely related in terms of functional area, objectives, and recipient governmental jurisdictions. The commission called for elimination of programs that (1) have a federal share that is 10 percent or less of total grant funds or combined state-local outlays; (2) do not embody essential national objectives; (3) are too small to address the need for which they were established; (4) have high administrative costs; (5) receive most of their funding from state and local budgets or from service fees, and (6) could be shifted to the private sector.[35]

Criteria for Decision Making

The upward or downward movement of functional responsibility in the federal system has been influenced more by the pragmatism of intergovernmental grant and regulatory policy than by theories of sorting-out based on underlying principles. In fact, grants and mandates have helped forestall making difficult trade-offs involved in separating responsibility.[36] Instead, critics have pointed to the opportunities for "pass the buck" federalism inherent in a system that emphasizes sharing rather than separation of responsibility. Another factor, in the view of Harold Hovey, former Illinois and Ohio budget director, is: "Sometimes critics say that the wrong level of government is making a decision when what they really mean is they do not like a particular decision and think it would be made more in their favor by some other level of government."[37] This tendency has been apparent in the debates over school choice, national educational proficiency standards, Medicaid costs and mandates, and national health insurance.

The blurring effects of contemporary intergovernmental approaches should not suggest, however, that rational decision making criteria are lacking. On the contrary, the literature of political science, public administration, and public finance—as well as reports by a multitude of task forces and commissions—contains a rich variety of criteria, which occasionally have been drawn upon in the consideration of public policy options responding to four basic questions associated with functional assignment decisions:[38]

- Who provides (or should provide) the service?
- Who supervises and controls (or should supervise and control) provision of the service?
- Who pays (or should pay) for the service?
- Who is held accountable (or should be held accountable) for provision of the service?

Within the framework of these questions, consideration of sorting out has generally focused on four criteria:

1. Efficiency, in terms of assigning functions to achieve economies of scale and acceptable levels of pricing;
2. Effectiveness, in terms of assigning functions to encompass sufficient geographic area for service delivery, ensure adequate legal and administrative capacity of the responsible jurisdiction, and promote interlocal functional cooperation;
3. Equity, in terms of assigning functions to achieve adequate fiscal capacity for financing service responsibilities, to encompass costs and benefits of a function, and to compensate other jurisdictions for spillover costs, as well as to provide for interpersonal and interjurisdictional equity; and
4. Accountability, in terms of assigning functions to maximize conditions conducive to active citizen participation and control of services and oversight of policymakers.

Appendix 7.B shows the results of three decades of work by the ACIR to distill and define these terms. Appendix 7.C reveals a somewhat more refined scheme, developed in a 1989 report published by the National Governors' Association (NGA), which differentiates equity, efficiency, and accountability in terms of the basic policy, funding, and implementation actions of government.

These criteria are deceptively simple. In applying them to address the key questions about functional assignment raised previously, for example, it is likely that decision makers would generally sort out functions to the local level if they sought to attain such values as diversity, fiscal and programmatic accountability, responsiveness, and administrative efficiency. On the other hand, those favoring uniformity, redistribution, disparity reduction, and economies of scale would likely support national or state assumption of financial and service responsibility.

In applying these criteria to different levels of government, difficulties soon become apparent. With respect to equity, for example, both the states and federal government have roles to play, as described by De Witt John in the report for the NGA:

On the ... dimension of ... fiscal equity between individuals, states, regions, and communities, there are important differences in the capacities of different levels of government. As with equal treatment of minorities, the equitable sharing of the costs of government between individuals is a proper concern for all levels of government. However, the fiscal capacity of states and communities varies. The costs of providing service are higher in some jurisdictions, and the need for governmental services is greater in some places; some states and local governments have access to a smaller tax base than others. States can and do provide assistance to individual communities, but only the national government can equalize the capacity of states to provide public services.[39]

As Harold Hovey has pointed out with respect to the economy of scale criterion, "Economies of scale often give absolutely no indication about who should pay for services, who should control the provision of the service, or what tax or user charge base would stand behind it."[40] While in theory the political accountability value is best maximized by assigning functions to the grass-roots level, historically many local governments and some states were not representative of, or responsive to, racial minorities, the poor, inner-city neighborhood residents, and other relatively powerless groups. As a consequence, beginning in the 1960s, presidents proposed and congresses enacted Great Society programs, civil and voting rights legislation, and federal grant programs targeted to disadvantaged people and places. As a result, "actual provision of service may also have moved to higher levels even though no economies of scale and some loss of voter control may have been involved."[41]

The various decision-making criteria are also weighted differently by different policymakers and analysts. Some might well agree with Alan Campbell that equity should be the central value.

Public sector benefits should be based more directly on need rather than on what each individual's pocketbook permits him to acquire. Whether it be education services, police protection, sanitation services, or any other public services, the amount received should be related to the need for that service. Such equity should relate to both interpersonal and interjurisdictional distribution of services.[42]

The debate over access to and affordability of health care raises significant equity issues. Others, however, might stress efficiency or accountability. In education, proponents of magnet schools, parental choice, site-based management, and school-based social services would likely embrace one or more of these criteria.

In the context of particular functions or services, therefore, sorting out can become even more complex. As indicated in earlier chapters of this book, financial responsibility for elementary and secondary education has increasingly moved from local school districts to the state level and has been accompanied by a stronger state policy role involving such matters as graduation requirements; class size; school year length; student testing; teacher pay, pensions, and qualifications; mandatory kindergarten; and course electives. Since the 1980s, the federal government has become more involved in national curriculum standard setting and assessments, as well as promotion of local experimentation and parental choice arrangements. Emphasis has been placed on more national uniformity and, due to judicial involvement, on greater equalization of expenditure, which have shifted responsibility to the state and national levels. At the same time, diversity and flexibility have been emphasized, which have spurred efforts to empower teachers and school systems. As a result of these upward and downward pressures, clear delineations of roles and responsibilities in public education are difficult if not impossible.

In the case of health care, efficiency, effectiveness, and equity, considerations have produced a greater degree of consensus over the assignment of financial responsibility. Access to adequate and affordable health care has been considered a national issue warranting a single, stable, unified response through national health insurance; "pay or play" plans; federalization of Medicaid; caps and freezes on doctors' fees, prescription prices, and insurance rates; and other approaches under debate. Continuation of a widely varying, 50-state approach—replete with interstate gaps in Medicaid coverage, growth in the numbers of uninsured or underinsured citizens, uneven regulation of health care providers, excessive administrative and service costs, and other problems—is considered unsatisfactory by the Clinton administration, state and local elected officials, the business community, and the general public.

For most functions, neither clarity nor consensus is evident. In the view of the Task Force on State-Local Relations of the National Conference of State Legislatures, answers to the four sorting-out questions posed earlier in this section will vary on a state-by-state basis: "There is no single correct solution to this issue of 'sorting-out' responsibilities, since it depends on a state's size, diversity, wealth, and the desire, of citizens, among other factors."[43] The task force offered five guidelines for reviewing state service delivery systems as part of formulating a sorting-out scheme:

1. The state should consider why each major program to aid local government was created and whether those reasons are still valid.
2. The state should determine the goals of specific programs and whether changes in the structure of a program would help achieve those goals more effectively or at lower cost.
3. The state should strive to simplify the state-local system, with some programs expanded, others contracted, and still others combined or eliminated. This may involve shifting some programs from the state to the local level while others are transferred in the opposite direction.
4. Responsibility should be assigned to the lowest level of government unless there is an important reason to do otherwise.
5. Poverty-related services should be financed by the highest level of government possible, although local administration may or may not be desirable.[44]

The Sorting-Out Record

The difficulties just described have stalled national and state efforts rationally to sort out responsibilities. The realignments that have occurred are attributable to the incremental effects of budget pressures, regulatory policy, and intergovernmental lobbying rather than systematic consideration. This de facto approach is especially apparent in federal domestic budget and block grant policies during the 1980s, which succeeded in reducing the federal financial role in many domestic program areas and increasing the amount of discretion and flexibility accorded state and local recipients. To a greater degree than prior to 1980, these decremental and decentralizing efforts have helped clarify some of the confusion over intergovernmental roles noted by the ACIR and have lessened the number of cries of alarm that the federal system was "out of control." On the other hand, some observers have concluded that the effects of these developments on pinpointing responsibility have been offset and overshadowed by "reregulation" of the public sector through federal mandates and preemption.[45]

At the state level, de facto sorting out has accompanied the trend toward greater financial centralization for such local or state-local functions as courts, corrections, highways, and mental health, as well as elementary and secondary education. The track record of task forces and commissions set up more systematically or comprehensively to address the reassignment of functional responsibilities has not been impressive. A 1979 report by the Florida Advisory Council on Intergovernmental Relations reviewed the work of such bodies in seven states: "While the commissions' budgets ranged from $88.5 thousand to $1.2 million with working time frames of eight months to three years, only minor legislation was passed in New York, despite recommendations made by all commissions."[46]

THE "DIVISION SOLUTION": UPWARD OR DOWNWARD?

As the American federal system approached the twenty-first century, there was renewed interest in what an article by Alice Rivlin in the *Washington Post* called the "division solution."[47] This interest was prompted by a number of factors, including (1) concerns about massive federal budget deficits and the substantial costs of debt service, which constrained the federal government's ability to provide financial support for state and local services; (2) globalization of the world economy, which underscored the need for the United States to speak with one voice on financial, regulatory, and economic development matters; (3) the fiscal shocks of the severe national recession during the early 1990s, which impaired the service delivery capacities of states and localities; (4) technological advances in medicine, transportation, communications, and other fields, which were most effectively managed by larger, more authoritative, and fiscally strong units of government; (5) regionalization of services and functions—such as housing, transportation, health care, growth and development policy, and environmental protection—which called for multicounty or statewide delivery systems; (6) increased concerns on the part of the business community with the weak competitive position of the nation's work force, compared with that of other countries, and the high costs of remedial actions, which led to greater private sector interest and involvement in partnership arrangements with government agencies; (7) court decisions requiring states to equalize spending for public education, which increased both state fiscal centralization and policy control; (8) the modernization of state executive, legislative, and judicial branches over the past 25 years and willingness of many states to serve as "laboratories of democracy," which have equipped the states to assume greater responsibilities, enhanced their capacity to manage traditional functions, and encouraged them to launch innovative programs and to experiment with new approaches to meeting public needs; and (9) the antitax and anti-incumbent mood of the public, which emphasized the need to make the most efficient use of tax dollars, reduce overlapping or duplication of services, and curb administrative costs and bureaucracy.

As the sorting-out debate intensified, two dominant themes emerged. These were the top-down public sector approach and horizontal grass-roots, public-private approach.

The Top-Down Approach

The leading proponents of the top-down approach have been U.S. senator Charles Robb and Office of Management and Budget deputy director Alice Rivlin. In a June 1991 speech to the National Academy of Public Administration (NAPA), Senator Robb called for a "New Federalist Papers," derived from a series of first principles.

Six years earlier, Senator Robb had cochaired with Washington senator Daniel Evans a Committee on Federalism and National Purpose, which was convened under the auspices of the National Conference on Social Welfare's Project on the Federal Social Role. In its report entitled *To Form a More Perfect Union*, the committee offered recommendations for reforming intergovernmental programs, particularly Aid to Families with Dependent Children and Medicaid, which at that time accounted for 25 percent of federal spending through the intergovernmental system. Using criteria discussed previously that called for federal involvement where uniformity and redistribution were sought and for state and local participation where diversity and experimentation were sought, the following division of labor was proposed:[48]

Welfare

1. The federal government should establish national minimum benefit levels and eligibility standards for the AFDC and Medicaid programs. In the case of AFDC it should establish a national floor that, when combined with food stamps, is between 75 percent and 90 percent of poverty-level income.

2. It should assume full policy responsibility for these programs, as well as 90 percent of the financial responsibility up to the minimum benefit levels.

3. States should maintain administrative responsibility for AFDC and Medicaid.

4. The employment programs supporting AFDC should be strengthened by expanding education, training and placement activities. . . . Welfare systems should be converted into job systems.

5. The long-term care component of Medicaid should be converted into a federal block grant to states, indexed for changes in the program's cost and population it serves.

Devolution

1. States and localities should assume full financial, policy and administrative responsibilities for many community development, local infrastructure and social service programs.

2. States and localities should address more effectively the agenda of unresolved issues between them, such as state mandates, regulation and local revenue-raising options.

Fiscal Support for States and Localities

1. The federal government should provide general support grants targeted to states with very low fiscal capacity.

2. A transitional federal assistance program should be established, administered by states and targeted by them to localities with the greatest problems of fiscal capacity.

Intergovernmental Programs

1. Remaining shared programs should be better targeted to the most needy beneficiaries and localities. More reliance should be placed on states to accomplish this targeting.

2. Greater use should be made of incentives rather than sanctions to hold states and localities accountable.

3. Many of the more than 200 intergovernmental programs funded by the federal government at under $100 million should be consolidated into block grants or folded into existing programs.

Instead of debating "pie cutting," as had been done by the Committee on Federalism and National Purpose, in 1991 Senator Robb argued to NAPA that a New Federalist Paper, or *"Perestroika* for America," should design the best governance structure for the nation and not be bound by the programmatic status quo or the demands of "piranha pluralism."

In Senator Robb's view, "The principal measure by which we ought to evaluate the appropriate level at which to deliver a service should be *efficiency.*"[49] By this standard, embracing cost and uniformity factors, welfare, environmental protection, and labor law enforcement would be federal responsibilities, while education, infrastructure, and some business regulation would be handled subnationally because of the need to recognize different standards and priorities from state to state.[50] In the absence of compelling reasons such as standardization and interstate disparity elimination, "the default should always be that a program is executed at the lowest level" since "state and local jurisdictions can generally accomplish given tasks with less overhead and—importantly—more sensitivity to the people they serve than the federal government could ever hope to achieve."[51]

A more elaborate "division solution" was proposed by Alice Rivlin in 1992, as a response to the twin challenges of reviving the American economy and making government work better. Like Senator Robb, for Dr. Rivlin this area was not new terrain. In August 1983 the Congressional Budget Office, which

Dr. Rivlin directed at that time, issued a report entitled *The Federal Government in a Federal System*, which was prepared at the request of the U.S. Senate Subcommittee on Intergovernmental Relations. While the study offered no recommendations, it reviewed the federal role in public works infrastructure and development programs; education, employment, and social service programs; and income security and health programs from the standpoints of whether federal involvement was necessary and, if so, what form it should take. Each of these program areas was examined in terms of the rationale for national involvement and the effects of modifying existing programs by implementing three options: eliminating federal funding, changing funding provisions, and changing program rules.[52]

Nearly a decade later Dr. Rivlin recognized that many of the steps needing to be taken to meet the challenges confronting the nation's economy were of a "bottom-up" nature, in the sense of requiring experimentation and adaptation. These functions include education (especially improvement of the capacity of public schools to produce youth who have the attitudes and skills necessary to make a successful transition to the workplace), crime and drug abuse prevention, housing and community development, infrastructure renewal, and prevention of teenage pregnancy. In her judgment, these are examples of problems the federal government "can deplore but cannot fix. . . . Federal grants can help defray the costs, but at the price of confusing the issue of who is responsible and who needs to take action."[53] In the case of education, for instance, while President George Bush considered himself the "Education President" and used the visibility of his office to call attention to problems and propose remedial actions, such as America 2000 and parental choice, "he risks diluting state and local responsibility by implying that Washington can actually produce change."[54] The Head Start program is another example where the federal government's involvement since the Great Society has caused some local and state officials to believe that preschool education is a federal responsibility—not theirs. "Change could come more rapidly if concerned citizens, parents, and educators worked to improve their own preschools instead of lobbying Washington to allocate more funds for Head Start."[55]

On the other hand, the case for a "top-down" sorting out is compelling, beyond the needs to speak with one voice on national defense and foreign affairs, deal with interstate costs and benefits spillovers, and establish nationwide uniformity. These include the need to (1) increase national saving through the Social Security system and use these funds to finance investment rather than reduce "on paper" the size of the federal deficit; (2) free up more revenue to eliminate the deficit, balance the budget, and meet new or expanded responsibilities through load-shedding to the states and/or raising taxes; and (3) promote public understanding of governmental roles and clarify the linkage between taxes and the services provided with these revenues.

Dr. Rivlin contends that realigning functions would go a long way toward strengthening the economy and bolstering public confidence. In *Reviving the*

American Dream, she recommended a five-part strategy for dividing the tasks of domestic governance:[56]

1. Health care financing: The federal government should assume responsibility for providing all Americans with basic health insurance coverage and for controlling the escalation of health care costs. This move would ensure that there would be universal coverage through national health insurance or a combination of private and public insurance, that benefits would be consistent, and that fees and reimbursement rates for doctors, hospitals, and other medical service providers would be coordinated and controlled via a negotiated formula. From a state vantage point, an especially attractive feature would be relief from the escalating fiscal burdens of the Medicaid program, which would be financed from a health insurance trust fund. Tax increases necessary to finance the expanded federal health care role would be earmarked for this purpose.

2. Devolution: The federal government should terminate most of its involvement in programs not requiring nationwide uniformity and spillover containment, which can be better handled at the subnational level. These include education, housing, highways, social service, community economic development, and job training, producing a $75 billion reduction in federal domestic spending.

3. A "productivity agenda": States should "take charge of the primary public investment needed to increase productivity and raise incomes, especially to improve education and skill training, provide child care, promote economic development, and modernize infrastructure."[57]

4. Common shared taxes: States should strengthen their revenue by working together to levy and impose one or more taxes with a common base and rate—such as a value added (national sales) tax, a corporate income tax, or a gasoline tax—with proceeds to be shared on a formula basis. The federal government could enact the national tax or encourage states to do so through tax credits. The states could also accomplish this via interstate compact. Such a system is common in Germany and other federal systems, where the federal government collects most taxes and then distributes them to state-equivalent bodies. In the United States, the high degree of mobility of individuals and business activities across state borders, the dysfunctional effects of interstate tax competition, and the internationalization of the economy are trends that support greater coordination of state tax policy.

5. Federal budget surplus: partially due to devolution and load-shedding, the federal government should run a budget surplus (including Social Security), which should reduce funding for debt service and increase funding for investment in research and development, new technologies, certain infrastructure improvements, and skill development.

The Rivlin scenario for "dividing the job" may seem optimistic in view of the unimpressive track record of previous sorting-out proposals. Yet, it rests on at least five assumptions that were more powerful in the 1990s than in previous decades. First, federal system cannot "go back home again," in the sense of return to the Great Society of the sixties. Both the fiscal wherewithal and public support for a significant and widespread expansion of federal domestic involvement are lacking. Therefore, since the federal government is unable simultaneously to reform the health care system, balance the federal budget and create a surplus, and "fix" education, infrastructure, housing, and other important services, the responsibilities must be divided in accordance with the "strengths" of each level of government. Second, unlike the era when states were governed by "good-time Charlies,"[58] as a result of reapportionment, reorganization, and tax reform, the states are better equipped to manage and finance public services than they ever have been. Public opinion polls have revealed that the states are more trustworthy and give their citizens more for their money than the federal government.[59] Third, the focal points of much of the lobbying associated with domestic programs have shifted from Washington to the state capitals. This includes responsibility for traditional "development" programs (i.e., hospitals, highways, vocational education), in which federal-state cooperation has been extensive, and the "redistributive" programs (i.e., compensatory education, rent subsidies, antipoverty efforts), where the federal government once bypassed states due to fears that they would redirect funds to other interests or areas that were better represented in the capitals and more compatible with their political cultures.[60] Fourth, while the public is generally averse to new or higher taxes, revenue increases are more acceptable where they are tied to particular needs rather than general spending, budget balancing, or deficit reduction. Public comprehension of, and support for, governmental activities would be enhanced by separating and simplifying roles and "demystifying" decision-making processes. Fifth, the 1990s business revolution—with its emphasis on entrepreneurship, clearly defined missions, flatter hierarchies and leaner middle management ranks, team building and participatory management, total quality management, customer orientation, decentralized operations, and empowered workers—has carried over into the public sector.

As a result of these developments and trends, organizations at all levels are under pressure to revitalize and "reinvent" themselves. In Dr. Rivlin's judgment, "One ingredient should be a major effort to sort out functions of government—both between the federal government and the states and within the states—to clarify missions and make sure everyone knows who is responsible for which activities."[61] From the standpoints of work force skill preparation and the transition from school to work, areas where the United States has lagged in comparison with Japan and Germany, among other countries, these needs might well receive more serious and sustained attention as a consequence of a clearer focus of responsibility at the subnational level, where resources and results would be closer linked. Similarly, federalizing health care would not only free up state revenues for other purposes but also encourage development of more comprehensive approaches to related nutritional, health and social services, child care, and income needs of welfare parents and at-risk children.

The Grass-roots Approach

While much of the sorting-out literature has called for a "top-down" division of labor, probably due to the mounting concerns about the deteriorating fiscal and managerial capability of the federal government, similar efforts at the grass-roots level have also been chronicled. A landmark book embodying this approach is David Osborne's and Ted Gaebler's 1992 work, *Reinventing Government*. The basic message of this book relates to a sixth assumption made by Alice Rivlin, that the public sector will be greatly affected by the transformation of the private sector.

Basically, *Reinventing Government* calls upon government leaders at all levels, especially local and state, to deliver entrepreneurial government that would foster competition and focus on results, not rules and regulations. Public officials should steer the ship of state but leave much of the rowing to the private sector, volunteer organizations, and individual citizens. A key role of government should be to leverage change by using market mechanisms, always with the needs of citizens-customers, rather than the bureaucracy, at the forefront.[62]

The message conveyed in this book is powerful and popular. It calls for a "new paradigm" or governance model. From a federalism standpoint, the "rule of thumb" should be: "Unless there is an important reason to do otherwise, responsibility for addressing problems should be with the lowest level of government possible."[63] This message, of course, is not new. But how Osborne and Gaebler propose to carry it out is a significant contribution.

In their view, the traditional "government by program" is as out of date for the public sector as "ham and eggs" are for a cholesterol-conscious citizenry. When compared with markets, traditional government programs—"monpolistic organizations, normally of public employees, that spend appropriated money to deliver a service"—have several flaws:[64] (1) they are driven by the desires of constituency groups rather than the demands of customers; (2) they are subject to political pressure, which waters down and blurs goals, not to rational policy; (3) they devote too much attention to turf-and-custody battles over programs and clientele and not enough to effective management; (4) they fragment service delivery systems, each of which has its own procedures, and none of which is user-friendly; (5) they have no self-correcting mechanisms when results are not being achieved; (6) they tend to live on forever, regardless of whether the goals they were established to achieve have been accomplished; (7) they rarely achieve a fiscal magnitude that is necessary to attain their goal; and (8) they function on a command-control, rather than an incentive basis, and often the commands are difficult to enforce.

As shown in previous chapters, both public education and health care delivery have some of the above characteristics. For example,

- Head Start, the most successful long-term preschool program, still serves only one of every three children who are eligible.

- Many schools and school systems operate on the "command-control" model, resulting in teacher frustration and parental alienation.

- The goals of the post–1983 education reform movement have often been vague and sometimes contradictory.

- There have been few incentives offered to teachers and principals to improve schools by making fundamental departures from past methods. Similarly, there have been few incentives offered to doctors and other health services providers to contain treatment costs.

- Politicians have sought "quick fixes" of the educational system through raising standards but not through sustained investment of public funds. In health care, similar "quick fixes" have been sought by advocates of national health insurance or federal assumption of Medicaid.

- Both the education and health care systems have been overwhelmed by paperwork required to document compliance with rules and regulations.

- In public education and health care programs, politicians have frequently used mandates to help ensure attainment of goals, often with inadequate funding, producing resentment and resistance.

- In health care, too much of the "steering" role has been abdicated to providers (insurance companies, hospitals, health maintenance organizations, and the medical profession) while in the case of public schools too much has been ceded to education professionals.

- "Customers" have limited choice in the education and health care marketplace. In education parents and students may choose among a wide range of usually costly private schools or among a few public elementary and secondary schools, provided magnet school and similar arrangements are authorized. In health, except for managed care plans, patients have limited choices as to particular treatments or procedures, despite the wide range of physicians and other providers.

- There is strong competition among HMO providers, partly due to the federal government's impetus, to help improve services and reduce costs and moderate competition among insurance companies and other third-party payers, and as a result, in health care, competition has not necessarily kept costs low and quality high. In education there is moderate competition among public schools and little competition between public and private schools.

- Health, social, educational, and other services to at-risk youth and their families are often administratively and financially uncoordinated, and spatially separated.

- The intergovernmental and individual consequences and costs of various education and health reforms often have not been adequately considered, nor is sufficient time allowed for attainment of goals.

- In both education and health, rapidly rising public expenditures have not been accompanied by significant improvements in performance or achievement of desired results, and administrative systems are neither efficient nor streamlined.

In response to these criticisms of traditional programs, Osborne and Gaebler offer 10 principles that serve as the foundation for establishing entrepreneurial public organizations: (1) government should steer rather than row and choose alternatives to "in-house" delivery (i.e., policy formulation and oversight rather than implementation); (2) professional administrators should empower communities to participate in the delivery of services through management teams and councils; (3) competition should be encouraged within the public sector (i.e., bidding for tasks), as well as between government and the private sector; (4) agencies should be driven by mission rather than rules; (5) agencies and administrators should be "outcome"- and results-oriented instead of "input"- and process-oriented, and performance and funding should be based on the former; (6) clients should be considered customers, and their needs taken into account in determining service priorities and approaches; (7) agencies should earn money through user fees and profit centers as well as spend money; (8) prevention should be an objective in addition to amelioration or remediation; (9) authority should be decentralized; and (10) governments should leverage the marketplace (e.g., incentives for investment) rather than just create public programs to solve problems.[65]

The Clinton administration has embraced the spirit and much of the substance of "reinventing government." Vice President Albert Gore spearheaded a "National Performance Review," organized shortly after Clinton's inauguration, which over a 6 month period focused on ways federal agencies could improve their responsiveness, quality of management and services, and cost-effectiveness by incorporating the Osborne-Gaebler principles into their mission statements, operations, and personnel systems.[66]

Although education and health care have many trappings of monopolistic organizations, there are examples in both cases of the "new paradigm." In education, it is embodied in magnet and charter schools, as pioneered in Minnesota, and parental choice plans, especially where there is an option for sending children to private schools. The Bush administration's proposal to provide parents with $1,000 vouchers for each child, which could then be applied to the costs of public or private schooling of their choice, closely reflected the entrepreneurial and competitive thrust of the new paradigm. In health care, proposals to encourage competition among prepaid plans via vouchers, to allow patients greater choice over doctors and hospitals, to revise insurance plans to emphasize prevention as well as cure, and to require insurers and prepaid plans to cover high-risk as well as low-risk patients move in this direction.

The new paradigm called for by Osborne and Gaebler would have relevance for sorting out responsibilities. The federal and state governments would assume greater "steering" responsibilities, leaving much of the "rowing" to local units and the private sector. The federal government's funding and policy roles would continue, especially in such areas as:[67]

- Policies that transcend state and local borders and capabilities (i.e., international trade, macroeconomic policy, environmental protection).
- Antipoverty policy, especially where equalization is called for.
- Social insurance programs (i.e., Social Security and unemployment compensation) where equal benefits are sought despite interstate wealth differentials.
- Investments requiring larger tax increases (i.e., for health care), which might affect business location decisions if made at the subnational level.

However, even in these areas, states and localities would be accorded significant flexibility in tailoring programs to their priorities and needs, as well as in determining the providers of the services.

For example, an article on education and training by Richard Murnane and Frank Levy in the Brookings Institution's 1992 *Setting National Priorities: What Can Government Do?* volume concluded that the federal government had four key roles to pay in these areas: (1) promoting high-quality educational opportunities for disadvantaged children and youth; (2) recruiting and training qualified and motivated teachers; (3) supporting and coordinating development and implementation of both national standards and assessment methodologies, as well as state school reform efforts; and (4) sponsoring research and monitoring systemic reform implementation.[68]

A Sorting-Out Framework

To sum up, the preceding review of the sorting-out record and recent top-down and grass-roots proposals underscores that there is no "one best way" to rationalize the intergovernmental division of labor. De facto realignments of responsibility have occurred since the early 1980s and more than likely will continue. In both health care and education, fiscal and policy centralization have occurred at the national and state levels, respectively, even though service delivery has been decentralized.

The prospects for a more systematic approach to functional assignment are difficult to assess, although the Robb, Rivlin, and Osborne-Gaebler proposals have reopened the debate, and President Clinton has embraced the Osborne-Gaebler paradigm as a blueprint for reinventing government. The stakes are higher in the 1990s than they have been previously, given the mood of the public, fiscal constraints and demographic trends, and the challenges our nation faces in international competition.

As the future directions of sorting out are considered, they will be guided by the principles that have been developed in the literature and in practice. Following is a range of potential criteria that might be considered for application in a three-tier federalist system.

Responsibility could be placed at the national level when:

- A problem, issue, or need transcends state boundary lines;
- Interstate commerce is burdened by a diversity of state laws;
- A nationwide minimum level of effort and standard of service or a uniform national response is needed;
- Highly technical information or scientific expertise is needed;
- It is probable that industry will "forum shop" among the states, seeking the lowest common denominator of regulation;
- Interstate regulatory agencies are unable adequately to address the situation;

- The protection of civil and political rights and liberties is involved;
- It is necessary to ensure the protection of citizens' safety and welfare;
- It is more feasible for federal authorities to take the "political heat" for a programmatic regulatory initiative; and
- Competition among, lack of unified response by, or inaction on the part of, subnational units will impede the resolution of a nationwide problem.

States or regional bodies could assume responsibility when:

- A problem, issue, or need transcends the boundaries of a substantial number of local units and those of some states;
- A statewide minimum level of effort and standard of service is needed;
- The national government vacates the field;
- The situation can be adequately addressed through interstate action;
- The exercise of state police powers is involved;
- The costs of compliance are significantly beyond the fiscal capacity of individual local governments or consortia of such jurisdictions;
- The private sector does not have to achieve a uniform compliance or operational level across the 50 states;
- Competition among, lack of unified response by, or inaction on the part of, local units will impede the resolution of a statewide problem; and
- There is a desire to experiment and test the workability of new approaches.

Responsibility could be placed at the local level when:

- A problem, issue, or need can be contained within local boundaries;
- The situation can be adequately addressed through interlocal action;
- Diverse community values, standards, preferences, or conditions should be recognized and maintained;
- Competition among local units, or those providing services, would be likely to produce beneficial results; and
- Citizen participation and accountability in decision making and public access to information and decision makers are sought.

SERVICE INTEGRATION

The previous sections of this chapter have focused on the performance of functions through intergovernmental programs and proposals to separate more clearly responsibilities for services in accordance with considerations of efficiency, effectiveness, equity, and political accountability. In addition to these efforts to sort out responsibilities vertically through the federal system, since the early 1960s there have been several attempts to coordinate and integrate better the delivery of services funded by intergovernmental programs horizontally within each level of government. The federal government played a leadership role in these efforts.

The Federal Role

The intergovernmental human services system for children is expensive and fragmented. According to the National Commission on Children, in 1989 federal, state, and local expenditures on behalf of children totaled some $278.4 billion, of which $239.8 billion were actual outlays and $38.6 were federal tax expenditures for dependent exemptions, earned income credits, disability benefits, employer health coverage, and other purposes. The federal government accounted for $98.13 billion of the outlays, which were made in the following general areas: income support, $20.74 billion; nutrition, $13.49 billion; education, $9.09 billion; health, $5.11 billion; social services, $4.43 billion; housing, $4.37 billion; and training, $2.26 billion.[69]

While this investment is substantial, the growth of the federal government's domestic role beginning in the 1960s through grants-in-aid was accompanied by significant administrative problems. As discussed earlier in this chapter, the proliferation of programs created a functional fragmentation and overlapping that led the ACIR and others to conclude the system was "out of control." Programs serving similar purposes were focused on different missions and clienteles, were administered by different agencies, and had different eligibility criteria and administrative and matching requirements. The grant system was afflicted by a serious disease—"hardening of the categories."

The resulting pattern of intergovernmental relationships was labeled "picket fence federalism" by former North Carolina governor Terry Sanford in his 1967 book, *Storm over the States*.[70] Basically, the picket fence structure featured vertical program arrangements being orchestrated by technical specialists, with little effective coordination provided by administrative generalists or elected officials. From a public official's standpoint the effects were interpreted by Professor Deil S. Wright:

These interlevel loyalties were . . . criticized by elected officials as "vertical functional autocracies." Other epithets used to label these patterns are balkanized bureaucracies, feudal federalisms, and bureaucratic baronies. These terms emphasize both the program specialists' degree of autonomy from policy control by political generalists and also the separateness and independence that one program area has from another. Hence, interprogram, interprofessional, and interagency competition was fostered.[71]

The specific complaints about the intergovernmental system, from a human services delivery perspective, included:

• The lack of a "one-stop shop" or single point of access at the community level.

• The inability of undimensional programs to respond to clients having multiple needs, such as income maintenance, health care, employment counseling, and job training. An inner-city family might have one or more at-risk children needing drug abuse counseling and preschool social services, while the parents need food stamps, income support, and rent assistance, and an elderly grandparent needs medical services. The typical welfare agency or school could not deal with all of these needs.

- The persistence of gaps in service coverage, such as between the completion of federally sponsored job training programs and commencing of employment.

From a client's standpoint, linking needs with available funds was much like finding one's way through a maze. Professor Robert Agranoff, an expert on service integration, has described the barriers clients confront:

Clients do not easily articulate all of their problems. Even if they are able to identify all their needs, client advocates face a host of barriers in developing access to needed services: incompatible federal and/or state eligibility standards or other rules, funding limitations, professional dislike of working with certain clients, restrictive agency operating policies, and lack of available services. The agencies present barriers because they are usually at separate locations posing distance problems, have different intake procedures, and often choose to protect their resources by refusing to coordinate with other agencies. To compound these problems, agencies are funded by programs that generate these barriers because public policy is addressed to meet single (or related) problems that somehow have to be meshed when the service and client converge. Thus, the task in developing means to meet multiple needs is one of the most difficult challenges for those who work in the human services.[72]

In the view of critics of the grant-in-aid system of the 1970s, these barriers were largely due to the pervasive influence of what Daniel Patrick Moynihan, then President Nixon's domestic affairs adviser, called "paragovernments:" "the great number of ad hoc, quasi-governments spawned by the grant programs enacted in the 1960s, semi-public agencies that operate the local projects funded by the categoricals. Typically, these agencies are nonprofit and operate independently of general-purpose local government."[73] As former U.S Department of Health, Education, and Welfare (HEW) assistant secretary William A. Morrill characterized the system:

This system costs hundreds of billions of dollars in public and private expenditures. Despite these expenditures, in the United States little effort has been made to maintain a comprehensive human services delivery system that can meet the spectrum of individual and family needs. Instead, the penchant, at least through the mid 1970s, was to create new programs for each new social problem, an approach that only further fragmented the service systems.[74]

According to Lisbeth Schorr, bringing these programs together to serve clients in a comprehensive way "takes the combined talents of Mother Theresa, Machiavelli, and a C.P.A."[75]

The federal response to the fragmentation of education, health, employment, and social services has taken three forms. Beginning in the 1960s, some programs were established, among other purposes, to serve as the vehicles for coordinating the delivery of federally funded services at the community level. Chief among these were the Community Action Agencies, created pursuant to the Economic Opportunity Act of 1964, and the City Demonstration Agencies, organized in accordance with the Model Cities Program in 1966–67. In both cases the neighborhood-based bodies, whose policy boards were comprised of significant numbers of residents of the affected areas, were to marshal resources from a variety of federal, state, and local programs, coordinate their delivery, and ensure they were accurately targeted. In most cities, however, neither program attained these goals due largely to political distance between board members and local elected officials, the effects of competition and confrontation politics within the community agencies and between them and local office holders, and the administrative fragmentation of intergovernmental programs.[76]

The second response, beginning in 1966 with the enactment of the Partnership for Health Act and in 1968 with the enactment of the Omnibus Crime Control and Safe Streets Act, was the block grant. As noted earlier in this chapter, one of the aims of this instrument has been to enable recipients to tailor funds that are authorized for a broadly defined functional area to their particular needs and priorities. Yet, while 14 more block grants have been established since the 1960s, their fiscal magnitude is relatively small, accounting for only an estimated 14.5 percent of total federal grants in 1991. Moreover, in general, as block grants have matured, they have been "recategorized." Congressional authorizing committees have earmarked funds for particular purposes or established special program emphases. This "second-guessing" has been done in response to criticisms of the program priorities of state and local recipients, pressure from interest groups for statutory assurances that their concerns will be addressed, and worries about gaps in coverage.[77] For these reasons, block grants have not been effective vehicles of promoting service coordination or integration and reducing the fragmentation inherent in the categorical grant system.

A third approach has focused on the administration, rather than the structure, of federal programs. In response to the fragmentation of programs and clienteles, in the early 1970s the former Department of Health, Education, and Welfare (HEW) under the leadership of then secretary Elliot Richardson and Richard Darman, launched a "service integration" program, defined as follows:

Service integration refers primarily to ways of organizing the delivery of services to people at the local level. Service integration is not a new program to be superimposed ... rather, it is a process aimed at developing an integrated framework. Its objectives must include such things as (a) the coordinated delivery of services for the greatest benefit to people; (b) a holistic approach to the individual and the family unit; (c) the provision of a comprehensive range of services locally; and (d) the rational allocation of resources at the local level so as to be responsive to local needs.[78]

The main features of this initiative were a Service Integration Targets of Opportunity (SITO) Program—involving 45 research and demonstration projects funded between 1972 and 1975—and a Partnership Program—involving 84 projects funded between 1974 and 1977.[79] No new federal funding was made available; rather, research and demonstration monies from HEW constituent agencies—such as the Social and Rehabilitation Service—were redeployed. Generally, they sought to improve the planning and management capabilities of state, county, and city recipients, coordinate the core services available to clients at the local level, and encourage the establishment of comprehensive human resources programs and umbrella agencies to administer them.[80]

For the most part, these experiments were short-lived due to opposition from program administrators and clientele groups.[81] Another reason was the "top-down" approach: "Changes were dictated from the federal government to state and local governments and programs; the clients—individuals and families—had little choice or decision-making control."[82]

By the late 1970s, federal interest in, and support for, service integration projects had waned. While a strong case had been made for the need to link programs and services together to deal with multifaceted clientele problems in an effective and efficient manner, and a number of promising experiments had been conducted, the intergovernmental administrative system, or "vertical functional autocracies," had successfully resisted change. When the Reagan administration's New Federalism initiative was announced, interests in Washington shifted to decrementalism and decentralization. In the states and localities, elected and appointed officials focused attention on the impacts of federal grant-in-aid reductions and consolidation of categorical programs into block grants on their constituents. Even though federal funding for many programs was reduced or eliminated, fragmentation at the delivery level persisted.

Nevertheless, according to Agranoff, the principles of service integration were embodied in federal initiatives during the 1980s to target resources on particular problems or population groups. Chief among these were the Family Support Act of 1988, which sought to take people off welfare by providing education, training, and employment services through the Job Opportunities and Basic Skills (JOBS) program. Support services like child care and transportation were also provided to eligible welfare recipients to facilitate their progress toward self-sufficiency. A small-scale Services Integration Pilot Project program was created to handle management of cases where a multifaceted service approach was needed.[83] Another important congressional action was the 1988 Comprehensive Child Development Centers Act, which provided direct funding to support local efforts to establish or coordinate neighborhood child development program networks.

These developments kindled a renewed interest in service integration in the 1990s, albeit with somewhat different emphases. An additional factor was the influential 1988 book *Within Our Reach: Breaking the Cycle of Disadvantage*, by Lisbeth B. and Daniel Schorr, which concluded that the vicious cycle of poverty and disadvantage could be successfully broken through interventions that offer a broad spectrum of services on a flexible basis, consider children in the context of their families, demonstrate professional respect for clients, and are easy for clients to understand and use. The authors recommended that successful programs like Head Start and WIC be extended to all who are eligible, barriers to coordinated approaches be removed, and governments at all levels be willing to invest in first-class services for disadvantaged children.[84]

The revised version of service integration builds on the traditional emphasis on the development of holistic, comprehensive approaches to client educational, health, and social service needs and the overcoming of administrative, programmatic, and professional obstacles to successful outcomes. It includes the following components:

- A more person than place orientation, with client groups such as AIDS victims, the homeless, mentally ill, and long-term unemployed.[85]
- A more aggressive and intensive intervention than simply providing information and referrals, involving needs assessment and direct provision of services.[86]
- A two-pronged enabling strategy, ''not only to improve program outcomes (such as sustained employment and improved health), but also to increase family self-sufficiency through direct involvement of the family in the planning and evaluation of services.''[87]

As a practical matter, the management of integrated services involves three components:

First is the attempt to develop policies or strategies that will support integration at the services and program implementation levels. Second is the attempt to forge operating plans that position programs so that case-by-case service level integration is externally supported. Third is the development of local systems, with various service interfacing, at the level where the client potentially receives services.[88]

As was the case during the 1970s, the renewed federal interest in service integration has not been accompanied by an infusion of significant new funding. Instead, consistent with the previous discussion of sorting-out criteria, the federal role has largely involved promoting local and state experimentation, providing seed money for demonstration projects, supporting research, and facilitating the dissemination of information on innovations. The Bush administration's HHS initiative involved:[89]

- Establishment of a resource center within the department, funded at a level of $300,000, to provide information, advice, and technical assistance to state and local agencies that are interested in restructuring their program delivery system in order to accommodate integration of related services.
- Provision of financial support for the Family Academy Program sponsored by the Council of Governors' Policy Advisors, which is working on integration projects in 16 states.

- Awarding $600,000 in the summer of 1991 to support comprehensive school-based and public housing–based children's programs through urban and rural community consortia.

- Providing consulting assistance to local school systems and state education departments engaged in developing school health and early childhood health programs, which are partially financed by Medicaid, the Maternal and Child Health Services Block Grant, and federal categorical programs.

- Funding the Community Coalition Demonstration Program for Minority Males, totaling $3 million, which seeks to offer a range of community and school-based health, education, and social services to educationally, criminally, and otherwise at-risk minority males. These programs are closely tied to schools and emphasize developing positive attitudes toward work and independent living.

- Funding for the Healthy Start program, administered by the HHS Health Resources and Services Administration, which provides comprehensive maternal and infant care services, including family planning, home visitation, pregnancy testing, prenatal care, risk assessment, nutrition, and other assistance. Communities with very high infant mortality rates are targeted.

- Participation in the Service Integration Work group of the president's Empowerment Task Force, established in 1990, which, among other projects, is setting up a user-friendly, computer-based information system to facilitate officials' and families' gaining knowledge of, and access to, federal services, benefits, and programs. A major objective of the task force is to remove statutory, regulatory, and administrative barriers to innovative and integrative efforts at the state and local levels.

- Cosponsorship of the School Readiness Initiative demonstration program, in conjunction with the Department of Education and other federal agencies and private foundations, to help implement the fourth national goal agreed to at the Charlottesville education summit and later embodied in America 2000—that communities become places where learning can happen—by furnishing children integrated nutrition, preventive and environmental health, welfare, and other services vital to their successful preparation for, and participation in, school.

The department has also joined with private foundations to provide seed money for the National Center for Service Integration (NCSI), which is a joint collaborative venture among Mathtech, Inc., based in Princeton, New Jersey, and Falls Church, Virginia (which serves as the lead organization and chief technical assistance network contact); the Child and Family Policy Center in Des Moines, Iowa; the National Center for Children in Poverty at Columbia University's School of Public Health; the National Governors' Association and Policy Studies Associates, Inc., in Washington, D.C.; and the Bush Center on Child Development and Social Policy at Yale University. Established in late 1991, the basic purposes of NCSI are to stimulate and support service integration through serving as an information clearinghouse and a source of technical assistance and research.[90]

State and Local Responses

While the federal government has played a valuable leadership role over the years in encouraging service integration experiments through information, technical assistance, and seed money, responsibility for designing and implementing "cross-servicing" approaches has fallen on the shoulders of state and local officials. However, their capacity to do so has been conditioned by structural, professional, and programmatic constraints.

Structurally, a considerable amount of reorganization activity has taken place in states, counties, and cities in the past quarter-decade. Some of these efforts have been influenced by reorganizations at the national level. The federal departments of Transportation, Housing and Urban Development, Health and Human Services, and Energy, as well as the Environmental Protection Agency, have counterparts in many states. In the human services area, a 1986 survey by Keon Chi for the Council of State Governments found that over half of the states had established agencies that administered public assistance and social services in tandem with at least three of the following: health, mental health, mental retardation, adult corrections, youth institutions, vocational rehabilitation, and employment services.[91]

One of the most closely studied reorganizations has been Florida's 1975 merger of its human services programs into a comprehensive Department of Health and Rehabilitative Services (DHRS). Contrary to the "categorical imperatives" of federal grants-in-aid at that time, authority was taken from program specialists in federally defined "single state agency" units and decentralized to regional management generalists. Human services, however, did not include K–12 education. This departure from traditional ways of doing intergovernmental business generated controversy between federal HEW and state DHRS officials, which led to a court suit and subsequent decision supporting the federal program statutory and administrative requirements. In 1986 the National Academy of Public Administration (NAPA) released a report summarizing its previous assessments and reevaluating Florida's approach to service integration and gave it a mixed review. While the new structure was credited with facilitating the response to clients with multiple needs, and substantial progress was reported over a decade of experience, the centrifugal forces of separately authorized federal categorical grants and the program "blinders" of professional staff impeded accomplishment of the integration goal. Moreover, within DHRS, inconsistent and sometimes insufficient delegated authority to regional managers and problems with intake and case management were noted by the NAPA study.[92]

At the local level, a 1987 survey by Robert Agranoff for the International City/County Management Association found that half of the counties and one-fourth of the cities over 50,000 had set up an umbrella department for managing two or more human services programs. With respect to their common characteristics: "Most of these departments initially concentrated on making structural reorganization work, particularly through administrative support consolidation, such as in information systems, training, budgets, evaluation, and property management. Recently, departments have focused more efforts on selective program coordination."[93]

At the substate level, councils of governments have been involved in the planning, coordination, technical assistance, and certain aspects of service delivery. These efforts have been across local jurisdictions as well as between localities and state agencies. During their "heyday" in the seventies, regional councils were generally active in such work force—related programs as the Comprehensive Employment and Training and Social Services block grants and health planning programs. As a result of the Reagan administration's "decrementalism" efforts, the number, staffing, and budgets of regional councils were reduced, and their planning and coordination efforts were more jurisdictionally and programmatically focused. In the early 1990s, although there was considerable variation from state to state, the 529 regional councils were still involved in some aspects of social services planning and in coordinating and facilitating activities of Private Industry Councils Under the Job Training Partnership Act (the successor to the Comprehensive Employment and Training Act of 1973).[94] However, the integrative capabilities of most regional councils have not been significant.

Other Constraints. In Agranoff's judgment, many of the state umbrella agencies emphasize consolidation of budgeting, planning, coordination, and other staff functions. Policymaking by, and service delivery through, line units were carried out more in accordance with traditional categorical channels. Coordination in these matrix-managed organizations was sought through interagency task forces, interdisciplinary project teams, and special issue or function cabinets or subcabinets.[95]

In addition to the structural, professional, and programmatic barriers, efforts to better coordinate and integrate services have also encountered political obstacles. At the state level, for example, the policy direction of education, social welfare, and human services agencies, among others, has historically been provided by boards or commissions that are independent from the governor. Agency heads are appointed by, and accountable to, these bodies. While reforms since 1965 aimed at reducing the "long ballot" of separately elected state officials, merging agencies into larger departments, curbing the independence of certain agency heads, and strengthening the chief executive's formal authority as chief administrator have streamlined the executive branch, fragmentation of structure and authority persists in some states.[96] By the early 1990s, 15 states still had publicly elected education secretaries, and 19 states had a board or commission that appointed the agency head.[97]

At the local level, schools have often been the focal points for integrative initiatives. As at the state level, where the historic desires to check gubernatorial authority reinforced fragmentation of contemporary administrative authority and accountability, in many cities and countries the desire to keep schools insulated from the corrosive effects of partisan politics and patronage created fragmentation of services. As Michael Usdan, president of the Institute for Educational Leadership, put it in 1991:

The result of our century-long effort to keep the abuses of patronage politics out of schools has been to recreate them as public entities totally separated from general-purpose government, social service and health agencies, and the juvenile justice system. Moreover, school board elections are separated from general elections, with an amplification of the apathy expressed by low voter participation in political institutions. The separation is now dysfunctional. If 40 percent of children under six are growing up in poverty and need a set of comprehensive and integrated services, the disjointed and fragmented services now being offered them—without coordinated and systematic case management—must be re-evaluated. General government, including mayors and city councils, must become as aggressive in educational issues as the governors during the past five to eight years. The issues, of course extend beyond education to include poverty. The earlier we intervene in the poverty and school-preparedness lifecycle—prenatal would be ideal—the better off we will be as a society, and the greater return we will derive from our "investment," to couch the issue in crass economic terms, rather than terms of morality, equity and equalization.[98]

Success Stories. Despite these impediments, service integration success stories can be found. At the state level, service integration has received bipartisan support. Governors have used their leadership to push for integrating health, mental health, and social services in public schools. In January 1991, for example, California governor Pete Wilson (R) signed an executive order creating the cabinet-level position of secretary of Child Development and Education. In May 1991, Florida governor Lawton Chiles (D) stated, "I look forward to the time when we keep schools open to 10 o'clock every night, have them going 12 months a year, make them a place where poor families can pick up Food Stamps and their food from the WIC program and their AFDC checks, and where they can sign up for job training."[99]

Among the most notable innovations are the following:

- Kentucky's Education Reform Act of 1989 mandated the establishment of Family Resource and Youth Service Centers in or near all schools where 20 percent or more of the children were eligible for free or reduced-cost lunches. The types of services provided are substance abuse prevention, child care, health and education for expectant parents, parenting skills, referrals to social services, employment counseling and placement, and summer and part-time job development. Some $9.5 million was appropriated to create 134 centers serving 232 schools in 1991–92; by 1995 full implementation is anticipated, with possibly 1,200 schools establishing centers. State funding levels will reach $16 million by 1992–93 and $26 million by 1993–94. Grants ranged from $10,000 to $90,000 per school.[100] This program built on a 1988 joint effort between the State Department of Education and the Governor's Human Resources Cabinet to help coordinate local social service delivery at school sites, called the Kentucky Integrated Delivery System (KIDS).[101]

- New Jersey has a similar program, School Based Youth Services, which provides a variety of services to 13- to 19-year-old youth, including employment and training, health care, and counseling. In 1990, 18,000 students were involved in after-school or recreational activities that were the locus for these services, as well as related programs intended to reduce student conflict and intergroup tensions, encourage attendance, and deal with abused or homeless children.[102]

- Tennessee has established a program in which school districts can receive up to $50,000 to create family resource centers, which coordinate the delivery of state and local services. State funding may be used for such purposes as assistance to pregnant teen-agers, learning centers in urban housing projects, programs for parents of preschool at-risk children, and parent involvement in elementary schools. Tennessee also has adopted a statewide Children's Plan, targeted to those in state custody, or at risk of being so, under which the Department of Finance and Administration handles cross-services coordination of managed care, which includes home-based family preservation services. Tennessee also has a commission on Children and Youth, which acts as an advocate and information resource.[103]

- In Virginia, the General Assembly created a Council on Coordinating Prevention in 1987, composed of 12 state agencies and 5 private citizen representatives, to provide information, monitor legislation, and assist communities related to implementation of the *1992–2000 Comprehensive Prevention Plan for Virginia*. Three years later an Interagency Council on Community Services for Youth and Families was created, composed of 145 public and private leaders, parents, and service providers, to rec-ommend ways to coordinate the delivery of services to at-risk children and youth and their families. In 1993 a Comprehensive Services Act for At-Risk Youth and Families went into effect. The act decentralized greater responsibility for assessing needs and developing responses to the local level. It consolidated nine separate programs targeted on at-risk youth and their families that were previously administered by four agencies. Under the consolidated arrangement a team of representatives from all relevant agencies consults with families about the problems confronting their child and then decides on appropriate remedial actions. Architects of the plan hope both to render more compre-hensive and cost-effective services and to slow the rate of growth of public spending on the at-risk population.[104]

- In West Virginia, in 1990 the legislature authorized the Governor's Cabinet on Children and Youth Families to develop comprehensive services to children and families through community-based Family Resource Networks, a toll-free service available for parents and children to obtain information and referrals. These networks are funded by six federal and state programs. The cabinet also administers a Children's Fund, which supports child abuse prevention through contributions and a National Center on Child Abuse and Neglect challenge grant. Also, the West Virginia School Health Committee has developed an eight-component school health program that is being carried out in four counties.[105]

- The Caring Communities Program in St. Louis has provided support to the Walbridge Elementary School since 1989. A joint venture involving the state departments of education, mental health, and health and social services, the school district, and the Danforth Foundation, the program provides screening, case management, and referrals to keep children in functional home environments and out of the juvenile justice system.[106]

- In Maryland, school districts have joined forces with the federal-state Job Training Partnership Act to establish the Tomorrow Program, which seeks to reduce dropouts and increase the number of high school students who go on to postsecondary education, through early identification of potentially at-risk students (usually in the eighth grade) and provision of a range of services. Each school district must offer skill and personal development and transition assistance and encourage parental and business involvement.[107] Another Maryland integrated services experiment, based in Baltimore, has concerned establishing family development centers to help AFDC mothers and homeless families find work; combining school and neighborhood efforts to prevent drug abuse; providing child care and remedial education at public housing sites; and encouraging homeless persons to participate in educational job training.[108]

- The Massachusetts Employment and Training ("ET" CHOICES) Program, set up in the early 1980s, is one of the nationally better-known integration efforts, due to the 1988 presidential campaign. "ET" CHOICES has as its core a voluntary Family Independence Plan, worked out by client and caseworker, which draws on a wide range of services. It is predicated on the assumption that welfare recipients will prefer employment to welfare if support services like education, transportation, day care, and job placement are provided. In his 1991 book, *Leadership Counts*, Professor Robert D. Behn concluded, with some qualifications, that the program managers at the Massachusetts Department of Welfare "solved the coordination, motivation, technical, budgetary, overhead-agency, and political problems required to make ET CHOICES work."[109]

- In New Jersey, the School-Based Youth Services Program provides funding for 20 "one-stop shops," which coordinate education and human services programs on a year-round basis, after regular school hours, and on weekends. Local agencies have considerable flexibility in designing programs, which are available to all students, not just those at risk. In addition to the usual range of employment counseling, health services, child care, family planning, and other needs are addressed. The budget for the program is $6 million in state funds; 10,000 students were served in its first year.[110]

- Minnesota governor Arne Carlson has proposed merger of the departments of Education and Higher Education Coordinating Board into a Department of Children and Education Services, to provide childrens' programs from birth through higher education.[111]

- California's 1991 Healthy Start Support Services for Children Act established a statewide school-based health and social services program targeted to schools in which half or more of the enrolled students come from welfare families, have limited English-speaking capabilities, or qualify for free or reduced-cost meals. By June 1992, 110 schools had received planning grants and another 40 had been awarded operational grants. The legislature appropriated $20 million for the first year and $13 million for the second; community service organizations and foundations are expected to provide financial and other assistance. The heads of seven major state agencies are involved in program planning, coordination, and implementation. A Foundation Consortium for School-Linked Services works with state agencies to ensure that the school-based programs have adequate technical support.[112]

To summarize, the rich diversity of service integration experiments is beginning to yield useful data about the requisites for program success. For school-site based efforts, the Center for the Future of Children has concluded that the following criteria are among the essential components:

1. For school-linked efforts to be effective, the participating agencies will have to change how they deliver services to children and families and how they work with each other.
2. Planning and implementation should not be dominated by any one institution—schools or health or social services agencies.
3. Services should be comprehensive and tailored to the needs of individual children and their families.
4. Each agency participating . . . should redirect some of its current funding to support the new collaboration.
5. Service efforts should involve and support parents and the family as a whole.
6. Service efforts should collect data about what is attempted and achieved and at what cost.
7. Service efforts should be able to respond to the diversity of children and families.[113]

Overcoming Barriers. It is one thing to posit the conditions under which integration of health, education, and social services can succeed. It is another strategically to overcome the intergovernmental and interagency barriers identified earlier to achieve holistic goals on a long-term basis. In Agranoff's view, the track record is not inspiring:

Experience suggests that efforts that have merely created a set of services linkages without strategic and policy support have resulted in each problem and community effort being created *de novo*. Working at the operational level exclusively has meant there is no top support (authority to coordinate) nor service follow-through. Those efforts that have started at the "top," so to speak, without addressing service delivery or program commitments, find SI [service integration] to be hollow, or nothing but paper agreements. For example, many states have moved their "lines and boxes" into units that were more proximate, and then hoped that integration would somehow "fall into place." More must be done.[114]

To deal with these limitations, Agranoff has called for a new "transorganizational paradigm" that moves beyond the rhetoric of coordination and cooperation. Traditional organizational structures would not necessarily be disrupted or destroyed. Instead, the paradigm would broaden the public administrator's responsibilities by involving "interdependent (interunit/interorganization) efforts to forge directions by joint decisionmaking, engaging in goal-directed planning and programming, and in developing operating agreements executed by the mutual actions of disparate parties."[115]

An example of efforts to overcome the barriers to effective remedial action is the Education and Human Consortium, a "loose-knit coalition" of 22 national organizations. The membership is diverse—including groups representing state and local elected officials, educators, health and social welfare officials, women's and children's interests, and the business community—but united in its concerns about the need to connect families and children with a comprehensive range of services through interagency partnerships. To the consortium, comprehensive service delivery has five components:

• Easy access to a wide array of prevention, treatment, and support services.
• Techniques to ensure that appropriate services are received and adjusted to meet the changing needs of children and families.
• A focus on the whole family.
• Agency efforts to empower families within an atmosphere of mutual respect.
• An emphasis on improved outcomes for children and families.[116]

   To encourage collaborative efforts, the consortium has developed guidelines for agencies to use to evaluate their readiness for change, based on successful experiences across the country with school- and community-based service delivery. It also publishes case studies of these efforts and provides information on contacts. The consortium has been funded by the W. T. Grant Foundation Commission on Work, Family and Citizenship and is based at the Institute for Educational Leadership in Washington, D.C.
   A more specific illustration of the steps that policymakers could take to bring about greater collaboration through mandated, rather than voluntary, actions has been offered by Elizabeth C. Reveal, former budget director of the District of Columbia. In a paper prepared in 1991 for "The Children's Initiative," launched by the Center for Assessment and Policy Development, Dr. Reveal identified the following governance options as offering promise of overcoming legal, fiscal, and other constraints on public sector interventions to reorganize and realign service delivery to children.

Mandated/Legislated Collaboration between Existing Independent Agencies

1. Interstate juvenile justice compacts.
2. Legislatively created "superagencies" or "supersecretaries," with line authority over previously independent agencies.
3. Legal requirements for information system consistency or case tracking.
4. Legislated standards for intake eligibility or minimum treatment standards across departments.
5. Budgetary consolidation or transfer or functions.

Mandated/Legislated Collaboration Through New Parallel or Supplementary Agencies

1. Legislative creation of Office for Children and Families.
2. Legislatively mandated central intake or case management systems.
3. Legislative establishment of co-located, school-based family service centers.
4. Creation of central data processing or management information systems by statute.

Mandated Administrative or Programmatic Integration: New Parallel or Supplemental Systems

1. Statutory creation of a central case management and tracking agency to provide single point of contact for all families and children.

2. Statutory or regulatory broad-banding of line worker job descriptions and/or mandatory rotation among and between public agencies. . . .

3. Statutory expansion of mandatory preschool from kindergarten to nursery school.

4. Requirements for universal screening and immunization.

Mandated/Legislated Administrative or Programmatic Integration: Replacing Existing Systems

1. Statutory creation of "superagencies" . . . merging health, human services, and mental health into a new public agency.

2. Shifting service delivery and oversight responsibility from one level of government to another and combining it with new functions. . . .

3. Eliminating independent boards of education and merging them into new consolidated executive branch departments.

In contrast with voluntary approaches, these mandatory strategies have the potential advantages of a longer life span, more fundamental and effective reforms, fewer bureaucratic turf battles, reduced administrative costs, and greater operational efficiency. At the same time, their very strengths may be considered weaknesses since they are more threatening to traditional administrative boundaries, structures, and procedures. In fact, the organizational and personnel costs of disrupting the bureaucratic and program status quo by mandated collaboration and consolidation efforts may outweigh the gains, at least in the short run.[117]

Nevertheless, this review of the history of services integration suggests the need to approach the educational, health, employment, and social service needs of children and youth in a less fragmented and piecemeal manner—with the objective of serving people, not funding streams or agency turf. Designing and implementing the new paradigms, however, will clearly take patience and persistence.

PUBLIC-PRIVATE PARTNERSHIPS

The previous chapters of this book have documented the frustrations and failures that have often accompanied efforts to prepare the nation's current and future work force through educational and health care reform. A number of experiments, innovations, and other success stories have also been reported.

Much of the blame for poor results or unintended consequences has fallen on federal, state, and local authorities. Yet, public accountability in only part of the picture. The responsibility for developing an educated, skilled, healthy, and motivated work force—and society—that can compete in a global economy also rests with the family and the individual. In this sense, the ability of governmental intervention alone to achieve employability and productivity goals is limited. While sorting-out and integrating public services are useful steps, they do not go far enough or deep enough.

Increasingly, it is recognized that the private sector—especially corporations, small businesses, and foundations—is a key stakeholder in the reform movement. The rationale for business involvement is evident in the following statements by executives in large and small companies:

- From David T. Kearns, former chairman and chief executive officer of the Xerox Corporation and undersecretary of Education in the Bush administration:

  The American workforce is running out of qualified people. If current demographic and economic trends continue, American business will have to hire a million new workers a year who can't read, write, or count. Teaching them how—and absorbing the lost productivity while they're learning—will cost industry $25 billion a year for as long as it takes. And nobody I know can say how long that will be. Teaching new workers basic skills is doing the schools' product-recall work for them. And frankly, I resent it.[118]

- From Paul O'Neill, chairman of Alcoa: "It makes me angry to go to business meetings and find that my colleagues don't know about the President's education goals. And it makes me very angry to find that we're spending 95% of our time bashing each other about the things we disagree on and maybe 5% working on the things we agree on."[119]

- From Ian Rolland, chief executive officer of the Lincoln National Insurance Company: "We really have not done a very good job of telling the educational community what we expect—maybe because we're not sure."[120]

- From Louis Gerstner, Jr., chairman of RJR Nabisco: "We have reached this point of dismal academic performance because we as a country stopped demanding excellence. If we accept second rate, we will become second rate. We must demand the best, because you never get more than you demand. . . . For business, for all of us, this is not a matter of philanthropy. This is a matter of preserving our democracy and our standing in the world."[121]

- From William S. Woodside, chairman of Sky Chefs, Inc.: "Nothing business hopes to achieve in the areas of school reform and building a better-skilled work force will happen unless it starts paying attention to early childhood development."[122]

- From entrepreneur Chris Whittle: "We are all seriously kidding ourselves if we believe that business-led charity is the answer to the current crisis. It costs $250 million per hour to run American K–12 education. That means all the money business currently spends annually on philanthropy could run our schools for about 90 minutes."[123]

From these statements, it is clear that many of the business concerns about the inadequate quality of the nation's work force have focused on the public education system. However, organizations representing business interests—such as the Committee for Economic Development and the Business Roundtable— have called for a broad definition of "education system" to include a lifelong process of learning, personal development, and skill development. This "single system" ranges from prenatal and infant care, to early childhood development, to K–12 education, to entry-level work force training, to higher education, to continuous work force training, to adult learning. It also includes related health care and social services.[124] This next section reviews the types of actions taken by the private sector, in partnership with educators and other government officials, to serve as change agents and participants in a reformed education system.

Business-Education Partnerships: Support and Skepticism

In its 1984 report, *High School*, the Carnegie Foundation for the Advancement of Teaching concluded that business–public school partnerships had been helpful in making improvements and identified four lessons from experience: (1) business should enrich, but not control programs; (2) realistic goals should be established for collaborative efforts; (3) a clear division of responsibility should be established, drawing on the strengths of each partner, and (4) cooperation should be rooted in mutual respect.[125]

Seven years later, according to the 1991 annual poll of the chief executive officers of the *Fortune* Industrial 500 and Service 500 companies, "Corporate America's commitment to reading, writing and arithmetic . . . was bigger, broader, and better than ever."[126] Perhaps this should come as no surprise, as a 1991 survey by the Committee for Economic Development found that 12 percent of the employers believed high school graduates had good writing skills, and 22 percent felt they had a good mastery of mathematics.[127] Table 7.1 shows how the 1992 responses from 342 companies compared with the 1991 and 1990 replies from 301 and 305 companies, respectively.

Among the highlights of these surveys are the findings that (1) 84 percent of the companies reported that their top management was "very" or "fairly" involved in educational reform, compared with 70 percent in 1990; (2) the percentage of respondents who indicated they felt corporate involvement had not had any or much impact on school reform decreased from 55 percent to 35 percent, while at the same time, only 11 percent believed it had made a big difference; and (3) the greatest percentage increases in corporate contributions were to elementary schools, preschool programs, and junior high schools. The extent of change in the above survey results from year to year was less significant between 1991–92 than between 1990–91.

Fortune's analysis of the responses from individual companies revealed growing recognition that the sooner children's educational and related needs are addressed, the brighter the prospects for success. Hence, the increase in business support for early education. With respect to financial contributions, companies reporting donating $1 million or more to public schools rose from 18 percent in 1990 to 24 percent in 1991 to 28 percent in 1992, while those giving less than $100,000 declined from 41 percent to 29 percent over this period. The median 1992 contribution was $355,000, compared with $344,000 in 1991 and $173,000 in 1990.[128] The national leaders were IBM and Exxon, each of which contributed $24 million, followed by Ford Motor Company ($22 million) and General Electric ($17 million).[129]

Table 7.1
How Business Helps the Schools: Results of *Fortune*'s Annual Education Poll, 1990–92

HOW INVOLVED IS TOP MANAGEMENT?	1992	1991	1990
Very Involved	45%	41%	32%
Fairly Involved	39%	42%	38%
Not too Involved	14%	14%	25%
Not at all Involved	3%	3%	5%

HAS CORPORATE INVOLVEMENT MADE ANY DIFFERENCE?	1992	1991	1990
Big Difference	11%	10%	6%
Fair amount of Difference	50%	46%	33%
Not much Difference	34%	37%	48%
No Difference	1%	2%	7%
No answer	5%	5%	6%

WHERE CORPORATE CONTRIBUTIONS GO? *	1992	1991	1990
Preschool	36%	31%	14%
Elementary School	65%	64%	27%
Junior High School	56%	58%	32%
High School	75%	78%	58%
Vocational School	45%	45%	38%
College	87%	87%	81%
Graduate School	55%	62%	52%

* Figures do not add to 100%, as companies were allowed to choose more than one answer.

Source: Keehn, J. "How Business Helps the Schools," *Fortune*, October 21, 1991, p. 161; and Ramsey, N., "How Business Can Help the Schools," *Fortune*, November 16, 1992, p. 147.

Not all observers of the business-education partnership have been as sanguine. Some critics, for example, have argued that corporate executives have used the failures of the public schools as a smoke screen to cover their own poor management decisions and "escape any real economic policies that might disrupt business as usual."[130] As Stanford University economist Henry Levin has asserted: "The easiest way to take the pressure off of themselves for producing a lousy product with too many middle managers, too high executive salaries and too little creativity is to say, 'How can we do it? We have a lousy work force.' "[131]

Despite complaints about the costs of having to provide remedial education to their employees and meet needs for "upskilling" of their work force, the corporate commitment to productivity improvement through these means does not run very deep. A September 1991 survey of 402 companies by Louis Harris and Associates found that only 14 percent had a job training program that included reading, writing, and mathematics basics. Two-thirds said they had made no major changes to accommodate the growing demands of technology upon the work force, and three-quarters had not made major changes to adapt to the lower caliber of recent graduates.[132] According to the American Society for Training and Development (ASTD), by 1993 American companies were spending a total of only $30 billion annually on training, most of which is accounted for by fewer than 10 percent of the companies.[133] Moreover, about two-thirds of those receiving training were college graduates and executives, rather than high school graduates working in lower-skill positions. ASTD estimates that just 1 in 14 workers has received any employer-provided training.[134] According to U.S. secretary of labor Robert Reich, "Training . . . is typically provided to those who need it least."[135] As a result, the salary and benefits gaps between college- and noncollege-educated workers will continue to grow, exacerbating the "two-tier" work force in the United States.[136]

A 1989–90 survey by the Virginia Occupational Information System (VOIS) of the University of Virginia's Center for Public Service sheds more light on these general findings. The 249 employer respondents from private and public firms (one-third employed fewer than 25 employees, one-third had 50–249 employees, and one-third had 250 or more employees) were "not particularly concerned about the skills and educational level of their employees."[137] Only 21 percent were dissatisfied with the educational preparation of their employees. While they supported training, the commitment was to providing employees with skills directly related to their job, which probably could not have been acquired elsewhere. There was little interest in training to promote cultural and ethnic diversity, to facilitate worker empowerment or participatory management, to establish quality programs, or to improve the competitive position of Virginia's work force. Rather, the employer's orientation was to the short-term "bottom line" to "enhance skills, morale, and promotability—and to help recruitment. These benefits in turn enhance efficiency, productivity, and profitability, all of which help to ensure the survival of their organization."[138]

The findings can be explained in at least four ways. First, the absence of strong employer dissatisfaction with the education preparation of their own employees reflected that they had a sizable pool of prospective qualified workers to draw from. Those who were not hired, due to educational or skill deficiencies, were another matter. Second, many employers—especially smaller companies— are reluctant to invest in training for their employees because they fear that the upskilled workers will be lured away by higher wages offered by other firms. In this sense, employer-provided training can be a "lose-lose" investment resulting in a loss of newly trained workers or in a loss of profits attributable to meeting their demands for salary increases as a condition of remaining with the firm. Third, employers remain skeptical of the long-term success of government-sponsored programs to train disadvantaged workers. Fourth, the VOIS study confirmed the national finding by the Commission on the Skills of the American Workforce that "the reason we have no skills shortage is that we are using a turn-of-the-century work organization" in many companies, modeled after Henry Ford's system based on large numbers of limited or unskilled workers, mass production, breaking complex jobs into relatively simple tasks, and relying on management to make decisions and labor to execute them. In this traditional context, the challenges of computer technology and robotics were largely irrelevant to many Virginia employers.[139]

Many Japanese companies spend as much as 6 percent of payroll on training their employees. Some 100 to 200 American firms like Xerox, IBM, Hewlett-Packard, Aetna, and Motorola spent 2 percent or more, but most spend considerably less.[140] In response to inadequate corporate investments in this area, during the 1992 presidential campaign Governor Clinton proposed that all companies with 100 or more workers be required to spend 1.5 percent of their revenues for training. Those who fail to do so should contribute an equivalent amount to regional training centers, which would provide such services. The ASTD estimates that compliance would cost companies $21 billion a year and might produce short-run negative effects on hiring and wages. The long-term (3 to 5 years) impact of wage hikes and productivity gains resulting would be positive, however, creating $63 billion in new economic activity and 2.5 million new jobs.[141] In view of negative reactions from corporate leaders, the Clinton administration made the 1.5 percent figure a goal rather than a mandate.

The public sector's commitment to training also has been questioned. Too often, training programs are among the initial candidates for cutback during lean financial periods, and both the quantity and quality of course offerings vary widely. In its first report, *Hard Truths/Tough Choices*, the National Commission on the State and Local Public Service expressed the belief "that states and localities should aim for a stable learning budget set at at least *three percent of total personnel costs.*" Investment of these learning dollars in upgrading the skills of employees would enable them to build 5 types of competencies identified by the commission as "essential for performance": team-building, communication, involvement of employees, cultural awareness, and quality.[142]

A third source of skepticism of the business commitment to education reform comes from economists, who are concerned about corporate property taxes. Labor secretary Robert Reich, for instance, in his 1991 book, *The Work of Nations*, criticized companies for decreasing their contributions to education and for lobbying local governments for abatements and other incentives for relocating to the locality or remaining in it. (In addition to tax abatements, these incentives commonly include free or low-cost infrastructure, building and land for the facility, and tailored employee training programs provided largely at government expense.) In contrast with the results of the *Fortune* magazine survey, Reich's figures indicate that following annual giving increases averaging 15 percent during the 1970s, the growth rates slowed dramatically in the 1980s, for example, to 5.1 percent between 1986 and 1987 and 2.4 percent between 1987 and 1988.[143] Most of these monies went to colleges and universities, often those of which corporate executives were alumni. By 1989, merely 1.5 percent of corporate contributions went to K–12 schools.[144]

With respect to tax breaks, Reich points out that the corporate share of local property tax revenue has declined from 45 percent in 1957 to about 16 percent 30 years later. The property tax is not only the mainstay of local finance but the largest source of public school budgets. Tax breaks, while beneficial to companies, have detrimental effects on the education system; a *New York Times* article on General Motors negotiations with officials of Tarrytown, New York, reported that abatements and other tax concessions reduced revenues by $2.81 million in 1990, resulting in the firing of teachers.[145]

Despite these concerns, business-education partnerships are on the upswing. According to the Committee for Economic Development, in 1992 30,000 elementary and secondary schools had established 140,000 partnership arrangements with business. While these figures suggest considerable activity, the extent and impact of these arrangements are unclear. Nor is systematic attention given to diffusion of information about innovative and successful partnerships. As Harold Stevenson, coauthor of *The Learning Gap*, has observed, "We have all these thousands of points of light—but no illumination."[146]

These partnerships have been encouraged by groups representing business interests. The Business Roundtable, an association of chief executive officers of the nation's largest corporations, has developed the following checklist to guide business involvement in state education reform efforts:

1. Approach education reform in the broad context of human resource, workforce, and economic development.

2. Comprehend the state role, including responsibility for education and related areas and the state-local relationship, and place it in the context of national goals.

3. Mobilize business potential by building both internal capacity within the firm, and external capacity through business associations.

4. Take careful account of reform efforts already undertaken, their results, and their current status.

5. Develop a realistic vision of the new education system, and the strategic changes required to achieve it.

6. Consider each of the ten channels for business involvement, and set priorities accordingly.

7. Distinguish between business's role as a change-agent to help achieve the new education system, and the role that business will play in that new system.

8. Concentrate on the key, high-leverage opportunities for systems reform.

9. Prepare realistically for the magnitude and duration of commitment to reform in keeping with The Business Roundtable ten year campaign to support state education reform.[147]

The Roundtable has published a nine-point school restructuring agenda for its members and other business organizations to use in lobbying state legislatures.

1. Assumptions: All students can learn at high levels; we know how to teach them; curriculums must be demanding but flexible; every child needs an advocate.
2. There should be accountability based on outcomes.
3. There should be diverse methods of assessment.
4. Schools should be rewarded for success, helped to improve and penalized for failure.
5. Shared decision making between schools and the central office, as well as between teachers and administrators, should be encouraged.
6. Staff training must be comprehensive.
7. Quality preschool programs are necessary.
8. Health and other social services should be used to reduce barriers to learning.
9. Imaginative use of technology as a learning tool should be developed.[148]

The Committee for Economic Development (CED) also has long advocated greater business involvement in schools. As indicated in previous chapters, since 1985 CED has released three major reports proposing recommendations for responding to the needs of educationally disadvantaged children, for a competitive work force, and for an equitable and effective public education system. It also published two reports in 1991 dealing with education and child development linkages. In CED's view: "The business community's experience with managing people is relevant to the problems of teacher quality and school effectiveness. We recommend that links be created between schools and businesses for the purpose of transferring this understanding."[149] The next section reviews the ways that business has been involved in partnerships with public schools.

Extent and Types of Business Involvement

Chapter 5 of this book described three major "waves" of education reform since the early 1980s—standards, schools, and students. Chapter 6 examined the surge of interest in the 1990s in parental choice, which some consider a fourth "wave." The extent and types of business involvement in partnership arrangements with public schools have been influenced by these waves.

Table 7.2, which has been adapted from a table appearing in CED's 1985 report *Investing in Our Children*, reveals the range of business involvement in public schools. The major additions since then have been in the "structural reform" column, particularly choice plans and privatization experiments and the call for higher standards and a core curriculum.

A more recent typology of business involvement in public schools appeared in a September 1992 *Business Week* cover story on "Saving Our Schools." The four stages of this relationship are:[150]

Table 7.2
Types of Private Sector Involvement in Public Education

Type of Involvement	Strategies		
	System Support	Structural Reform	Incremental Change
Funding	Donation of Equipment Public Relations Campaigns	Public Education Funds Teacher Recognition Programs Minigrants Programs	Support of Major Research Privatization of Schools
Program Involvement	Career Days Speaker's Programs	Adopt-A-School Programs Management Training Early Childhood Education Magnet School Development School-to-Work Programs	Choice Plans for Students and Teachers
Policy Involvement	Local School Board Participation	State-Mandated Core Curriculum State Education Task Forces	Major State Policy Initiatives CED Statement on National Policy

Source: Adapted from Committee for Economic Development, *Investing in Our Children: Business and the Public Schools* (Washington, D.C.: The Committee, 1985), p. 87.

- Adopt-a-school, the most popular program, which is under way in 40 percent of the elementary schools, where companies provide services, goods, or personnel. Good relationships rather than basic reforms often are the by-product.

- Project-driven, where business undertakes to improve one aspect of schools such as management training or student school-to-work experiences. While these approaches are helpful, they may become too dependent on outside funding.

- Reform-oriented, where companies work with educators to improve programs in a school district. These approaches are essential but may produce short-lived results or may be too limited by education administrators' desire for self-protection or to retain control.

- Policy change, where statewide reform is accomplished through legislative and gubernatorial lobbying. Macrolevel changes are often desirable, but results usually take more time, which may frustrate business leaders.

The Traditional Partnership: "Doing" Improvements

Over the years businesses formed a wide variety of partnerships with the schools to help make improvements in the educational system or in the student body—so-called "high tech" and "high touch," respectively. These approaches have generally been "win-win" situations for all concerned.

As indicated in Table 7.2, the donation of equipment is a common business contribution to schools. In the Baltimore, Maryland–Washington, D.C., metropolitan area, for example, the Giant and Safeway food chains have set up receipt collection programs under which family grocery receipts are collected by students and exchanged for computers and other equipment. There is evidence of richer neighborhoods' transferring receipts to school systems serving areas that spend less in these stores. Since September 1989, Giant has presented schools in these metropolitan areas with 45,000 free computers, television sets, videotape recorders, camcorders, musical instruments, microscopes, and physical education equipment.[151]

Other types of business involvement benefiting the schools include:

- Raising funds for school facility and equipment improvements, support of education bond issues, awards recognizing outstanding teachers and principals, and making grants for special classroom projects.

- Adopt-a-school programs, where business representatives apply their management and technical skills to deal with appropriate problems and to train school personnel.

- Supporting "public service academies"—involving government agencies, nonprofit organizations, and universities—focusing on encouraging students to pursue public service careers through exposing them to role models, enrolling students in college- or university-level government courses, offering work-study programs, working with guidance counselors to prepare students for college placements, and offering curriculum development workshops for teachers. One of the exemplary academies was established in 1989 at Anacostia Senior High School, a largely black school in Washington, D.C. In 1992, 32 tenth graders, 21 eleventh graders and 40 twelfth graders participated. In addition to public agency, university, and individual contributions, the $72,000 annual budget has been supported by American Express, among other corporations.[152]

- Serving on private industry councils established pursuant to the Jobs Training Partnership Act (JTPA) to help coordinate education and training programs targeted to low-income, low-achieving youth.

- Forming compacts or collaboratives between entire school districts and companies under which business provides financial, managerial, program, and political help. The Boston Compact, which was launched in 1982 under the auspices of the City's JTPA Private Industry Council, has involved the agreement on the part of over 350 private employers to give full-time jobs to high school graduates who have passing grades and a good attendance record, provided the schools also achieve certain goals like reduced dropout rates and higher student test scores. The results have been mixed.[153]

- Participating on local school boards, task forces and study commissions, and stay-in-school, antidrug, and similar campaigns.

- Providing funding to support implementation of school reform innovations. One of the leading contributors has been RJR Nabisco, Inc., which will donate a total of $30 million in three-year grants to 45 schools through out its Next Generation Schools project. Those reforms that seem especially amenable of transfer elsewhere will receive small ($100,000) replication grants. The project's motto is "Changing Education One School at a Time." In December 1993 publisher Walter H. Annenberg announced a $500 million multi-year donation to public schools, the largest such gift in history; 30 percent will go to the 9 largest public school systems.[154]

With respect to student-oriented programs, typical examples include:

- Sponsoring career days, speakers programs, and mentoring arrangements to help students identify positive role models, learn about the world of work, identify career choices, hone job-related skills, sharpen job search and interview techniques, and engage in other activities intended to facilitate the transition from school to work.

- Establishing youth apprenticeship programs aimed at students who do not plan to go to college to give them the opportunity while in high school to develop good work habits and marketable skills, learn first-hand about the workplace, and make personal contacts that could lead to after-school and full-time job opportunities.[155] In Maine, for example, Governor John McKernan supported expansion of apprenticeships, and companies like Blue Cross/Blue Shield, Parker Hannifin (auto parts), and UNUN (insurance) have responded. Beginning in the fall of 1992, 50 students entered pilot programs featuring 20 weeks of school followed by 30 weeks of training. Employers pay the apprentices minimum wage rates.[156]

- Funding college students to serve as tutors, especially of disadvantaged children,[157] and guaranteeing college scholarships to inner-city students who achieve scholarship goals or commit to a teaching career upon graduation.[158]

- Providing classroom space and equipment in company buildings in which public schooling as well as child care and social services are offered to those who otherwise might drop out, such as teenage mothers, and coupling a flexible and supportive learning environment with internships and counseling. The New Vistas program, a partnership between Honeywell, IBM, and the Minneapolis school system since September 1990, focuses on students who have completed ninth grade, live in low-income neighborhoods near Honeywell, and have children or are pregnant. The early results of this experiment have been encouraging in terms of mothers graduating, going on to college, obtaining employment, and staying off welfare.[159]

• Sending engineers, scientists, and other experts to schools to meet with gifted and high-achieving students to share with them information about the world of work, new technologies, and job opportunities.

• Supporting state and local workplace education programs to provide on-site training and adult education and literacy opportunities to workers.[160]

• Sponsoring Junior Achievement programs, one of the oldest partnerships, to acquaint high school students with business practices.

• Offering prizes and awards to students who demonstrate good study and health habits. In Des Moines, Iowa, for example, Principal Financial Group gives backpacks, watches, and a chance to win a bicycle to second and fifth grade students who read books, brush their teeth, play sports, attend all classes, and avoid video games. Parents monitor their children's progress.[161]

• Supporting early childhood development programs so that, consistent with the first national education goal, children enter school healthy and ready to learn. A noteworthy effort launched in Minneapolis–St. Paul in 1988 is "Success by 6." Major employers, including Honeywell, General Mills, Dayton Hudson, and American Express—working in conjunction with United Way, local governments, and nonprofit organizations—provide funding for prenatal care, immunization, nutrition, and childrearing skill development. A communications campaign informs the broader community of the importance of properly caring for children. Twenty-five other cities have launched similar programs with their corporate community.[162]

These and other partnership arrangements have undoubtedly been helpful to school systems and students cross the country. They exemplify what David Kearns calls "feel-good" relationships in which educators define the problem and set the agenda, business gets involved in a supportive and sustaining, rather than a critical or combative, way, and everybody comes away with "warm, fuzzy" feelings about having accomplished something worthwhile.[163]

The Rochester Partnership. An example of a business-education partnership that has evolved since the mid–1980s is in Rochester, New York, where Eastman Kodak Co., has become a major player in school reform. Beginning with employee volunteers helping students with mathematics and science, the program—called Kodak's 21st Century Learning Challenge—has 800 volunteers, six staff members, and a 10-year corporate commitment of $4.5 million. Other Kodak divisions are following suit. Kodak also has set up training institutes for mathematics and science teachers and early childhood education centers.

Building on this impressive, but traditional, partnership, Kodak has launched programs to help schools improve their management. Since the career path for principals and superintendents often is teaching rather than management, not surprisingly there is considerable room for improvement. Kodak has responded by supplying experts on total quality management to the schools.

A third step in the Rochester school reform effort was the creation of the

Rochester Business Education Alliance, comprised of 25 companies, including Xerox Corporation. In addition to providing further help to school management improvement through corporate strategic planners, the group has begun to lobby in the state capitol in behalf of state education policy reforms, as well as before the city council and Monroe County Board of Supervisors at budget time.

The fourth stage of the partnership's development has involved results, what Marc Tucker—head of the Rochester-based National Center on Education and the Economy—calls "school-leaving standards." Former Kodak CEO Kay Whitmore negotiated with school officials over the standards. High school graduates who attain them will receive hiring preference and higher salary.[164]

Shifting Emphasis. As the education reform movement entered its fourth wave—restructuring—some observers reported that these "feel-good" responses were not only insufficient but counterproductive. This "fuzzy altruism," in the judgment of Ted Kolderie, "is roughly the equivalent of doing your daughter's homework. It is a kindness, but a misdirected kindness. Business should help the schools. But not that way."[165] Osborne and Gaebler have noted: "Business leaders rarely focus on the incentives built into the education system. Instead they create 'partnerships' and sponsor projects."[166]

The previous approaches, "doing" improvement, had built much goodwill but had not resulted in lasting system improvements or significant student benefits. Moreover, business not only accepted the ineffective status quo but helped sustain it by not applying to the public education system the same fundamentals that would be drawn on in a business setting:

Stripped to its essentials, the situation is this: an old institution, long accustomed to stability, now faces growing outside competition, major changes in the nature of its customers, and a deepening internal crisis in the quality of its professional work force. Its managers' response has essentially been to point to outside changes beyond their control, to resist changing the nature of the operation, and to insist that problems could be resolved if only they could have loyal support and additional resources.

Faced with this situation most business executives would probably prescribe a hard challenge to the traditional ways of thinking, followed quickly by decisive action to change the basics of the operation. Very little of the present business involvement in public education, however, can be called either challenging or decisive. Rather, partnerships are the order of the day. Business has come in offering to help and wanting to be liked. So the problem gets framed by the people who run the schools. And business gets involved not with the central issues in education but with a classroom here, a school there, a district somewhere else.[167]

As a result of these concerns, beginning in the late 1980s business involvement in public education moved beyond the "system support" and "incremental change" categories. More and more attention was devoted to structural reform and the appropriate roles for business to play in system change. Chris Pipho called attention to this changing mood in a summary of the dialogue at a session on "Business Speaks to Education" at the August 1988 annual meeting of the Education Commission of the States:

The case that these leaders made for changing the education system makes the old "first wave" prescriptions for school reform, with their top-down mandates, look like a Sunday school picnic. In fact, if the scene painted by these business leaders were suddenly understood and accepted by all business leaders across the country, the separate waves of education reform would suddenly merge into one big tidal wave, and all of education would be in for some big changes.[168]

The New Partnership: Restructuring and Reform

The post–1980s business agenda for education reform has been ambitious. In their book *Winning the Brain Race*, Kearns and Doyle called for six fundamental changes in the ways schools "do business": (1) parental and student choice plans, which would break the public school's monopoly over students in their district and force them to compete with one another for "customers" in the public education marketplace; (2) establishment of year-round magnet schools to promote specialization in areas like science, mathematics, and the arts, as well as give students more instructional options and provide matching funds to districts that undertake experiments in teaching and school organization; (3) teacher choice plans, which would release them from being assigned to a specific school and enable teachers to market their services to any school in their district or region; (4) greater teacher professionalism achieved through hiring standards that emphasize substance over methodology, elimination of undergraduate degrees in education, and mandatory internships prior to entering the classroom; (5) state-mandated core curricula for all students, including foreign language, music, and geography at the elementary level, and no promotions to higher levels unless students demonstrate competency; and (6) more and better early childhood education, especially implementation of CED's 1987 recommendation in its *Children in Need* report calling for full funding of the Head Start and Chapter 1 programs.[169]

The type of partnerships envisioned by Kearns, Doyle, Kolderie, and others is much different from the "doing" improvement model. Business becomes a proactive, rather than reactive, player in school reform. Corporate representatives are visible rather than behind the scenes. They are advocates and critics rather than complacent supporters. The role of business becomes more of a change agent than check writer. In carrying out these new roles, business must have its own agenda for school reform and not be a captive of the "education establishment." According to Kearns: "Business will have to force the agenda for school reform, or business will have to set its own agenda. Force it or set it—either way—we've got to make it our agenda. There's good reason for that. The new agenda for school reform will be driven by market forces and accountability—unfamiliar ground for politicians and educators. That's an important distinction."[170]

A consequence of this new role will be conflict among business representatives, educators, and politicians. But, as Kolderie has stated: "Business has to decide whether it is serious or not. If the central issues are going to be raised and addressed, somebody is bound to be upset, and some conflict is inevitable. No pain, no gain."[171]

Reform Texas-Style. As indicated in Table 7.2, on the policy level, business can have important roles to play. One example given national publicity during the 1992 presidential campaign was Ross Perot's crusade for school reform legislation in Texas and greater state funding for K–12 education during the early 1980s.

In 1983 newly elected governor Mark White sought to keep a campaign promise to raise teacher salaries. Since the state's surplus had been eliminated by the recession, to pay for his 24 percent "emergency" pay hike, he proposed a plan to raise taxes on alcohol, cigarettes, gasoline, and video machines. The legislature was unsympathetic to both the salary increase and new taxes. As a compromise, Governor White called upon the legislature to approve a panel to study teacher salaries; the legislature responded by passing a concurrent resolution on the last day of the session establishing a Select Committee on Public Education (SCOPE) to conduct a broad study of issues and concerns in Texas education.[172] The panel was comprised of legislators and statewide officials, but no teachers were appointed. Governor White appointed Perot chairman. The SCOPE budget was $68,500; it is estimated that Perot spent $2 million on the study. A wide-ranging investigation was launched, which put the problems of Texas schools in the headlines, partly due to Perot's charges that they were "places dedicated to play," because of the amount of school resources and student time devoted to extracurricular activities (athletics, clubs, band and drill teams, pep squads). Teachers, administrators, the state board of education, and education schools were blasted, as were students. No one was immune from SCOPE's scathing criticism.

Perot crossed the state holding hearings and site inspections and meeting with the press, business leaders, and local politicians. His efforts "moved education from the sports page to the front page."

After more than a year of work, SCOPE issued a report with over 140 wide-ranging and controversial recommendations, including proposals to lengthen the school year by 10 days, keep schools open from 7:00 A.M. to 6:00 P.M., limit class sizes, eliminate extracurricular activities from the school day and establish a "no-pass, no-play" policy, put principals on one-year contracts, raise passing grades and promotion standards, establish teacher career ladders and tie increased salary to performance, give students standardized tests each year, and reorganize the state board of education.

Governor White called a special session to act on SCOPE's recommendations. Even though the reform package was strongly supported by statewide officials and the legislature's leadership, considerable maneuvering by state officials, the business community, and Perot was necessary to achieve passage and signature of the 226-page Education Opportunity Act of 1984 (BH 72) on July 13. Nearly all of the SCOPE proposals were approved.

Cincinnati's Efforts. A more recent example of business leadership occurred in Cincinnati in 1990, where troubled schools, a growing dropout population, and a bankrupt school district were greeted with parent dismay and voter disdain. At the request of the superintendent, a team of corporate leaders headed by Clement L. Buenger, chairman of Fifth Third Bancorp, conducted an evaluation and issued a report with reform recommendations, calling for major central office staff reductions and decentralization of decision making to nine minidistricts. An intense lobbying campaign was launched by Mr. Buenger and his colleagues. In November 1990, two months after release of the report, the voters approved a $9 million school reform tax. In 58 days, the Ohio legislature passed an emergency bill permitting the school district to refinance its debt.[173]

Other Examples. More typically, business representatives are appointed to commissions and task forces examining public education concerns. In this context as well, business has played a more aggressive, proactive role in "hastening history." For instance:

• In the 1980s, the Minnesota Business Partnership funded a study that recommended fundamental redesign of elementary and secondary education, including site management, choice, grade level reorganization, and diagnostic testing and measurement. Governor Rudy Perpich endorsed the recommendations and included them in his open-enrollment bill. Business leaders lobbied in support of its adoption, and the partnership continues to advocate components not adopted by the legislature.[174]

• Since the early 1990s, the Massachusetts Business Alliance for Education Reform has been advocating an educational reform plan that includes school-based management, public school choice, receiverships for failing schools, and elimination of teacher tenure. The alliance has worked with Governor William Weld to obtain support for reform; however, the governor has not endorsed the alliance's call for revising Proposition 2½ to allow local governments to raise more funds for schools.[175]

• In South Carolina, the corporate community lobbied hard for passage of education reform legislation in 1990. The textile industry was a particularly strong advocate and has established a permanent education improvement committee.[176]

These and other examples show how business is working within the system to initiate and influence change. Summarizing the general nature of the partnership in the early 1990s, *Governing* magazine reported:

Across the country, business leaders are reaching out to schools. And they are not just giving money or computers or school band uniforms anymore. They are investing their political influence. Business executives are walking the hallways of high schools these days, but they are also walking the hallways of state capitols—lobbying on behalf of structural change and more funding. At a time when state and local budgets are tight and the federal government is mired in debt, business is the one element of the education coalition that seems to have both the motivation and the resources to do something.[177]

Privatization

The general nature of the school reforms advocated by business since the late 1980s has mirrored the direction of corporate reorganization: decentralized structures, empowered employees, flexible working conditions, accountability for results, and competition. While business leaders often assert that they are partners in education reform for the long haul, in view of the discussion of deterrents in chapters 3 and 5, the potential for frustration is high. Not surprisingly, then, some have urged privatization as an alternative to working within the system and the expectation for incremental change.

For many years, of course, private nonprofit organizations have played important roles in health care, social services, and public education. Similarly, these bodies have been active in a variety of areas related to work force preparation and performance, including training and retraining, counseling, placements, child care, and other services.

An example of how business leaders can get involved in education and youth service activities is Cities in Schools (CIS), a national nonprofit program that focuses on preventing dropouts through providing school-based health and human services to at-risk children and their families. Public-private partnerships have been established in 400 schools located in 22 states and 127 communities, and over 36,700 students and their families have been served. Business leaders, local officials, educators, health and social welfare administrators, career counselors, and others work together under CIS auspices to bring comprehensive, coordinated services to the schools and to overcome the fragmentation and frustration often present in traditional delivery systems. Financially, the approach has proven quite cost-effective, with a $100,000–$150,000 annual investment—some of which may come from JTPA funding—leveraging as much as $750,000 in reassigned personnel and in-kind contributions (volunteer counselors and mentors, office space and equipment, and so on).[178]

Since the election of Ronald Reagan to the presidency, interest in "privatization" has surged. This term refers to both load-shedding by governments divesting themselves of servicing responsibilities, with the private non- and for-profit sectors assuming a delivery role, as well as public agencies contracting out to the private sector responsibility for service provision. In the latter case, policy control and regulatory and pricing authority are retained by the public entity.[179]

Chapter 6 reviewed recent developments on this front, including the Bush administration's ill-fated proposal for parental choice arrangements involving private schools. One area of growing business activity is the management of public schools under contract. An emerging leader in this area is Education Alternatives, Inc. (EAI) of Minneapolis, a corporation run by former school administrators. It was created in 1986 after Control Data Corporation sold EAI its research on curriculum and school operations that they had spent two years and $1 million developing. EAI has formed consortia with KPMG Peat Marwick for accounting services and with Johnson Controls for management and maintenance. EAI's first contracts were to build and operate a private 220-student school in Eagan, Minnesota, in 1987 and a school in Paradise Valley, Arizona, in 1988. In 1989 EAI contracted to run the existing 650-student South Pointe Elementary School in Dade County, Florida. The county and its teachers' union operate the school and provide much of the budget; EAI furnishes student teachers, teacher training, and computers for a $1.2 million fee. The instructional approach features individualized, self-directed learning to achieve goals established in a "personal education plan" developed between teachers and each parent. Teacher-student ratios are small, about half those in private schools, and there are no tests and few textbooks.

Results from Minnesota and Arizona have shown that students advanced a half grade higher than otherwise would have been expected. However, the company has not been profitable. Significant savings have not yet materialized from contracting out maintenance, transportation, and food services. In the long term, EAI expects higher revenues from management contracts, consulting fees, and sales of proprietary products.[180] In 1992, EAI contracted with the Duluth, Minnesota, school board to develop a budget, hire a permanent superintendent, and manage school closings.[181] In Baltimore, it has entered into a five-year agreement to manage as many as nine public schools; EAI receives $26.6 million from the school system, the average annual cost per student ($5,542), which it uses to operate the schools. In the first year EAI used its own funds for a $6.2 million lease-purchase of 1,106 computers and software, which are being used to implement new teaching techniques. The results of the initial year were mixed, and it is too early to evaluate the experiment. In December 1993 the superintendent of the 165-school District of Columbia public system proposed turning over 10 to 15 schools where students were performing poorly to EAI.[182]

A second example of partnerships are academies set up by companies to offer educational alternatives to at-risk students. These "academy projects" are usually offered as electives during school hours. Students also may participate in paid summer internships. Sears, Roebuck and Co., Burger King Corporation, and Rick's Department Store (a part of Campeau), among others, have opened schools, often on their premises. American Express has sponsored academies on finance, travel, and tourism. The local public schools supply teachers, counselors, and social service professionals, and the company employees serve as tutors and mentors and assist in curriculum development.[183] In the judgment of Osborne and Gaebler, "These students were failing in the standard system, but having chosen a school that made real-world sense to them, they took it very seriously." Ninety percent of the first American Express Academy of Finance graduates went on to college.[184]

A third example of business involvement is vouchers. In the absence of congressional and state legislative approval of parental choice, some firms are giving low-income students vouchers to enable them to attend private schools. In Indianapolis, the business-funded Golden Rule program has given 900 such students vouchers worth up to $800; 71 private and parochial schools participate.

Subsequently, the school board approved a choice plan limited to public schools since, among other factors, the loss of 400 students to private schools proved to be a costly state aid reduction. Eli Lilly and Co. pledged $1.2 million to support Golden Rule. One motivation for this program was expressed by J. Patrick Rooney, chairman of Golden Rule: "I just don't think our inner-city schools are fixable."[185] By business's funding such vouchers, constitutional issues that have arisen in other states that have attempted to pass choice plans including private schools have been avoided.[186]

A fourth example is the plan by Channel One founder and entrepreneur Christopher Whittle to establish a chain of for-profit schools across the country. Whittle's "Edison Project" (named for inventor Thomas Edison), proposed in 1992, would entail opening 100 schools in 1996, followed by 1,000. Tuition would be $5,500 annually, and there would be open admissions. The schools would be open 12 hours a day year-round and operate on a staggered schedule. The curriculum and teaching would be "state-of-the-art," and parents as well as infants would be involved. Whittle's plans have met with skepticism, especially when the number of schools to be opened initially was scaled back to from 200 to 100 and projected tuition was raised to $9,000. In August 1993 another revision of the plan was announced, in which the project's focus was shifted from building new schools to managing existing ones, which would reduce the projected $2.5 billion cost of the initial proposal by some 80 percent. The president of the National Education Association has called the Edison Project a "con job."[187]

To sum up, this section has reviewed a wide range of approaches to business-school partnerships. The major shift in the nature of these arrangements since the late 1980s has been more proactively on the part of business in calling for fundamental reforms and supporting alternatives to traditional public schools. Seeking to inject more competition and a marketplace spirit into educational systems that have proven resistant to change over the years will be a stiff—but worthy—challenge.

FROM BIRTH TO WORK: CRITICAL TASKS AHEAD

This chapter has examined several approaches to improving America's future work force through education and health care reform and facilitating the transitions from birth to work. Sorting out public sector responsibilities, integrating the delivery of services, forming public-private partnerships, and using alternative human services delivery methods are neither new nor novel. Increasingly, government officials, professionals, and business leaders are turning to them in recognition that traditional, incremental responses have proven inadequate. Each of these approaches threatens the organizational status quo and established modes of behavior. Each requires new ways of looking at, and responding to, old problems. Their implementation will require patience and courage. Clearly, there are many critical tasks ahead.

There is no "one best way" to achieve the goal of increased employability of American youth through health and education reform. More experimentation, demonstration, innovation, and "reinvention" are necessary at all levels of government, as well as in the private sector, to arrive at better understandings of which approaches offer promise—and which do not. Research on causality and outcomes is a vital component of this effort.

Approaching the mid-nineties, America faced the most serious socioeconomic condition in several decades: doubts of its ability to maintain its economic leadership in a global economy; in its inner cities, the deadly combination of widespread drug addition, with the highest homicide rates in the industrial democracies; a fragmenting family structure combined with severe poverty among many mother-headed households; health and education systems under growing strain and public dissatisfaction; and racial tensions building dangerously in many localities.

These conditions pose severe challenges on many fronts, several being squarely within the broad public policy arenas of health and education. The nation's ability to withstand and excel in global economic competition depends upon a skilled labor force, which rests in turn upon effective linkages between school and work. To succeed in school, the growing child must acquire and follow healthy habits and life-styles.

To meet these challenges, specific actions such as the following must be taken: preventive health care for all mothers and growing children; early identification of, and assistance to, at-risk families and children; mastery by students not only of basic cognitive and social skills but of a sense of human values, community service ideals, and explicit knowledge of the risks associated with drugs, sex, and violence; a transformation of America's prisons and jails into institutions that are correctional in fact as well as name; and the provision of drug treatment, random testing, and probationary supervision until cured. Finally, American public opinion must begin to think broadly instead of compartmentally, especially in issues affecting generations other than one's own—the generation to come and its successors.

A 1992 *Fortune* magazine poll of workers in their 20s found that they were surprisingly optimistic about their careers and financial prospects. Yet, in pursuing their dream to do as well as, or better than, their parents and in overcoming such obstacles as high housing and college education costs, the respondents identified a number of "big threats" to the American way of life. These were drugs, 81 percent responding; troubled educational system, 74 percent; damage to the environment, 73 percent; crime, 72 percent; America's economic malaise, 52 percent; foreign economic competition, 45 percent; racial problems, 38 percent; global political and military unrest, 31 percent.[188]

In working to identify and implement effective remedial actions, government and business leaders, educators, public and private employment agencies, child welfare and correctional workers, health care providers, parents, and others must strive to maintain or restore a sense of community.[189] The issues discussed in this book are difficult and often divisive. They need to be addressed by those involved in a spirit of cooperation rather than confrontation, characterized by a willingness to support the exploration of options that may prove to be valuable solutions to the problems affecting America's work force and society.

NOTES

1. Reagan, M.D., *Regulation: The Politics of Policy* (Boston: Little, Brown, 1987), 18.

2. U.S. Advisory Commission on Intergovernmental Relations, *Regulatory Federalism: Policy, Process, Impact and Reform* (Washington, DC: U.S. Government Printing Office, February 1984), 65–68.

3. Nathan, R. P., "The Role of the States in American Federalism," in Van Horn, Carl E. (ed.), *The State of the States* (Washington, DC: Congressional Quarterly, 1989), 28–29.

4. Stenberg, C. W., "Beyond the Days of Wine and Roses: Intergovernmental Management in a Cutback Environment," *Public Administration Review*, January/February 1981, 10.

5. U.S. Advisory Commission on Intergovernmental Relations, *Regulatory Federalism*, 93–94.

6. Broder, D. S., "The Governors, Feeling Burned," *Washington Post*, August 24, 1980.

7. U.S. Advisory Commission on Intergovernmental Relations, *An Agenda for American Federalism: Restoring Confidence and Competence* (Washington, DC: U.S. Government Printing Office, June 1981), 101. See also U.S. Advisory Commission on Intergovernmental Relations, *The Federal Role in the Federal System: The Dynamics of Growth* (10 vols.) (Washington, DC: U.S. Government Printing Office, 1981); Walker, D. B., *Slouching toward Washington: Rebirth of Federalism* (Chatham, NJ: Chatham House Publishers, 1993).

8. U.S. Advisory Commission on Intergovernmental Relations, *An Agenda for American Federalism*, 112.

9. Vogel, D., "The 'New' Social Regulation in Historical and Comparative Perspective," in McGraw, T. K. (ed.), *Regulation in Perspective* (Cambridge, MA: Harvard University Press), 175–76.

10. Harris, R. A., and Milkis, S. M., *The Politics of Regulatory Change: A Tale of Two Agencies* (New York: Oxford University Press, 1989), 11.

11. Wright, D. S., "New Federalism: Recent Varieties of an Older Species," *American Review of Public Administration*, Spring 1982, 56–74; Conlan, T., *New Federalism: Intergovernmental Reform from Nixon to Reagan* (Washington, DC: Brookings Institution, 1988); Walker, D. B., "American Federalism: From Reagan to Bush," *Publius*, Winter 1991, 105–19; Elazar, D. J., "American Federalism Today: Practice Versus Principles," in Hawkins, R. B., *American Federalism: A New Partnership for the Republic* (New Brunswick, NJ: Transaction Books, 1982); Wright, D., "Policy Shifts in the Politics and Administration of Intergovernmental Relations, 1930's–1990's" *The Annals of the American Academy of Political and Social Science*, May 1990, 68.

12. See U.S. General Accounting Office, *Education Block Grant Alters State Role and Provides Greater Local Discretion* (Washington, DC: U.S. General Accounting Office, November 19, 1984); U.S. General Accounting Office, *Education Block Grant:*

How Funds Reserved for State Efforts in California and Washington are Used (Washington, DC: U.S. General Accounting Office, May 1986). See also U.S. General Accounting Office, *Department of Education, Long-Standing Management Problems Hamper Reforms* (Washington, DC: General Accounting Office, May 1993).

13. U.S. Advisory Commission on Intergovernmental Relations, *Federal Statutory Preemption of State and Local Authority: History, Inventory, and Issues* (Washington, DC: U.S. Government Printing Office, September 1992), 9. See also U.S. Advisory Commission on Intergovernmental Relations, *Federal Regulation of State and Local Governments: The Mixed Record of the 1980s* (Washington, DC: U.S. Government Printing Office, July 1993); Zimmerman, J. F., "Regulating Intergovernmental Relations in the 1990s," *The Annals*, 48–59; Zimmerman, J. F., *Federal Preemption: The Silent Revolution* (Ames: Iowa State University Press, 1991), 12. For case studies of deregulating the airlines, telecommunications, and trucking industries, see Derthick, M., and Quirk, P. J., *The Politics of Deregulation* (Washington, DC: Brookings Institution, 1985).

14. U.S. Advisory Commission on Intergovernmental Relations, *Characteristics of Federal Grant-in-Aid Programs to State and Local Governments: Grants Funded FY 1991* (Washington, DC: U.S. Government Printing Office, March 1992), 12.

15. Ibid., 15.

16. Stenberg, C. W., "States Under the Spotlight: An Intergovernmental View," *Public Administration Review*, March/April 1985, 319–26; Colman, W. G., *State and Local Government and Public-Private Partnerships: A Policy Issues Handbook* (New York: Greenwood Press, 1989).

17. Nathan, R. P., Doolittle, F. C., and associates, *Reagan and the States* (Princeton, NJ: Princeton University Press, 1987), 362.

18. National Association of State Budget Officers, *State Aid to Local Governments: The Shining Star of Intergovernmental Finance* (Washington, DC: National Association of State Budget Officers, March 1990).

19. U.S. Advisory Commission on Intergovernmental Relations, *Fiscal Management of Federal Pass-Through Grants: The Need for More Uniform Requirements and Procedures* (Washington, DC: U.S. Government Printing Office, September 1981), 22–23.

20. See Kee, J. E., and Shannon, J., "The Crisis and Anticrisis Dynamic: Rebalancing the American Federal System," *Public Administration Review*, July/August 1992, 321–29.

21. U.S. Advisory Commission on Intergovernmental Relations, *An Agenda for American Federalism: Restoring Confidence and Competence* (Washington, DC: U.S. Government Printing Office, June 1981), 111.

22. Kincaid, J., "Is Education Too Intergovernmental?" *Intergovernmental Perspective*, Winter 1992, 28–34.

23. The Commission on Intergovernmental Relations, *A Report to the President for Transmittal to the Congress* (Washington, DC: U.S. Government Printing Office, June 1955).

24. Joint Federal-State Action Committee, *Reports to the President of the United States and to the Chairman of the Governor's Conference* (Washington, DC: U.S. Government Printing Office, 1957–61).

25. U.S. Advisory Commission on Intergovernmental Relations, *The Federal Role in the Federal System: The Dynamics of Growth* (10 vols.) (Washington, DC: U.S. Government Printing Office, 1981); *Performance of Urban Functions: Local and Areawide* (Washington, DC: U.S. Government Printing Office, 1963).

26. California Council on Intergovernmental Relations, *Allocation of Public Service Responsibilities*, June 1970.

27. Commission on Intergovernmental Relations, 65.

28. Ibid., 64.

29. Ibid., 194.

30. Ibid., 252.

31. Ibid., 270, 275. See also the commission's reports, *Federal Responsibility in the Field of Education*, *Federal Aid to Public Health*, and *Federal Aid to Welfare*, all published by the U.S. Government Printing Office in June 1955.

32. U.S. Advisory Commission on Intergovernmental Relations, *An Agenda for American Federalism*, 111.

33. U.S. Advisory Commission on Intergovernmental Relations, *State Aid to Local Government* (Washington, DC: U.S. Government Printing Office, April 1969), 14.

34. U.S. Advisory Commission on Intergovernmental Relations, *An Agenda for American Federalism*, 111.

35. Ibid., 111–12.

36. Pagano, M. A., *City Fiscal Conditions in 1992* (Washington, DC: National League of Cities, 1992).

37. Hovey, H. A., "Analytic Approaches to State-Local Relations," in Liner, E. B. (ed.), *A Decade of Devolution: Perspectives on State-Local Relations* (Washington, DC: Urban Institute Press, 1989), 163.

38. See ibid., 164; Stenberg, C. W., "Beyond the Days of Wine and Roses," 11 14.

39. John, D., *Shifting Responsibilities: Federalism in Economic Development* (Washington, DC: National Governors' Association, 1989), 13.

40. Hovey, 167.

41. Ibid., 181.

42. Campbell, A., "Functions in Flux," in U.S. Advisory Commission on Intergovernmental Relations, *American Federalism: Toward a More Effective Partnership* (Washington, DC: U.S. Government Printing Office, 1975), 37.

43. Gold, S., *Reforming State-Local Relations: A Practical Guide* (Washington, DC: National Conference of State Legislatures, 1989), 95.

44. Ibid.

45. See Zimmerman, J. F., *Federal Preemption: The Silent Revolution* (Ames: Iowa State University Press, 1991).

46. Florida Advisory Council on Intergovernmental Relations, *A Comprehensive Review of Local Government Service Delivery in Florida: Service Scope, Intensity, and Dominance* (Tallahassee: The Council, November 1991), 9.

47. Rivlin, A. M., "The Division Solution; Stop Sending the Feds to Do the States' Job," *Washington Post*, June 14, 1992, C1, C4.

48. The Committee on Federalism and National Purpose, *To Form a More Perfect Union* (Washington, DC: National Conference on Social Welfare), 9–10.

49. Robb, C. S., "Making Federalism Work: Perestroika for America?" the First Elmer Staats Lecture, National Academy of Public Administration, Austin, TX: June 7, 1991, 5.

50. Ibid.

51. Ibid., 6.

52. See U.S. Congress, Congressional Budget Office, *The Federal Government in*

a Federal System: Current Intergovernmental Programs and Options for Change (Washington, DC: U.S. Government Printing Office, August 1983).

53. Rivlin, A. M., *Reviving the American Dream: The Economy, the States and the Federal Government* (Washington, DC: Brookings Institution, 1992), 12.

54. Ibid., 11.

55. Ibid., 12.

56. Ibid., 16–19.

57. Ibid., 17.

58. See Sabato, L., *Good-bye to Good-Time Charlie: The American Governorship Transformed* (Washington, DC: Congressional Quarterly Press, 2nd ed., 1983).

59. See U.S. Advisory Commission on Intergovernmental Relations, *Changing Public Attitudes on Governments and Taxes: 1992* (Washington, DC: U.S. Government Printing Office, 1992).

60. See Peterson, P. E., Rabe, B. G., and Wong, K. K., *When Federalism Works* (Washington, DC: Brookings Institution, 1986); U.S. Congressional Budget Office, *The Federal Role in Improving Elementary and Secondary Education* (Washington, DC: U.S. Government Printing Office, May 1993), 49–69.

61. Rivlin, 181.

62. Osborne, D., and Gaebler, T., *Reinventing Government: How the Entrepreneurial Spirit Is Transforming the Public Sector* (Reading: MA: Addison-Wesley, 1992). For critiques, see Frederickson, H. G., "Painting Bull's Eyes Around Bullet Holes," *Governing*, October 1992, 13; Goodsell, C. T., "Reinvent Government or Rediscover It?" *Public Administration Review*, January/February 1993, 85–87.

63. Ibid., 277.

64. Ibid., 285–90.

65. Ibid., 25–310.

66. National Performance Review, *Creating a Government That Works Better and Costs Less* (Washington, DC: U.S. Government Printing Office, September 7, 1993); Barr, S., "On the Road to 'Reinventing Government,' " *Washington Post*, June 3, 1993, A23; Barr, S., "From Gore, Clues About New Directions," *Washington Post*, August 3, 1993, A15. See also Dilulio, J. J., Garvey, G., and Kettl, D. F., *Improving Government Performance: An Owner's Manual* (Washington, DC: Brookings Institution, 1993).

67. Osborne and Gaebler, 277–78.

68. Murnane, R. J., and Levy, F., "Education and Training," in Aaron, H. J., and Schultze, C. L. (eds.), *Setting Domestic Priorities: What Can Government Do?* (Washington, DC: Brookings Institution, 1992), 211.

69. National Commission on Children, *Beyond Rhetoric, a New American Agenda for Children and Families* (Washington, DC: U.S. Government Printing Office, 1991), 315.

70. Sanford, T., *Storm over the States* (New York: McGraw-Hill, 1967), 80.

71. Wright, D. S., *Understanding Intergovernmental Relations*, 3d ed. (Pacific Grove, CA: Brooks/Cole, 1988), 84.

72. Agranoff, R., "Human Services Integration: Past and Present Challenges in Public Administration," *Public Administration Review*, November/December 1991, 534.

73. *National Journal*, March 1973, 48.

74. Morrill, W. A., "Overview of Service Delivery to Children," in Center for the Future of Children, *The Future of Children* (Los Altos, CA: The David and Lucile Packard Foundation, Spring 1982), 33.

75. Cited in Sawhill, I. V., "Toward More Integrated Services for Children: Issues

and Options," statement before the Subcommittee on Children, Family, Drugs, and Alcoholism, U.S. Senate Committee on Labor and Human Resources, May 7, 1991.

76. See Sundquist, J. L., and Davis, D. W., *Making Federalism Work: A Study of Program Coordination at the Community Level* (Washington, DC: Brookings Institution, 1969).

77. U.S. Advisory Commission on Intergovernmental Relations, *Characteristics of Federal Grant-in-Aid Programs to State and Local Governments*, 5. See also U.S. Advisory Commission on Intergovernmental Relations, *Block Grants: A Comparative Analysis* (Washington, DC: U.S. Government Printing Office, October 1977).

78. Quoted in Gerry, M. H., and Certo, N. J., "Current Activity at the Federal Level and the Need for Service Integration," in Center for the Future of Children, *The Future of Children* (Los Altos, CA: David and Lucile Packard Foundation, Spring 1992), 121.

79. Ibid., 120–21. See also *National Journal*, March 1973, 65–67.

80. Agranoff, 534.

81. See U.S. Department of Health and Human Services, Office of Inspector General, *Service Integration: A Twenty-Year Retrospective* (Washington, DC: U.S. Government Printing Office, 1990).

82. Gerry and Certo, 121.

83. Agranoff, 535–37. See also Rom, M., "The Family Support Act of 1988," *Publius*, Summer 1989, 57–73.

84. Schorr, L. B., with Schorr, D., *Within Our Reach: Breaking the Cycle of Disadvantage* (New York: Anchor Press, 1988).

85. Agranoff, 535.

86. Ibid.

87. Gerry and Certo, 121.

88. Agranoff, 535.

89. Gerry and Certo, 122–26.

90. See National Center for Service Integration (NCSI), *NCSI News*, Spring 1993, 3; Chaudry, A., Maurer, K. E., Oshinsky, C. J., and MacKie, J., *Service Integration: An Annotated Bibliography* (New York: NCSI, 1993); NCSI, *Directory of Federally Funded Resource Centers—1993* (New York: NCSI, March 1993).

91. Chi, K., "What Has Happened to the Comprehensive Human Service Agency?" *New England Journal of Human Services*, Fall 1987, 25.

92. National Academy of Public Administration (NAPA), *Reorganization in Florida: How Is Services Integration Working?* (Washington, DC: NAPA, 1977); *Human Services Coordination: A Panel Report and Accompanying Papers* (Washington, DC: NAPA, 1982); *After a Decade: A Progress Report on the Organization and Management of Florida State Department of Health and Rehabilitative Services* (Washington, DC: NAPA, 1986).

93. Agranoff, 539.

94. U.S. Advisory Commission on Intergovernmental Relations, *Regional Organizations in the 1990s: An Update* (Washington, DC: U.S. Government Printing Office, forthcoming).

95. Agranoff, 539.

96. Conant, J. K., "Executive Branch Reorganization in the States, 1965–1991," in Council of State Governments, *The Book of the States 1992–93 Edition* (Lexington, KY: Council of State Governments, 1992), 64–73.

97. Council of State Governments, *The Book of the States: 1992–93 Edition*, 74–77.

98. Usdan, M., "Emerging Leadership Needs in Education," *National Civic Review*, Winter 1991, 48.

99. Cited in Center for the Future of Children, *The Future of Children*, 6.

100. Farrow, F., and Tom, J., "Financing School-Linked Integrated Services," in Center for the Future of Children, *The Future of Children*, 63. See also Appalachia Educational Laboratory, *The Link*, Summer 1992, 11.

101. Melaville, A. I.,, with Blank, M. J., *What It Takes: Structuring Interagency Partnerships to Connect Children and Families with Comprehensive Services* (Washington, DC: Education and Human Services Consortium, 1991), 45–46.

102. Appalachia Educational Laboratory, 3.

103. Ibid., 11–12.

104. Ibid., 12–13; *Governing*, July 1993, 20–21.

105. Appalachia Educational Laboratory, 13.

106. Ibid., 2–3.

107. Ibid., 3.

108. Agranoff, 540.

109. Behn, R. D., *Leadership Counts: Lessons for Public Managers from the Massachusetts Welfare, Training, and Employment Program* (Cambridge: Harvard University Press, 1991), 218. See also Agranoff, 537.

110. Melaville, 47.

111. *Chronicle of Higher Education*, January 27, 1993, A32.

112. NCSI, *NCSI News*, Spring 1993, 6.

113. Center for the Future of Children, *The Future of Children*, 9–12. For examples, see Chira, S., "Poverty's Toll on Health Is Plague of Schools," *New York Times*, October 5, 1991, A1, A6; Lear, J. G., and Porter, P. J., "Help Our Children: Bring Health Care into the Schools," *Washington Post*, December 1, 1991, C5; Taylor, P., "Bringing Social Services into Schools, *Washington Post*, May 2, 1991, A1, A34.

114. Agranoff, 540. See also Armstrong, B., *Making Government Work for Your City's Kids: Getting Through the Intergovernmental Maze of Programs for Children and Families* (Washington, DC: National League of Cities, 1992). For a review of state experiences and experiments with overcoming the challenges to service integration, see National Governors' Association (NGA), *Changing Systems for Children and Families* (Washington, DC: NGA, 1994).

115. Ibid., 541.

116. Melaville, 36.

117. Reveal, E. C., "Governance Options for the Children's Initiative: Making Systems Work," June 1991, 9–10, 23–24. See also Education Commission of the States (ECS), *Confidentiality and Collaboration: Information Sharing in Interagency Efforts: A Joint Publication of Joining Forces, American Public Welfare Association, Center for Law and Social Policy, Council of Chief State School Officers and Education Commission of the States* (Denver: ECS, 1992).

118. Kearns, D. T., "An Education Recovery Plan for America," *Phi Delta Kappan*, April 1988, 566.

119. Perry, N. J., "Where We Go from Here," *Fortune*, October 21, 1991, 114.

120. Ibid.

121. Ibid., 114–15, 129.

122. Richman, L. S., "Struggling to Save Our Kids," *Fortune*, August 10, 1992, 36.

123. Perry, 124.

124. See Fosler, R. S., *The Business Role in State Education Reform* (New York: Business Roundtable, 1990), 4. See also the following reports by the Business Roundtable: *The Business Roundtable Participation Guide: A Primer for Business on Education* (1991): Essential Components of a Successful Education System (1990).

125. Boyer, E. L., *High School: A Report on Secondary Education in America* (New York: Harper and Row, 1983), 279–80.

126. Keehn, J., "How Business Helps the Schools," *Fortune*, October 21, 1991, 161.

127. "Saving Our Schools," *Business Week*, September 14, 1992, 70.

128. Keehn, 161; Ramsey, 147–74.

129. Keehn, 161–80. See also Perry, N. J., "School Reform: Big Pain, Little Gain," *Fortune*, November 29, 1993, 130–62.

130. Weisman, J., "Skills and Schools: Is Education Reform Just a Business Excuse?" *Washington Post*, March 29, 1992, C4.

131. Ibid.

132. Ibid.

133. *Business Week*, February 22, 1992, 76.

134. Liddell, S. A., "Putting the Future on the High (Skills) Road," *State Legislatures*, May 1993, 22.

135. Reich, R. B., *The Work of Nations: Preparing Ourselves for 21st Century Capitalism* (New York: Alfred A. Knopf, 1991), 259. See also Stone, N., "Does Business Have Any Business in Education?" *Harvard Business Review*, March–April 1991, 46 62.

136. *Fortune*, March 8, 1993, 11.

137. Martin, J. H., and Carrier, A. H., "Training & Education: The Virginia Employer's View," *University of Virginia Newsletter*, April 1991, 7; Martin, J. H., Tolson, D. J., and Carrier, A. H., *Meeting Needs: Education and Training for Virginia's Adults* (Charlottesville: Center for Public Service, University of Virginia, September 1992).

138. Martin and Carrier, 4.

139. See Commission on the Skills of the American Workforce, *America's Choice: High Skills or Low Wages* (Rochester, NY: National Center on Education and the Economy, 1990), 3; Murnane and Levy, 218–21.

140. Stone, 48.

141. *Business Week*, February 22, 1993, 76.

142. National Commission on the State and Local Public Service, *Hard Truths/ Tough Choices: An Agenda for State and Local Reform* (Albany: The Nelson A. Rockefeller Institute of Government, 1993), 42–44.

143. Reich, 280–81.

144. See Council of Economic Priorities, "Corporate America in the Classroom," January 1990, cited in Reich, 281.

145. Rubenstein, C., "The Deadbeat of America," *New York Times*, March 17, 1990, A22, cited in Reich, 281.

146. "Saving Our Schools," *Business Week*, 70, 72.

147. Fosler, 29.

148. Sylvester, K., "Business and the Schools: The Failure and the Promise," *Governing*, September 1992, 24. See also Daranbeim, R., *Corporate Support of National Education Goals* (New York: Conference Board, 1991).

149. Committee for Economic Development (CED) *Investing in Our Children: Business and the Public Schools* (Washington, DC: CED 1985), 79. See also the following reports published by CED: Timpane, P. M., *Business Impact on Education and Child*

Development Reform (1991); *The Unfinished Agenda: A New Vision for Child Development and Education* (1991).

150. "Saving our Schools," *Business Week*, 70–71.

151. "Business Help for the Schools," *Washington Post*, August 23, 1992.

152. Newcomer, K. E., "Building Partnerships: Public Service Academy," *The Bureaucrat*, Winter 1991–1992, 33–34.

153. Sylvester, K., "The Strange Romance of Business and the Schools," *Governing*, April 1991, 67–68. See also Useem, E. L., "Improving Values Through School-Business Alliances," *Curriculum Review*, March/April 1987, 18.

154. "Saving Our Schools," 74–78; Jordan, M., "Annenberg's Education Gift Will Fund Electronic Library," *Washington Post*, December 18, 1993, A2.

155. See Wartzman, R., "Learning by Doing: Apprenticeship Plans Spring Up for Students Not Headed to College," *Wall Street Journal*, May 19, 1992, A1, A5.

156. *Fortune*, June 28, 1992, 16.

157. See Raspberry, W., "And a Plan That Just Might Work," *Washington Post*, June 19, 1991, A19.

158. See Kotlowitz, A., "A Businessman Turns His Skills to Aiding Inner-City Schools," *Wall Street Journal*, February 25, 1992, A–1; Gugliotta, G., "Operation Exodus's Path Is Education," *Washington Post*, March 16, 1993, A1, A6.

159. See Kilborn, P. T., "In Unique High School, Young Mothers Thrive," *New York Times*, November 30, 1991, A1, 27.

160. For examples of successful programs, see Sachar, S. F., *From Homes to Classrooms to Workrooms* (Washington, DC: National Governors' Association, 1992), 67–71.

161. *Fortune*, February 24, 1992, 10.

162. Richman, 38. See also Koprowicz, C., and Myers, J., *Getting on Board: The Private Sector and Learning Readiness* (Denver: National Conference of State Legislatures, July 1992).

163. Kearns, D. T., "An Education Recovery Plan for America," *Phi Delta Kappan*, April 1988, 565.

164. Sylvester, "Business and the Schools," 25–28.

165. Kolderie, T., "Education That Works: The Right Role for Business," *Harvard Business Review*, September-October 1987, 56.

166. Osborne and Gaebler, 307.

167. Kolderie, 56.

168. Pipho, C., "The Wave Theory of Education Reform," *Phi Delta Kappan*, October 1988, 102.

169. Kearns, D. T., and Doyle, D., *Winning the Brain Race: A Bold Plan to Make Our Schools Competitive* (Washington, DC: Institute for Contemporary Studies, 1988).

170. Kearns, "An Education Recovery Plan for America," 566.

171. Kolderie, 60.

172. For an excellent account of the Texas school reform "crusade," see Toch, T., *In the Name of Excellence* (New York: Oxford University Press, 1991), 72–95. This summary is based on chapter 3 of this book.

173. "Saving Our Schools," *Business Week*, 78.

174. Kolderie, 60–61.

175. *Governing*, June 1992, 40.

176. Sylvester, "The Strange Romance of Business and the Schools," 64.

177. Ibid., 64, 66.

178. Morris, J., "Encouraging Collaboration to Keep Kids in School," *Public Management*, September 1992, 3–10.

179. See Savas, E. S., *Privatizing the Public Sector: How to Shrink Government* (Chatham, NJ: Chatham House, 1982); Donahue, J. D., *The Privatization Decision: Public Ends, Private Means* (New York: Basic Books, 1989).

180. "The Green in the Little Red Schoolhouse," *Business Week*, October 14, 1991, 68–69.

181. Wilkerson, I., "A City Is Letting a Company Run a School District," *New York Times*, April 22, 1992, B8.

182. *Wall Street Journal*, June 10, 1992; Valentine, P. W., "Baltimore's Corporate Classrooms," *Washington Post*, June 14, 1993, B1, B5; "Private Firm Proposed for D.C. Schools," *Washington Post*, December 8, 1993, A1, 16, 18–19.

183. Stout, H., "Firms Help Set Up, Run Public Schools," *Wall Street Journal*, April 18, 1991, B1, B7; Sylvester, K., "The Strange Romance of Business and the Schools," 67.

184. Osborne and Gaebler, 185.

185. "Saving Our Schools," *Business Week*, 73.

186. Stout, H., "Business Funds Program in Indianapolis Letting Poor Children Flee Public Schools," *Wall Street Journal*, February 27, 1992, B1, B5.

187. Jordan, M., "For-Profit Schools Plan Math Is Faulty, Critics Say," *Washington Post*, February 8, 1993, A1, A6. See also Truehart, C., "A New Thought of School," *Washington Post*, July 21, 1992, B1–B2; "Whittle's Lesson Plan for the Public Schools," *Wall Street Journal*, June 2, 1992, A15; Jordan, M., "Whittle to Revamp Plan to Build Chain of For-Profit Private Schools," *Washington Post*, August 2, 1993, A6.

188. Deutschman, A., "The Upbeat Generation," *Fortune*, July 13, 1992, 52.

189. See Kordesh, R., "Community for Children," *National Civic Review*, Fall 1991, 374–80.

Appendixes

Appendix 1.A
Projected Population, by Age Group, 1995–2080 (numbers in millions; includes armed forces overseas)

1989 Projections:						Age					
Year	Total	Under 5	5-13	14-17	18-24	25-34	35-44	45-64	65 & Over	85 & Over	Median Age
1995											
Low	255.2	16.4	33.1	14.4	23.9	40.1	41.9	52.2	33.3	3.2	35.0
Middle	260.1	17.8	33.9	14.5	24.3	41.0	42.3	52.6	33.8	3.9	34.7
High	265.2	19.5	34.7	14.7	24.7	41.7	42.6	53.0	34.3	4.0	34.4
2000											
Low	259.6	14.9	31.3	15.1	24.7	36.0	43.0	60.6	34.0	4.3	36.3
Middle	268.3	16.8	33.5	15.3	25.2	37.1	43.9	61.4	34.9	4.6	36.4
High	278.2	19.4	36.1	15.6	25.9	38.4	44.6	62.2	36.1	4.9	35.8
2020											
Low	264.5	13.0	25.3	11.7	21.5	35.7	35.5	73.5	48.2	5.4	41.9
Middle	294.4	17.1	31.7	14.1	25.0	39.1	37.5	77.7	52.1	6.7	40.2
High	335.5	23.3	41.0	17.4	29.8	43.6	40.0	81.9	58.0	8.6	38.0
2040											
Low	245.7	10.6	20.8	10.1	19.0	29.1	30.3	67.0	58.8	9.2	45.9
Middle	301.8	16.2	30.2	14.0	25.4	37.1	36.5	74.2	68.1	12.3	42.6
High	388.1	26.1	46.2	20.4	35.5	49.0	45.2	83.1	82.6	17.9	38.7
2050											
Low	230.2	9.7	19.3	9.2	16.9	27.0	28.8	62.0	57.2	10.7	46.4
Middle	299.8	15.9	30.1	13.8	24.1	36.9	37.2	73.1	68.5	15.3	42.7
High	413.6	27.7	49.6	21.7	37.0	52.6	49.4	88.2	87.4	24.1	38.6
2080											
Low	184.6	7.5	15.0	7.2	13.2	20.9	22.6	48.6	49.5	9.8	47.5
Middle	292.2	15.0	28.3	13.1	23.3	34.8	35.6	70.6	71.6	17.0	43.9
High	501.5	32.4	58.2	25.6	43.9	61.5	58.9	107.0	113.9	33.9	39.9

Appendix 1.A (continued)

Year	Total	Under 5	5-14	15-19	20-24	25-34	35-54	55-64	65-74	74-84	85 & Over	Median Age
1992 Projections:						**Age**						
1995	264.3	19.4	38.4	17.8	17.8	41.7	74.0	21.4	19.0	10.9	3.9	34.4
2000	276.4	19.4	40.0	19.4	18.1	38.3	81.9	24.3	18.3	12.0	4.6	35.7
2005	288.5	19.9	40.5	20.4	19.7	37.6	84.0	29.9	18.5	12.6	5.3	36.5
2010	301.1	21.1	40.9	21.0	20.7	39.5	82.7	35.7	21.2	12.3	6.1	37.0
2015	314.1	22.4	42.9	20.9	21.1	42.0	79.5	40.1	26.2	12.6	6.6	37.0
2020	327.0	23.2	45.2	21.5	21.2	43.4	78.1	41.9	31.3	14.6	6.7	37.2
2030	350.6	24.2	48.6	24.0	22.9	45.1	83.2	36.6	36.7	21.7	8.2	37.5
2040	372.4	25.9	51.0	25.4	25.1	48.7	88.1	37.9	32.4	25.6	12.4	37.2
2060	417.2	28.8	57.2	28.6	27.9	54.4	100.7	42.7	37.2	24.2	15.3	37.2
2080	470.5	32.0	63.9	31.6	30.8	60.8	112.1	50.0	42.2	28.1	19.0	37.7

Percent of Total Population, 1992 Projections:

Year	Total	Under 5	5-14	15-19	20-24	25-34	35-54	55-64	65-74	74-84	85 & Over
						Age					
1995	100	7.3	14.5	6.7	6.7	15.8	28.0	8.1	7.2	4.1	1.5
2000	100	7.0	14.5	7.0	6.5	13.9	29.6	8.8	6.6	4.3	1.7
2005	100	6.9	14.0	7.1	6.8	13.0	29.1	10.4	6.4	4.4	1.8
2010	100	7.0	13.6	7.0	6.9	13.1	27.5	11.8	7.0	4.1	2.0
2015	100	7.1	13.7	6.7	6.7	13.4	25.3	12.8	8.3	4.0	2.1
2020	100	7.1	13.8	6.6	6.5	13.3	23.9	12.8	9.6	4.5	2.0
2030	100	6.9	13.9	6.8	6.5	12.9	23.7	10.4	10.5	6.2	2.3
2040	100	7.0	13.7	6.8	6.7	13.1	23.7	10.2	8.7	6.9	3.3
2060	100	6.9	13.7	6.9	6.7	13.0	24.1	10.2	8.9	5.8	3.7
2080	100	6.8	13.6	6.7	6.5	12.9	23.8	10.6	9.0	6.0	4.0

Sources: Bureau of the Census: *Projections of the Population of the United States, By Age, Sex, and Race: 1988 to 2000*. Series P-25, No. 1018, Tables D and F. January, 1989, p. 7. Bureau of the Census, Series P-25, No. 1018 (Supplement, Series 18), Table 6. March 1992, unnumbered pages.

Note: The 1018 Supplement, Series 18 was a revision of the earlier projections. In a "User Note on Recommended Alternatives to the Middle Series of National Population Projections" it was noted that Series 18 (high fertility and high immigration assumptions) more accurately tracked recent past trends than those of the middle series and that the revised set of projections would be published later in 1992.

527

Appendix 1.B
Employment Status of the Civilian Noninstitutional Population (NIP) and of the Civilian Labor Force (CLF), by Age Group, Sex, and Race, July 1992

Total; Race, Sex and Age	CIP No.	CLF		Employed		Unemployed		Total		Not in Labor Force (NILF) and Reasons Therefor							
										Keeping House		School		Health		Other*	
		No.	% of CIP	No.	% of CLF	No.	% of CLF	No.	% of NIP	No.	% of NILF	No.	% of NILF	No.	% of NILF	No.	% of NILF
1	2	3	4	5	6	7	8	9	10	11	12	13	14	15	16	17	18
(in millions)																	
Total, All 16 & Over	191.62	129.60	67.6	119.75	62.5	9.85	7.6	62.02	32.4	24.87	40.1	2.59	4.2	3.89	6.3	30.66	49.4
16-19	13.12	8.53	65.1	6.84	52.2	1.70	19.9	4.58	34.9	.60	13.1	1.02	22.3	.03	0.7	2.92	63.9
20-24	17.76	14.54	81.8	12.91	72.6	1.63	11.2	3.22	18.2	1.31	40.7	.79	24.3	.12	3.7	1.01	31.3
25-64	130.00	103.05	79.3	96.68	74.8	6.37	6.2	26.96	20.7	14.99	55.6	.79	2.9	2.46	9.1	8.72	32.3
65 & Over	30.74	3.48	11.3	3.33	10.8	.15	4.2	27.26	88.7	7.97	29.2	—	—	1.29	4.7	18.01	66.1
(in thousands)																	
Total, White 16 & Over	162,682	110,481	67.9	103,201	63.4	7,280	6.6	52,202	32.1	21,319	40.8	1,777	3.4	2,932	5.6	26,175	50.1
Men, 16+	78,364	61,066	77.9	57,095	72.9	3,972	6.5	17,297	22.1	357	2.1	813	4.7	1,556	9.0	14,570	84.2
16-19	5,293	3,783	71.5	3,138	59.3	644	17.0	1,510	28.5	31	2.1	339	22.5	10	0.6	1,131	74.9
20-24	7,157	6,495	90.7	5,901	82.5	594	9.1	662	9.2	7	1.1	251	37.9	64	9.7	340	51.4
25-64	54,390	48,959	90.0	46,280	85.1	2,680	5.5	5,431	10.0	208	3.8	221	4.1	1,083	19.9	3,918	72.1
65+	11,523	1,829	15.9	1,776	15.4	53	2.9	9,694	84.1	112	1.2	1	N	3,994	4.1	9,182	94.7
Women, 16+	84,319	49,414	58.6	46,106	54.7	3,308	6.7	34,904	41.4	20,961	60.1	963	2.8	1,376	3.9	11,604	33.2
16-19	5,166	3,359	65.0	2,812	54.4	547	16.3	1,807	35.0	379	21.0	365	20.2	13	0.7	1,050	58.1
20-24	7,375	5,763	78.1	5,229	70.9	534	9.3	1,612	21.9	958	59.4	278	17.2	27	1.7	349	21.7
25-64	55,846	39,993	71.6	36,842	66.0	2,152	5.4	16,853	29.7	12,499	74.2	320	1.9	720	4.3	3,313	19.7
65+	15,932	1,299	8.2	1,223	7.7	76	5.8	14,633	91.8	7,125	48.7	—	—	616	4.2	6,893	47.1

Total, Black 16 & Over	21,966	14,428	65.7	12,283	55.9	2,145	14.9	7,538	34.3	2,628	34.9	490	6.5	841	11.2	3,578	47.5
Men, 16+	4,891	7,134	72.1	6,041	61.1	1,093	15.3	2,757	27.9	140	5.1	219	7.9	446	16.2	1,952	70.8
16-19	1,026	578	56.3	360	35.1	217	37.6	448	43.7	27	6.0	99	22.1	6	1.3	315	70.3
20-24	1,165	928	79.6	687	59.0	241	25.9	237	20.3	15	6.3	73	30.8	22	9.3	127	53.6
25-64	6,635	5,484	82.7	4,854	73.2	631	11.5	1,152	17.4	66	5.7	47	6.1	317	27.5	721	62.6
65+	1,065	145	13.6	140	13.1	4	2.9	921	86.5	32	3.5	—	—	101	11.0	788	85.6
Women, 16+	12,075	7,294	60.4	6,242	51.7	1,052	14.4	4,781	39.6	2,488	52.0	271	5.7	395	8.3	1,627	34.0
16-19	1,041	523	50.2	318	30.5	204	39.1	518	49.8	126	24.3	116	22.4	—	—	277	53.5
20-24	1,336	860	64.4	644	48.2	216	25.1	476	35.6	278	58.4	73	15.3	5	1.1	120	25.2
25-64	8,139	5,777	71.0	5,154	63.3	623	10.8	2,362	29.0	1,547	65.5	82	3.5	238	10.1	494	20.9
65+	1,560	134	8.6	126	8.1	8	5.9	1,425	91.3	538	37.8	—	—	152	10.7	735	51.6
Other Races 16 & Over	6,974	4,691	67.3	4,270	61.2	420	9.0	2,283	32.7	924	40.5	327	14.3	121	5.3	910	39.9
Men, 16+	3,308	2,561	77.4	2,319	70.1	241	9.4	748	22.6	32	4.3	150	20.0	55	7.4	512	68.4
16-19	299	151	50.5	112	37.5	41	27.2	148	49.5	7	4.7	54	36.5	2	1.4	85	57.4
20-24	362	270	74.6	235	64.7	35	13.0	92	25.4	1	1.1	46	50.0	—	—	45	48.9
25-64	2,362	2,695	88.7	1,930	81.7	163	7.8	268	11.3	18	6.7	52	19.4	51	19.0	150	55.9
65+	285	45	15.8	42	14.7	4	8.9	239	83.9	4	1.7	—	—	2	0.8	233	97.4
Women, 16+	3,666	2,131	58.1	1,952	53.2	179	8.4	1,536	41.9	893	58.1	178	11.6	67	4.4	398	25.9
16-19	291	144	49.5	101	34.7	44	30.6	147	50.5	31	21.1	50	34.0	—	—	66	44.9
20-24	369	223	60.4	208	56.4	14	6.3	146	39.6	53	36.3	64	43.8	—	—	30	20.5
25-64	2,632	1,739	66.1	1,620	61.6	118	6.8	892	33.9	656	73.5	64	7.2	43	5.4	124	13.9
65+	374	25	6.7	23	6.1	2	8.0	350	93.6	153	43.7	—	—	19	5.4	178	50.9

Source: Employment and Earnings July 1992, Table A-4, 9-11.

Note: * A further breakdown of the "Other" category of reasons for not being in the labor force appears in text Table 1.5

529

Appendix 1.C
Employed Civilians, Age 16 and Over, in Selected Occupations, by Sex, Race, and Hispanic Origin, Annual Averages, 1992 (numbers in thousands)

Occupation	Total Employed	Men	Women	Percent Distribution Women	Black	Hisp.	Illustrative Detailed Occupations Included in Field
1	2	3	4	5	6	7	8
Total, all occupations	117,598	63,805	53,793	45.7	10.1	7.6	
Managers and Professionals	31,153	16,416	14,736	47.3	6.5	3.9	
Exec., admin., managerial	14,767	8,641	6,126	40.0	5.7	3.9	Private & public sector admin. & personnel mgt.
Professionals	16,386	7,775	8,611	51.2	6.7	3.4	Several not listed (e.g. legal, social sciences)
Natural scientists	459	334	124	27.2	3.0	3.0	Physical, biological, life/medical scientists
Math & computer scientists	935	622	313	33.5	6.8	3.1	
Engineers	1,751	1,603	147	8.5	3.9	2.9	
Health assessmnt/treatment	2,517	332	2,184	86.8	8.5	3.4	Physicians, dentists, nurses, pharmacists, etc.
Teachers excl. college	4,216	1,062	3,154	73.7	8.7	3.5	
Writers, artists, athletes	2,019	1,066	953	47.2	4.9	4.5	
Technical, Sales, Admin. Sup.	36,808	13,269	23,539	64.7	9.2	5.8	
Technicians; related support	4,253	2,169	2,084	49.2	9.1	4.3	Health, engr. sciences techs.; computer programmers
Sales occupations	13,919	7,252	6,667	49.2	6.4	5.3	
Admin./clerical support	18,636	3,848	14,788	79.8	11.4	6.5	
Secretaries, typists	4,315	70	4,245	98.3	8.6	5.4	
Financial records procsrs.	2,335	219	2,117	91.6	6.2	5.1	
Service occupations	16,096	6,494	9,602	60.1	17.3	11.2	
Private household service	876	37	840	96.3	24.7	19.7	
Protective service	2,096	1,745	351	14.6	16.6	5.9	Police, fire, correctional, detective, etc.

Food prep. & service	5,459	2,243	3,215	59.5	12.4	12.5	Supervisors, cooks, waiters, bartenders
Health	2,105	237	1,868	90.2	26.3	6.4	Dental assistants, non-nurse aides
Building services	2,988	1,760	1,228	44.0	22.4	16.7	Includes supervisors, maids, janitors, cleaners
Personal services	2,573	473	2,100	81.6	12.0	7.3	Barbers; recreation/child care, other attendants
Precision production, craft, repair	13,128	12,000	1,128	8.5	7.3	8.5	
Mechanics & repairers	4,441	4,293	147	3.3	8.3	7.2	Masons, painters, plumbers, carpenters, etc.
Construction trades	4,790	4,702	89	1.9	7.3	9.5	
Precision production	3,897	3,005	892	22.3	8.5	9.8	Tool/die makers, machinists, metal workers,etc.
Operators/fabricators/laborers	16,957	12,720	4,237	25.5	15.0	12.2	Includes inspectors, testers, scanners
Machine operations/assemblers	7,524	4,535	2,989	40.0	14.4	13.9	
Transport'n/material moving	4,878	4,451	427	9.0	15.4	8.5	
Handlers/cleaners/laborers	4,556	3,734	821	17.7	15.7	12.9	Includes wide variety of helpers
Farming, forestry, fishing	3,456	2,905	551	16.0	6.1	14.2	
Farm operators/managers	1,232	1,042	190	15.7	0.9	1.7	
Other farm/fishery workers	2,224	1,864	361	17.1	9.1	22.8	

Source: Bureau of Labor Statistics, *Employment and Earnings.* January, 1993, Tables 20, 22, pp. 193-200.

Appendix 1.D
Persons Not in Labor Force (NILF) for Ages 16 and Over, by Reason, Sex, Race, and Hispanic Origin, Annual Averages, 1992 (numbers in thousands)

Reason	Total No.	Total %	White Male No.	White Male %	White Female No.	White Female %	Black Male No.	Black Male %	Black Female No.	Black Female %	Hispanic Male No.	Hispanic Male %	Hispanic Female No.	Hispanic Female %
1	2	3	4	5	6	7	8	9	10	11	12	13	14	15
Total Persons NILF	64,593	100	18,521	100	35,610	100	2,997	100	5,070	100	1,478	100	3,659	100
Does not Want Job Now:	58,413	90.4	16,867	91.1	32,768	92.0	2,473	82.5	4,168	82.2	1,218	82.4	3,179	86.9
School Attendance	6,723	10.4	2,469	13.3	2,607	7.3	521	17.4	581	11.5	319	21.6	375	10.2
Ill, Disabled	5,101	7.9	2,008	10.8	1,957	5.5	485	16.2	516	10.2	237	16.0	204	5.6
Keeping House	21,705	33.6	272	1.5	18,599	52.2	96	3.2	1,951	38.5	35	2.4	2,119	57.9
Retired	20,240	31.3	10,346	55.9	7,719	21.7	926	30.9	776	15.3	417	28.2	307	8.4
Other	4,644	7.2	1,772	9.6	1,886	5.3	444	14.8	345	6.8	209	14.1	174	4.8
Wants Job Now but Not Looking:	6,181	9.6	1,657	8.9	2,837	8.0	524	17.5	903	17.8	262	17.7	480	13.1
School Attendance	1,601	2.5	550	3.0	568	1.6	168	5.6	221	4.4	79	5.3	100	2.7
Ill, Disabled	1,078	1.7	391	2.1	410	1.2	113	3.8	131	2.6	55	3.7	56	1.5
Home Responsibility	1,236	1.9	—	0.0	911	2.6	—	0.0	282	5.6	—	0.0	174	4.8
Other	1,169	1.7	389	2.1	534	1.5	98	3.3	107	2.1	56	3.8	61	1.7
Thinks Cannot Get a Job Because:	1,097	1.7	328	1.8	415	1.2	144	4.8	162	3.2	71	4.8	88	2.4
Personal Factors	326	0.5												
Too young, too old	128	0.2	52	0.3	55	0.2	8	0.3	9	0.2	9	0.6	8	0.2
Lacks education or training	130	0.2	34	0.2	61	0.2	9	0.3	17	0.3	11	0.7	13	0.4
Other personal handicap	68	0.1	24	0.1	27	0.1	7	0.2	6	0.1	2	0.1	4	0.1
Job Market Factors	771	1.2												
Could not find work	484	0.7	121	0.7	149	0.4	90	3.0	106	2.1	32	2.2	43	1.2
Thinks no job available	287	0.4	97	0.5	123	0.3	29	1.0	23	0.5	18	1.2	19	0.5

Source: Bureau of Labor Statistics, Employment and Earnings January, 1993. Tables 35, 36, 37, pp. 214-216.

Appendix 1.E
Percent Distribution of the Civilian Labor Force, Ages 25 to 64, by Educational Attainment, Sex, and Race, for Period 1970–90 (numbers in thousands)

Year, Sex, and Race	Total Civilian Labor Force	Percent Distribution of Educational Attainment			
		Less than High Sch.	High Sch. Only	Coll. 1-3 Yrs.	College 4 Yrs. +
Total					
1970	61,765	36.1	38.1	11.8	14.1
1975	67,774	27.5	39.7	14.4	18.3
1980	78,010	20.6	39.8	17.6	22.0
1985	88,424	15.9	40.2	19.0	24.9
1990	99,981	13.3	39.4	20.8	26.5
Men					
1970	39,303	37.5	34.5	12.2	15.7
1975	41,628	28.9	36.1	14.8	20.2
1980	45,417	22.2	35.7	17.7	24.3
1985	49,647	17.7	36.9	18.3	27.1
1990	55,049	14.9	37.3	19.8	28.0
Women					
1970	22,462	33.5	44.3	10.9	11.2
1975	26,146	26.3	45.5	13.9	14.1
1980	32,593	18.4	45.4	17.4	18.7
1985	36,779	13.7	44.4	19.9	22.0
1990	44,932	11.2	42.1	22.1	24.6
White					
1970	55,044	33.7	39.3	12.2	14.8
1975	60,026	25.7	40.6	14.7	19.0
1980	60,509	19.1	40.2	17.7	22.9
1985	76,739	14.7	40.7	19.1	25.6
1990	85,882	12.5	39.4	20.8	27.3
Black					
1970	6,721	55.5	28.2	8.0	8.3
1975	7,586	41.9	33.1	12.4	12.6
1980	7,731	34.7	38.1	16.3	11.0
1985	9,157	26.2	39.5	19.2	15.0
1990	10,711	19.4	43.0	21.8	15.8

Source: Pre-1990 data from BLS, *Handbook of Labor Statistics*, Table 65, 1980, 280-281. 1990 data from BLS, Unpublished Tabulations from the Current Population Survey, 1990 Annual Averages, Table 1. 1991, 2, 9, 16.

Appendix 1.F

1990 Educational and Employment Status of Civilian Labor Force (CLF) Members, Ages 16 to 24, for School Enrollment, Employment, and Years of School Completed, by Race and Hispanic Origin (numbers in thousands)

Status	Civilian NIP	In CLF No.	In CLF % CLF	Not in CLF No.	Not in CLF % NIP	Employed No.	Employed % NIP	Unemployed (seeking) Total	Unemployed (seeking) F.T.	Unemployed (seeking) P.T.	Unempl. Rate*
Population Categories	31,593	21,252	67.3	10,341	32.7	18,883	59.8	2,369	1,582	787	11.1
Enr. in School, Total	12,824	6,203	48.4	6,621	51.6	5,528	43.1	675	136	539	10.9
High School	6,381	2,572	59.7	3,809	59.7	2,154	33.8	419	57	362	16.3
College	6,443	3,631	56.4	2,812	43.6	3,374	52.4	256	79	177	7.1
Full Time	5,419	2,732	50.4	2,687	49.6	2,523	46.6	209	54	156	7.7
Part Time	1,024	899	87.8	125	12.2	852	83.2	47	25	22	5.2
Not Enrolled, Total	18,769	15,049	80.2	3,720	19.8	13,355	71.2	1,694	1,446	248	11.3
Less than 4 yrs. H.S.	5,278	3,340	63.3	1,938	36.7	2,675	50.6	667	538	129	20.0
H.S. Only	8,664	7,309	84.4	1,355	17.6	6,650	75.6	758	674	84	10.4
1-3 Years' College	3,304	2,950	89.3	354	10.7	2,756	83.4	193	161	32	6.6
4 or More Years' College	1,524	1,451	95.2	73	4.8	1,375	90.2	76	73	3	5.2
Not Enrolled, White	15,457	12,730	82.4	2,727	17.6	11,542	74.7	1,189	1,011	178	9.3
Less than 4 yrs. H.S.	4,233	2,820	66.8	1,413	33.2	2,342	55.5	478	386	92	17.0
H.S. Only	7,057	6,088	86.3	969	13.7	5,576	79.0	512	454	58	8.4
1-3 Years' College	2,793	2,509	89.8	284	10.2	2,373	85.0	135	111	25	5.4
4 or More Years' College	1,375	1,314	95.6	61	4.4	1,251	91.0	63	60	9	4.8

Not Enrolled, Black	2,736	1,898	69.4	838	30.6	1,439	52.6	459	396	63	24.2
Less than 4 yrs. H.S.	866	424	49.0	442	51.0	252	29.1	171	138	33	40.4
H.S. Only	1,385	1,050	75.8	335	24.2	819	59.1	231	207	23	22.0
1-3 Years' College	393	340	86.5	53	13.5	291	74.0	49	43	6	14.3
4 or More Years' College	90	85	94.4	5	5.6	77	85.6	8	8	0	9.8
Not Enrolled, Hispanic	2,349	1,739	73.7	618	26.3	1,530	65.1	201	178	23	11.6
Less than 4 yrs. H.S.	1,260	837	66.4	423	33.6	720	57.1	117	104	13	13.9
H.S. Only	817	657	80.4	160	19.6	592	72.5	65	57	8	9.9
1-3 Years' College	225	194	86.2	31	13.8	178	79.1	16	14	2	8.3
4 or More Years' College	47	43	91.5	4	8.5	39	83.0	4	4	0	8.3

Source: Bureau of Labor Statistics, *Employment and Earnings*, Table 6. January 1991, 169-170.

* Indicates number of unemployed as percent of CLF.

Appendix 1.G

Educational Attainment of Persons in 25–64 Age Group Not in Labor Force (NILF) or Unemployed, in 1990, by Sex, Race, and Hispanic Origin (numbers in thousands)

Sex and Race	NIP No.	NILF No.	% NIP	Below H.S. No.	% NILF	% Below Gr. 8	HS Only No.	% NILF	1-3 Yrs. Coll. No.	% NILF	4 or more years' college No.	% NILF	4 yr. %	5 + %	MSYC*
Not in Labor Force:															
Total, All Persons	126,722	26,742	21.1	8,348	31.2	14.9	10,846	40.6	4,125	15.4	3,423	12.8	8.3	4.5	12.5
White, Total	107,994	22,112	20.5	6,294	28.5	13.7	9,242	41.8	3,563	16.1	3,012	13.6	8.9	4.7	12.5
Male	53,152	5,245	9.9	1,878	35.8	19.8	1,932	34.9	777	14.8	757	14.4	7.7	6.7	12.4
Female	54,842	16,867	30.8	4,416	26.2	11.8	7,409	43.9	2,786	16.5	2,225	13.2	9.2	4.1	12.5
Black, Total	14,207	3,496	24.6	1,652	47.3	19.3	1,250	35.8	425	12.2	168	4.8	2.9	1.9	12.1
Male	6,381	1,083	17.0	554	51.2	25.9	350	32.3	127	11.7	52	4.8	2.6	2.2	11.8
Female	7,826	2,413	30.8	1,098	45.5	16.2	901	37.3	298	12.3	117	4.8	3.1	1.7	12.1
Hispanic, Total	9,863	2,542	25.8	1,587	62.4	43.6	605	25.4	194	7.6	116	4.6	2.8	1.7	9.9
Male	4,890	521	10.7	338	64.9	45.9	114	21.9	39	7.5	30	5.8	3.3	2.3	9.6
Female	4,924	2,022	40.7	1,249	61.8	43.1	531	26.3	155	7.7	87	4.3	2.7	1.5	9.9

Unemployed:	CLF	Unempl.	% Unempl.												
Total, All Persons	99,981	4,396	4.4	1,126	25.6	9.3	1,914	43.5	17.5	770	17.5	587	13.4	8.5	4.9	12.6
White, Total	85,882	3,298	3.8	808	24.5	10.0	1,421	43.1	17.5	578	17.5	491	14.9	9.3	5.6	12.6
Male	47,907	1,865	3.9	501	26.9	11.2	784	42.0	16.2	303	16.2	277	14.9	9.3	5.6	12.6
Female	37,975	1,433	3.8	308	21.5	8.3	637	44.5	19.2	275	19.2	214	14.9	9.4	5.6	12.6
Black, Total	10,711	921	8.6	275	29.9	6.5	438	47.6	17.2	158	17.2	50	5.4	4.0	1.4	12.4
Male	5,298	475	9.0	146	30.7	7.2	225	47.4	16.2	77	16.2	27	5.7	4.0	1.7	12.4
Female	5,413	446	8.2	129	28.9	5.6	213	47.8	18.2	81	18.2	23	5.2	4.0	1.1	12.4
Hispanic, Total	7,321	502	6.9	282	56.2	37.5	146	29.1	9.8	49	9.8	26	5.2	3.6	1.6	10.9
Male	4,369	297	6.8	173	58.2	39.7	83	27.9	8.8	26	8.8	16	5.4	3.4	1.7	10.7
Female	2,952	205	7.0	109	53.2	34.1	63	30.7	11.7	24	11.7	10	4.9	3.4	1.5	11.3

Source: Bureau of Labor Statistics, Unpublished tabulations from the *Current Population Survey*, 1990 Annual Averages, Table 1 (Labor Force Status of the Civilian Noninstitutional Population, uncomposited annual averages).

* Indicates median school years completed

Appendix 1.H

Current and Projected Employment and Educational Status of Major Occupational Groups and Selected Occupations Thereunder, 1990–2000

Occupation	Total Empl'd	% of Total	1990 Percent Distribution Education Level				Year 2000 Projection			Illustrative Detailed Occupations Included in Field
			Below H.S.	H.S. Only	1-3 yrs. Coll.	Coll. 4 + yrs.	No.	%	% Change 1990-2000	
Total, all occupations	117,905	100	15.2	39.3	21.6	24.0	136,211	100	15.5	
Managers and Professionals	30,732	26.1	2.6	17.2	20.0	60.2	32,899	24.2	7.1	
Exec., admin., managerial	14,899	12.6	4.0	26.6	24.0	45.4	14,762	10.8	-0.1*	Private/public sector admin. & personnel mgt.
Professionals	15,833	13.4	1.3	8.3	16.3	74.1	18,137	13.3	14.6	
Natural science, math, engr	3,150	2.7	0.8	8.3	17.4	73.6	2,928	2.1	-7.0*	Math. & computer scientists; chemists, geologists, life scientists; engineers; architects
Health diagnosis/treatment	3,195	2.7	0.7	6.0	24.9	68.3	3,871	2.8	21.2	Physicians, dentists, nurses, pharmacts., etc.
Teachers excl. college	3,989	3.4	1.1	6.4	8.8	83.6	5,026	3.7	26.0	
Other professionals	5,505	4.7	2.2	10.8	16.0	71.0	6,312	4.6	14.8	Lawyers, artists, soc. & relig. workers; college faculty, librarians, soc. scientists, etc.
Technical, Sales, Admin. Sup.	36,582	31.0	7.9	43.6	29.2	19.2	44,566	32.7	21.8	
Technicians; related support	3,836	3.3	2.5	28.1	36.8	32.5	5,089	3.7	32.7	Health, engr. sci. techs.; computer progmrs.
Sales occupations	14,168	12.0	12.1	38.8	25.0	24.1	15,924	11.7	12.4	
Admin./clerical support	18,578	15.8	5.9	50.5	30.8	12.8	23,553	17.3	26.8	
Secretaries, typists	4,641	3.9	3.2	52.9	33.6	10.3	4,991	3.7	7.5	
Service occupations	15,769	13.4	29.0	45.5	19.2	6.4	22,651	16.6	43.6	
Private household service	798	0.7	49.7	36.2	9.5	4.4	860	0.6	7.8	
Protective service	1,990	1.7	9.0	42.3	33.7	15.0	2,610	1.9	31.2	Police, fire, correctional, detective, etc.
Food prep. & service	5,344	4.5	35.7	42.5	17.0	4.9	9,227	6.8	73.0	Supervisors, cooks, waiters, bartenders
Health	2,083	1.8	19.1	51.9	23.5	5.5	2,450	1.8	17.6	Dental assts. non-nurse aides
Building services	3,110	2.6	40.5	45.4	10.9	3.2	3,960	2.9	27.3	Includes supervisors, maids, janitors, cleaners
Personal services	2,444	2.1	18.0	52.2	22.1	8.1	2,625	1.9	7.4	Barbers;recreation/child care, other attendants

Precision production, craft, repair	**13,654**	**11.6**	**21.1**	**53.0**	**19.7**	**6.2**	**15,563**	**11.4**	**14.0**	Masons, painters, plumbers, carpenters, etc.
Mechanics & repairers	4,446	3.8	18.5	53.6	22.3	5.6	5,471	4.0	23.1	
Construction trades	5,158	4.4	25.1	51.3	17.9	5.7	4,423	3.2	-14.2	Tool/die makers, machinists, metal wkrs.,etc.
Precision production operators	4,051	3.4	19.0	54.3	19.4	7.4	NA			
Operators/fabricators/laborers	**17,754**	**15.1**	**30.7**	**52.3**	**13.5**	**3.6**	**17,198**	**12.6**	**-3.1**	Includes inspectors, testers, scanners
Machine operations/assemblers	8,056	6.8	30.7	53.8	12.0	3.6)	7,048	5.2	-12.5	
Transportation/material moving	4,853	4.1	26.2	54.1	15.3	4.3	5,154	3.8	6.2	
Handlers/cleaners/laborers	4,845	4.1	35.2	47.9	14.1	2.8	4,995	3.7	3.2	Includes wide variety of helpers
Farming, forestry, fishing	**3,414**	**2.9**	**36.7**	**40.8**	**14.3**	**8.2**	**3,334**	**2.4**	**-2.3**	
Farm operators/managers	1,238	1.0	20.2	48.5	17.2	14.1	NA			
Other farm/fishery workers	2,176	1.8	46.0	36.5	12.6	4.9	NA			

Source: 1990 data from BLS unpublished data from *Current Population Survey*, 1990 Annual Averages. Year 2000 projections from "Projections of Occupational Employment 1988-2000," Table 2, *Monthly Labor Review*, November, 1989, 45.

* By 1990, Year 2000 projections had already been exceeded.

Appendix 2.A
Percentage of Persons in Poverty, by Race, Hispanic Origin, and Asian/Pacific Islander, and by Definition of Income, 1990

Definition of Income	All Races	White Origin	Black	Hispanic	Asian/Pac.Isl.
All Income Levels					
All persons (thousands)	248,644	208,611	30,808	21,405	7,014
In Poverty					
Income before taxes:					
1. Money income excl. capital gains (current measure)	13.5	10.7	31.9	28.1	12.2
2. Definition 1 less gov't. cash transfers	20.5	17.7	39.7	33.7	16.9
3. Def. 2 plus capital gains	20.4	17.6	39.7	33.4	16.8
4. Def. 3 plus health insurance supplements to wage/salary income	19.9	17.1	38.6	32.5	16.3
Income after taxes:					
5. Def. 4 less Soc. Sec. payroll taxes	20.9	18.0	40.2	34.7	17.3
6. Def. 5 less federal income taxes excl. EITC	21.1	18.2	40.5	35.3	17.4
7. Def. 6 plus earned income tax credit (EITC)	20.6	17.8	39.7	34.2	16.9
8. Def. 7 less state income taxes	20.8	18.0	39.9	34.5	16.9
9. Def. 8 plus nonmeans-tested government cash transfers	14.7	11.7	34.4	30.4	14.5
10. Def. 9 plus the value of Medicare	14.3	11.3	33.6	29.6	14.0
11. Def. 10 plus value of regular priced school lunches	14.3	11.3	33.6	29.6	14.0
12. Def. 11 plus means-tested government	13.2	10.6	30.8	27.9	11.3
13. Def. 12 plus value of Medicaid	12.4	10.0	28.9	26.3	10.8
14. Def. 13 plus value of other means-tested government noncash transfers	11.0	9.0	24.3	22.7	9.3
15. Def. 14 plus net imputed return on home equity	9.8	7.9	22.3	21.4	8.8

Source: Replicated from U. S. Bureau of the Census, *Measuring the Effects of Benefits and Taxes on Income and Poverty: 1990*. Current Population Reports, Consumer Income, Series P-60, No. 176RD, Table H. August 1991, 13.

Notes: Persons of Hispanic origin may be of any race.

Appendix 2.B

Children Under 18 Living with One Parent, by Marital Status of Parent, by Race and Hispanic Origin of Child (numbers in thousands)

Subject	Number				Per cent distribution			
	1990	1980	1970	1950	1990	1980	1970	1960
Total children	15,857	12,466	8,199	5,829	100.0	100.0	100.0	100.0
Marital status of parent:								
Divorced	6,122	5,281	2,473	1,543	38.6	42.4	30.2	23.0
Married, spouse absent	3,767	3,898	3,521	2,700	23.7	31.3	42.9	46.3
Separated	3,222	3,327	2,484	1,608	20.3	26.7	30.3	27.6
Other	545	571	1,037	1,092	3.4	4.6	12.6	18.7
Widowed	1,125	1,469	1,649	1,543	7.1	11.8	20.1	26.5
Never married	4,853	1,820	557	243	30.6	14.6	6.8	4.2
White children	9,869	7,901	5,110	3,392	100.0	100.0	100.0	100.0
Marital status of parent:								
Divorced	4,847	4,106	1,997	1,118	49.1	52.0	39.1	28.4
Married, spouse absent	2,356	2,243	1,822	1,515	23.9	28.4	35.7	41.1
Separated	1,982	1,817	1,111	779	20.1	23.0	21.7	19.8
Other	373	426	711	836	3.8	5.4	13.9	21.3
Widowed	774	1,000	1,160	1,139	7.8	12.7	22.7	29.0
Never married	1,894	552	131	61	19.2	7.0	2.6	1.6
Black children[1]	5,484	4,297	2,995	1,897	100.0	100.0	100.0	100.0
Marital status of parent:								
Divorced	1,117	1,078	438	225	20.4	25.1	14.6	11.9
Married, spouse absent	1,251	1,573	1,651	1,085	22.8	36.6	55.1	57.2

Appendix 2.B (continued)

Subject	Number				Per cent distribution			
	1990	1980	1970	1960	1990	1980	1970	1960
Separated	1,125	1,463	1,343	829	20.5	34.0	44.8	43.7
Other	125	110	308	256	2.3	2.6	10.3	13.5
Widowed	278	411	482	405	5.1	9.6	16.1	21.3
Never married	2,839	1,235	423	182	51.8	28.7	14.1	9.6
Hispanic children[2]	2,154	1,152	NA	NA	100.0	100.0	NA	NA
Marital status of parent:								
Divorced	574	353	NA	NA	26.6	30.6	NA	NA
Married, spouse absent	728	468	NA	NA	33.8	40.6	NA	NA
Separated	577	400	NA	NA	26.8	34.7	NA	NA
Other	151	68	NA	NA	7.0	5.9	NA	NA
Widowed	149	103	NA	NA	6.9	8.9	NA	NA
Never married	703	228	NA	NA	32.6	19.8	NA	NA

Source: Census Bureau, *Marital Status and Living Arrangements: March 1990.* P-20, No. 450, Table F. May 1991, 6. 1960 data: 1960 Census of Population, *Persons by Family Characteristics,* tables 1 and 19.

1. Nonwhite in 1960.
2. Persons of Hispanic origin may be of any race.
Notes: NA indicates data not available.

Appendix 2.C
Public and Private Effects Associated with Paternity Establishment

Domain	Indicator	Measure
Public	Change in male out-of-wedlock behavior	Reduction in the number of out-of-wedlock births (through either lowering of the birthrate or an increase in the marriage rate)
	Encourages idea that unmarried men are responsible for their behavior and discourages the idea that the out-of-wedlock child is solely the mother's responsibility	Increase in the number of men who voluntarily admit paternity
Private	Legal effects on the father if paternity is established	
	Establishes a right to custody of child if the mother dies or loses custody	Whether father's right to custody of the child is exercised and recognized at custody hearing
	Establishes a right to custody of the child if mother wishes to place child for adoption or give up custody	Whether father's right of parental consent is exercised and recognized at custody hearing
	Psychological and social effects on the father if he acknowledges paternity	

Appendix 2.C (continued)

Domain	Indicator	Measure
	Effect on his desire to assume coresponsibility for the child	Whether the father initiates contact with the child An increase in frequency of father's visit to the child. A change in duration of visits. Whether the father promotes contact between the child and the paternal family. An increase in the regularity of financial support.
	Social effects of public disclosure of paternity	Whether the father experiences public support or public condemnation for disclosure. Whether, if married, his marriage experiences disruption or increased tension.
	Psychological and social effects on the child if paternity established	
	Effects on level of identification between child and father	Whether the child knows the biological father's name Whether child accepts the biological father and identifies with him in a familial sense Level of child's self-esteem
	Effects on level of involvement of paternal family in support and care of the child	Whether paternal family members assume responsibility for child care/support The number of paternal family members who assume this responsibility. Frequency of contacts between paternal family members and the child. Whether child acknowledges this support network to be based on a paternal link.
	Effects on extent and nature of father-child contacts	Whether or not father initiates contact with the child. An increase in the number of visits to the

	child. The duration of visits. Whether or not child characterizes such contacts as supportive or stressful.
Effects on child's health prospects (in cases of genetic disease)	Whether the child's health is improved because a linkage with an inherited disease was established.
Psychological and social effects on the mother if paternity is established	Whether or not mother has sense of relief or intrusion about the prospect of mutual obligation and shared contact
Effects of acknowledgment of mutual obligation and father-child contact	
Effects of the prospect of contact with the father	Whether the mother encourages contacts with the father. Whether mother seeks to establish a "good-cause" claim during intake process in AFDC (for AFDC cases only). Whether the mother moves out of the area in order to avoid contact with father Whether the mother seeks to deny visitation by the father. Number and types of contacts encouraged.
Involvement with the parental family	Whether the mother supports contact with the parental family. Number and types of contacts encouraged between child and the paternal family.
Psychological and social effects on purported father when paternity claim is not established	If married, whether his marriage experiences disruption or increased tension. Whether the alleged father experiences public condemnation through presumption of responsibility.

Source: Replicated from: U.S. General Accounting Office (GAO) A Framework for Child Support Program. GAO/PEMD-91-6 (—1991), 36-37.

Appendix 3.A
Real National Health Expenditures by Payer and Type of Service, in Amounts and Percent Distribution, for Selected Years, 1961–91 (amounts in billions of 1991 dollars)

Service Type	All Payers			Consumer Out-of-Pocket			Private Health Insurance			Other Private Payers*			Government Total			Federal Government			State and Local Government		
	1961	1975	1991	1961	1975	1991	1961	1975	1991	1961	1975	1991	1961	1975	1991	1961	1975	1991	1961	1975	1991
Amounts:																					
Total	121.1	322.1	751.8	56.9	93.4	144.3	27.7	79.7	244.4	6.0	15.4	33.2	30.5	133.6	330.0	13.9	88.2	222.9	16.6	45.4	107.1
Hospitals	42.2	126.9	288.6	8.1	10.6	9.9	15.7	43.7	101.5	0.6	3.5	14.7	17.8	69.2	162.7	7.5	48.1	119.2	10.3	21.1	43.5
Physicians	23.0	56.4	142.0	13.8	18.5	25.7	7.5	22.2	66.8	n	n	0.1	1.8	15.7	49.4	0.4	11.3	39.0	1.4	4.4	10.4
Nursing Homes	4.2	24.1	59.9	3.2	10.1	25.8	0.0	0.2	0.6	0.3	1.2	1.1	0.8	12.6	32.3	0.4	7.4	19.5	0.4	5.2	12.8
Drugs and Other Non-durables	18.5	31.5	60.7	18.0	27.1	44.3	0.2	2.0	9.0	0.0	0.0	0.0	0.4	2.4	7.3	0.2	1.2	3.6	0.2	1.2	3.7
Other**	33.1	83.1	200.5	13.9	27.0	38.5	4.3	11.7	66.5	5.1	10.7	17.3	9.8	33.7	78.3	5.4	20.2	41.6	4.4	13.5	36.7
Percents																					
Total	100.0	100.0	100.0	45.7	29.0	19.2	24.0	24.8	32.5	5.5	4.8	4.4	24.8	41.5	43.9	11.6	27.4	29.6	13.2	14.1	14.2
Hospitals	34.8	39.4	38.4	19.2	8.4	3.4	37.2	34.4	35.2	1.4	2.8	5.1	42.2	54.5	56.4	17.8	37.9	41.3	24.4	16.6	15.1
Physicians	19.0	17.5	18.9	60.0	32.8	18.1	32.6	39.4	47.0	—	—	—	7.8	27.8	34.8	1.7	20.0	27.5	6.1	7.8	7.3
Nursing Homes	3.5	7.5	8.0	74.4	41.9	43.1	—	0.8	1.0	7.0	5.0	1.8	18.6	52.3	53.9	9.3	30.7	32.6	9.3	21.6	21.4
Drugs and Other Non-durables	15.3	9.8	8.1	97.3	86.0	73.0	1.1	6.3	14.8	—	—	—	2.7	3.8	12.0	1.1	3.8	5.9	1.6	3.7	6.1
Other	27.3	25.8	26.7	42.0	32.5	19.2	13.0	14.1	33.2	15.4	12.9	8.6	29.6	40.6	39.1	16.3	24.3	20.7	13.3	16.2	18.3

Source: Congressional Budget Office (CBO), based on data from HHS, Health Care Financing Administration (HCFA), Office of the Actuary, 1992.

Notes: n = Less than $100 million; * includes philanthropic, uninsured employer, other; ** includes home health care, dental and other professional services, durable medical equipment, other personal health care, administration, and research.

The word "real" is used here to mean: adjusted for general inflation rather than for inflation in health care costs. Health expenditures are adjusted to 1991 dollars, using the consumer price index for all urban consumers (CPI-U).

Appendix 3.B

Health Care Insured and Uninsured Persons, by Selected Age Group, in Medicaid, Race and Ethnic Origin, Residence, and School Years Completed, 1989 (numbers in thousands)

Characteristics	All	Total Insured	Percent	Insured In Medicaid Number	Insured In Medicaid Percent	Uninsured Total Number	Uninsured Total Percent*	Uninsured White Number	Uninsured White Percent*	Uninsured Black Number	Uninsured Black Percent*	Uninsured Hispanic Orig. Number	Uninsured Hispanic Orig. Percent*
All Persons	246,191	212,807	86.4	21,185	8.6	33,384	13.6	25,857	12.5	5,842	20.6	6,933	33.4
White	206,983	181,126	87.5	12,779	6.2	25,857	12.5	25,857	12.5				
Black	30,392	24,550	80.8	7,123	23.4	5,842	19.2			5,842	19.2		
Hispanic Origin	20,779	13,846	66.6	3,221	15.5	6,933	33.4					6,933	33.4
Other Races	8,116	7,131	80.1	1,283	14.6	1,955	22.2	Age group, school years completed, and residence data not computed for this group					
Age Group:													
Under 65	216,625	183,549	84.7	18,608	8.6	33,076	15.3	25,643	99.2	5,783	99.0	6,891	99.4
Under 18	64,343	55,796	86.7	10,099	15.7	8,547	25.6	6,466	25.0	1,661	28.4	2,179	31.4
18-24	25,311	18,954	74.9	2,057	8.1	6,357	19.0	4,972	19.2	1,085	18.6	1,397	20.2
25 and over	156,537	138,057	88.2	9,029	5.8	18,480	55.4	14,419	55.8	3,096	53.0	3,355	48.4
School Yrs. Completed:													
8 Years or less	17,590	14,433	82.1	4,732	6.1	3,157	17.1	2,534	17.6	457	14.8	1,548	46.1
1-3 Yrs. H.S.	17,462	14,146	81.0	1,996	11.4	3,316	17.9	2,402	16.7	812	26.2	567	16.9
H.S. graduate	60,119	52,830	87.9	2,736	4.6	7,289	39.4	5,768	40.0	1,187	38.3	841	25.1
1-3 Yrs. College	28,075	25,300	90.1	775	2.8	2,775	15.0	2,180	15.1	453	14.6	250	7.5
4+ Yrs. College	33,291	31,347	94.2	304	0.9	1,994	10.5	1,535	10.6	187	6.0	150	4.5

Appendix 3.B (continued)

Characteristics	All	Insured Total Insured	Percent	In Medicaid Number	Percent	Uninsured Total Number	Percent*	White Number	Percent*	Black Number	Percent*	Hispanic Orig. Number	Percent*
Residence:													
In Metro Areas	191,315	165,672	86.6	16,253	8.5	25,643	76.8	19,499	75.3	4,737	81.1	6,371	91.9
In Central City	75,197	62,475	83.1	9,859	13.1	12,722	38.1	8,474	32.8	3,445	59.0	3,759	54.2
1 million or more	47,079	38,308	81.4	6,745	14.3	8,711	26.3	5,616	21.7	2,531	43.3	2,984	43.0
Below 1 million	28,118	24,167	85.9	3,114	11.1	3,951	11.8	2,859	11.1	912	15.6	775	11.2
Outside Cntrl City	116,118	103,198	88.9	6,394	5.5	12,920	38.7	11,004	42.6	1,292	22.1	2,613	37.7
Out of Metro A's	54,876	47,135	85.9	4,932	9.0	7,741	23.2	6,378	24.7	1,106	18.9	561	8.1
Non Farm	241,571	208,680	86.4	21,077	8.7	32,891	98.5	25,393	98.2	5,829	99.8	6,882	99.3
Farm	4,620	4,126	89.3	108	2.3	494	1.5	464	1.8	13	0.2	50	0.7

Source: U.S. Department of Commerce, Bureau of the Census, *Current Population Survey.* Unpublished Data, Table NC 6. Health Care Coverage of Persons, By Selected Characteristics, Type of Coverage, Race and Hispanic Origin, and Poverty Status, 1989. January 31, 1991, 1561-1583.

Notes: *For age group and residence, represents proportion of all uninsured persons within the respective total racial/ethnic category. For school years completed, represents proportion of persons in the respective 25 and over age group within each total racial/ethnic category.

548

Appendix 3.C

Rates and Percents, by State and Race, for Low Birth-Weight Babies (1990), Infant Mortality (1987–89 and 1991), Births to Single Mothers (1990), and Early Prenatal Care (1988)

Region and State	Low Birth Weight 1990 %			Infant Mortality Rates All			Race 1987-89		Births to Single Mothers 1990 %			Early Prenatal Care 1988 %		
	All	White	Black	1987-'88	'989	1991	White	Black	All	White	Black	All	White	Black[1]
U.S. Total	7.0	5.7	13.3	9.9	9.9	8.9	9.3	18.6	28.0	20.4	66.5	74.2	77.8	59.0
New England														
Maine	5.1	4.9	*	7.8	7.4	6.7	7.8	*	22.7	22.4	38.5	81.8	92.0	76.7
New Hampshire	4.9	4.9	*	8.0	8.0	6.1	8.0	*	16.9	16.9	37.2	82.9	83.2	67.8
Vermont	5.3	5.3		7.4	6.9	5.8	7.4	*	20.1	20.1	*	75.5	76.6	55.9
Massachusetts	5.9	5.3	10.5	7.6	7.7	6.6	6.8	16.7	24.7	20.7	60.9	83.0	83.5	62.2
Rhode Island	6.2	5.7	10.3	8.8	10.2	8.0	8.4	15.9*	26.3	22.6	63.0	83.2	85.5	68.3
Connecticut**	6.6	5.7	13.1	8.9	8.8	7.4	7.4	19.5	26.6	20.3	69.2	72.3	76.2	49.5
Middle Atlantic														
New York	7.6	6.0	13.4	10.7	10.6	9.4	9.7	18.7	33.0	24.3	67.4	70.6	32.3	51.0
New Jersey	7.0	5.5	13.0	9.5	9.3	8.7	7.3	19.2	24.3	15.6	63.6	77.1	82.0	50.0
Pennsylvania	7.1	5.7	15.1	10.1	10.2	9.1	8.0	22.9	29.6	20.2	77.5	77.8	82.8	51.8
East North Central														
Ohio	7.1	5.9	13.5	9.6	9.9	9.4	9.3	17.3	29.9	20.6	74.7	80.0	83.4	62.1
Indiana	6.6	5.8	12.5	10.4	10.2	9.1	9.3	20.5	26.2	20.3	73.9	76.2	78.7	58.0
Illinois	7.6	5.5	14.5	11.6	11.7	10.7	8.9	21.5	31.7	19.0	77.8	77.6	82.3	62.2
Michigan**	7.6	5.7	14.7	11.0	11.1	10.4	8.3	22.4	26.2	14.6	70.3	79.2	82.1	67.1
Wisconsin	5.9	4.9	14.3	9.7	9.1	8.3	7.9	17.0	24.2	17.7	80.7	82.8	85.9	63.7

Appendix 3.C (continued)

Region and State	Low Birth Weigh 1990 %			Infant Mortality Rates			Race '87-'89		Births to Single Mothers 1990 %			Early Pre-Natal Care 1988%		
	All	White	Black	All 87-'88	'89	'91	White	Black	All	White	Black	All	White	Black[1]
West North Central														
Minnesota	5.1	4.6	13.7	7.8	7.1	7.5	7.1	22.8	20.9	17.6	73.3	67.3	74.4	46.5
Iowa	5.4	5.2	13.0	8.7	8.3	8.0	8.2	22.6*	21.0	19.5	73.1	84.5	85.3	70.0
Missouri	7.1	5.8	13.3	10.1	9.9	10.2	8.7	17.5	28.6	18.8	76.0	78.5	81.4	64.4
North Dakota	5.5	5.5	#	9.1	8.0	8.1	8.4	#	18.4	14.0	#	81.1	83.3	79.6
South Dakota	5.1	5.1	#	9.9	9.6	9.4	8.1	#	22.9	14.5	#	76.3	80.4	69.6
Nebraska	5.3	4.9	11.8	8.5	7.9	7.6	7.7	20.6*	20.7	17.0	71.1	82.1	83.7	64.8
Kansas	6.2	5.7	12.0	8.7	8.8	8.9	7.8	18.9	21.5	17.5	62.8	79.7	81.5	66.6
South Atlantic														
Delaware	7.6	5.9	13.4	11.8	11.8	11.8	9.2	20.5	29.0	16.7	70.3	79.4	84.9	61.0
Maryland	7.8	5.4	13.0	11.0	10.3	9.2	8.3	17.7	29.7	16.2	60.2	77.4	84.3	63.6
Dist. of Columbia	15.1	7.3	17.5	21.9	22.9	21.0	14.4	25.3	64.9	19.3	76.0	60.7	85.6	56.3
Virginia	7.2	5.6	12.3	10.2	10.0	9.9	7.8	18.2	26.0	15.1	61.3	79.9	84.4	66.9
West Virginia	7.1	6.8	13.2	9.4	9.4	8.2	9.1	18.7*	25.4	23.8	68.0	69.5	70.3	51.8
North Carolina	8.0	5.9	12.8	11.9	11.3	10.8	9.1	18.8	29.4	14.2	64.4	75.4	82.3	60.1
South Carolina	8.7	6.1	12.9	12.6	12.8	11.3	9.4	17.9	32.7	14.7	61.8	64.0	74.6	47.9
Georgia	8.7	6.2	13.0	12.5	12.3	11.4	9.4	18.5	32.8	14.9	64.9	72.0	78.9	59.9
Florida	7.4	5.9	12.5	10.3	9.8	9.0	8.1	17.8	31.7	20.9	67.6	69.6	75.2	52.4
East South Central														
Kentucky	7.1	6.6	12.0	9.9	9.2	8.9	9.2	16.7	23.6	19.0	68.6	75.7	77.2	62.5
Tennessee	8.2	6.5	13.7	11.1	10.8	10.0	8.5	19.2	30.2	17.7	71.1	74.0	77.6	63.0
Alabama	8.4	6.2	12.6	12.1	12.1	11.2	9.1	17.9	30.1	12.0	64.7	72.3	79.9	57.9
Mississippi	9.6	6.5	12.9	12.5	11.6	11.4	9.0	16.4	40.5	13.3	69.9	75.3	85.1	64.8
West South Central														
Arkansas	8.2	6.6	13.2	10.4	10.2	10.2	8.6	16.6	29.4	17.1	69.6	65.2	71.3	46.3
Louisiana	9.2	6.0	13.8	11.4	11.4	10.5	8.4	16.1	36.9	15.6	67.2	74.0	84.4	59.6
Oklahoma	6.6	6.1	11.5	9.1	8.5	9.6	8.5	14.1	25.2	18.5	64.9	67.5	71.1	48.6
Texas **	6.9	6.0	13.0	9.1	9.2	7.7	8.1	15.8	17.5	12.8	48.3	65.3	66.8	55.4

Mountain														
Montana	6.2	6.2	#	10.0	11.3	7.0	9.1	#	23.7	18.0	#	76.5	79.6	70.5
Idaho	5.7	5.6	#	9.6	9.7	8.7	9.3	#	16.7	16.2	#	71.9	72.3	77.5
Wyoming	7.4	7.2	#	9.2	9.4	7.9	10.2	#	19.8	18.6	44.8	77.5	78.3	70.6
Colorado	8.0	7.5	15.8	9.4	8.7	8.4	9.1	16.5	21.3	19.2	54.6	76.7	77.7	65.8
New Mexico	7.4	7.5	12.0	8.9	8.5	8.1	8.3	22.6*	35.4	30.5	56.6	51.0	52.3	40.7
Arizona	6.4	6.2	11.5	9.5	9.2	8.6	8.9	21.4	32.7	28.9	61.2	66.3	68.5	58.7
Utah	5.7	5.7	12.8	8.3	8.0	6.1	8.0	#	13.5	12.6	52.7	81.1	82.2	64.6
Nevada	7.2	6.5	14.1	8.7	8.1	9.2	7.7	20.0	25.4	21.2	66.2	71.9	74.6	52.2
Pacific														
Washington	5.3	4.9	11.6	9.3	9.2	7.5	8.7	20.6	23.7	21.8	54.3	74.4	85.9	59.4
Oregon	5.0	4.8	10.2	9.3	8.9	7.3	9.1	21.4*	25.7	24.5	71.4	73.7	74.4	61.5
California**	5.8	5.1	12.5	8.7	8.5	7.6	8.0	18.8	31.6	30.7	62.3	74.2	74.6	67.9
Alaska	4.8	4.0	10.9	10.4	9.2	8.9	8.0	15.7*	26.2	17.2	30.1	78.2	82.0	79.3
Hawaii	7.1	5.6	12.1	8.1	8.3	7.4	5.5	14.4	24.8	14.5	17.7	71.5	80.6	80.1
Prior U.S. Totals														
1970	7.9	6.8	13.8	20.0	11.8	32.6			10.7	5.5	37.4	68.0	72.4	44.4
1980	6.8	5.7	12.5	12.6	11.0	21.4			18.4	11.0	55.2	76.3	79.3	62.7
1985	6.8	5.6	12.4	10.6	9.3	18.2			22.0	14.5	60.1	76.2	79.4	61.8

Sources: U. S. Department of Health and Human Services, U. S. Public Health Service, National Center for Vital Statistics: (1) *Vital Statistics of the United States 1988* vol. I: Natality, Sec. I, Table I-91, pp. 264-266; and vol. 3: Mortality, Sec. 2, Table 2-8, p. 8. (2) "Advance Report of Final Natality Statistics, 1989,"*Monthly Vital Statistics Report* (39:4), Tables 6 and 16, August 15, 1990, 21, 30. (3) "Advance Report of Final Mortality Statistics, 1989," *Monthly Vital Statistics Report* (39:7 S), Table 13, November 28, 1990, 2. (4)"Advance Report of Final Mortality Statistics, 1991," *Monthly Vital Statistics Report* (42:2S), Table 24, August 31, 1993, 53. (5) USPHS, *Health USA 1991*, Table 7, March 1991, 58. See also, for analysis and comment, Center for the Study of Social Policy, *Kids Count Data Book 1991* (Greenwich, CT: Annie F. Casey Foundation 1991).

Notes: † indicates low birth weight and prenatal care.

* indicates data for states with fewer than 5,000 live births over 3-year period considered by NCHS as unreliable but still shown.

** indicates NCHS notes that in these states, marital status of mother is not shown on birth certificate, in contrast to other states and the District of Columbia; Marital status is inferred from comparison of child's and parent's surnames.

# indicates state groups with fewer than 1,000 live births considered by NCHS to be highly unreliable and not shown.

Infant mortality rates: Number per 1,000 live births in each race group and state; unmarried mothers and early prenatal care (during first trimester) shown in percents of total live births in each state race category. Low birth weight: Below 2,500 g. (5 lbs., 8 oz.).

Appendix 3.D

Congressional Expansion of Mandates and State Options for Expansions in Medicaid Coverage, 1984–90

1984: 1. (M) Required coverage of all children born after (PL 98-369) 9/30/83 that meet state AFDC income and resource standards, regardless of family structure.

2. (M) Required coverage from date of medical verification of pregnancy, providing they would qualify for AFDC once child was born or they would qualify for AFDC-UP* once child was born regardless of whether state had Up program.

3. (M) Required automatic coverage of infants for 1 year after birth if mother already receiving Medicaid and remains eligible, and infant resides with her.

1985 1. (M) Required coverage of pregnant women if family income (PL 99-272) and resources below state AFDC levels, regardless of family structure.

2. (M) Required coverage of postpartum women for 60 days if eligibility was pregnancy-related.

3. (O) Allowed extension of 1984-required coverage of infants and children up to age 5 immediately, instead of requiring phase-in by birth date.

4. (M) Required coverage of adoptive and foster children even if adoption/foster agreement was entered into in another state.

5. (M) Required coverage of children with special needs covered, regardless of income/resources of adoptive or foster parents.

1986: 1. (O) Created new optional categorically needy group for (PL 99-509) pregnant women and infants with income below 100% of poverty, with women to receive pregnancy-related services only; for this new category assets tests would be dropped.

2. (O) Allowed presumptive eligibility to pregnant women for up to 45 days to be determined by qualified provider.

3. (O) Allowed guarantee of continuous eligibility to pregnant women through postpartum period.

Appendix 3.D (continued)

4.   (O) Allowed phased-in coverage of children up to age 5, if household income below 100% of poverty.

5.   (M) Required continuation of eligibility for those infants and children who otherwise would become ineligible if they are hospital patients when age limit is reached.

1986:   (M) Required provision of emergency and pregnancy-related (PL 99-603) services to newly legalized aliens if otherwise eligible.

    Also required full coverage for eligibles under 18.

1986:   (M) Required state to provide proof of eligibility for (PL 99-570) persons otherwise eligible (homeless or having no permanent address).

1987:   1.   (O) Allowed coverage to pregnant women and infants if income (PL 100-203) level below 185% of poverty.

  2.   (O) Allowed immediate extension to children of 1906 coverage up to 100% of poverty line up to age 5.

  3.   (O) Clarified that states could provide in-home services for qualified disabled children.

  4.   (O) Allowed coverage for children age 5-7 up to state AFDC level (phased in by age).

  5.   (O) Allowed coverage for children below age 9, up to 100% of poverty (phased in by age).

1987:   (M) Required increase in period of Medicaid coverage for (PL 100-485) families if AFDC cash assistance is lost due to earnings.

    Implementation beyond 9/30/89:

1989:   1.   (M) Required coverage of pregnant women and infants if (PL 101-239) income below 133% of poverty.

  2.   (M) Required coverage of children up to age 6, if income below 133% of poverty.

  3.   (M) Required provision of all Medicaid-allowed treatment to correct problems identified during EPSDT screenings even if treatment is not covered otherwise under state's Medicaid plan.

Appendix 3.D (continued)

4. (Prior O now M) Required interperiodic screenings under EPSDT when medical problem is suspected.

1990:   1. (M) Required coverage of children up to age 18 if income (PL 101-508 below 100% of poverty (phased in by age).

2. (Prior O now M) Rquired continuous eligibility of pregnant women through postpartum period.

3. (M) Required extention of presumptive eligibility for pregnant women before written application submittal.

4. (M) Required states to receive and process Medicaid applications at convenient outreach sites.

5. (M) Required continuous eligibility for infants if (a) born to Medicaid-eligible mother who would remain eligible if pregnant and (b) remaining in mother's household.

Notes: * AFDC-UP is the
M indicates mandate to state governments to take specified action as condition of continued financial assistance for Medicaid.
O indicates option for states to adopt; if adopted, would be partially reimbursed in accordance with particular state's federal matching share.

Source: U.S. General Accounting Office, *Medicaid Expansions: Coverage Improves but State Fiscal Problems Jeopardize Continued Progress.* GAO/HRD-91-78, Appendix I. June, 1991, 40-42.

Appendix 3.E

Death Rates for Selected Causes of Death, by Sex and Race, for Age Groups 1–4 and 5–14 in 1950, 1970, and 1988 (deaths per 100,000 population of age group)

Causes	Under 1 White '50	'70	'88	Under 1 Black '50	'70	'88	Age 1-4 White '50	'70	'88	Age 1-4 Black '50	'70	'88	Age 5-14 White '50	'70	'88	Age 5-14 Black '50	'70	'88
	2	3	4	5	6	7	8	9	10	11	12	13	14	15	16	17	18	19
Males:																		
Motor Vehicle Accidents	9.1	9.1	5.8	NA	10.6	7.7	13.2	12.2	6.9	NA	16.9	9.2	12.0	12.6	8.7	9.7	16.1	9.5
Malignant Neoplasms	9.6	4.3	2.3	NA	5.3	2.7	13.1	8.5	3.9	NA	7.6	3.4	7.6	7.0	3.7	5.8	4.8	3.1
Heart Diseases	4.1	12.0	21.2	NA	33.5	43.0	1.1	1.5	1.9	NA	3.9	4.5	1.7	0.8	1.0	6.4	1.4	1.8
Cerebrovascular Disease	5.9	4.5	3.1	NA	8.5	12.3	1.1	1.2	0.3	NA	1.4	0.5	0.5	0.8	0.2	0.7	0.8	0.2
Suicide	—	—	—	NA	—	—	—	—	—	NA	—	—	0.3	0.5	1.1	—	0.1	0.6
Homicide and Legal Intervention	4.3	2.9	5.6	NA	14.3	19.3	0.4	1.4	2.2	NA	5.1	7.5	0.4	0.5	1.0	1.8	4.2	4.2
HIV Infection			1.1			8.1			0.4			3.2			0.2			0.4
Females:																		
Motor Vehicle Accidents	7.8	10.2	5.3	NA	11.9	5.5	10.1	9.6	6.2	—	12.6	7.5	5.6	6.9	6.2	6.2	9.3	5.6
Malignant Neoplasms	7.8	5.4	2.2	NA	3.3	3.4	11.3	6.9	3.7	—	5.7	3.8	6.3	5.4	2.6	3.9	4.0	2.8
Heart Diseases	2.7	7.0	16.8	NA	31.3	39.9	1.1	1.2	2.2	—	4.2	4.1	1.9	0.7	0.7	8.8	1.8	1.0
Cerebrovascular Disease	2.9	3.2	2.8	NA	9.1	8.2	0.6	0.6	0.3	—	1.4	0.7	0.4	0.6	0.2	0.6	0.8	0.4
Suicide	—	—	—	NA	—	—	—	—	—	—	—	—	—	0.1	0.1	0.4	0.2	0.5
Homicide and Legal Intervention	3.9	2.9	6.0	NA	10.7	23.5	0.6	1.2	1.6	NA	6.3	6.3	0.4	0.5	0.8	1.2	2.0	3.1
HIV Infection			0.7			7.5			0.4			2.8			0.1			0.5

Notes: NA = Not available; data breakdown by race for these Under 1 and 1-5 age groups not initiated until 1960s.
Sources: *Health USA 1990*, Tables 27, 28, 29, 33, 34, 35, 36, 85-90, 95-101, *Vital Statistics of the U.S. 1988*, vol. IIA, Table 1-9,16, 18, 22, 28, 34, 36.

Appendix 4.A
Major Health Insurance Reform Proposals as of Early 1992

	Coverage				Services		
	Uninsured	Aged	Currently Insured	Long-Term Health	Complete Coverage	Pharmaceutical	Managed Care
Urban Institute	X			X	X		X
Brookings Institution	X		X	X	X		X
Heritage Foundation	X	X	X	X	X	X	X
Blue Cross/Blue Shield	X				X	X	X
Mitchell	X				X		X
Rostenkowski	X				X	X	
Canadian NHI	X	X	X	X	X	X	X
AARP*	X	X	X	X	X	X	

	Financing					Costs Control		
	Pay-or-Play	Payroll Taxes	Trust Fund/ General Fund	Copayments, Deductibles	Medicaid Medicare	Third Party Insurance	Provider Costs/ Revenue Control	Capital Expend Control
Urban Institute	X	X		X	X	X		
Brookings Institution	X	X	X	X	X	X	X	X
Heritage Foundation		X		X	X	X		
Blue Cross/Blue Shield					X			
Mitchell	X	X						
Rostenkowski	X	X	X	X		X	X	X
Canadian NHI		X	X	X			X	X
AARP*		X	X	X	X	X		X

Source: U.S. Advisory Commission on Intergovernmental Relations, "Overview of the U.S. Health Care Industry and Analysis of Major Reform Proposals" (staff memorandum), November 15, 1991, p. 2 of attachment thereto; American Association of Retired Persons, AARP Bulletin, March 1992, 1, 7-8.

Notes: * = American Association of Retired Persons; plan still under consideration by membership.
X = Change from current system.

Appendix 4.B
1992 State Legislative Initiatives for Expanding Coverage of the Uninsured

State	Incentives for Expanding Small Employer Coverage			Universal Employer Based	Universal Publicly Financed	Health Insurance Risk Pools	Access Commissions, Task Forces, Studies
	Basic/Limited Benefit Plan	Regulation of Small Group Market	Tax Incentive				
Alabama	BI	BI			BI	BI	BI
Alaska		BI			RA/BI	BI	BI
Arizona	AP/A	BI	BI			BI	AP
Arkansas	AP	AP	BI				AP
California	BI	LA	BI	BI on ballot	BI	AP	BI
Colorado	AP/A	AP/A		County Demonstrat[1]		AP/A	LA
Connecticut	AP	AP/A	BI		BI	AF	LA
Delaware	LA	AP/A					LA
Florida	AP/A	AP/A		Comp. Reform[2]		AP	AP
Georgia	AP	AP	BI		BI	AP	LA
Hawaii			BI	AP	RA		LA
Idaho	BI	BI			BI	BI	AP
Illinois	AP			BI	BI	AP/A	AP
Indiana	BI	LA	AP/A		BI	AP	BI
Iowa	AP/A	AP/A			BI	AP	
Kansas	AP/A	AP/A	AP	BI	BI	LA	AP
Kentucky	AP	BI	AP	BI	BI	BI	BI
Louisiana	BI	AP			RA	AP/A	AP/A
Maine	LA	AP/A		BI	BI	AP/A	AP
Maryland	AP	BI	BI	AP	BI	BI	LA
Massachusetts	AP	AP	BI		BI	BI	BI
Michigan	BI		BI		BI	BI	
Minnesota	LA	LA	BI	Comp. Reform		LA	
Mississippi	LA	BI	LA			AP	

557

Appendix 4.B (continued)

State	Incentives for Expanding Small Employer Coverage			Universal Employer Based	Universal Publicly Financed	Health Insurance Risk Pools	Access Commissions, Task Forces, Studies
	Basic/Limited Benefit Plan	Regulation of Small Group Market	Tax Incentive				
Missouri	AP/A	LA	BI	BI	BI	AP	LA
Montana	AP		AP			AP	
Nebraska	AP	AP		BI	RA	AP/A	AP/A
Nevada	AP						
New Hampshire	BI	LA	BI	BI	BI		AP/A
New Jersey	AP	LA	BI		BI	AP	AP
New Mexico	AP	AP	BI	BI	BI	BI	AP/A
New York	BI	LA	BI	BI	BI		BI
North Carolina	AP	AP	AP	BI	BI		AP
North Dakota	AP	AP	BI			AP	
Ohio	BI	LA	BI	BI	BI	BI	AP
Oklahoma	AP	AP/A	BI			BI	AP/A
Oregon N	AP	AP	AP	AP		AP	LA
Pennsylvania	BI	BI	BI		RA		LA
Rhode Island	AP/A	AP/A	BI		RA		AP/A
South Carolina		AP				AP/A	
South Dakota	BI	AP				BI	LA
Tennessee	LA	LA				AP/A	AP/A
Texas	BI	BI	RA	BI		AP	AP/A
Utah	BI	AP/A	BI	Comp. Reform	BI	AP	LA
Vermont		LA					AP/A
Virginia	AP/A						AP/A

558

Washington	AP	BI	BI	BI	AP
West Virginia	AP	AP	AP	BI	AP
Wisconsin	LA	AP/A	BI	BI	AP/A
Wyoming	LA	LA			BI AP/A LA

1 Feasibility study for county demonstrations of ColoradoCare passed.

2 Three states, Florida, Minnesota and Vermont, have enacted a universal system that is based on a combination of public and employer based financing. Therefore, the chart double codes them as both publicly financed and employer based.

KEY

BI	Bill introduced in 1992
LA	Law adopted in 1992
AP	Adopted prior to 1992
AP/A	Law adopted prior to 1992 and amended or expanded in 1992
RA	Resolution adopted
N	States that did not have a session in 1992

Source: Intergovernmental Health Policy Project, "Major Health Legislation in the States: '92. " (Washington, DC: George Washington University, January 1993), Chart I.

Appendix 4.C
Summary of Those Recommendations of the 1991 Advisory Council on Social Security Relevant to Perinatal, Young Child, and Adolescent Health Care

GENERAL OBJECTIVES

Improve access to health care
Significantly reduce rate of health care cost growth
Fundamentally reform many of the basic institutions involved
   in health care delivery and financing
Fully involve the American people in commitment to change by
   the year 2000

SPECIFIC ACTIONS

Improvement of Access

- Assist state departments of health to establish *school-based clinics* for primary care services for children
- Assist states in offering *school-based major medical insurance* to complement/supplement care provided by the school clinics
- Expansion of *community and migrant health center programs*
- Commitment to *reduce infant mortality* through consolidated efforts by all levels of government

Correction of Private Health Insurance Flaws

- Improve *private insurance portability*
- Enact new rules for insurance *sold to small employers*
- Disallowance of state-mandated benefits for small employer core benefit plans
- *Preemption of state laws limiting* use of managed care in health benefit plans

Reducing Growth Rate in Health Care Costs

- Actions to *promote healthy life-styles*
- *Education programs on alcohol/drug prevention and treatment* introduced in preschool through K-6
- Conduct of massive public education campaign on *prevention of disease*

Appendix 4.C (continued)

- Installation of model secondary school course for *Family Financial Management and Planning*, including saving for, and investing in, health care
- Installation of federal *alternative procedure to adjudicate malpractice claims* and companion bill for consideration by states
- *Reform of health care institutions*
- *Standardization of health care claim forms*
- Revision of antitrust rules to *permit hospital mergers and joint ventures*
- Facilitation of *technology assessment and data pooling* to better manage technology
- Basic and applied *research to improve health outcomes* while reducing costs
- *Long-term development of new health care system*
- Develop prototype of various approaches—insurance market reform; all payer model; employer mandate (play or pay); public-private partnership, etc.
- Test and evaluate prototypes
- Enactment of new overall plan by national government by 2000

Source: U.S. Department of Health and Human Services, 1991 Advisory Council on Social Security, *Commitment to Change: Foundations For Reform.* (Washington, DC: December, 1991), 14-20.

Appendix 5.A

Source of School District Revenues, Selected Years, 1959–60 to 1989–90

	Percentage of Funds from Each Source											
State	1959-60			1969-70			1979-80			1989-90		
	Federal	State	Local	Federal	State	Local	Federal	State	Local	Federal	State	Local
1	2	3	4	5	6	7	8	9	10	11	12	13
United States	3.7	39.5	56.8	7.2	40.9	51.8	9.2	48.9	42.0	6.1	47.2	46.6
Alabama	8.1	69.3	22.6	15.2	63.3	21.5	12.6	69.0	18.4	11.2	60.0	28.8
Alaska	17.9	50.0	32.1	27.1	53.3	19.6	13.0	70.2	16.9	12.8	62.4	24.8
Arizona	6.8	39.5	53.7	8.2	46.4	45.4	11.1	41.6	47.3	7.9	43.5	48.6
Arkansas	8.0	47.7	44.3	18.2	44.5	37.3	14.5	53.0	32.5	9.6	56.8	33.6
California	3.6	42.7	53.7	5.3	37.3	57.4	8.7	71.2	19.1	6.6	66.9	26.5
Colorado	5.7	19.9	74.4	7.6	27.8	64.5	6.1	41.0	52.9	4.8	38.1	57.1
Connecticut	3.0	26.8	70.2	2.1	25.2	72.8	6.1	31.5	62.5	4.6	43.1	52.3
Deleware	2.2	78.9	18.9	7.4	71.3	21.3	13.0	64.7	22.3	7.3	66.8	25.9
District of Columbia	0.8	N/A	99.2	30.2	N/A	69.8	15.8	N/A	84.2	9.8	N/A	90.2
Florida	2.2	57.7	40.1	9.5	55.7	34.8	11.0	55.2	33.7	6.2	51.2	42.5
Georgia	11.1	62.8	25.1	10.5	58.3	31.1	11.8	57.6	30.6	6.3	53.1	40.5
Hawaii	13.6	69.9	16.5	9.7	87.2	3.2	12.5	85.2	2.4	10.1	87.3	2.6
Idaho	5.8	33.2	61.0	8.4	37.8	53.8	9.5	55.0	35.5	8.0	60.2	31.8
Illinois	2.7	18.9	78.4	5.7	34.6	59.5	12.8	41.2	46.0	5.9	32.8	61.3
Indiana	3.1	29.8	67.1	6.8	39.4	53.8	6.9	56.1	37.0	4.9	57.7	37.4
Iowa	2.9	12.1	85.0	3.6	28.0	68.4	6.7	42.2	51.0	4.9	49.1	46.0
Kansas	5.3	21.5	73.2	5.9	31.2	62.9	6.9	43.3	49.8	5.0	44.2	50.9
Kentucky	4.7	44.9	50.4	13.6	56.2	30.2	12.5	69.7	17.8	9.8	68.5	21.6
Louisiana	2.4	67.7	29.9	11.9	56.4	31.7	14.8	54.4	30.8	10.1	55.5	34.4
Maine	4.0	30.6	65.4	6.7	32.5	60.8	9.6	48.9	41.5	5.4	53.1	41.4

State												
Maryland	6.9	36.4	56.7	6.4	35.2	58.4	8.0	40.2	51.8	4.6	37.7	57.7
Massachusetts	2.0	20.5	77.5	6.0	20.0	74.0	6.5	36.3	57.2	4.7	34.5	60.8
Michigan	2.8	43.8	53.4	3.9	45.1	51.0	7.4	42.7	49.9	5.7	26.8	67.4
Minnesota	2.7	38.2	59.1	5.3	46.0	37.3	6.1	56.6	37.3	4.1	52.4	43.5
Mississippi	9.2	52.4	38.4	21.4	53.1	22.8	24.1	53.1	22.8	15.5	56.2	28.3
Missouri	4.8	30.5	64.7	7.9	33.7	58.4	9.7	36.7	53.6	5.5	40.0	54.4
Montana	3.7	25.4	70.9	8.5	25.4	66.2	8.4	49.3	42.2	9.0	45.9	45.1
Nebraska	4.3	4.3	91.4	6.4	17.6	76.0	7.9	18.2	73.9	5.9	23.1	71.0
Nevada	9.4	56.4	34.2	8.8	36.5	54.7	8.6	58.5	32.9	4.2	38.0	57.8
New Hampshire	4.6	5.3	90.1	5.1	8.3	86.7	5.1	6.8	88.1	2.8	8.4	88.8
New Jersey	1.5	24.1	74.4	5.4	27.0	67.6	4.1	40.4	55.5	3.8	39.8	56.4
New Mexico	15.2	69.4	15.4	17.7	61.9	20.4	16.6	63.4	20.0	12.3	72.9	14.8
New York	1.2	39.3	59.5	4.7	46.4	48.9	5.0	40.6	54.4	5.1	40.7	54.1
North Carolina	4.7	68.3	27.0	15.6	65.7	18.7	15.2	62.4	22.3	6.4	66.8	26.8
North Dakota	1.7	31.3	67.0	9.3	25.7	65.0	7.7	46.5	45.7	9.8	44.8	45.5
Ohio	2.8	30.3	66.9	5.0	28.3	66.7	7.7	40.6	51.6	5.4	43.6	51.1
Oklahoma	7.2	42.2	50.6	11.8	43.8	44.4	11.8	43.8	44.4	5.6	57.0	37.4
Oregon	4.5	29.5	66.0	6.0	20.8	73.2	9.9	35.5	54.6	6.1	25.1	68.8
Pennsylvania	1.8	50.2	48.0	6.2	46.2	47.6	8.5	45.0	46.5	5.2	43.6	51.2
Rhode Island	4.0	18.1	77.9	5.9	38.8	55.4	5.9	38.8	55.4	4.9	43.1	52.0
South Carolina	5.8	70.9	23.3	14.0	59.5	26.4	14.9	56.8	28.3	8.0	50.0	41.9
South Dakota	5.3	8.6	86.1	11.7	13.1	75.2	13.9	20.8	65.3	11.5	25.9	62.6
Tennessee	3.7	54.0	42.3	11.9	48.0	40.1	14.0	48.3	37.7	9.0	45.8	45.2
Texas	4.6	49.9	45.5	9.3	46.4	44.3	11.0	50.1	38.9	7.3	41.9	50.8
Utah	5.3	41.9	52.8	7.6	52.8	38.2	7.8	54.0	38.2	6.6	56.6	36.8
Vermont	0.8	23.1	76.1	2.9	37.1	60.0	7.7	28.0	64.2	4.3	32.2	63.4
Virginia	9.5	36.5	54.0	11.1	36.4	52.5	9.5	40.9	49.6	5.3	33.1	61.7
Washington	5.7	61.1	33.2	6.6	39.4	36.8	8.6	70.8	20.6	5.8	71.6	22.6
West Virginia	4.2	54.2	41.6	12.4	48.2	39.4	10.6	60.1	29.3	7.5	65.7	26.8
Wisconsin	2.9	21.3	75.8	2.5	31.6	65.9	5.5	37.6	56.8	4.1	40.2	55.7
Wyoming	5.7	45.7	48.6	20.2	24.8	55.0	6.6	29.6	63.8	5.0	51.2	43.8

Source: Advisory Commission on Intergovernmental Relations, *Significant Features of Fiscal Federalism*, 1992 Edition, Vol. II (Washington D.C., September, 1992), Table 138, p. 265.

Appendix 5.B
Current Expenditure per Pupil in Average Daily Attendance in Public Elementary and Secondary Schools, by State, 1959–60 to 1989–90

State or other area	Unadjusted dollars				Constant 1989-90 dollars [1]			
	1959-60	1969-70	1979-80	1989-90	1959-60	1969-70	1979-80	1989-90
1	2	3	4	5	6	7	8	9
United States	$375	$816	$2,272	$4,960	$1,547	$2,618	$3,546	$4,960
Alabama	241	544	1,612	3,327	995	1,745	2,516	3,327
Alaska	546	1,123	4,728	8,374	2,253	3,601	7,380	8,374
Arizona	404	720	1,971	4,057	1,665	2,310	3,077	4,057
Arkansas	225	568	1,574	3,485	929	1,821	2,458	3,485
California	424	867	2,268	4,391	1,749	2,782	3,540	4,391
Colorado	396	738	2,421	4,720	1,634	2,367	3,779	4,720
Connecticut	436	951	2,420	7,604	1,799	3,052	3,778	7,604
Deleware	456	900	2,861	5,696	1,880	2,888	4,466	5,696
District of Columbia	431	1,018	3,259	8,904	1,778	3,267	5,088	8,904
Florida	318	732	1,889	4,997	1,310	2,349	2,949	4,997
Georgia	253	588	1,625	4,187	1,045	1,886	2,537	4,187
Hawaii	325	841	2,322	4,448	1,339	2,697	3,624	4,448
Idaho	290	603	1,659	3,078	1,195	1,935	2,590	3,078
Illinois	438	909	2,587	5,118	1,808	2,918	4,038	5,118
Indiana	369	728	1,882	4,549	1,521	2,336	2,939	4,549

State								
Iowa	368	844	2,326	4,453	1,517	2,708	3,632	4,453
Kansas	348	771	2,173	4,752	1,434	2,474	3,392	4,752
Kentucky	233	545	1,701	3,675	961	1,749	2,656	3,675
Louisiana	372	648	1,792	3,855	1,534	2,079	2,798	3,855
Maine	283	692	1,824	5,373	1,166	2,222	2,847	5,373
Maryland	393	918	2,598	6,196	1,620	2,946	4,056	6,196
Massachusetts	409	859	2,819	6,237	1,687	2,756	4,401	6,237
Michigan	415	904	2,640	5,546	1,712	2,900	4,122	5,546
Minnesota	425	904	2,387	4,971	1,754	2,899	3,726	4,971
Mississippi	206	501	1,664	3,096	849	1,607	2,597	3,096
Missouri	344	709	1,936	4,507	1,419	2,273	3,023	4,507
Montana	411	782	2,476	4,736	1,694	2,503	3,866	4,736
Nebraska	337	736	2,150	4,842	1,390	2,363	3,356	4,842
Nevada	430	769	2,088	4,117	1,775	2,469	3,260	4,117
NewHampshire	347	723	1,916	5,304	1,432	2,320	2,991	5,304
New Jersey	388	1,016	3,191	7,991	1,598	3,260	4,982	7,991
New Mexico	363	707	2,034	3,518	1,496	2,268	3,175	3,518
New York	562	1,327	3,462	8,062	2,316	4,257	5,405	8,062
North Carolina	237	612	1,754	4,268	979	1,955	2,739	4,268
North Dakota	367	690	1,920	4,189	1,512	2,212	2,998	4,189
Ohio	365	730	2,075	5,136	1,506	2,342	3,239	5,136
Oklahoma	311	604	1,926	3,512	1,284	1,939	3,007	3,512
Oregon	448	925	2,692	5,521	1,849	2,967	4,202	5,521
Pennsylvania	409	882	2,535	6,061	1,689	2,829	3,957	6,061
Rhode Island	413	891	2,601	6,249	1,705	2,859	4,060	6,249

Appendix 5.B (continued)

State or other area	Unadjusted dollars					Constant 1989-90 dollars [1]			
	1959-60	1969-70	1979-80	1989-90	1959-60	1969-70	1979-80	1989-90
1	2	3	4	5	6	7	8	9
South Carolina	220	613	1,752	4,088	908	1,965	2,735	4,088
South Dakota	347	690	1,908	3,732	1,430	2,213	2,978	3,732
Tennessee	238	566	1,635	3,664	982	1,816	2,553	3,664
Texas	332	624	1,916	4,150	1,371	2,002	2,991	4,150
Utah	322	626	1,657	2,730	1,330	2,009	2,586	2,730
Vermont	344	807	1,997	6,227	1,419	2,590	3,118	6,227
Virginia	274	708	1,970	4,612	1,131	2,271	3,075	4,612
Washington	420	915	2,568	4,681	1,734	2,937	4,009	4,681
West Virginia	258	670	1,920	4,359	1,066	2,149	2,998	4,359
Wisconsin	413	883	2,477	5,524	1,704	2,832	3,867	5,524
Wyoming	450	856	2,527	5,577	1,858	2,746	3,944	5,577

[1] Based on the Consumer Price Index, prepared by the Bureau of Labor Statistics, U.S. Department of Labor, adjusted to a school year basis. These data do not reflect differences in inflation rates from State to State.

[2] Estimated by the National Center for Education Statistics.

Source: U.S. Department of Education, National Center for Education Statistics, *Statistics of State School Systems*; and Common Core of Data survey. Cited in U.S. Department of Education, *Digest of Education Statistics: 1992*, p. 161.

Appendix 5.C

Highlights of Federal Children's Program Cost-Effectiveness, 1990

	BENEFITS FOR CHILDREN	COST BENEFIT	SCOPE/PARTICIPATION
WIC - SPECIAL SUPPLEMENTAL FOOD PROGRAM FOR WOMEN, INFANTS AND CHILDREN	Reduction in infant mortality and births of low birthweight infants; reduced prevalence of anemia; improved cognitive skills.	$1 investment in prenatal component of WIC has saved as much as $3 in abort-term hospital costs, as much as $3.13 in Medicaid costs for newborns and mothers, and up to $3.90 for newborns only.	4.5 million participants - 50%-60% of those eligible - received WIC services in March 1990, up by 1.4 million since Spring 1983.
PRENATAL CARE	Reduction in prematurity, low birthweight births and infant mortality; elimination or reduction of diseases and disorders during pregnancy.	$1 investment can save $3.38 in cost of care for low birthweight infants.	24% of live births in 1988 were to mothers who did not begin prenatal care in the first trimester of pregnancy. The rate for white births was 21%, for black births 39%. Figures reflect essentially no change since 1982.
MEDICAID	Decreased neonatal and infant mortality, and fewer abnormalities among children receiving EPSDT services.	$1 spent on comprehensive prenatal care added to services for Medicaid recipients has saved $2 in infant's first year; lower health care costs for children receiving EPSDT services.	In FY 1989, an estimated 10.6 million dependent children under 21 were served by Medicaid, including 2.5 million screened under EPSDT. Figures reflect an increase of approximately 600,000 served under Medicaid and 400,000 served under EPSDT since 1986. In calendar year 1989, there were 12.8 million related children under 21 in families below the poverty line, compared with 13.0 million in 1986.
CHILDHOOD IMMUNIZATION	Dramatic declines in incidence of rubella, mumps, measles, polio, diphtheria, tetanus and pertussis.	$1 spent on Childhood Immunization Program saves $10 in later medical costs.	No data available on percent of children immunized since 1985. In 1985, percent of children ages 1-4 immunized ranged from 73.8 for rubella to 87.0 for diphtheria-tetanus-pertussis. For those ages 5-14, percent immunized ranged from 85.3 for rubella to 93.0 for DTP. Increasing incidence of certain diseases has been reported.

567

Appendix 5.C (continued)

	BENEFITS FOR CHILDREN	COST BENEFIT	SCOPE/PARTICIPATION
PRESCHOOL EDUCATION	Increased school success, employability and self esteem; reduced dependence on public assistance	$1 investment in quality preschool education returns $6 because of lower costs of special education, public assistance, and crime.	In Oct. 1989, there were 11.1 million children ages 3-5. 6.03 million of them were enrolled in public and non-public pre-primary programs. 450,970 children - fewer than 1 out of every 5 eligible - were participating in Head Start in FY 1989. Head Start participation dropped by 1,000 since 1985.
COMPENSATORY EDUCATION	Achievement gains and maintenance of gains in reading and mathematics.	Investment of $750 for year of compensatory education can save $3700 cost of repeating grade.	In 1987, 4.92 million children - an estimated 50% of those in need - received Chapter 1 services under the LEA Basic Grant Program. Figure reflects essentially no change since 1985.
EDUCATION OF CHILDREN WITH DISABILITIES	Increased number of students receiving services in regular school setting; greater academic and employment success.	Early educational intervention has saved school districts $1560 per student with disability.	During School Year 1988-89, 4.587 million children ages 3-21 were served under the State Grant Program, up approximately 466,000 children served in 1985-86. The prevalence of disabilities in the population under age 21 is estimated to be 11.4% (9.5-10 million children).
YOUTH EMPLOYMENT AND TRAINING	Gains in employability, wages, and success while in school and afterwards.	Job Corps returned $7,400 per participant, compared with $5,000 in program costs (in 1977 dollars). FY 1982 service year costs for YETP $4,700; participants had annualized earnings gains of $1810.	During 1989 program year, 68,068 youths were enrolled in Job Corps; 334,380 served under JTPA Title 11A; 639,900 youths participated in summer youth programs. The annualized number of unemployed persons 16-21 years old in 1989 was 1,719,000 (13.2% overall, 29.4% black, 13.7% white, 20.9% Hispanic).
CHILDHOOD INJURY PREVENTION	Reduced risk of injury and less severe injuries; increased safety knowledge and behavior.	Savings from use of child restraint devices estimated to exceed $2 million in one state over two years.	Annually, more than 22,000 children ages 0-19 die from injuries. For each injury death, an additional 45 children are hospitalized and 1,300 visit emergency room for treatment of non-fatal injuries.

LEAD SCREENING AND REDUCTION	Early detection of elevated blood lead levels with treatment and abatement reducing exposure to and effects of lead poisoning, including poor birth outcomes and impaired cognitive functioning.	Savings from reduction of effects of lead on U.S. children estimated at $500 million annually.	An estimated 3 to 4 million preschool children have blood lead levels associated with adverse effects, and 400,000 infants are born with toxic blood levels every year.
SMOKING CESSATION PROGRAMS FOR PREGNANT WOMEN	Quit rates ranging from 6% to 32% with reduced prenatal, neonatal and postnatal problems pre- and postnatally, including reduced infant mortality, fewer low birthweight births, lowered risk of SIDS and other complications.	Smoking cessation to some 350,000 pregnant smokers estimated at $1.75 million compared with more than $37 million in costs of low-birth-weight births.	An estimated 21-32 percent of U.S. pregnant women smoke during their pregnancies.
HOME VISITING	Early outreach to families with needed preventive services, such as prenatal care, social supports, skills training and preschool education; improved birth outcomes; reduced likelihood of maltreatment.	Costs of home visiting range from $100 to $3,400 per family per year; annual savings estimated at $487 million in prevention of hospitalizations, rehabilitation, special education.	Currently more than 4,500 efforts under way with services ranging from prenatal support to child development education.

Source: U.S. House of Representatives, Select Committee on Children, Youth, and Families, *Opportunities for Success: Cost-Effective Programs For Children Update, 1990* (Washington, D.C.: U.S. Government Printing Office, October 1990), pp. 6-10.

Appendix 5.D
National Education Goals

Readiness for School

GOAL 1: By the year 2000 all children in America will start school ready to learn.

Objectives:

- All disadvantaged and disabled children will have access to high-quality and developmentally appropriate preschool programs that help prepare children for school.

- Every parent in America will be a child's first teacher and devote time each day helping his or her preschool child learn; parents will have access to the training and support they need.

- Children will receive the nutrition and health care needed to arrive at school with healthy minds and bodies, and the number of low birth-weight babies will be significantly reduced through enhanced prenatal health systems.

High School Completion

GOAL 2: By the year 2000, the high school graduation rate will increase to at least 90 percent.

Objectives:

- The nation must dramatically reduce its dropout rate and 75 percent of those students who do drop out will successfully complete a high school degree or its equivalent.

- The gap in high school graduation rates between American students from minority backgrounds and their nonminority counterparts will be eliminated.

Student Achievement and Citizenship

GOAL 3: By the year 2000, American students will leave grades 4, 8, and 12 having demonstrated competency in challenging subject matter including English, mathematics, science, history, and geography; and every school in America will ensure that all students learn to use their minds well, so they may be prepared for responsible citizenship, further learning, and productive employment in our modern economy.

Appendix 5.D (continued)

Objectives:

- The academic performance of elementary and secondary students will increase significantly in every quartile, and the <u>distribution of minority students</u> in each level will more closely reflect the student population as a whole.

- The percentage of students who demonstrate the ability to reason, solve problems, apply knowledge, and write and communicate effectively will increase substantially.

- <u>All students</u> will be involved in activities that promote and demonstrate good citizenship, community service, and personal responsibility.

- The percentage of students who are competent in more than one language will substantially increase.

- All students will be knowledgeable about the diverse cultural heritage of this nation and about the world community.

Science and Mathematics

GOAL 4: By the year 2000, U.S. students will be first in the world in science and mathematics achievement.

Objectives:

- Math and science education will be strengthened throughout the system, especially in the early grades.

- The number of teachers with a substantive background in mathematics and science will increase by 50 percent.

- The number of U.S. undergraduate and graduate students, <u>especially women and minorities</u>, who complete degrees in mathematics, science, and engineering will increase significantly.

Adult Literacy and Lifelong Learning

GOAL 5: By the year 2000, every adult American will be literate and will possess the knowledge and skills necessary to compete in a global economy and exercise the rights and responsibilities of citizenship.

Appendix 5.D (continued)

Objectives:

- Every major American business will be involved in strengthening the connection between education and work.

- <u>All workers</u> will have the opportunity to acquire the knowledge and skills, from basic to highly technical, needed to adapt to emerging new technologies, work methods, and markets through public and private educational, vocational, technical, workplace, or other programs.

- The number of quality programs, including those at libraries, that are designed to serve more effectively the needs of the growing number of part-time and mid-career students will increase substantially.

- The proportion of those qualified students, <u>especially minorities</u>, who enter college; who complete at least two years; and who complete their degree programs will increase substantially.

- The proportion of college graduates who demonstrate an advanced ability to think critically, communicate effectively, and solve problems will increase substantially.

Safe, Disciplined, and Drug-Free Schools

GOAL 6: By the year 2000, every school in America will be free of drugs and violence and will offer a disciplined environment conducive to learning.

Objectives:

- Every school will implement a firm and fair policy on use, possession, and distribution of drugs and alcohol.

- Parents, businesses, and community organizations will work together to ensure that schools are a safe haven for all children.

- Every school district will develop a comprehensive K-12 drug and alcohol prevention education program. Drug and alcohol curriculum should be taught as an integral part of health education. In addition, community-based teams should be organized to provide students and teachers with needed support.

Source: U.S. Congressional Budget Office, <u>The Federal Role in Improving Elementary and Secondary Education</u> (Washington, D.C.: U.S. Government Printing Office, May 1993), 10 - 11.

Appendix 6.A
Nine Phony Assertions About School Choice: Answering the Critics!

ASSERTION # 1: THE UNDERMINING-AMERICA ARGUMENT.
Choice will destroy the long tradition of common schools in America by subsidizing private schools at the expense of public schools. These schools, which embody the classless and democratic principles of the United States are enshrined in the public school system.

RESPONSE:
Choice, in fact, affords Americans the best chance of re-creating the common school by returning all children to a level playing field and ensuring the schools are representative of diverse communities. Parents of all colors, socioeconomic levels, and classes should be able to choose among the widest range of schools possible, rather than being segregated out of a particular school because its cost may be prohibitive.

ASSERTION #2: THE CREAMING ARGUMENT.
Choice will "leave behind" the poor and most difficult to educate, while good students will be "creamed" into the best schools.

RESPONSE:
This criticism overlooks one of the most fundamental dynamics of choice: the ability of parents to choose schools forces existing public schools to change. Another dynamic is that good schools expand and new schools emerge. If bad schools cannot or will not improve, their students can go elsewhere.

ASSERTION #3: THE INCOMPETENT PARENT ARGUMENT.
Since some parents are truly incapable of making choices, such as those who abuse drugs, some parents also are incapable of wisely exercising their choice option, thus consigning their children to substandard education.

RESPONSE:
Choice plans would require parent information centers and parent liaisons to help parents who need assistance in making choices. But even if such source information were not available, the worst that could happen is that children for whom no choice is made would be assigned to a school--which is not different from what occurs today.

ASSERTION #4: THE NONACADEMIC PARENTAL NEGLECT ARGUMENT.
Parents will use such criteria as a school's location or its athletic facilities, rather than the quality of the education it provides, in deciding what school their child will attend.

RESPONSE:
Even with clear performance testing and with precise information on which to make choices, some parents may decide that a neighborhood school or a school with an emphasis on team sports is better for their child than one that excels in mathematics. But that should be their choice to make as parents. It is a choice made routinely by affluent parents. Choice plans allow poor parents the chance to make that same decision.

ASSERTION # 5: THE SELECTIVITY ARGUMENT.
Private schools in the choice plan will admit only easy-to-teach children, leaving difficult, less academically gifted children in the public schools. Such selectivity is the reason for the private schools' vaunted ability to outperform public schools.

RESPONSE:
The selectivity issue argument challenges choice advocates. Few are willing to deny a private school the right to set admissions standards. But while some private schools set high admission requirements, the fact is that parochial schools— the private schools serving most children in cities with or considering choice plans—actually are less selective than public schools.

ASSERTION #6: THE RADICAL SCHOOLS SCARE.
A choice system will lead to fly-by-night schools, which take public funds without providing adequate education. Worse still, schools espousing radical or extremist dogmas would emerge, perhaps even those run by the Ku Klux Klan or by black extremists.

RESPONSE:
Most states have imposed minimum academic standards on private, as well as public, schools. Most education choice proposals, moreover, require the government to play some role in enforcing federal antidiscrimination laws and ensuring contractual obligations to students.

Appendix 6.A (continued)

ASSERTION#7: THE CHURCH-STATE PROBLEM.
Choice plans that include private, religious schools are unconstitutional because they violate the First Amendment's establishment clause.

RESPONSE:
In practice, as long as a school choice program puts the decision of where the funds are spent in the hands of individual students or parents, and as long as the program does not discriminate in favor of religious schools, the program is likely to survive any constitutional challenge.

ASSERTION #8: THE PUBLIC ACCOUNTABILITY ARGUMENT.
Private and parochial schools in a choice system would not be regulated by state and federal laws, and therefore would not be accountable to public authority.

RESPONSE:
All constructive choice proposals require that schools follow legal accountability requirements and federal antidiscrimination laws.

ASSERTION #9: THE CHOICE IS EXPENSIVE ARGUMENT.
There are large hidden costs associated with school choice programs. Transportation costs, for instance, would be so prohibitive as to offset benefits.

RESPONSE:
Choice does not imply higher costs, even higher transportation costs for large districts.

Source: J. Allan, "Nine Phony Assertions about School Choice: Answering the Critics!" *Heritage Foundation Backgrounder*, September 13, 1991.

Appendix 7.A

Number of Categorical and Block Grant Programs, Selected Fiscal Years, 1975–91

	1975	1978	1981	1984	1987	1989	1991
	1	2	3	4	5	6	7
Block	5	5	5	12	13	14	14
Categorical	422	492	534	392	422	478	543
Total	427	497	539	404	435	492	557

Source: ACIR tabulation based on *Catalog of Federal Domestic Assistance, United States Code,* and federal agency contacts. U.S. Advisory Commission on Intergovernmental Relations, *Characteristics of Federal Grant-in-Aid Programs to State and Local Governments: Grants Funded FY 1991* (Washington, D.C.: U.S. Government Printing Office, March 1992), p. 1.

Appendix 7.B
Which Level Should Do What? Criteria for Decision Making

I.   Public Finance Criteria

     A.   Production Efficiency: Assign functions to jurisdictions that are large enough to realize economies of scale.

     B.   Trade-offs Among Complementary Services: Assign a function to a level of multi-purpose jurisdictions that can choose among the variety of service alternatives for meeting similar objectives.

     C.   Optimum Levels of Service: Assign functions to governments geographically large enough to encompass the geographic scope of benefits received and costs incurred from a public policy. If the jurisdiction is too small for the extended benefits, the service will be under-provided; if the jurisdiction is too small to encompass the full costs or adverse side effects of the program, the program will be too large. If scope of benefits and costs match, the government responsible for the service should be fully responsible for financing for it—i.e., fiscal accountability.

     D.   Fiscal Capacity: Given an assignment of taxing authority—constitutional, statutory, or de facto—assign service financing responsibility to a level with adequate taxing authority and taxing capacity.

II.   Political Criteria

     A   Political Accountability: Functions should be assigned to jurisdictions that are controllable by, accessible to, and accountable to their residents, to jurisdictions that maximize the conditions and opportunities for active and productive citizen involvement including full representation for minorities.

     B.   Matching Desired Services to Public Preferences: Functions should be assigned to a level that will provide diversity and a tailoring of services to community preferences. Under these circumstances, individuals will be able to pick among jurisdictions so as to best match their preferences to service and tax levels.

     C.   Responsiveness: Assign functions to levels that respond readily to changes in public preferences among types of services or taxes and their levels.

     D.   Individual Freedoms: Assign functions so that checks and balances on the power of government will operate.

III.   Equity Criteria

     A.   Redistribution of Income: To redistribute income successfully by means of an expenditure program or tax instrument, the jurisdiction must be large enough to prevent those from whom resources would be taken from leaving and outsiders to whom resources might flow from immigrating.

     B.   Minimizing Tax or Service Disparities: Assign a function to a level and among jurisdictions so that disparities in resources with which public services can be financed will either be minimal or have minimal effects on the level of service provided.

IV.   Administrative Efficiency Criteria

     A.   Capacity: Assign functions to levels that articulate program goals, evaluate programs, assess needs, and have adequate legal authority and management capability.

     B.   Effectiveness: Assign functions to levels that can effectively carry out the program with the least overhead and with the least amount of fraud, waste, and abuse.

Source: Advisory Commission on Intergovernmental Relations, *Intergovernmental Perspective*, Spring 1982, p. 17.

Appendix 7.C
Criteria for Sorting-Out Roles

Dimension of Government Action	Equity	Efficiency	Accountability
Policy	Federal role as a countervailing power, advocate for the average citizen and protector of minorities.	Unity of the national economy. Diversity	Responsiveness to public concerns and to social problems and opportunities. Overload and congestion of the federal agenda.
Funding	Fiscal equity	Spillovers	Fiscal accountability
Implementation	Equal treatment of all citizens	Economies/diseconomies of scale	Complexity, workability of the federal-state system. Clarity.

Source: John, D. *Shifting Responsibilities: Federalism in Economic Development* (Washington, D.C.: National Governors' Association, p. 20.

Bibliographical Essay

The primary focus of this reference work is a collection of major public and private sector policy issues confronting the adequacy of the nation's labor force, as they pertain to early education and training and the health care of American youth. These issues concern not only national, state, and local governments and their school districts and public health agencies but private employers, large and small, and the multitude of private and nonprofit organizations that provide and otherwise participate in the delivery of health, training, and other educational services. Finally, they concern every family and parent with growing children, in the arrangements for their children's education and appropriate health care, including the examples they set for those children in their own behaviors. Policy options—not prescriptions or recommendations—are presented, along with contrasting views on each side (or several sides) of the respective issues.

The materials used in the preparation of this book comprise the following categories: (1) aggregated national data in the labor market, education/training and public health fields from the national government, interstate instrumentalities of the state governments, and other public and nonpublic agencies and organizations; (2) substantively oriented (labor market, health, education) issue analyses based on individual and institutional research; (3) conceptual underpinnings for particular policy approaches and evaluative studies of *outcomes* of specific policy initiatives. A summary of some major sources in these three categories follows, together with a listing of a number of periodic publications of organizations and agencies involved in the policy areas dealt with in this book.

STATISTICS AND SURVEYS

For aggregated national data, major sources used have been the following:

Labor Market Trends, Composition, Unemployment Rates, and Associated Aspects

1. U.S. Department of Labor (DOL), Bureau of Labor Statistics (BLS), through its monthly report *Employment and Earnings* and annual averages carried in that publication in January of each year; and *Monthly Labor Review*, published by BLS, carrying a combination of statistical data and associated trend and other analyses. Also published by the DOL at multiyear intervals is the *Handbook of Labor Statistics*, which brings together an array of governmental and other national data on labor-associated matters from nongovernmental sources.

2. U.S. Department of Commerce, Bureau of the Census, through its decennial census of population, quinquennial censuses of manufactures, wholesale and retain trade, and selected services, showing employment by occupation and geographic distribution, among other factors. The bureau's quinquennial *Census of Governments* includes volumes on organizational structure, public employment, and similar topics; it publishes annual volumes on *Government Finances* showing federal, state, and local revenues, expenditures, and debt, among other fiscal topics. Finally, through its *Current Population Reports* and other surveys, the bureau publishes data at varying intervals on household and family characteristics and participation by individuals in various governmental assistance programs. The U.S. Advisory Commission on Intergovernmental Relations (ACIR) also publishes an annual two-volume report, *Significant Features of Fiscal Federalism*, containing data on revenues, expenditures, budget processes, and tax systems, as well as special reports from time to time.

Education and Training

1. U.S. Department of Education, which publishes several sets of data, including the *Digest of Education Statistics*, which is issued annually by the National Center for Education Statistics. The *Digest* is a comprehensive compilation of data from public and private sources covering kindergarten through graduate school. Another useful source of statistical information from the center is the edition of *Projections of Education Statistics to 2002*, covering K–12 and higher education institutions.

2. Each year the National Assessment of Educational Progress (NAEP) releases a report, "The Nation's Report Card," prepared by the Educational Testing Service with financial support from the National Center for Education Statistics. The NAEP statistics measure academic achievement levels of fourth, eighth, and twelfth grade public and private school students in reading, writing, mathematics, science, history, civics, and geography.

3. Aggregated national data on K–12 education, as well as status reports on state reform efforts, are published by the Education Commission of the States. Regional data on various aspects of public education finance, standards, and innovations are provided by the Southern Regional Education Board and the Western Interstate Commission on Higher Education.

   Through occasional nationwide sampling surveys of private employers, the American Society for Training and Development publishes data on employer-provided basic and advanced skills, as well as managerial training. Similarly, from state education agencies and other sources, enrollment, financial, and other data are assembled and published by the two major teachers' organizations, the National Education Association and the American Federation of Teachers. The Council of the Great City Schools publishes national totals on the 30 largest city school districts. An especially useful source of information on the public's attitudes on current issues in education is the annual Gallup Poll published in *Phi Delta Kappan*. This magazine also covers trends, developments, and emerging issues in public education, such as the status of state school finance equity cases. The Carnegie Foundation for the Advancement of Teaching has conducted and supported several surveys of teachers and teaching, released periodically as "report cards."

Health Care

Most official health care data emanate from the US. Public Health Service in the Department of Health and Human Services. Much of these data are collected from the vital statistics agency in each of the 50 states, the District of Columbia, and territorial governments. Through the Centers for Disease Control (CDC) and its statistical arm, the National Center for Health Statistics (NCHS), four annual vital statistics reports are published, usually for the second or third year back from data of publication. *Vital Statistics of the United States* comprises Vol. 1, Natality; Vol. 2, Mortality, Part A; Vol. 2, Mortality, Part B; and Vol. 3; Marriage and Divorce. A *Monthly Vital Statistics Report* carries monthly and cumulative data on births, deaths, marriages, divorces, and infant deaths by state. NCHS publishes occasional reports on different subjects. The CDC publishes a weekly, *Morbidity and Mortality Report*. Finally, an annual comprehensive volume, *Health USA*, is issued by NCHS.

Qualitative and quantitative information and analyses on particular policy areas are originated and published under the sponsorship of numerous governmental agencies, academic institutes, foundations, or special interest groups. Illustrative examples in the health and behavioral areas are the American Medical Association, Childrens' Defense Fund, Intergovernmental Health Policy Project of George Washington University, Institute of Medicine of the National Academy of Sciences National Research Council, and the Institute for Research on Poverty, University of Wisconsin. For education, the National Governors' Association has monitored state progress toward achieving the national education goals and issued annual status reports. The National Conference of State Legislatures also collects and interprets data on school expenditures and related subjects. The National League of Cities has established an ongoing "Children and Families in Cities Project" to encourage local elected officials to help children and families in need through direct and networking assistance, research, and policy analysis. Other organizations that provide information and analysis pertaining to K–12 education are the Education Commission of the States, Twentieth Century Fund, Committee for Economic Development, and Business Roundtable.

EVALUATIONS

The public policy evaluation area, covering all three aspects of this book, includes the Advisory Commission on Intergovernmental Relations, American Enterprise Institute, Brookings Institution, Carnegie Foundation, Heritage Foundation, Hudson Institute, Rand Corporation, and Urban Institute. The national government maintains several evaluative agencies. On the executive side, evaluations outside the particular operating health, education, or other agency usually are carried on by appointed study commissions. Within the Congress, four agencies conduct studies and evaluations, the results of which have been cited extensively in this book. They are (1) General Accounting Office (GAO); (2) Office of Technology Assessment (OTA); (3) Congressional Budget Office (CBO); and (4) Congressional Research Service (CRS).

GENERAL REFERENCE WORKS

Following is a summary listing of monthly or other periodical publications, with the sponsoring organization, that deal with the labor market, education/training, and health care policy areas covered in this work.

- Advisory Commission on Intergovernmental Relations (ACIR), *Intergovernmental Perspective* (quarterly)
- American Association of Retired Persons (AARP), *News Bulletin* (monthly)
- American Enterprise Institute (AEI), *Regulation* (monthly)
- American Medical Association, *JAMA* (*Journal of the American Medical Association*) (four times monthly)
- American Public Welfare Association (APWA), *Public Welfare* (quarterly)
- American Society for Training and Development (ASTD), *Training and Development Journal* (quarterly)
- Annie B. Casey Foundation, *Kids Count* (annual)
- Brookings Institution, *Brookings Review* (quarterly)
- Children's Defense Fund (CDF), *State of America's Children* (annual)
- Council of Chief State School Officers (periodic reports)
- Council of State Governments (CSG), *State Government News* (monthly) and *Spectrum* (quarterly)
- Economic Policy Institute, *Economic Journal* (three times annually) and *Annual Report*
- Education Commission of the States (ECS), *State Education Leader* (quarterly)
- General Accounting Office, *Health Report* (monthly)
- *Governing* magazine (monthly)
- Heritage Foundation, *Policy Review* (quarterly)
- Hudson Institute, *Hudson Institute Report* (quarterly)
- Institute for Research on Poverty, *Focus* (quarterly)
- Intergovernmental Health Policy Project, *State Health Notes* (monthly), *State Health*

Legislation (annually), and *Journal of Education Finance* (quarterly) and *Health Project Supplement* (biweekly)

- National Center for Health Statistics (NCHS), *Monthly Vital Statistics Report* (monthly)
- National Center for Service Integration (NCSI), *NCSI News* (quarterly)
- National Conference of State Legislatures, *State Legislatures* (monthly)
- National Governors' Association (NGA), *Governors' Bulletin* (weekly)
- National League of Cities, *Nation's Cities Weekly* (weekly) and reports issued periodically through its Children and Families in Cities Project
- National School Boards Association (NSBA), *National School Board Journal* (monthly)
- National Science Foundation (NSF), *Annual Report* (available mid-year)
- *Phi Delta Kappan* (monthly)
- Rand Corporation, Rand Drug Policy Research Center, *DPRC Issue Paper*
- Southern Regional Education Board (periodic reports)
- U.S. Conference of Mayors (USCM), *Mayor* (weekly)
- Urban Institute (UI), *Policy and Research Report* (quarterly)

Index

About the Authors

CARL W. STENBERG III, director of the Center for Public Service at the University of Virginia, was formerly the executive director of the Council of State Governments and president of the American Society for Public Administration. He has written at length about intergovernmental management.

WILLIAM G. COLMAN, author of *State and Local Government and Public Private Partnerships: A Policy Issues Handbook* (Greenwood Press, 1989), an award-winning academic reference book, has written at length on public policy issues and government management. Formerly he was executive director of the Advisory Commission on Intergovernmental Relations.